Managerial Accounting: Tools for Business Decision Making

Managerial Accounting: Tools for Business Decision Making

Edited by **Terry Ness**

Willford Press

New York

Published by Willford Press,
118-35 Queens Blvd., Suite 400,
Forest Hills, NY 11375, USA
www.willfordpress.com

Managerial Accounting: Tools for Business Decision Making
Edited by Terry Ness

International Standard Book Number: 978-1-68285-263-7 (Hardback)

Printed in China.

Contents

Preface

This book has been a concerted effort by a group of academicians, researchers and scientists, who have contributed their research works for the realization of the book. This book has materialized in the wake of emerging advancements and innovations in this field. Therefore, the need of the hour was to compile all the required researches and disseminate the knowledge to a broad spectrum of people comprising of students, researchers and specialists of the field.

Managerial accounting refers to creation of various financial databases and reports that are used by officials and managers to evaluate the financial performance of an organization and take future decisions. The main objectives of managerial accounting are cost estimation, planning financial budgets, analysis of expenditure and profit, performance management, etc. The topics included in this book like cost finding, tax accounting, analysis of transactions and events, core financial statements, and credit & debit rules are of utmost significance and bound to provide incredible insights to readers. This book, with its detailed analyses and data, will prove immensely beneficial to professionals and students involved in this area at various levels.

At the end of the preface, I would like to thank the authors for their brilliant chapters and the publisher for guiding us all-through the making of the book till its final stage. Also, I would like to thank my family for providing the support and encouragement throughout my academic career and research projects.

Editor

Attitudes toward learning accounting by computers: The impact on perceived skills

Husam Aldeen Al-Khadash[1*] and Sulieman Al-Beshtawi[2]

[1]Department of Accounting, Hashemite University, P.O. Box 330125, Postcode 13133, Hashemite University, Zarqa, Jordan.

[2]Department of Accounting, Al-Mafraq, University, Zarqa, Jordan.

Accountancy has been significantly affected by information technology. Accounting education curricula, however, still largely ignore the use of computers as tools in the learning process, mainly because of budgetary and timetable constraints. This study investigates the impact of learning accounting by computers on students' perceived skills. The aim of our study was to determine the effectiveness of teaching undergraduate accounting students courses in using computer in accounting, Four hundred and sixty-three accounting students were included in the study, a multiple choice question survey was performed after finishing a course offered to teach students computer skills in accounting . The results showed that such course has an impact on attitudes towards the perceived skills from using computers for accounting purposes. After the course, no gender differences with respect to attitudes towards the perceived skills were found, but males report shows slightly more computer experience than females.

Key words: Information technology, using computer in accounting, learning skills, gender.

INTRODUCTION

The proliferation of personal computers throughout business environments will continue to place demands on workers at all levels to develop proficient computer skills. In accounting, the accounting profession recognizes that individuals entering the profession must have sufficient knowledge of computer skills to be successful because of its pervasiveness in business activities (Elliott, 1997). Using computer in accounting is an integral means for helping students to provide needed skills and it is vitally important that accounting students have the proper experience and a positive attitude towards computers because of the relationship between attitudes towards computers and motivation and performance (Mcdowall and Jackling, 2006; Mills, 1997; Igabaria et al., 1990; Eason and Damodaran, 1981, Shneiderman, 1979). Because of the importance placed on computer skills by the profession, it is important to determine the impact of teaching computer skills that accounting have on accounting students in terms of the perceived skills.

*Corresponding author. E-mail: husam@hu.edu.jo.

Many studies investigated the relationship between students' perceptions toward computer skills in accounting and students attitudes and some other variables such as gender or prior experience in using computer. Gender differences have been reported in literature as affecting perceptions in general (Hackett et al., 1991). Consequently, gender was included as a matter of understanding if differences of perceptions toward using technology occurred between male and female respondents. Experience with the computer skills was included because research has documented the relationship between experience and user acceptance of technology in general (Koohang, 1989). The more experience a user has with technology the more he or she tends to accept it. Therefore, user's acceptance may in turn promote learning.

Because of these critical professional and educational issues, this study provides an investigation on the impact of studying a course in using computers for accounting purposes on attitudes towards the skills perceived in general and further to know to what extent this impact is affected by prior experience and gender. Accounting students are surveyed in this course at the end of a semester with respect to their experience and attitudes towards computers for determining the impact of the course on those surveyed. Survey responses at the end of the semester are further analyzed to determine whether differences exist by gender after attending the course.

Literature review

For over twenty years, accounting researchers have been studying the cognitive effects of a variety of techniques for integrating computers into the accounting curriculum; however, the results are frequently contradictory. After a comprehensive review of the studies concerning computer used in accounting instruction, Ng and Er (1989) opined that based on existing evidence "computing is irrelevant to the learning of accounting concepts". Earlier than this, Baxter (1974) and Arnett (1976) examined differences in examination scores between experimental groups, which used template programs, and control groups, which did not use computers. In both studies, no differences were found in examination scores between control and experimental groups, leading them to conclude that the use of computers did not enhance accounting proficiency.

Research outside the accounting discipline is also inconsistent and thus largely inconclusive. Kulik and Kulik, (1986) in a meta analysis of 101 studies across disciplines found a significant overall positive learning effect attributed to computer use. On the other hand, Norris (1987) reported that studies in various disciplines at six universities had failed to establish a correlation between learning and computer use. An extensive study at Dartmouth conducted in 24 introductory courses found no difference in grades between computer owners and non-owners in 21 of the 24 courses (Norris, 1987).

In the 1980s as computers became common, the American Accounting Association (AAA) recognized the growing pressure on accounting educators to integrate computer technology into accounting education. In an early report, the AAA (1985) identified these pressures as emanating from three primary sources. Firstly, the AACSB reviews computer use in accounting courses as part of its accreditation evaluation of accounting programs. Secondly, the widespread use of computers in accounting practice has pressured accounting departments to produce computer literate graduates to enhance their employability. Thirdly, computer use in secondary education has increased the expectations and desires of students to use computers in college (AAA, 1985).

While recognizing the value of computers to accounting practice, the AAA was concerned about the efficacy of using computer technology to educate accounting students. Contradictory results from earlier studies such as Baxter, (1974) and Arnett, (1976), which indicated that using a computer in a course did not necessarily improve student performance, and studies which did find learning effects (Groomer, 1981; Friedman, 1981) prompted these concerns. As a result of concerns by its membership, the AAA formed the committee on integrating the microcomputer into undergraduate financial accounting to promote the study of ways to effectively integrate computer technology into accounting curriculum (AAA, 1985).

Concurrent as the microcomputer use is becoming widespread, accounting researchers were already exploring a variety of ways to use computers in accounting education. This research, similar to the research a decade earlier, primarily explored the cognitive effects of different techniques for incorporating computers in accounting courses and attempted to measure the effects by measuring the student's perceptions.

Borthick and Clark (1986), while studying cognitive effects broadened the search for the effects of computers on students beyond the cognitive and into the affective domain with an investigation of attitudinal effects. While they did not detect performance differences, they found that student enthusiasm for using computers declined. Similarly, Dickens and Harper (1986) examined the effects of computer use on student achievement and attitudes in an intermediate accounting course. They required students to use an interactive computer program to solve either an inter-period tax allocation problem or an earning per share problem. Examination performance of students who used computer and those who did not was the same. However, contrary to Borthick and Clark's (1986) results, they reported that students reacted positively to using computers.

Austin (1989) examined the performance and behavioral effects of using computers and spreadsheets in the introductory financial accounting course. He found no performance differences on examinations of either problems or essay questions between the control and experimental groups; however, he detected a decline in enthusiasm for using computers.

Kachelmeier et al. (1992), using a spreadsheet based template for pension accounting, observed a performance difference on examinations between the students who used the spreadsheet program and those who did not. They noted that the students in the study had been extensively exposed to computers in other classes so discounted the novelty effect of sparking interest in the subject matter which might be manifested in heightened interest in the subject matter. Despite finding cognitive effects, they cited the lack of a measurement of the attitudinal effects as a limitation of their study.

The impact of studying a course in using computers in accounting on students' skills and link with gender was also important to study. Many studies, in general, report that males tend to have more experience and more favorable attitudes towards computers than females. Daigle and Morris (1999), however, found results for accounting students contrary to most findings for students in general. Based on a survey given to students in four courses across an accounting curriculum at the beginning of a semester, Daigle and Morris, (1999) failed to find an attitude or experience difference towards computers based on gender amongst students later in an accounting curriculum after finding some minor differences amongst students early in an accounting curriculum. Daigle and Morris (1999) also failed to find a difference in attitudes or experience based on gender of students who had been selected to emphasize their studies in studying computer in accounting course.

Daigle and Morris (1999) results indicate that gender differences for experience and attitudes towards computers may not exist because of a self-selection bias when choosing a major and in choosing an area of emphasis within accounting. However, if gender differences in experience and attitudes towards computers do in fact exist /with regard to accounting students, accounting programs and the profession should seek to ensure that gender differences not exist amongst those choosing careers in accounting because of the relationship between attitudes towards computers, motivation and performance. Therefore, further research is definitely needed to determine if using computer in accounting courses change the attitudes and experience towards computers by gender. The importance of this research is magnified since more than 40% of today's accounting students are female and because of the increasing importance of computer competencies within the accounting profession. This study provides the first formal look at the impact of computer skills in accounting course on the experience and attitudes towards computers of accounting students in general and further by gender in the Jordanian universities.

Wet and Niekerk (2001) concluded that computer assisted learning packages were suitable means of communicating many instructor materials to students. Also Mcdowall and Jackling (2006) examined students' perceptions at the usefulness of computer assisted leaving packages in learning accounting concepts in terms of the influence on academic performance. They concluded that gender, prior studies at accounting and computing systems were not significant on academic influence on academic performance.

Mohd et al. (2007) investigated that students with different backgrounds and attitudes towards computers influence their levels of computer skills. All Form Five (GCE 'O' Level equivalent) students from three different types of schools in the rural district of Segamat, Malaysia were sampled. The t-test and ANOVA results show that there were significantly different influences of the types of schools they enrolled in, their computer ownership, computer club memberships and their computer skills. The findings also revealed significant correlation between the same computer attitude subscales and the students' computer skills.

Research questions

This study measures the impact of studying a course in using computers for accounting purposes and attitudes towards the computer skills perceived by accounting students. The authors hypothesized that exposure to computers might similarly produce behavioral effects and influence perceptions. This supposition leads to the following exploratory research questions:

1) What are the students' attitudes toward using computers?
2) Are student's attitudes toward using computers differing by gender?
3) Is there a value added in student's computer skills after studying an introductory course in accounting which offers some computer skills?
4) Do accounting students have pervious experience in using computer?
5) What are the factors affecting the students' perceived skills in using computers for accounting purposes?

METHODOLOGY

In study, students were enrolled in an introductory course in accounting which offers some computer skills. Such course offered in many Jordanian universities. The aim of this course is to make accounting students able to use computers as tools to record and analyze financial transactions and to have some needed skills such as using spread sheets and excel functions in accounting. Also in some universities such course covers the skills of building a database for accounting purposes. The outcomes based nature at this course could contribute to the preparation of students at workplace. Since the beginning of 2000 a decision result were taken by high education ministry in Jordan that all students at Jordanian universities have to take at least two primary computer courses as part at the first year course (computer skills 1 and 2). More courses in computer skills are offered in many Jordanian Universities. For accounting majors all accounting students are required to study a course on introductory accounting which offers some computer skills, the course might be offered in different names but the content is almost same.

This study uses a survey design, using a combination of a modified version of the Adapted Bath County Computer Attitude Scale of some attitude and experience questions (Qureshi and Hoppel, 1995). Another experience questions were included from a study by Lowe and Krahn, (1989). The First Section of the survey instrument asks for demographic data regarding gender, class status, major, concentration area of current interest in accounting and GPA. The Second Section of the instrument was designed to evaluate the students' responses toward attitude questions of using computers in general. Section three was added to collect information about students experience in using computers. Finally section four is also included to collect information regarding students' responses toward the perceived skills after study-

Table 1. Mean response rate for all students to attitude questions toward using computers.

Question	Mean response
Working problems on a computer is fun.	4.00
It is easy to get tired of using a computer.	3.10
Studying computers in university would be a good idea.	4.40
People who use computers in their occupations are the only people who need to study about computers.	1.20
Learning about computers is interesting.	3.90
University would be a better place without computers.	1.30
I enjoy using a computer.	4.52
Computers are boring.	1.20
Working on a computer is a good way to spend spare time.	4.20
Using a computer becomes boring after about 30 minutes.	2.00
Learning about computers is something I can do without.	1.55
Computers are not exciting.	1.80
Studying about computers is a waste of time.	1.51
It is fun to figure out how computers work.	4.21
Computers help people think.	3.54
Classroom discussions about the uses of computers in society are a waste of time.	2.09
Learning about the different uses of computers is interesting.	3.45

Table 2. Mean response rate by gender for attitude questions found significant

Question	Mean Response For Females	Mean Response for Males
It is easy to get tired of using a computer.	3.12	3.06
Learning about computers is something I can do without.	2.85	3.05

ing a course in using computers for accounting purposes. The subjects of this study are students who enrolled in a course covers computer skills in accounting at five Jordanian universities.

RESULTS FROM TESTING RESEARCH QUESTIONS

Students enrolled in the course of the study completed the survey at the last week of the semester, the semester is sixteen week time, and the survey was completed in week fifteen. Only surveys from students who completed a survey are used in the analysis. This results in a useable sample of 463 surveys. Males completed 270 and females 193. The gender make up of the sample is consistent with the current trend that more males than females are studying accounting at Jordanian universities.

The first research question was about the students' attitudes toward using computers. Table 1 show that students' attitudes towards computers are very positive. To interpret the mean responses, the direction of the question and the mean response shown in Table 1 must be considered together. As examples, a question says computers are not exciting has a mean response of 1.80 indicating that subjects tended to disagree with the statement, while a question says computers help people think has a mean response of 3.54 indicating that the subjects tended to agree with the statement. These mean responses show a favorable attitude towards computers.

The mean responses shown in Table 1 illustrate that the students surveyed generally have a positive attitude towards computers. Of the attitude questions all responses are either positive or neutral, with the majority being positive. The mean responses suggest that, in general, those surveyed have an overall positive attitude towards using computers.

Second research question deals with the effect of gender on the attitudes towards computers. The research questions are important because of the possibility that the course impacts experience and attitudes towards computers differently for males and females. But in this current study no significant interaction between genders is found for attitude questions at a level significance of 0.05. These results indicate a failure to find significant changes in the attitudes towards computers of those surveyed after taking the course, based on gender. But as shown in Table 2, only two questions point a significant difference by gender at the end of the semester. Therefore, only these two questions require further consideration for

Table 3. Mean response rate for all students to the value added of studying computer skills in accounting

Reading and talking about how computers might be used in the future is boring.	2.00
Learning about the using of Excel in accounting is interesting.	3.41
Learning about using computers as tools to record and analyze financial transactions is interesting.	2.89
Learning about using accounting commercial programs is interesting.	3.59
I enjoy learning about how computers are used in accounting profession.	4.12
Studying about the uses and misuses of computers in accounting issues will help me to be a more responsible accountant.	4.11
I wish I had more time to use computers in doing accounting issues.	4.25
Taking a computer related course can have a positive impact on my attitude towards using computers in accounting.	4.36
It is fun to figure out how computers are used by accountants	4.22
I wish I had more courses about using computer in accounting	3.98

Table 4. Mean response rate for all students to experience questions

Question	Mean response
If you have access to a personal computer at home, how often do you use it?	3.10
If you do not have a personal computer, but had the ability to get one, would you acquire one?	1.90
How often do you use the college computer labs?	2.90
If you have access to a computer at work, how often do you use it?	3.20
Before entering college, did you ever take a course that met six times or more to learn about computers?	1.90
Approximately how many such courses did you take before entering college?	0.20
How many such courses have you taken in college?	1.50
Besides this course, are you enrolled this semester in a computer-related course?	1.10
Which of the following skills do you have with using a computer?	mean
(The scale yes:1 and No: 2)	
Playing games	1.90
Data entry	2.00
Word processing	1.80
Spreadsheets	1.00
Programming	1.00
Statistical analysis	1.02
Database management	1.01

determining whether attitudes of those surveyed differ by gender.

None of the mean responses in Table 2 show an unfavorable attitude towards computers by gender. The mean responses for females and males for questions shown in Table 2 are essentially neutral. Therefore, based on the results from Tables 1 and 2, one can conclude that both males and females generally have an overall favorable attitude towards computers after taking a course in computer in accounting. As shown in Table 3 students attitudes toward the value added of studying computer skills in accounting is very strong, which means that this course is very beneficial to the accounting students. Consequently in regards to research question number 4 and as shown in Table 4, it might be concluded that positive attitudes towards computers are related to experience with computers, the positive attitudes of the students in this survey can likely be explained by examining the student's experience with computers. Therefore, the mean responses to experience questions for all the students surveyed are provided in Table 4.

The mean responses to the experience questions generally show that students would use the computer many times if they have access to a personal computer at home or at work. The mean responses in Table 4 show that students have not taken many computer courses in college or before entering college. Specific mean responses in Table 4 of interest are those related to students skills in using computers playing games, data entry and word processing are general level of skills that all or most

Table 5. Bivariate correlations of the predictors with students' perceived skills in using computer for accounting purposes (predicted variable).

Predictor	Correlation with the predicted variable
Gender	-0.006
Age	-0.055
Grade-Point Average (GPA)	-0.063
Attitudes toward using computers	0.280*
Prior Experience in using computer	0.223*

*p < 0.001

Table 6. Results of stepwise regression analysis using five variables as predictors.

			Regression			
Steps	**Variable**	**R**	**R square**	**R square change**	**F change**	**Sig. Fchange**
1	Prior experience	0.223	0.050	0.050	23.011	0.001
2	Attitude towards using computers	0.340	0.115	0.066	32.359	0.001
			ANOVA			
Steps	**Variable**			**Df**	**F**	**Sig. F**
1	**Prior experience**					
	Regression			1	23.011	0.001
	Residual			438		
	Total			439		
2	**Attitude toward using computer**				28.509	0.001
	Regression			2		
	Residual			437		
	Total			439		

of students have but skills with using spread sheets and statistical analysis are too low even such skills are very important to accountants in their work life.

Correlation analysis

In order to answer question 5, the results of the correlation analysis associated with the stepwise regression analysis are displayed in Table 5. The bivariate correlations of the possible predictors (gender, age, GPA, attitudes toward using computers and prior experience) with the predicted (dependent) variable, students' perceived skills in using computer for accounting purposes are listed in the second column. It is interesting to note that the correlations between each of gender, age, GPA and the predicted variable are negative, relatively small and statistically not significant. However, the other two predictors (attitudes toward using computers and prior experience) proved to be significant. In fact, the strongest correlation existed between the predicted variable and prior experience in using computer (r =.223).

Multiple regression analysis stepwise approach

Table 6 shows the results of the stepwise regression analysis using five variables as predictors. Step one of the analysis revealed that prior experience in using computers is a significant predictor of students' perceptions toward the value added of studying computer skills in accounting course, r2 = 0.05, F(1,438)=23.01, p<0.001. This result is supported by the close moderate correlation between the two variables (r=.223). Approximately 5% (r2) of the variance of the students' perceptions variable was accounted for by its linear relationship with students' prior experience in using computer.

Step two of the stepwise regression analysis indicated that the attitudes toward using computers variable did add significantly to the prediction of students' perceptions toward the value added of studying computer skills in accounting r2 change=0.066, F(1,437)=32.359, p<0.001.

The same step also showed that the linear combination of the two variables (prior experience with the computer and attitudes toward using computers was significantly related to the students' perceptions variable, r2 =.115, F

(2,437) = 28.509, p<.001. This means that almost 11.5% of the variance of the students' perceptions variable was accounted for by its linear relationship with students' attitudes toward using computers and prior experience.

Conclusion

As Jordanian institutions of higher education enforced to teach computer skills in accounting for their accounting students, it is imperative to understand and predict students' perceptions toward the value added of studying such course. By being able to predict students' perceptions, instructors and decision makers can improve and enhance students' learning experience.

The purpose of this study was to determine the extent to which age, gender, grade point average (GPA), prior experience in using computers and attitudes toward using computers could predict students' perceptions toward the value added of studying computer skills in accounting.

The findings of the study determined that age, gender and GPA have no positive and significant relationship with the students' perceptions toward the value added of studying computer skills in accounting. Furthermore, the findings showed that students' prior experience in using computers and their attitudes toward using computer course may act as predictors of their perceptions toward the value added of the course. More precisely, the study showed that approximately 11.5% of the variance of students' perceptions was accounted for by its linear relationship with both students' prior experience and their attitudes toward using the computers.

REFERENCES

American Accounting Association (1985). "Report of Committee on Integration of the Microcomputer into the Financial Accounting Curriculum" (August 1985).

Austin WW (1989). A Study of the Effects of Integrating Microcomputers into the Introductory Financial Accounting Course. Working Paper. University of Georgia, Athens.

Baxter CA (1974). The Effects of Computer Augmented Instruction on Achievement in the Collegiate Principles of Accounting Course. Working Paper University of Georgia, Athens.

Borthick AF, Clark RL (1986). "The Role of Productive Thinking in Affecting Student Learning with Microcomputers in Accounting Education. Account. Rev. January: 143-157.

Daigle RJ, Morris PW (1999). Gender Differences in Accounting Student Attitudes and Experience Towards Computers. Rev. Account. Inf. Syst. (3): 75-84.

Dickens T R, Harper R M (1986). "The Use of Microcomputers in Intermediate Accounting: Effect on Student Achievement and Attitudes, J. Account. Edu. Spring. 127-146.

Eason KD, Damodaran I (1981). The Needs of the Commercial User. In Coombs MJ Atly JI (Eds.). Computer Skills and the User Interface,. New York: Academic Press. pp. 115-139.

Elliott RK (1997). Assurance Service Opportunities: Implications for Academia. Account. Horizons, 11(4) Dec: 61-74.

Er MC, Ng AC (1989). "The Use of Computers in Accountancy Courses: A New Perspective," Account. Bus. Resour. autumn: 319-326.

Friedman ME (1981). The Effect on Achievement of Using the Computer as a Problem Solving Tool in the Intermediate Accounting Course, Account. Rev., Jan.137-143.

Groomer SM (1981). An Experiment in Computer-assisted Instruction for Introductory Accounting, The Accounting Review, Oct. 931-941.

Hackett E, Mirvis P, Sales A (1991). Women's and men's expectation about the effect of new technology. Group and Organizational Studies, 16(1): 60-85.

Igabaria M, Parasuraman S, Pavri F (1990). A Path Analytic Study of the Determinants of Microcomputer Usage. J. Manage. Syst. 2 (2), 1-14.

Kachelmeier SJ, Jones JD, Keller JA (1992).Evaluating the Effectiveness of a Computer Intensive Learning Aid for Teaching Pension Accounting, Issues in Accounting Education, Fall, 1992: 164-178.

Koohang A (1989). A study of attitudes toward computers: Anxiety, confidence, liking, and perception of usefulness. J. Resour. Comp. Edu. 22 (2): 137-150.

Kulik CC, Kulik A J (1989). Effectiveness of Computer-based Education in Colleges, AEDS .J. Winter/Spring: 81-108.

Lowe G S, Krahn H (1989). Computer skills and use among high school and university graduates. Canadian Public Policy 15 (June): 175-188.

Mcdowwall T, Jackling B (2006). The Impact of computer – Assisted learning on Academic Grades: An A ssessmont at students, Per - ceptions. Account. Educ. 15 (4): 377 – 389.

Mills TA (1997). An Examination of the Relationship Between Accountants' Scores on Field Independence and Use of and Attitude Toward Computers. Perceptual and Motor Skills, 81: 715-20.

Mohd D, Chong S, Azizah A, Salwani M, Rafidah K, Ruhana Z (2007). The effects of students' backgrounds and attitudes on computer skills in Malaysia. Inter.J. Manage. Educ. 1 (4): 371-389.

Norris W (1987). "Micro Boom Begins to Loose its Byte," Times Higher Education Supplement, February 6.

Shneiderman B (1979). Human Factors Experiments in Designing Interactive Systems. Computer, 12 (9): 24.

Perception towards the importance and knowledge of information technology among auditors in Malaysia

Noor Azizi Ismail* **and Azlan Zainol Abidin**

College of Business, Universiti Utara Malaysia, Sintok 06010 Kedah, Malaysia.

This paper reports the results of a study that investigates the level of IT knowledge and also IT importance in the specific context of audit work in Malaysia. Results of this study is based on data collected from 95 audit firms via mailed questionnaires. The results suggested information systems audit in Malaysia is still at the infant stage. IT knowledge level among the auditors is lower than their perception towards the importance of the technologies. Twelve technologies are considered relevant in the context of audit work in Malaysia, while only 5 technologies are considered knowledgeable by the responding auditors. On average, General Office Automation receives the highest mean value for both importance and knowledge, whilst system development and installation receives the lowest mean value. Overall, responding auditors perceived their overall IT knowledge as adequate, while the current practice of information systems audit is less than adequate. Findings from this study are significant to the standards setters regulating the audit profession, academicians designing university courses and audit practitioners evaluating their own IT knowledge. The findings can be used to gauge the relevant IT in the specific context of audit work and also the IT knowledge level of the auditors not just in Malaysia but also other developing countries.

Keywords: Auditors, auditing, external auditing, information systems auditing, developing economies.

INTRODUCTION

Competence in information technology (IT) is crucial for the professional accountants due to its pervasive use in the business world (IFAC, 2001). Today, almost every aspect of the accounting profession is being pervasively affected by advances in IT (Elliot, 2002). The extent, mode and quality of IT adoption in most enterprises have becoming more sophisticated and complicated, hence introduces new challenges and risks to the professional accountants (Scapens and Jazayeri, 2003).

The integrated nature of Enterprise Resource Planning System (ERPS), for example, has not only changed the traditional role of accountants (Scapens and Jazayeri, 2003; Caglio, 2003) but has substantial impact on the internal controls of the adopting companies (Sayana, 2004). Undoubtedly, in the light of large scale business failure such as Enron, MCI-WorldCom and Parmalat, one of the most critical roles is auditing. To be effective, auditors need to embed technology in everything they do during the audit process, similar to the practices of their clients (Winograd et al., 2000; Janvrin et al., 2008).

The increasing dependence of businesses on computerized information systems such as ERPS and e-business requires external auditors to evaluate the reliability of computer generated data supporting financial statements and analyze specific programs and their outcomes (Abu-Musa, 2004). This is important as audit judgment influences the quality and effectiveness of audit (Bonner, 1999), while decisions tools may influence audit judgment (Janvrin et al., 2008). Hence, to effectively audit on-line systems, auditors need to incorporate on-line audit software as their primary audit tool and gather evidence electronically (Bierstaker et al., 2001).

Auditors will no longer able to perform audit around the computer but to use new technology to gain audit efficiency and effectiveness. In addition, IT auditors need to examine the adequacy of controls in information systems and related operations to ensure systems effectiveness (Zhao and Yen, 2004). Therefore, auditors would normally be expected to have higher level of IT knowledge and skills than the average accountants since

*Corresponding author. azizi833@uum.edu.my.

they must audit the work of many different clients with diverse information systems (Greenstein-Prosch et al., 2005).

Despite auditors' IT knowledge is required by the professional standards, comprehensive reviews of audit literature indicate that very few studies have examined the use and perceive importance of IT among the auditors (Janvrin et al., 2008) especially those in developing economies like Malaysia. The possible reason is that companies in most developing countries use less complicated IT systems (Sanggaran, 2001), thus IT audit is viewed as less relevant by auditors in those countries. Even results from prior research studies of external auditors in the Western countries like Norway, German and United States (e.g. McKee, 2000; Greenstein-Prosch and McKee, 2004; Greenstein-Prosch et al., 2005) indicated a relatively low level of IT knowledge.

McKee's (2000) study was the earliest that investigated IT knowledge among auditors in Norway. Extending McKee's (2000) study, Greenstein-Prosch and McKee (2004) investigated appropriate ITs for auditing professors and audit practitioners and their self-perceived knowledge of these technologies. In another study, Greenstein-Prosch et al. (2005) compared the level of IT knowledge among auditors in Germany and United States. More recently, Janvrin et al. (2008) examined perceived importance and use of IT audit across a diverse group of audit firms in the United States and found extensive use of variety of audit applications among the auditors.

Applying the theory of task-technology fit (Goodhue and Thompson, 1995), this study extends Greenstein-Prosch et al. (2005) and Janvrin et al.'s studies by exploring not only the level of IT knowledge but also the auditors' perception toward the importance of the technologies. More specifically, this study attempts to achieve three objectives: first, to examine the knowledge level of IT audit applications; second, to examine the auditors' perception toward the importance of the technologies and finally, to examine the fit between knowledge possessed by auditors and the relevance of IT audit applications in the context of auditors' work in Malaysia.

Finding from this study is important as it would extend the existing literature on auditors' ITs knowledge levels. In addition to the auditors' knowledge level, this study would identify the auditors' perception towards the importance of recent ITs in their audit works in the specific context of Malaysia. This is important as IT sophistication levels are different in different countries.

Therefore, findings from studies in advanced countries might not be applicable in the context of developing economies like Malaysia. For example, Sangaran (2001) found the sophistication of IT adoption among businesses in Malaysia is still lagging of those in developed countries. Therefore, it is expected that the level of IT audit practices is also lower in Malaysia compared to those countries. This argument is in tandem with the task-technology fit theory which postulates that IT is more likely to have a positive impact on individual performance and be used if the capabilities of the IT match the task that the user must perform (Goodhue and Thompson, 1995).

The remainder of the paper is organized as follows. The next section reviews literature relating to the impact of IT on the accounting and audit profession. Next, the paper discusses the methodology and presents the results of the study. Finally, the paper provides a brief conclusion of the study, discusses its limitations and offers important implications for future research.

Literature review

The IFAC Education Committee (2001) has stated that "information technology is pervasive in the world of business. Competence with this technology is imperative for the professional accountant" (p. 6). Chang and Hwang (2003), however, questioned whether professional accountants including auditors are competence in IT. They argued that "given the dynamic nature of IT and its widespread adoption in business organizations, many in the accounting profession have voiced concerns over whether college education and professional training effectively and efficiently prepare accountants to meet these challenges" (p. 441). Their concern is supported by Chen's (2005) study which revealed that accountants in Taiwan, on average, are proficient with the general computer and the professional accounting software skills. Despite this encouraging result, Chen (2005) argued that accountants' capability in performing managerial, advisory and evaluative roles of IT deployment is still an issue of great concern. These arguments raised the issue of the perceived value of various IT knowledge and skills by audit practitioners (Greenstein-Prosch and McKee, 2004; Hall, 2004).

According to IFAC (2001), the accounting profession performs many roles where IT is used. First, as user of information systems, accountants must be able to clearly convey their needs to the IT professionals who design the system. Being information-oriented professionals, accountants should actively participate in systems development projects to ensure appropriate systems design. Second, as designer of information systems, accountants are responsible for the conceptual system which determines the nature of the information required, its sources, its destination and the accounting rules that must be applied. Third, as manager of information systems, accountants must be able to perform appropriate analyses of IT investments, understand IT related benefits and risks and stimulate and manage organizational change. Finally, as auditor of information systems, the role of accountants encompasses the function of internal audit, external audit and other evaluative roles. Greenstein-

Prosch et al. (2005) suggested that "IT knowledge requirements for independent auditors are higher than average accountant since they typically serve a wide variety of clients" (p. 4).

The rapid growth of technology and the use of computers in business result in more IT auditing and internal control standards and guidelines to assist auditors in their roles and responsibilities. IT audit can be defined as the process of collecting and evaluating evidence to determine whether a computer system has been designed to maintain data integrity, safeguard assets, allows organizational goals to be achieved effectively and uses resources efficiently (Yang and Guan, 2004).

Several organizations such as the American Institute of Certified Public Accountants (AICPA), the Information Systems Audit and Control Association (ISACA) and the IFAC have issued standards in this area to be observed by their members in performing an IT audit. SISA 040: Competence issued by ISACA (1997), for example, requires information systems auditor to be technically competent, having the skills and knowledge necessary to perform the auditor's work. It also requires that the auditor maintains technical competence through appropriate continuing professional education.

The AICPA, in addition to issuing several standards for IT-related auditing, also publishes Top 10 Technologies list annually to build member awareness about important and emerging technologies that will contribute to the profession. Auditor knowledge levels are clearly specified in the International Standard on Auditing (ISA) 401, paragraph 4, (IFAC, 1999) which states that the auditors should have sufficient knowledge of the computer information system (CIS) to plan, direct, supervise and review the work performed.

Auditors need, among others, obtain sufficient understanding of the accounting and internal control systems affected by the CIS environment; determine the effect of the CIS environment on the assessment of overall risk and of risk at the account balance and class of transaction level; design and perform appropriate tests of control and substantive procedures and if specialized skills are needed, the auditor would seek the assistance of a professional possessing such skills, who may either on the auditor's staff or an outside professional. If the use of such a professional is planned, the auditor should obtain sufficient appropriate audit evidence that such work is adequate for the purposes of the audit, in accordance with ISA "Using the Work of an Expert". In the Malaysian context, the same standard applies since the Malaysian Institute of Accountants (MIA) has determined to adopt the ISA as the basis for approved standards on auditing.

Reviews of literature indicated that several studies have attempted to investigate the gap between the desired and the actual level of IT knowledge among auditors. Lymer and Debrecency (2003), for example, discussed issues about the role of auditors in providing assurance on corporate reporting via the Internet. They find gaps between IT utilization and professional responses and conclude that, "...the actual pronouncements made thus far by the various bodies around the world fall considerably short as a response to the challenges that arise from current and future Internet reporting technologies" (p. 103). Chen, Tseng and Chang (2005) found that only half of the accounting firms in Taiwan used the Internet in business-related activities. They argued that, if the firms do not implement the internet, while the firms' clients have transmitted their data through Internet to the firm, then the auditors' ability to assist clients in enhancing added value is questionable.

McKee's (2000) study is probably the earliest that investigate IT knowledge among auditors when he surveyed Norwegian practicing auditing profession during the late 1998 and early 1999. Major findings from this survey include: a large number of professionals indicated either no knowledge or relatively low levels of knowledge for the 25 technologies surveyed; 71% of the respondents believed they had received less than adequate coverage of ITs in their college or university careers; 17.3% of the respondents self-rated their overall knowledge of IT as either low or very low and "Big 5" audit firm respondents self-rated their overall knowledge of IT higher than did other respondents.

Greenstein-Prosch and McKee (2004) extended McKee's (2000) study by investigating appropriate ITs for auditing professors and audit practitioners and their self-perceived knowledge of these technologies. The study found a relatively low level of knowledge for e-commerce and advanced technologies and audit automation by both educators and practitioners. The study, however, found a relatively high level of knowledge for office automation and accounting firm office automation constructs.

Greenstein-Porsch et al. (2005) conducted a survey similar to McKee (2000) and Greenstein-Porsch and McKee (2004) but among the German and United States auditors during 2000 - 2001. Their study revealed a relatively low level of knowledge for the general constructs of e-commerce, systems design and implementation and audit automation technologies for both German and US auditors. The knowledge of German auditors were found to be higher for e-commerce technologies than US auditors, while the knowledge of US auditors were found to be higher for systems design and implementation and office automation technologies than German auditors. Importantly, the study revealed that more than one-fourth of the respondents in both countries rated their overall IT knowledge as "less than adequate".

Interestingly, results from a more recent study by Janvrin et al. (2008) revealed that auditors in the United States extensively use a variety of audit applications such as analytical procedures and electronic working papers. However, while auditors perceive several sophisticated audit applications as important, they use them infrequently.

The above discussions suggest that the audit profession is having a problem adjusting to the rapidly changing technology landscape. Thus, it is interesting to investigate whether the level of IT knowledge and usage among auditors found in the Western countries is also applicable here. The auditing profession in Malaysia and other developing countries with similar characteristics can benefit by identifying relevant technologies and conducting self-assessment to learn how knowledgeable its members are about these technologies.

METHODS

A questionnaire survey was undertaken to gather data relating to this research. However, prior to the actual survey, the questionnaire was pre-tested with 10 audit and accounting information systems lecturers and 10 practicing auditors. The main purpose of the test is to achieve more clarification regarding the wording of both questionnaire instructions and questions (Oppenheim, 1992).

A total of 100 firms were then randomly selected for the pilot survey. A total of 9 questionnaires were returned after duration of about one month. This represents a response rate of 9% since no reminders had been issued, this return rate was considered sufficient to continue with the main survey. However, no alterations were made to the questionnaire since the overall impression from the answers given by the 9 respondents was that the questionnaire was satisfactory.

The questionnaires were finally delivered to the partner of 1110 audit firms listed in Malaysia Institute of Accountants (MIA) Member Firms Directory during October to December 2007. Of the 1110 questionnaires distributed, 20 were returned unopened, stamped on the envelope 'addressee has moved' or 'ceased operation'. Following Churchill's (1999) suggestions, these 20 questionnaires were excluded from the calculation of the response rate.

After duration of about three months and two reminders including random phone calls, 95 usable questionnaires were returned, representing about 8.7% response rate. While the percentage is considered low which would affect generalization of the findings, it is still reasonable in the context of Malaysia. According to PricewaterhouseCoopers (2002), the average response rate to postal surveys in Malaysia is about 16% and much less for audit firms. For example, Md Salleh et al. (2002) study on the state of IT consulting services among audit firms in Malaysia received quite a response rate of 9%.

Definition and categories of IT

The IFAC defines IT as: "...hardware and software products, information systems operations and management processes, and the human resources and skills required to apply those products and processes to the tasks of information production and information systems development, management and control" (IFAC, 2001, p. 9). McKee (2000) argued that the definition is too broad as it includes "human resources and skills" in addition to "hardware and software" products (McKee, 2000). Chang and Hwang (2003) also raised about the difficulty in assembling a complete list of IT topics that are important to accounting professionals due to the dynamic nature and broad spectrum of IT.

Following McKee (2000), Greenstein-Prosch and McKee (2004), Greenstein-Prosch et al. (2005) and Janvrin et al. (2008) this study narrows the IT definition by focusing only on the hardware and software products. The instrument for this study is adapted from prior researches such as Greenstein-Prosch et al. (2005) and Janvrin et al. (2008). In addition, a literature search which includes the latest IFAC and AICPA publications was also carried out to ensure that all latest technologies relevant to accountants are included in the questionnaire. The original lists comprise of 40 technologies but reduced to 35 technologies after it was pre-tested with academicians and practitioners. These 35 technologies were grouped into five categories: general office automation, accounting firm office automation, audit automation, e-commerce tecnologies and system design and implementation.

DEMOGRAPHIC RESULTS

Table 1 indicates that about 91% of the respondents are working with the national or local audit firms, while the remaining 9% are working with the big-four firms. Seventy-three percent of firms are located in the central region. The results in Table 2 shows that only 16% of the responding firms provide information systems audit and assurance services, while Table 3 indicates that only 21% use generalized audit software. Similar to the results of prior studies conducted in developed countries such as McKee (2000), Greenstein and McKee (2004), Greenstein et al. (2005) and Janvrin et al. (2008), results of this study also suggest that information system audit among audit firms in Malaysia is still at the minimum level.

The results in Table 4 exhibit the profile of respondents. While the questionnaires were originally addressed to the firms' partners, only 55% of the respondents are partners. When asked their age range, about 82% of the respondents stated that they are in the category of 30 years old and above. The respondents were also asked to indicate the audit experience. Results show that the respondents' experience ranges from 1 to 37 years, with a mean experience level of 14 years. The demographic data suggest that the responding auditors are quite experienced in their career, thus are able to give meaningful answers to the questions.

Importance and knowledge of information technology

To identify relevant IT in the context of audit work in Malaysia, the first part of the questionnaire asked respondents to rank their perception toward the importance of 35 technologies in the context of their audit work on a 1 to 4 scale, where 1 = not important and 4 = very important. The questionnaire then asked respondents to rank their own knowledge of the same 35 technologies on a 1 to 4 scale, where 1 = very little knowledge and 4 = expert knowledge. The mean value of the responses for each category of the 35 technologies is shown in Table 5 below.

The results in Table 5 show that the mean value of the perception of the importance of technology items ranges from 2.01 to 3.84. Twelve technologies received a mean value of 3.00 and above, thus can be considered as relevant in the context of audit work in Malaysia. The technologies are word-processing, electronic spreadsheet, email, electronic search and retrieval, electronic working papers, small business accounting software, tax

Table 1. Category of Firms.

Category	Frequency	Percent
Big four and its affiliates	9	9.5
Non big four	86	90.5
Total	95	100

Table 2. Services provided.

Services	Frequency	Percent
Audit	95	100
Tax advisory	81	86.3
Business advisory	52	54.7
Financial advisory	45	47.4
Information systems audit and assurance	15	15.8
Others	18	18.9

Table 3. Types of technology used.

Technology	Frequency	Percent
Accounting-based application	86	90.5
Office support system	84	88.4
Local area network	78	82.1
Decision support system	75	78.9
Database system	54	56.8
Generalized audit software	20	21.1
External network	52	54.7

Table 4. Profile of respondents.

Position	Frequency	Percent
Partner	51	55.4
Audit manager	14	15.2
Senior auditor	19	9.8
Auditor	16	17.4
Audit trainee	2	2.2
Total	94	100
Age range	**Frequency**	**Percent**
20 – 29	17	18.3
30 – 39	36	38.7
40 – 49	23	24.7
50 and above	17	18.3
Total	93	100
Location	**Frequency**	**Percent**
Central region	69	73.4
Southern region	16	17.0
Northern region	8	8.5
Eastern region	1	1.1
Total	94	100

return preparation software, time management and billing

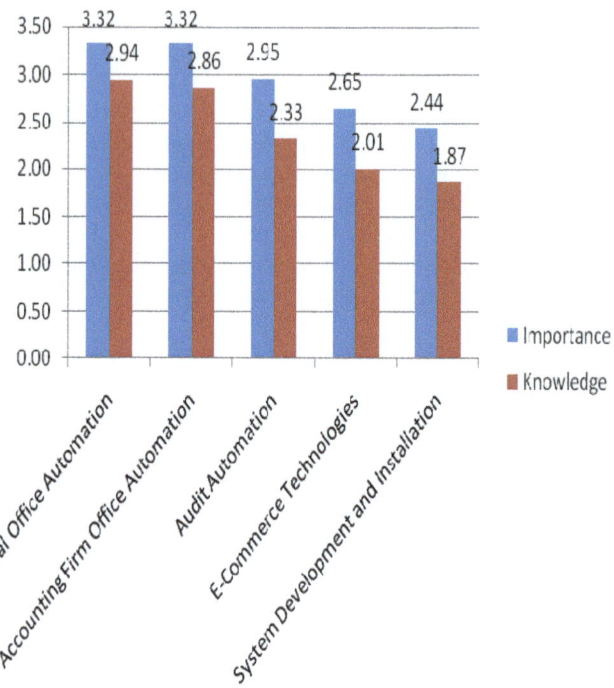

Figure 1. Average mean value of importance and knowledge for each category of technologies.

systems, image processing, generalized audit software, firewall hardware/software and external network configurations.

In terms of knowledge, the results in Table 5 show the mean value for the self-perceived IT knowledge items ranges from 1.35 to 3.49, which is lower than the mean value range for their perception towards the importance of IT (2.01 to 3.84). This suggests that the responding auditors perceived their IT knowledge are less than what they perceived as important in their audit work. Only five technologies received a mean value of 3.00 and above, thus can be considered as knowledgeable by the responding auditors. The technologies are word-processing, email, electronic spreadsheet, electronic search and retrieval and small business accounting software.

Figure 1 below summarizes the average mean value for each category of technologies. General Office Automation receives the highest mean value for both importance and knowledge of technology, whilst system development and installation receives the lowest mean value for both importance and knowledge of technology.

The alignment between IT importance and IT knowledge

The previous discussion explored IT importance and IT knowledge without employing a specific analytical scheme of measuring alignment. This section describes the matching approach for measuring AIS alignment. According to Venkatraman (1989), one of the analytical

Table 5. Mean ratings and rankings of importance and knowledge of IT.

Category/Technology	Importance		Knowledge		Matching
	Mean	Rank	Mean	Rank	Mean
General office automation:					
Word processing	3.84	1	3.49	1	0.35
Electronic spreadsheets	3.75	2	3.29	3	0.46
E-Mail	3.66	3	3.46	2	0.46
Internet search and retrieval	3.55	4	3.26	4	0.22
Image processing	3.05	9	2.68	8	0.77
Electronic presentations	2.84	16	2.49	9	0.58
Groupware	2.58	24	1.93	24	0.71
Accounting firm office automation:					
Small business accounting software	3.47	6	3.17	5	0.49
Tax return preparation software	3.41	7	2.93	7	0.54
Time management and billing systems	3.08	8	2.49	9	0.86
Audit Automation:					
Electronic Working Papers	3.52	5	2.98	6	0.34
Generalized Audit Software	3.05	9	2.42	11	0.78
Embedded Audit Modules/Real-time audit modules	2.64	21	1.95	22	0.43
Expert systems	2.59	23	1.96	21	0.63
E-Commerce Technologies:					
Firewall software/hardware	3.02	11	2.31	14	0.74
External network configurations	3.00	12	2.41	12	0.78
User authentication systems	2.98	13	2.21	16	0.62
Internal network configurations	2.87	14	2.18	18	0.64
Intrusion detection and monitoring	2.86	15	1.95	22	0.64
Wireless communications	2.76	17	2.36	13	0.66
Digital communications	2.74	18	2.24	15	0.74
Encryption software	2.39	28	1.68	32	0.84
EDI-traditional	2.33	30	1.82	27	0.82
Agent technologies	2.14	33	1.59	33	0.73
EDI-web based	2.01	35	1.35	35	0.64
Systems Design and Implementation:					
Cooperative client/server environment	2.74	18	2.21	16	0.68
Test data	2.73	20	2.05	19	0.75
Database search and retrieval	2.62	22	2.05	19	0.62
Flowcharting/data modeling	2.44	25	1.90	25	0.69
Enterprise resource planning	2.43	26	1.77	30	0.58
Simulation software	2.41	27	1.73	31	0.66
Workflow technology	2.34	29	1.86	26	0.82
Database design and installation	2.31	31	1.79	29	0.95
Application service providers	2.30	32	1.80	28	0.76
Case tools	2.09	34	1.49	34	0.80

schemes that can be used for the matching perspective is the deviation score analysis. This method is based on a premise that the absolute difference between the standardized scores of two variables indicates a lack of fit.

For the purpose of this study, the deviation score analysis is adopted and the measure of alignment is computed as the absolute difference between the rating for IT importance and the rating for IT knowledge. A low value for the difference indicates that the alignment between the two variables is high, while a high value for the difference implies that there is a high degree of misalignment. The mean difference for each type of technology is calculated by summing up the absolute difference for all responses and divided by the number of responses. A mathematical representation of the above is as follow:

Mean Difference = Σ ABS (IT importance rating – IT knowledge rating) / N

The results for all 35 technologies are presented in column 6 Table 5. A low mean indicates that there is a high degree of alignment between the paired IT importance-IT knowledge items. From Table 5, it appears that Internet search and retrieval, electronic working papers, word-processing, embedded audit modules/real-time audit modules, electronic spreadsheets, email and small business accounting software are most aligned with IT knowledge for the responding auditors. The greatest mismatch is observed for more advanced technologies such as database design and installation, time management and billing systems, encryption software, EDI-traditional, workflow technology and CASE tools.

Finally, the respondents were asked to rate, based on a five-point scale, their current overall knowledge of IT and their perception toward current practice of information systems audit in Malaysia. The results indicate that the responding auditors perceived their overall IT knowledge as adequate (mean = 3.04), while the current practice of information systems audit is less than adequate (mean = 2.74).

Conclusions, Limitations and Future Research

This study aims to achieve three objectives. The first objective is to identify relevant technologies from the perspective of external auditors in Malaysia. Twelve technologies are rated as important by the responding auditors, thus considered relevant in the specific context of audit work in Malaysia. It is interesting to note that while only 21% of the participating firms use generalised audit software and only 16% provide information systems audit and assurance services, the responding auditors perceived generalized audit software knowledge as important in their audit work. Twenty-three technologies perceived as less important and thus considered less relevant by the responding auditors are more advanced technologies.

The second objective is to identify the level of IT knowledge among the Malaysian external auditors. The responding auditors considered themselves as having good knowledge of 5 technologies, little knowledge on 15 technologies and very little knowledge on the remaining 15 technologies. The technologies that responding auditors are good at are in the category of General Office Automation and Accounting Firm Office Automation. Most auditors considered themselves as having poor knowledge of more sophisticated technologies especially technologies in the E-Commerce and Systems Design and Installation categories.

The less complicated information systems adopted by Malaysian companies and thus less demand for external auditors to acquire the knowledge might also explain the finding. However, considering that many companies are moving toward digital transactions, lack of auditors' knowledge on audit automation and e-commerce technologies such as encryption software, intrusion detection and monitoring and embedded audit modules and real-time audit modules skills may affect the reliability of audit works. Despite this, it is interesting to note that the low level of advanced technologies' knowledge among the responding Malaysian auditors is consistent with those found in other studies like McKee (2000), Greenstein and McKee (2004), Greenstein et al. (2005) and Janvrin et al. (2008).

The third objective is to examine the fit between IT importance and IT knowledge among the Malaysian external auditors. A comparison between the mean value of the perceived importance of technologies and their respective knowledge indicate that IT knowledge items always received a lower mean rating than the IT importance items. The findings suggest a lack of alignment between what the responding auditors perceived as important and their knowledge of the technologies.

To further explain the findings, a matching technique was used to examine the alignment between the importance of ITs and the actual levels of knowledge possessed by the responding auditors regarding these technologies. With the exception of embedded audit modules and real-time audit modules, the results suggest that the most aligned technologies are common technologies like Internet, email, electronic working papers, word-processing, spreadsheets and small business accounting software.

The greatest mismatch between ITs importance and knowledge items among the responding auditors are observed for more advanced technologies like database design and installation, encryption software, EDI-traditional, workflow technology and CASE tools. It can be concluded from the findings that while more advanced technologies are deemed as less important in the context of audit work in Malaysia by the responding auditors, their knowledge regarding the technologies is much less.

In a nutshell, an important contribution of this study is that the findings would initiate discussion, debate and action that will lead to positive changes in the Malaysian auditing profession and other developing countries as they move forward in today's technology-intensified environment. It is hoped that the survey results will help not only the practitioner but also academicians to focus on the development on necessary IT skills of accounting graduates. Considering the effort of Malaysian government to speed up the development of the country's IT infrastructure, it is also expected that Malaysian companies would also adopt more sophisicated information systems especially among large companies. Therefore, Malaysian Institute of Accountants (MIA) must introduce a policy which requires auditors to possess a minimum set of knowledge and skills to audit computerized accounting systems.

As is common with all types of research, this study has few limitations that may limit the validity of its results. One possible limitation of survey research is non-response bias, especially one with low response rate such as this study. This occurs when the perception of persons not responding to the questionnaire are significantly different from those individuals who responded (Greenstein-Porsch and McKee, 2004). Since a comparison between respondents and non-respondents is not possible, the alternative solution is to compare early versus late respondents (Lindner et al., 2001).

In this case, t-test is conducted comparing early (first 30 respondents) versus late respondents (last 30 respondents) for each of the 35 technologies for both IT importance and IT knowledge. The results indicate that only 3 of the 70 items had response differences that were statistically significant at the 0.05 level. The nonresponse bias for this survey can be considered mild and not to be significantly affect the results of the survey (Ismail and King, 2005).

Second, the 35 technologies examined in this research were mostly adopted from previous studies. Therefore, some equally significant technologies may have been inadvertently overlooked in the literature and thus are not included in this research. Finally, it is important to note about the respondents' self-reported views about their perception toward ITs. They may hold incorrect views about their perception of the importance and knowledge of these technologies, hence their actual knowledge may be higher or lower than what was reported.

Furthermore, future research could examine how audit complexity and decision-making activities impact the use of IT audit applications. Despite these limitations, this study is the first that provides important insights about auditors' perception toward the level of importance and knowledge of IT in the specific context of audit work in Malaysia. The findings of this study could also benefit and can be used as a benchmark by audit and accounting profession in other developing countries especially those with similar IT development.

REFERENCES

Abu-Musa AA (2004). "Auditing e-business: New challenges for external auditors" J. Am. Acad. Bus. 4(1/2): 28-42.

Bierstaker JL, Burnaby P, Thibodeau J (2001), "The impact of information technology on the audit process: An assessment of the state of the art and implications for the future", Manage. Audit. J. 16(3): 159-164.

Bonner SE (1999). Judgment and decision making research in accounting, Account. Horiz. 13: 385-398.

Caglio A (2003). "Enterprise Resource Planning systems and accountants: towards hybridization?" Eur. Account. Rev. 12(1): 23-153.

Chang CJ, Hwang NR (2003). „Accounting education, firm training and information technology: A research note", Account. Educ. 12(12): 441-450.

Chen M, Tseng CY, Chang J (2005). "A survey investigation into the use of the Internet among accounting firms", Int. J. Manage. 22(4): 649-660.

Chen YF (2005). "Prepare for e-generation: The fundamental computer skills of accountants in Taiwan", J. Am. Acad. Bus. 7(1): 131-135.

Churchill Jr. GA (1999). Marketing Research: Methodological Foundations, 7th Ed., London: Harcourt College Publishers.

Elliot RK (2002). "Twenty-first century assurance", Auditing: J. Pract. Theor. 21(1): 139-148.

Goodhue DL, Thompson RL (1995). "Task-technology fit and individual performance", MIS Q. 19(2): 213-236.

Greenstein-Prosch M, McKee TE (2004). "Assurance practitioners' and educators' self perceived IT knowledge level: An empirical assessment", Int. J. Account. Info. Syst. 5: 213-243.

Greenstein-Prosch M, McKee TE, Quick R (2005). "A comparison of the information technology knowledge of United States and German auditors", paper presented at the 8th European Conference on Accounting Information Systems, Goteborg, Sweden.

Hall JA (2004). Accounting Information Systems, 4th ed. Singapore: Thomson South-Western.

International Federation of Accountants (IFAC) (1999). "ISA 401: Auditing in a Computer Information Systems Environment", available at www.elearning.strathmore.edu/.../Auditing_in_a_computerised_Environment.pdf (accessed 20 February 2007).

International Federation of Accountants (IFAC) (2001). "Information technology in the accounting curriculum", IFAC Education Committee Guideline 11, available at www.ifac.org/store/Details.tmpl?SID=303859141967 (accessed 1 March 2007).

International Federation of Accountants Education Committee (IFAC) (2001). "Information Technology for Professional Accountants", available at https://www.imanet.org/pdf/ITPA.pdf (accessed 2 February 2007).

ISACA (1997). "Standards for Information Systems Auditing 040: Competence", Rolling Meadows, IL.

Ismail NA, King M (2005). "Firm Performance and AIS Alignment in Malaysian SMEs", Int. J. Account. Info. Syst. 6(4): 241-259.

Janvrin D, Bierstaker J, Lowe DJ (2008). An examination of audit information technology use and perceived importance, Account. Horiz. 22(1): 1 – 21.

Lindner JR, Murphy TH, Briers GE (2001). "Handling nonresponse in social science research", J. Agric. Educ. 42(4): 43-53.

Lymer A, Debrecency R (2003). "The auditor and corporate reporting on the Internet: Challenges and institutional responses", Int. J. Audit. 7: 103-120.

McKee TE (2000) "Accounting/auditing technology in Norway: An investigation of the Norwegian accounting/auditing professional knowledge and views on information technologies", Norwegian Institute of Public Accountants (DnR), Oslo, Norway.

Md Salleh MS, Ismail NA, Ibrahim MA (2002). The State of IT Consulting Services among Local Audit Firms in Malaysia, Working Paper Series No. 52, College of Business, Universiti Utara Malaysia.

Oppenheim AN (1992). Questionnaire Design, Interviewing and Attitude Measurement, New Ed. London: Printer Publishers.

PricewaterhouseCoopers. (2002). Market Readiness for Disclosure-Based Regulation, Highlights from survey on the readiness for the Malaysian Market Capital participants for DBR. Kuala Lumpur: Securities Commission.

Sangaran S (2001). "ICT adoption to ensure competitiveness of SMIs", Computimes Malaysia June, p. 1.

Sayana SA (2004). "Auditing security and privacy in ERP applications", available at http://www.isaca.org/Content/NavigationMenu/Students_and_Educators/IT_Audit_Basics/IT_Audit_Basics_Auditing_Security_and_Privacy_in_ERP_Applications.htm (accessed 12 July 2007).

Scapens RW, Jazayeri M (2003). "ERP systems and management accounting change: opportunities or impacts? A research note", Eur. Account. Rev. 12(1): 201-233.

Venkatraman N (1989). "The concept of fit in strategy research: Toward verbal and statistical correspondence", Acad. Manage. Rev. 14(3): 423-444.

Winograd BN, Gerson JS, Berlin BL (2000). "Audit practices of Pricewaterhouse Coopers", Auditing: J. Pract Theor. 19(2): 175-182.

Yang DC, Guan L (2004). "The evolution of IT auditing and internal control standards in financial statements audits", Manage. Audit. J. 19(4): 544-555.

Zhao V, Yen DC (2004). "Auditing in the e-commerce era", Information Manage. Comput. Secur. 12(5): 389-400.

The relative informativeness of GAAP and *pro forma* earnings announcements in France

Francois Aubert

Faculté des Sciences Économiques et de Gestion, Université d'Auvergne Clermont 1, B. P. 54, 41 Bd. Francois Mitterrand, 63002 Clermont-Ferrand Cedex, France. E-mail: francois.aubert@u-clermont1.fr.

This paper addresses the main problem raised by *pro forma* (or "street") earnings. The aim is to help investors find their focus as they rely on *pro forma* earnings figures to make decisions on investing in French publicly-traded securities. We study 116 *pro forma* earnings announcements made over the period 1996 - 2006 to investigate why French traded corporations use *pro forma* reporting in their annual earnings announcement press releases. Interestingly, the study finds that managers use *pro forma* earnings numbers strategically to report better corporate performance than numbers based on GAAP earnings metrics. In 79% of the cases we identified, *pro forma* numbers are higher than GAAP numbers, suggesting that managers have significant motives for reporting a profit that would be higher than under GAAP-based numbers and higher than in analysts' forecasts. Furthermore, about 82% of *pro forma* announcements should have disclosed bad news that would have been revealed by releasing GAAP earnings. Finally, we show that *pro forma* numbers are much more informative than GAAP earnings.

Key words: *Pro forma* reporting, street earnings, non-GAAP earnings, abnormal stock returns, analysts' forecasts, discretionary earnings, informative content.

INTRODUCTION

In recent years, corporate earnings statements have provided the financial community with obscure and discretionary definitions of earnings metrics called *pro forma* earnings or *street* earnings, collectively referred to as 'non-GAAP (for 'non-generally accepted accounting principles') earnings. Indeed, managements are increasingly turning to reports of a distinctive measure of corporate profitability made up of such ad-hoc metrics, which are un-audited financial measures that do not comply with domestic or international GAAP but which capital market regulators (including the American SEC and the French AMF) claim are accepted definitions for financial reporting purposes. *Pro forma* earnings refer to non-GAAP figures as "street earnings," "core earnings," "adjusted earnings," "recurring earnings," or "ongoing earnings" [1]. All these alternative *ad hoc* earnings definitions systematically exclude nonrecurring, extra-ordinary, non-cash items and other expenses such as goodwill amortization or tax expenses [2]. Critics assume

1. 'Street' earnings, 'pro forma' earnings or 'non-GAAP' earnings measures share a great deal of overlap. All three terms are used at different points to qualify the phenomena of heterodox announcements resulting from discretionary releasing of ad hoc earnings undefined by any financial reporting standards or regulations. For instance, the proof of this phenomenon is that all of the basic EPS forecasted by any brokers included in the Factset/JCF consensus are based upon the criterion of EPS before goodwill amortization. Furthermore, the "convergence consensus" issued afterwards cancels out the impact of some accounting methods at the time the earnings are calculated, as financial analysts need to use their own calculus to revise their forecasts. The I/B/E/S database also provides users with 'adjusted' forecasts.

2. For instance, Vivendi Universal has been announcing its annual earnings on a pro forma basis for a few years. The corporation then reconciles its pro forma and GAAP earnings in their financial statements. Its pro forma earnings measures, called 'adjusted net income, group share', are systematically higher than earnings computed under GAAP (i.e., 'net income, group share'). The most astonishing point is the type of items excluded. The reconciliation statement included in the annual report conspicuously excluded important operational and economic expenses such as 'non-recurring expenses', 'gains/losses on disposals', 'financial provisions' and even 'goodwill amortization and income tax'.

that pro forma numbers are '*fantasy*' ad hoc figures, self-serving to managers and misleading to financial investors. Consequently, *pro forma* figures may trigger unorthodox investor decisions, as they can skew users' perceptions of a firm's current financial status. However, while the GAAP earnings system is deemed good, it also carries a number of disadvantages in that it includes extraordinary, nonrecurring items that are transitory in nature - a feature that hampers assessments of future earnings.

This article investigates the effectiveness of *pro forma* (that is, 'street') earnings released by French listed companies compared with earnings calculated by applying local GAAP standards [3]. Alternatively, the question of whether or not companies report non-GAAP numbers in order to sway investors' perceptions has prompted investigations from both regulatory bodies and researchers, notably to determine whether publicly-held companies may be using *pro forma* numbers to mislead investors. The main issue is that *pro forma* earnings prevent a useful comparison of profits on a fiscal year-by year basis (Grant and Parker, 2001), and instead aim to beat market expectations, above all when earnings levels are low (Doyle and Soliman, 2002; Lougee and Marquardt, 2004). If managements are voluntarily announcing *pro forma* results, then it is imperative to prevent investors from suffering or share prices from being driven up. Conversely, if *pro forma* disclosure is not being used extensively or to misinform, then there is little justification for further regulation. Obviously, earnings disclosures participate in enhancing the function of capital markets. Efficient markets are built on earnings statements that are informative, that is, both relevant and credible. Furthermore, earnings must be financially standardized in order for investors to trust in the comparability of information across industries and fiscal-years, and in the financial condition and results of operations of the issuer under GAAP. Market authorities therefore require listed organizations to reconcile *pro forma* earnings numbers with operating and net income figures calculated in application of GAAP, and to provide these GAAP figures for auditing by statutory auditors.

Responding to these assertions, this article contributes to recent literature documenting the increasing differences between GAAP-defined earnings and strategically-defined 'alternative' profits numbers by examining the French context. Our empirical results provide several interesting insights. First, we show that *pro forma* earnings report significantly higher abnormal equity returns than earnings prepared in accordance with French GAAP, thus documenting how investors over-react to *pro forma* announcements. Furthermore, we find that *pro forma* earnings announcements enable French corporations to opportunistically inflate positive *pro forma* forecast error and downplay negative reported *pro forma* forecast error. This results in (1) cosmetically enhancing the economic performance of the firm. Indeed, over 82% of the *pro forma* reports would have reported negative news if they had regularly released their GAAP earnings (*versus* 45.97% of GAAP reporters)[4]. We provide strong evidence that *pro forma* reporting enables firms to exceed analysts' forecasts, while GAAP-based earning metrics do not permit to meet these expectations. Consistent with findings by Entwistle et al. (2005), 79% of *pro forma* statements report a *pro forma* income superior to GAAP-based income (2) enabling them to report surprise positive earnings instead of releasing bad news. In addition, we find that *pro forma* users report a GAAP-based loss more frequently than GAAP reporters (10.6% vs. 9.3%). (3) In contrast, on a *pro forma* basis, earnings announcements reduce the percentage of losses to only 5.4%. This prompts the conclusion that firms use 'street' earnings announcements to transform GAAP losses into *pro forma* profits. Finally, *pro forma* announcements generate higher abnormal daily returns than GAAP earnings announcements. Also, when regressing CAR (centered on a three-day-window) on forecast error in GAAP and *pro forma* earnings (that is, earnings surprises), empirical results suggest that *pro forma* figures are more informative and more relevant than GAAP earnings because they reveal a positive association between cumulative abnormal returns and both pro-GAAP and non-GAAP earnings forecast error. These findings provide strong evidence that investors assign more value to *pro forma* numbers for security pricing.

The article is organized as follows. The first section documents previous research in this area and introduces French regulations on corporate *pro forma* announcements. The second section examines the hypotheses, sample design, and data. The third section presents the empirical results. The article ends with concluding remarks.

BACKGROUND

Previous research

In recent years, there has been a wide-reaching debate over whether the intention of managements reporting *pro forma* numbers is to better inform investors or, conversely, to mislead them. These two competitive alternative assumptions are summed up in the *opportunism vs. signaling* hypothesis. Indeed, most empirical investigations have emphasized the manipulative component of *pro forma* reporting, considering that enables corporate managements to play number games in order to prevent investors from fully measuring the firm's performance. On the other hand, *pro forma* reporting is also seen as flagging the need to make financial numbers more relevant (Dumontier, 2003). Empirical studies testing for assumptions of misleadingness or informativeness in *pro forma* disclosure, presentation and classification of financial accounting

3. In terms of establishing consolidated statements, GAAP refer to accounting systems resulting from regulation #CRC 99-02 enacted by the French Accounting Regulator.

4. GAAP reporters refer to other companies belonging to the SBF 250 index, once pro forma adopters are excluded, as a fair benchmark of GAAP reporters.

information have reported mixed evidence. Lougee and Marquardt (2004), Bowen et al. (2005) and Frankel et al. (2008) find evidence of *pro forma* reporting decisions being strategically rather than opportunistically motivated.

Even though the adoption of Sarbanes-Oxley led the SEC to enact specific rules on *pro forma* earnings, managers apparently still enjoy considerable flexibility in presenting *pro forma* results (Entwistle et al., 2004, 2005). For instance, Entwistle, et al. (2004) documents that 77% of all US S&P 500 companies report *pro forma* earnings. In addition, empirical investigations suggest that when *pro forma* earnings are disclosed, they are more likely to be of greater relevance than GAAP earnings numbers because they are more informative. Managers mostly argue that in doing this, they are providing market participants with value-relevant information rather than intentionally trying to manipulate the perceptions of financial statement users. Empirical surveys generally document that *pro forma* earnings are more "permanent" than GAAP earnings, since they are more closely related to stock price and more predictive of future earnings. Nonetheless, the expenses/gains excluded from GAAP earnings are not positively associated with future stock returns. Another motive for disclosing *pro forma* earnings is to provide more profitable performance figures or to artificially create a perception that the company has "met or exceeded" GAAP-based earnings forecasts. Thus, there is evidence that managers exclude small amounts of "non-recurring"/"non-cash" expenses in order to beat earnings analysts' predictions. Conversely, researchers have found that sophisticated investors (that is, analysts) were not disturbed by *pro forma* earnings[5].Bradshaw (2003) and Bhattacharya et al. (2003a) identified earnings announcements in press releases and showed that *pro forma* earnings had a higher informative content than accounting earnings. They observed that companies reporting *pro forma* metrics generally belong to the high-tech sector and announce accounting losses more often.

Furthermore, these *pro forma* earnings are much more informative than operational profits computed in application of local GAAP. Investors consider "street'" earnings a more accurate estimate of true firm performance than earnings calculated in compliance with accounting standards. Given that about 70% of the time, *pro forma* EPS exceed GAAP-reported EPS, the authors concluded that managers strategically highlighted their preferred earnings figures by reporting them first in press releases (87% of 1,149 quarterly *pro forma* press releases). Brow and Sivakumar (2003) and Bradshaw and Sloan (2002) reported similar findings.

Nevertheless, in these circumstances, investors find *pro forma* announcements less informative than accounting announcements, notably when disclosed *pro forma* earnings are above market expectations while GAAP earnings fall below (Ciccone, 2002). However, investors and financial analysts seem more skeptical of *pro forma* announcements that aim to confuse investors' understanding, especially when *pro forma* profits cover up a net loss. Accordingly, a review of 185 quarterly earnings announcements by James et al. (2003) shows that any *pro forma* earnings reported were almost always (88% of the time) higher than GAAP earnings numbers. The net effect of *pro forma* reporting for the 58 companies that made *pro forma* announcements was to increase net earnings by $11.4 billion over GAAP earnings. Furthermore, companies reporting a GAAP loss were more likely to state *pro forma* earnings amounts than companies posting a GAAP profit (40% vs. 27%). There seems to be support for the contention that GAAP losses are often recast as pro forma profits [6]. Pro forma indicators are useful for investors in that they are aware of expenses (or gains) excluded from *pro forma* earnings (Lougee and Marquardt, 2004; Doyle et al., 2003), and markets appear to interpret the release of these profit numbers as bad news.

Johnson and Schwartz (2005) reported that although many companies switched their accounting losses to *pro forma* profits, investors were not subsequently misled by *pro forma* announcements, particularly when a description of expenses or applied principles was excluded. In contrast, Frederickson and Miller (2004) and Bhattacharya et al. (2007) assumed that *pro forma* disclosures affect individual (read: 'less informed') investors more than the better-informed institutions or financial analysts. Individual investors overreact to *pro forma* earnings that are generally more favorable than accounting earnings, while sophisticated investors' responses are based more on other information sources available (Andersson and Hellman, 2007). Firms may alter naïve investors' perceptions in disclosing *pro forma* profits while reporting a net GAAP loss (Elliott, 2006). *Pro forma* announcements mainly seem to involve young companies from high-tech industries that are less profitable. Thus, *pro forma* disclosures are more important for firms for which high debt-to-equity ratios, price-earnings, and book-to-market ratios are important (Bhattacharya et al. 2004). Overall, the frequency of *pro forma* disclosure increases as stock prices decline.

AMF regulations

Accounting regulators, capital market authorities and other critics usually assume that *pro forma* numbers are "fantasy" figures - self-serving to managers and misleading to financial investors (e.g., Derby, 2001; Dreman, 2001; Elstein, 2001; Standard and Poor's, 2002; Federal Reserve Bank of Cleveland, 2003). In the French context, the *Autorité des Marchés Financiers* (AMF)[7] (formerly the COB - *Commission des Opérations de Bourse*) has to ensure that investors are able to clearly understand how 'street' financial numbers differ from income numbers prepared in accordance with GAAP prior to investing in stocks. The AMF has subsequently been adamant that *pro forma* earnings must be systematically reconciled to GAAP metrics in press releases, as presenting *pro forma* earnings without any precise adjustments "would make the presentation of the material non-GAAP measure misleading". Surprisingly, French companies had been reporting *pro forma* earnings in their press releases for years, prompting the AMF to endorse guidelines on which firms are no longer allowed to disclose *pro forma* metrics without presenting a reconciliation statement though a press release occurring one day after the *pro forma* earnings announcements. Despite this guidance, *pro forma* financial information was reported with increasing frequency over the late 1990s. As a result, in June 2002 and September 2005[8], the AMF issued two formal warnings to public companies on the use of non-GAAP reporting. While few restrictions were placed on reporting *pro forma* information, the AMF expressed concern that such information could mislead investors because it departs from well-established French GAAP, making it harder to make comparisons across reporting periods and with other companies. The AMF asserted that this situation stemmed from the 2005 switch to IFRS, which is not well standardized in terms of performance results presentation. Consequently, the AMF announced that

5. This is why most brokers included in consensus adopt different ways of measuring forecasted earnings and provide adjusted aggregated earnings after the announcements, by providing their own reported numbers in application of their specific calculations. They re-calculate their forecasts taking into account the EPS announced.

6. *"This may be due to the fact that in November and December 2001, 41% of companies with a GAAP loss attributed it to the effects of the September 11 terrorist attacks, thereby giving them less incentive to use pro forma reporting to excuse net losses".*

7. The COB (*Commission des Opérations de Bourse*) became the AMF (*Autorité des Marchés Financiers*) after merging with the CMF (*Conseil des Marchés Financiers*).

8 AMF Press release dated September 20, 2005 entitled "Financial reporting of listed firms: the case of earnings announcements" following on from the June 24, 2002 release entitled and "Warning on non-GAAP reporting".

non-GAAP results will be deemed misleading unless the basis of presentation is fully disclosed. The French authority required companies to pay attention to the nature of items omitted from a *pro forma* presentation. While *pro forma* information may be literally correct, *pro forma* disclosure may be misleading if recurring items are omitted without providing explanations of the nature and size of the omissions. Finally, the AMF required that any public press release of non-GAAP financial information should also disclose how it deviates from GAAP, and the amounts involved. The AMF is tasked with implementing these requirements, and if any non-GAAP financial measures not directly reconciled to the most comparable GAAP metrics are published, the AMF immediately requires the company to report the information reconciled to the most comparable GAAP earnings measure[9].

The AMF, in accordance with the International Organization of Securities Commissions (IOSCO)[10], thus enacted corporate disclosure regulations. Accordingly, the AMF requires firms to immediately provide a press release that: (1) does not include any investor-misleading information that does not reconcile to the GAAP earnings, and (2) makes explicit the complete reconciliation between *pro forma* numbers and GAAP metrics if a GAAP-reported figure has been published (recently or in the fiscal year prior to comparison). Other regulatory bodies, including the IOSCO, have required companies to disclose their earnings prepared in accordance with GAAP to ensure that information is comparable across industries.

In comparison, section 401 of the Sarbanes-Oxley Act (SOX) amends the Securities Exchange Act of 1934 by specifying the principle underlying *pro forma* financial information disclosures. It stipulates that "*pro forma* financial information included in any periodic or other report filed with the Commission pursuant to the securities laws, or in any public disclosure or press or other release, shall be presented in a manner that:

(1) Does not contain an untrue statement of a material fact or omit to state a material fact necessary in order to make the *pro forma* financial information, in light of the circumstances under which it is presented, not misleading; and
(2) Reconciles it with the financial condition and results of operations of the issuer under generally accepted accounting principles."

Hypotheses formulated and description of the variables

We sought to investigate research hypotheses in which equity investors were assumed likely to be the main targets of managers' strategic announcements attempting to influence their perceptions of firm performance. We therefore addressed the following questions:

1. How do *pro forma* earnings differ from GAAP numbers?
2. How different are GAAP and *pro forma* earnings in terms of their informativeness to market participants?

We test in this paper whether pro forma disclosures are more informative than GAAP numbers in the French context. If *pro forma* information is really misleading or more useful and informative to investors than GAAP earnings are (Bhattacharya et al., 2003), then *pro forma* earnings surprise would be significantly associated with abnormal stock returns around the announcement date. Thus, we argue:

H1a: Ceteris paribus, positive (negative) GAAP forecast errors are associated with positive (negative) abnormal stock returns.

Under market efficiency, investors are supposed to incorporate misleading information into their response and react in the opposite direction of the manipulation. Then, under the opportunism/inefficiency hypothesis, we would expect CAR to be negatively related to *pro forma* forecast error. However, under the signaling/efficiency hypothesis, we would expect a positive association between CAR and *pro forma* forecast error.

H1b: Under the opportunism hypothesis, ceteris paribus, positive (negative) *pro forma* forecast errors are associated with negative (positive) cumulative abnormal stock returns;

H1c: Under the signaling hypothesis, ceteris paribus, positive (negative) *pro forma* forecast errors are associated with positive (negative) cumulative abnormal stock returns.

When the press release containing GAAP and *pro forma* reconciliation is disclosed, at days t+1 or t+2 the market participants would be expected to react to both GAAP and *pro forma* earnings surprises[11]. Prior literature suggests *pro forma* results can provide higher-quality earnings measures than GAAP. Brown and Sivakumar (2003) acknowledge that if markets are not efficient, then investors would erroneously focus on lower-quality earnings numbers. Bradshaw and Sloan (2002a) provide evidence that *pro forma* measures have become the primary determinant of security prices compared to GAAP and are perceived by market participants as more value-relevant. While their findings suggest investors may see 'street numbers' as a better indication of long-run recurring performance, Bhattacharya et al. (2003) report similar findings indicating that investors see *pro forma* earnings as more informative than GAAP earnings.

If non-GAAP earnings are more relevant than GAAP measures, then *pro forma* earnings surprises would be more closely correlated with abnormal security returns that GAAP earnings surprises are. We test whether coefficients of *pro forma* earnings surprises are significantly higher than the coefficient of GAAP earnings surprises, and we test whether the R-squared of apparent earnings surprise, that is, its capacity to explain abnormal equity returns surrounding the announcement, is significantly better than the R-squared of GAAP earnings surprises. Then, if *pro forma* reporting aims at either misleading investors (opportunism hypothesis) or signaling private information about future prospects and future performance [Dumontier, 2003; Lougee and Marquardt (2004), Bowen et al. (2005) and Frankel et al. (2008)],. If markets are efficient, then investors would react in the opposite direction of the *pro forma*

[9] Accordingly, the AMF considers that these nonstandardized and nonaudited definitions of earnings stand in contrast with the historical and traditional conception of pro forma earnings that represented earnings under the assumption that two firms had been merged in prior years.

10. OISCO (2004), "Mise en garde sur les indicateurs de résultats non conformes aux principes comptables généralement admis (GAAP)", press release, 3 p.
AMF (2004), press release on earnings communication as of June 26th, 2004 related to the presentation of the 2006 AMF annual report, 4 p.
AMF (2005), "Communication des émetteurs sur leurs résultats", September 20th, 2005, 2 p.

11. Indeed, we had factor in two French calendar events directly related to financial reporting. [1] Firstly, at the date of the annual earnings announcements on day t, firms disclose their pro forma earnings metrics without providing any reconciliation statement. [2] Secondly, the new press release detailing adjustments of excluded items follows on, providing earnings computed under GAAP requirements. Where this press release could not be found in any databases, it is assumed the adjustments occurred on day t+1 and t+2 at the latest. Investors only find out 'street' measures, after which they are able to identify GAAP and/or pro forma surprises. On the other hand, we may have considered the full set of financial statements published in the B.A.L.O. (*Bulletin des Annonces Légales et Obligatoires*, an Appendix of the French Official Journal) as the date financial reports are released, providing users with GAAP and non-GAAP adjustments.

forecast error. Alternatively, if they react in the same direction, they may see street earnings as being a signal. If markets are not efficient, then positive coefficients of $FE_{PROFORMA}$ may suggest that investors erroneously focus on lower quality earnings numbers, and have been misled.

Under the opportunism/inefficiency hypothesis or under the signaling/efficiency hypothesis, depending on literature findings, we expect a higher coefficient of *pro forma* forecast error than GAAP forecast error.

Then: 2: Ceteris paribus, when regressing CAR on forecast errors, the coefficient of *pro forma* earnings surprises is higher than the coefficient of GAAP-reported earnings surprises.

Independent variables

Institutional ownership

Institutional owners are often characterized as sophisticated investors who have advantages over individual investors in acquiring and processing value-relevant information (e.g., Lev, 1988; Shiller and Pound, 1989; Hand, 1990; Jiambalvo et al., 2002). Hence, institutions can potentially monitor abuse of accounting discretion by managers. Under the opportunism hypothesis, we expect manipulations of earnings to be negatively associated with the INSTIT variable, measured from the FactSet LionShares database as the proportion of a firm's shares held by top-10 institutional investors.

However, according to Bowen et al. (2008), another body of literature has argued that institutional investors are "transient owners" who are overly focused on short-term earnings and thus pressure managers to deliver consistently higher earnings, even if it entails abuse of accounting discretion (Porter, 1992; Bushee, 1998; Graham et al., 2005). From this perspective, we expect to find a negative association between cumulative abnormal returns and INSTIT.

Audit quality

Prior research (Craswell et al., 1995) argues that audit quality increases with auditor's market share, and that discretionary accruals are lower for firms audited by a Big 4 firm. To construct a proxy for auditor reputation, we use a dummy variable AUDIT, equals to 1 if audited by a BIG4, zero otherwise. We expect the sign of the coefficient to be negative.

Growth opportunities

Skinner and Sloan (2002) observe that the market severely penalizes growth firms for negative earnings surprises. Therefore, growth firms have relatively strong incentives to meet earnings benchmarks, perhaps to avoid increases in the cost of capital or to maintain access to capital. Furthermore, growth firms have an incentive to smooth earnings via accruals, since earnings volatility increases perceived firm risk (Beaver et al., 1970) which, in turn, adversely affects the cost of the capital needed to fund new projects (Minton and Schrand, 1999). Thus, growth firms have relatively strong incentives to announce *pro forma* earnings metrics to meet earnings benchmarks. We proxy for growth opportunities with the market-to-book ratio (MBR), and expect a negative association between CAR and MBR.

Size

Watts and Zimmerman (1990) argue that larger firms face more political costs and hence have incentives to exercise accounting discretion to reduce unwanted political visibility. We use the natural logarithm of net sales (LnSALES) to proxy for size, and expect a positive association between accounting discretion and LnSALES.

Analyst coverage

To reflect the research findings of Healy and Palepu (2001), Dyck et al. (2006) and Yu (2008), we include in our model the regressor of analyst coverage captured by the number of analysts participating in the consensus forecast. Each of the studies cited above found that financial analysts following a firm affect the earnings management behavior of a firm through their role as external monitors, with a firm's accounting discretion behavior becoming increasingly curtailed as a function of the number of analysts following its increases.

Litigation costs

Skinner (1994) argued that the threat of lawsuits arising from large negative earnings surprises gives managers strong motives for pre-announcing information to reduce litigation costs. Consistently with this assumption, Kaznik and Lev (1995) had used this variable to capture litigation risk. They found that TECH firms are more likely to warn investors of an earnings surprise, thus adding support to the argument that litigation risk provides incentives for early disclosures. The variable is also similar to the classification used in Francis et al. (1994) to identify firms facing high litigation risk. If TECH effectively captures litigation risk and firms perceive *pro forma* reporting to reduce potential litigation costs, CAR should be negatively associated with TECH. Hence, we used the two following TECH measures to capture litigation costs:

TECH = 1 if the firm belongs to ICB sectors (Industry Classification Benchmark codes) classified as Pharmaceutical (ICB sector code 4577), Computer Services (9533), Electronic Equipment (2737), Telecommunications Equipment (9578), Software (9537), Aerospace (2713), Computer hardware (9572), Biotechnology (4573), Internet (9535) or Defense (2717); 0 otherwise

Sample design and data

We collected press releases on annual earnings from companies traded on NYSE-Euronext Paris over the period 1996 - 2006. Our initial sample was composed of 119 *pro forma* press releases. Our final sample consists of 116 *pro forma* announcements after dropping three observations whose forecasted earnings were missing. Whereas a large number of press releases issued in the US mention *pro forma* earnings measures, there is less evidence of its use in France. Press releases were extracted using the Factiva database that details any press releases covering any field of interest over the past 25 years relating to financial reporting. Firms used different nomenclature to disclose *pro forma* data that my methodology restrictively defined. *Pro forma* indicators are any indicators not covered under the French GAAP definition of earnings. We decided to search for *pro forma* earnings by using keywords found in the title or the content of the press release. We used keywords to highlight the nature of *pro forma* figures by looking up "net profit before goodwill amortization," "adjusted net profit," "net income excluding extraordinary expenses", "*pro forma* income", "*pro forma* EPS", "EPS before amortization" or "EPS excluding." Many press releases indicate that the firm has arrived at *pro forma* earnings by making multiple adjustments from GAAP. The most popular adjustment consists of announcing a net income before extraordinary items or before goodwill amortization, or announcing ordinary earnings, recurring earnings, or pro forma income. There is considerable interest in how financial analysts and broker tracking services such as FactSet, First Call, I/B/E/S or Zack have become increasingly reliant on adjusted definitions of GAAP earnings measures (Bradshaw and Sloan, 2002; Gu and Chen, 2004). The evidence suggests that press releases often report net profit on a gross basis rather than on a per share basis, yet at the same time, earnings per share (EPS) are also disclosed on a *pro forma* basis [12]. Each press release was fully analyzed to make sure that no GAAP-based earnings were specified. Unless the press release specified that earnings were prepared in accordance with French GAAP, it was considered as a *pro forma* press release. Except where several press releases were identified from different press agencies, data homogeneity was insured by cross-checking that different press releases gave the same information. Consequently, to consider an announcement a *pro forma* earnings announcement, two criteria had to be met. First, the press release had to provide a non-GAAP measure of annual earnings, either on a gross or a per share basis. Second, this alternative measure had to be associated with annual announcements rather than quarterly or semi-annual announcements. In most cases, the firm expressed the non-GAAP metric as unique performance measure, making no mention of any GAAP earnings or references to GAAP adjustments. In a handful of cases, a firm published both accounting and street earnings. The *pro forma* press releases were further analyzed to assess the number, nature, and income effect (both direction and magnitude) of the adjustment(s) to GAAP earnings used in determining the firm's *pro forma* measure.

Factiva contains any press releases provided by information agencies like Reuters, Bloomberg or domestic economic and financial press from French newspapers. Then, for a few firms, another press release reporting the GAAP earnings (that is, the regulatory press release) was supposed to be published one day later, that is, at day t+1, in another source.

Therefore, it is assumed that the reconciliation of *pro forma* and GAAP earnings appears one day after the *pro forma* release. *Pro forma* earnings are those mentioned in the press releases, corresponding to the official date of annual announcements taken from Factiva, after first controlling for coherence with the dates indicated in the FactSet Research System database. Forecasted GAAP earnings consist of median Basic EPS before extraordinaries, as gauged by financial analysts based on the latest estimates provided by brokers within the forty-five days immediately preceding earning announcements. The forecasted 'Adjusted Net Income' is the proxy collected from FactSet Estimates that captures the forecasted *pro forma* earnings figure. This item refers to recurrent earnings that do not comply with GAAP accounting earnings definitions because it excludes non-recurring items, exceptional items and other specific expenses. Given that the item is not standardized, each company's managers use their discretion in disclosing 'Adjusted Net Income'. In other words, it is the most reliable and accurate proxy for expected *pro forma* earnings.

EMPIRICAL RESULTS

Descriptive statistics on *pro forma* earnings metrics

Table 1 presents the initial sample of 116 *pro forma* press releases that report *pro forma* earnings to communicate their annual financial performance. Panel A tabulates the most commonly reported *pro forma* measure (around39% of the sample): "Net profit before goodwill amortization." This terminology adopts several variants, as in 6.9% of cases, the firm gave net income excluding goodwill amortization, while one press release specified the net profit excluding goodwill amortization. Further-more, in 3.4% of cases, firms excluded extraordinary items, thus improving their result significantly by reporting a *pro forma* number inflated by around 16.25, 19.89, and 12.9% respectively, compared with classically-calculated GAAP income. These results indicate expenses excluded from the calculation of GAAP earnings that represent significant amounts, expressed in relative value. Further-more, the "net earnings excluding non-recurring/unusual expenses" item is also often employed (7.8% of the sample) to disclose annual economic performance to the market. In only two cases (1.7% of the whole *pro forma* disclosures population), firms explicitly used "pro forma" terminology. Panel B in Table 1 illustrates that, on average, *pro forma* earnings amounted to about €689 thousand while GAAP earnings are worth about €612 thousand. Additionally, median *pro forma* numbers are above median GAAP numbers. The figures for total weighted mean (median) adjustments between GAAP and non-GAAP earnings reported in Panel C of Table 1 highlight that excluded items represent about 14.53% (18.59%) of the gross value of net income prepared in accordance with French accounting principles. Consequently, *pro forma* earnings are aimed at inflating reported numbers, making *pro forma* an income-increasing method.

Pro forma reporting widely remains an attempt to disclose biased information in order to influence investors' beliefs. Harvey Pitt, former SEC chairman, had declared that behind pro forma, reporting is often "a legitimate desire by companies to demystify mandated financial statements disclosures." *Pro forma* earnings reports are not audited by anyone prior to their release, so there is no assurance on the reasonableness of the items the reporting management chooses to exclude. As a result, there is no consistency in the calculation of *pro forma* earnings, and neither regulatory guidance nor standard definitions. The specific expenses or gains excluded from the calculation of *pro forma* EPS (that is, net income) vary from company to company, often within the same industry, making it very difficult to run reliable comparisons between two companies. More disturbing is the fact that items excluded from *pro forma* earnings sometimes vary from one period to the next, based upon what the company's management chooses to emphasize. In the U.S. most *pro forma* press releases appeared after the Enron collapse, which in itself documents how the financial community no longer trusts financial reporting. Indeed, one analyst argued that "the reported classical (GAAP) profits figure is now considered an accounting fiction", because it often includes nonrecurring items and unspecified accrual accounting distortions. We observed that *pro forma* releases were on the increase from 1996 – 2001 and declined thereafter. It thus becomes clear that, except for 2001 where 34 *pro forma* announcements were

12. Indeed, the dilutive problem is due to the number of outstanding shares integrated into the calculation of the reported EPS denominator. The number in the denominator could differ while analysts are forecasting the EPS measure.

Table 1. Characteristics of *pro forma* earnings in Reuters press releases disclosed by French listed-companies from January 1997 to July 2006.

	Firms number*	(%**)
Panel A. Description of *pro forma* earnings (% of the sample): comments appearing in the press releases (Reuters)		
Net profit, group share* in a separate press release, where the firm mentions that its earnings are before goodwill amortization	8	6.9
Net profit excluding extraordinary items	19	16.4
"Pro forma" earnings	2	1.7
Ordinary earnings, group share	5	4.3
Net profit, group share excluding "purchase/acquisition costs"	2	1.7
Operational profit, group share	16	13.8
Net earnings before recurring/unusual items	9	7.8
Adjusted net profit	10	8.6
Net profit before goodwill amortization	33	28.4
Net profit before goodwill amortization and extraordinary expenses	4	3.4
Net profit before disposals gains/losses (PMV)	3	2.6
Net profit before restructuring costs	1	0.09
Net earnings with specific GAAP (including changes in accounting procedure/specific consolidation method within a subsidiary)	4	3.4
Total of observations	116	
Panel B. Annual *pro forma* and GAAP earnings as reported by sample firms (in thousands of €)	**Mean**	**Median**
Pro forma earnings figures	689.240	205.600
GAAP earnings figures	612.053	193.394
Panel C. GAAP items excluded from *pro forma* earnings (% of GAAP net income)	**Mean**	**Median**
Net profit, group share* in a separate press release, where the firm mentions that its earnings are before goodwill amortization	16.25	17.00
Net profit excluding extraordinary items	-27.06	5.89
"Pro forma" earnings	35.28	NA
Ordinary earnings, group share	0.33	-0.20
Net profit, group share excluding " purchase/acquisition costs"	3.5	NA
Operational profit, group share	5.79	5.89
Net earnings before recurring/unusual items	23.06	10.08
Adjusted net profit	-9.62	-5.32
Net profit before goodwill amortization	19.89	14.45
Net profit before goodwill amortization and extraordinary expenses	12.90	10.53
Net profit before disposals gains/losses (PMV)	14.34	8.56
Net profit before restructuring costs	7.67	7.67
Net earnings with specific GAAP (including changes in accounting procedure/specific consolidation method within a subsidiary)	-41.19	NA
Total *pro forma* adjustments of sample firms (weighted)	14.83	18.59

* Some observations aggregate different items ranging from "*pro forma* earnings before recurring expenses and goodwill amortization" or "ordinary earnings reported on a *pro forma* basis" to "*pro forma* earnings before extraordinary components.
** Percentages are computed on number of items based on 116 observations.

identified, the numbers of *pro forma* announcements are limited annually. These phenomena are recurring, since the 116 "heterodox" announcements recorded over ten fiscal-years concerning only 66 firms. Over the period studied, non-GAAP earnings measures were released six times by both Zodiac and L'Oreal, five times by Total and

Sanofi, and four times by Carrefour. Most firms announced a non-GAAP earnings measure once or twice at some point in the study period, documenting that *pro forma* reporting practices are not widely used by all French SBF 250 firms but, rather, are used recurrently by certain firms.

Firms' incentives to disclose *pro forma* earnings measures

Comparisons of GAAP and pro forma earnings forecast errors

Table 2 presents a comparison of earnings forecast errors reported either according to GAAP measures or on a *pro forma* basis. The descriptive statistics point out many interesting trends in terms of managerial behavior and the incentives for revealing non-GAAP earnings. In all cases, the only expectation arising from analysts is the accounting [GAAP] net income forecasted. When firms announce a *pro forma* earnings measure generating apparently good news, the mean *pro forma* forecast error amounts to +20.39%, whereas the GAAP number that should have been disclosed would have led to a negative GAAP forecast error of just -9.04%.

The motives for disclosing valuable positive *pro forma* earnings leads to reporting an inflated earnings surprise that improves on earnings that had been eroded due to the announcement of GAAP figures. There evidence strongly suggests that the reason managers choose to disclose negative *pro forma* earnings is that they are looking to reduce the extent of the negative *real* surprise that would have provoked a slide in stock price. Panel B shows that *pro forma* adopters report a mean negative *pro forma* surprise of -3.67% when their GAAP forecast errors should have been estimated at -29.5%. These statistics show that managers try to enhance a firm's financial performance by issuing *pro forma* numbers instead of disclosing GAAP earnings. In addition, the sub-sample of firms that announced legal GAAP (Panel C) earnings had an average positive (negative) forecast error of about +15.67% (-22.08%).

As shown in Panel D, *pro forma* announcers use ad hoc numbers to exceed median analyst forecasts by announcing good news of about +5.7% whereas their GAAP forecast error would, on average, have been negative (-13.00%)[13]. These results are consistent with Johnson and Schwartz (2005) who found that GAAP-reported earnings surprises (averaging out at +6.32%) are lower than pro forma-reported surprises (that is, +16.11%). Consistent with findings by Entwistle et al. (2005), our results show that 79% of companies reporting *pro forma* earnings had results superior to GAAP-based earnings. The descriptive statistics show that, on average, FEPROFORMA (0.091) is higher than FEGAAP (0.0097); (Table 4: matrix correlation in notes/appendix)

Are *pro forma* earnings used to beat markets' expectations or report a profit?

We also focus on the frequency with which these two types of earnings calculations i) report a profit/loss or ii) meet analysts' expectations. Figure 1 shows that GAAP announcers meet analysts' expectations in 54% of identified cases, while *pro forma* adopters exceed analysts' predictions about 84% of the time when they use a *pro forma* definition of earnings but only 21% of the time if they use a GAAP definition. These observations show that firms tend to adopt a non-GAAP definition in their reported earnings mainly to meet median analysts' earnings forecasts, whereas their results defined in compliance with GAAP would not allow them to exceed the forecasts.

Figure 2 also shows that over 82% of *pro forma* announcers should have announced bad news if they had released GAAP-based earnings figures (compared with 46% of GAAP reporters). Thus, our study provides strong evidence that *pro forma* reporting enables firms to exceeded analysts' forecasts, while GAAP-based earnings metrics do not allow firms to meet these forecasts. Companies whose accounting earnings announcements result in negative surprises tend to disclose *pro forma* earnings more often (82%). These findings demonstrate the discretionary willingness of managers to mislead investors using *pro forma* numbers. Furthermore, while only 18% of *pro forma* reporters succeed in beating market expectations of their earnings prepared in compliance with GAAP, this figure jumps to 79% in reporting *pro forma* earnings measures, a figure fairly similar to the 70% found by Bhattacharya et al. (2003).

Figure 3 illustrates that GAAP announcers report a profit in 90.7% of identified cases. *Pro forma* adopters report a *pro forma* profit about 94.6% of the time when they should have reported a profit only about 89.4% of the time if publishing their earnings in accordance with accounting principles. Our results therefore indicate that French companies can disclose street earnings in order to turn GAAP losses into *pro forma* profits. This evidence is consistent with the notion that managers are often under extreme pressure to report earnings that are equal to or above the median analysts' expectations (e.g. Burgstahler and Dichev, 1997; Skinner and Sloan, 2002). Therefore, *pro forma* earnings disclosures may often be motivated by managers' moves to meet targets and avoid reporting a loss. In addition, we found that *pro forma* announcers more frequently report a loss than GAAP

13. To enhance these results, an analysis of both pro forma and GAAP forecast error distributions of ad hoc reporters (not tabulated here) showed, first, that their GAAP earnings errors are left-tailed (negatively) distributed while their pro forma earnings errors are right-tailed (positively) distributed. Thus, most firms use pro forma earnings metrics to exceed median brokers' predictions and release good news so as to avoid triggering the price slide that would occur if they reported the bad news resulting from announcing GAAP earnings that fall below the analysts' forecasts.

Table 2. *Pro forma* versus GAAP earnings per share (EPS) measure forecasts errors.

Pro forma and GAAP earnings measures forecast error (FE)				
	Pro forma FE		GAAP FE	
	Mean	Median	Mean	Median
Panel A. *Pro forma* earnings releases - Good news (N = 88)	0.1839	0.1160	-0.07	-0.0255
Panel B. *Pro forma* earnings releases - Bad news (N = 28)	-0.0367	-0.0245	-0.295	-0.1375
Panel C. GAAP Earnings releases only (N = 1456)	0.1567	0.0423	-0.2208	-0.0986
Panel D. *Pro forma* Earnings releases only (N = 113)	0.057	0.0218	-0.13	-0.4988

Pro forma FE = Reported *pro forma* earnings – Forecasted GAAP earnings.
GAAP FE = Reported GAAP earnings - Forecasted GAAP earnings.

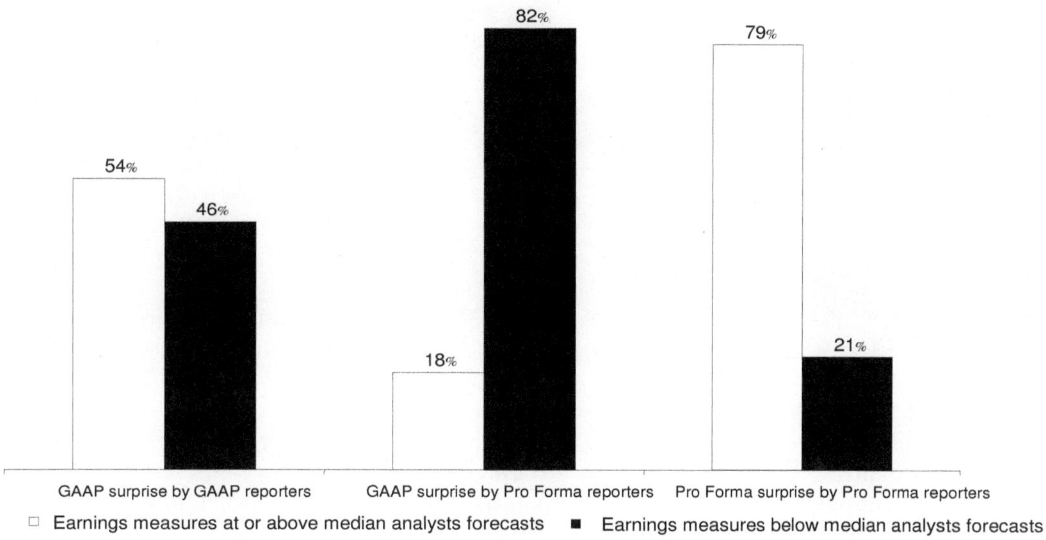

Figure 1. Earnings measures above versus below median analysts' forecasts.

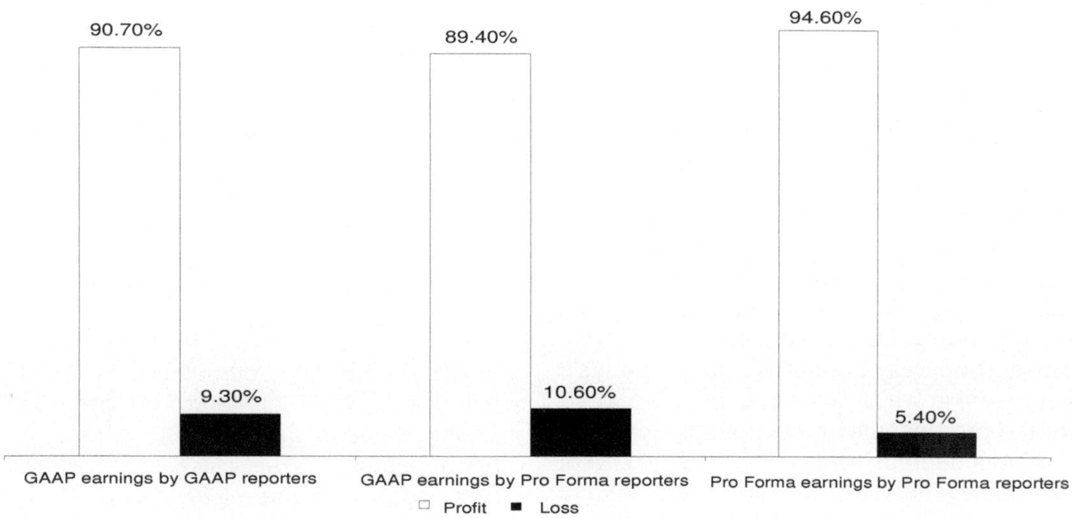

Figure 2. Percentages of profit versus loss.

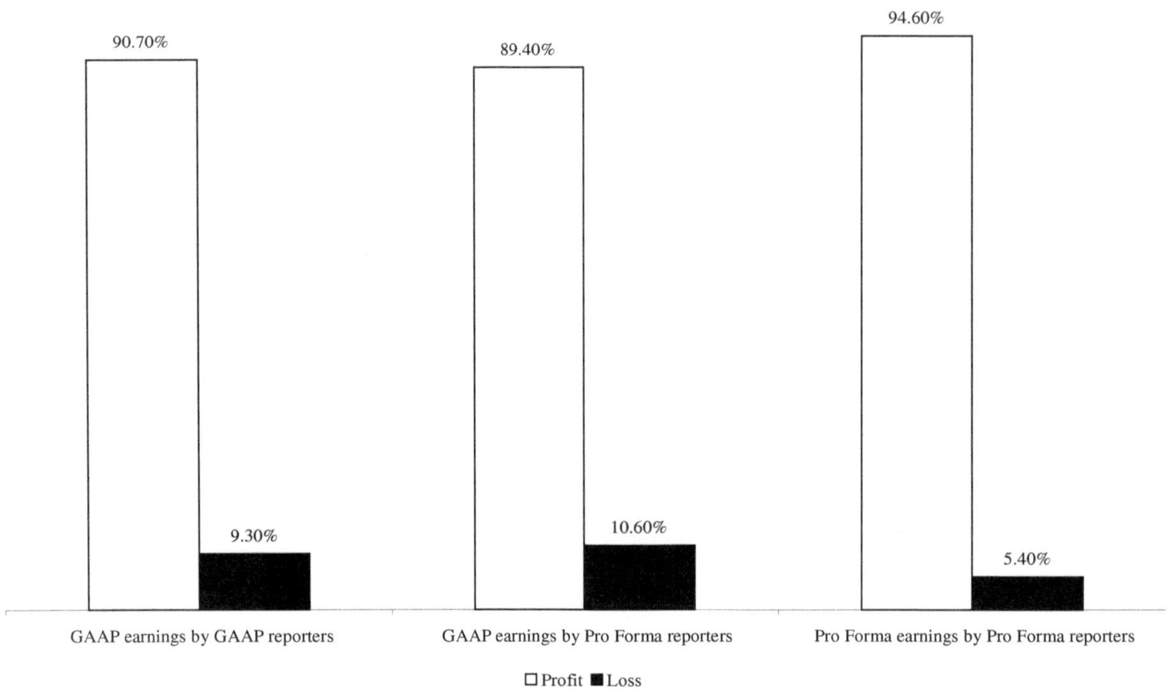

Figure 3. Percentages of profit versus loss.

reporters (10.6% vs 9.3%) when the announcement is based on earnings prepared in accordance with accounting principles. Furthermore, on a *pro forma* basis, announcers reduce the percentage of losses at only 5.4%. Hence, descriptive statistics show that French firms use "street" announcements to transform GAAP losses into non-GAAP profits. Our findings converge at and towards the conclusion that companies tend to use *pro forma* earnings to meet analysts' expectations and downplay negative earnings news. This is consistent with the conclusions drawn by Bhattacharya et al. (2004).

Relative informativeness of *pro forma* and GAAP earnings metrics

We went on to examine whether *pro forma* earnings surprises were comparatively more informative than GAAP earnings numbers. To test this point, we regressed short-window abnormal returns separately, then together, on earnings surprise measures based on each of the two earnings metrics, that is, *pro forma* or GAAP earnings, denoted as $FE_{PROFORMA}$ and FE_{GAAP}, respectively. We ran an event study based on daily abnormal returns analysis using the market model in which we compute the model's parameters over the pre-announcement period [-250;-11], 0 being the announcement date. The results (not tabulated here) show that, on average, announcing positive (negative) *pro forma* earnings generates a positive - and significant - abnormal return of around +3.27% (-0.53%). In comparison, positive (negative) GAAP earnings announcements lead to a positive response of +1.20% (-0.71%), both of which are statistically different from zero. The difference in means is statistically significant, suggesting that *pro forma* earnings announcements induce higher returns movements. As outlined below, we tested the following three regression models:

$$CAR_{[0,2]} = \alpha_0 + \alpha_1 FE_{PROFORMA} + \alpha_2 ANALYSTS + \alpha_3 INSTIT + \alpha_4 BIG4 + \alpha_5 MBR + \alpha_6 TECH + e''$$

(Equation 1)

$$CAR_{[0,2]} = \alpha_0 + \alpha_1 FE_{GAAP} + \alpha_2 ANALYSTS + \alpha_3 INSTIT + \alpha_4 BIG4 + \alpha_5 MBR + \alpha_6 TECH + e''$$

(Equation 2)

$$CAR_{[0,2]} = \alpha_0 + \alpha_1 FE_{GAAP} + \alpha_2 FE_{PROFORMA} + \alpha_3 ANALYSTS + \alpha_4 INSTIT + \alpha_5 BIG4 + \alpha_6 MBR + \alpha_7 TECH + e''$$

(Equation 3)

In which CAR is the cumulative abnormal returns over the two-day window centered on the *pro forma* earnings announcement date (0;+2), where 0 is the date of announcement, $FE_{PROFORMA}$ is the difference between the reported pro forma EPS and the forecasted EPS excluding extraordinary items resulting from the median analysts' consensus, scaled by the closing stock price as of December 31 of preceding year, and FE_{GAAP} is the final GAAP EPS reported by the firm minus the forecasted EPS excluding extraordinary items, scaled by the closing stock price as of December 31 of last year. Integrating the annual average number of shares outstanding taken from FacstSet Excel Connect, we divided any *pro forma* income identified by the annually - weighted average number of shares outstanding, which gives any EPS disclosed on a *pro forma* basis.

Daily returns were calculated as the firm-specific daily return minus the expected daily return on that day as computed through the market model. The earnings response coefficient and the adjusted R^2 value, capturing the overall explanatory power of the earnings surprise measure, provide measures of the informativeness of the analyzed earnings metrics (e.g. Brown et al., 1987; Brown and Sivakumar, 2003). Similarly, we estimated the following models with standardized variables using variables for which the distribution of each is transformed so that the mean is zero and the standard deviation is one. Therefore, we directly compared the respective earnings response coefficients, that is, α_1 versus α_2[15].

These models provide direct empirical evidence on whether *pro forma* figures are significantly more informative to information users than GAAP numbers. Table 3 shows that the $FE_{PROFORMA}$ (α_1) coefficient is greater than the FE_{GAAP} (α_2) coefficient [16]. Multivariate analysis allows us to directly compare the earnings response coefficient of $FE_{PROFORMA}$ (α_1) against the coefficient of FE_{GAAP} (α_2).

These results indicate that pro forma-based earnings measures are significantly much more informative to investors than earnings prepared in compliance with GAAP. In univariate analysis, the coefficient of FE_{GAAP} (.04) is lower than the coefficient of $FE_{PROFORMA}$ (.52). The coefficient on the *pro forma* forecast error in equation 1 is not significant, while the coefficient on the GAAP forecast error in equation 2 is still significantly positive.

However, in equation 3, the coefficients on *pro forma* and GAAP forecast errors are significant at the 0.05 level and positive, at .69 and .044, respectively, suggesting street earnings are more value relevant than the GAAP performance measure. Our findings are consistent with previous studies suggesting *pro forma* results can provide higher-quality earnings measures than GAAP.

The findings reported by Brown and Sivakumar (2003) state that if markets are not efficient, then investors may erroneously focus on lower-quality earnings numbers. A study by Bradshaw and Sloan (2002a) on the magnitude of the difference between *pro forma* earnings reported by analysts' tracking services (that is, I/B/E/S) and GAAP earnings reported an increasing tendency to exclude significant and allegedly non-recurring expenses from *pro forma* measures. The authors provide evidence that *pro forma* measures have outstripped GAAP as the primary determinant of stock prices and are perceived by investors to be more value-relevant. While their findings suggest investors may perceive 'street earnings' as a better indication of long-run recurring performance, Bradshaw and Sloan (2002b) put forward an alternative theory that investors are getting "hoodwinked". Bhattacharya et al. (2003) also provide evidence that investors view *pro forma* earnings as more informative than GAAP earnings. However, results obtained by Philbrick and Ricks (1991) indicated that matching analysts' forecasts to actual earnings figures reported by the same tracking service provides a more accurate, that is, less 'noisy' measure of forecast error[18]. Thus, in equation 3, empirical results corroborate that *pro forma* earnings are more informative to market participants than GAAP measures. Coefficients on forecast errors are predicted to be positive, suggesting we focus on managerial opportunism. Despite the difficulties in discriminating between efficient contracting and opportunism, our results provide strong evidence that if markets are efficient, *pro forma* numbers are informative about future prospects (signaling hypothesis), whereas if markets are not efficient, *pro forma* numbers mislead investors. For control variables, only INSTIT and MBR are negative and statistically significant. The coefficient on ANALYSTS is not significant, except in equation 2 where, as expected, it turns out negative. Our results are robust, since there were no multicolinearity biases (Table 5: matrix correlation in notes/appendix).
The limits of this research stem from the difficulty in distinguishing between opportunism and. efficiency, and from the sample size, which is smaller in this study than in empirical American studies. These limits may create a statistical bias in the robustness of results, especially since regression estimates are highly sensitive to sample size. However, in terms of data representation, we have taken into account nearly all of the *pro forma* announcements in France over the period under study.

---

15. Indeed, in classical OLS estimation, examining the values of the estimates does not definitively conclude that the explanatory variable with the largest estimated coefficient has the greatest explanatory power for the response variable, since the magnitudes of the control variables are directly sensitive to the units used to assess the respective powers of the variables. However, standardizing the variables makes their scale irrelevant, and consequently places the explanatory variables on "equal footing" in terms of explanatory power. As a result, the response coefficient on standardized estimated earnings can be considered the number of standard error changes in the dependent variable resulting from a standard error change in the independent variable. Hence, coefficients measure the effects of each variable in standard deviation units as opposed to the gross initial units of the regressors employed within the classical OLS models. Therefore, OLS estimation using standardized variables is a better-adapted technique when the the researcher aim' is to accurately determine the respective relative power of any control variables in explaining variations in the response variable (e.g. Wooldridge, 2000).

16. We winsorized each of the variables used in the regression models at the 5th and 95th percentiles to reduce the influence of outliers on the results.

18. Therefore, by design, FE_{GAAP} is less noisy than the 'street' forecast error ($FE_{PROFORMA}$) measure since the pro forma forecasts provided by FactSet JCF exclude goodwill amortization expenses while the regular criterion for earnings metrics supplied by Compustat may exclude or include extraordinary items in specific cases. Furthermore, EPS forecasted by financial analysts are generally based on the EPS excluding extraordinary items.

Table 3. Relative informativeness of *pro forma* and GAAP earnings.

Dependent variable	**CAR[0;2]**	**CAR[0;2]**	**CAR[0;2]**
Independent variables	**Coefficient (Prob.)**	**Coefficient (Prob.)**	**Coefficient (Prob.)**
	0.156104* **	**0.157427*** **	**0.214061** **
Intercept	(0.0023) 0.516554*	(0.0036)	(0.0114) 0.689471*
$FE_{PROFORMA}$	(0.1072)	0.039697*	(0.0347) 0.044584*
FE_{GAAP}	-0.001445	(0.0642) -0.002652*	(0.0308) -0.027645
ANALYSTS	(0.2731) -0.003436***	(0.0832) -0.004183***	(0.2493) -0.004938***
INSTIT	(0.0097) 0.012105	(0.0055) 0.027943	(0.0013) 0.019901
BIG4	(0.6055) -0.007460	(0.3074)*** -0.000433	(0.4093) -0.007672*
MBR	(0.0624)* 0.008656	(0.8429) -0.020287	(0.0541) 0.012462
TECH	(0.7970) 101	(0.4969) 101	(0.6508) 101
Observations	0.405861	0.365432	0.518100
R^2	0.207815	0.198440	0.319671
Adjusted R^2	(0.072965)*	(0.098461)*	(0.050218)**
Prob(F-statistic)			

* Significant at the 0.10 level (two-tailed); ** Significant at the 0.05 level (two-tailed); *** Significant at the 0.01 level (two-tailed). $FE_{PROFORMA}$: Reported *pro forma* income (per share) – Forecasted adjusted net income (per share) deflated by lagged stock price; FE_{GAAP} : Reported net income (per share) – Forecasted basic EPS before extraordinaries deflated by lagged stock price; ANALYSTS: number of analysts contributing to the consensus (EPS estimates); INSTIT: percentage of firm's shares held by institutional investors; BIG4: dummy variable = 1 if the firm is audited by a BIG4, zero otherwise; MBR: Market-to-Book ratio; TECH = 1 if the firm belongs to technological ICB sector classifications, zero otherwise. Ln(SALES) was removed as the coefficient was insignificant and highly correlated with BIG4 and ANALYSTS, consequently multicolinearity problems.

Table 4. Descriptive statistics on the variables.

	CAR[0;2]	**ANALYSTS**	**BIG4**	**MBR**	**INSTIT**	**TECH**	**$FE_{PROFORMA}$**	**FE_{GAAP}**
Mean	0.036027	28.88000	0.520000	5.814516	13.48120	0.200000	0.091496	0.009797
Median	0.021856	31.00000	1.000000	4.119750	10.58400	0.000000	5.57E-05	-0.000739
Maximum	0.143910	40.00000	1.000000	27.15530	37.54400	1.000000	3.013763	0.314407
Minimum	-0.051302	5.000000	0.000000	1.339590	2.391000	0.000000	-0.593635	-0.076623
Std. Dev.	0.055330	9.301971	0.509902	5.164328	9.372667	0.408248	0.620715	0.065645
Skewness	0.211415	-1.230301	-0.080064	3.006165	1.265185	1.500000	4.375140	4.145350
Kurtosis	2.059608	3.760595	1.006410	12.84678	3.875082	3.250000	21.38767	20.25504
Obs.	101	101	101	101	101	101	101	101

Table 5. Correlation matrix (common samples).

	ANALYSTS	BIG4	CAR[0;2]	FE_{GAAP}	INSTIT	MBR	$FE_{PROFORMA}$	TECH
ANALYSTS	1							
BIG4	0.4617	1.0000						
CAR[0;2]	-0.1434	0.0530	1.0000					
FE_{GAAP}	-0.1417	-0.2752	-0.0822	1.0000				
INSTIT	-0.2664	-0.1627	-0.3939	0.2137	1.0000			
MBR	0.0290	-0.1833	-0.2093	0.8249	-0.0152	1.0000		
$FE_{PROFORMA}$	-0.0842	-0.1781	0.1170	-0.1624	0.4867	-0.2651	1.0000	
TECH	-0.2238	0.2802	0.0763	-0.1945	-0.1361	0.0098	-0.0943	1.0000

SUMMARY AND CONCLUSION

Non-GAAP financial measures, frequently called "pro forma" numbers, are performance measures created and disclosed by managers that are not calculated in accordance with GAAP (Generally Accepted Accounting Principles). Bowen et al. (2005) found that managers emphasize the metric (GAAP or pro forma) that best portrays firm performance. Elliott's (2006) experimental evidence reveals that when press releases give more prominence to non-GAAP measures than GAAP measures, nonprofessional investors become more reliant on non-GAAP values, which consequently affects their judgments and decisions. This financial reporting research stream emphasizes that *pro forma* disclosures ultimately misinform capital market participants by disclosing financial indicators that do not comply with generally accepted accounting principles, mainly for the purpose of cosmetically improving the financial results of the company and making the firm more financially attractive and profitable for investors.

This empirical study is the first to focus on *pro forma* reporting in the French context, and provides evidence that French companies use "street" earnings in their annual press releases. However, these practices are proportionally less common in France than in the U. S., where most of the S&P 500 companies disclose their earnings on a *pro forma* basis through their annual earnings announcements.

Consequently, this work reveals several relevant trends. (1) Discretionary *pro forma* earnings are more informative than GAAP earnings metrics because they more closely reflect abnormal daily returns. These findings show that alternative definitions of profits are more useful and relevant than results computed in accordance with accounting principles in terms of assessing future security values. Indeed, GAAP earnings encompass extraordinary items or "non-recurring" expenses that are irrelevant to forecasts on future earnings. Attempts to corroborate efficiency (signaling) or inefficiency (opportunism) gave mixed results. (2) Forecast errors are biased in favor of non-GAAP earnings. (3) Approximately 5.4% of *pro forma* adopters have reported a loss expressed on a non-GAAP basis, whereas only 9.30% of GAAP earnings figures actually resulted in a loss. (4) Approximately 89.4% of *pro forma* earnings announcers met or exceeded median analysts' forecasts, whereas only about 18% of them met or beat analysts' forecasts based on GAAP income numbers. (5) Finally, analyzing the magnitude of biased and unbiased forecast errors, we demonstrate that *pro forma* reporting is principally aimed at improving apparent positive earnings surprises so as to report similar surprises to those posted by firms reporting standard GAAP results. Conversely, announcing a negative *pro forma* earnings surprise enables firms to reduce their apparent forecast errors significantly, so that their reported performance would be similar to that shown by GAAP earnings reporters. *Pro forma* measures make earnings announcements difficult to interpret, and research should be extended to focus on the possible existence of *pro forma* reporting in semi-annual financial statements as well.

ACKNOWLEDGEMENTS

The author is grateful to Monique Marcelet, Account Manager for *Factiva*, a Dow Jones & Reuters Company, for providing data collected from the Reuters Business Briefing database, and Phourasamy Maokhamphiou for opening access to the *Factiva* database. I thank Factset for providing financial data as and accounting data taken from Compustat Global. I gratefully thank the International Business Economics and Accounting Collaborative Network (iBEACON) at the San Diego State University School of Accountancy (College of Business Administration) where additional data were collected during summer 2006, and the French-American Fulbright Commission for awarding the 2006/2007 postdoctoral scholarship. The author is unwilling to share this data.

REFERENCES

Andresson P, Hellman N (2007). Does *pro forma* reporting bias analyst forecasts, Eur. Acctg. Rev., 2: 277-298.

Aubert F (2005a). L'incidence des annonces hétérodoxes de résulta sur

la réaction des investisseurs. AFFI Conf., June 27-28.
Bagnoli M, Eskew R, Watts SG (2001). Earnings surprises when firms choose what matters. Purdue University Work. Pap.
Beaver W, Kettler P, Scholes M (1970). The association between market-determined and accounting-determined risk measures, Acctg. Rev., 45(4): 654–682.
Bhattacharya N (2001). Investors' trade size and trading responses around earnings announcements: an empirical investigation. Acct. Rev., 7: 221–244.
Bhattacharya N, Black E, Christensen T, Mergenthaler R (2004). Empirical evidence on recent trends in *pro forma* reporting. Acct. Hor., 18 : 27 – 43.
Bhattacharya N, Black E, Christensen T, Larson C (2003). Assessing the relative informativeness and persistence of *pro forma* earnings and GAAP operating earnings, J. Acct. Econ., 36: 285–319.
Bhattacharya N, Black E, Christensen T, Alle C (2007). *Pro forma* disclosure and investor sophistication: external validation of experimental evidence using archival data. Acctg. Org. Soc., 32-36.
Biddle GC, Seow GS, Siegel A (1995). Relative versus incremental information content, Cont. Acct. Res., 12: 1-23.
Bowen RM, Davis AK, Matsumoto DA (2005). Emphasis on *pro forma* versus GAAP earnings in quarterly press releases: determinants, SEC intervention, and market reactions, Acctg. Rev., 80(4): 1011-1038.
Bradshaw MT, Sloan RG (2002). GAAP versus the street: an empirical assessment of two alternative definitions of earnings., J. Acct. Res., 40: 41–66.
Bradshaw MT (2003). Discussion of 'Assessing the relative informativeness and persistence of *pro forma* earnings and GAAP operating earnings', J. Acct. Econ., 36: 321-335.
Bray C (2001). SEC looking at *pro forma* earnings with 'purpose News., November in mind'. D. J., 8-12.
Brown LD, Sivakumar K (2003). Comparing the quality of three earnings measures, Rev. Acctg. Stud., 8: 561-572.
Brown LD, Griffin PA, Hagerman RL, Zmijewski ME (1987). An evaluation of alternative proxies for the market's assessment of unexpected earnings, J. Acct. Econ., 9: 159–193.
Burgstahler D, Dichev I (1997). Earnings management to avoid earnings decreases and losses, J. Acctg. Econ., 24: 99-126.
Ciccone S (2002). GAAP versus street earnings: making earnings look higher and smoother, Acct. Enq., 11: 155-186.
Collins DW, DeAngelo L (1990). Accounting information and corporate governance: market and analyst reactions to earnings of firms engaged in proxy contests, J. Acct. Econ., 13: 213-247.
D'Avolio G, Gildor E, Shleifer A (2001). Technology, information production, and market efficiency. Harvard University Work. Pap.
Dechow PM (1994). Accounting earnings and cash flows as measures of firm performance, J. Acct. Econ., 18: 1-42.
Derby MS (2001). Investors getting more data, but is it the News. September right data, D. J., 3:10.
Dow Jones, Company Inc. (2001). SEC probes 4 firms for possible abuses of pro-forma results News. June D. J., 19-22.
Doyle J, Lundholm R, Soliman M (2003). The predictive value of expenses excluded from 'pro forma' earnings. Rev. Acct. Stud. Dreman D (001).antasy earnings. Forbes, October 1(8): 145 – 174.
Easton PD, Zmijewski ME (1989). Cross-sectional variation in the stock market response to accounting earnings announcements, J. Acctg. Econ., 1: 117-41.
Elliott B (2006). Are investors influenced by *pro forma* emphasis and reconciliations in earnings announcements? Acct. Rev., 81.
Elstein A 2001). Waste management excludes some expenses in accounting. The Wall Str. J. Aug. 23 : 17 – 18.
Frankel R, McVay SE, Soliman MT (2008). Street earnings and board independence. SSRN Work. Pap. Ser. at http://ssrn.com/abstract=994914.
Frederickson J, Miller J (2004). The effects of *pro forma* earnings disclosures on analysts' and nonprofessional investors' equity valuation judgments. Acct. Rev., 79 : 667 – 686.
Grant J, Parker L (2001). EBITDA. Res. Acct. Reg., 15: 205-211.
Gu Z, Chen T (2004). Analysts' treatment of non-recurring items in street earnings, J. Acct. Econ., 38: 129-170.
Hayn C (1995). The information content of losses. J. Acctg. Econ., 20: 125-153.
James K, Michello F (2003). The dangers of *pro forma* reporting. CPA J.
Johnson W, Schwartz W. (2005). Are investors misled by 'pro forma' earnings, Cont. Acct. Res., p. 24.
Kaznik R, Lev B (1995). To warn or not to warn: management disclosures in the face of an earnings surprise Acct. Rev., 70: 113–134.
Kevin L, Michello F, Colson R (2003). The dangers of *pro forma* reporting. CPA J., 73: 65-67.
Lambert R (2004). Discussion of 'analysts' treatment of non-recurring items in street earnings and loss function assumptions in rational expectations tests on financial analysts' earnings forecasts. J. Acctg. Econ., 38: 205-222.
Lougee B, Marquardt C (2004). Earnings informativeness and strategic disclosure: an empirical examination of 'pro forma' earnings, Acct. Rev., 79(3): 769-795.
Minton B, Schrand C (1999). The impact of cash flow volatility on discretionary investment and the costs of debt and equity financing. J. Fin. Econ., 54(3): 423–60.
Securitiesm Exchange Commission (2001). Cautionary advice regarding the use of "pro forma" financial information in earnings releases. Release Nos. 33-8039. 34-45124, FR-59.
Skinner D, Sloan RG (2002). Earnings surprises, growth expectations, and stock returns, or don't let an earnings torpedo sink your portfolio, Rev. Acct. Stud., 7(2–3): 287–312.
Vuong QH (1989). Likelihood ratio tests for model selection and non-nested hypotheses, Econ., 57: 307-333.
Weil J (2001a). Companies pollute earnings reports leaving p/e ratios hard to calculate. The Wall Str. J. Aug. 21: 17.
Weil J (2001b). 'EPS' means different things in different earnings reports. The Wall Str. J. Oct. 16: 19.
Wallace W (2002). *Pro forma* before and after the SEC's warning: A quantification of reporting variances from GAAP. (FEI Research Foundation, Morristown, N.J). pp. 1-14.
Wooldridge JM (2000). Introductory Econometrics: A Modern Approach. South-Western College Publishing, Cincinnati, OH. pp. 1-778.

Political stewardship accounting for good governance in Ekiti state, Nigeria

Anthony Adekunle Owojori[1]*, Ishola Rufus Akintoye[2] and Felix Adidu[3]

[1]Department of Educational Foundations and Management, Faculty of Education University of Ado-Ekiti, Nigeria.
[2]Department of Accounting, Olabisi Onabanjo University, Ago-Iwoye, Ogun State, Nigeria.
[3]Department of Business Administration, Delta State University, Abraka, Delta State Nigeria.

This paper aimed at analyzing the importance of stewardship accounting in government ministries in Ekiti State and the causes of mismanagement in government-sector finance. The population comprised four thousand principal officers in the sixteen local governments of Ekiti State of Nigeria out of which four hundred were stratifiedly selected from each local government. The data were gathered through questionnaires while frequency counts, percentage scores and factor analysis were used to analyze the data. The findings showed that stewardship accounting promotes good management of public funds, increases accountability and probity in the public sector and discourages embezzlement of public funds and promotes economics growth. It was therefore recommended that the government should make sure that stewardship accounting should be set up and strictly implemented for better reconstruction of good governance so as to guide against mal-administration of the public funds by public officers; and the ascertainment of proprietary of transactions and their conformity with established rules.

Key words: Politics, stewardship accounting, good governance.

INTRODUCTION

Glymn (1985) stated that the theme of accountability is crucial to the operation of both the private and public sectors. It is a fundamental concept that can be traced back to earliest times. In the New Testament, Mathew (25 Vs 14 - 30) relates the parable about the man who entrusted his property to three servants. Two of the servants doubled the funds entrusted to them and were praised for their efforts. The third servant simply buried the funds entrusted to him in a hole in the ground for safe keeping and was condemned for his worthlessness because he had not even taken the (virtually riskless) alternative of leaving the money on deposit with bankers. Even earlier, Aristotle wrote in the politics. "To protect the treasury from being defrauded, let all public money be issued openly in front of the whole city and let copies of the accounts be deposited in the various wards" Sinclair (1984). Both of these references relate to one particular concepts of accountability, namely that of "financial accountability". The former reference can be thought of as a private sector illustration of financial accountability. The master expected his servant to increase his own personal wealth, a situation that is exactly analogous with the generally accepted micro-economic concept that management should seek to maximize the wealth of their ordinary (equity) shareholders. The latter question is, obviously a reference to public sector financial accounting, which is, in practice a vaguer and less tangible concept. Public accountability is an essential component for the functioning of our political system.

Glym (1985) also stated that "Public sector accountability means that those who are charged with drafting and or carrying out policy should be obliged to give an explanation of their actions to their electorate: - the electorate being a composite group then includes clients employees and tax payers.

The growth in the public sector, both in terms of its scale and the diversity of its activities, has outstretched the traditional machinery of public accountability which is

*Corresponding author. E-mail: adekunleowojori@yahoo.com.

heavily dependent upon the formal relationship between the executive and the legislative. There have emerged alternative views of what accountability entails, involving different answers to both the substance and form of the account. The concepts of accountability, which now dominate the debate, are political accountability, managerial accountability and legal accountability.

Adolph (1983) discovered the "Law of ever-increasing stated Activity" upon surveying the public expenditure records of several advanced countries. He based his law on the pressure for social progress and resulting changes in the relative spheres of private and public economy.

Peacock and Wiseman (1992) found that expenditures grow because revenues grow, rather than the other way round. A given tax system with constant tax rates yields more money as the economy grows, and governments, like most of us, somehow spend their income. Furthermore, the cost of providing public service grows with the nation. There is usually a substantial gap between people desires for expenditures and their tolerance levels of taxation. The pressures for larger budgets are always immense to the extent that revenues are available; the guardians of the public purse (the conservative politicians, budget bureaus, and treasuries of the world) have little power to refuse requests. Only when action is required to raise tax rates to finance new spending can they say "No!" and make it slick.

Akachi (1988) stated that, the stewardship accounting also has its origin in the fact that wealthy men employed "stewards" to manage their properties, the steward rendered their account periodically of their stewardship and this notion is still the root of financial reporting today. In addition, Folorunso (1991) also stated that accountability may be defined, as the rendering of returns on stewardship relating to the management of funds and other assets of which individuals or institutions had been custodians. One would be concerned, when considering accountability within the public sector, as to reliance (in terms of their regularity, timeliness and accuracy) than may be placed on returns rendered. Public sector organizations such as the universities, NEPA, NITEL, the various government department, the Federal, the State and the Local government, which is the lowest and third tier of the government, have not met the requirements for true accountability.

Oke (1988) defined "account" as meaning: (1.) To finish a reckoning (to someone) of money received and paid out, and (2.) To give satisfactory reasons or explanation...."

Following the above definition and given the political socio-environment of Africa and other less developed countries, Chartey (1987) defined accountability as furnishing (to someone) satisfactory, reliable and accessible records, reasons and explanations, for actions of those having custody of power, human resources public money and other resources.

He further implied in this definition, the requirement to identify the party who has to render the accounts, the party to receive them, and the reasons for preparing and receiving the accounts.

Statement of the problem

Nigerian politicians face many problems in rendering their political stewardship in the country. These could be summarized as follows:

Political and economic instability: The political and economic instability in Nigerian political system had led to absence of planning that has slowed down economic growth and development. The instability, according to Owojori (2006) is evidenced in four civilian Republics that were sandwiched with eight military regimes in Nigeria.

Constitutional framework: The absence of a stable constitution was also a significant factor to the problem of revenue allocation in Nigeria. In a country where there is no permanent legal structure, the political field was opened only to money-bag heavy weights that decide whatever they wish.

Financial weakness: Since most of the physical units were created without a guided political and economic philosophy, they are financially very weak to stand on their own. This led to sharing of the proceeds of the federation.

Insincerity: The insincerity on the part of the judiciary, legislature and the executive arms of government to address the problem of revenue sharing led to the destruction of the various structures put in place by the preceding regimes and governments.

Qualified personnel problems: At times, qualified personnel is not employed or chosen to man the government work for effective and efficient job performances. It is not uncommon to appoint someone who is not finance or accounting person to be the head of finance and budget or the minister of finance.

Lack of political objectives: The politicians always forget their political objectives and promises in their manifestoes the moment they were voted in as power corrupts absolute and absolute power corrupts absolutely.

The purpose of this paper therefore is to analyze the importance of political stewardship accounting in government parastatals in Nigeria and the causes of mismanagement in government sector in general as well as proffering plausible suggestions and recommendations for sustainable good governance.

The following null hypotheses, which were tested at 0.05 level of significance, were formulated: (1) Stewardship accounting does not bring about good governance by the politicians as a result of their inability to remit or or give proper account of the funds entrusted to them; (2) There is no relationship between statement of income and expenditure: The statement of income is not regarded as the management expenses to generate a given level of income; (3) The task of making life worth living for people at the grass-root is not an easy task because of over increasing demand for all sorts of welfare packages, and (4) Political stewardship accounting is not the sole determinant responsible for increase in good governance and at times it causes political imbroglios among the politicians in the country.

Review of related literature

Nature of stewardship accounting: Good governance, according to Odozi (1999), is the act of ensuring accountability in the public sector which involves the critical examination of procedures, records and transactions by well trained and properly qualified personnel in order to minimize the degree of misappropriation of fund in public sector organizations. Johnson (1971) said that historically the emphasis in Britain has been almost exclusively on procedures which would enable parliament to exercise a post-facto check on the manner in which monies had been spent for the purpose it was approved.

Nomanton (1971) pointed out that public accountability is an open source of knowledge about how government services function in actual practice and hence of ideas about how they ought to function.

Glym (1985) stated that 'public sector accountability means that those who are charged with drafting and or carrying out policy should be obliged to give an explanation of their actions to their electorate, that is the tax-payers and employees. It is not unusual to request a public servant to give an account of how he has managed the public fund entrusted to his care especially by the electorates. Rendering of political stewardship accounting is better when one is made to give the account of his stewardship when he is still in power than to be re-called to face a difficult situation after leaving the office.

Chartey (1987) defined accountability as 'furnishing (to someone) satisfactory, reliable, verifiable and accessible records, reasons and explanations for actions of those having custody of power, human resources, public money and other resources' implied in this definition is the requirement to identify the party who has to render the accounts, the party to receive them, and the reasons for preparing and receiving the accounts.

Oke (1988) stated that, what accountability does then is to provide answers to the interrogatory questions related to stewardship – what, why, who, whom, whose, which and how. Examples of questions that need answers are: What has to be accounted for; who has to account for it; why it should be submitted; who is responsible for various segments of activity in the society; does responsibility go with commensurate authority; how are governments and public officers to be elected or appointed? These and other enormous numbers of related questions are not easy to answer. The answers become even more elusive when they have to be provided to unspecified diverse groups with different needs and interests that accountability reports are intended to cater for.

Government and politics: Afeniforo (1982) stated that government can be used to refer to the working of the three organs of the state - Legislature, Executive and judiciary. In the actual sense, the Executive arm is particularly identified as the real government. Therefore, government means the group of people that rules the state at a particular time. In a democratic state, the government is formed by the political party that wins the majority in a general election. The cabinet or the council of ministries is often referred to as the government. In a military administration, the supreme military council acts as the government. He further stated that, the word is often used to describe the political order that exists in a state. Thus, a state that is based on popular sovereignty is said to be a democratic government while a state that is ruled by a person is referred to as an autocratic government.

David (1980) attempted to find a working definition for the word 'politics'. In his book 'The political system' He described politics as the authoritative allocation of values for a society" in this sense, politics is regarded as the process of deciding how resources are distributed. David (1980) therefore, saw politics as the process of deciding how resources are distributed. Thus, activities connected with the formation of political parties' selection of candidates, election campaigns, voting, debates passing of bills and assents of the chief Executive revolve on politics as they deal with decision making on how the resources of the state are to be allocated.

Harold (1980) in his own contribution, defined politics as who gets what, when, How? In this sense, politics is seen involving power struggle and competition in the distribution process. In actual sense, government is a product of politics, while 'politics' includes all activities connected with the affairs of the state. Thus, while a vast number of the citizens participate in the politics of the state, only a small group controls the legal government.

Political stewardship accounting in good governance in Nigeria

The political stewardship accounting in good governance in Nigeria can be classified and divided into two prospective aspects, they are: Political stewardship accounting and good governance. Each concept shall be critically worked into as follow.

Political stewardship accounting concepts

Amongst the political stewardship accounting concepts

are as follows: Alimi (1988) categorically stated as follows the concepts of political stewardship Accounting.

The political objectives on manifesto

Before a candidate emerged as a winner, there must be political objectives or manifesto which will comprise how and manner the candidate is proposing to satisfy the electorate. The Objectives are:

Free education at all levels: In a democratic system of government, one of the manifestoes of the aspirant is free-education for the country. It has become the idea of the politicians to encourage the voters by convincing them during campaign that the government will embark on free education should they given him the mandate to rule.

Health services for the people: Another important point is Health services for all. The electorates are always interested on any candidate who is proposing to include free health services in his/her manifestoes.

Transpiration services: The electorates also buy this idea and the politician always includes this to their manifestos.

Accountability and probity: This is also one of the manifestoes that interest the public during the campaign rally.

Revenue generation

Under this sub-heading, Alimi (1988) stated that, financial business in the public sector is similar to that applicable to the private sector. In the public sector, the government has to live and perform its duties to the Nation; as a result, there must be a means of livelihood called money. The money required by the government to perform its duties must be obtained from some where and utilized on something. Thus the government's financial problems falls under the areas which are: i) Where to get the money? ii) How to keep the money? iii) How to utilize the money?

These problems are more compounded because; the state in a modern time has many functions to perform. Its activities are no longer confined to mere maintenance of peace, order and security. Importantly, economic, industrial and social schemes form part and parcel of the activities of a modern state.

Sources and classification of government revenue

Alimi (1988) stated that the federal government derives its revenue from different sources, paid into the consolidate Revenue fund. Prior to 1989 budget, the federal government derives its revenue through the following heads:

Head 1 -Indirect Taxes.
Head 2 -Direct Taxes.
Head 3 -License and internal Revenue.
Head 4 -Mining.
Head 5 -Fees.
Head 6 -Earning and sales.
Head 7 -Rent of government property.
Head 8 -Interest and repayment (General).
Head 9 -Interest and repayment (State).
Head10 -Reimbursements.
Head 11 -Armed Forces.
Head 12 -Miscellaneous.

With effect from 1989 Budget, the Federal Government Revenue was classified into two groups, viz.

- Federal Accounts Revenue Head
- Federal Government Accounts Revenue Heads.

Accountability

Oke (1988) defined accountability as the rendering of returns on stewardship relating to the management of funds and other assets of which individuals or institutions had been custodians. One is concerned, when considering accountability within the public sector, as to the reliance that may be placed or returns rendered. Reliance in terms of their regularity, timeless and accuracy.

Oke (1988) further said that the important thing is that the whole citizenry, policy makers, public officers, politicians, social scientists, professional, renders and the general public should:

i) Appreciate the potency of accountability for development.
ii) Realize the need to be accountable and expect others to be accountable for public office, trust and property.
iii) Recognize when to utilize professional services and advice to achieve accountability.
iv) Realize that accounting transcends the boundaries of measuring and communicating financial information and that, working in collaboration with social scientists (Lawyers and other professionals), accountants can assist in providing the data based needed to install the culture of accountability and this bring about political and social-economic transformation in the country.

Record keeping

Nomston (1971) stated that the activities of organizations have to be kept accordingly, for the accounting users e.g. accounting reports and financial memoranda.

For more clarity, the following are five distinct internal and external users of government financial reports and the purpose for which the reports are required:

Internal users

a) The executives and their advisers.
b) Top administrations of government departments.
c) Managers of government units.
d) Sub-ordinates who are delegated with control tasks.
e) Various hoe and other committees set up by Government to examine a specified functions.

External users

a) The legislative houses.
b) The general public.
c) Researchers and representative of the media.
d) Sectional group within the population such as trade unions, political parties, etc
e) Foreign interests, such as foreign friendly country/ countries, foreign investors and creditors.

Purposes for which the reports are required

(1) Planning: To serve as a basis for planning
(2) Controlling: To serve as a basis for controlling.
(3) Decision making: To serve as a basis for decision making
(4) To give evidence of financial accountability.
(5) To ascertain the propriety of transactions and their conformity with establishes rules.
(6) To serve as a basis for appraisal of the performance of management and staff of government.

Good governance concepts

Full employment

Glym (1985) stated that, full employment is a concept that cannot be precisely defined. Full employment does not mean that everyone has a job. This is because there shall always be people, such as babies, under-aged kids, very old people who cannot work even if they are willing to do so.

This situation makes every government to define its full employment level e.g. in United States full employment level is 97%. In Canada it is 96% then the balance being the unemployment rate. In Nigeria, however, full employment policy has not been given a place of prominence and specific target has to been mentioned. Unemployment is a welfare loss to the society in terms of total output that is being forgone. It is equally a welfare burden borne by individuals. To achieve good governance there must be adequate employment opportunity for the masses.

Price stability

Odozi (1999) also stated that price stability refers to a situation where the general level of process of goods and services changes very little or no changes at all. Price level stability exists when the annual rate of increases in price measured by appropriate indexes is less than 2%. Common measures of price stability are: 1) Consumer price index. 2) Wholesale price index. 3) National product deflator.

Economic growth

Alexander (1985) stated that economic growth can be defined as an increase in a country's physical output over a long period of time. A country is said to have experience economic growth, when the real output of goods and services is increasing at a fastest rate than the rate of growth of its population. Countries pursue economic growth in order to enjoy the benefit of a greater output, hence improve their standard of living.

Economic development

Another important concept is good governance in the country which is part of economic development; this can be defined according to Alimi (1988) as the elimination or reduction in poverty, inequality and unemployment within the context of a growing economy. There may be growth without economic development and a good administrator should take note and promote evenly growth of economic and development in the country.

Balance of payment equilibrium

Balance of payment equilibrium, as stated by Alimi (1988), provides an indicator for a country's international trade; balance of payment equilibrium becomes an important objective of economic stabilization policy and good governance.

Equitable distribution of incomes

Anthony (1977) stated that, this has to do with how income is being distributed in the economy in a fair and equitable manner. Unfortunately in less developed countries, the income distribution pattern are asymmetrically one, that is, it is not evenly distributed. This accounted for the widespread property in Nigeria.

The policy investment usually used to achieve the above objectives or concepts are:

The monetary policy is a measure designed to influence cost allocation and distribution of credit in order to change the level of money supply in the economy.

The fiscal policy refers to the deliberate action which the government for a country takes in areas spending money and / or levying taxes with the objectives of achieving macro-economic variable

The income policy on the other hand relates to the regulation of the rewards that goes to the factors of production such as labour (minimum wage legislation). It equally includes the regulation of product prices (minimum and maximum price legislation).

Budgeting

The Institute of cost and management Accountant gives the following definition of budget. "A plan quantified in monetary terms, prepared and approved prior to a defined time, usually showing planned income to be generated and/or expenditure to be incurred during that period and the capital to be employed to attain a given objectives"

Brown and Howard (1984) also defined a budget as a "predetermined statement of management policy - during a given period which provides a standard for comparison with the results actually achieved.

Harper (1982) defined a budget as a quantitative economic plan in respect of a period of time. He however, explained the key words of his definition as follows:

(a) **Quantitative:** A budget must comprise quantities. An enterprise many plan to build up a reputation for fair-trading but it is not possible to budget for such a reputation since this is an intangible that cannot be quantified.
(b) **Economic:** To be a budget, a plan must be in economic terms. An enterprise may plan to make the strongest steel in the world but such a plan cannot be properly referred to as a budget.
(c) **Plan:** A budget is a plan; it is not a hope or a forecast but an authoritative intention. A forecast is a prediction of what will happen as a result of a given set of circumstances while a budget is a planned result that an enterprise aims to attain.
(d) **Time:** A budget is always in respect of a period of time. Budgets are five yearly: yearly, quarterly, weekly, daily or other time period.

Types of budgeting

Armey and Egginton (1979) stated that there are three main types of budgeting systems;

- The Traditional budgeting
- The zero based Budgeting
- The Programmed planning and budgeting systems.

Adams (1987) stated that to achieve good governance in stewardship accounting there should be budgeting and the preparation of the budget.

Budget cycle

See below the budget cycle according to Alimi (1988)

Stage 1

Call circular: Horne (1986) stated that all the arms of government do prepare budget, that is, Federal, State and the Local Government, which is the third tier of the arms of government. He further said, the president articulate the government objectives in terms of economy social and other welfare parameter. The government through budget planning ministries sends circular to all ministries and parastatal. The department of parastatal submits advance proposal of their estimate for the text fiscal year informs of draft estimate.

Stage 2

Budget preparation in the ministry and government agency: Horne (1986) further stated that, each ministry would then send the circular with the little addition to the objective and the policy of the government.

Stage 3

Budget defense Committee: The composition of the committee are made up of the following: 1) Head of government (president in federal level governor in the state and chairman in the local government level). 2) Finance minister. 3) Justice Minister and attorney general of the federation 4) Director of budget.

Stage 4

Budget hearing by the house: Okigbo (2001) explained that, during this stage the president, present his appropriation bills to the houses (budget estimate) the budget will contain (a) Review of economy; (b) Policy of the following year. E.g. Government may decide not to import 'Tokunbo' vehicles or the importation of certain goods or foodstuff should be abolished; (c) Source of funds; (d) Recurrent of capital expenditure; (e) Fiscal and monetary policies of the government.

Stage 5

Debate and approval of the budget: This is the stage when the house will come together and debate in the proposed budget and delete or add if it is necessary before the approval of the house of assembly (state).

Stage 6

Budget speech: Harper (1982) stated that whenever the house approve the budget, the head of state or president (Federal Government) will now broadcast the approval of the house to the nation for awareness.

State 7

Implementation of the budget: Harper (1982) stated that, in the course of implementation of the Budget, warrant is issued to individual ministries for implementation. The cheques needed for the implementation of the budget are sent and each ministry would now send their expenditure return (transcript) to the ministry of finance.

Stage 8

Budget control: This is the final stage, it is constituted through committee and sub-committee and finally the call circular would therefore be formulated again for the fiscal year.

Importance of stewardship accounting

For proper accountability in the public sector the under listed points are the importances of stewardship accounting according to Fayemi (1980). These are:

i) To ascertain the propriety of transactions and their conformity with established rules. This means that the historical accounting information should depict the extent of compliance with the various rules and regulation applicable to the organization be it government or organized private sector. It also showed whether the transactions are proper in relation to the object clause of the organization as any business outside the object clause is regarded as utra-vires.
ii) To give evidence of financial accountability, here we need to actually ascertain how transparent the government management is in relation to financial probity. That is the government/ management has a liability to reveal justify and explain what they did with the funds entrusted to them. Have they utilized the money in the best interest of the general public or they have utilized it in the best interest of their pockets.
iii) To serve as a basis for planning it is crystal clear that the futures are laden with series of uncertainty. Without adequate planning, a business organization which can be likened to various ministries and department many not be able to forge ahead effectively and efficiently, planning is therefore of almost importance to every business organization or government parastatal in other to reduce the uncertainty associated with the future. The historical accounting record of the past events can be used to postulate into the future.
iv) To serve as a basis for controlling. Here if the various business activities are not adequately controlled, it could lead to problem in the future as the main object of our plans may not be realized. Controlling is one of the key managerial functions, which must be critically examined. When there is adequate too much from our plans. It is therefore every important that all activities should be controlled to achieve our targets/objectives.
v) To serve as a basis for decision making. At all levels of business activities, decision making is very crucial, failure to make adequate and informed decision at the right time could lead to business failure and or in calculate losses to the organization. The various accounting information, which are historical events of the past, provided a basis for such decision making in the future.
vi) To serve as a basis of appraisal of the performance of management. The importance of appraisal cannot be over-emphasized, through appraisal, lapses will be discovered which may warrant urgent attention of management. Through appraisal, financial viability, probability, efficiency and liquidity could be ascertained which should be used for future decision making.

Growth of government spending

Adolph (1983) thought he had discovered the "law of Ever-increasing State activity" upon surveying the public-expenditure records of several advanced countries in the nineteenth century. He based his "law" on the pressure for social progress and resulting changes in the relative spheres of private and public economy". History has certainly born him out, although war and its aftermath have cost more than social progress.

Reason for increase in government expenditure

Brownwhich (1976) stated the main reasons why government expenditure is increasing often and then. The traditional functions of government such as defense, maintenance of law and order, e.t.c are becoming extensive and cumbersome. Defense is becoming expensive more than ever. Within the country administrative set up is increasing both in coverage and intensity, that is, government machinery has to be manned by experts in their respective fields. In addition, various complexities of economic and social measures develop which make an efficient administration complex and expensive as well.

Besides the traditional functions of the state, there is growing awareness of additional responsibilities. The government is expending its activities in the area of various welfare measures which include measures to enrich the cultural life of the society and those designed to provide social securities to the people such as pensions, old peoples' home e.t.c.

Increasing population may also be a determinant of public expenditure growth. The share scales of various public goods and services have to rise in conformity with the growth of population. The need for more schools, hospitals and such likes cannot be over-emphasized in the light of increasing population.

It has been suggested that urbanization and the resulting congestion has increased the need for more infrastructure and public goods and services. Also quite a number of incidental services like those connected with traffic, roads, pedestrian bridge e.t.c have to be provided.

The tendency for prices to go up has equally contributed to the growth of public expenditure. The increase in prices of input and other goods purchased by public sector has resulted in an increase in public expenditure. It is the responsibility of the government to protect the citizenry against the evils of price mechanism. Consequently, anti-cyclical and other regulatory measures are put in place. Efforts are made to deduce income and wealth in equalities and bring about social and economic justice.

Increasing public expenditure can also be explained in terms of increasing cost of debt servicing. Since states are related to one another through various economic transactions, there are tendencies to run into debts which must be settled.

Public debt

Byrne (1986) stated that, public debt is the totality of debt owned both internally and externally by the government of a country. Internal debts are those owned by the government to the residents of a country while external debts are those debts owned to overseas government and international institution.

Alimi (1988) further stated that Debt management represents the action of government or the central Bank to influence the composition of debt. In respect of internal debt, it is issues new securities, either to replace those maturing or to raise additional money to the government treasury. It makes use of treasury bills, treasury certificates development stocks and ways and means, advances as instruments. Internal debt includes trace-related debts owned directly to banks, contractors and suppliers.

Nigeria's external debts stock comprises:

i) Project tied debts.
ii) Trade - related debts.
iii) Balance of payments support loan.

The following are the amount of Nigeria's external debt.

Year	Amount $
1976	1.27b
1986	18.6b
1991	33.2b
1995	32.6b
1996	28.2b
1997	27.04b

Causes of Nigeria's debt crisis

Dawson (1993) stated the causes of Nigeria's debt crisis as follows:

Change in economy

Nigeria enjoys oil boom in the 70s and what followed was excessive supply of crude petroleum which led to oil glut in the world market causing the price of oil to fall rapidly.

This was sequel to the discovery and exploitation of oil in North Sea, Egypt, Malaysia and Mexico, which drastically reduced the oil price from $36 to $10 per barrel in 1990s. This external development led to a substantial reduction in oil revenue and the inability to reduce expenditure led to heavy debt accumulation.

Nature of Nigerian economy

Bluceh (1991) stated that, Nigerian economy is heavily dependent on one or few agricultural or mineral, commodities. Our manufacturing sector is mostly at infant stage and relies heavily on imported inputs. Nigeria equally depends on advanced countries for the supply of other imports and finance needed for economic development. All these made Nigeria to incur heavy debts and at the same time vulnerable to external shock.

Problem of committing short and median term loans to long-term projects

Fayemi (1980) also stated that, in a situation in which it is difficult to complete these projects before amortization is due, problem of this nature will no doubt aggravated debt service Borden.

Low level of savings

He further stated that, the low level of saving and high propensity to consume foreign goods and services is another factor that has contributed to the Nigeria debt crises and this has led to the emergence of trade areas.

The shift from official to private sources of credit also contributed to the problem being experienced by Nigeria in the area of external loan. For a private loan, interest rate would be higher and the period of maturity very short while the reverse is the case in respect of official loan.

Solutions to external debt problems

According to Alimi (1988) the following were stated as the solutions to external debt problems:

Debt rescheduling

This involves the re-arrangement of payment terms of debt in terms of the adjustment of interest rate grace period principal repayment, and maturity. The strategy does not cause a reduction in the stock debts rather it facilitates management of debts by providing relief. For instance, Nigeria negotiated series of rescheduling arrangements with the Paris club of creditors between 1986 and 1991 to which more than half the external debt is owned. However, the use of this method has been argued against because it will only lead to the postponement of the evil day of the debtor nation.

Debt - Equity conversion

Brown and Howard (1984) further stated that Nigeria government is currently applying debt equity swap. It is an ideal of converting foreign debt into equity in local companies. This will make the economic environment attractive for foreign investment.

Debt forgiveness

Hongrene (1980) also stated that Debt forgiveness must take with consideration. This arises when the creditor nation decides to forget or write off the debt of the debtor nation. This option has been taken by Paris club in favour of some debtors. However, Nigeria will not benefit because these debts have not been used to alleviate poverty. Another reason why Nigeria could enjoy this opportunity is the position of Nigeria among the oil producing countries.

Debt repudiation

This involves disallowing the debt completely. Castro (1980) in his own contribution does not see any sense in developing countries paying back the debt because through colonialism African countries had more than paid for the debts. However, there is possibility of sanction from (IMF) International monetary fund and World Bank if Nigeria should repudiate.

Roles of the accountant in political stewardship accounting in Nigeria

Harper (1982) stated that, an accountant is a person whose profession is to keep and examine business accounts with a view to reporting on them for the benefit of all interested groups.

These groups of interested persons include managers, owners/shareholders, investors, creditors, employees, and even governments. Accountant therefore, occupies a place of pride and accountability. He is found in all human organizations including clubs and societies, He further said, that Jesus Christ had an 'accountant' among the disciples in the person of Judas Iscariot who kept their funds.

The main or traditional roles of accountant

Keeping of business records

The primary function of accounting and the accountant is to keep systematic records of all monetary transactions of the organization, entering them in a prescribed manner and leading to the preparation of financial statements.

Protection of the organizations assets or funds from misappropriation or misapplication

Oke (1988) lamented on this and said it is a cardinal function of the accountant and the strict adherence to this that has led to the accountant being branched 'conservative' of course, this is in the interest of his employer and his; (with his employers) expectations since no one would want to entrust his assets, particularly cash, into the hands of someone whose integrity is questionable. Essentially, the accountant keeps all the financial records or books of account of the organization and institutes controls to check authorizations and compliance with laid-down policies so as to forestall fraud and misappropriation.

Provision of financial information

The accountant provides financial information about the performance of a business and its financial position. Oke (1988) stated also that, performance is measured in terms of profits and profit and loss Accounts is designed to describe the overall performance of a business over a period of usually one year. The financial position of the business is measured in terms of assets and liabilities, which the Balance sheets disclose. Those who would be interested in such financial information include managers, creditors, investors, bankers, employees, and the government to mention a few.

Ensuring compliance with legal requirements

Oke (1988) stated that, this is mother important role played by the Accountant and his profession. He (Accountant) ensures that the business keeps within the laws governing the operations of business. Some of the legal requirements a business must comply with are the submission of tax returns, preparation of prospectus for publics offer etc.

Financial regulations

Brown and Jackson (1983) stated that financial regulations are issued matters of the Federal Government, in accordance with and under the authority of the finance (control and management) Act, 1958 as amended.

He further stated that, financial regulations are internal regulations that are intended to provide a framework of financial control and place prime responsibility for elementary control and anti-fraud duties on executive departments, whilst recognizing the role of internal audit.

They are useful in the following ways:

i) They outline good systems, organization and procedures of basic financial management.
ii) They give backing to internal audit and establish it as a "tool of management", this avoids the function being, viewed as a "tool of an interfering treasurer".
iii) They help internal audit allocate responsibility and maintain its "independence", making a clear separation between departmental and audit duties.
iv) They ensure that operations remain within the law and reduce the scope for fraud.

Financial Regulations should seek to outline the system of financial administration to operate at departmental level, without necessarily setting out in detail arrangements and system that might be in corporate in separate codes or manuals of financial procedures and instructions.

Supply procedure

Bird and Morgan (1981) stated that, National Assembly maintains control of central government expenditure by what is know as "supply procedure. This operates as follows.

(a) Each governments department submits "estimates" for expenditure in the new financial year to the budget ministry for approval. After negotiation, the agreed estimates are presented to the National Assembly, thus, satisfying the condition that no money shall be withdrawn from any public fund of the federation unless the issue of those moneys has been authorized by an Act of the National Assembly. If necessary, supplementary estimates can also be presented during the year.
(b) National Assembly examines the estimates, when they are divided into 'Votes' for particular items of expenditure. Each vote gives details of the services which will be provided, when approve, in a standard form.
John (1991) further stated the introduction. Description of the expenditure, and comparison with the budgeted and actual expected amounts for the previous year.

Part I: The "ambit" of the vote, being a brief description of the services to be financed.

Part II: Detailed analysis of the amounts to be provided, divided, divided first according to which expenditure programme the vote relates to (e.g. defense, transport, etc) and subdivided into subheads savings encountered on one subhead may be applied with permission from the Budget ministry, to meet excesses on another subhead - this process is know as virement.

Part III: Details of receipts expected which will be paid into the consolidated Revenue Fund.

Part IV: Further analysis of the expenditure e.g. between capital and current expenditure.

(c) When approved, the votes are included in the appropriation Act.
(d) The appropriation accounts are audited by the Auditor General of the federation. He is appointed by the president on the advice of the civil service commission, and his independence is further assured by his salary being paid straight from the consolidated Revenue fund, and his freedom from dismissal except on a motion passed by both Houses of Assembly.
(e) There may be expenditure, not previously authorized by the National Assembly, which is needed urgently but for which there is no time to be granted parliamentary authority. Such expenditure, which may be taken from the contingencies fund, but any expenditure which is met from this fund must be authorized in arrears by the National Assembly and charged to the vote for which the expenditure is then authorized. It is an "imprest" fund financed by the consolidated Revenue fund.
(f) The Auditor - General of the federation will report any material irregularities to the public Accounts committee.

Cash accounting

Harper (1982) stated that, a cash accounting is restricted to measuring the change in cash payments from cash receipts. Cash accounting records transaction in the period in which the related cash receipts and payment occur and is really only useful for short term financial control.

Expenditure is recognized as cash paid out, which may be before or after the time when the resource (cost) was consumed and any benefit received. Similarly, revenue on income is recognized as it is received in the form of cash. On this basis, revenue expenditure, revenue income and capital income are all treated in the same way. An account is no more than an analysis and summary of the cash book.

Accruals and commitment accounting

Alimi (1988) stated that, the difference between the accruals and commitment system of accounting is in the time at which the expense is recognized as an operation statements produced under the commitment accounting system which includes not only expenditure which has actually taken place but also expenditure to which the organization has become committed, e.g. by placing an order for goods and services.

RESEARCH DESIGN AND METHODOLOGY

The population comprised of four hundred (400) key officers in the (16) sixteen local governments of Ekiti State of Nigeria out of which (100) hundred were selected at random. The data used were gathered through questionnaire and were analyzed using frequency counts, percentage scores and factor analysis.

RESULTS, SUMMARY AND DISCUSSIONS OF FINDINGS

The following were the summary of the findings which were derived from the results of the analysis of the questions in the questionnaire.

1) Stewardship accounting promotes good management of public funds.
2) Stewardship accounting promotes economic growth in the country.
3) Political stewardship accounting increases standard of living.
4) Good governance in public sector discourages embezzlement.
5) Political Stewardship increases probity and accountability.
6) There is no relationship between income and expenditure.
7) The expenditure is always more than income in preparation of public accounts.
8) Public account is not properly prepared like the private company's account.
9) There is unnecessary expenditure, which brings public debt.
10) The public account does not correct perceived inequalities.
11) Public sector is to provide services for all citizens e.g. education good roads, health services and so on.
12) Public sector is to provide services beyond the private means of people using those services.
13) Public sector should provide benefit to everyone within socially acceptable norms.
14) Public sector ensuring constant approach to certain practices.
15) Public sector substitutes central or local planning in place of consumer choice.
16) Political stewardship account is the main determinant responsible for increasing in good governance and did not bring political imbroglio.
17) Political stewardship disallowed political stability in the country.
18) Political stewardship account aids good governance in public sector.
19) Political stewardship accounting is the quickest way to manipulate the implementation of policies and plans for effective management in Nigeria.
20) Political stewardship accounts bring probity and accountability.

Conclusion

It was therefore concluded that:

1) There is no increase in volume of good governance in the management of public funds.
2) There is a negative relationship between statement of income and expenditure.
3) The tax of making life worth living for people at the grass-root is not an easy task because of over increasing demand for all sorts of welfare packages.
4) Political stewardship account is not the sole determinant responsible for increase in good governance and it causes political unrest.

Recommendations

The following recommendations are made:

1) The country as a whole should make sure that political stewardship accounting system should be set up and strictly embarked, so as to guide against maladministration by the public officers and politicians that are currently affecting every individual in the country.
2) The ascertainment of the propriety of transactions and their conformity with established rules should be taken into consideration in order to comply with the rules and regulations applicable to the organization, be it government or organized private sector in the country.
3) There must be an evidence of financial accountability. We need to actually ascertain how transparent the government management is in relation to financial probity. That is to say, political stewardship accounting would enable the government that has a liability to reveal, justify and explain what it did with the funds entrusted to it. Has it utilized the money in the best interest of the general public or the officials have utilized it in the best interest of their pockets.
4) Political stewardship serves as a basis for planning. The historical accounting record of the past events can be used to postulate into the future; that is to say, that planning is a crystal ball that the future is laden with series of uncertainty. As a result of this, without adequate planning, government which can be likened to various ministries and department may not be able to forge ahead effectively and efficiently.
5) Political stewardship accounting can serve as a basis for control. If the various public organizations are not adequately controlled; it could lead to problem in the future as the main object of our plans may not be realized. As we all know that, controlling is one of the key managerial functions which must be strictly examined. When there are adequate control measures we are not likely to deviate too much from our plans. It is therefore important that all activities should be controlled to achieve our objectives/targets in the country (Nigeria).

REFERENCES

Adams JL (1987). Conceptual Black-bursting. Penguin publisher London.
Adolph I (1983): http://internet search.
Afeniforo PO (1982). Questions and answers on Government. Omolayo

Standard Press Nigeria Ltd.
Akachi U (1988). : http:// internet search.
Alexander L (1985). Successfully implementing Strategic Decision. Long range Planning, 18(3).
Alimi RA (1988). Public sector accounting. Corporate Ventures, Lagos.
Anthony RN (1977). Zero-Base Budgeting, a useful fraud? Govern. Account. J. Summ. pp. 19-26.
Armey B, Egginton DA (1979). : http://. Internet search.
Bird P, Morgan JP (1981). Financial reporting by charities. London ICAEW.
Bluceh D (1991). 'Poll Tax Review: The parties Go on the record'. Public Finance and accountancy, 15th Edition. London.
Brown J, Jackson M (1983). : http://. Internet search.
Brown JL, Howard LR (1984). Managerial Accounting, & Finance M&E, Fourth Edition.
Brownwich M (1976). The economics of capital Budgeting, Harmondsworth, Penguin.
Byrne T (1986). Local Government in Britain. Harmedworth Penguin.
Castro F (1980). : http://. Internet search.
Chartey BC (1987). :http://. Internet search.
David FA (1980). : http:// internet search.
Dawson T (1993). Principles and practice of Modern Management. Tudor Publishing Company.
Fayemi DO (1980). Principles of local government accounting. Chapter Ten, Lagos.
Folorunso OO (1991). http:// internet search/.
Glymn JJ (1985). Public sector financial control and accounting 2nd edition.
Harold (1980): http://. Internet search.
Harper A (1982): http://. Internet search.
Hongrene BC (1980) 'Cost Accounting' A managerial Emphases. Penguin, London.
Horne JV (1986). Financial management and policy. Tudor publishing company.
Jackson PM (1983). Public sector Economics (second edition). Oxford martin Robertson London.
John OC (1991). : http://. Internet search.
Johnson AA (1971). : http:// internet search.
Nomanton DT (1971). : http:// internet search.
Odozi VA, Victor A (2001). Implementation of Policies and plans for effective Management. Niger. Inst. Manage. Vol. 37.
Oke EF (1988). The concept of accountability. ICAN J. Vol. xxi (4).
Okigbo PHC (2001). Essays in the public philosophy of development Vol.2.
Owojori AA (2006). Monogram on Political Stewardship and Accountability in Nigeria.
Peacock WZ, Wiseman J (1992). : http://internet search.
Sinclair AD (1984). :http:/ internet search/.
The finance (control) and management Act (1958). Federal Government of Nigeria.

5

The factors influencing bank credit risk: The case of Tunisia

Nabila Zribi[1]* and Younes Boujelbène[2]

[1]Faculty of Economics and Management of Sfax. University of Sfax-Tunisia. Route Saltania 4 Km, 3081 Sfax-Tunisia.
[2]Faculty of Economics and Management of Sfax. University of Sfax-Tunisia. Higher Institue of Business Administration of Sfax. Route from the Areport 4 Km, Sfax. BP1013-3018 Sfax-Tunisia.

This paper aims to examine the determinants of bank credit risk in Tunisia, being an emergent country. Our sample includes ten commercial banks over the period of 1995 to 2008. The paper takes into account both macroeconomic factors and microeconomic variables that are likely to influence credit risk. Overall, the results show that the main determinants of bank credit risk in Tunisia are: ownership structure, prudential regulation of capital, profitability and macroeconomic indicators.

Key words: Bank credit risk-taking, bank's characteristics, ownership structure, capital regulation, emerging country.

INTRODUCTION

Over the last few years, the Tunisian banking sector has become more and more market oriented, competitive, attractive for foreign investors and not immunized against diffusion of new technologies of information and communication. In consideration of this new open and turbulent environment and in view of minimizing all kinds of risks or signs of fragility, the Central Bank of Tunisia has made it mandatory for the banks to respect restrictive reforms.

These reforms are centred around five axes: improving prudential regulation, opening the financial sector to foreign investors, promoting the equity market, implementing new indirect monetary policies and liberating the interest rates and the allocation of credits. All these changes will certainly have implications on the risk taken by the Tunisian banking industry. In this setting, our paper aims to analyse the factors that are likely to influence the level of bank credit risk.

Three main factors lie behind this research: First, the competitive and regulated environment in which Tunisian banks operate. Second, the increase of the potential of moral hazard and agency problems between different actors in the Tunisian banks due to the lack of transparency. Finally, the gap we have noticed in the literature about the analysis of the key factors influencing credit risk of banks in emerging countries.

This research paper is organized as follows. Subsequently, a review of the literature and hypotheses was done, after which the study focused on Tunisian banking literature. This was followed by a description of the methodology and the empirical results. Finally, the study was concluded.

RELATED LITERATURE AND HYPOTHESES

Two trends in the literature have focused on the main factors that are likely to influence bank credit risk. One trend appears to suggest internal variables as potential determinants of credit risk. The other trend highlights changes in external variables in the prudential regulation and economic conditions affecting the bank credit risk. The main results of this literature provide evidence of a close relationship among internal variables, external variables and bank credit risk.

A large part of the literature highlights that the ownership structure might play a role in influencing credit risk and a particular focus is put on the relationship between public ownership or State-owned banks and their levels of risk. Generally, it is assumed that State-owned banks take more risks than the private and foreign capital requirements and bank risks in complete markets.

*Corresponding author. E-mail: nabila1zribi@gmail.com

Their results have shown that with a flat insurance banks. In this context, Micco and Panizza (2004) have found that public banks are exposed to more risk than other banks since they play an important role in the facilitation of the credit policies and their loans are less sensitive to macroeconomic shocks in comparison with private banks. Sapienza (2004) has also found such a relationship. He explains this result by three alternative views. From the social view, he has shown that the State interferes in banks in order to correct the market failure caused by private banks. According to the political view, he demonstrates that the State-owned banks are a mechanism for pursuing politicians' private interests, such as doing favours for political protégés.

Finally, in relation to the agency view, he has shown that State-owned banks are basically benevolent maximizers of social welfare but they are plagued by corruption and misallocation. In a recent research from industrialised countries, De Nicolo (2001) and Giuliano et al. (2007) have suggested that state-owned banks typically exhibit higher risk than other types of banks. In Russian banks over the period 1999 to 2007, Zuzana and Laura (2008) have found that the effect of state ownership on banks' insolvency risk is positive. They explain this result by the fact that state-controlled banks tend to be more stable. In order to investigate this result more closely, they add an interaction term of size and state control to their model. This interaction makes the coefficient of state controlled variable become negative, which indicates that only large state-controlled banks are more stable than other state-controlled banks. In the context of a sample of 423 banks in transition countries (Russia, Ukraine, Hungary, Czech Republic etc), Rainer and Paul (2007) have found no indication of excessive risk taking by any specific ownership or size categories of transition banks. Generally, studies in the context of transition countries have not been conclusive about the sign of state-controlled banks. So, following theoretical literature, we expect to find a positive relationship between state-owned banks and the level of bank credit risk.

Hypothesis 1: State owned-banks take more risks than other banks

As for the prudential regulation of capital, it might also help to explain why banks take risks. The common belief, at least among regulators, is that higher capital requirements result in a higher stability of the banking sector and consequently in lower levels of bank risk-taking. However, the literature analysing the relationship between bank capital regulation and the level of risk is ambiguous and is not conclusive about the sign (positive or negative) of this relationship. Kahane (1977) and Sharpe (1978) have analysed the relationship between premium, banks have incentives to increase risk-taking. Similar results have been reached by Koehn and Santomero (1980). These authors have analysed the impact of capital ratio (equity capital to total assets without taking into consideration the inherent risk of different assets) on bank risk-taking. Their results show that higher capital requirements lead banks to revise the composition of their portfolios.

This composition is characterized by the detention of riskier assets in comparison with those before the amendment of the regulation. Kim and Santomero (1988) have criticized the researches of Kahane (1977) and Koehn and Santomero (1980). They have propose the ratio of equity capital to risk-weighted assets as a regulator ratio. Their results have shown that a regulator ratio adjusted to risk leads the banks to change the compositions of their asset portfolios in favour of less risky assets and thus a less bank risk-taking. Similar results have been found by Furlong and Keely (1989, 1990) and Dothan and Williams (1980) suggesting that the prudential regulation of capital leads banks to reduce their potential of bank risk-taking. For empirical researches, Shrieves and Dahl (1992) represent the reference point of all the empirical studies. Shrieves and Dahl (1992) have studied the impact of regulation of equity capital on the bank risk-taking decisions in the context of 1800 U.S. banks over the period 1983 to1987. Based on a simultaneous equation model, these results show a positive association between changes in equity capital and the level of risk, particularly for over-capitalized banks. In the same context, Jacques and Nigro (1997) have shown that the introduction of capital based on risk has led to higher capital ratios and a lower risk portfolio of banks.

Hussain and Hassan (2004), in the context of 11 developing countries have also shown a negative relationship between capital ratio and portfolio risk. In the European context and especially in Switzerland, Rime (2001) has examined the relationship between regulatory capital and risk-taking by banks. She has concluded that the regulatory pressure has induced Swiss banks to increase their capital levels while keeping stable levels of risk-taking. Nor and Mohamed (2007) have presented a comparative study of all factors contributing to the credit risks of commercial banks in a multi-country setting: Australia, France, Japan and the U.S. represent developed economy banking systems while emerging ones are represented by India, Korea, Malaysia, Mexico and Thailand. They have found that the regulatory capital is an important factor influencing the credit risk of any banking system that offers a range of services. This study also highlights that the credit risk in emerging economy banks is higher than that in developed economies and that risk is formed by a larger number of bank-specific factors in emerging economies compared to their counterparts in developed economies.

Marina and Svetlana (2001) have studied the main The Tunisian banking sector has received a part of the factors influencing excessive risk in transition banks with a special emphasis on Russian banks. They have found that many banks in Russia have violated prudential ratios in a forbearance environment or when the value of license is low and the probability of success in a risky project is relatively high. In the context of emerging countries, Goldlewski (2004) have found that the regulation of capital and risk are negatively related. In summary, as the ratio of capital and its regulation aim to reduce the levels of bank risk-taking, we expect to find a negative relationship between these two variables.

Hypothesis 2: There is an inverse relationship between capital regulation and bank credit risk

Another part of the literature has been interested in the analysis of the theoretical arguments based on the relationship between the bank size and bank risk-taking. It suggests a negative relationship between these two variables. Such a relationship is justified by the most natural argument that is diversification by size. Indeed, larger banks are expected to have lower risks because they have the capability of holding more diversifiable portfolios. In this respect, many researches have been conducted. According to the researches of Saunders et al. (1990), Chen et al. (1998), Cebenoyan et al. (1999) and Megginson (2005), there is a negative relationship between bank risk and bank size. They explain this result by the fact that larger banks are likely to be more skilled in risk management and have also better diversification opportunities. Thus, we expect to find that the bank size is negatively related to the level of risk.

Hypothesis 3: The bank size affects the level of risk negatively

Moreover, macroeconomic indicators can also influence bank risks. These indicators are those at the origin of banking crises: inflation rate of growth GDP, interest rate and exchange rate. In this setting, many researches have been conducted to analyse the relationship between these indicators and the occurrence of banking crises. The findings in this respect indicate that there is a close relationship between macroeconomic indicators and banking crises and excessive risk(Angeloni and al (2009), Olga Bohachova (2008), Buch and al (2010). We will test if these variables influence the levels of credit risk in the Tunisian context.

Hypothesis 4: Macroeconomic factors affect bank credit risk

The Tunisian banking sector has received a part of the littérature.

One part of this literature has been interested in the analysis of banking performance, banking efficiency, banking stability and banking governance. Another part of the literature focuses on some phenomena characterizing the Tunisian banking industry like restructuring, liberalisation and privatisation. In this context, Mohamed (2002) has studied the impact of alternative ownership structures on Tunisian firm performance and managerial behaviour with special emphasis on institutional and managerial ownerships. His results have suggested a positive relationship between institutional ownership and the value of the firm explained essentially by internal mechanisms of control. He has also found that the higher the managerial ownership is the lower institutional ownership.

Abdelwahed (2003) has studied the impact of the different variables of corporate governance on the performance of 43 quoted Tunisian firms during the period 1995 to 2000. His study has shown that there is a statistically significant relationship between corporate governance systems and performance. Samy (2003) has investigated the impact of banks' characteristics, financial structure and macroeconomic indicators on banks' net interest margins and profitability in the Tunisian banking industry over the 1980 to 2000 period. His results have shown that individual bank characteristics are main factors that determine bank interest margins and net profitability. Other important internal determinants of banks' interest margins are bank loans which have a positive and significant impact. The size has mostly negative and significant coefficients on the net interest margins. He has also found that the macroeconomic indicators such as inflation and growth rates have no impact on banks' interest margins and profitability. Then, turning to the financial structure and its impact on banks' interest margins and profitability, he has found that concentration is less beneficial to the Tunisian commercial banks than competition.

Wade et al. (2005) have been interested in the analysis of the impacts of financial liberalization on the efficiency of the banking system in Tunisia, using various DEA models and Panel data covering the period 1992 to 1997. Also, Zaghla and Boujelbene (2008) have analysed the determinants of efficiency of the banking system in Tunisia. Their empirical results have revealed pronounced differences in efficiency depending on the size and structure of bank ownership. In addition, the preponderance of credit activity relative to other outputs represents a source of efficiency. Then, there is a negative relationship between the ratio of equity to total assets and bank efficiency, suggesting that banks are engaged in risky activities. Finally, the share of non-performing loans represents a source of inefficiency since the charges for bank increase with these types of loans, especially for large banks.

Studies on bank risk-taking decisions in the Tunisian banking sector are limited. In this context, we can cite the

Table 1. List of the Tunisian banks.

Banks abbreviation in French	Full name of banks	Ownership structure (Period: 1995 to 2008)	Specialisation
AB	Amen Bank	Private	No specialisation
ATB	Arab Tunisian Bank	Private	No specialisation
BH	Bank of Housing	State	Estate-field
BIAT	International Arab Tunisian Bank	Private	No specialisation
BNA	National Agricultural Bank	State	Agriculture
BS	South Bank or Attijari Bank	State (95 to 05) Private (06 to 08)	No specialisation
BT	Bank of Tunisia	Private	No specialisation
STB	Tunisian Company Banking	State	No specialisation
UBCI	Industrial and Commercial Bank Union	Private	No specialisation
UIB	International Bank Union	State (95 to 02) Private (03 to 08)	No specialisation

research of Hamza (2009) and Mnasri and Abaoub (2010). Hamza (2009) has investigated the effects of ownership structure, as an internal control mechanism of agency problem, on corporate governance. He has focused especially on the impact of the size, number and type of blockholders on the performance and the risk-taking of the Tunisian listed companies over the period 2001 to 2004. The main result of his study indicates that the presence of controlling shareholders affect performance and risk-taking and play an important role in corporate governance. However, we assume that the control contest of the leading shareholder is not conclusive but it indicates a form of coalition and agreement effect to share private benefits. In the same way, Mnasri and Abaoub (2010) have empirically analysed the determinants of risk-taking in Tunisian commercial banks, with a special emphasis on the ownership structure, the acceptance of government officials on banks' boards, the capital adequacy requirements and the franchise value. Using a sample of ten commercial banks for the period from 1997 to 2006, they have found that the acceptance of government officials on banks' boards reduces bank risk.

The relationship between the managerial holdings and total risk and firm specific risk is non-linear; the risk increases initially with the ownership by managers and then decreases as the effect of managerial entrenchment dominates the effects of interest alignment on bank risk. In contrast, systematic risk is unrelated to ownership and franchise value does not affect bank risk. Following these researches, our research aims to analyse the determinants of bank credit risk in relation with microeconomic factors, macroeconomic factors, ownership structure and bank prudential regulation.

METHODOLOGY

Sample and data

The purpose of this paper is to analyse the internal and external factors determining the levels of bank credit risk-taking in Tunisia. Our sample consists of a panel of 10 commercial banks that are listed on the Stock Exchange of Tunis (Table 1) over the period 1995 to 2008. The data used in this paper are collected from the annual reports of the Professional association of the Tunisian banks and financial establishments; the activity reports of the Banks, the guides of the Tunis stock exchange, the Documents of the council of financial market and the Web sites news of the companies, the stock exchange and the central bank of Tunisia.

Variables' measures

First, following Shrives and Dahl (1992), Jacques and Nigro (1997), Rime (2001) and Hussain and Hassan (2004) among others, we employ the ratio of risk-weighted assets to total assets as a measure of bank credit risk. This measure is justified by the fact that the allocation of bank assets across different categories of risk is the major determinant of bank risk. Second, we define banks' characteristics in the following manner:

1. Ratio of profitability: Return on assets "ROA" is measured as the ratio of net income to total assets.
2. Ratio of capital: CAP- is defined as the ratio of equity capital to total assets.

Thirdly, we also measure ownership structure (GOV) by a dummy variable that equals 1 if it is the case of State-controlled banks' (Public Ownership) and 0 otherwise (Private and Foreign ownership).

Fourth, we use one proxy for regulation. Our measure of bank regulation (REG) is a dummy variable that captures the degree of respect to the regulation by banks. It takes one if the bank respects the minimum threshold of 5% before 1999 and 8% after 1999 and 0 in other cases. So, if the solvency ratio of the bank (the ratio

Table 2. Descriptive statistics.

	Risk	COV	REG	ROA	CAP	LN size	% GDP growth	Inflation	Exchange rate	Interest rate
Mean	0.904493	0.435714	0.885714	0.007809	0.092806	14.47209	4.99285	3.442857	1.169456	6.053482
Median	0.915310	0.000000	1.000000	0.008680	0.090960	14.41782	5.15000	3.150000	1.281053	5.875000
Maximum	0.995856	1.000000	1.000000	0.035006	0.194211	16.28021	7.10000	6.300000	1.436490	8.812500
Minimum	0.660699	0.000000	0.000000	-0.103505	-0.010985	13.37246	1.70000	1.900000	0.000000	5.000000

Table 3. Regression results.

Credit risk	Coefficient	Z	P› |Z|
GOV	0.180684	2.27	0.023**
REG	-0.029004	-3.22	0.001***
ROA	0.893013	4.47	0.000***
CAP	-0.3494283	-3.17	0.002***
LN size	0.0001677	0.03	0.977
GDP growth	-0.005324	-4.98	0.000***
Inflation	-0.0083063	-4.72	0.0000***
Exchange rate	-0.022998	-2.58	0.0100***
Interest rate	-0.016921	-5.55	0.0000***
Constant	1.149065	12.33	0.0000***

*** Significant at the 1% level. ** Significant at the 5% level.

Of equity-capital to risk-weighted assets) is superior to the minimum required by the regulator variable it takes the value of 1 and 0 otherwise.

Fifth, we use four macroeconomic indicators that can influence banks' risk: inflation, growth rate of GDP, interest rate and exchange rate. Finally, we define one control variable: Bank size (LNSIZE) measured as the natural logarithm of total assets.

Empirical model

The estimation model is written as:

$$CreditRisk_{i,t} = \alpha + \varsigma_{it} Z_{i,t} + \delta_{it} COV_{i,t} + \varphi_{it} REG_{i,t} + \eta_{it} V_{i,t} + \beta_{it} LTA_{i,t} + \varepsilon_{it} \quad (1)$$

Where for each individual bank (i), at time (t): RISK *i, t:* ratio of risk-weighted assets to total assets in bank i for period t, Z *i, t:* matrix of the bank's characteristics variables, COV *i, t:* ownership structure variable, REG *i, t* : regulation variable, V *i, t:* matrix of macroeconomic variables, LTA*it:* bank size, α, β, δ, ς, η, φ: Parameters to be estimated; ε: Error term.

Estimation method

In order to analyse the determinants of Tunisian bank credit risk-taking, we adopt Panel data. This econometric method permits to control the heterogeneity of the observations in their individual measurements, either by taking into account a specific stationary effect (Fixed effect) or by considering a non-observable specific effect (Random effect). In order to identify the specific effect, we resort to Hausman test. We resort also to Breusch-Pagan test and Wooldridge's test for testing serial correlation and heterosedasticity. The model specified is a random effect model which takes into account the existence of heterosedasticity and correlation (Table 3).

EMPIRICAL RESULTS

Descriptive statistics

The descriptive statistics for the dependent, independent and control variables are provided in Table 2. First of all, the descriptive statistic of the variable of risk demonstrates that the average bank risk is 0.9044, which means that 90.44% of total assets are risk-adjusted assets. Second, the descriptive statistic of the ownership structure variable shows that the mean of ownership held directly by the State, the public and semi-public establishments is on average equal to 43.57%. This result shows that despite the encouragement of the participation of foreign and private investors in the Tunisian banking sector, the State continues until now the control of the three major Tunisian banks (BNA, BH and STB) by the support of public and semi-public establishments. Third, the descriptive statistic of bank regulation demonstrates that 88.57% of the Tunisian banks respect the regulatory threshold, which illustrates the capacity of the regulatory authorities in Tunisia to control the banking system. Fourth, the descriptive statistic of banks' characteristics

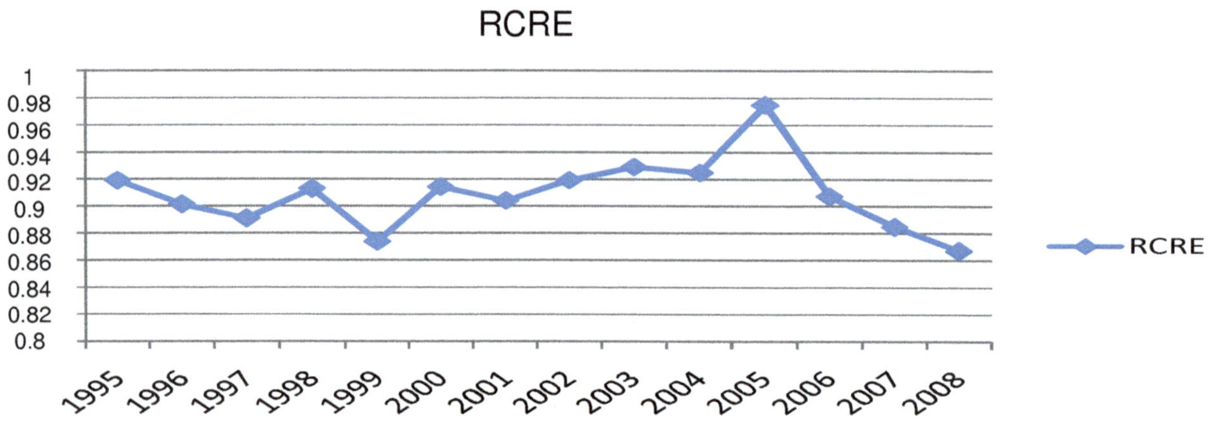

Figure 1. Evolution of mean of credit risk in Tunisia over 1995 to 2008 periods.

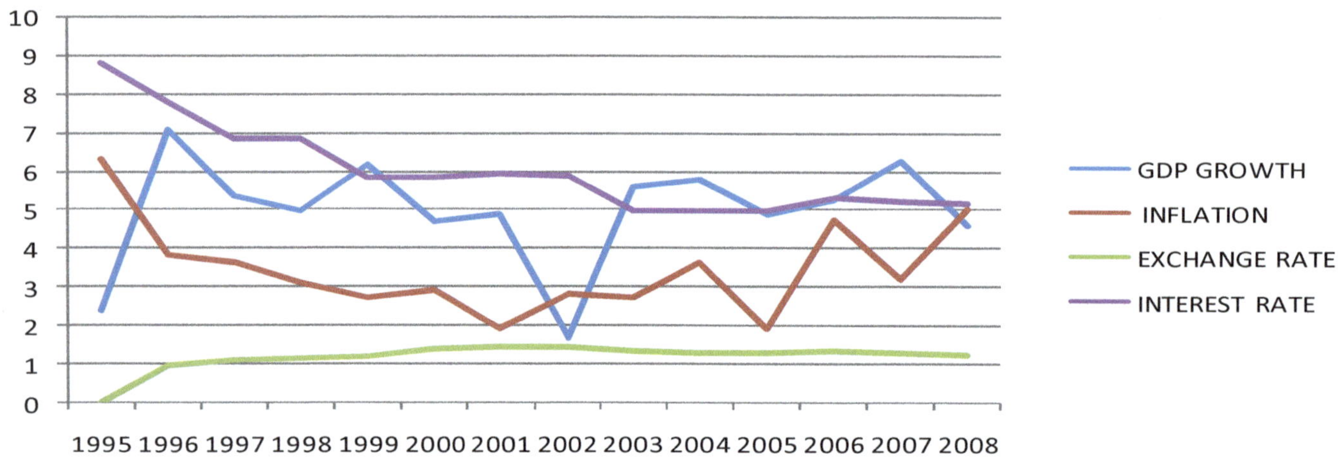

Figure 2. Evolution of mean of macroeconomics variables in Tunisia during 1995 to 2008 periods.

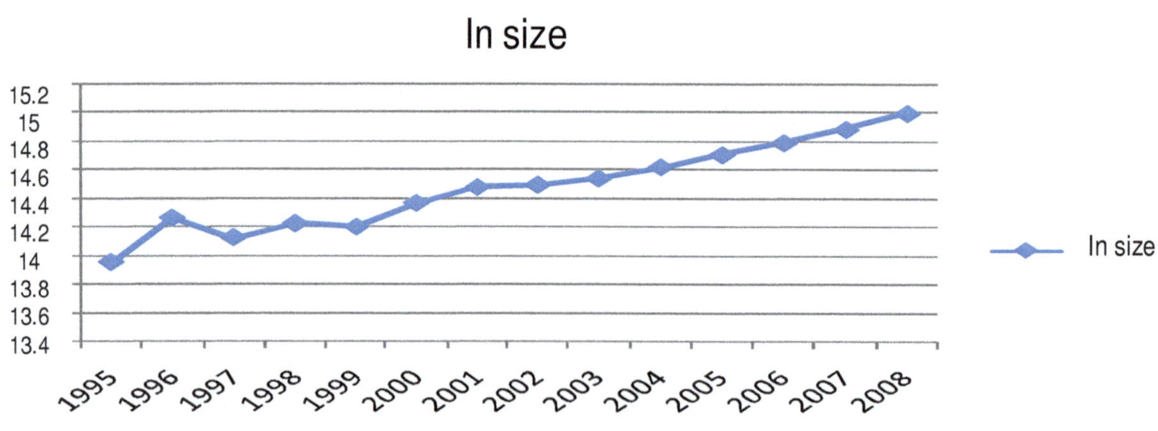

Figure 3. Evolution of mean size of Tunisian commercial banks over 1995 to 2008 period.

show that the mean of the ratio of return on assets is about 0.78%, which means that the average net income of Tunisian banks represents 0.78% of their total assets.

Also, the mean of the ratio of capital is about 9.28%, which shows that on average the Tunisian banks capital represent 9.28% of their total assets. Fifth, the descriptive

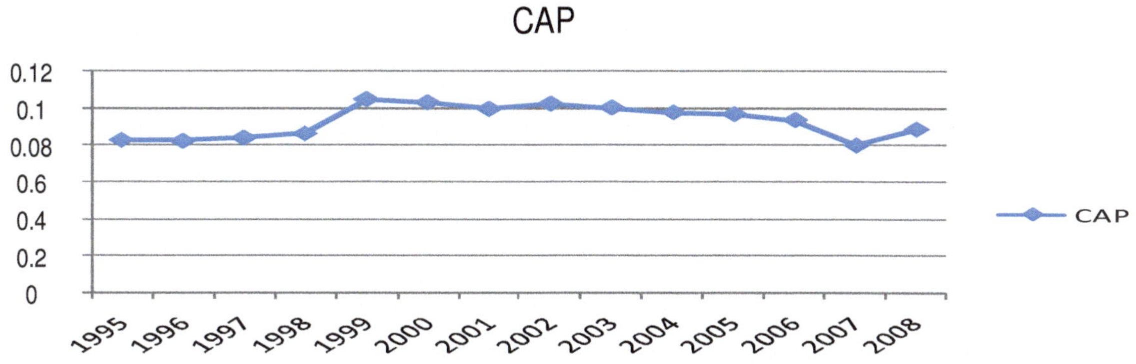

Figure 4. Evolution of the mean capital ratio in Tunisian commercial banks over 1995 to 2008 period.

statistic of the control variable indicates that the mean of banks size is about 1,447,209 Tunisian Dinars. Finally, the descriptive statistic of macroeconomic variables indicates that the mean of GDP growth is about 4.99, the mean of inflation is about 3.45 and the mean of interest rate and exchange rate are around 6 and 1.17, respectively. To have an idea about the tendencies of some of these variables during the period of the study (Figures 1, 2, 3 and 4).

Regression results

The credit risk is one of the main risks that seriously affect banks' stability. The credit risk in banking is commonly defined as the probability of a borrower defaulting his loan commitments. The main goal of a bank is to manage this type of risk because effective management of credit risk is a critical component of a comprehensive approach to risk management and essential to the long-term success of any banking organisation. In this respect, it is essential to identify the main factors causing this risk in order to manage it. In the following, we present the regression results of the main factors influencing bank credit risk in Tunisia. So, Table 3 indicates the results of GLS estimation of regression of Equation 1. Overall, the results of the model show that:

1. The ownership structure influences the risk taken by Tunisian banks. Indeed, consistent with expectation, the coefficient of GOV is positive and statistically significant with the bank credit risk. This result is coherent with the research of Sapienza (2004) and La Porta et al. (2002) who have found that the public ownership is positively related to the bank risk. They explain this result by the fact that the State acquires the control of the banks to direct their resources towards the financing of political and social projects. In the Tunisian context, this result can be explained by the fact that the public banks (BH, STB and BNA) have strengthened their efforts in financing projects in the estate, the tourist and the agricultural fields. These sectors play a leading role in the economic development in Tunisia because of their contribution to cover the trade deficit and the resolution of unemployment problems. However, these sectors show a risky character since they are associated with numerous contingencies. For example, the tourist sector is affected by a seasonal character since the Tunisian tourism attracts more tourists in the high season and results in an under-use of the tourist facilities off-season which leads to a limited performance of this sector and this makes it vital for the State to interfere to revive it. Moreover, the agricultural sector strongly depends on the climatic conditions (drought, flood, rainfall variability etc) that can affect its performance and can justify the tendency of the state to come to the finance of this risky sector. The interference of the State to finance these risky sectors explains the positive relationship between State ownership and Tunisian bank credit risk-taking.
2. The prudential regulation of banks' capital also influences the level of banks' risks. Indeed, the coefficient of REG is negative and statistically significant with risk at a level of 1%. This result shows that the introduction of the capital adjusted to risks has led to a significant increase in capital ratios and a lower risk in the portfolios of banks which have already respected the regulations requirements. This result converges with from the literatures supporting that the over-capitalized banks force the under-capitalized banks to reduce their potential of credit bank risk taking (Kim and Santomero (1988); Furlong and Keely (1989, 1990); Jacques and Nigro (1997); etc). This result can be also explained by the efforts made by the Central Bank to make the Tunisian banks at the same level as their foreign counterparts by imposing a new prudential regulation. Indeed, the new prudential regulation in Tunisia was born with the circular of the Central Bank no. 91 to 24 of December 17th, 1991. The main important reforms of this circular are:

1. The net capital of a bank always has to represent 5% of the total of its risk-weighted assets (article 4 of thiscircular).
2. Since 31 December 1999, the solvency ratio has

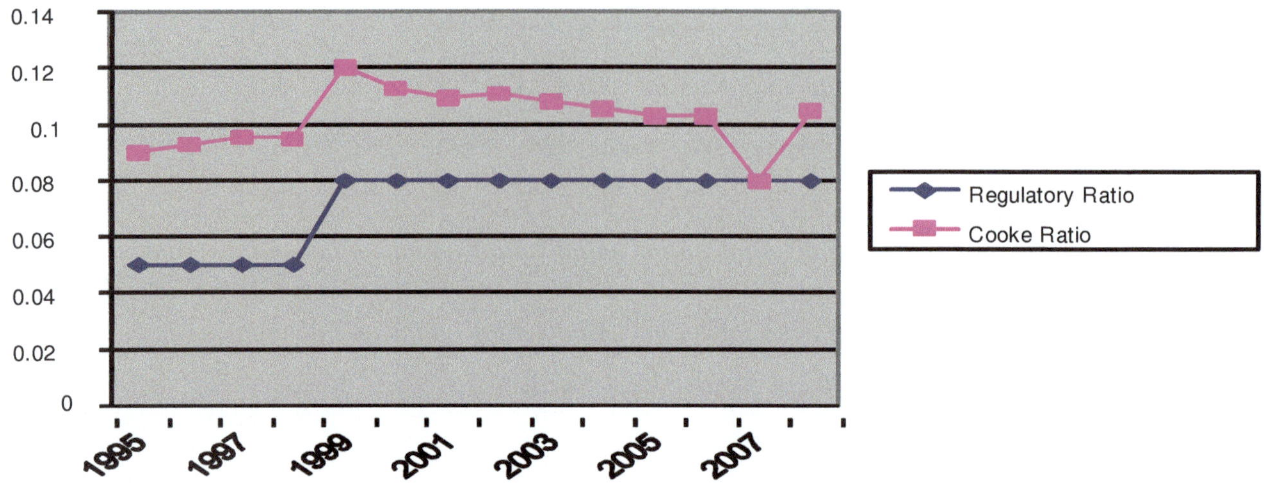

Graph 1. Evolution of mean ratio of solvency and regulatory threshold. (Regulatory Threshold = 5% before 1999 and 8% from 1999 to 2008).

increased from 5 to 8%.

The negative association between the bank risk and the prudential regulation of capital make it necessary to analyse of the tendencies of the ratio of solvency of Tunisian banks during the period of the study (Graph 1).

From this graph, we can notice that the Tunisian commercial banks have respected the reglementation threshold over 1995 to 2008 period. These tendencies show that the capital regulation is effective in the Tunisian banking sector and this can reduce the risks taken by these banks.

The banks' characteristics are also important factors influencing the level of the Tunisian bank credit risk-taking. Indeed, the ratio of profitability also influences bank risk taking decisions. Since the coefficient of return on assets (ROA) is positive and statistically significant with risk. This result shows that the most profitable banks are the riskiest banks. The ratio of capital CAP is negative and statistically significant with risk. This result indicates that over-capitalized banks are less risk-taker compared with under-capitalized banks. Contrary to expectation, the coefficient of bank size is insignificant with bank credit risk. This result diverges from the results obtained by Saunders and al. (1990), Chen and al. (1998), Cebenoyan et al. (1999) and Megginson (2005). This result can be explained by the fact that Tunisian banks have almost similar sizes and the majority of them conform to banking regulation and these show that the bank size have a minor influence on the level of credit risk.

Finally, the results indicate that the macroeconomic indicators are determinant factors that influence Tunisian bank credit risk-taking decisions. Indeed, the coefficients of rapid growth of GDP, inflation, exchange rate and interest rate are statistically significant at a level of 1% with bank credit risk.

Conclusion

This paper has empirically examined the determinants of credit risk held by Tunisian banks over 1995 to 2008 periods. This study takes its importance from the numerous structural changes in the Tunisian banking sector (globalization, deregulation, internationalization, technologies of information and communication) that have exposed them to a number of risks and stated important challenges for their stability. The empirical results of this study show that the public ownership increases the bank credit risk. Moreover, the prudential regulation of capital decreases the credit risk taken by Tunisian banks. This result accounts for the willingness of these banks to respect the bank regulations. Besides, the banks' characteristics are also important factors influencing the levels of risks taken by Tunisian banks. Indeed, the ratio of return on assets is positively related with credit risk and the ratio of capital adequacy is negatively associated with credit risk. Then, the results indicate that the bank credit risk-taking decisions are also related to bank macroeconomic indicators.

REFERENCES

Abdelwahed O (2003). Governance systems and performance of Tunisian firms. French Review. Management. 29 (142) : 85-102.

Angeloni I, Faia E (2009). A tale of two policies prudential regulation and monetary policy with fragile banks. Kiel Institute for die World Economy. Kiel Working Papers 1569. Kiel.

Buch CM, Eickmeier S, Prieto E (2010). Macroeconomic factors and micro-level bank risk. Deutsche Bundesbank Discussion Paper Series 1. Economic Studies20.

Cebenoyan AS, Cooperman ES, Register CA (1999). Ownership structure charter value and risk-taking behavior of thrifts Financial Management, 28 (1): 43-60.

Chen C, Steiner T, Whyte, A (1998). Risk-taking behavior and management ownership in depositors institutions. J. Fin. Res.. 20: 1-16.

De Nicolo G (2001). Size, charter value and risk in banking: An

international perspective. Board of Governors of the Federal Reserve System. International Finance Discussion Paper, P. 689.
Dothan U, Williams J (1980). Banks, bankruptcy, and public regulation. J. Banking. Fin., 4: 65-87.
Furlong FT, Keeley MC (1990). A reexamination of mean- variance analysis of bank capital regulation. J. Banking. Fin., P. 14.
Giuliano I, Giacomo N, Andrea S. (2007). Ownership structure, risk and performance in the European banking industry. J. Banking. Fin., 31: 2127-2149.
Goldlewski (2004). Capital regulation and credit risk-taking: empirical evidence from banks in emerging market economies. Finance 0409030, EconWPA.
Hamza T (2009). Controlling shareholders, performance and risk-taking of Tunisian's Listed Firms. Corporate Ownership. Control, 7(1).
Hassan MK, Hussain ME (2004). Basel capital requirements and bank credit risk taking in developing countries, University of New Orleans/Drexel University, LeBow College of Business, Department of Economics and Finance, Working Paper.
Jacques KT, Nigro P (1997). Risk-based capital portfolio risk and bank capital a simultaneous equations approach. J. Econs. Bus., 49: 533-547.
Kahane Y (1977). Capital adequacy and the regulation of financial intermediaries. J. Banking. Fin., 1: 207-218.
Keeley MC, Furlong FT (1989). Capital regulation and bank risk-taking: a note. J. Banking. Fin., 13: 883-891
Kim D, Santomero AM (1988). Risk in banking and capital regulation. J. Fin., 43: 1219-33.
Koehn M, Santomero AM (1980). Regulation of bank capital and portfolio risk. J. Fin., 35: 1235-1244.
La Porta R. Lopez-de-SF, Shleifer A (2002). Government ownership of banks. J. Fin. 57(1): 265-301.
Marina M, Svetlana P (2001). The Determinants of excessive risk-taking by banks in transition. Economics Education and Research Constoruim-Russia and CIS.
Megginson WL (2005). The economics of bank privatization. J. Banking. Fin., 29: 1931-1980.
Micco A, Panizza U (2004). Bank ownership and lending behaviour. Inter-American developement. bank. Research Department, Working Paper no. 520.
Mnasri k, Abaoub E (2010). Corporate governance, regulation and risk-taking behaviour in the banking industry. the Tunisian evidence. Intl. J. Acct. Audit. Performance Eval., 6(4): 422-450.
Mohamed AO (2002). Role of institutional investors and performance of Tunisian firms. Rev. Manage. Sci., pp. ?????.
Nor HA, Mohamed A (2007). Multi-country study of bank credit risk determinants. Intl. J. Banking. Fin., 5(1): 135-152.
Olga Bohachova (2008). The impact of macroeconomic factors on risks in the banking Sector: A cross-Country empirical assessment. Paper provided by Institut für Angewandte Wirtschaftsforschung (IAW) in its series IAW Discussion Papers with no. 44.
Rainer H, Paul W (2007). Risk taking by banks in the Transition countries. Comparative Economic Studies. Forthcoming.
Rime B (2001). Capital requirements and bank behaviour empirical evidence for Switzerland. J. Banking. Fin., 789-805.
Samy BN (2003). The Determinants of the Tunisian Banking Industry Profitability. Panel evidence. Annual Conference ERF.
Sapienza P (2004). The effect of government ownership on bank lending. J. Fin. Econs., 72: 357-384.
Saunders A, Strock E, Travlos NG (1990). Ownership structure deregulation and bank risk taking. J. Political Econs., 78: 1-26.
Saunders A, Strock E, Travlos NG (1990). Ownership structure, deregulation, and bank risk taking. J. Fin., 45(2): 643-654.
Sharpe, William F (1978). Bank capital adequacy, deposit insurance and security values. J. Fin. Quantitative Analysis, Cambridge University Press, 13(04): 701-718.
Shrieves RE, Dahl D (1992). The Relationship between risk and capital in commercial banks. J Banking Fin., 16: 439-457.
Wade DC, Moez H, Liang L (2005). Financial Liberalization and Efficiency in Tunisian Banking Industry: DEA Test. Int. J. Infor. Techno & Decision. Making, 4(3): 455-475.
Zaghla A, Boujelbene Y (2008). Explanatory factors of X-efficiency in the Tunisian Banks: a stochastic frontier approach, MPRA Paper No. 12437, Online at http://mpra.ub.uni-muenchen.de/12437.
Zuzana F, Laura S (2008). Determinants of bank interest margins in Russia: Does bank ownership matter. BOFIT Discussion Papers.

The challenge of risk management in Nigerian banks in the post consolidation era

Adekunle A. Owojori[1]*, Ishola R. Akintoye[2] and Felix A. Adidu[3]

[1]Accounting and Business Education, University of Ado-Ekiti, Ado-Ekiti, Ekiti State, Nigeria.
[2]Department of Accounting, Banking and Finance, Osun State University, Nigeria.
[3]Department of Business Administration, Western Delta University, Oghara, Delta State, Nigeria.

Many empirical literature showed several attempts at explaining and measuring risk-taking behaviour in banks to incentives created by safety-net programmes such as the fixed-rate deposit insurance system which though arguably, engenders cross-subsidization by creating avenues to take on risk inefficiently; the so-called moral hazard problem. The moral hazard view of risk taking in banks assumes that shareholders make the lending and investment decisions and therefore take a risk to maximize the value of insurance if they so desire. The foregoing discussion becomes even more imperative with the on-going reforms in the Nigerian banking industry. This paper attempts to provide an overview of risk management practices in insured banks in Nigeria. As we are now in the post consolidation era, consistent with the efficiency argument of a market economy, the need to foster healthy competition amongst fewer, mega banks becomes pertinent. Amongst the host of risks envisaged, those risks considered most important are identified, and their management and mitigating factors are analyzed. The risks relating to mergers and acquisitions (M&As) were also mentioned. The study employed trend analysis of variables to derive its results and concluded by pointing to some steps that would help to preserve the banking system and sustain its impact on our fragile economy.

Key words: Risk management, post-consolidation, mergers and acquisition, banking, moral hazard, insurance.

INTRODUCTION

Banking crises in Nigeria have shown that not only do banks often take excessive risks but the risks differ across banks. Some banks engage in more risks than their capital could bear. Other banks are more prudent and would be able to contain a banking crisis. As a way to stem the tide, the Central Bank of Nigeria (CBN) on July 6, 2004, introduced measures to make the entire banking system a safe, sound and stable environment that could sustain public confidence in it. According to the Bank's Governor at the time, Charles Chukwuma Soludo, "it is now time to set up a structure that creates a strong base relatives to the kind of economy we are operating where banks become channels to do proper intermediation (The Obasanjo Economic Reforms on the Banking Sector, 2005)."

As a follow-up, the CBN further announced a 13-point agenda to stabilize the base of the banking industry. The key elements in the agenda included the compulsory re-capitalization requirement of N25 billion for a commercial bank operating in the country (this requirement, it stressed, must be complied with by December 31, 2005). The essence of the reform policy was to consolidate the banking institutions through mergers and acquisitions (The Obasanjo Economics Reforms, 2005). While initially the policy seemed to have raised some dusts and generated some debates among different strata of the Nigerian society, it is to be seen that at the end of the day, 25 of the 89 commercial banks operating in the country emerged consolidated through re-capitalization to the tune of N25 billion. More than 50% of the new banks came to their present position through mergers and acquisitions.

It may be necessary, at this point, to stress that since the emergence of 25 consolidated commercial banks in

*Corresponding author. E-mail: adekunleowojori@yahoo.com

Nigeria in 2005, the industry players and other stakeholders have been faced with how best to manage the post-consolidation challenges, that confront the Nigerian banking industry and the economy. This perhaps is the compelling reason operators of the banking system in Nigeria are challenged to take more seriously the important issue of risk acceptance/rejection, which is often the point at which bankers fall into or escape the trap of greed (Adedipe, 2005). The end of risk management for operators is risk mitigation, which emphasizes the protection of the bank's assets and by extension depositors' funds and capital. Our effort in this paper is directed at discussing the risk that bankers face and how such risks are managed as well as those risks associated with consolidation.

A REVIEW OF RISKS IN BANKING

The banking business by its nature is a high risk environment. It is risky in the sense that it is the only business where the proportion of borrowed funds is far higher than the owners' equity. A high level of financial leverage is usually associated with high risk. This can easily be seen in a situation where adverse rumours, whether founded or precipitated financial panic and by extension a run on a bank. According to Umoh (2002) and Ferguson (2003} few banks are able to withstand a persistent run, even in the presence of a good lender of last resort. As depositors take out their funds, the bank hemorrhages and in the absence of liquidity support, the bank is forced eventually to close its doors. Thus, the risks faced by banks are endogenous, associated with the nature of banking business itself, whilst others are exogenous to the banking system.

The risks that arise in the course of business which bankers should be able to control include, amongst others, credit risk, liquidity risk, reputation risk, legal risk, operational risk, customer satisfaction risk, leadership risk and information technology risk. On the other hand, the risks that are exogenous to the banking system which tend to pose the greatest control problem to bankers include regulatory risk, industry risk, government policies risk, sovereign risk and market risk. Other important ones, as added by Umoh (2002), include competition risk, human resources risk and fraud risk.

Credit default risk

Available statistics from the liquidated banks clearly showed that inability to collect loans and advances extended to customers and directors or companies related to directors/managers was a major contributor to the distress of the liquidated banks. At the height of the distress in 1995, when 60 out of the 115 operating banks were distressed, the ratio of the distressed banks' non-performing loans and leases to their total loans and leases was 67%. The ratio deteriorated to 79% in 1996; to 82% in 1997; and by December 2002, the licences of 35 of the distressed banks had been revoked.

In 2003, only one bank (Peak Merchant Bank) was closed. No bank was closed in the year 2004. Therefore, the number of banking licences revoked by the CBN since 1994 remained at 36 until January 2006, when licences of 14 more banks were revoked, following their failure to meet the minimum re-capitalization directive of the CBN. At the time, the banking licences were revoked, some of the banks had ratios of performing credits that were less than 10% of loan portfolios. In 2000 for instance, the ratio of non-performing loans to total loans of the industry had improved to 21.5% and as at the end of 2001, the ratio stood at 16.9%. In 2002, it deteriorated to 21.27%, 21.59% in 2003, and in 2004, the ratio was 23.08% (NDIC Annual Reports- various years).

In a collaborative study by the CBN and the Nigeria Deposit Insurance Corporation {NDIC} in 1995, operators of financial institutions confirmed that bad loans and advances contributed most to the distress. In their assessment of factors responsible for the distress, the operators ranked bad loans and advances first, with a contribution of 19.5%. The relevant question now is: What lesson can be learned from the experiences of the liquidated banks in this regard? To answer this question, one needs to examine the administration of loans and advances which contributed to the crisis as well as possible mitigation that could have been applied. Banks are expected to have credit policies which should guide the bank in credit administration. Section 18(1b) of the Banks and Other Financial Institution Act (BOFIA) of 1991, as amended, forbids a bank from granting any advance, loan or credit facility to any person, unless it is authorized in accordance with the rules and regulations of the banks. The section also directs a bank to obtain adequate securities for advances, loans or credit facilities. In addition, section 18(1a) of the Act prohibits a manager or any other officer of a bank from having "personal interest in any advance, loan or credit facility; and if they do, such shall be declared.

Available evidence has, however, showed that most of the liquidated banks' officers flouted these provisions with impunity and some still in operation are allegedly not obeying these provisions (Umoh, 2002). Loans were granted without collateral; when taken, not adequate and when adequate, not perfected. Such officers of the liquidated banks are known to have faced the Failed Bank Tribunals for loans granted improperly with the result that the loans were irrecoverable. Furthermore, loan disbursements in many instances were known to have been effected even before conditions precedent to draw down were met. Some banks were (and some are still) reckless in disbursing facilities before loan applications and /or acceptance letter were received. How can such customers be made to repay if the simple but important contract documents were not executed at the onset of a credit relationships? Section 20{1} {a} of BOFIA as amended seeks to limit the credit exposure of banks to single obligors as a means of avoiding undue credit concentration thereby mitigating credit risk.

Evidence from the liquidated banks is that most of the banks violated 20% of shareholders' funds unimpaired by losses limit. Although, the guidelines on Universal Banking that were issued by the CBN have raised the limit to 35%, some banks are known to have been exceeding the limit without seeking approval from the CBN as required by law. Such practice does not indicate that the affected banks have learned any lessons in this regard from the experiences of the failed banks. By wantonly exceeding the limit without approval, such banks have unwillingly laid foundations for distress, in addition to the stigma of being labelled as non-compliant. Directors of banks are also not permitted to have outstanding unsecure loans, advances or unsecure credit facilities in their names and/or in the name of associated companies without "prior approval in writing of the bank {CBN}", (BOFIA). The code of conduct for directors of licenced banks issued by the CBN and endorsed by every bank director warns that a director shall "be disqualified if any of his loans in a bank is classified lost by the Bank Examiners of The Regulatory Authorities". The provision of the Act and those of the conduct are intended to keep directors above board in their banks' credit administration. The directors are expected to be shining examples in this important aspect of banking operations.

However, available evidences are to the contrary. In the Liquidated Financial Merchant Bank Limited for example, all the loans in the bank were insiders-related. In Group Merchant Bank Limited, also liquidated, 80% of the loans were extended to directors and in the liquidated Credit Bank Nigeria Limited; the ratio was 76%. To the extent that such loans were not performing, it would have been a miracle for the banks to survive. In view of the importance of credit allocation in a bank and the potential risks associated with credit, most banks have credit committees with the board having the highest level, but short of the banks' single obligors limit. Unfortunately, in some banks the board credit committees had been chaired by the board chairmen until the CBN stopped the practice in August, 2002. Such an arrangement amounted to the board chairmen reporting to them, and to a great extent, it effectively compromised the independent appraisal of credit that the committee would have given the board. In spite of the major reason of speed of credit approval adduced to justify the practice, it could not have been in the best overall interest of the banks that had the practice. Senior management oversight of the leading function, involving regular and periodic loans review, done independently of the lending officers, is a good credit risk litigant. Such credit review can reveal weaknesses inherent in outstanding facilities and could allow for quick intervention or remedial measure to prevent loan losses or at worse, minimize such losses. Although, many banks set up credit review committees, nothing concrete is known to have been done to implement the committee's recommendations. As a matter of fact, rather than make provisions for loan losses as prescribed by the committees, many banks are known to have sidelined such recommendations in favour of year-end profits.

The credit risk management bureau of the CBN, that provides information on prospective borrowers can be a viable medium for credit risk mitigation. The information from the bureau is intended to assist lending officers in forming opinions as to the credit worthiness of intending borrowers. Unfortunately, some banks have refused to avail themselves of the services provided by the medium. Similarly, such banks fail to provide credit information to the bureau. It is obvious that the services provided by the bureau, which in any case is owned by bankers, are to assist banks to fight the menace of 'professional' borrowers who move from bank to bank securing credit facilities with no intention to repay. There is also the use of risks quality ratings of both internal and external rating systems to provide some information on the risk quality of bank borrowers. Internal rating systems entail ranking customers in accordance with information available to the banker about the credit quality of the customer, whereas external rating usually relies on published information. With the proposed implementation of the New Basel Capital Accord, credit rating agencies will need to be actively encouraged in Nigeria.

Besides, the new capital accord expects every bank to ultimately establish an internal rating-based approach, to the measurement of capital requirement. In that regard, it would be each bank's responsibility to determine the rating to be given to every credit booked, subject, of course, to a supervisory review process. Banks are, therefore, advised to begin to put in place necessary tools for the establishment of reliable internal rating systems which would enable them to determine the riskiness of their credit portfolio and the set asides for risk weighted capital ratio. The BASEL 11 Accord provides for an arrangement that allows for demands for loan supervision and proactive credit dispute management system as the lifeblood to effective credit management. Perhaps the most widely used method of credit risk mitigation is asset securitization. Asset securitization is a process that involves the packaging of individual loans and other debt instruments, converting the package into security or securities, and enhancing their credit status/rating to facilitate their sale to third-party investors. A critical element of asset securitization is the creation of a special entity called the special purpose vehicle (SPV) to purchase loans and issue asset-backed securities on their collateral. The SPV may be a subsidiary of the originator of the loan or, of the investment bank that underwrites and distributes the securities. The whole essence of an SPV is to create a clean and legal break in the transaction for it to be regarded as asset sale without recourse.

The practice, till date, appears not to be well understood in Nigeria and those who understand it, appear to blatantly misapply it. For example, some bankers simply repackage their loans as Bankers' Acceptances (BA) or Commercial Papers (CPs). Or "Asset Sale" matches them with equal amount of deposit and transfers same off balance sheet. Thus, they have not transferred the credit risk on such loans but have only succeeded to illegally understate the volume of loans and deposits of their banks. Nigerian banks have been enjoined to seek ways of setting up SPVs for the dual benefit of credit risk mitigation and deepening the financial market (Umoh, 2002). It has now become fashionable for banks to place huge sums of money with discount houses for on-lending or investment in commercial papers. Such placements are sometimes presented as off-balance sheet engagements by the discount houses. One implication of such accounting treatment is that the discount houses are not the primary obligors but the banks. In the event of default, the bank would be in trouble because it would not have direct access to the obligors. A way to mitigate such risk is to set limits to placements with a discount house, if such placement is not supported by treasury bills. The bank can also beef up its capital base, if it wants to expand its credit profile instead of doing it through a third party who, though carrying no risk, derives huge income benefit.

Operational risk

This is the risk of direct and indirect loss resulting from inadequate or failed internal processes people and systems or external threats generate. Operational risk may include frauds. By this we mean a situation where customers and/or bank staff intentionally falsify information or present forged documents. It may also include technology risk which refers to the risk of inadequate or ineffective operating and information technology infrastructure to support the business of the bank. Other examples are system failures, losses due to natural disasters, and accidents involving key management staff of the bank. But the question may arise as to how well banks prepared to meet the challenges of operational risk in the post-consolidation era, especially now that master forgers present and obtain value on cheques with the same characters like genuine ones issued to customers? What are banks doing to address the problems of insiders' frauds, weak internal controls and unprotected IT systems? Besides, how many banks recall their data tapes that are stored in off-site locations for regular revalidation and testing to ensure that such data can be relied upon at times of emergency?

One of the manifestations of high operational risk in Nigerian banks is the volume of frauds and forgeries. In compliance with the requirement of sections 39 and 40 of the NDIC Act No.22 of 1988 (as amended), banks render monthly returns on frauds and forgeries and also notify the corporation about terminations and dismissals of staff (Table 1). Similarly, in compliance with Section 32 of the Act, insured banks are expected to provide fidelity bond insurance to cover frauds and forgeries committed by banks' staff. During the year 2004, the average number of reporting banks stood at 77 as against 79 for the previous year. Reported cases of fraud have increased significantly over the year and stood at a total of 1,133 in 2004, showing about 33.29% increase relative to the 2003 figure which totaled 850.

Post consolidation experience

Operational risk became more pronounced in the post-consolidation era as losses are now running into about three billion naira in each case (Table 5). These losses arise principally from weak internal controls and the retention of staff with high propensity for fraudulent practices. Invariably, banks with high volume of losses from frauds tend to have these two factors and often the weak internal control manifests in such ways as preponderance of un-reconciled items, non-segregation of active from dormant balances, lack of dual control of strong room, lack of online auditing for banks that are online, etc. An analysis of the types of frauds and forgeries perpetrated showed that the commonest types were the following:

a. Presentation of forged cheques;
b. Granting of unauthorized credits;
c. Posting of fictitious credits;
d. Fraudulent transfers/withdrawals;
e. Cheque and cash defalcation;
f. Loss of money to armed robbers; and
g. Outright theft of money.

The frequency, amount of money involved and expected losses are presented in Tables 2a and 2b. It is pertinent to note that the greater percentage of those involved in frauds and forgeries are in the higher echelon of the management\cadre. In fact, as shown in Table 4, increasing number of managers is entrapped in this crime. The fidelity insurance policy, as required by Section 32 of the NDIC Act No. 22 of 1998 (as amended), covers frauds and forgeries committed by staff of insured banks. The insurance policy is intended to reduce the adverse effect of insiders' frauds and forgeries on the banks. In this wise, therefore, all insured banks are expected to take up the fidelity insurance cover and renew same on an annual basis. The required minimum coverage for each bank is fixed at 15% of its paid-up capital as at 31st December of the preceding year. Table4 shows banks' response to the insurance coverage

Table 1. Returns of commercial banks frauds and forgeries.

Quarter	Year	Average no. of banks rendering returns	Total no. of fraud cases	Total amount involved (N'm)	Total expected loss (N'm)	Proportion of total expected loss to amount involved (%)
	2004	78	235	989.69	238.06	24.05
	2003	79	238	2,144.68	104.72	4.89
1st	2002	78	165	6,556.32	235.25	3.59
	2001	75	297	5,313.9	251.60	4.73
	2000	67	45	381.41	37.62	9.79
	2004	70	247	2,477.01	511.17	20.64
	2003	78	218	1,221.45	311.54	25.51
2nd	2002	77	233	1,224.2	471.94	3.86
	2001	74	176	612.90	111.1	18.13
	2000	66	156	360.48	124.17	34.44
	2004	84	366	3,133.99	524.16	16.72
	2003	81	263	1,146.65	213.39	18.61
3rd	2002	78	266	4,596.73	410.69	8.93
	2001	77	229	1,572.65	273.4	17.38
	2000	67	151	1,459.70	738.75	50.01
	2004	76	285	1,709.14	531.06	31.07
	2003	76	131	4,870.89	277.81	4.67
4th	2002	73	132	872.3	181.51	2.08
	2001	75	241	3,744.49	270.2	7.22
	2000	64	51	653.75	180.03	27.54

Source: NDIC Annual reports and accounts – various years.

Table 2a. Types of Major Frauds and Forgeries Up to 2007.

General nature of fraud	Frequency of expected loss occurrence	Amount involved (N'm)	%	N'm	%
General unauthorized loans/overdrafts	25	702.97	11.32	59.15	3.28
Presentation of forged cheques	368	1,759.90	28.33	547.02	30.31
Posting fictitious credit	58	311.10	5.01	88.75	4.92
Loss of money to armed robbers	55	33.87	5.37	296.39	16.42
Fraudulent transfers and withdrawals	309	2382.48	38.36	560.45	31.06
Outright theft	49	188.45	3.03	45.56	2.52
Suppression of cash/cheques	201	532.57	8.57	207.10	11.48
Total	1,065	6,211.34	100.00	1,804.42	100.00

Source: NDIC Annual reports and accounts – various years.

guideline.

According to the proposal in the new Basel Capital Accord, banks are required to provide capital for operational risk. This requirement must have been part of what spurred the Nigerian Regulatory Authority to raise the minimum capital base for banks. Banks are enjoined to develop viable internal approaches to the measurement of operational risks and to put in place operational risk management and control processes, which should cover the design, implementation and review of operational risk methodology. The banks' internal audit groups are expected to conduct regular reviews of the operational risk management involvement of the board of directors, and senior management of banks are expected in risk management. In the final analysis, the most important factor in mitigating operational risk is good management. A good management team would ensure that the internal control process in the bank is effective. Offences such as rendering of false returns to supervisory/regulatory authorities, manipulating customers' accounts on month-end and non-rendition of VAT/Withholding tax to government would have the moral high ground to sanction staff engaged in malpractices to the detriment of

Table 2b. Frauds and forgeries as per totals for 2001 – 2007.

Year	Frequency of occurrence	Amount involved (N'm)	Expected loss (N'm)
2007	1,553	10,000.00	2,870.00
2006	1,193	8,000.00	2,700.00
2004	1,065	6,211.34	1,804.42
2003	773	8,377.93	857.46
2002	696	8,291.23	1,299.19
2001	714	3,616.22	847.55

Source: NDIC Annual reports and accounts – various years.

Table 3. Banks' staff involved in frauds and forgeries between 2000 and 2007.

Rank	No	%	No	%	No	%	No	%	No	%
Supervisor and managers	132	26.8	55	36.18	16	18.80	25	23.58	157	40.99
Assistant	101	20.5	60	39.47	48	56.50	41	38.68	129	33.68
Clerks and cashiers	137	27.8	30	19.74	13	15.30	25	23.58	61	15.93
Typists, technicians and stenographers	20	4.1	-	-	-	-	-	-	18	4.70
Messengers, drivers, cleaners, security guards and stewards	81	16.4	5	3.29	4	4.70	7	6.60	15	3.92
Temporary staff	8	1.6	2	1.32	4	4.70	8	7.55	3	3.78
Uncategorized staff	14	2.8	-	-	-	-	-	-	-	-
Total	493	100.0	152	100	85	100	106	100	383	100

Source: NDIC Annual reports and accounts – various years.

the bank.

Reputational risk

There is no doubt that trust and confidence are crucial factors in banking and the chance or probability that the public may lose these essentials in a banking institution constitutes reputational risk. Where a bank faces reputational risk, such a bank will have difficulty attracting and keeping deposits. Its dealings with other banks will also suffer, and in a matter of time, the bank would be out of business. Consequently, banking institutions are expected to cultivate and safeguard the confidence reposed in them by the public. However, such trust and confidence is bound to suffer, if any or all of the following take place:

a) The bank levied excessive charges on customers;
b) Customers are unduly delayed in the course of effecting deposits/withdrawals and other transactions;
c) The staff of the bank are rude towards customers;
d) The bank has known incidents of frauds, forgeries and unwholesome insider dealings;
e) There is publicized instability in the board and management of the bank; and
f) The bank is known not to be a good corporate citizen obeying laws and regulations.

Whilst the list cannot be said to exhaust all possible reasons for a bank's loss of trust and confidence, the list, however, includes some of the major reasons in the Nigerian banking environment. Some of the items on the list deserve further comment. In an effort to reduce deposit insurance premium, meet required liquidity ratio, capital adequacy, some banks, have been found to engage in unwholesome practices that are capable of denting their image before the regulatory authorities and the public. Such banks have been found to repackage non-performing credits as Banker' Acceptances (BAs) and Commercial Papers (CPs) then reporting them as Off Balancing sheet Engagements (OBS). Sometimes, the items are not reflected in the bank's books except in memorandum records. Some other banks are known to adopt the practice of crediting debtors' accounts whilst the corresponding debits are warehoused in impersonal accounts in a bid to reduce non-performing loans and hence required provision on such credits. Still, some banks take deposits from customers and rather than record same in their books as deposits, convert them to investment in CPs and treat them as contingent liabilities.

In addition, some banks capitalize as fixed assets such items as hotel, travel and training expenses in a bid to spread such expenses over time and thus enhance current profit through reduced expenditure. Given the increased demand for foreign exchange (forex), and the

Table 4. Banks response to NDIC fidelity insurance cover guideline.

Year	No. of Banks in operation	No of Banks that responded	% of total
2007	24	3	10
2006	24	3	10
2004	89	29	32.58
2003	89	56	63.0
2002	90	74	82.2
2001	90	81	90.0
2000	88	17	19.1

Source: NDIC Annual reports and accounts (various years).

Table 5. Post consolidation experience.

Year	Reported frauds and forgeries	Actual loss in N
2006	1,193	2.7bn
2007	1,553	2.87bn

drive by some banks to make billion naira profits, a number of banks had been found by the regulatory authorities to have engaged in unwholesome practices. For example, the banks needed their customers' namesto bid for forex without the knowledge of such customers and the forex so acquired were sold in the parallel market. Such a malpractice, generally referred to as "round-tripping", was frowned at by the authorities, which quickly suspended the affected banks from the foreign exchange market. Although, such banks had since been recalled to the market only to be involved again in forex malpractices, the stigma of the suspensions remains and cannot be said to be healthy for a bank in a competitive environment. It is difficult to alter a first impression.

In spite of the provisions of Section 41 of the NDIC Act, which prohibits rendition of false returns to the authorities, some banks willingly pay penalties rather than render accurate returns. Even when onsite bank examiners ask for certain information which should allow the examiners determine the true condition of an examined bank, some banks' management is known to have denied the examiners the requested information. Again, such bank managers would willingly pay penalties for the infraction. These situations are clearly undesirable and do not portray such banks as law-abiding. Before the new millennium, the absence of ethics and professionalism in some banks was a serious matter of concern to the public, bank customers, the regulatory authorities and the Bankers' Committee. However, on 19th December 2000, the Bankers' Committee established a sub-committee on Ethics and Professionalism "to sanitize the practice of banking and finance in Nigeria and instill discipline in the profession." The sub-committee has since come up with a Code of Conduct which is to enable all operators and supervisors "know in clear terms what acts, conducts, omissions and practices are considered unethical, and the appropriate sanctions that would apply for non-compliance with the code". It is hoped that this step to instill sanity will continue in the post consolidation period.

Human resources risk

This is the risk that a bank may not have adequate human resources in terms of number, qualification and experience, to pursue its mandate. The risk should also cover losses to the bank occasioned by errors of commission and omission by staff. In addition, it includes losses to the banks arising from outright theft, frauds and forgeries. Human resources risk in the Nigerian banking industry caught the attention of many people, perhaps for the industry in 1987. In the course of deregulation, the issuance of banking licences was liberalized. The newly licensed banks had to compete for staff with the many finance houses in particular, that were similarly licensed. The result was high staff turnover in the existing banks. Management quality also deteriorated. It was no surprise, therefore, that the distress plagued the industry, culminating in the liquidation of 34 banks between 1994 and 2000 as a result of the poor quality of management in the affected banks.

In addition to the CBN/NDIC (1995) study on the distress already cited, an NDIC research team conducted a manpower survey of the banking industry in 1991. That survey found out dearth of skilled manpower, high labour turnover, staff poaching and recruitment of inexperienced staff as responsible factors. In the commercial banks surveyed, professional staff defined as those who were members of professional bodies such as the Chartered Institute of Bankers of Nigeria (CIBN) and the Institute of

Chartered Accountants of Nigeria (ICAN) represented only 1.8% of total staff, whilst in the merchant banks the proportion was high as 10.4%. Similarly, staff with degrees was only 9.3% of total staff in the commercial banks surveyed, whilst in the merchant banks the proportion was as high as 34.7%. Thus, over ambitious young bankers as well as those with proven bad records are allegedly recycled into the system. No doubt, this practice does not augur well for the industry. The management of banks has a responsibility to assist the regulatory authorities to sanitize the banking industry in this regard for the benefit of all (NDIC, 1991).

Risks associated with mergers and acquisition (M&A)

M&A entail both risks and opportunities for banks. With regard to risks, three aspects are relevant. First, M&A entail an operational risk owing to the difficulty of integrating different risk management systems as well as different accounting and control procedures. Second, the problem of reconciling the different corporate cultures, including difference in work cultures and practices among the staff and business units of the two or various entities, entail the risk of a loss of key employees and/or clients. Third, there is the risk of failing to achieve the expected rationalization gains owing to the complexity of the operation as well as for other reasons, including labour market rigidities (Agbakoba, 2005). In this context, there is the risk that the structure of financial services groups may become less transparent. Besides, there may emerge initial skepticisms amongst merging entities as well as incoherent business activities too difficult to manage.

SUMMARY AND CONCLUDING REMARKS

There is obviously much concern in banks for return (profitability) without as much concern for risk even though the latter necessarily accompanies the former. A better understanding and appreciation of risk are desirable in banking business where one transaction or series of transactions can put the bank out of business as the Barings case and similar other exposures had shown. Nonetheless, enshrouded in this thick mist of argument is the issue of adequate legal and institutional framework that facilitate consolidation and risk management and by extension the health of the banking and financial sector. This is self-evident as we consider the emerging practice, the Basel II Accord on credit risk management, the issue of corporate governance, etc. as earlier observed, and the practice of securitization being a vital element in mitigating credit risk in an impoverished Nigeria. It sometimes could take a year to perfect an average mortgage agreement. This is the situation with other credit securitization processes. The credit Risk Management Committee of the Basel Accord had suggested that in order to protect credit through securitization, title should pass effectively and the process of recovery must be efficient.

Other legal inadequacies include lack of a comprehensive insolvency/bankruptcy law that is effective as well as lack of seamless credit information sharing amongst banks. Also, mortgage is non-existent and the mortgage institution Act has little or no relevance to today's housing reality. In addition, there is little to say about leasing. These are the very bases upon which a modern credit structure is built; the absence of these has continued to hamstrung the efforts of banks to capitalize adequately. These loopholes are continuously usurped by "system viruses". The Basel Committee listed some of the responsibilities expected of the regulators under the new Accord to include amendments to existing banking legislations, supervisory policies and guidelines; increased monitoring of the banks; re-training for supervisors and bank examiners on the new requirements of risk management. These should be *primus* in the reform process.

In Nigeria, it is common for bankers to overlook some risks and even ignore regulatory guidelines meant to mitigate such risks. A good number of banks have failed and some are distress, because of management's poor attitude towards risk, particularly credit default risk. Bankers have a responsibility to identify their key risks, their source and then map out strategies towards their mitigation. The risk management structure and culture should be well understood and imbibed by all, starting from the board of directors. It is, of course, not enough to have a structure in place but there must be enough courage and will to implement the structure efficiently and effectively. The result might not be mega profits but the survival of the banking institution in an increasingly competitive industry. The regulatory structure should, in addition, incorporate close monitoring of the banks to avoid the emergence of different monsters that engage in unwholesome activities to stifle competition or create non-beneficial oligopoly. Sectoral consolidation and reduction in competition suggest no immediate benefits for customers or employees who find themselves in the frontline rationalization and having to bear the brunt of costs.

Consistent with the findings of many experts, a study by the Bank for International Settlements (BIS) reports the experience of the majority of mergers as "disappointing", with organizational problems almost inevitably underestimated and most acquisitions overpriced, noting the creation of bank "too big to fail". These banks eventually become complacent and overconfident and still face insolvency.

On the issue of employment, it would appear that a merger in many ways invalidates the employment contract thereby exacerbating human resources risk: the worker is now working for someone else, but without having taken any steps to change employers. It brings home in the most emphatic manner the one-sidedness of the employment relationship and the fact that workers have no control over the decision of their employer.

Mergers and Acquisitions have sometimes been described as a legitimate means for breaking implicit contracts in order to restructure (Agbakoba, 2005). Given this description, the firm is seen as a nexus of implicit and explicit contacts, which only work on the basis of trust between managers and workers; it is underpinned by beliefs and assumptions regarding mutual responsibility between the employer and the employee (the "psychological contract"). Job security derives more from assumptions which M & A have the effect of disrupting. We must rise up now to tackle the trickle effect of the new structures we nurse today in order to forestall stillbirths.

REFERENCES

Adedipe B (2005). "Post-consolidation challenges." CBN Bullion, 29(2): 37-41.

Agbakoba O (2005). "Issues on bank consolidation and recapitalization." CALAD National, Lagos.

CBN/NDIC (1995). "Distress in the Nigerian Financial Services Industry." CBN/NDIC Collaborative study.

Ferguson RE (2003). "Basel II: A case study in Risk Management." Risk Management Workshop for Regulation, Washington D.C.

NDIC (2007). Annual Reports and Accounts of Banks submitted to NDIC.

NDIC (1991). "Report on manpower satiation in the Nigerian naming Industry." NDIC Annual Report.

The Obasanjo Economic Reforms on Banking Sector (2005). Abuja: Federal Ministry of Information and National Orientation.

Umoh PN (2002). "An overview of Risk management Practices in the Nigeria Banking Industry." NDIC Q., 12(4): 36-48.

7

Comparative analysis of the impact of mergers and acquisitions on financial efficiency of banks in Nigeria

Okpanachi Joshua

Department of Economics and Management Sciences, Faculty of Arts and Social Sciences, Nigerian Defence Academy, Kaduna, Nigeria. E-mail: okpasmg@yahoo.com.

Mergers and acquisitions in the Nigerian banking sector are reform strategies recently adopted to reposition the banking sector. These were done to achieve improved financial efficiency, forestall operational hardships and expansion bottlenecks. It is against this backdrop that the paper made a comparative analysis of the impact of mergers and acquisitions on financial efficiency of banks in Nigeria. This paper used gross earnings, profit after tax and net assets of the selected banks as indices to determine financial efficiency by comparing the pre-mergers and acquisitions' indices with the post-mergers and acquisitions' indices for the period under review. For this paper, three Nigerian banks were selected using convenience and judgmental sample selection methods. Data were collected from the published annual reports and accounts of the selected banks and were subsequently analyzed applying t-test statistics through statistical package for social sciences. It was found that the post-mergers and acquisitions' period was more financially efficient than the pre-mergers and acquisitions period. However, to increase banks financial efficiency, the study recommend that banks should be more aggressive in their profit drive for improved financial position to reap the benefit of post mergers and acquisitions bid.

Key words: Banks, financial efficiency, mergers and acquisitions.

INTRODUCTION

Banks play a crucial role in propelling the entire economy of any nation, of which there is need to reposition it for efficient financial performance through a reform process geared towards forestalling bank distress. In Nigeria, the reform process of the banking sector is part and parcel of the government strategic agenda aimed at repositioning and integrating the Nigerian banking sector into the African regional and global financial system. To make the Nigerian banking sector sound according to Akpan (2007), the sector has undergone remarkable changes over the years in terms of the number of institutions, structure of ownership, as well as depth and breadth of operations. These changes have been influenced mostly by the challenges posed by deregulation of the financial sector, operations globalization, technological innovations, and implementation of supervisory and prudential requirements that conform to international regulations and standards.

Similarly, a strong and virile economy depends to a very large extent on a robust, stable and reliable financial system including the banking sector. This explains the frequency with which the Nigerian banking sector has witnessed repeated reforms aimed at fine-tuning it to meet the challenges for economic stability and developmental goals which are not only limited to domestic savings mobilization and financial intermediation, but also the elimination of inefficiency to enhance financial efficiency. The financial efficiency parameters are determined and measured by gross earnings, profit after tax and net assets.

Soludo (2004) opined that, the Central Bank of Nigeria (CBN) chose to begin the Nigerian banking sector reforms process with the consolidation and recapitalization policy through mergers and acquisitions. This is done in order to arrest systems decay, restoration of public confidence, building of strong, competent and competitive players in the global arena, ensuring longevity and higher returns to investors. Considering the inability of most Nigerian banks to perform well due to operational hardship, expansion bottlenecks as a result of heavy fixed and operating costs coupled with volatility between deposits and lending rates, the present banking sector reforms in Nigeria was announced by Professor Chukwuma Soludo, the then CBN governor on July 6th, 2004 with the objective of creating a sound and more secure banking system that depositors can trust through mergers and acquisitions which enhanced operational capital base. These and many more, act as a spring board to achieving improved efficiency.

Ajayi (2005), Garba (2006) and Augustine (2007) stated that, other programmes in the Nigerian banking sector reforms agenda includes; ensuring exchange rate and price stability, managing interest rate for stability and development, macro economic coordination, improvements of the payment system and financial sector diversification to avoid a situation of boom and bust that can result to bank distress. This, Walter and Uche (2005) supported. The current reforms framework anchored on two critical pillars; firstly, to provide effective protection against systemic financial crises in the interest of the depositors; and secondly, to fast track the growth and development of the national economy.

However, for Akpan (2007), recapitalization through mergers and acquisitions is not a new development in the Nigerian banking sector but a chain of similar events that have been on since 1952. For instance, between 1952 and 2005, there have been nine (9) re-capitalization requirement targets that banks were made to achieve. The first was in 1952, and the second in 1964 which both minimum capital base were pegged at thousand brackets. The million bracket capital base was introduced in 1988 when banks were made to capitalize at N10 million while the existing capitalization is N25 billion. According to Rewane (2004) and Sobawale (2004), recapitalization through mergers and acquisitions has however generated a lot of controversies in the Nigerian banking sector. Most of the key players in the sector saw the time frame within which to meet the requirements as unrealizable. For Walter and Uche (2005), the timing of the exercise was also seen as unfavorable given the current economic condition, the prevailing business atmosphere of inflation and diminishing savings and investments.

Nevertheless, it is in record that between 1990 to date, Nigeria witnessed several mergers and acquisitions arrangement. This trend dramatically changed particularly from 1995. In 1997 alone, about 10 mergers and acquisitions bids was recorded, whereas, as at 31st December 2005, the Nigerian banking sector witnessed 25 mergers and acquisitions activities (Okpanachi, 2007). For this, mergers and acquisitions is not a new scheme geared towards business survival but more importantly assist in repositioning business for more efficiency and reliability which it has done to the Nigerian banking sector through strengthening the industry with its position multiplier effects on the economy. The incidence of distressed and technically insolvent banking institutions has been with us for quite some time. Umoh (2004) noted that the unprecedented liquidation of twenty-six (26) Nigerian banks in 1998, in addition to the earlier closure of five (5) banks in 1994/95, did not put an end to the distress syndrome. This, recently manifested when in August 14th, 2009 the CBN declared five Nigerian banks illiquid as a result of inadequate capital ratio due to reckless lending, followed by two others on 2nd October, 2009 which resulted to the immediate sacking of the affected banks' Managing Directors.

According to Umoh (2004), mergers and acquisitions are expected to address the problem of distress among insolvent banks without an initial resort to liquidation. For the Nigerian banking sector, out of the 89 banks that were in existence before 31st December 2005, it is only 25 banks that met the consolidation requirements through mergers and acquisitions arrangement. Currently, only 24 banks exist in Nigeria due to the merger between Stanbic bank Ltd and IBTC Chattered bank Plc which became effective on 24th September, 2007, at a shareholders' meeting held on 12th December, 2007 to effect the change of name to Stanbic IBTC bank Plc. Also, as at 1st January 2009, Bank PHB Plc acquired Spring Bank Plc, but each bank is operating differently on the basis of name and identity under BankPHB group over an integration period of less than two years. Again, as at 5th February 2009, the CBN restored the operational licence of Savannah Bank of Nigeria Plc which was closed down on 15th February 2002 as a result of liquidity problem. The new capitalization policy of the Nigerian government on banking sector reform had forced many banks to merge or be acquired which resulted to the formation of Mega banks.

For Muhammed (2005), most Nigerian banks were becoming personalized in ownership and management structure which made the banks incapable to finance large scale and long term projects due to limited liquidity at their disposal. The sector was characterized with import financing rather than encouraging domestic growth in the economy; there was loss of public confidence due to fear of liquidation, customer dissatisfaction on banking services as well as some obnoxious, unprofessional and other sharp practices within the industry. All these caused great distortion in the financial system resulting to financial inefficiency, which made investors not to get constant and high dividends as a result of inefficiency in terms of gross earnings, profit after tax and net assets. In line with the aforementioned, the following null hypotheses were formulated and tested:

H_{01}: There is no significant difference in the pre and post mergers and acquisitions periods of banks in terms of gross earnings.

H_{02}: There is no significant difference in the pre and post mergers and acquisitions periods of banks in terms of profits after tax.

H_{03}: There is no significant difference in the pre and post mergers and acquisitions periods of banks in terms of net asset.

Consequently, it is against this background that the paper attempts to make a comparative analysis of the impact of mergers and acquisitions on financial efficiency of banks in Nigeria.

Literature review and theoretical framework

Mergers and acquisitions are a global business terms used in achieving business growth and survival. Merger entails the coming together of two or more firms to become one big firm while acquisition is the takeover or purchase of a small firm by a big firm; which are both pursuing similar motives (Gaughan, 1999; Amedu, 2004; Bello, 2004; Katty, 2005). Accordingly, Soludo (2004) opined that mergers and acquisitions are aimed at achieving cost efficiency through economies of scale, and to diversity and expand on the range of business activities for improved performance.

Numerous studies have empirically examined whether mergers and acquisitions are solutions to bank problems. The studies of Cabral et al. (2002), Carletti et al. (2002) and Szapary (2001) provided the foundation for a research on the linkage between banks mergers and acquisitions and profitability. Evidence as provided by Calomiris and Karenski (1996), De-Nicolo (2003), and Caprion (1999) suggested that mergers and acquisitions in the financial system could impact positively on the efficiency of most banks. Surprisingly, the available empirical evidence suggests that mergers and acquisitions operations in the United States banking industry have not had a positive influence on performance in term of efficiency (DeLong and Deyoung, 2007; Amel et al., 2004; Berger et al., 1999). Overall of these studies provide mixed evidence and many fail to show a clear relationship between mergers and acquisitions and performance. Some of the previous literature has examined the impact of mergers and acquisitions operation on cost efficiency as measured by simple accounting cost ratios (Rhoades, 1990, 1993; Pilloff, 1996; DeLong and DeYoung, 2007), the impact on cost X-efficiency (Berger and Humphrey, 1992; DeYoung, 1997; Peristiani, 1997; Berger, 1998; Rhoades, 1998).

Also, evidence supporting mergers and acquisitions to achieve cost saving and efficiency gain is sparse (Kwan and Elsenbeis, 1999). Akhavein et al. (1997) analysed changes in profitability experienced in the same set of large mergers as examined by Berger and Humphrey (1992). They found that banking organizations significantly improved their profit efficiency ranking after mergers. De Young (1993) does find that when both the acquirer and target were poor performers, mergers resulted in improved cost efficiency. Healy et al. (1992) examined all commercial banks and bank holding company mergers and acquisitions occurring between 1982 and 1986. They found that mergers and acquisitions did not reduce non-interest expenses that could have led to improved efficiency. According to Pilloff and Santomero (1997), there is little empirical evidence of mergers achieving growth or other important performance gains. Their findings undermine a major rationale for mergers and consequently raised doubt about other benefits mergers and acquisitions may provide to businesses.

However, Cornett and Tehranian (1992) and Kay (1993) find some evidence of superior post merger period because of the merged firms' enhanced ability to attract loans. They also show increased employee productivity and net asset growth. Also, this is evident in the Nigeria's banking industry (Okpanachi, 2006). Walter and Uche (2005) posited that mergers and acquisitions made Nigerian banks more efficient. They used table to present their data which was analyzed using simple percentage. Akpan (2007), using chi square to test his stated hypothesis found that the policy of consolidation and capitalization has ensured customers' confidence in the Nigerian banking industry in term of high profit. But, for Sobowale (2004) and Osho (2004), it is expected that the value of the companies that participated in mergers and acquisitions activities would be higher than before because future dividends and earning streams are expected to rise and subsequently improves efficiency.

Similarly, Uchendu (2005) and Kama (2007) opined that, the bank consolidation which took place in Malaysia facilitated banks expansion which led to growth. In a related study of the Chilean banking industry, Kwan (2002) found that the high rate of economic activities experienced in Chile was mainly from productivity's improvement from the large banks formed as a result of mergers and acquisitions. The studies by Berger and Mester (1997) and Stiroh (2002) using data on United States banks suggested that, there may be more substantial scale efficiency from larger sizes of banks as a result of mergers and acquisitions. But for Straub (2007), mergers and acquisitions have often failed to add significantly to the performance of the banking sector. Surprisingly, the majority of studies comparing pre and post mergers performance found that, these potential efficiency derived from mergers and acquisitions rarely materialize (Piloff, 1996; Berger et al., 1999). Towards this end, Beitel et al. (2003) found no gain effect due to mergers and acquisitions, but for Yener and David (2004), mergers and acquisitions played an important role in improving after merger financial performance which is a stimulus for efficiency. Most of the studies examined found that mergers and acquisitions add significantly to the profits of the banking sector, except for Straub (2007) and Rhoades (1993) that have contrary views.

Table 1. Access Bank Plc extracted financial efficiency parameters (2002 to 2008).

Period	Pre mergers/acquisition			Base year	Post mergers and acquisitions		
Years	2002	2003	2004	2005	2006	2007	2008
				Naira (Million)			
Gross earnings	2,604,378	4,367,887	5,515,086	7,494,855	13,360,358	27,881,451	57,627,098
Profit after tax	(55,245)	556,573	637,473	501,515	737,149	6,083,439	16,056,464
Net assets	1,943,784	2,365,357	2,702,830	14,071,924	28,893,886	28,384,891	171,002,026

Source: Researchers' computation from the published annual reports and accounts, various issues.

Table 2. First Bank of Nigeria Plc extracted financial efficiency parameters (2002 to 2008).

Period	Pre mergers/acquisition			Base year	Post mergers and acquisition		
Years	2002	2003	2004	2005	2006	2007	2008
				Naira (Thousand)			
Gross earnings	46,267	50,597	51,318	49,475	61,243	79,299	130,600
Profit after tax	4,776	11,010	11,483	12,184	16,053	18,355	30,473
Net assets	19,406	27,006	41,605	48,726	64,277	83,627	351,854

Source: Researchers' computation from the published annual reports and accounts, various issues.

METHODOLOGY

For this paper, the population is all the twenty one (21) banks currently quoted in the official daily lists of the Nigerian Stock Exchange (NSE) market as at 30th October, 2009 making up the Nigerian banking sector. Three banks namely; Access Bank Plc, First Bank of Nigeria Plc and Wema Bank Plc were chosen as sample for the study using convenient and judgmental techniques of sample selection. To be selected as a sample, the banks must meet the following criteria:

1. They must retain their identities prior to and after the mergers and acquisitions activities.
2. End of accounting year must be 31st March, which made their published annual reports and accounts available.
3. Members of the group as a result of mergers and acquisitions bid must not exceed three (3).
4. Their Managing Directors were never sacked by the CBN governor under the current reform process.

The paper made use of secondary data obtained and computed from the banks' published annual reports and accounts covering the periods from years 2002 to 2008 in Tables 1, 2 and 3. Years 2002 to 2004 is the pre mergers and acquisitions period and 2005 is the base year, while 2006 to 2008 is the post mergers and acquisitions period. This we did to compare if there is any significant difference accruing to efficiency in terms of gross earnings, profit after tax and net assets. The collected data were analysed using t - test statistic at 5% level of significant with the aids of statistical package for social sciences (SPSS) version 15 which is an improvement on the ordinary student t-test as used by Adereti and Sanni (2007). The t - test statistic formula is given as:

$$t = \frac{\sum (X - \mu)}{SE\ X} \sim t_{n1-2}$$

where, X = Sample mean; μ = Hypothesized mean; SE = Standard error, and n_1 = Sample size.

Decision rule

Reject Ho if the t – calculated value is greater than the t – tabulated value at 5% level of significance.

RESULTS AND DISCUSSION

Here, the study extracted the gross earnings, profits after tax, and net assets from the published annual reports and accounts of the three sampled banks in order to test the formulated hypotheses and make analyses for interpretation of the results.

The tables showed the financial efficiency parameters in terms of gross earnings, profit after tax and net assets extracted from the annual reports and accounts of the three selected banks. From the tables, all the selected banks witnessed improved financial performance as a result of mergers and acquisitions activities leading to more financial efficiency. To test the stated hypotheses, the study applied the t-test statistic which produced results as shown in Tables 4 and 5.

Tables 4 and 5 show the computed t-test from the SPSS output of the sampled banks financial efficiency parameters prior to and after mergers and acquisitions activities. It clearly depicted the combined means, standard deviations and the calculated t-value. Of the three banks after mergers and acquisitions bids, their combined means for gross earnings increased and that of profit after tax declined as a result of high tax charges and increased depreciation charges while the net assets recorded a tremendous increase due to investment in more fixed assets.

Table 3. Wema Bank Plc extracted financial efficiency parameters (2002 to 2008).

Period	Pre mergers/acquisition			Base year	Post mergers and acquisition		
Years	2002	2003	2004	2005	2006	2007	2008
				Naira (Million)			
Gross earnings	7,919,749	9,716,374	12,856,096	15,287,866	14,836,623	26,430,982	51,279,366
Profit after tax	1,481,667	1,477,775	967,148	844,285	(6,601,961)	2,554,098	4,217,641
Net assets	3,768,119	7,215,393	8,040,348	24,258,860	20,540,001	25,182,705	31,061,406

Source: Researchers' computation from the published annual reports and accounts, various issues.

Table 4. t-test descriptive measures of financial efficiency parameters before and after mergers and acquisitions.

VAR00014	N	Mean	Std. deviation	Std. error mean
VAR00015				
Pre M and As	9	18799494	41524345.054	13841448
Post M and As	9	21291086	21600435.453	7200145.2
VAR00016				
Pre M and As	9	590321.44	626797.62666	208932.54
Post M and As	9	2569043.2	6163011.3543	2054337.1
VAR00017				
Pre M and As	9	13603679	23468095.032	7822698.3
Post M and As	9	33913089	53094556.803	17698186

Source: SPSS output.

Table 5. t - Value statistic of financial efficiency parameters for analytical comparison between the pre and post mergers and acquisitions periods.

		N	Mean	Std. deviation	t -value	Prob.	Remark
Gross earnings	Before M and As	9	18799493.6	41524345.1	-01.60	0.875	NS
	After M and As	9	21291086	21291086			
Profit after tax	Before M and As	9	590321.4	590321.4	-0.958	0.352	NS
	After M and As	9	2569043.2	2569043.2			
Net assets	Before M and As	9	13603679	13603679	-1.050	0.310	NS
	After M and As	9	33913088.7	33913088.7			

Source: SPSS output.

Looking critically at the results of the t-test, one is made to conclude that bank' mergers and acquisitions exercise has no significant impact on the financial efficiency of the selected banks. This arose from the fact that, the calculated t-values is less than the t-critical value at 5% level of significance; hence, there is no significant difference between the pre and post mergers and acquisitions periods in term of gross earnings, profit after tax and net assets. However, the post mergers and acquisitions periods have a higher performance in gross earnings; profit after tax and net assets has a better performance than the pre mergers and acquisitions periods. Based on the aforementioned, the null hypotheses are rejected. But for Sanni (2009), there was a significant increase in profitability of the four banks used in his study after the consolidation exercise in the Nigerian banking sector while the profitability of other thirteen banks significantly decreased.

CONCLUSION AND RECOMMENDATIONS

The paper attempted to make a comparative analysis of the impact of mergers and acquisitions on financial efficiency of selected banks in Nigeria. The results showed an enhanced financial performance leading to improved financial efficiency, but the t-test statistic result of the three selected banks as contained in the SPSS output depicted an increase in their combined means for gross earnings and net assets while profit after tax recorded a decline.

There are mixed evidences from researchers on the relationship between mergers and acquisitions, financial efficiency, profitability and performance. Calomiris and Karenski (1996), Caprion (1999), De-Nicolo et al. (2003) are of the opinion that mergers and acquisitions in the financial system could impact positively on both the financial and operational efficiency of most banks. But De Long and De Young (2007) suggested that mergers and acquisitions in the United States banking sector did not have a positive influence on performance in term of improved financial efficiency while Humphrey (1992) found that banks significantly improved their profit efficiency after mergers whereas Healy et al. (1992) found that mergers and acquisitions in the banking sector did not lead to improved financial efficiency which Straub (2007) supported by saying that mergers and acquisitions have often failed to add significantly to the performance of the banking sector.

However, it is still impossible to clearly state whether mergers and acquisitions in the Nigerian banking sector lead to improved financial efficiency. This is because mergers and acquisitions in the Nigerian banking sector is a continuous scheme and the sector is still undergoing reforms as a result of global economic meltdown which affected profits. Also, most of the conclusion reported by researchers on performance pattern of Nigerian banks as a result of mergers and acquisitions concentrated on using similar variables with fewer numbers of banks as population samples for their studies. They could have been differences in results and findings if all the twenty one (21) banks currently quoted in the official daily lists of the Nigerian Stock Exchange (NSE) market as at 30th October, 2009 making up the Nigerian banking sector were used as the population sample for the study.

This study concludes that though there is no significant difference between the pre and post mergers and acquisitions period in terms of gross earnings, profit after tax and net assets as the calculated t-values is less than the t-critical value at 5% level of significant. Also, the study found that the post mergers and acquisitions periods has a higher performance in gross earnings and low performance in profit after tax while net assets has a better performance than the pre mergers acquisitions period. The finding in this paper is quite in agreement with the work of Calomiris and Karenski (1996), Caprion (1999) Nicolo et al. (2003) and Sanni (2009). Therefore, the paper recommends that banks should be more aggressive in financial products marketing to increase financial efficiency for an improved financial position in term of gross earnings, profit after tax and net assets in order to reap the benefit of post mergers and acquisitions bid in the Nigerian banking sector.

REFERENCES

Access Bank Plc. Published Annual Reports and Accounts, Various Issues (2008).

Adereti A, Sanni MR, (2007). The Effects of Mergers and Acquisitions on Corporate Performance. Knowl. Rev., 15(9): 81-87.

Ajayi M, (2005). Banking Sector Reforms and Bank Consolidation. C.B.N Bullion Abuja, 29(2a).

Akhavein JD, Berger AN, Humphrey DB (1997). The Effects of Megamergers on Efficiency and Prices: Evidence from a Bank Profit Function. Rev. Ind. Org., p. 12.

Akpan AB (2007). Effectiveness of Bank Capitalization and Consolidation in Building Market Confidence: An Assessment of Customers Perception in Nigeria. Abuja J. Bus. Admin., 1(2), December.

Amedu S (2004). Corporate Takeover, Acquisition and Merger. The Nigerian Stockbroker, the Official J. Chartered Inst. Stockbrokers, January – March.

Amel D, Barnes C, Panetta F, Salleo C (2004). Consolidation and Efficiency in the Financial Sector: A Review of the International Evidence. J. Banking Finan., 28(10): 2493-2519.

Augustine NK (2007). Impact of Nigeria's Bank Consolidation on Shareholder's Return. African Institute for Economic Development and Planning.

Beitel P, Schiereck D, Wahrenbur M (2003). Explaining the M&A-Success in European Bank Mergers and Acquisitions. Center for Financial Studies Working Paper Series, Johann Wolfgang Geoth University.

Bello MS (2004). Mergers and Acquisitions as a Strategy for Business Growth in Nigeria. Nig. J. Acct. Res., 1(1).

Berger AN (1998). The Efficiency Effects of Bank Mergers and Acquisitions: A Preliminary Look at the 1990s Data. In Amihud Y, Miller G. (eds.), Bank Mergers and Acquisitions. Kluwer Academic Publishers: Boston, pp. 79-111.

Berger AN, Demsetz RS, Strahan PE (1999). The Consolidation of the Financial Services Industry: Causes, consequences and implications for the future. J. Banking Finan., 23 (2-4).

Berger AN, Humphrey D (1992). Megamergers in Banking and the Use of Cost Efficiency as an Antirust Defense. Antitrust Bull., p. 37.

Berger AN, Mester LJ (1997). Banking Consolidation: What is a Small Business to do? Bus. Rev., January/February.

Cabral I, Dierick F, Vesala J (2002). Banking Integration in the Euro Area. Eur. Central Bank Occasional Pap., (6).

Calomiris C, Karenski J (1996). The Bank Merger Wave of the 1990s: Nine Case Studies. University of Illinois.

Caprion L (1999). The Long term Performance of Horizontal Acquisitions. INSEAD Work. Pap., 99/24/SM, April.

Carletti E, Hartmann P, Spagnolo G (2002). Bank Mergers, Competition and Financial Stability. Committee of the Global Financial System Conference 2, Part 2.

Cornett MM, Tehranian H (1992). Changes in Corporate Performance Associated with Bank Acquisitions. J. Finan. Econ., April.

De Long G, De Young R (2007). Learning by Observing: Information Spillovers in the Execution and Valuation of Commercial Bank Merger and Acquisitions. J. Finan., 62: 181-216.

De-Nicolo G (2003): Bank Consolidation, Internationalization and conglomeration: Trends and Implications for Financial Risks. IMF Work. Pap., 03/158.

De Young R (1997). Bank Mergers, X-Efficiency, and the Market for corporate control. Manage. Finan., 23: 32-47.

First Bank of Nigeria Plc. Published Annual Reports and Accounts, Various Issues (2008).

Garba AA (2006). Recent Reforms in the Nigerian Banking Industry. Issues and Challenges. The Financier, A.B.U Zaria.

Gaughan PA (1999). Mergers and Acquisition. New York, Harper Collins.

Healy PM, Palepu KG, Ruback RS (1992). Does Corporate Performance Improve after Mergers? J. Finan., Econ., 31.

Kama U (2007). Bank Post Consolidation, Issues and Challenges in Malaysia and India: Lessons of Experience. Bullion, Central Bank of Nigeria, Abuja, 31(4).

Kathy L (2005). Mergers and Acquisitions – Another Tool for Traders. Investopedia.

Kay JA, (1993). Foundations of Corporate Success. Oxford University Press.

Kwan SH (2002). Operational Performance of Banks among Asian

Economies: An International and Time Series Comparison. HKIMR Work. Pap., 13, June.

Kwan SH, Eisenbeis RA (1999). Mergers of Publicity Traded Public Organization Revisited. Econ. Rev., Federal Reserve Bank of Atlanta, 4th Quarter.

Mester LJ (1996). A Study of Bank Efficiency Taking into Account Risk-Preference. J. Banking Finan., 20: 1025-1045.

Muhammed R (2005). Understanding Mergers and Acquisitions. Business Day Newspaper February 17th.

Okpanachi J (2006). Effects of Financial Products Marketing Management on Profitability of Some Banks in Nigeria. ABU J. Mark. Manage., 1(II), June.

Okpanachi J (2007). Global Syndromic Nature of Bank Distress: the Nigerian Perspective. Acad. J. Defence Stud., p. 14, February.

Osho M (2004). Consolidation through Mergers and Acquisitions: The African Experience. Conference Proceedings on Consolidation of Nigeria's Banking Industry, Central Bank of Nigeria, Abuja.

Peristiani S (1997). Do Mergers Improve the X-Efficiency and Scale Efficiency of U.S. Banks? Evidence from the 1980s. J. Money Credit Banking, 29(3): 326-337.

Pilloff SJ, Santomero AM (1997). The Value Effects of Bank Mergers and Acquisitions. Work. Pap., Financial Institution Centre, University of Pennsylvania, pp. 97–107.

Rewane B (2004). Stakeholder Perspective on N25 Billion Banks Capital Base. Financial Standards, August.

Rhoades SA (1993). The Efficiency Effects of Bank Mergers: An Overview of Case Studies of Nine Mergers. J. Banking Finan., 22: 273-291.

Rhoades SA (1990). Billion Dollar Bank Acquisitions: A Note on the Performance Effects. Working Paper, Board of Governors of the Federal Reserve System, Washington, DC.

Rhoades SA (1993). Efficiency Effects of Horizontal (in-market) Bank Mergers. J. Banking Finan., 17: 411–422.

Sanni MR (2009). Short Term Effect of the 2006 Consolidation on Profitability of Nigerian Banks. Nig. Res. J. Accountancy, Inst. Chartered Account. Nig., 1(1), October.

Sobowale D (2004). Soludo's Revolution and N25 billion Capital Base Policy, The Grave Danger Ahead; Mergers, Acquisitions and Recapitalization Options, How Feasible. Weekend Vanguard, July.

Soludo C (2004). Consolidating the Banking Industry to Meet Development Challenges. Discussion Paper, http:/www. thisday online.com/business.

Stiroh K, (2002). Diversification in Banking: Is Non-interest Income the Answer? Staff Reports, Federal Research Bank of New York, (154). September.

Szapary G (2001). Banking Sector Reform in Hungary: Lessons Learned Current Trends and Prospects. In Current Issues in Emerging Market Economies Organized by the Croatian National Bank on 28th – 30th June.

Straub T (2007). Reasons for Frequent Failure in Mergers and Acquisitions – A Comparative Analysis. Deutscher Universitats Verlag, Wiesbaden.

The Nigerian Stock Exchange (2009). NSE Fact Book.

Uchendu OA (2005). Banking Sector Reforms and Bank Consolidation: the Malaysian Experience. Bullion, Central Bank of Nigeria, Abuja, 29(2), April/June.

Umoh PN (2004). Capital Restructuring of Banks: Conceptual Framework. Conference Proceedings on Consolidation of Nigeria's Banking Industry, Central Bank of Nigeria, Abuja.

Walter CN, Uche U (2005). New Capitalization for Banks: Implication for the Nigerian Economy. Adamawa State Univ. Bus. J., 1(1), January.

Wema Bank Plc. Published Annual Reports and Accounts, Various Issues (2008).

Yener A, David MI (2004). Mergers and Acquisitions and Banks Performance in Europe: The Role of Strategic Similarities. Eur. Central Bank Work. Pap. Ser., (398), October.

Divergences between the BR GAAP and US GAAP

Ilse Maria Beuren* and Roberto Carlos Klann

Universidade Regional de Blumenau – PPGCC/FURB, Rua Antonio da Veiga, 140, Sala D 202, Bairro Victor Konder – Caixa Postal 1507, CEP 89012-900 – Blumenau/ SC, Brasil.

The objective of this paper is to analyze impacts of the divergences between Brazilian accounting standards (BR GAAP) and 'generally accepted accounting principles' in the United States (US GAAP) in accounting recognition, measurement and disclosure. Seventeen Brazilian companies listed on the São Paulo stock exchange (BOVESPA) that negotiated American depositary receipts (ADRs) on the New York stock exchange (NYSE) were selected, using as a reference financial statements. Results demonstrate that the principal groups of accounts affected by divergences were long term realizable assets (assets and equity realizable over a long term), long term exigible liability (long term debts) and operational profit. The principle divergences observed in explanatory notes were those relative to '*goodwill*' and structure of the balance.

Key words: Divergences, BR GAAP, US GAAP, financial statements, disclosure, Brazilian companies.

INTRODUCTION

One of the challenges faced by regulatory accounting agencies worldwide is how to reduce or even eliminate the asymmetry of information evidenced in reports produced according to the standards of different countries. Various international agencies like the International Accounting Standards Board (IASB), the International Federation of Accountants (IFAC), the United Nations Conference on Trade and Development (UNCTAD) and the International Organization of Securities Commission (IOSCO) have made an effort to develop high quality international accounting standards. In doing so, they seek to promote the convergence of various local standards into an international harmonization on accounting. The 'international financial reporting standards' (IFRS) are rapidly gaining worldwide acceptance. In January 2005, approximately 7,000 companies listed with the European Union converted their statements to the IFRS requirements (Cummings; Brannen, 2005). Approximately, 113 countries around the world currently require or permit IFRS reporting for domestic listed companies (International Accounting Standard Board – IASB, 2009).

In the United States, the 'securities and exchange commission' was voted in August 27th, 2008 to publish for public comment a proposed 'roadmap' that could lead to the use of IFRS by U.S. issuers beginning in 2014. The 'commission' would make a decision in 2011 on whether adoption of IFRS is in the public interest and would benefit investors (U.S. Securities and Exchange Commission - SEC). In November 14th, 2008, the 'commission' proposed a 'roadmap' for the potential use of financial statements prepared in accordance with IFRS as issued by the IASB by U.S. issuers (U.S. Securities and Exchange Commission - SEC).

In Brazil, the efforts of the 'committee on accounting pronouncement' (CPC), has contributed to the convergence process of Brazilian accounting standards with the international accounting standards of the IASB. The CPC is made up of representatives from the 'Brazilian association of publicly owned companies' (ABRASCA), the 'association of analysts and professionals from the capital investments market' (APIMEC), the São Paulo stock exchange (BOVESPA), the 'federal accounting council' (CFC), the 'foundation institute of accounting, actuarial and financial research' (FIPECAFI) and the 'institute of independent auditors of Brazil' (IBRACON).

The Brazilian government has also given signals that it supports this process. Proof of which was in the

*Corresponding author. E-mail: jlklein@uol.com.br, ilse@furb.br.

promulgation of Law n. 11.638, of 28 December 2007, which alters various dispositives factors related to the accounting section of Law n. 6.404/76 (Law on Shareholder Organizations) and n. 6.385/76, introducing significant advances to accounting in Brazil and allowing adoption of international accounting standards starting in 2008. The major objective of these efforts is to reduce asymmetry of information among various users of financial statements, thereby increasing the trust that investors place in Brazilian companies and mainly among foreign investors.

Asymmetry in information provided to users, provoked by differences in accounting standardization between countries, can prejudice the decisions of investors and other decision makers. In a globalized economy, accounting information from companies is analyzed by different users from all over the world. In particular, minimizing or eliminating these differences can help investors in the analysis of this information, in any market where the company's shares are traded. Despite all the efforts made towards international harmonization of accounting standards, it is possible that a company, for example, presents favorable performance indicators according to local accounting standards, but does not present the same performance when the indicators are calculated based on financial statements prepared according to the standards of another country. Thus, the objective of this article is to analyze the impacts of the divergences between Brazilian accounting standards (BR GAAP) and the 'generally accepted accounting principles' in the United States (US GAAP) in accounting recognition, measurement and disclosure. It seeks to identify the variations provoked in the account groups of the balance sheet and in operational profit and liquid profit in statement of fiscal period.

It is assumed that not found significant differences in accounting recognition, measurement and disclosure on the account groups of the financial statements prepared according to the Brazilian and American accounting standards due to historical events that influenced the Brazilian accounting process. In Brazil, there was a strong influence of the Anglo-American audit firms in the past, which came to the country bringing a strong tradition of audit procedures and manuals, and the habit of giving training courses in companies on accounting standards and procedures (Iudícibus, 2004). These aspects gave to the accounting procedures adopted in Brazil, certain similarities to the ones established in the US GAAP.

The goal of this study is to reinforce the importance of professionals in the accounting area and its regulatory agencies to promote the convergence of local standards to the IFRS. The United States (whose economy is among the largest ones in the world) and Brazil (whose emerging economy has potential signs for growth) realized, rather than many other countries, that market globalization requires the convergence of local accounting standards to IFRS. Even though researches (Cia et al., 2008; Lemes and Carvalho, 2009) are questioning the effects and implications of the divergence of local standards to US GAAP, the results indicated that there are differences in profits, which were reported by Brazilian companies in BR GAAP and US GAAP and the researches suggested additional studies to identify specific differences. Thus, this research analyzes the impact of the adoption of different accounting standards (Brazil versus United States) in the groups of accounts of the 'balance sheet', operating profit and net profit of Brazilian companies with ADRs on the NYSE. These companies were selected because they are required to submit financial statements to BOVESPA in Brazil GAAP and to NYSE in the U.S.

ACCOUNTING DISCLOSURE

Lopes and Martins (2005) state that the accounting process is characterized by three phases: recognition, measurement and disclosure. The accounting process and its stages are the result of the social, economic and political environment that surrounds them. In this context, the different accounting standards adopted by various countries can affect one or all of the stages of this process, resulting in asymmetry of information among the various users of accounting information.

The disclosure consists of demonstrating the process of recognition and measurement realized to outside users of the organization. There have been various studies and discussions about what should be disclosed by organizations. Radebaugh and Gray (1977) understand that disclosure of information does not necessarily need to be legal or enforced; it can be voluntary or informal. What is important is that it should be the same for everybody, thus avoiding the potential problem of inside information. Choi and Mueller (1992) point out that accounting disclosure is influenced by four main factors:

(a) The environment in which the company is inserted (the stage of economic development of the home country, colonial history, etc.
(b) The market for capital (competition for resources of less cost).
(c) Non-financial influences (like unions).
(d) The corporate demand for greater transparency.

Therefore, the level of disclosure will be more or less elevated in accordance with these characteristics. Companies from countries with a more developed economy and capital markets would tend to realize more transparent disclosure than companies from countries with less developed economies and more closed markets. An example of this environmental and market influence on the level of disclosure is presented by Hendriksen and Van Breda (1992), who note that in the United States, it is common for reports to be prepared by shareholders, creditors and other investors. In Europe, the vision is a bit wider, since the interests of employees and the state is placed on the same level of shareholders' interests.

Whatever the forms or methods of disclosure used, the information produced by accounting must be disclosed in accordance with the interests and possibilities of understanding each user, with the goal of helping them in the decision making process. Hendriksen and Van Breda (1992) note that those companies that end up having a greater dependence on foreign capital tend to provide disclosure that is more appropriate to the markets where they intend to capture resources. However, whether the greater quality of disclosure is due to the competition for funds or to the desire to look for resources in the American and British markets, which possess rigorous regulations for disclosure, is not known.

The strongest argument for voluntary disclosure on the part of companies is the strengthening of their image in the stock exchange markets. This contributes to a greater financial evaluation of a company, resulting in less cost of capturing resources, greater return and less fluctuation in the price of its shares on the market (Malacrida and Yamamoto, 2006). A study made by Price Waterhouse Coopers with institutional investors and analysts points out five benefits of greater disclosure: increased credibility of managers, more long-term investors, greater monitoring on the part of analysts, better access to new capital and better evaluation of the share price (Eccles et al., 2001).

According to Hendriksen and Van Breda (1992), there also exist companies that resist increasing the degree of accounting disclosure unless there is pressure from the accounting community or from public agencies. They allege that greater disclosure will help competitors to the detriment of shareholders and will give unions an advantage in negotiating wages. Investors do not understand accounting policies and procedures and as a result, this will confuse them. They also alleged that there exist other sources of available information at a much lower cost and finally, that the needs of investors are not known.

Wong and Ho (2003) understand that compulsory disclosure and spontaneous disclosure complement each other, thereby enhancing the total functioning of the market. Despite the increase in voluntary disclosure, Carvalho et al. (2004: 265) point out that as a result of the recent scandals involving large companies, the relationship between investors and companies has become less solid and has given way to mistrust: "Consequently, there is an elevated demand for more relevant information, which further increases the importance of transparency in financial statements". To meet this demand, regulatory agencies have made efforts to determine the information that must be disclosed by publicly owned companies. Obligatory disclosure has become more and more detailed by regulating agencies. This is done in order to return credibility to financial statements for the sake of investors. However, this credibility still cannot be achieved in relation to the global market due to the divergences among international accounting standards, which can cause asymmetry of information about what is disclosed in different markets.

DIVERGENCES IN WORLD ACCOUNTING STANDARDS

Differences in accounting standards between countries require different practices of recognition, measurement, accounting and disclosure in business, which is reflected in the financial statements available to the public. Tarca (2004) points out that two types of non-domestic use of non-national patterns in the consolidated accounts presented to the public may be considered: adoption of international standards in replacing national standards and supplement use when international standards are used in conjunction with national standards. These two methods have been considered by countries in the convergence to 'international financial reporting standard' (IFRS).

The accounting systems and information to be shown will be heavily impacted in the convergence of local rules of each country with the international accounting standards. However, Soderstrom and Sun (2007) believe that differences in the quality of accounting disclosure between countries can be maintained by the adoption of 'international financial reporting standard' (IFRS) because they understand that quality is an overall institutional positioning of the company, including the legal and political systems of the country where the company is. Studies on the causes of divergences in accounting standards between countries almost point in the same direction, citing the characteristics of the legal system of each country involved. Castro Neto (1998), commenting on the probable causes of the different accounting practices of member nations of the European Union, lists the following reasons: the historical formation of the country, cultural influence, level of governmental control, structure of property and raising of capital and peculiarity of accounting principles.

According to Weffort (2005), the causes of different accounting practices can be classified into: characteristics and necessities of users and preparers of information, the manner in which the society is organized, cultural aspects and other external factors. Table 1 shows the association of these causes and some of the more frequent reasons as they appear in the literature according to Weffort.

To Weffort (2005: 42), "the reasons often complete, overlap and even confuse things among themselves and are clearly interdependent". In regard to this point, Niyama (2005: 21) comments; "considering that each country has its own set of laws, rules, philosophies, procedures and objectives (they look to protect their own national interests), it is reasonable to suppose that the

Table 1. Summary of the principle reasons for difference in accounting standards and practices.

Generic reasons	Examples of specific reasons
Characteristics and needs of users of financial statements	Level of education and sophistication of users (especially in terms of business management and the financial community) Type of capital investment system Characteristics of the company: size, complexity, multi-nationality, debts, etc.
Characteristics of preparers of financial statements (accountants)	Professional education system of accountants Status, age and size of the accounting profession
Way in which the society is organized and the accounting method that develops from this organization	Political system Economic system and level of development Juridical system Fiscal system
Cultural aspects	Cultural values Religion Language
Other external factors	Historical events (principal invasions and colonial heritage) Geographical factors Political and economic ties

Source: Adapted from Weffort (2005, p. 42).

accounting systems of each country have been impacted by such measures". Therefore, divergences among accounting standards between countries do not originate in one factor only, but in a set of factors that range from cultural aspects to technical differences in recognition, measuring and disclosure. The principle divergences in accounting recognition and measurement observed by Niyama (2005) and PriceWaterHouseCoopers (2006) in relation to Brazilian and North American accounting standards are presented in Table 2. The divergences shown in Table 2 referent to the recognition and measurement of accounting elements can impact the constant values in financial statements. Therefore, the same company can present different compositions of assets and liabilities, beyond divergent results, in disclosing financial statements prepared from these different starting points. Consequently, asymmetry of information can occur if the statements were sent to different countries or stock markets.

RESEARCH METHODS AND PROCEDURES

The present research is characterized as a descriptive one and it used a quantitative approach. Gil (2002) notes that the objective of a descriptive research is to describe the characteristics of a determined population or phenomenon, or to establish relationships between variables. In this sense, this research seeks to describe the principle divergences observed between Brazilian and American accounting standards and the respective variation in balance account groups and the results of companies involved in the study. In regard to a quantitative approach in descriptive research, Boudon (1973: 24) affirms; "quantitative research can be defined as that which allows collection, within a set of elements, of information comparable between one element and another". Therefore, the existence of a set of more or less comparable elements is indispensable to the adoption of the quantitative approach.

In regard to the procedure used in data collection, this research prioritized document analysis, using as a reference financial statements from 2004 and 2005 sent by companies to BOVESPA (www.bovespa.com.br) and the NYSE (www.nyse.com), and their explanatory notes were included in the Form 20-F submitted by companies to NYSE. Document research is characterized by Gil (2002) as that which is based on material that has yet to receive any analytical treatment or that which can be re-elaborated in terms of research objectives.

The study is transversal or sectional cut, as the focus of analysis covers financial statements referent to 2004 and 2005. With these financial statements as references, the principal adjustments made by companies to the 'balance sheet' and to the 'statement of result of the fiscal period' and which were disclosed in the explanatory notes of financial statements were analyzed. In selecting Brazilian companies, the option was made to work with companies listed according to the 'corporate governance' of BOVESPA, by considering that these companies had greater commitment to transparency and responsibility for the information submitted. Thus, there was greater ease in access to data and greater reliability in using them. The population thus consisted of 81 Brazilian companies listed in levels 1 and 2 of the 'new market' of corporate

Table 2. Principal differences between the BR GAAP and US GAAP in the recognition and measurement of accounting elements.

Divergences	Recognition and measurement
Research and development expenses	BR GAAP – must be capitalized as an asset and amortized during the expected period of future economic benefits, no longer than ten years. US GAAP – all research and development expenses must be taken to a result immediately, without exceptions (SFAS 2).
Re-evaluation of assets	BR GAAP – permits re-evaluation, including negative. The proposal to modify the corporate law foresees re-evaluation only in cases of corporate re-organization. US GAAP – prohibits any type of re-evaluation.
Accounting of financial leasing	BR GAAP – are accounted for as rent, in compliance with fiscal legislation, both for the lessee and the leaser. US GAAP – the essence must prevail over the form. The asset must be registered by the leaser as a fixed asset in correspondent with a liability obligation. In this case, the contract must have at least one of these requirements: transference of the property of the asset to the leaser, a bargain buying price, the contractual period must be greater than 75% of the useful economic life of the asset or the present value of the minimum leasing payments must be greater than 90% of the marker value of the asset leased on the date when the operation began (SFAS 13).
Accounting of 'goodwill'	BR GAAP - treated as a premium, must be declared an asset and amortized according to its useful life, not longer than ten years. Fiscal legislation permits the inclusion of goodwill as an asset that must be amortized in up to five years. US GAAP – must be capitalized as an asset and subjected annually to the impairment test, taking it as the result of the difference between the determined value of the goodwill and what is effectively capitalized (SFAS 142).
Actualization of stock via the LIFO method	BR GAAP – the LIFO is not admitted fiscally, hence leading companies use the average or the FIFO (first in first out). US GAAP – allows adoption of the LIFO (last in first out) for fiscal and corporate purposes.
Deferred taxes	BR GAAP – legislation requires accounting for the effects of temporary differences, such as tax credit, the asset and provisions for deferred income tax. FASB – determine the recognition of deferred taxes for corporate effects, accounted for in the same accounting period in which the expenses and receipts were recognized (SFAS 109).
Responsibilities for employee retirement benefit plans	BR GAAP – essentially observes IAS 19, starting in 2001, but only for public companies authorized by the SEC (Deliberation 371/00). Others adapt a cash basis. UG GAAP – accounts through competence regime, with recognition of a passive actuarial and a financial asset evaluated by a fair value, similar to the IAS 19 (SFAS 87 e SFAS 88).
Financial instruments	BR GAAP – only financial institutions are subordinate to the control and inspection of the Central Bank's adopted international accounting rules. Public companies are subjected only to disclosure by explicative notes of market values, that is, for options, futures, terms and swaps. Other anonymously owned companies, subordinate to Law n. 6.404/76, are not obligated for any kind of disclosure of these instruments. US GAAP – are norms identical to the IASB (SFAS 133). Derivatives must be registered as resources items in the balance sheet, as assets and liabilities by fair value. Usually, adjustments to fair value must be recognized in that they occur as a result, except those derivatives classified as hedges (IAS 39).

Source: Adapted from Niyama (2005, pp. 55-83) and Price Water House Coopers (2006, pp. 12-25).

governance of BOVESPA. The listings considered are from October 2006. The sample is of the intentional type, with the selection criterion being companies that negotiated American depositary receipts (ADRs) on New York stock exchange (NYSE) in January 2007. Based on this criterion, 19 Brazilian companies were selected, with two being discarded because of a lack of information sent to the NYSE in the period researched, leaving a total sample of 17 companies.

In the data analysis, the differences between BR GAAP and US GAAP have been identified from the reconciliation of net income and the PL, based on the notes on the Form 20-F submitted by companies to NYSE. Then, the differences were found in the 'balance sheet' groups, as well as in the operating profit and net profit of the 'statement of results' of the year of each company. The

Table 3. Sum total of account groups in the year 2004 in BR GAAP and US GAAP from Brazilian companies.

Indicator	CA	LTRA	PA	CL	LTEL	NW	OP	NP
BR GAAP	329.191	100.096	69.017	277.666	147.633	73.004	19.305	12.419
US GAAP	350.398	46.466	77.558	166.123	231.112	77.184	36.975	14.891
Difference	6%	-54%	12%	-40%	57%	6%	92%	20%
ANOVA (standard error)	1717839138	7308831	1581204	74356242	40830170	1836244	810261,4	120636,8
ANOVA(t statistics)	9.4963^{e-06}	-0.00056	0.000416	-0.00012	0.000157	0.000175	0.001678	0.001576

Table 4. Sum total of account groups in the year 2005 in BR GAAP and US GAAP from Brazilian companies.

Indicator	CA	LTRA	PA	CL	LTEL	NW	OP	NP
BR GAAP	374.844	119.431	69.433	290.359	191.618	81.734	25.161	18.286
US GAAP	419.613	49.153	80.269	186.509	275.418	87.203	43.603	19.335
Difference	12%	-59%	16%	-36%	44%	7%	73%	6%
ANOVA (standard error)	234511357	10127801	1552162	82912735	63393409	2576871	1420494	284230,4
ANOVA(t statistics)	1.4685^{e-05}	-0.00053	0.000537	-9.6^{e-05}	0.000102	0.000163	0.000999	0.000284

differences between BR GAAP and US GAAP were calculated using the sum of the respective groups of all accounting firms. Having established the differences in each group of accounts, ANOVA was performed to verify whether the percentage differences found are statistically significant.

DESCRIPTION AND ANALYSIS OF DATA

Presented in the description and analysis of data are the adjustments to accounts from the 'balance sheet' to the operational profit and net profit, based on the financial statements from 2004 to 2005 sent by these companies to the São Paulo stock exchange (BOVESPA) and the New York stock exchange (NYSE), because of divergences between the BR GAAP and the US GAAP.

Analysis of the variations in relation to account groups of financial statements

To begin this analysis, it can be stated that there exist variations in the groups of the 'balance sheet' as well as in the operational profit and net profit of the 'statement of results for the fiscal period'. The differences between the BR GAAP and US GAAP, beginning with the sum total of the respective account groups of all the companies, are presented in Table 3. These are considered, in a global way, to be the values of the groups: Current Asset – CA (assets and short term equity), Long Term Realizable Asset – LTRA (assets and equity realizable over a long term), Permanent Asset – PA (assets and equity of permanent character in the company), Current Liability – CL (short term debts), Long Term Exigible Liability – LTEL (long term debts) and Net Worth – NW (capital invested by shareholders and bond investors). In other words, they comprised the whole items from the 'balance sheet' and two items from the results statement, operational profit (OP) and net profit (NP). Besides the percentage differences between the groups of accounts, ANOVA was performed to verify whether they are statistically significant (Table 3). ANOVA is a resource used to determine the likelihood of having differences in averages of different groups occurring only due to sampling error. To conduct the test, the significance level of 0.05 was chosen. To determine the t_{crit},, the distribution t 13 - 1 degree of freedom (k - 1) and α = 0.05 was applied, having t_{crit}, = 1.782. Table 3 reveals that the percentage difference in operational profit between the implementation of BR GAAP and US GAAP is 92% in the companies analyzed for the year 2004, considering the sum of the net income values in BR and US accounting standards of all companies. Other groups that presented high variations were 'long term realizable assets' (-54%), 'current liability' (-40%) and 'long term exigible liability' (57%).

The ANOVA test shows that the percentage differences found in comparing the sum of the values of accounts' groups based on BR GAAP and US GAAP for all companies surveyed, are mostly in groups; 'long term realizable assets' (LTRA), 'current liability' (PL), 'long term exigible liability' (LTEL) and 'operational profit' (OP), although none of the groups had t_{crit}, = 1,782. Therefore, for this analysis, it cannot be said that the differences found between the implementation of BR GAAP and US GAAP are statistically significant. The other groups in the financial statements did not present relevant differences, varying from 6 - 20% points. Similar procedures were adopted to analyze the figures of the year 2005, whose results are shown in Table 4. Analyzing Table 4, the set of 17 companies, shows that the principal variations in relation to BR GAAP versus US GAAP are found in 'long term

realizable assets' (-59%), 'active liability' (-36%) and 'long term exigible liability' (44%). Besides these variations, there was also a variation of 73% in 'operational profit' in comparing the values found in BR GAAP and US GAAP. In the other groups of financial statements, the differences observed can be considered minimal, varying from six to sixteen percentage points.
The ANOVA test shows, as in the previous year, that although the percentage differences were found in comparing the sum of the values of accounts' groups based on BR GAAP and US GAAP for all companies surveyed, none of the groups had $t_{crit,}$ = 1,782. Therefore, it can not be said that the differences found are statistically significant. It can not be stated that the differences between BR GAAP and US GAAP have statistically affected the values of accounts' groups of the 2004 and 2005 financial statements of these companies in a significant manner. However, the explanations for the variations are found in the fact that some companies were more heavily impacted accounting groups by differences in accounting standards, particularly in the case of transactions that affected the value of 'long term realizable assets' (LTRA), 'current liability' (CL), 'long term exigible liability' (LTEL) and 'operational profit' (OP) of the analyzed companies. Differences observed in groups of accounts as a result of the implementation of the BR GAAP and US GAAP indicates that users of accounting information may come to different conclusions of the assets and economic-financial evaluation of a company's situation. Depending on the accounting standard that is being considered (BR GAAP or US GAAP) in the financial statements published, one can apply different evaluations to the same company. Doing so could negatively interfere in these organizations´ decisions about investments, thereby losing potential investors. It could also harm investors that expected to derive profit from the values invested and felt punished by the information asymmetry caused by the differences in the accounting standards applied. After the classification of variations in the principal accounts of the 'balance sheet' and the 'statement of result of the fiscal period', analysis was made of the principal adjustments disclosed in the explanatory notes of financial statements sent to the NYSE.

Analysis of variations by account group, based on explanatory notes

The variations in the groups of accounts of the 'balance sheet' and 'statement of results' above resulted from the adjustments made in the following accounts: Research and development expenses, re-evaluation of assets, financial leasing of accounting, accounting of goodwill, stock update via LIFO method, deferred taxes, responsibilities for employee retirement benefit plans and financial instruments. The adjustments observed in the explanatory notes, with the corresponding asset item or the result affected, are displayed in Table 5. Table 5 shows that of the divergences between Brazilian and American accounting practices, the ones most observed in the financial statements of the Brazilian companies investigated were related to 'goodwill' (stated in 14 of the 17 companies analyzed) and those related to the structure of the balance sheet (present in nine of the 17 companies analyzed). Other explanatory notes, which will be addressed in the specific chart, were found in the reports of all analyzed companies.

On the other hand, the divergences least observed in the explanatory notes of Brazilian companies were those related to re-evaluation of assets and expenses in research and development, observed in only three companies. When confronting the findings of this research to the main differences between BR GAAP and US GAAP in the recognition and measurement of accounting elements, identified by Niyama (2005) and PricewaterhouseCoopers (2006), as discussed in the theoretical basis of this study, there are some aspects that deserve to be highlighted. Although, the structure of the balance sheet is not an item indicated by these authors as having differences between BR GAAP and US GAAP, nine companies mentioned something about the notes. Moreover, stock update via the LIFO method and differed taxes were pointed out by the authors as evidence of differences, but differences in the notes of the companies surveyed were not indicated.

During the analysis of the notes, some items appeared in a more dispersed way among the companies and were not discussed in the references. So, this set of differences was named "others". Besides these divergences that are constant with the reference table, others were also seen in analysis of the explanatory notes. Those found are listed in Table 6. In Table 6, 'other' divergences can be seen between Brazilian and American accounting standards observed in the explanatory notes that are not part of the reference table. These are highlighted because they affected a greater number of account groups, that is, those oriented towards adjustments relative to the conversion of local currency *(reais)* to dollars, deferred taxes and the appraisal of fair value for assets and liabilities. The number of companies affected by the divergence in "others", highlighted as shown in Table 6, is presented in Figure 1. Figure 1 shows that 14 of the 17 Brazilian companies investigated suffered alterations in their financial statements when converted to US GAAP because of adjustments related to deferred taxes. This adjustment is derived from other adjustments such as goodwill, impairment, patrimonial equivalence and recognition of receipts, among others. Every adjustment that alters the value of the result ends up impacting the calculation of tax on this same result, being deferred in the conversion. Besides deferred taxes, other adjustments can be highlighted, such as patrimonial equivalence and the impairment test, observed in seven companies, as well as monetary actualization and the recognition of receipts, which appeared in six companies.

Other adjustments pointed out in Table 6 appeared in a maximum of five companies, in which divergences were observed in just one of the 17 companies investigated. The survey results confirm what Soderstrom and Sun (2007) believe can happen even adopting IFRS rather than local standards. Their belief was that the differences in the quality of accounting disclosure between countries can be maintained because they understand that the quality depends on the overall institutional positioning of the company. Within, the companies surveyed were found in the explanatory notes about the differences between BR GAAP and US GAAP not covered in the literature and the reverse was also found, that is, items addressed in the literature and not found in the explanatory notes of the companies, although they have affected their financial statements.

Conclusions

The objective of this paper is to analyze impacts of the divergences between Brazilian accounting standards (BR GAAP) and the generally accepted accounting principles in the United States (US GAAP), in the recognition, measurement and disclosure of financial statements. Seventeen Brazilian companies listed on BOVESPA, that negotiated American depositary receipts (ADRs) on the New York stock exchange (NYSE) in January 2007, were selected, in order to analyze the impacts in financial statements from 2004 and 2005 sent by companies to BOVESPA and the NYSE. Based on analysis of the values in the 'balance sheet' and the 'statement of results for the fiscal period' from the years 2004 and 2005, it can be stated that the groups most affected were the 'long term realizable asset', the 'current liability' and 'the long term exigible liability', along with the operational profit of these organizations. It can be inferred from what was

Table 5. Variations, in relation to account groups, in financial statements.

Companies	Groups of accounts affected by divergences from the table of reference																										
	CA and CL				**LTRA and LTEL**				**PA**					**PL**							**OP and NP**						
	3	5	6	7	3	5	6	7	1	2	3	4	8	1	2	3	4	5	6	8	1	2	3	4	5	6	8
Aracruz Celulose S/A										x		x	x		x		x			x		x		x			x
Banco Bradesco S/A	x	x		x	x	x		x			x	x	x			x	x	x		x			x	x	x		x
Banco Itaú Holding Financeira S/A				x				x				x	x				x			x				x			x
Brasil Telecom Participações S/A	x	x	x		x	x	x				x	x	x			x	x	x	x	x			x	x	x	x	x
Braskem S/A		x				x						x	x				x	x		x				x	x		x
Cia. Brasileira de Distribuição	x		x		x		x				x	x	x			x	x		x	x			x	x		x	x
Cia. Energética de Minas Gerais – CEMIG				x				x					x							x							x
Cia. Saneamento Básico do Estado de São Paulo – SABESP		x				x			x				x	x				x		x	x				x		x
Cia. Vale do Rio Doce				x				x				x	x				x			x				x			x
CPFL Energia S/A	x	x	x		x	x	x			x	x	x	x		x	x	x	x	x	x		x	x	x	x	x	x
Gerdau S/A		x	x			x	x					x	x				x	x	x	x				x	x	x	x
Gol Linhas Aéreas Inteligentes S/A				x				x					x							x							x
Perdigão S/A			x	x			x	x	x			x	x	x	x		x		x	x	x			x		x	x
Sadia S/A		x	x	x		x	x	x				x	x				x	x	x	x				x	x	x	x
Ultrapar Participações S/A			x				x		x	x		x	x	x	x		x		x	x	x	x		x		x	x
Unibanco Holdings S/A			x	x			x	x				x	x				x		x	x				x		x	x
Votorantim Celulose e Papel S/A		x		x		x		x				x	x				x	x		x				x	x		x
N°. of observations	4	8	8	9	4	8	8	9	3	3	4	14	17	3	4	4	14	8	8	17	3	3	4	14	8	8	17

Legend:		
	Re-evaluation of assets	Employee benefit plans
	Research and development expenditures	Financial assets
	Leasing financing	Balance sheet structure
	Goodwill	Others

was discussed that these differences can lead to asymmetry of accounting information and can prejudice the analysis of a company's performance indicators (mainly those indicators involving profitability and debt). This in turn can prejudice investor decisions or the decisions of other users of this accounting information in relation to these companies. However, despite the differences found in the comparative percentage of the sum of the groups' values of accounts based on BR GAAP and US GAAP in all com-panies surveyed, the ANOVA test indicates that none of the groups had t_{crit}, = 1.782, so it cannot be stated that the differences are statistically significant.

In regard to analysis of explanatory notes, it was observed that the divergences most found were related to 'goodwill' and to the structure of the balance sheet. These divergences mainly affected the groups of 'permanent assets' (goodwill), 'current assets', 'long term realizable assets', 'active liability' and 'long term exigible liability'. One consequence of this is that they also ended up affecting the 'net worth' and 'net profit' of the companies analyzed. This fact was pointed out in

Table 6. Account groups affected by other divergences.

Divergences	Account groups affected by other divergences not found in the reference table							
	CA	LTRA	PA	PL	LTEL	NW	OP	NP
Conversion	x	x	x	x	x	x	x	x
Monetary actualization			x			x		x
Deferred taxes	x	x		x	x	x		x
Treatment of financial expenses as operational or non-operational							x	
Interest on own capital				x		x		x
Adjustments from patrimonial equivalence			x			x		x
Adjustments by gains/losses in the sale of available assets	x					x		x
Classification of receipts and expenses into operational and non-operational							x	x
Provision for corporate res-structuring				x		x		x
Different criteria of capitalization and amortization of loans and financial expenses (SFAS 34)				x	x	x	x	x
Classification of dividends and interest on the NW				x	x	x		
Classification of certain fiscal incentives directly on the NW or on the result from the period						x		x
Classification of the participation of employees in profits as an operational expense or as an appropriation of profit at the end of the period						x	x	x
Valorization of long term assets (impairment test)			x			x		x
Recognition of receipts				x	x	x	x	x
Classification of pre-operational costs			x			x	x	x
Accounting of obligations regarding environmental assets (SFAS 143)				x	x	x		x
Capitalization of operational costs			x			x	x	x
Depreciation			x			x	x	x
Capitalization of financial costs in constructions underway			x			x	x	x
Effects in the acquisition of businesses (evaluation of fair value versus cost value)			x			x		x
Allocation of employee participation in profits of stock	x					x		x
Evaluation of fair value for assets and liabilities	x	x	x	x	x	x	x	x
Treatment of expenses with public stock offerings						x	x	x
Classification of export notes as a reducer of asset or as liability	x	x		x	x			
Minority participation					x	x		x
Anticipated expenses	x					x		x

the prior analysis, when the values of respective account groups from the 'balance sheet' and from the 'statement of results for the fiscal period' were compared and prepared based on the BR GAAP and US GAAP. Therefore, the assumption that significant differences would not be found in the account groups of the financial statements prepared according to the Brazilian and American accounting standards has not been confirmed._In conclusion, generally speaking, it can be stated that the divergences between BR GAAP and US GAAP can cause asymmetry of accounting information between what is published for different users that are spread throughout the world. Depending on the statement that is

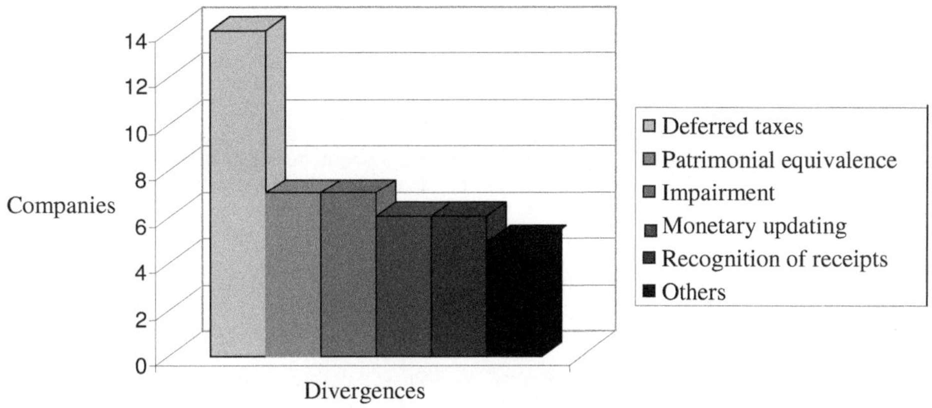

Figure 1. Number of companies affected by 'other' divergences observed in explanatory notes of financial statements of Brazilian companies.

being analyzed, based on BR GAAP or US GAAP, these users can make different decisions on the same company. The consequences could be investors mistrusting and weakening of the capital market.

Although, it is necessary to look carefully to the results of this paper, it can be considered that an exploratory study will work as the base for future studies on the subject. The results also reinforce the importance of the international organizations' efforts such as IASB in creating global accounting standards and the discussion on the convergence of accounting standards in each country for the global accounting standards. It is emphasized that the United States and Brazil, and most of other countries in the world, are already promoting the convergence of local standards to IFRS, which will minimize differences like the ones presented in this study. As a matter of fact, the number of countries making the decision of adopting the IFRS has a long way to go in achieving the desired convergence. As already warned by Tarca (2004), the adoption of international standards in replacing national standards is possible, but there is also the option of using it as a supplement or making changes in local rules by using IFRS as a parameter. Each of these strategies will have implications on the quality of the accounting information and its comparability in different countries. Another relevant aspect is the time required for regulatory agencies to define the form and content of agreements and for companies to adjust to the new accounting standards. In 2008, the U.S. Securities and Exchange Commission decided to implement IFRS in 2014, but the discussion about form and content is still in an embryonic stage. In Brazil, the 'Accounting Announcements Committee' (CPC) was formed in 2005 to make the convergence of local standards to IFRS, making it mandatory for companies in 2010.

Choi and Mueller (1992) have already warned that the accounting disclosure is influenced by the environment, the capital market and the corporate response. However, another factor that was found in this study is the impact of applied accounting standards. The requirement of a single accounting language to strengthen and expand international relations has become more widely discussed from the globalization of markets and the consolidation of economic blocks. Even though there is a strong trend of adopting IFRS to having a universal accounting language, refinement studies will be needed to address specific issues that affect the accounts of each accounting group. Considering the limitations of the present study, it is recommended that future research should investigate other companies in order to determine the differences in account groups of the 'balance sheet' and the 'statement of result of the fiscal periods' in the conversion of their statements from BR GAAP and US GAAP to IFRS. Analysis of an historical series of financial statements can also lead to different results. It is also recommended that other differences in the identification and measurement of events, resulting from the diversity in accounting standards among countries, should be investigated and consequently, other affected account groups should be considered as well.

REFERENCES

Bolsa de Valores de São Paulo (BOVESPA). Listed companies. Available as of January 05th, 2007, at http: <http://www.bovespa.com.br>.

Boudon R (1973). Les méthodes em sociologie. Paris: P.U.F.

Carvalho LNG, Trapp ACG, Chan BL (2005). 'Disclosure e risco operacional: uma abordagem comparativa em instituições financeiras que atuam no Brasil, na Europa e nos Estados Unidos', Revista de Administração da USP, v. 39, n. 3, p. 264-273, jul./set.

Castro NJL (1998). Contribuição ao estudo da prática harmonizada da contabilidade da União Européia, Tese de doutorado não publicada, Faculdade de Economia, Administração e Contabilidade da Universidade de São Paulo, São Paulo, Brasil.

Cia JNS, Santos ES, Cia JC (2008). US GAAP x normas contábeis dos países da américa latina: há diferenças significativas no valor do lucro reportado pelas empresas com ADRs na NYSE? In: Congresso USP de Controladoria e Contabilidade, 8., 2008, São Paulo. Anais ... São Paulo: FEA/USP. CD ROM.

Choi FDS, Mueller GD (1992). Int. accoun. 2. ed. Prentice Hall.

Eccles RG et al. (2001). The value reporting revolution: moving beyond the earnings game. PriceWaterhouseCoopers. New York: John Wiley & Sons, Inc.

Cummings J, Brannen L (2005). 'Waking up to global gaap', Bus. Finance. J.

Financial Accounting Standards Board (FASB). SFAS 2 Accounting for Research and Development Costs, Available as of April 20th, 2008, at http://www.fasb.org/st/summary/stsum2.shtml.

Financial Accounting Standards Board (FASB), SFAS 13 Accounting for Leases, Available as of April 20th, 2008, at http://www.fasb.org/st/summary/stsum13.shtml.

Financial Accounting Standards Board (FASB), SFAS 39 Offsetting of Amounts Related to Certain Contracts - an interpretation of APB Opinion No. 10 and FASB Statement No. 105, Available as of April 20th, 2008, at http://www.fasb.org/st/summary/finsum39.shtml.

Financial Accounting Standards Board (FASB), SFAS 87 Employers' Accounting for Pensions, Available as of April 20th, 2008, at http://www.fasb.org/st/summary/stsum87.shtml.

Financial Accounting Standards Board (FASB), SFAS 88 Employers' Accounting for Settlements and Curtailments of Defined Benefit Pension Plans and for Termination Benefits, Available as of April 20th, 2008, at http://www.fasb.org/st/summary/stsum88.shtml.

Financial Accounting Standards Board (FASB), SFAS 109 Accounting for Income Taxes, Available as of April 20th, 2008, at http://www.fasb.org/st/summary/stsum109.shtml.

Financial Accounting Standards Board (FASB), SFAS 133 Accounting for Derivative Instruments and Hedging Activities, June 1998, Available as of April 20th, 2008, at http://www.fasb.org/pdf/fas133.pdf.

Financial Accounting Standards Board (FASB), SFAS 142 Goodwill and Other Intangible Assets, Available as of April 20th, 2008, at http://www.fasb.org/st/summary/stsum142.shtml.

Gil AC (2002). Como elaborar projetos de pesquisa. 4. ed. São Paulo: Atlas.

International Accounting Standard Board (IASB), IAS 19 Employee benefits, Available as of April 20th, 2008, at http://www.iasplus.com/standard/ias19.htm.

Iudícibus, S. (2004) Teoria da contabilidade. 7. ed. São Paulo: Atlas.

Hendriksen ES, Van BMF (1992). Accounting theory. 5 ed. Hemewood, Illinois: Rchard D. Irwin.

International Accounting Standard Board (IASB), Use of IRFS by jurisdiction, Available as of January 20th, 2009, at http://www.iasplus.com/country/useias.htm.

Lemes S, Carvalho LNG (2009). Comparabilidade entre o resultado em BR GAAP e US GAAP: evidências das companhias brasileiras listadas nas bolsas norte-americanas. Revista Contabilida & Finanças, n. 50, maio/ago.

Malacrida MJC, Yamamoto MM (2006). 'Governança corporativa: nível de evidenciação das informações e sua relação com a volatilidade das ações do Ibovespa', Caderno de Estudos, FIPECAFI, Edição Comemorativa, set.

New York Stok Exchange (NYSE). Information for listed companies. Available as of January 05th, 2007, at http: <http://www.nyse.com/audience/listedcompanies.html>.

Niyama JK (2005). Contabilidade internacional. São Paulo: Atlas.

PriceWaterhouseCoopers (PWC). Semelhanças e diferenças IFRS x US GAAP x práticas contábeis adotadas no Brasil. Available as of November 21th, 2006, at em http://www.pwc.com.br.

Radebaugh LH, Gray SJ (1997). International accounting and multinational enterprises. 4. ed. Boston: Wiley & Sons.

Soderstrom NS, Sun KJ (2007). IFRS adoption and accounting quality: a review. Eur. Account. Revi. 16(4): 675-702, Dec.

Tarca A (2004). International convergence of accounting practices: choosing between IAS and US GAAP. J. Int. Financ. Manage. Account. 5(1): 60-91.

U. S. Securities and Exchange Commission (SEC). SEC proposes roadmap toward global accounting standards to help investors compare financial information more easily. Available as of January 12th, 2009, at http://www.sec.gov/news/press/2008/2008-184.htm.

Weffort EFJ (2005). O Brasil e a harmonização contábil internacional: influências dos sistemas jurídico e educacional, da cultura e do mercado. São Paulo: Atlas.

Wong KS, Ho SSM (2003). 'Preparer's perceptions of corporate reporting and disclosures', Int. J. Disclosure. Governance. 1(1).

Corporate social responsibility: A study on awareness of managers and consumers in Vietnam

PHAM Duc Hieu

University of Commerce, Ha noi, Vietnam. E-mail: hieuphamduc@gmail.com.

This paper aims to examine how executives and managers from different Vietnamese enterprises represent their awareness and their perceptions of corporate social responsibility (CSR), as well as whether the attitude of Vietnamese consumers towards CSR is positive. Based on the quantitative analysis, the paper provides evidence that while a large proportion of managers express a highly positive attitude towards CSR and its reporting, consumers' perception is at low state and questionable. But the hypothesis testing shows that there seems to be a discrepancy between what managers say they do and what they actually do. Nevertheless, the willingness to learn and gain more knowledge about CSR found from the survey has drawn a bright future for CSR implementation and CSR disclosure in Vietnam.

Key words: Corporate social responsibility (CSR), Vietnam, perception, awareness.

INTRODUCTION

Corporate social responsibility (CSR), also known as social responsibility of business, is no stranger to the developed world. It becomes a contemporary issue not only for companies but also for consumers in the world. In fact, there have been a number of suggestive examples, such as Nike Corporation which was ostracized for harsh working conditions in the East and Southeast Asia, and GAP which was attacked for using child labor or any acts causing environmental pollution that can also damage the reputation of a big company.

CSR can be defined as "the obligation of a firm to use its resources in ways to benefit society, through committed participation as a member of society, taking into account the society at large and improving welfare of society at large independent of direct gains of the company" (Kok et al., 2001). This definition raises two important points: firstly, a company should conduct its business which is socially responsible to society as an integral part of its ongoing strategy; and secondly, it is implied that a business cannot be separated from societal issues such as community and environment. Conse quently, these two points lead to the basic premise that a company is responsible, not only to maximize profits, but also to protect the environment and to contribute to the well-being of society.

Whilst there has been increased public attention to CSR worldwide, most CSR studies conducted so far have been in the context of developed countries such as Western Europe, the USA and Australia (Gray et al., 1995; Gray, 2008). There have been relatively few empirical studies on CSR practices in developing countries (Hopper and Hoque, 2004). Two interesting issues of CSR are: to understand which stakeholder group has been perceived as the party that most influence the company in disclosing its CSR activities and to find what motivation a company has to disclose its CSR activities, since this practice is voluntary. These two main objectives have been the basis to answer the research question of this paper: "Which stakeholder groups influence, and what is the major motivation for CSR practices in Vietnam?"

The remainder of this paper is organized as follow: The first part is CSR in the context of Vietnam; the second part is the theoretical framework and research hypothesis development; the third describes the research methodology and data collection process; the fourth presents the results of hypothesis testing and discussions; the last part is the recommendations and implications for future research.

CORPORATE SOCIAL RESPONSIBILITY (CSR) IN VIETNAMESE CONTEXT

CSR in Vietnam

CSR is firstly introduced by international corporations

sourcing in Vietnam under the form of Code of Conduct or social standard requirements. According to Professor André Schmitt, Director of CFVG, "Current financial crisis shows that Vietnam Economy was depended on supply chains of the world. Vietnam economy can not evade the global competitive pressures. Thus, the task of implementing CSR is as difficult as it is in any developed countries" (CSR Vietnam Forum, 2009). Presently, events such as pollution in Thi Vai River by Vedan Vietnam, conflict between workers and their bosses have proved that implementing CRS is necessary for sustainable economy of the country.

Government actions

"Sustainable development and protecting the environment" is the commitment of Vietnam government set in the national strategy, which goes along with most nations in the world (O'Rourke, 1995). The 'Doi Moi'[1] and open-door policies, implemented since 1986, have helped Vietnam to achieve high economic growth; however major social problems still remain. In order to tackle those problems, Vietnamese government had issued new regulations, Environmental protection law and the Vietnam agenda 21 for sustainable development. Other legislative tools also include labor code enforcement and labor inspection. Besides, the government also established environmental police and special fees levied on the emission of wastewater to strengthen enforcement measures against companies that pollute. Moreover, the government strongly expresses its commitment and puts effort in calling on companies to protect the environment and promote safety and health in the workplace (Civil Law Network, 2009). The violations of the labor law and environmental law would cause company to incur cost of monetary penalties, to be suspended, or in severe case, to be imprisonment. However, there is no requirement from government for the companies to formally issue CSR reporting.

Vietnamese Accounting Standards (VAS)

In February 12, 1999, the Vietnam accounting standards board (VASB) was established by the Ministry of finance (MOF). Presently, based on the International accounting standard (IAS), the VAS is set up by the MOF through the accounting policy department. With the IAS base, Vietnamese considerations are used to adjust economic, finance and accounting issues when Vietnam accounting standards (VAS) is drafted.

There are some differences in disclosure requirements between two standards. Under the VAS 21 Presentation of financial statement, which is derived from IAS 1, bonuses and welfare funds for employees are not required to disclosure.

In Vietnam, retirement benefits are paid by companies under compulsory levy, the companies charge this contribution against operating costs. Besides, comparing to the IAS 19 Employee Benefits, there are no other disclosure requirements for retirement benefits in VAS. Moreover, Vietnam does not have standard specifically addressing areas which are established under IAS 26 accounting and reporting by retirement benefit plans. Thus, it can be seen that VAS does not have any special requirement for enterprise to disclose employee benefits. Also, the VASB does not require the company to disclose CSR information (Vietnamese Accounting Standards, 2006).

CSR practice and challenges

From 2005, Vietnam has had CSR Awards, which was organized by Vietnam chamber of commerce and industry (VCCI), ministry of labor-invalids and social affairs, Vietnam ministry of industry and trade, together with Vietnam Leather and Footwear Association, and the Vietnam national textile and garment group, in order to honor enterprises in CSR implementation in the context of global integration. In 2006, 50 companies of Vietnam leather and footwear association, and the Vietnam national textile and garment group took part in this prize. According to Vice-Director of Vietnam chamber of commerce and industry "CSR has become necessary requirement for each company, if the company does not embrace CSR, they can not approach the global market" (Saga Vietnam, 2008).

However, in Vietnam, there are still lots of challenges in implementing CSR. Firstly, there is lack of law enforcement as well as cooperation. The evaluations of CSR effectuation are set in code of conduct and standards such as SA 8000, WRAP, ISO 14000, GRI, etc. However, the standards are not in agreement with Government regulations in international convention. Thus, ties are only among export or import companies or companies' rules. Secondly, the companies' knowledge about CSR is still limited. They consider that CSR is only charity rather than the needs from inside of the company. Thirdly, companies are lack of money and technique to apply CSR criteria, specially, for small and medium companies (Saga Vietnam, 2008). Moreover, the awareness and demand for CSR information of Vietnamese are also not strong, giving less incentive for companies to embrace CSR and disclose CSR information.

There are some companies that have started to produce clean vegetables, clean aquaculture, clean coal, etc.; however, those actions have compelled or unprompted nature rather than in a voluntary basis that associate with the business activities and company's

[1] In Vietnamese, the word 'Doi Moi' means reform

image.

LITERATURE REVIEW AND HYPOTHESIS

Theory framework

The conceptualization of CSR is based on two key questions: what are corporations responsible for? and to whom are they responsible? (Friedman, 1970). These questions have engendered much philosophical and legal debate. A precise, universally accepted definition of CSR is therefore difficult to achieve, with views on where a firm's responsibility to society starts and finishes as various as the names given used to describe such a notion, including corporate citizenship (Maignan et al., 1999), stakeholder management (Freeman, 1984), corporate social responsiveness (Miles, 1987), corporate social performance (Wood, 1991), and corporate social responsibility (Carroll, 1979).

For the purpose of this study, the term corporate social responsibility (CSR) will be used to describe how business acts to implement the broad societal responsibility of going beyond economic criteria, such as creating products, employment, and profits, to meet broader social and environmental expectations. The term CSR is preferred as it maintains the focus on the issue of responsibility to society as a whole, and it is a term that corporations are increasingly using, both internally and in their communication efforts with external audiences.

According to the World business council for sustainable development (2004), CSR is expressed as: "the commitment of business to contribute to sustainable economic development, working with employees, their families, the local community and society at large to improve their quality of life, in ways that are both good for business and good for development". This position is generally interpreted as business' commitment to minimizing negative externalities and maximizing beneficial impacts on society (Mohr et al., 2001).

Various theories about CSR have been introduced, of which are emerged two important theories for this study, namely: the Triple bottom line (Elkington, 1997) and the Stakeholder theory (Freeman, 1984).

Elkington's (1997) triple bottom line

The triple bottom line theory introduced by Elkington (1997) is known as a common way for companies to conceptualize CSR. The concept of triple bottom line captures an expanded spectrum of values and criteria for measuring organizational success: economic, environmental and social. In practical terms, triple bottom line means expanding the traditional reporting framework to take into account ecological and social performance in addition to financial performance.

The triple bottom line demands that a company's responsibility lies with stakeholders rather than shareholders. Accordingly, the business entity should be used as a vehicle for coordinating stakeholder interests, instead of maximizing shareholder profit. For these reasons, the triple bottom line theory sets directions and principles to evaluate and report companies' CSR achievements.

Stakeholder theory

The stakeholder theory, originally detailed by Freeman (1984), is a theory of organizational management and business ethics that addresses morals and values in managing an organization. In this theory, the concept "stakeholders" refers to any group or individual who is influenced, either directly or indirectly, by the actions of the firm. In the traditional view of the firm, the shareholders view, the shareholders or stockholders are the owners of the company, and the firm only addresses the needs and wishes of its owners.

However, stakeholder theory argues that there are other parties involved, including governmental bodies, political groups, trade associations, trade unions, communities, associated corporations, prospective employees, prospective customers, and the public at large. From the ethical perspective, organizations have an obligation to treat fairly among stakeholders (Deegan, 2009); that is, organizations are not managed the interest of shareholders alone, but a wide range of stakeholders who have a legitimate interest in the corporation as well. In the case of stakeholder conflict of interest, business has a duty to attain optimal balance among them.

Based on the Freeman's theory, Baron (1995) had divided the stakeholders into two groups, called market and non-market. While customers, competitors, employyees, partners and suppliers are often seen as the market group; NGOs, government, regulators, environmental safety and standards organizations, media, society or community are consider as the non-market group.

Both these groups exert their influences at different levels on the social responsibility pressures or motivations of the company. From this perspective, many activities taken by the company are related to stakeholder's expectations (Friedman and Miles, 2002). It is meaningful to see that the concerning and satisfying the interest of stakeholders help to improve corporate governance and accountability that includes stakeholder communication and CSR reporting.

Hypothesis

Managers' perception of CSR and CSR reporting

Hill and Jones (1992) describe the relationship between managers and stakeholders as "Managers are the only group of stakeholders who enter into a contractual relationship with all other stakeholders. Managers are also the only group of stakeholders with direct control over the decision making process of the firm". From this perspective, the stakeholders' point of view to some extent is affected by the managers' behavior. In essence, for the CSR issues, it is necessary to have managers' agreement and commitment to conduct and improve CSR initiative.

There are many responsibility pressures which influence the managers' attitude. Such pressures come from the profitability incentive goals or from a high level of expectations of investors or significant creditors. Besides, managers are also influenced by community pressures that require them to meet the expectations set up by the community.

In the context of Vietnam, two questions of management perception are crucial with respect to CSR initiative: Do they consider sustainability as an important part of doing business? and why do managers address CSR as their strategic integration and competitiveness? From the foregoing discussions, the first hypothesis is formulated:

H_1: In the context of Vietnam, CSR practice and reporting is influenced by management perception.

Consumers' perception of CSR and CSR reporting

CSR has recently shifted to the field of marketing, and in particular the CSR-consumer relationship, to understand how firms social, ethical, and environmental initiatives can influence marketplace outcomes. Marketplace evidence suggests CSR is becoming a more salient purchase criterion among consumers who not only expect businesses to be socially responsible, but also want to be informed about what firms are doing, and will support firms that pursue CSR initiatives.

A 23-nation poll of public attitudes to CSR, for example, found that Australians have amongst the highest CSR expectations of business (Environics, 1999): 45% of those surveyed believed the role of large companies in society was to "set higher ethical standards and help build better society", while only 8% believed that their role is to "make profit, pay taxes, create jobs, and obey the law", and 43% believed companies "should operate somewhere between the two positions".

Cone Inc (2004) found that 86% of American respondents wanted companies to tell them how they supported social issues. In the UK 74% of respondents indicated that more information on a company's social and ethical behavior would influence their purchasing decisions, and 86% thought companies should actively communicate their CSR activities (Dawkins, 2004).

This study investigates how Vietnamese consumers are informed about the social and environmental conditions under which products have been produced. Drawing from the previous argument, the second hypothesis is formulated:

H_2: In the context of Vietnam, consumer's behavior is influenced by companies' CSR practices and disclosures.

RESEARCH METHODOLOGY

A structured questionnaire was used to collect the necessary data whereby it will serve as primary data to answer the research questions and objectives pertaining to CSR practices and reporting in Vietnam. The questionnaire comprises two patterns: one for management in 30 selected companies operating in three main sectors, namely Banking, Brewery, and Clothing and Textiles; another for consumers of these selected companies.

Each pattern of survey questionnaire consists of 8 statements pertaining to the relationship between CSR perceptions and CSR practice and reporting. In view of time and cost constraints, a convenience sampling method was used to collect data mainly from the companies and consumers in Ha noi and Ho Chi Minh cities which have more concentration on CSR issues. Even though the sampling method adopted has limitations in terms of generalisability compared to other method of sampling, it is assumed that the sample represents the whole population of companies and consumers in Vietnam.

The survey was conducted mainly via face-to-face interviews, also administered through e-mail and postage service. The two patterns use Likert five-point interval scale that provides a battery of attitude statements. The respondents then say how much they agree or disagree with each statement (the scale ranges from (5) denoting "strongly agree" to (1) denoting "strongly disagree"). These results will be answered by the depth of their thought about the CSR value.

RESULTS AND DISCUSSION

Management survey

With the selected sample size, 100 questionnaires for management have been distributed. However, only 32 responses were considered complete and valid for data analysis. This represents a success rate of 32%, which is considered to be good in view of time and cost constraints. The Table 1 details the management responses.

Table 2 represents a list of statements, while Figure 1 illustrates the percentage of response distribution. Tables 3 and 4 show descriptive statistics including median and mode. The results of the Table 2 and Figure 1 show that five of the eight statements have scores of more than 50% agreement or endorsement of CSR. About 75% respondents think organizing and participating in public welfare activities are the social responsibility of the company. Moreover, 75% of managers confirm that their company has spent extra costs improving working environment quality. The majority of respondents (68%) think that engaging CSR, firm could get a favorable image within the public, only 28% still wonder how CSR could impact on the image of companies, and very few respondents (6%) do not believe that CSR will bring them

Table 1. The number of management responses.

Management pattern	Sample	Number of response
Banking	30	9
Brewery	35	11
Clothing and textiles	35	12
Total	100	32

Table 2. Distribution of managers' responses towards the statements.

S/N	Statements	5	4	3	2	1
1	Organizing and participating in public welfare activities are the social responsibility of the company.	8	16	7	1	0
2	Company has incurred extra costs for health and safety working environment.	11	13	7	1	0
3	CSR provides a favorable public image.	7	14	9	2	0
4	Involvement in improving community's quality of life will also improve long run profitability of the company.	2	12	10	7	1
5	Firm perceived as being socially responsible can improve industry-labor relationship.	2	16	10	4	0
6	CSR is good for strategic competitive advantage.	0	8	12	8	4
7	CSR reporting will have positive impacts on investor's decision.	2	7	10	13	0
8	CSR reporting will become general practice in near future.	8	12	2	10	0

Note: 5, strongly agree; 4, agree; 3, neutral; 2, disagree; 1, strongly disagree.

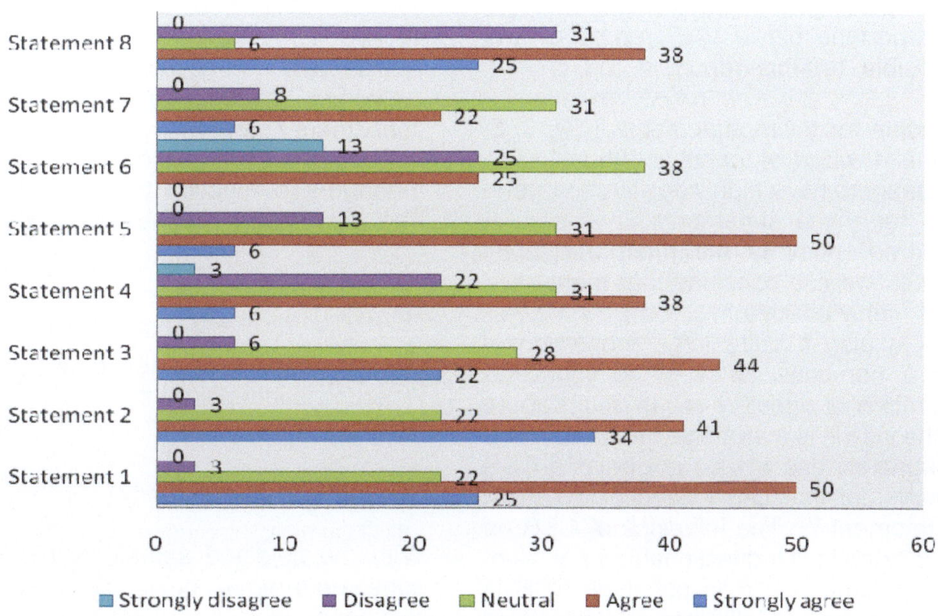

Figure 1. Percentage of managers' responses towards CSR by five scale.

Table 3. Descriptive statistics from management survey (1).

S/N	Statements	Median	Mode
1	Organizing and participating in public welfare activities are the social responsibility of the company.	4	4
2	Company has incurred extra costs for health and safety working environment.	4	4
3	CSR provides a favorable public image.	4	4
4	Involvement in improving its community's quality of life will also improve long run profitability of the company.	4	4
5	Firm perceived as being socially responsible can improve industry-labor relationship.	4	4
6	CSR is good for strategic competitive advantage.	3	3
7	CSR reporting will have positive impacts on investor's decision.	3	2
8	CSR reporting will become general practice in near future.	4	4

Note: 5, strongly agree; 4, agree; 3, neutral; 2, disagree; 1, strongly disagree.

Table 4. Descriptive statistics from management survey (2).

Statements	Median			Mode		
	Banking	Brewery	Clothing and textiles	Banking	Brewery	Clothing and textiles
1	4	4	4	4	4	4
2	4	4	4	4	4	4
3	4	4	3	4	4	4
4	3	4	3	2	4	4
5	4	4	4	4	4	4
6	2.5	3	3	3	3	3
7	4	3	4	2	4	2
8	4	4	3	3	4	4

any beneficial outcomes. Besides, more than half of managers (56%) agree that being socially responsible will raise industry-labor relationship. Furthermore, 63% of those express their belief on the bright future of CSR practice and CSR reporting. It means that managers have realized the important role of CSR reporting, and they will be responsible for this report in the coming years.

Moreover, the median for these statements 1, 2, 3, 5, and 8 has the value 4 where 4 denotes "agree". The results show that managers have highly positive answers. Besides, the mode for these statements is also 4; it means that the "agree" point is the most frequently happened. As a result, we can conclude that managers' perception of CSR is highly positive.

In contrast, there is also a quite large proportion of managers express a non-consistency in opinion. Statement 6 represents 25% of directors still in doubt about the role of CSR in the view it is a strategic integration and competitive for companies, and 8% do not believe CSR reporting is important tool that can influence investors' decision-making (statement 7). The influence of CSR on investors' decision-making is still questionable as 31% of respondents remain neutral. They do not think CSR is really important, so it has limited influence on investment decisions of investors.

The analysis of median and mode showed that there were no significant differences in the perception of managers working in Banking, Brewery, and Clothing and Textiles towards CSR. But managers in Brewery indicate stronger positive attitude in comparison with other two sectors. The reason may come from the product features of that business because it has long been regarded as consumer goods, directly and quickly affected to consumers health.

The Chi-square is used to test the relationship between managers' perception towards CSR and CSR reporting. The Chi-square value is 7.10 ($\chi^2 = 7.10$) while $\chi^2_{\alpha,(r-1)(c-1)} = \chi^2_{.05,6} = 12.59$ ($\alpha = 0.05$ and $df = 6$). Since $\chi^2 < \chi^2_{\alpha,(r-1)(c-1)} = \chi^2_{.05,6}$, the hypothesis H1 is rejected. In other words, management's awareness of CSR and CSR reporting is independent.

Customers' survey

With the selected sample size, 200 questionnaires for consumers have been distributed. However, only 97 responses were considered complete and valid for data analysis, representing a success rate of 48.5%. The

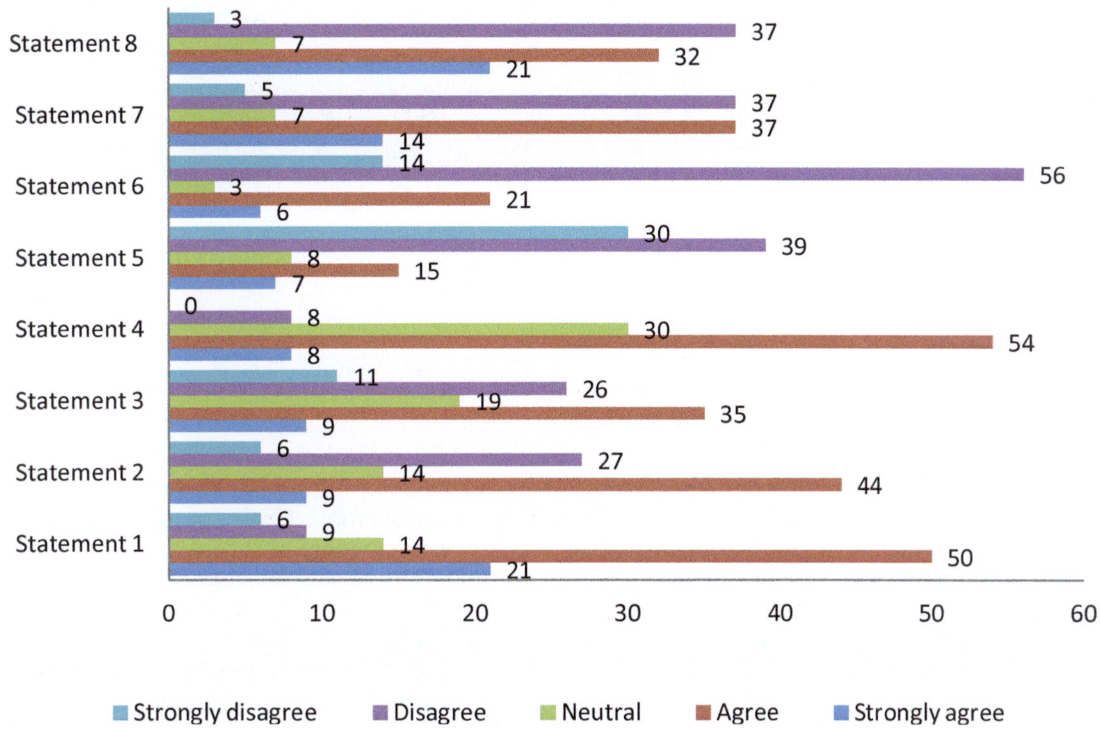

Figure 2. Percentage of consumer's responses towards CSR by five scales.

Table 5. Distribution of consumers' responses towards statements.

S/N	Statements	5	4	3	2	1
1	You know the meaning of the term "Corporate Social Responsibility".	20	48	14	9	6
2	Companies should conduct social responsibility initiatives.	9	43	14	25	6
3	Donations to charitable and public welfare organizations are obligations of a company.	9	34	18	25	11
4	If I bought products of a company with good social responsibility practices, I would be more likely to continue buying that company's products.	8	52	29	8	0
5	I would avoid buying products from immoral companies.	7	15	8	38	29
6	I am willing to pay a premium for goods/services from socially responsible companies.	6	20	3	54	14
7	I think it is important to examine companies' CSR strategies	14	35	7	36	5
8	I will make some changes in behavior for social responsibility.	20	31	7	36	3

Table 6. Descriptive statistics from consumer survey (1).

S/N	Statements	Median	Mode
1	You know the meaning of the term "Corporate Social Responsibility".	4	4
2	Companies should conduct social responsibility initiatives.	3	4
3	Donations to charitable and public welfare organizations are obligations of a company.	3	4
4	If I bought products of a company with good social responsibility practices, I would be more likely to continue buying that company's products.	4	4
5	I would avoid buying products from immoral companies.	2	2
6	I am willing to pay a premium for goods/services from socially responsible companies.	2	2
7	I think it is important to examine companies' CSR strategies	4	2
8	I will make some changes in behavior for social responsibility.	4	2

Table 7. Descriptive statistics from consumer survey (2).

Statements	Median					Mode				
	A1	A2	A3	A4	A5	A1	A2	A3	A4	A5
1	4	4	3	4	3	4	4	3	4	3
2	4	3	4	4	4	4	4	3	5	4
3	2	3	3	4	4	4	4	4	4	4
4	3	4	3	3	3	2	4	2	4	4
5	3	2	3	4	3	2	2	2	4	3
6	4	2	4	4	4	3	4	2	2	2
7	4	4	3	4	2	2	4	3	2	2
8	3	4	4	3	2	3	2	2	2	4

Note: A1= 20-30, A2= 30-40, A3= 40-50, A4= 50-60, A5=above 60 (years old).

Table 5 details the consumer responses.

The results in the Table 5 and Figure 2 show that six of the eight statements have scores of more than 50% agreement. About 71% of respondents know the meaning of "Corporate social responsibility". It reflects the fact that SCR is familiar to consumers. Furthermore, nearly 52% mentioned that companies should conduct social responsibility initiatives.

A majority of consumer (62%) express their want of buying products of a company with good social responsibility practices. In addition, 51% of those surveyed think it is important to examine companies' CSR strategies. And 53% of respondents said they would make some changes in behavior for social responsibility.

However, these results above are not meaning that consumers have strong support for companies' practices as about 69% of respondents still buy products from immoral companies. And a majority either say "disagree" (56%) or "strongly disagree" (14%), for a total of 70% are aware that they are not willing to pay a premium for goods/services from socially responsible companies.

Table 6 represents the median and mode from which further analysis of the research would be explored. The first four statements have mode of 4, showing that there is a positive attitude toward CSR from consumers. This means that CSR is familiar and important thing to consumer. However, their support for efforts of companies to be responsible is not so strong. Preliminary findings in the previous section portray a large of consumers failed to recognize the importance of CSR, and they are not willing to pay a premium for goods/services from socially responsible companies. Those surveyed respondents are too focused on price of the product rather than its quality and its friendliness to environment.

Dividing respondents into five ranges of age as presented in Table 7 gives some interesting results. Overall, the descriptive statistics suggest that the young customers show the higher positive attitude toward CSR than olders. Many of them are students and young workers with better education so they pay more attention to companies' CSR strategies. Young customers, however, are not willing to pay a premium for goods or services from responsible companies. The reason is due to their low financial status that does not allow them to buy products with high quality but high price.

The Chi-square is used to test the relationship between consumers' perception towards CSR and CSR reporting. The Chi-square value is 163.91 ($\chi^2 = 163.91$) while $\chi^2_{\alpha,(r-1)(c-1)} = \chi^2_{.05,12} = 21.03$ ($\alpha = 0.05$ and $df = 12$). Since $\chi^2 > \chi^2_{\alpha,(r-1)(c-1)} = \chi^2_{.05,12}$, the hypothesis H2 is accepted. In other words, consumers' awareness of CSR and CSR reporting is interdependent.

Conclusion

The research results have provided interesting findings on two factors affecting CSR implementation and CSR reporting of enterprises in Vietnam. For managers, a high level of awareness towards CSR may not be a factor to ensure that enterprises will fulfill their CSR obligations and requirements. For consumers, although they do not have a clear attitude, the research results show that the awareness of Vietnamese consumers and their purchasing decisions influence significantly on the CSR implementation as well as CSR disclosure of companies.

Although firms commit to provide high quality products and services at reasonable price as important factors in being socially responsible, there are also gaps in CSR disclosure and management belief. Due to the fact that there were lack of national standards and requirements from investors and customers, Vietnamese companies are not willing to report their CSR activities. Therefore, customers do not have or have very limited information about CSR implementation and CSR achievement of companies; as a result, they do not realize the importance and benefits of CSR. The majority of consumers focus on the price of products rather than CSR when making purchasing decisions. However, a large proportion of consumers mentioned that in the course of integration Vietnamese companies would change their behaviors, undertaken actions and show their responsibility for society. Moreover, if government pays more attention to CSR, there will be a bright future for CSR to become general practices in Vietnam.

Those findings have challenged for companies to solve CSR issues in which how to operate effectively to bring added-value to customers, and how to improve the attitude and awareness of customers towards CSR to gain their loyalty. In order to achieve these target objectives, CSR should build on:

1 Social Responsibility: offer safety products and services, provide health and safety working environment, ensure human rights, improve customers and employees satisfaction, and establish good relationships with government and community...
2. Environmental Responsibility: protect and improve environment, reduce resources consumption (materials, water, electricity etc), improve waste management (3Rs strategies)...
3. Economic Responsibility: support the investors, pay taxes, create jobs, and improve risk management...

The results of the research indicate that there is a perception gap in CSR issues between managers and customers. The positive management awareness of CSR is essential but not enough for the success of CSR implementation and practices. Therefore, consumers that have ability to "influence the profits of competing firms, and indirectly also the direction of the economy" need to pay more attention on whether companies' activities are responsible to society or not (Hansenand Schrader, 1997). If the public have strong feeling and sensitive for CSR issues, the environmental and social scandals might be prevented. Public positive awareness of CRS also encourages firms to act and to behave responsibly and ethically.

Since, the study focuses on a small sample of companies in Hanoi and Ho Chi Minh cities, the generalisability of the research findings is restricted. Theses limitations provide a basis for further research, especially appropriately designed quantitative in combination with qualitative studies, to be conducted to verify the findings of this study.

REFERENCES

Baron DP (1995). Integrated strategy: Market and nonmarket components. California Manage. Rev., 37(Winter) 47-65.

Carroll A (1979). A three-dimensional conceptual model of corporate performance. Acad. Manage. Rev., 4(4): 497-505.

Cone Inc, 2004. Cone Corporate Citizenship Study. Boston, MA.

CSR Vietnam Forum, 2009. Social responsibility of enterprises in Vietnam: from theory to practice. Available at http://www.vietnamforumcsr.net/default.aspx?portalid=1&tabid=17&itemid=4703 [Retrieved on 17th March, 2010].

Dawkins J (2004). The Public's views of Corporate Responsibility, 2003. White Paper Series, MORI.

Deegan C (2009). Financial Accounting Theory. 3rd Edition. McGraw-Hill Australia Pty Ltd.

Elkington J (1997). Cannibals with forks: The triple bottom line of 21st Century business. Oxford: Capstone.

Environics (1999). The Millennium Poll. from http://www.globescan.com [Retrieved on 17th October, 2010].

Friedman M (1970). The social responsibility of business is to increase profits. New York Times Magazine, (September 13) 32-33, 122, 126.

Friedman A, Miles S (2002). Developing stakeholder theory. J. Manage. Stud., 39(1): 1-21.

Freeman E (1984). Strategic management: A stakeholder approach. Pitman Publishing, Bostom.

Gray R (2008). Social and environmental accounting and reporting: From ridicule to renovation? From hope to hubris?- A personal review of the field. Soc. Environ. Accounting. 2(1): 3-18.

Gray R, Kouhy R, Lavers S (1995). Corporate social and environmental reporting: A review of the literature and longitudinal study of UK disclosure. Accting. Audit. Acctability. J., 8(2): 47-77.

Hansen U, Schrader U (1997). A modern model of consumption for a sustainable society. J. Consumer Policy, 20(4): 443-68.

Hill CW, Jones TM (1992). Stakeholder-agency theory. J. Manage. Stud. (March), pp. 131-152.

Hopper T, Hoque Z (2004). Introduction: changing form of accounting and accountability within emerging countries, in Hopper, T. and Hoque, Z. (Eds), Accounting and Accountability in Emerging and Transition Economies, Elsevier, London, pp. 1-18.

Kok P, Wiele T, McKenna R, Brown A (2001). A Corporate Social Responsibility Audit Within a Quality Management Framework. J. Bus. Ethics, 31(4): 285-297.

Maignan I, Ferrell OC, Hult GTM (1999). Corporate citizenship: Cultural antecedents and business benefits. J. Academy Marketing Sci., 27(4): 455-469.

Miles RA (1987). Managing the Corporate Social Environment. Prentice-Hall, Englewood Cliffs, NJ.

Mohr LA, Webb DJ, Harris KE (2001). Do consumers expect companies to be socially responsible? The impact of corporate social responsibility on buying behavior. J. Consumer Affairs, 35(1): 45-75.

O'Rourke D (2004). Opportunities and obstacles for corporate social responsibility reporting in developing countries. The World Bank and IFC (March 2004).

Saga Vietnam, 2008. Social responsibility of business: Van de son nguyen appeal. Available at http://www.saga.vn/view.aspx?id=9582 [Retrieved on 17 March 2010].

Vietnamese Accounting Standard (VAS, 2006), He thong Vietnam accounting standard. Publisher Financing.

Wood JD (1991). Corporate social performance revised. Acad. Manage. Rev., 16(4): 698-718.

World Business Council for Sustainable Development (2004). Cross Cutting Themes – Corporate Responsibility, Retrieved 30 November 2009, from http://www.wbcsd.org.

Disclosure frequency and earnings management: An analysis in the Tunisian context

Youssef RIAHI* and Mounira BEN ARAB

Department of Finance and Strategy of Businesses, Institute of Higher Management of Tunis, University of Tunisia, 23 Impasse 5 Rue 4267 DEN 2011, Tunis- Tunisie.

The aim of this paper is to study the relationship between information disclosure by quoted Tunisian firms and earnings' management. Our survey has been achieved on a sample of 19 firms listed in the Tunis stock exchange over a period spanning from 1999 to 2008. The results confirm the existence of a negative and significant relationship between disclosure by firms which constitute this study's sample and earnings management. This study's survey shows that information disclosure related to financial decisions and performances constitute a constraint to the proliferation of earnings' management.

Key words: Disclosure frequency, financial information, disclosure score, earnings management, transparency.

INTRODUCTION

Most studies carried out about the relationship between earnings' management and information disclosure frequency are divided into two trends. The first indicates, forecasting earnings and voluntary information disclosure, which encourages firms to manage earnings (Graham et al., 2005; Rahman et al., 2007); whereas the second foresees that information disclosure exposes earnings management and helps investors to detect this phenomenon (Lobo and Zhou, 2001; Hunton et al., 2006; Jo and Kim, 2007).

Beyer (2008) concluded that analysts have some incentives to disclose forecasts that foresee earnings correctly and directors have some incentives to disclose earnings that match or go beyond the predicted outcome yielded by analysts. Then, financial analysts can encourage earnings' management, by setting targets of earnings that are difficult or impossible to meet. Likewise, according to Rahman et al. (2007), the press in Singapour[1] reported the concern that with more frequent disclosures under a quarterly reporting regime, firms will focus on short-term earnings and engage in earnings management on a more frequent basis. Contrarily, other researches emphasize that disclosure strategy enables the improvement of the transparency of publications, thereby facilitating the detection of earnings' management practice. Indeed, Lobo and Zhou (2001) stress the existence of a negative correlation between disclosure quality and earnings' management. The former demonstrated that corporate managers who disclose more information have less management flexibility.

Hunton et al. (2006) examined the scale at which the transparency of financial publications affects attempt of earnings management whether during an upward trend or a downward trend. In fact, they found that the increased transparency reduced but did not eliminate managers' attempt to enter into the practice of earnings' management. Jo and Kim (2007) show that disclosure increases transparency and therefore reduces incentives

*Corresponding author. E-mail: youssef.riahi@gmail.com

[1] The Business Times, 2 November, 2002b; The Business Times, 21 August 2002c.

to manage earnings because increased transparency helps investors to detect earnings' management. Greater disclosure frequency exposes earnings management, and accordingly, disclosure frequency and earnings' management are negatively associated. Within sight of all this, we notice that the role of information disclosure in the reduction of information asymmetry received a meaningful attention in the literature, but as ascertained by Cormier and Martinez (2006), in spite of this vast literature, the politics of disclosure is not again completely included.

The objective of this paper is to enrich the debate on this issue while studying the impact of information disclosure on earnings' management in the Tunisian context.

Our survey has been motivated by the following incentives: first, to know the reforms and mutations in the Tunisian context which remain a field of investigation and not exploration; secondly, the impact of disclosure frequency on earnings management is not, until our days, especially explained completely in the emergent countries; thirdly, we want to study the specific distinct feature of Tunisian firms as compared to firms in other countries, such as US, England and other Asian countries.

In order to test this study's hypotheses, we constituted a sample of 19 non-financial firms that are listed on the Tunisian Stock market (BVMT) over the 10-year period (1999 to 2008). It is necessary however, to note that the estimations of our model are made on panel data since the regressions are about two dimensions: temporal and individual, which enables some tests to be checked. These tests are essentially Pearson test and vifs of independent variables. To detect the multicollinearity between these variables, test of the presence of individual effect, Hausman test and heteroscedasticity test were used.

INFORMATION DISCLOSURE, TRANSPARENCY AND EARNINGS' MANAGEMENT: LITERATURE REVIEW

Beforehand, it is not clear, whether the highest disclosure and the transparency of a country should increase or reduce the level of earnings' management. On the one hand, high disclosure and transparency exercise strong pressures on firms to communicate voluntary information, which brings them to manage earnings (Degeorge et al., 1999, 2005; Iatridis and Kadorinis, 2009), while on the other hand, in countries with high disclosure, investors and financial analysts can be disincentives to earnings' management because they can get information easily on firms (Baber et al., 2006; Yu, 2008; Allayannis and Simko, 2009).

In their effort to meet financial analysts' forecasts and the expectations of investors, firms find earnings management as a good solution (Linen et al., 2006; Rees and Sivaramakrishnan, 2007; Chevis et al., 2007). The failure to meet analysts' forecasts and the expectations of investors can be catastrophic for firms in terms of access to funds and growth opportunities (Graham et al., 2005; Bergstresser and Philippon, 2006). Firms in countries with higher disclosure have a stronger propensity to manage earnings to meet financial analysts' forecasts. That makes disclosure not to be credible. Degeorge et al. (2005) found in their survey on a sample of 51401 observations for 10866 non-financial firms in 26 countries from 1994 to 2002 that firms in transparent countries use short-term earnings' management techniques to reach the consensus analyst forecast. In opaque countries, analyst follow-up neither act as a curb on total earnings management, nor create any short-term pressure to manage earnings.

Degeorge et al. (1999) indicate that analysts can exert pressure on managers to handle earnings. They indicate that firms do not have analysts' forecasts undergo a fall in the prices of its shares. Yu (2008) found in his survey on a sample of French firms that firms with analysts following have lower levels of the discretionary accruals than those firms without cover. Similarly, Allayannis and Simko (2009) indicate that financial analysts play an important role in limitation of earnings' management. They are more efficient controllers in transparent environments than in opaque environments. Besides, the more the country is transparent, the more the reduction of earnings management is bound by analysts following.

Baber et al. (2006) analyzed the reaction of share prices to the practice of accounting manipulation, when some supplementary information are disclosed voluntarily. Their results show that investors penalize the practice of accounting manipulation, when supplementary information is disclosed. The credibility of disclosures can be checked by comparison forecast earnings to real earnings, the market react positively to the forecast if the earnings achieved increase, but react negatively to the forecast if the earnings achieved decreased (Iatridis and Kadorinis, 2009).

MATERIALS AND METHODS

This study's empirical approach is based on the model of Jo and Kim (2007) that consists of studying the impact of information disclosure on earnings' management. We begin in a first time, by putting forward some hypotheses. On the basis of these hypotheses, we shall present the model and measures of the variables used. Then, we shall display descriptive statistics. Eventually, we will show and interpret our findings.

Hypotheses development

Schipper (1989) puts forward that information asymmetry and the lack of full communication allow managers to deal with earnings. It implies that earnings management is more unlikely for firms that disclose more information, because transparency lowers information asymmetry and helps investors to detect earnings management. Inversely, incentives of earnings' management are likely to increase for firms where there is information asymmetry and limited disclosure. The hypothesis that is tested is as follows:

H_1: Earnings' management is a decreasing function for the level of disclosure.

Iatridis and Kadorinis (2009) indicated that the main objective for providing voluntary disclosure of accounting information is to give explanations to agents interested in the financial picture and performance of the firms and to remove the scepticism that can hinder the growth of firms. The availability of an informative accounting and the transmission of a good accounting quality of information reduce the extent of earnings' management (Lobo and Zhou, 2001; Jo and Kim, 2007).

The disclosure of financial information is tremendous and essential for protecting investors against fraud and for the good financial market operation. Indeed, the free access to the news relative to the situation of firms and their incorporation into decision-making constitutes the underpinnings of the financial markets' management. In accordance with these works, we presume:

H_2: The disclosure of financial information decreases the extent of earnings' management.

Data sources and sample

This study's survey is conducted on a sample of 19 non-financial firms that are listed on the Tunisian Stock market (BVMT) over the 10-year period (1999 to 2008). The selection of the sample was achieved on a two-criterion basis:

1. The financial institutions are excluded because the nature of these firms' accruals differs from that of other firms.
2. A set of financial data such as the accounts of result and balance sheets, the leaflets, the annual reports of these firms are available in the data base that was collected.

The data were collected by BVMT Financial Market Council and from the following website: www.tustex.com.

Model specification

The model used to examine the effect of information disclosure (PR) on earnings' management (AD) was inspired by the survey of Jo and Kim (2007). A regression that has relation discretionary accruals with other explanatory variables and controls was led by this study. The dependent variable in this regression is discretionary accruals calculated from the model of Kothari et al. (2005), as long as the explanatory variable is the disclosure frequency (PR). Moreover, the financial performance, the institutional investment, the external auditing, the size, the liabilities, the managerial ownership as well as block ownership were kept as control variables.

In a second stage, this study's analysis was further deepened to know what type of information (strategic information, financial information and non-financial information) had an impact on earnings' management. That is why we measured the quality of disclosure by the score disclosure of Eng and Mak (2003) in a first step. Then, we proceeded to subdivision of the total score of disclosure between the three types of scores: the score relative to the financial information (FI), the score relative to the non financial information (NFI) and finally, the score relative to the strategic information (SI).

To answer the objectives set and to test the formulated hypotheses, the following two panel models were used:

$$AD_{i,t} = a + b1\ PR_{i,t} + b2\ PPE_{i,t} + b3\ ROA_{i,t} + b4\ IINST_{i,t} + b5\ AUD_{i,t} + b6\ CF_{i,t} + b7\ SIZE_{,t} + b8\ LEV_{i,t} + b9\ INSD_{i,t} + b10\ BLOCK_{i,t} + \varepsilon_{i,t} \quad (1)$$

$$AD_{i,t} = a + b1\ FI_{i,t} + b2\ NFI_{i,t} + b3\ SI_{i,t} + b4\ PPE_{i,t} + b5\ ROA_{i,t} + b6\ IINST_{i,t} + b7\ AUD_{i,t} + b8\ CF_{i,t} + b9\ SIZE_{,t} + b10\ LEV_{i,t} + b11\ INSD_{i,t} + b12\ BLOCK_{i,t} + \varepsilon_{i,t} \quad (2)$$

With:

$AD_{i,t}$: Discretionary accruals for firm i in year t; $PR_{i,t}$: press releases for firm i in year t; $FI_{i,t}$: Score relative to financial information for firm i in year t; $NFI_{i,t}$: Score relative to non financial information for firm i in year t; $SI_{i,t}$: Score relative to strategic information for firm i in year t; $PPE_{i,t}$: Net property, plant and equipment for firm i in year t; $ROA_{i,t}$: Return on assets for firm i in year t; $IINST_{i,t}$: Institutional ownership in firm i in year t; $AUD_{i,t}$: Quality of auditors for firm i in year t; $CF_{i,t}$: Operating cash flows for firm i in year t; $SIZE_{,t}$: Size of firm i in year t; Lev: Level of debt for firm i in year t; $INSD_{i,t}$: Insider ownership for firm i in year t; and $BLOCK_{i,t}$: Percent of equity held by those owning more than 5% of a class of the company's equity securities.

Variables' measures

Discretionary accruals (AD)

We adopt the definition of discretionary accruals of Kothari et al. (2005) to measure earnings management. So Kothari et al. (2005) add the variable ROA to Jones model (1991). We used this model, because it showed its robustness to detect earnings management, especially in performance firms and we found that on average the Tunisian firms are successful. However, this model proved to be more adaptable to the Tunisian context:

$$(TAcc_{i,t} / AT_{i,t-1}) = w_0 + w_1\ (1/ AT_{i,t-1}) + w_2\ (\Delta\ REV_{i,t} / AT_{i,t-1}) + w_3\ (PPE_{i,t} / AT_{i,t-1}) + w_4\ ROA_{i,t-1} + \varepsilon_{i,t} \quad (3)$$

where: $TAcc_{i,t}$: Total accruals[2] for firm i in year t; $AT_{i,t-1}$: Total assets for firm i in year t-1; $\Delta\ REV_{i,t}$: Revenues for firm i in year t with less revenues for year t-1; $PPE_{i,t}$: Net property, plant and equipment for firm i in year t; $ROA_{i,t}$: Return on assets for firm i in

[2] Estimation of total accruals:
$TAcc_{i,t} = \Delta\ CA_{i,t} - \Delta\ cash_{i,t} - \Delta\ CL_{i,t} - \Delta\ DEPN_{i,t}$ where:
$\Delta\ CA_{i,t}$: firm i's change in current assets;
$\Delta\ cash_{i,t}$: firm i's change in cash;
$\Delta\ CL_{i,t}$: firm i's change in current liabilities;
$\Delta\ DEPN_{i,t}$: firm j's depreciation and amortization expense;

year t; and $\varepsilon_{i,t}$: A residual term that captures discretionary accruals.

Thus, the parameters obtained for the estimation of regression (3) are used in determination of non discretionary accruals (AND) scaled by lagged total asset:

$$AND_{it} = \hat{w}_0 + \hat{w}_1 (1/AT_{i,t-1}) + \hat{w}_2 (\Delta SA_{i,t} / AT_{i,t-1}) + \hat{w}_3 (PPE_{i,t} / AT_{i,t-1}) + \hat{w}_4 \ ROA_{i,t-1} \quad (4)$$

Therefore, discretionary accruals (ADi, t) are determined by the difference between TAcci, t / ATi,t-1 and ANDi,t.

Press releases (PR)

Press releases (it is the variable proxy of disclosure frequency) are the mandatory and voluntary publications communicated by the firm about a one year-business activity. It is necessary to indicate that in calculating this variable, we resorted to the review of the empirical and theoretical literature. Thus, we identified the number of press releases while looking into the information disclosure by firms on www.tustex.com, www.bvmt.com and www.cmf.com, and expected a negative relationship between disclosure frequency and earnings management.

The disclosure score

At the time of development or adoption of a disclosure score, it is necessary to take account of the features of the market and firms operating on this market and also the specificities of the sectors. Indeed, the industrial sector does not have the same features as the financial sector. So, for the industrial sector, we are compelled to foresee items that have a relation with the effort provided concerning research and development and the protection of the environment. These types of communication are not indeed very applicable for the financial sector because the latter provides services. In our investigation, we opted for the same methodology of determining the disclosure score of Eng and Mak (2003) as it includes the different types of information disclosed by firms and it proved to be that this method is more adaptable in the Tunisian context.

The disclosure score is measured by the report between the total number of points assigned to the firm and the number of possible maximum points. However, the two authors took into consideration three categories of information that appear in the annual reports:

1. Strategic information: Brief history of the company, organizational structure, general description of business, principal products, principal markets, current and future strategy and its future perspectives.
2. Non financial information: Number of employees, compensation per employee, value-added per employee and productivity indicator.
3. Financial information: Performance indicators (not from financial statements), financial ratios and useful projected information.

A point is assigned to every firm for any information disclosed by each category. A supplementary point is granted if the information disclosed includes a non recoverable quantitative data from the basis of the financial statements. The firm that does not present any disclosure for these different categories will have 0. Then we proceeded with the subdivision of the disclosure score between the three types of scores: the score relative to the financial information (FI), the score relative to the non financial information (NFI) and the score relative to the strategic information (SI).

As regards the choice and measures of the variables of control (Net property, plant and equipment, performance, institutional investment, audit quality, cash flows, size, lev, INSD and block), we based on the review of the empirical and theoretical literature and more exactly on the study of Jo and Kim (2007).

Net property, plant and equipment

Net property, plant and equipment are scaled by lagged total asset. Firms use the amortization like a means to manage earnings, then firms that invest more in net property, plant and equipment have more flexibility to manage earnings. A positive relationship is considered between discretionary accruals and net property, plant and equipment.

Performance

Managers of profitable firms have several methods to manage earnings. So a positive relationship is anticipated between ROA and discretionary accruals. Performance was measured by return on assets ratio (ROA):

ROA = earnings / total assets.

Institutional investment

The role of an institutional investor in controlling managers has been stated in the financial literature. Rajgopal et al. (1999) showed the efficiency of institutional investment to discipline managers and to avoid their manipulation for numbers of accountants. According to this argument, we expect a negative relationship between the part of shares held by institutional and earnings management. The retained institutional investors are banks, societies of investments and the companies of insurances.

IINST = Number of shares detained by institutional investors / total number of shares.

Audit quality

A better quality of audit services would be able to restrict the tendency of managers to manipulate their earnings (Kim et al., 2003). This quality of audit is feared by the adherence of external auditors to BIG[3]. In order to measure the control performed by auditors, we use an indicator variable that equals one if the firm's auditor is one of the BIG accounting firms, and zero if otherwise. Thus, we expect a negative relationship between earnings' management and the quality of external auditors.

Cash flows

Cash flows can be defined as being the difference between returns of operation and operation expenses, scaled by lagged total asset.

[3] Evolution of the big international accounting firms passage of the "BIG8" in the "BIG4". End of the years 1970: BIG8; 1989: BIG6; 1998: BIG5; 2002: BIG4.

Table 1. Definition and measurement of variables.

Variable	Abbreviation	Measurement
Dependent variable		
Discretionary accruals	AD	Discretionary accruals calculated from the model of Kothari et al. (2005).
Independent variables		
Disclosure frequency	PR	Mandatory and voluntary publications communicated by firms for about one year.
	FI	Score relative to financial information.
Quality of disclosure	NFI	Score relative to non financial information.
	SI	Score relative to strategic information.
Control variables		
Net property, plant and equipment	PPE	Level of net property, plant and equipment in firm.
Performance	ROA	Earnings / total assets.
Institutional investment	IINST	Number of shares detained by institutional investors / total number of shares.
Audit quality	AUD	Indicator variable that equals one if the firm's auditor is one of the BIG accounting firms, and zero if otherwise.
Cash flows	CF	CF = R – E
Size	Size	Logarithm (assets).
Debt	Leverage ratio	Total Debt /Total assets.
Managerial ownership	INSD	Number of shares detained by insiders / total number of shares of firm.
Block	Block ownership	The percent of equity held by those who own more than 5% of a class of the company's equity securities.

No prediction is considered between discretionary accruals and cash flows.

Size

In general, the big firms cause the public interest. They are followed minutely by financial analysts, as well as the economic and financial press. Indeed, the large-size firms are, by definition, committed in several activities rather than those of small size. Following this volume and this diversity of activities, firms of large size will have a need of credible information. Then we expect a negative relationship between the size variable and discretionary accruals.
Size = logarithm (assets).

Lev

Firms that are greatly indebted operate earnings' management in order to negotiate contracts of loans in more advantageous conditions. Proximity to contractual terms' limits that are generally based on accountants' figures incite managers to select accountants' procedures which increase profit (Watts and Zimmerman, 1986). Then a positive relationship is anticipated between these two variables.

Lev = total Debt /Total equity.

INSD

The insider ownership is measured by the percentage of shares detained by insiders. These shareholders are those that detain some shares in the capital of firms while participating in decisions and management. In the setting of this survey, we considered insiders, administrators, the president general (director) and the general manager of the firm.
INSD = Number of shares detained by insiders / total number of shares of the firm.

Block

Lennox (2005) indicates that block ownership could give some incentives to the main shareholders to direct decisions of managers and also expropriate the minority shareholders while hiding the true performance of the firm. No prediction is considered between the discretionary accruals and block ownership. This variable is measured as follows (Table 1): BLOCK = the percentage of equity held by those who own more than 5% of a class of the company's equity securities.

Descriptive statistics

Table 2 provides the descriptive statistics (mean, standard deviation, minimum and maximum) of every variable used in the

Table 2. Descriptive statistics.

Variable	Mean	Std dev	Min	Max
AD	0.0191	0.1137	-0.3877	0.5639
PR	8.1315	4.7093	1.0000	26.0000
FI	0.1626	0.0947	0.0234	0.9342
NFI	0 .0885	0.0809	0.0134	0.2962
SI	0.1202	0.0575	0.0123	0.3498
PPE	0.3714	0.1768	0.0528	0.8412
ROA	0.0446	0.0682	-0.2160	0.2670
IINST	0.1345	0.1983	0.0000	0.8165
AUD	0.2631	0.4415	0.0000	1.0000
CF	0.0687	0.2605	-3.1282	0.6044
Size	7.6019	0.4670	6.4483	8.9190
Lev	0.4343	0.2346	0.013	0.951
INSD	0.0314	0.0560	0.0000	0.2000
Block	0.7272	0.1301	0.4621	0.9613

This table presents descriptive statistics of variable studied (dependent, independent and control). The sample covers 19 Tunisians firms during the period of 1999 to 2008. Ad: Discretionary accruals calculated from model Kothari et al. (2005), PR = Mandatory and voluntary publications communicated by firm about one year, FI : Score relative to financial information, NFI : Score relative to non financial information, SI : Score relative to strategic information, PPE : Level of net property, plant and equipment in firm, ROA = Earnings / total assets, IINST = Number of shares detained by institutional investors / total number of shares, AUD : Indicator variable that equals one if the firm's auditor is one of the BIG accounting firms, and zero otherwise, CF = R-D, Size = logarithm (assets), Debt = Total Debt /Total assets, INSD = Number of shares detained by insiders / total number of shares of firm, Block = The percent of equity held by those owning more than 5% of a class of the company's equity securities.

study's analysis. According to Table 2, the mean value of (AD) is 0.0191. This enables us to notice that the level of earnings' management in the firms which constitute our sample is not raised; otherwise, the managers of these firms show evidence of a weak intensity of earnings management. The positive sign indicates that on average, the earnings management of the sample's firms tentatively increased.

The mean value of press releases is 8.1315, which permits the conclusion that firms of our sample do not disclose a lot of information. It can be accounted for on the one hand, by blockholder ownership (investors who hold a high percentage of shares and who can get information directly from the firms) and on the other hand, by the weakness of institutional ownership, since according to the literature, the presence of institutional investors can urge managers to do frequent disclosures. Its standard deviation (4.7093) permits the study to notice that this indicator varies between the different firms that compose its sample.

The profitability of assets varies between a negative performance of 21.6% and an extreme value positive of 26.7%, with an average of 4.4%. The mean value of the variable net property, plant and equipment is 0. 3714. This shows that firms that constitute the study's sample dedicate a tremendous part of their funds to investment in assets, plant and equipment. Institutional investment is weak in American firms (13.45%) as compared to 35.86% in the survey of Rajgopal et al. (1999) and 53.1% in the survey of Hartzell and Starks (2008); but standard deviation (19.83%) shows that this indicator varies in a considerable manner between the different firms that compose the sample of the study. More than 50% of the sample's firms are not audited by BIG accounting firms, since the mean value is 0.2631.

The value of cash flows is on average with a positive value of 0.0687. This variable has a standard deviation of 0.2605, which shows that cash flows vary considerably for firms that constitute our sample. The mean size of the sample's firms is 7.6019; and it varies between 6.4483 and 8.9190. It permits us to conclude that the Tunisian firms are of average mean size. However, we notice that the volatility of this variable is not very elevated (0.4670). This value implies that the size of firms measured as logarithm of total assets does not vary in a significant manner inside the sample.

According to the mean value of leverage ratio (43.43%), we can say that the debt constitutes a very important financing source for Tunisians firms. This value is nearly the duplicate of that found by Kumar (2004), which returned a mean leverage ratio of 24.09% for the case of India. The mean value of managerial ownership is 3.14%, which is weaker than institutional ownership (13.45%), American managerial ownership [20% in the survey of Dennis and Kruse (1999); 12.2% in the study of Holderness et al. (1999) and 12.4% in the survey of Cho (1998)], British and Australian firms [16.7% reported in the survey of Faccio and Lasfer (1999) and 10.65% in the survey of Braislford et al. (1999)] and even of Indian businesses [17.29% according to Kumar (2004)].

Finally, the ownership structure is very concentrated (since the mean value is 72.72%).

Tests on panel data

It is necessary however, to note that the estimations of our model are made on panel data since the regressions that enable us to check for some tests are in about two dimensions: one temporal and the other individual. These tests are essentially Pearson test and vifs of independent variables, to detect the multicollinearity between these variables, test of the presence of individual effect, Hausman test and heteroscedasticity test.

Test of the presence of the individual effect

Since the study's data are penalized, it is worth to identify the effect

Table 3. Result of test presence individual effect.

Chi test (2)	28.97 (0.0013)

Table 4. Result of Hausman test.

Chi test (2)	7.67 (0.6610)

associated to every individual, otherwise it would be an effect that does not vary with time, but varies with one individual to the other. This effect can be within or in random effect. The test of existence of the individual effect rejects the hypothesis of the individual effects absence (Table 3). Therefore, we are going to test hypothesis H0 against hypothesis H1.

H_0: Absence of individual effect.
H_1: There is individual effect.

Results of the test individual effect indicated that individual effects exist.

Hausman test

Since our model is of the effect, it is necessary to choose what modelling is best suitable for our data: within or random modelling of these effects, that is, these effects can be either within or random. Thus, we resort to Hausman test (Table 4).

The results of Hausman test indicate that we must turn towards a random modelling of effects. In other words, the consideration of individual specificity of firms is under the shape of an uncertain effect which provides significant statistically better results in comparison to a model that is within individual effect.

Pearson correlation matrix and vifs

Before moving to the regression, it is essential to establish the correlation matrix between the variables in order to test the possible relationship between the independent variables and to avoid the problems of multicollinearity.

The multivariate analysis helps to carry out the simultaneous treatment of a set of variables. In our survey, the linear regression requires the absence of multicollinearity problem between the independent variables introduced in the same model. We verify this condition while resorting to Pearson correlation matrix and vifs. Table 5 shows the results yielded by this test. The positive coefficients (negative) indicate positive relationships (negative) between the explanatory variables. According to these results, although Pearson's correlation coefficients are not raised[4], we can put forward that a certain interdependence exists between the different independent variables kept in our survey. Consequently, the absence of autocorrelation between the explanatory variables is shown. The absence of the multicollinearity problem between the variables is also justified by Vifs test in which all the variables have a value lower than 3 with a global mean equal to 1.49.

[4] Kervin (1992) foresees an r = 0.7 to be pronounced on a problem serious of colinearity between two independent variables included in a model of regression.

Heteroscedasticity test

Besides, we took care to verify the hypotheses of homoscedasticity[5] while using Breush-Pagan test (Table 6). The rationale behind these tests is to verify if the square of the residues can be explained by explanatory variables of the model. In other words, the variance of the residual term is bound then to the values of the explanatory variable, if it is the case when we have a problem of heteroscedasticity.

H_0: Homoscedasticity.
H_1: Heteroscedasticity.

The results of Breush-Pagan test verify the absence of heteroscedasticity problem.

RESULTS

After carrying out the econometrics tests: Pearson test and vifs of the independent variables test of individual effect presence, Hausman test and the heteroscedasticity test were discriminated to present the results of our models. Table 7 presents the results of the equation's estimation, in which the relationship between the disclosure frequency and earnings management was tested, the variables' coefficients, the expected sign as well as the associated probabilities. The findings show that the relationship between the disclosure frequency and earnings management is negative and significant. This confirms the study's hypothesis which shows that earnings management is a decreasing function for the disclosure level. Indeed, disclosure decreases asymmetry information and increases transparency, and thereafter firms have less incentive to manage their earnings. This result is coherent with the one of Jo and Kim (2007) in the American context, which shows that a bigger disclosure frequency exposes earnings' management, and that of Ambrose and Bian (2009), which assert that the availability of a great deal of information on the financial market can contradict the phenomenon of earnings management. This result is also coherent with the one of Li (2010) which shows that the biggest disclosure helps the investors to detect earnings management by the real activities.

Unlike the positive theory and the results of Iatridis and Kadorinises (2009), in our survey, the level of debt (LEV) is influenced negatively and significantly at 10% level of discretionary accruals. This result shows that the level of debt constitutes a constraint to the managerial discretion and thus represents a means to fight against the growth of earnings' management. As advanced by Jensen and Meckling (1976), one can say then that the debt is a

[5] The homoscedasticity qualifies a constant variance of the residues of data composing the sample. To the inverse, one says that there is homoscedasticity when the variance of the residues of the model is not constant, that is to say that the value predicted by the estimator doesn't converge toward the value in the population.

Table 5. Pearson correlation matrix and vifs.

	AD	PR	FI	NFI	SI	PP	ROA	IINST	AUD	CF	Siz	Lev	INSD	Block	Vif
AD	1.00														
PR	0.01	1.00													1.07
FI	-0.20	0.11	1.00												1.67
NFI	0.08	0.02	-0.34	1.00											1.46
SI	-0.01	0.07	0.40	0.21	1.00										1.55
PP	-0.05	-0.01	-0.07	-0.01	-0.04	1.00									1.66
ROA	0.19	0.05	-0.09	-0.07	-0.10	-0.30	1.00								1.93
IINST	-0.07	-0.05	-0.03	0.01	-0.12	0.32	-0.45	1.00							1.49
AUD	-0.17	0.03	0.02	0.03	0.03	0.21	0.07	0.02	1.00						1.20
CF	-0.10	0.09	0.03	0.03	-0.07	-0.09	0.27	-0.10	0.09	1.00					1.17
Siz	0.03	0.16	0.02	-0.17	-0.10	0.09	0.27	-0.11	0.31	0.08	1.00				1.36
Lev	-0.19	-0.04	0.08	-0.06	-0.07	0.43	-0.54	0.38	-0.03	-0.18	-0.02	1.00			1.80
INSD	0.10	0.05	-0.01	0.20	0.14	-0.46	0.09	-0.21	-0.09	0.10	-0.24	-0.29	1.00		1.52
Block	-0.04	0.02	0.14	-0.15	-0.03	-0.02	-0.01	-0.15	-0.03	0.14	0.06	0.12	-0.15	1.00	1.18

Ad : Discretionary accruals calculated from model Kothari et al. (2005), PR = mandatory and voluntary publications communicated by firm about one year, FI : score relative to financial information, NFI : score relative to non financial information, SI : score relative to strategic information, PPE : Level of net property, plant and equipment in firm, ROA = earnings / total assets, IINST = number of shares detained by institutional investors / total number of shares, AUD : indicator variable that equals one if the firm's auditor is one of the BIG accounting firms, and zero otherwise, CF = R-D, Size = logarithm (assets), Debt = total debt /total assets, INSD = number of shares detained by insiders / total number of shares of firm, Block = the percent of equity held by those owning more than 5% of a class of the company's equity securities.

Table 6. Result of Breush-Pagan test.

Chi test (2)	0.8 (0.3696)

means that permits the alleviation of agency conflicts between the shareholders and managers and the reduction of the costs of asymmetry information.

As for the profitability of assets (ROA) which is positive and statistically significant at a 5% level, this result is consistent with the predictions of several researchers who affirm that earnings' management is operated in the case where an extreme performance is achieved. In other words, profitable firms arrange several methods to manipulate earnings (Dechow et al., 1995). Regarding the quality of auditor, the relation with (AD) is negative and statistically significant at a 1% level; in other words, the level of earnings management is bigger in firms not audited by BIG accounting firms. This result is compatible with the results of other studies, like Chtourou et al. (2001), Francis et al. (1999) and Becker et al. (1998), which show that firms audited by BIG accounting firms, that is, Big6[6] type (or Big5 according to the time) have relatively less elevated discretionary accruals than firms audited by non Big accounting firms. This shows that for the Tunisian firms, while providing services of better quality, the BIG reduce the discretionary latitude of managers.

The relative coefficient to managerial ownership (INSD) for its part is positive and significant at a 10% level. Such a result is in favor of the thesis of managerial entrenchment, suggesting that the more the managerial ownership is raised, the more it has divergence of interests and the more the managers will be driven to manage earnings in order to generate private advantages. We corroborate this result with that of the studies of Jo and Kim (2007), Bowmen et al. (2005), Klein (2000) and Peasnell et al. (1998). The estimation of the coefficient relative to the variable size of (Size) gives a positive and significant relation at a 10% level. This result is also coherent with the idea of Watts and Zimmerman (1990) according to

[6] These are very well-known accounting firms to USA: Ernst &Young, Arthur Andersen, Deloitte Touch, Price Waterhouse, KPMG and Coopers & Lybrand.

Table 7. Results of regression.

Variable	Expected sign	Coefficient	Probability
PR	-	-0.0035***	0.052
PPE	+	-0.18***	0.093
ROA	+	0.3877**	0.023
IINST	-	-.00436	0.362
AUD	-	-0 .0502*	0.008
CF	?	-0.0756**	0.020
Size	-	0.0222***	0.065
LEV	+	-0.0568***	0.071
INSD	+	0.1558***	0.085
BLOCK	?	-0.0002	0.997

$AD_{i,t} = a + b1\ PR_{i,t} + b2\ PPE_{i,t} + b3\ ROA_{i,t} + b4\ IINST_{i,t} + b5\ AUD_{i,t} + b6\ CF_{i,t} + b7\ SIZE_{,t} + b8\ LEV_{i,t} + b9\ INSD_{i,t} + b10\ BLOCK_{i,t} + \varepsilon_{i,t}$. With: Ad : Discretionary accruals calculated from Kothari et al. (2005) model, PR = mandatory and voluntary publications communicated by firm about one year, PPE : level of net property, plant and equipment in firm, ROA = earnings / total assets, IINST = number of shares detained by institutional investors / total number of shares, AUD : Indicator variable that equals one if the firm's auditor is one of the BIG accounting firms, and zero otherwise, CF = R-D, Size = logarithm (assets), Debt = Total Debt /Total assets, INSD = number of shares detained by insiders / total number of shares of firm, Block = percent of equity held by those owning more than 5% of a class of the company's equity securities. Wald chi (2) = 28.97; prob = 0.0013; within = 0.0581; between = 0.5943; overall = 0.1393; *, **, *** Significant at 1, 5 and 10% level, respectively.

which the biggest firms are incited to exercise practices of earnings management[7] in order to reduce their political visibility. The relationship between discretionary accruals and cash flows is negative and significant at a 5% level. This result corroborates with the results of Jo and Kim (2007), Becker et al. (1998) and Burgstahler and Dichev (1997), and it permits us to conclude that the results are managed in order to avoid losses and negative changes.

As far as the variable net property, plant and equipment in the firm are concerned, the outcomes show that it has a positive and significant impact at a 10% level on the level of earnings management. In other words, firms that invest more in net property, plant and equipment better manage their earnings. Since firms that constitute our sample are on average profit, we can say that these firms use amortization to inflate loads and thereafter minimize political costs. In fact, public authorities can interpret the results raised of firms as an indicator of performance and of the existence of monopolistic practice. Hence, they are going to implement regimentation under the shape of price control or increased taxes. It was found that institutional investment does not have an effect on earnings' management in the firms that constitute our sample, since the relationship between these two variables is non-significant. This result is compatible with the survey of Dey (2004) that found a non-significant relationship between artificial smoothing and institutional investment. Eventually, the results show that a non-significant relationship exists between block ownership and earnings' management. This result is compatible with that of Park and Shin (2004), in which it was found that block ownership did not affect earnings management. In fact, our survey highlights that block ownership in Tunisia does not have an effect on the practices of earnings' management. Subsequently, we found that the biggest disclosure exposes earnings' management and helps the investors to detect this phenomenon; thus, we tested accurately in a second stage what type of information has an impact on earnings' management.

Table 8 presents the results of the equation's estimation, in which the relationship between earnings management and the scores ofdisclosure was tested: that is, the coefficients of variables, the expected sign as well as the probabilities associated. The results show that the score relative to the financial information affects negatively the level of discretionary accruals, considering a negative and statistically significant coefficient at a 5% level. In other words, the disclosure of financial information exposes the practices of earnings' management by firms, but the other information, which is either strategic or has a non-financial characteristic do not have an effect on earnings management since their coefficients are non significant.

DISCUSSION

About the relationship between the disclosure information and earnings management, the study's result is in favor of the signalling theory and the agency theory, because the signalling theory stipulates that the disclosure of voluntary information aims at the reduction of informational asymmetry between the managers of firms (insiders) and external investors (outsiders). The agency theory foresees the voluntary disclosure not only as an important and efficient means to protect shareholders

[7] Enron that was classified recently among the ten big American firms, made bankruptcy December 2, 2001, being a matter for an extreme practice of earnings management.

Table 8. Results of regression.

Variable	Expected sign	Coefficient	Probability
FI	-	-0.2146**	0.043
NFI	?	0.0461	0.692
SI	?	0.1314	0.437
PPE	+	0.7957***	0.083
ROA	+	0.3195**	0.045
IINST	-	0.0413	0.390
AUD	-	-0.0595*	0.002
CF	?	-0.0712**	0.028
Size	-	0.9248***	0.096
LEV	+	-0.0746***	0.094
INSD	+	0.2381***	0.065
BLOCK	?	0.0470	0.471

$AD_{i,t} = a + b1\ FI_{i,t} + b2\ NFI_{i,t} + b3\ SI_{i,t} + b4\ PPE_{i,t} + b5\ ROA_{i,t} + b6\ IINST_{i,t} + b7\ AUD_{i,t} + b8\ CF_{i,t} + b9\ SIZE_{,t} + b10\ LEV_{i,t} + b11\ INSD_{i,t} + b12\ BLOCK_{i,t} + \varepsilon_{i,t}$. With: Ad : Discretionary accruals calculated from model Kothari et al. (2005), FI : Score relative to financial information, NFI : score relative to non financial information, SI : score relative to strategic information, PPE : level of net property, plant and equipment in firm, ROA = earnings / total assets, IINST = Number of shares detained by institutional investors / total number of shares, AUD : Indicator variable that equals one if the firm's auditor is one of the BIG accounting firms, and zero otherwise, CF = R-D, Size = logarithm (assets), Debt = total debt /total assets, INSD = number of shares detained by insiders / total number of shares of firm, Block= The percent of equity held by those owning more than 5% of a class of the company's equity securities.

from managerial latitude, but also to protect the minority shareholders from the risk of expropriations on behalf of the majority shareholders.

The results of this study are consistent with the theoretical predictions and empirical findings of the preceding research. They provide evidence on how management may use the flexibility provided to exercise discretion in reporting earnings. This has implications for the interpretation of the information conveyed by reported accounting earnings. However, the result of this study is consistent with the results of Arthur Levitt (1998), which show that financial analysts and investors use better financial information in their decisions.

Conclusion

In this article, we studied on the one hand the type of relation that exist between the disclosure frequency and earnings management, and on the other hand, the relationship between the different scores of disclosures and earnings' management, after which a literature review was presented on disclosure information, transparency and earnings management. This literature allowed the empirical validation of 19 firms quoted in the B.V.M.T and earnings management in the setting of disclosure information in the Tunisian context (Appendix 1). The findings of the study's survey show that earnings' management is a decreasing function of the disclosure level; in other words, if the level of disclosure increases, earnings' management decreases. Our survey shows that disclosure of information about the financial decisions and performances constitute a constraint to the proliferation of earnings' management. In conclusion, the results of this study's survey suggest that information disclosure reduces incentives of earnings' management since it increases transparency and helps investors to detect this phenomenon.

REFERENCES

Allayannis G, Simko PJ (2009). Earnings Smoothing, Analyst Following, and Firm Value. www.ssrn.com.

Ambrose BW, Bian X (2009). Stock Market Information and REIT Earnings Management. www.ssrn.com.

Baber W, Chen S, Kang SH (2006). Stock Price Reaction To Evidence Of Earnings Management: Implications For Supplementary Financial Disclosure. Rev. Account. Stud., 11: 5-9.

Bergstresser D, Philippon T (2006). CEO Incentives And Earnings Management. J. Fin. Econ., 80: 511–529.

Beyer A (2008). Financial Analysts' Forecast Revisions And Managers' Reporting Behavior. J. Acct. Econ. 46: 334–348.

Burgstahler D, Dichev I (1997). Earnings Management To Avoid Earnings Decreases And Losses. J. Account. Econ., 24: 99–126.

Chevis GM, Das S, Sivaramakrishnan K (2007). Does It Pay To Consistently Meet Analysts' Earnings Expectations. www.ssrn.com.

Chtourou SM, Bédard J, Courteau L (2001). Corporate Governance And Earning Management. www.ssrn.com.

Cormier D, Martinez I (2006). The Association Between Management Earnings Forecasts, Earnings Management, And Stock Market Management. Account. Rev., 70: 193-226.

Dechow PM, Sloan RG, Sweeney AP (1995). Detecting Earnings Valuation: Evidence From French IPOs. Int. J. Account., 41: 209-236.

Degeorge F, Patel J, Zeckhauser RJ (1999). Earnings Management To Exceed Thresholds. J. Bus., 72: 1–33.

Degeorge F, Ding Y, Jeanjean T, Stolowy H (2005). Does Analyst Following Curb Earnings Management? International Evidence. www.ssrn.com.
Dey A, (2004). Income Smoothing and Sophisticated Investor Preferences. www.ssrn.com.
Faccio M, Lazfer MA (1999). Managerial Ownership, Board Structure And Firm Value: The UK Evidence . www.ssrn.com.
Eng LL, Mak YT (2003). Corporate governance and voluntary disclosure. J. Account. Pub. Pol., 22: 325–345.
Graham JR, Harvey CR, Rajgpal S (2005). The Economic Implications Of Corporate Financial Reporting. J. Account. Econ., 40: 3-73.
Hartzel JC, Starks LT (2008). Institutional Investors And Executive Compensation. www.ssrn.com.
Hunton JE, Libby R, Mazza CR (2006). Financial Reporting Transparency And Earnings Management. Account. Rev., 8: 135–158.
Iatridis G, Kadorinis G (2009). Earnings Management And Firm Financial Motives: A Financial Investigation Of UK Listed Firms. I. Rev. F. Anal., 18: 164–173.
Jensen MC, Meckling WH (1976). Theory Of The Firm: Managerial Behaviour Agency costs And Ownerships Structure. J. F. Econ., 3: 305-360.
Jo H, Kim Y (2007). Disclosure Frequency And Earnings Management. J. F. Econ., 84: 561-590.
Jones J (1991).Earnings Management During Import Relief Investigations.J. Account. Res., 29: 193–228.
Kim JB, Chung R, Firth M (2003). Auditor Conservatism, Asymmetric Monitoring And Earnings Management. Cont. Account. Res., 20: 323–359.
Klein A (2000). CEO power, board independence and CEO compensation: An empirical investigation. www.ssrn.com.
Kothari SP, Leone AJ, Wasley CE (2005). Performance Matched Discretionary Accrual Measures. J. Account. Econ., 39: 163–197.
Lennox CS (2005). Management Ownership And Audit Firm Size. www.ssrn.com.
Li X (2010). Accounting conservatism and the cost of capital: An international analysis. www.ssrn.com.
Linen S, Radhakrishnan S, Su L (2006). Earnings Management And Guidance For Meeting Or Beating Analysts' Earnings Forecasts. www.ssrn.com.
Lobo GJ, Zhou J (2001). Disclosure Quality And Earnings Management. As. Pa. J. Account. Econ., 8: 1-20.
Park YW, Shin HH (2004). Board Composition And Earnings Management In Canada. J. Corp. Fin., 10: 431-451.
Peasnell KV, Pope PF, Young S (1998). Outside Directors, Board Effectiveness, And Earnings Management. www.ssrn.com.
Rahman AR, Tay TM, Ong BT, Cai S (2007). Quarterly Reporting In A Voluntary Disclosure Environment: Its Benefits, Drawbacks And Determinants. Int. J. Account., 42: 416–442.
Rajgopal S, Venkatachalam M, Jiambalvo J (1999). Is Institutional Ownership Associated With Earnings Management And The Extent To Which Stock Prices Reflect Future Earnings. www.ssrn.com.
Rees L, Sivaramakrishnan K. (2007).The Effect Of Meeting Or Beating Revenue Forecasts On The Association Between Quarterly Returns And Earnings Forecast Errors. Cont. Account. Res., 24: 259–290.
Schipper K (1989) .Commentary On Earnings Management. Account. Horizons, 3: 91–102.
Watts R, Zimmerman J (1986).Positive Accounting Theory. Prentice-Hall, Englewood Cliffs, NJ (Chapter 8).
Watts RL, Zimmerman JL (1990). Positive Accounting Theory: A Ten Year Perspective. Account. Rev., 65: 131-156.
Yu F (2008). Analyst Coverage And Earnings Management. J. Fin. Econ., 88: 245–271.

Appendix 1. Disclosure index.

(SS) Score relative to strategic information	Score	
(S-1) General corporate information:		
Brief history of company	1	
Organizational structure/chart	1	
General description of business/activities	1	
Principal products	1	
Principal markets	1	
(S-2) Corporate strategy:		
Statement of corporate goals or objectives	1	
Current strategy	1	2
Impact of strategy on current results	1	2
Future strategy	1	2
Impact of strategy on future results	1	2
(S-3) Management discussion and analysis:		
Review of operations	1	2
Competitive environment	1	2
Significant events of the year	1	2
Change in sales/profits	1	2
Change in cost of goods sold	1	2
Change in expenses	1	2
Change in inventory level	1	2
Change in market share	1	2
(S-4) Future prospects:		
New developments	1	2
Forecast of sales/profit	1	2
Assumptions underlying the forecast	1	2
Order book or backlog information	1	
(S-5) Other useful strategic information:		
--	1	2
--	1	2
--	1	2
Sub total (A)	43	
(SNF) Score relative to non financial information		
(N-1) Employee information:		
Number of employees	1	
Compensation per employee	2	
Value-added per employee	2	
Productivity indicator	2	
(N-2) Other useful non-financial disclosure :	Score	
--	1	2
--	1	2
--	1	2
Sub total (B)	13	
(SF) Score relative to financial information		

Appendix 1. Contd.

(F-1) Performance indicators (not from financial		
Historical figures for last five years or more	2	
Turnover	1	
Profit	1	
Shareholders funds	1	
Total assets	1	
Earnings per share	1	
(F-2) Financial ratios:	Score	
ROE	1	
ROA	1	
Gearing ratio	1	
Liquidity ratio	1	
Other useful ratios:	Score	
---	1	
---	1	
---	1	
(F-3) Projected information:	Score	
Cash flow forecast	2	
Capital expenditures and/or R&D expenditures forecast	2	
Earnings forecast	2	
(F-4) Foreign currency information:	Score	
Impact of foreign exchange fluctuations on current results	1	2
Foreign currency exposure management description	1	2
Major exchange rates used in the accounts	1	
(F-5) Other useful financial information :	Score	
---	1	2
---	1	2
---	1	2
Sub total (C)	31	
Total (Company DScore)	87	

11

Priority sector advances: Trends, issues and strategies

R. K. Uppal

D. A. V. College, Malout (Punjab), India. E-mail rkuppal_mlt@yahoo.com.

An enunciation of the need to channelise the flow of credit to certain sectors of the economy, known as the priority sectors, in the largest interest of the country, can be traced to the Reserve Bank's credit policy for the year 1967 - 1968. The government initiated measures for social control over banks in 1967 - 1968 with a view to securing a better adaptation of the banking system to the needs of economic planning and it is playing a more active role in aiding sectors like agriculture and small scale industries (SSIs). The present study is an attempt to study the priority sector advances by the public, private and foreign bank groups. This study is based on the parameters like lending to priority sector by public, private sector and foreign bank groups, targets achieved by public, private sector and foreign bank group NPAs (Non-performing assets), while lending to priority sector. On the basis of these parameters, the study concludes that public sector banks have not achieved the target of 40% while private sector banks have achieved the overall target. No private sector bank could achieve the 10% target by lending to weaker section. On the other hand, foreign banks have achieved the small scale industries' export credit and overall target. NPAs of public sector banks have increased because of high priority sector advances. The paper also throw light on the problems or issues which arise due to priority sector advances and also suggest some strategies to sought out these issues. All the parameters have been analyzed for the period, 2006 - 2007.

Key words: Priority sector advances, targets achieved, issues, strategies.

INTRODUCTION

It has been in the post 1969 period that priority sector lending and social banking concepts have been crystallized and adopted for the purpose of credit deployment (Gupta S and Kumar S 2004). The term 'priority sector' indicates those activities which have national importance and have been assigned priority for development. Hence, the adoption of priority sector concept for the purpose of bank lending reflects the effort to synchronize the lending activities of each bank with the national priorities. These sectors, in particular agriculture, small industries and other small business were the neglected sectors and for the purpose of bank credit, they have been categorized as priority sector.

The priority sector advances has undergone several changes, since then, several new areas and sectors has being brought within the purview of this sector. While there has been continuous demand to include new areas such as infrastructure within the ambit of priority sector, there have also been suggestions that the focus on the needy sectors of economy and weaker sections of the society is getting lost because of such inclusions. A need has therefore, been felt to review the concept and the segments of priority sector. Consequently, in paragraph 89 of the Annual Policy Statement of Reserve bank of India for the year 2005 - 2006, it was stated that prescriptions relating to priority sector lending have been modified from time to time and generally, the eligibility criteria have been enlarged to include several new areas. In December 2004, it was decided that direct advances to priority sector will be encouraged, thus beginning a phased withdrawal of eligibility in special bonds of specified institutions.

At the second meeting of the national credit council in July 1968, the priority sector was defined to include only two activities, agriculture and small scale industries. A list indicating the type of advances which would be eligible for compliance with the lending targets for these sectors was sent out by RBI to the banks. For small scale

Abbreviations: NPA, Non Performing Assets; **RBI**, Reserve Bank of India; Public sector banks includes SBI and Associates banks and Nationalized banks; Indian private sector banks include old private sector banks and new private sector banks.

industries, no separate guidelines were issued, but it was indicated that direct loans granted to road transport operators would qualify for compliance with lending targets along with small scale industries. Financing of industrial estate was also to be included under small scale industries. Over a period of two decades, the composition of priority sector has undergone some modification in the activities covered, such as the addition of housing for weaker sections and pure consumption loans under the priority sector. (Vashisht, 2004) suggests Economic Reforms in the real sectors of an economy fail to realize their full potential without a parallel reform in the financial sector. The financial sector refers to a general improvement in the functioning and efficiency of the financial system as a whole and the removal of impediments to its long term developments. (Samal B, 2002) As a result of financial sector reforms, there is a shift in the focus from quantitative to qualitative growth and Indian banking should be subjected to rigors or prudential norms of operations and competitive environment. (Mujumdar NA, 2001), the deregulation, the vital component of the financial sector reforms, has increased the overall profitability of the banking industry. (Passah, 2002) analyzed the Indian financial system comprising the commercial banks, the financial institutions and the capital markets. He concluded that Indian banking has undergone a very rapid transformation in the past three decades. There is a sea change in the Indian banking sector in the post financial sector reforms'.

The scope and extent of priority sector lending has undergone a significant change in the post-reform period with several new areas and sectors being brought under its purview while there had been demands to include new areas, such as infrastructure, within the ambit of priority sector, there is apprehension that it will dilute the definition of the priority sector with the focus on the needy sectors of the economy and weaker section of society getting completely lost. Against this background, an internal working group was set up in the Reserve Bank (Chairman: shri C.S. Murthy) to examine the need for continuance of priority sector lending prescriptions, review the existing policy on priority sector lending, including the segments constituting the priority sector targets and sub-targets and to recommend changes, if any, required in this regard. Based on the draft technical paper submitted by the internal working group and the feedback received thereon, the guidelines were revised. The sectors of the society economy that impact large segments of the population, the weaker section and the sectors which are employment-intensive such as agriculture and micro and small enterprises, have been retained as priority sector in the revised guidelines, which came into effect from 30 April, 2007. Agriculture, small enterprises, micro credit, retail trade, education loans and housing loans up to 20 lakh are the broad categories included in the priority sector.

In the olden days, poor people borrowed money from indigenous banks to fulfill their needs. But as the time passes, banking as an institution, dealing with lending and collection of money came into existence. This type of banking is called simple banking. According to the changing requirements of time, simple banking transformed itself into commercial banking (Gujral N, 2003). Commercial banking, itself, has undergone numerous changes all over the world, during the last five decades. Now, the present day banking does not restrict itself to traditional deposit collection and money lending, encompassing a wide sphere of financial activity; lending still remains the primary activity. Most credit needs of the society, for carrying commercial activities are fulfilled by the banks (Prasad M., Sinha KK and Prasad KM, 2004). The conventional credit from the banking system to the commercial sector comprises bank loans and advances in the form of term loans, demand loans, cash credit, overdrafts, inland and foreign bills purchased and discounted as well as investments in instruments issued by non-government sector. But lending is not an easy task for the banks because it creates a big problem for the banks which is called non-performing assets (Chhimpa J, 2002). Non-performing asset generally refers to those assets which cease to provide any return to the bank. In the present time, NPAs is a big problem for the banks as it has ever been a major concern for the bank promoters and government. But efficient banks have no need to frighten from the NPAs because they can find some other sources of income to match these NPAs in the era of LPG.

Categories of priority sector advances

The broad categories of priority sector for all scheduled commercial banks are as under:

Agriculture (Direct and Indirect Finance)

Direct finance to agriculture includes short medium and long term loans given for agriculture and allied activities directly to individual farmer, self-help groups (SHGs) or joint liability groups (JLGs) of individual farmers without limit and to others (such as corporate partnership firms and institutions) upto Rs. 20 lakh for taking up agriculture allied activities. Indirect finance to agriculture includes loans given for agriculture and allied activities.

Small scale industries (Direct and Indirect Finance)

Direct finance to small scale industries (SSIs) includes all loans given to SSI units which are engaged in manufacture, processing or preservation of goods and whose investment are in plant and machinery (original cost) excluding land and building.

Small business/service enterprises

It includes small business, retail trade, professional and self employed persons, small road and water transport operators and other enterprises.

Micro credit

Provision of credit and other financial services and products of very small amounts not exceeding Rs. 50,000 per borrower to the poor in rural, semi-urban and urban areas, either directly or through a group mechanism, for enabling them to improve their living standards, constitutes micro credit.

Education loans

Education loans include loans and advances granted to individuals for educational purpose, upto Rs. 10 lakh for studies in India and Rs. 20 lakh for studies abroad and do not include those granted scholarship by the institutions.

Housing loans

Loans upto Rs. 15 lakh for construction of houses by individuals, (excluding loans granted by banks to their own employees) and loans given for repairs to the damaged houses of individuals upto Rs. 1 lakh in rural and semi-urban areas and upto Rs. 2 lakh in urban areas.

Policy measures by RBI

The description of the priority sector was formalized in 1972 on the basis of the report submitted by the informal study group on statistics relating to advances to the priority sector, constituted by the Reserve Bank. Although, initially, there were no specific targets fixed in respect of priority sector lending in November, 1974. Public sector banks were advised that their priority sector lending should reach a level of not less than one-third of the outstanding credit by March 1979. In November, 1978, the private sector banks were also advised to send a minimum of 33% of their total advances to the priority sector by the end of March 1980. Subsequently, the target was enhanced to 40% of aggregate advances. In achieving this overall target, sub-target for lending to agriculture sector and weaker section were also stipulated for the banks. At present, banks are required to lend at least 18 and 10% of their net bank credit (NBC) to the agriculture sector and weaker section of society, respectively.

Foreign banks operating in India were also advised to progressively increase their advances to the priority sector to reach a level of 15% of their NBC by end-March 1992. In April 1993, this ratio was further raise to 32% of NBC to be achieved by March 1994. Within the enhanced target of 32%, two sub-targets of 10% in respect of SSI and 12% for export were fixed. On the basis of revised guidelines on lending to the priority sector, the priority sector lending target/sub-target have now been linked to adjusted net bank credit (ANBC) or credit equivalent amount of off-balance sheet exposures, whichever is higher, with effect from 30 April, 2007.

OBJECTIVES AND RESEARCH METHODOLOGY

Objectives

1) To study and analyze the priority sector lending by various bank groups.
2) To analyze targets achieved by various bank groups.
3) To study the issues and prepare strategies to enhance the priority sector advances.

Research methodology

The research design of the study is priority sector advances of various banking groups. RBI has given several targets to banks to enhance loans in priority sector but out of these targets, banks have been succeeded to achieve only a few targets. Lending to priority sector has created the fear of NPAs among the banks. Profitability of the banks has also been adversely affected by the priority sector advances, because of low rate of interest on the priority sector advances.

The universe of the present study is banking industry of India. The Indian banking industry has been divided into three major bank groups namely: 1) Public Sector Bank Group (28)*; 2) Private Sector Bank Group (26); 3) Foreign Bank Group (30). * including IDBI Bank.

The study attempts to accomplish its objectives by making analysis on the basis of seven parameters: 1) Priority Sector Lending by Public Sector Bank Group; 2) Priority Sector Lending by Private Sector Bank Group; 3) Priority Sector Lending by Foreign Bank Group; 4) Targets Achieved by Public Sector Banks Under Priority Sector; 5) Targets Achieved by Private Sector Banks Under Priority Sector; 6) Targets Achieved by Foreign Banks Under Priority Sector; 6) NPAs while lending to Priority Sector.

All the parameters have been analyzed for the period, 2006 and 2007.

RESULTS AND DISCUSSIONS

Priority sector lending by public sector banks (G-I)

Table 1 indicates the priority sector advances by the public sector banks. The outstanding advances granted by public sector banks to the priority sector were at Rs. 5, 21 and 180 crore as on March 2007. Advances to agriculture constituted 15.6% of NBC during 2007, of which Indian Bank (21.0), State Bank of Saurashtra (18.8), Bank of India (18.4) gave more advances to agriculture (Appendix 1). Advances to small scale

Table 1. Priority sector lending by public sector banks (Amount in Cr).

Sector	2006		2007		Growth rate (%)
	Amount	Percentage to net bank credit	Amount	Percentage to net bank credit	
Priority Sector Advances	4,09,748	40.3	5,21,180	39.6	27.19
Agriculture	1,55,220	15.3	2,05,091	15.6	32.13
Small-Scale Industries	82,434	8.1	1,04,703	8.0	27.01
Other Priority Sector	1,63,756	16.1	2,01,023	15.3	22.76

Source: Report on Trend and Progress of Indian Banking, RBI, Mumbai, 2006 - 2007.

Appendix 1. Advances of public sector banks to priority sector percent.

Name of the Bank	Total agricultural advances	Weaker section	Total priority sector advances
	Percent to NBC	Percent to NBC	Percent to NBC
Public sector banks	15.6	7.2	39.6
Nationalized banks*	16.0	7.1	39.9
Allahabad Bank	18.3	6.6	39.6
Andhra Bank	18.5	9.5	41.1
Bank of Baroda	15.9	7.5	40.6
Bank of India	18.4	10.1	47.1
Bank of Maharashtra	14.0	5.2	41.7
Canara Bank	15.7	6.0	40.2
Central Bank of India	15.8	7.2	43.6
Corporation Bank	9.2	3.3	40.6
Dena Bank	15.2	5.0	42.0
Indian Bank	21.0	11.5	49.4
Indian Overseas Bank	18.7	10.2	40.9
Oriental Bank of Commerce	11.1	4.5	36.5
Punjab National Bank	18.9	11.0	41.9
Punjab and Sind Bank	16.0	5.6	42.8
Syndicate Bank	17.4	10.1	39.9
Union Bank of India	16.8	6.9	44.4
United Bank of India	12.0	8.0	41.7
UCO Bank	13.9	4.0	40.4
Vijaya Bank	12.4	5.8	41.0
IDBI Ltd.	2.2	0.3	15.2
State bank group	14.8	7.3	38.8
State Bank of India	14.5	7.6	38.4
State Bank of Bikaner and Jaipur	18.3	10.3	41.0
State Bank of Hyderabad	13.7	7.1	40.8
State Bank of Indore	17.2	10.0	40.0
State Bank of Mysore	13.8	9.7	38.3
State Bank of Patiala	15.8	1.1	36.3
State Bank of Saurashtra	18.8	6.8	42.2
State Bank of Travancore	12.6	5.4	41.0

Source: Same as Table 1.

industries by public sector banks were only 8.0% while advances to other priority sector were 15.3% during 2007.

Priority sector lending by private sector banks (G-II)

Priority sector lending by private sector banks can be

Table 2. Priority sector lending by private sector banks (Amount in Cr).

Sector	2006		2007		Growth rate (%)
	Amount	Percentage to net bank credit	Amount	Percentage to net bank credit	
Priority Sector Advances	1,06,586	42.8	1,43,768	42.7	34.88
Agriculture	36,712	13.6	52,056	12.8	41.80
Small-Scale Industries	10,421	4.2	13,063	3.9	25.35
Other Priority Sector	57,777	23.2	76,925	22.9	33.14

Source: Same as Table 1.

Appendix 2. Advances of private sector banks to priority sector percent.

Name of the Bank	Total agricultural advances	Weaker Section	Total priority sector advances
	Percent to NBC	Percent to NBC	Percent to NBC
Private Sector Banks	12.82	1.55	42.71
Axis Bank	14.09	1.11	42.58
Bank of Rajasthan	6.05	1.12	31.49
Bharat Overseas Bank	11.08	1.63	41.05
Catholic Syrian Bank	12.49	1.69	45.35
Centurian Bank of Punjab	14.63	0.53	38.35
City Union Bank	7.12	1.54	40.01
Development Credit Bank	13.67	3.29	41.57
Dhanalakshmi Bank	16.02	6.43	46.55
Federal Bank	15.80	6.50	44.37
Yes Bank	18.84	-	42.74
HDFC Bank	14.24	0.70	44.21
ICICI Bank	11.65	0.80	44.87
Indusind Bank	13.86	0.09	41.52
ING Vysya Bank	8.74	3.86	41.01
Jammu and Kashmir Bank	4.73	3.13	24.57
Karnataka Bank	8.16	1.37	35.11
Karur Vysya Bank	15.90	4.17	40.56
Kotak Mahindra Bank	16.26	-	41.25
Lakshmi Vilas Bank	18.19	6.59	41.08
Lord Krishna Bank	9.80	1.03	44.92
Nainital Bank	13.93	1.24	50.33
Ratnakar Bank	14.60	2.23	43.08
Sangli Bank	24.30	7.63	93.86
SBI Commercial and International Bank	8.76	-	42.37
South Indian Bank	17.23	4.05	41.56
Tamilnad Mercantile Bank	15.62	6.27	48.85

Source: Same as Table 1.

seen in Table 2. It is clear from the Table that priority sector advances extended by private sector banks in 2007 were at Rs. 1,43,768 crore, constituting 42.7% of NBC. Lending by private sector advances to the agriculture sector improved from 8.3% of NBC at the end of March, 2000 to 13.6% at the end of March, 2006, before declining to 12.8% of NBC as on March 2007. Lending to agriculture sector was more in Sangli Bank (24.30%), Yes Bank (18.84%) while it was least in Bank of Rajasthan (6.05%) and in City Union Bank (7.12&) (Appendix 2*)*. Of the overall advances, advances to small scale industries were the least that is 3.9% in 2007.

Priority sector lending by foreign banks (G-III)

Table 3 indicates that priority sector advances by foreign banks, having offices in India, increases from Rs. 30,439 crore to 37,835 crore as at 2007 which constituted 33.4% of net bank credit. The share of export credit in total net bank credit was 18.3% which is higher than the share of small scale industries in 2007.

Export credit was more in Mashreq bank (102.5%), Societe Generale Bank (177.1%) and least in American Express Bank (6.3%) and Mizuho Corporate Bank (9.5%) (Appendix 3).

Table 3. Priority sector lending by foreign banks (Amount in Cr).

Sector	2006		2007		Growth rate (%)
	Amount	Percentage to net bank credit	Amount	Percentage to net bank credit	
Priority Sector Advances	30,439	34.4	37,835	33.4	24.30
Export credit	17,326	19.6	20,714	18.3	19.55
Small-Scale Industries	8,430	9.5	11,648	10.3	38.17

Source: Same as Table 1.

Appendix 3. Advances of foriegn banks to priority sector percent.

Name of the bank	SSI advances	Export credit	Total priority sector advances
	Percent to NBC	Percent to NBC	Percent to NBC
Foreign banks	10.3	18.3	33.4
ABN Amro Bank	10.2	27.8	33.6
Abu Dhabi Commercial Bank	10.7	14.3	30.9
American Express Bank	43.0	6.3	48.6
Antwerp Diamond Bank	26.0	96.9	96.9
Arab Bangladesh Bank	23.4	16.1	39.5
Bank International Indonesia	719.7	-	719.7
Bank of America	10.6	20.5	32.4
Bank of Baharin and Kuwait	13.9	42.0	75.6
Bank of Ceylon	20.5	55.0	70.0
Bank of Nova Scotia	8.3	29.6	41.4
Bank of Tokyo-Mitsubishi	9.0	16.4	31.9
Barclays Bank PLC	12.2	22.8	35.0
BNP Paribas	11.3	13.0	33.8
China Trust Commercial Banks	15.8	16.4	37.3
Calyon Bank	12.9	17.9	38.7
Citi Bank	8.7	16.0	31.8
Deutsche Bank	10.3	23.3	34.1
Development Bank of Singapore	21.9	17.2	39.1
HSBC Ltd.	7.6	14.0	29.6
JP Morgan Chase Bank	9.5	23.3	32.8
Krung Thai Bank	38.9	16.1	85.7
Mashreqbank	14.2	102.5	116.8
Mizuho Corporate Bank	6.1	9.5	25.8
Oman International Bank	26.5	73.3	99.8
Shinhan Bank	9.5	13.1	33.2
Societe Generale	13.9	177.1	190.9
Sonali Bank	25.4	54.5	54.5
Standard Chartered Bank	11.4	14.6	34.1
State Bank of Mauritius	15.3	12.7	46.4

Source: Same as Table 1

Table 4. Targets achieved by public sector banks under the priority sector.

Name of the bank	Overall	Agriculture	*Weaker section*
Public Sector Banks			
Nationalized Banks			
Allahabad Bank			
Andhra Bank	√	√	
Bank of Baroda	√	√	
Bank of India	√		
Bank of Maharashtra	√	√	√
Canara Bank	√		
Central Bank of India	√		
Corporation Bank	√		
Dena Bank	√		
Indian Bank	√		
Indian Overseas Bank	√	√	√
Oriental Bank of Commerce	√	√	√
Punjab National Bank			
Punjab and Sind Bank	√	√	√
Syndicate Bank	√		
Union Bank of India			√
United Bank of India	√		
UCO Bank	√		
Vijaya Bank	√		
IDBI Ltd.			
State Bank Group			
State Bank of India			
State Bank of Bikaner and Jaipur			
State Bank of Hyderabad	√	√	√
State Bank of Indore	√		√
State Bank of Mysore	√		
State Bank of Patiala			
State Bank of Saurashtra	√	√	
State Bank of Travancore	√		

Source: Same as Table 1.

Targets achieved by public sector banks under the priority sector

Table 4 exhibits the targets achieved by public sector banks under the priority sector. The public sector banks, as a group, continued to meet the target till 2005 - 2006. Priority sector lending by the public sector bank group however marginally fell short of the target of 40% by 0.7% as at March, 2007. Seven PSBs (Allahabad Bank, Oriental Bank of Commerce, Syndicate Bank, IDBI Ltd., State Bank of India, State Bank of Mysore and State Bank of Patiala) did not achieve the priority sector lending target of 40% during 2007. Out of 28 PSBs, only eight banks (Allahabad Bank, Andhra Bank, Bank of India, Indian Bank, Indian Overseas Bank, Punjab National Bank, and State Bank of Bikaner and Jaipur and State Bank of Saurashtra) could achieve the agricultural lending target of 18%. In the case of lending to weaker sections, only seven PSBs (Bank of India, Indian Bank, Indian Overseas Bank, Punjab National Bank, Syndicate Bank and State Bank of Bikaner and Jaipur and State Bank of Indore) achieved the sub-target of 10% as at March 2007.

Targets achieved by private sector banks under the priority sector

Table 5 reflects the targets achieved by private sector banks under the priority sector. The private sector banks, as a group, were able to achieve the overall priority sector lending target in 2007. Out of 26 private sector banks, four banks (Bank of Rajasthan Ltd., Centurian Bank of Punjab Ltd., Jammu and Kashmir Bank Ltd. and Karnataka Bank Ltd.) did not achieve the target as at March 2007. Only three banks (Yes Bank, Lakshmi Vilas

Table 5. Targets achieved by private sector banks under the priority sector.

Name of the bank	Overall	Agriculture	Weaker section
Private Sector Banks	√		
Axis Bank	√		
Bank of Rajasthan			
Bharat Overseas Bank	√		
Catholic Syrian Bank	√		
Centurian Bank of Punjab			
City Union Bank	√		
Development Credit Bank	√		
Dhanalakshmi Bank	√		
Federal Bank	√		
Yes Bank	√	√	
HDFC Bank	√		
ICICI Bank	√		
Indusind Bank	√		
ING Vysya Bank	√		
Jammu & Kashmir Bank			
Karnataka Bank			
Karur Vysya Bank	√		
Kotak Mahindra Bank	√		
Lakshmi Vilas Bank	√	√	
Lord Krishna Bank	√		
Nainital Bank	√		
Ratnakar Bank	√		
Sangli Bank	√	√	
SBI Commercial and International Bank	√		
South Indian Bank	√		
Tamilnad Mercantile Bank	√		

Source: Same as Table 1.

Bank and Sangli Bank) was able to achieve the 18% sub-target for agriculture during 2007. Lending to agriculture by another six banks ranged between 15 and 18%. No private sector bank could achieve the 10% target for lending to weaker section.

Targets achieved by foreign banks under the priority sector

Target achieved by foreign banks under the priority sector depicts in Table 6. The share of export credit in total net bank credit at 18.3% was significantly above the prescribed sub-target of 12.0%. Foreign banks also reached the sub-target of 10.0% in respect of lending to small scale industries. Out of 29 foreign banks operating in India, five banks (Abu Dhabi Commercial Bank, Bank of Tokyo-Mitsubishi, Citi Bank, HSBC Ltd. and Mizuho Corporate Bank) could not achieve the priority sector lending target of 32% of NBC in March 2007. Seven foreign banks (Bank of Nova Scotia, Bank of Tokyo-Mitsubishi, Citi Bank, HSBC Ltd., JP Morgan Chase Bank, Mizuho Corporate Bank and Shinhan Bank) could not achieve the small scale industries lending targets at the end of March 2007, while three foreign banks (American Express Bank, Bank International Indonesia and Mizuho Corporate Bank) could not achieve the sub-target of lending for exports.

NPAs while lending to priority sector

Table 7 listed the NPAs in priority sector by three major bank groups. It clearly indicates that NPAs were more in public sector bank group while the least was in foreign bank group, because advances by public sector bank group to the priority sector were also high. NPAs in the public and private sector bank group were high mainly due to increase in NPAs in the agricultural sector.

Thus, it is concluded from all the tables that lending to priority sectors are higher by the public and private sector banks than the foreign banks. Public and private sector banks have achieved the overall target and sub-target but not as much as foreign banks. Non-achievement of

Table 6. Targets achieved by foreign banks under the priority sector.

Name of the bank	Overall	Agriculture	Weaker section
Foreign Banks	√	√	√
ABN Amro Bank	√	√	√
Abu Dhabi Commercial Bank		√	√
American Express Bank	√	√	
Antwerp Diamond Bank	√	√	
Arab Bangladesh Bank	√	√	√
Bank International Indonesia	√	√	√
Bank of America	√	√	
Bank of Baharin and Kuwait	√	√	√
Bank of Ceylon	√	√	√
Bank of Nova Scotia	√		√
Bank of Tokyo-Mitsubishi			√
Barclays Bank PLC	√	√	√
BNP Paribas	√	√	√
China Trust Commercial Banks	√	√	√
Calyon Bank	√	√	√
Citi Bank			√
Deutsche Bank	√	√	√
Development Bank of Singapore	√	√	√
HSBC Ltd.			√
JP Morgan Chase Bank	√		√
Krung Thai Bank	√	√	√
Mashreqbank	√	√	√
Mizuho Corporate Bank	√	√	√
Oman International Bank	√		√
Shinhan Bank	√	√	√
Societe Generale	√	√	√
Sonali Bank	√	√	√
Standard Chartered Bank	√	√	√
State Bank of Mauritius			

Source: Same as Table 1.

Table 7. NPA's while lending to priority sector per cent.

Sector	Public sector bank group	Private sector bank group	Foreign bank group
Priority Sector Advances	9.46	31.22	13.5
Agriculture	16.86	9.31	-
Small Scale Industries	15.14	6.98	2.2
Other Priority Sector	27.47	14.93	11.3

Source: Same as Table 1.

agriculture lending target by many public and private sector banks is due to low capital formation in agriculture resulting in poor credit absorption and write-off of non-performing loans leading to reduction in the outstanding advances in the case of some banks.

MAJOR ISSUES

Preferences of RBI to priority sector advances have created various issues for the Indian banking industry which need quick resolution. These issues are discussed below:

Low profitability

Profitability has been affected by a wide range of factors such as increasing proportion of deposit resources under statutory liquidity pre-emption at lower interest, the shift of savers' preferences to long-term deposits and the incidence of non-performing assets. Though banking is not a high profit area in most countries, profitability has been particularly low in India. One of the important reasons for declining profitability of banks has been their increasing involvement in providing mandatory credit entailing rigid target setting and the concessionality.

High NPAs

Persons who borrow from the bank do not repay the loan. This increases non-performing assets of the banks. Thus priority sector credit has created fear among banks and, discourages them to go slow in disbursement of credit.

Quantitative targets

The concerns for achieving quantitative targets within stipulated time frame irrespective of assessed demand or potential have caused an erosion of the qualitative aspects of lending which have an effect on the viability of the lending institutions.

Government interference

One of the major problems of bank is that the government interferes in the working of the banks especially in public sector banks. Therefore, loans are delivered in the hands of the rich rather than weaker section of the society.

Transaction cost

Sanctioning and monitoring of large number of small advances is time consuming and manpower intensive, thus adding to the transaction cost. The problem is further compounded by the deficiencies in pre-sanction and bunching of applications at the last moment by the sponsoring agencies in the case of lending under poverty alleviation programmes. These deficiencies have resulted in the lowering of the overall quality of credit and the effectiveness of its delivery.

STRATEGIES

Recovery of NPAs

For the recovery of NPAs, banks should follow the following measures: 1) Debt Recovery Tribunal should implement to recover the NPAs; 2) Banks should be very careful in considering settlement compromise proposals; 3) Banks should try to introduce a system of internal audit of sanction of loans before disbursements for large averages.

Rate of interest

Bank should follow the following guidelines of RBI for the rate of interest; 1) In respect of direct agricultural advances, banks should not compound the interest in the case of current dues, that is crop loans and installments should not fall due in respect of term loans, as the agriculturalist do not have any regular source of income other than sale proceeds of their crops; 2) When crop loans or installments under term loans become overdue, banks can add interest to the principal; 3) Where the default is due to genuine reasons, banks should extend the period of loan or reschedule the installments under term loan. Once such a relief has been extended, the overdues become current dues and banks should not compound interest.

Discretionary powers

All Branch Managers of banks should be vested with discretionary powers to sanction proposals from weaker section without interference of the government.

Qualitative targets

Bank should fix quantitative as well as qualitative targets so that viability of the banks can increase.

IMPLICATIONS

The main implication is that although RBI has fixed some targets regarding priority sector advances but many banks are not in position to achieve it. The implicit of the paper is that RBI should carry out strict measures against these banks that are not properly providing priority sector advances. In the era of global recession, our country RBI should redefine priority sector advances.

AREAS OF COMPREHENSIVE FUTURE RESEARCH

The following topics should be given top priority for future research:1) Extent of NPAs from different components of priority sector advances; 2) Rural-Urban gap in NPAs from priority sector advances; 3) Priority sector advances and efficiency of banks.

Conclusion

Thus, the study concludes that priority sector advances of all the banking groups are increasing. Inspite of increasing advances, Indian banks have not achieved some targets fixed by RBI. Lending to priority sector creates many problems for the Indian banks like low profitability, high NPAs, transaction cost etc. It is a need of the hour to find out solutions for these problems otherwise progress of the Indian banks will cease. If the proper priority sector advances are given they will be helpful in reducing the poverty level.

REFERENCES

Chhimpa J (2002). "Incremental NPA: Stem that Inflow", Vinimaya, 23 (3): 18-21.

Gujral N (2003). "NPA Blues and the Securitization Act", Vinimaya, 24(1): 13-23.

Gupta S, Kumar S (2004). "Dimensions and Prospects of Non-performing Assets: Challenges Before the Banking Sector Reforms in the New Millennium", Edited Book Banking in the New Millennium pp. 279-291.

Kumar R (2000). "NPA Management for Better Banking", Proceedings of the Bank Economist Conference 2000 pp. 68-73.

Prasad M, Sinha KK, Prasad KM (2004). "Post-reform Performance of Public Sector Banks with Special Reference to Non-performance Assets", Edited Book Banking in the New Millennium pp. 259-267.

Passah PM (2002). "Banking and Financial Sector Reforms in India – Rationale, Progress, Efficacy and Future Agenda" Edited book, Banking and Financial Sector Reforms in India New Delhi : Deep and Deep Publ. pp. 18-37.

Mujumdar NA (2001). "The New Architecture of the Rural Credit System", Prof. M.L. Dantwala Monograph Series, Department of Economics, University of Mumbai, of Indian Society of Agricultural Marketing at Vizag (A.P.)"

Samal B (2002). "The NPA Overhung: Magnitude, Solution and Legal Reforms", Vinimaya 23(3): 12-17.

Vashisht AK (2004). 'Commercial Banking in the Globalized Environment', Political Economy J. India 13(1& 2): 1-10.

12

An empirical assessment of the determinants of bank profitability in Nigeria: Bank characteristics panel evidence

Ani, W. U.[1]*, Ugwunta, D. O.[2], Ezeudu, I. J.[1] and Ugwuanyi, G. O.[3]

[1]Department of Banking and Finance, Michael Okpara University of Agriculture, Umudike, Abia State, Nigeria.
[2]Department of Banking and Finance, The Renaissance University, Enugu, Nigeria.
[3]Department of Accountancy, Institute of Management and Technology, Enugu, Nigeria.

Given the recent developments in the Nigerian banking industry, only a profitable banking sector is better able to withstand negative shocks and contribute to the stability of the financial system. This assertion compels an in depth investigation of the determinants of the profitability of deposit money banks in Nigeria. Our data set is made up of 147 bank level observations over a 10-year period from 2001 to 2010 in respect of 15 banks that satisfied the study requirements. Data were obtained from the annual reports and accounts of the sampled banks. Pooled OLS (Pooled ordinary least square) stated in a multiple regression form was used to estimate the coefficients. Major outcomes of the analysis include that increase in size (higher total assets) may not necessarily lead to higher profits due to diseconomies of scale; higher capital-assets ratio and loans and advances contribute strongly to bank profitability. Overall, the paper suggests bank size, capital and asset composition as the major endogenous determinants of bank profitability in Nigeria.

Key words: Profitability, bank size, asset composition, liquidity, capital adequacy.

INTRODUCTION

A profitable banking sector is better able to withstand negative shocks and contribute to the stability of the financial system. The profitability of a financial institution is affected by numerous factors. These factors include elements internal to each financial institution and several important external forces shaping earnings performance. In Nigeria, years 2004 and 2005 witnessed a forced consolidation exercise with a regulatory option of mergers and acquisitions. This exercise brought about a landmark change in the number of Nigerian banks as the banking system shrank to only twenty five banks from a whooping eighty nine banks before the consolidation exercise. It is therefore important to understand the determinants of banking sector profitability in Nigeria. This is essentially important in the light of the above notable changes that have occurred in the operating environment of banks in

*Corresponding author. E-mail: doctorani2010@gmail.com.

In banking, the determinants of profitability are well observed and explored as it is increasingly important to strengthen the foundations of domestic financial system as a way to buildup flexibility for capital flow volatility. In the past, researchers investigated the determinants of profitability in the banking sector. A good number of researchers considered only the banking characteristics, whereas others included the financial structure and macroeconomic factors as well. In all these studies, contributions had been made in determining the factors that shape the profitability of banks. More recent studies distinguish between managerial (internal) and environmental (external) factors that affect bank profitability. Literature has argued that financial market structure and entry barriers constitute the main external force driving bank profits. Financial market structure (represented by regulatory conditions or concentration) is one of the external influences that affect bank profitability; others include trade interdependence, economic growth, inflation, market interest rates and ownership structure. The internal factors according to past studies include capital ratio, credit risk, productivity growth and size of the bank (Smirlock, 1985; Bourke, 1989; Molyneux and Thornton, 1992; Stienherr and Huveneers, 1994).

A number of other studies have examined bank profitability in an effort to isolate the factors that account for differences in bank profitability. Studies have linked bank earnings and various aspects of bank operating performance to profitability. A second set of studies focused on the relationship between bank earnings performance and balance sheet structure and profitability. A third body of literature examined the impact of regulatory and macroeconomic factors on overall bank profitability. The main conclusion emerging from past studies is that internal factors explain a large proportion of banks profitability; nevertheless external factors have also had an impact on bank profitability. Overall, operational efficiency is the major factor in determining performance across banks. Among the internal factors are the management controllable factors which are the bank specific financial ratios representing cost efficiency, liquidity, asset quality, and capital adequacy. The objective of this paper accordingly is to determine the management controllable factors that determine bank's profitability in the context of the Nigerian banking industry using industrial data set from 2000 to 2010.

This paper contributes to literature in a unique way. Our dataset, made up of 147 bank level observations consist of 71.43% of banks operating in Nigeria. This enhances the generalization of our result to all the banks operating in Nigeria before and after the major changes in the Nigerian banking environment. The rest of the paper is divided as follows. Highlights on the review of related literature are presented. Second, Methodological issues are discussed, presentation of the data and results are then analysed. Finally, conclusions.

LITERATURE REVIEW

In principle a bank's capacity to absorb unforeseen losses determines its level of risk (Goddard et al., 2004). Several ratios are commonly used to proxy for risk, including the CAR and the liquidity ratio. In theory an excessively high CAR could signify that a bank is operating over-cautiously and ignoring potentially profitable investment opportunities. A bank holding a relatively high proportion of liquid assets is unlikely to earn high profits, but is also less exposed to risk; therefore shareholders should be willing to accept a lower return on equity (Goddard et al., 2004). An overview of previous studies indicates various ways that profitability was examined. Some studies were country specific and few of them considered panel of countries reviewing the determinants of profitability. Such empirical studies on bank profitability literature that focused mainly on specific countries include those of the US (Berger, 1995) Greece (Kosmidou, 2006); Australia (Pasiouras et al., 2005), Malaysia (Guru et al., 1999); Colombia (Barajas et al., 1999); and Tunisia (Naceur, 2003). Molyneux and Thorton (1992) were the first to investigate a multi-country setting by examining the determinants of bank profitability for a panel of European countries. This is followed by the study of Abreu and Mendes (2000), Staikouras and Wood (2003), and Pasiouras et al. (2005). Other multi-country studies include those of Hassan and Bashir (2003), who examined profitability for a sample of Islamic banks from 21 countries; and Demirguc-Kunt and Huizinga (1999) who considered a comprehensive set of bank specific characteristics, as well as macroeconomic conditions, taxation, regulations, financial structure and legal indicators to examine the determinants of bank net interest margins in over 80 countries. The main conclusion emerging from these studies is that internal factors explain a large proportion of banks profitability; nevertheless external factors have also had an impact on their performance.

The profitability of European banks during the 1990s was investigated by Goddard et al. (2004) using cross-sectional, pooled cross-sectional time-series and dynamic panel models. Their model for the determinant of profitability incorporates size, diversification, risk and ownership type, as well as dynamic effects. They found that despite intensifying competition there is significant persistence of abnormal profit from year to year. The evidence for any consistent or systematic size–profitability relationship is relatively weak. The relationship between the importance of off-balance-sheet business in a bank's portfolio and profitability is positive for the UK, but either neutral or negative elsewhere. The relationship between the capital–assets ratio and profitability is positive.

Javaid et al. (2011) analyzed the determinants of top 10 banks' profitability in Pakistan over the period 2004 to 2008. They focused on the internal factors only. Javaid et al. (2011) used the pooled ordinary least square (POLS) method to investigate the impact of assets, loans, equity, and deposits on one of the major profitability indicator of banks which is return on asset (ROA). The empirical results found strong evidence that these variables have a strong influence on profitability. How-ever, the results show that higher total assets may not necessarily lead to higher profits due to diseconomies of scales. Also, higher loans contribute towards profitability but their impact is not significant. Equity and deposits have significant impact on profitability.

Imad et al. (2011) studied a balanced panel dataset of Jordanian banks for the purpose of investigating the nature of the relationship between the profitability of banks and the characteristics of internal and external factors for 10 banks over the period 2001 to 2010. Using two measures of bank's profitability: the rate of return on assets (ROA) and the rate of return on equity (ROE), the results show that the Jordanian bank's characteristics explain a significant part of the variation in bank profitability. High Jordanian bank profitability tends to be associated with well-capitalized banks, high lending activities, low credit risk, and the efficiency of cost management. Results also show that the estimated effect of size did not support the significant scale economies for Jordanian banks. Due to the fact that some of the differential slope coefficients are statistically signifycant, they conclude that the estimation results indicate that individual effects on the profitability are present.

Scott and Arias (2011) developed an appro-priate econometric model whereby the primary deter-minants of profitability of the top five bank holding companies in the United States could be examined and understood. The econometric model was based on internal aspects of the banking organizations as they relate to their return on assets and external aspects of the environment in which they compete as measured by growth in GDP was developed based on guidance provided by economists and industry experts to determine the impact of the external national economy of these five leading banks according to their size as measured by total assets. The results show that profitability determinants for the banking industry include positive relationship between the return on equity and capital to asset ratio as well as the annual percentage changes in the external per capita income.

In another dimension, Gull et al. (2011) examined the relationship between bank-specific and macro-economic characteristics over bank profitability by using data of top fifteen Pakistani commercial banks over the period 2005 to 2009. The paper used the pooled ordinary least square (POLS) method to investigate the impact of assets, loans, equity, deposits, economic growth, inflation and market capitalization on major profitability indicators that is, return on asset (ROA), return on equity (ROE), return on capital employed (ROCE) and net interest margin (NIM) separately. The empirical results showed strong evidence that both internal and external factors have a strong influence on the profitability.

Seven years earlier, Goddard et al. (2004) had investigated the profitability of European banks during the 1990s using cross-sectional, pooled cross-sectional time-series and dynamic panel models. Models for the determinants of profitability incorporate size, diversification, risk and ownership type, as well as dynamic effects. They found that despite intensifying competition there was significant persistence of abnormal profit from year to year. Their results suggests that evidence for any consistent or systematic size–profitability relationship is relatively weak; the relationship between the importance of off-balance-sheet business in a bank's portfolio and profitability is positive for the UK, but either neutral or negative elsewhere. Furthermore the relationship between the capital–assets ratio and profitability was positive.

In a study on the determinants of the Tunisian banking industry profitability for 10 banks in Tunisia for the period 1980 to 2000, Naceur (2003) observed that high net interest margin and profitability are likely to be associated with banks with high amount of capital and large overheads. Further the paper also noted that other determinants such as loans has positive and bank size has negative impact on profitability.

Naceur and Goaied (2001) investigated the impact of banks' characteristics, financial structure and macro-economic indicators on banks' net interest margins and profitability in the Tunisian banking industry from 1980 to 2000. Individual bank characteristics explain a substantial part of the within-country variation in bank interest margins and net profitability. High net interest margin and profitability tend to be associated with banks that hold a relatively high amount of capital, and with large overheads. Size is found to impact negatively on profitability which implies that Tunisian banks are operating above their optimum level.

METHODOLOGICAL FRAMEWORKS

The large body of empirical literature, as earlier highlighted, propose that the determinants of bank profitability can be divided into two groups; internal and external factors. This study is limited to the internal drivers of bank profitability. Return on asset (ROA) was used as the major metric for measuring profitability while the endogenous drivers of bank profitability were used as the independent variables. Our sample consists of 15 deposit money banks, selected through a non-probabilistic sampling method (purposive sampling). The deposit money banks selected include stand-alone banks and banks that retained their brand names after the 2005 concluded bank consolidation exercise that have complete dataset for the period under review. The data set covers a 10-years period from 2001 to 2010 for fifteen Nigerian deposit money banks yielding 147 observations. Data concerning total asset, net profit, total loans and advances, total equity were obtained from the sampled banks annual reports of various years. The basic estimation strategy involved pooling the observations across the banking industry and estimating the determinants of bank profitability by means of regression analysis. The symbolic form of the model followed the earlier studies of Gull et al. (2011) and Javaid et al. (2011) and is as stated as follows:

$$Y_t = \beta_0 + \beta_1 X1_t + \beta_2 X2_t + \beta_3 X3_t + u_t$$

Where;

Y_t = ROA represents (return on asset); ROE (return on equity); NIM (net interest margin) for bank *i* at time *t*.
$X1_t$ = Log (TA) represents natural logarithm of total asset for bank *i* at time *t*.
$X2_t$ = TE/TA represents ratio of total equity to total asset for bank i at time *t*.
$X3_t$ = TL/TA represents ratio of total loans to total asset for bank i *at* time *t*.
u_t = Error term.

The advantage of pooling is that more reliable estimates of the parameters in the model can be obtained. It is a valid procedure where the relationship between the variables is stable across cross-section units and is as applied by Javaid et al. (2011) and Gull et al. (2011). Our data set gives evidence that Nigerian banks show similar response to cyclical movements. Therefore, we believed that the relationship between profitability and independent variables are stable across banks in 147 observations and that is why we applied POLS estimation method.

Table 1. Descriptive statistics.

	Mean	Std. deviation	N
ROA	.2299	1.87547	147
NLTA	7.4883	1.14236	147
TETA	3.5648	29.89715	147
TLATA	6.5539	53.65346	147

Source: Authors' SPSS output.

Endogenous drivers of bank profitability as detailed as follows were factored into the model.

Total assets (TA)

Total assets determine the size of a bank. Size is used to capture the fact that larger banks are better placed than smaller banks in harnessing economies of scale in transactions to the plain effect that they will tend to enjoy a higher level of profit. In most of the finance literature, the total assets of the banks are used as a proxy for bank size. Consequently, a positive relationship is expected between size and profits. Molyneux and Thornton (1992), Bikker and Hu (2002) and Goddard et al. (2004) find size to be positively related to profitability. The size of the bank is included as an independent variable in this study to account for size related economies and/or diseconomies of scale. However, since the dependent variable in the model (ROA) was deflated by total assets it would be appropriate to take the natural logarithm total assets before including it in the model to reduce the scale effect of numbers and be consistent with other ratios.

Total equity (TE) to total assets (TA)

Capital – assets ratio is taken as the ratio of equity capital to total assets. It's interesting to note that higher capital level breeds higher profitability level since by having more capital, a bank can easily adhere to regulatory capital standards so that excess capital can be provided as loans (Berger, 1995). The capital ratio (TE/TA), which is measured by total equity over total asset, reveals capital adequacy and should capture the general safety and soundness of the financial institution (Gull, 2011). It indicates the ability of a bank to absorb losses and handle risk exposure for shareholders. Previous studies have found a positive relationship between TE/TA and profitability (Hassan and Bashir, 2004). TE/TA is expected to have a positive relation with performance because well capitalized banks are less risky and more profitable (Bourke, 1989). TE/TA is included as an independent variable to examine banking profitability.

Total loans and advances (TL&A) to total assets (TA)

Asset composition of loans and advances are the main source of income and are expected to have a positive impact on bank performance. Other things constant, the more deposits are transformed into loans, the higher the interest margin and profits. However, if a bank needs to increase risk to have a higher loan-to-asset ratio, then profits may decrease. In addition, as bank loans and advances are the principal source of income, we expect that non-interest bearing assets impact negatively on profits (Gul et al., 2011). Asset composition (TL&A/TA), which is explained by total loans divided by total asset, provides a measure of income source and measures the liquidity of bank assets tied to loans (Javaid et al., 2011: 3798). TL/TA is included in the study of profitability as an independent variable to determine the impact of loans on banks' profitability.

Profitability is primarily measured by return on assets. The details of these metrics follow in the succeeding section. The ROA is a functional indicator of bank's profitability. It is a ratio calculated by dividing net income by total assets. ROA shows the profit earned per dollar of assets which reflects bank's management ability to utilize the bank's financial and real investment resources to generate profits (Naceur, 2003).

DATA AND RESULTS

The banks in the Nigerian banking industry include banks with very different sizes and business mixes as evidenced by the descriptive statistics shown in Table 1.

Table 1 shows the descriptive statistics for the variables. ROA (profitability), size (natural log of total asset), asset composition (ratio of total loans and advances to total asset) and capital adequacy (ratio of total equity to total asset) have a positive mean value which ranges from 0.2299 for profitability to 7.4883 in size. The banks in the Nigerian banking industry include banks with varying sizes and business mixes. Capital adequacy and asset composition has the highest standard deviation of 29.89 and 53.65 respectively. This indicates that the observations in the data set are widely dispersed from the mean. It means that all the banks in the industry are consistent with increase in total equity as a result of the 2005 forced consolidation by the regulatory authority in Nigeria. This also implies that the consolidation exercise provided the banks with a lot of loanable funds which resulted in increased loans and advances. Thus there is greater variation in the data set of capital adequacy and loans and advances because of the size differences of deposit money banks operating in the Nigerian banking industry. Relationships among the study variables were tested using Pearson correlation and the outcomes are presented in Table 2.

Model specification involves the determination of the dependent and explanatory variables which were included in the model and the expectations about the sign and the size of the parameters of the function (Koutsoyiannis, 2003; Onwumere, 2008).

The correlation matrix presented in Table 2 shows that size has a weak negative relationship with profitability (ROA) at -14.7%. This means that bigger banks have lower ROA. Capital adequacy and asset composition have a positive relationship with profitability. The strength of their relationship is indeed strong at 88.7 and 92.8% for capital adequacy and asset composition respectively. Although size has a negative relationship with profitability, the one tailed significance level 5% shows that all the independent variables are statistically significant. This result is strengthened as P* of 0.05 > .038, .000 and .000 for size capital adequacy and asset mix.

The size (nLog of total asset) has a significant negative relationship with profitability. This significant negative

Table 2. Correlations.

		ROA	NLTA	TETA	TLTA
Pearson correlation	ROA	1.000			
	nLogTA	-.147*	1.000		
	TETA	.887*	-.165	1.000	
	TLTA	.928*	-.164	.995	1.000
Significant (1-tailed)	ROA		.038	.000	.000
	NLTA	.038	.	.023	.024
	TETA	.000	.023	.	.000
	TLTA	.000	.024	.000	.

Source: Authors' SPSS output. * are significant at 5%.

Table 3. Regression coefficient.

Model		Unstandardized coefficient		Standardized coefficient	T	Sig.
		B	Std. error	Beta		
1	Constant	-.006	.051		-.124	.901
	nLogTA	.001	.007	.001	.146	.884
	TE/TA	-.234	.003	-3.735	-92.089	.000
	TL/TA	.162	.001	4.645	114.533	.000

R^2 =. 999; Adj. R^2 =. 998; Durbin Watson = 1.8; Sig. F-change = .000
Source: Authors' SPSS output.

relationship shows that the size of a bank could significantly affect the profitability of the bank negatively. This is in consonance with the findings of Berger et al. (1987), Boyd and Runkle (1993), Bourke (1989), Naceur (2003) and Javaid et al. (2011).

Asset composition (ratio of total loans and advances to total asset) shows a positive and significant relationship with profitability. This suggests that with increase in inflation in the economy, the banks interest rate on all kinds of advances would increase and in this way the bank's interest earnings would show significant increase. Assuming other variables remains constant, the higher the rate of transforming deposits into loans, the higher the profitability of the bank. Thus a positive relationship between the loans and advances of a bank with profitability is as expected and is as documented by Imad et al. (2011). This result is consistent with the study of Athanasoglou et al. (2006). Also, Abreu and Mendes (2000) found a significant and positive relationship between asset composition and profitability.

Capital adequacy (ratio of total equity total asset) shows a positive correlation with profitability (ROA). In the presence of asymmetric information and bankruptcy costs, the way the assets are funded could affect the banks value. A well-capitalized bank may send a good signal to the market regarding its performance (Imad et al., 2011). Our result is in consonance with the findings of (Goddard et al., 2004) that investigated profitability of European banks profitability.

The relatively high coefficient of multiple determination suggest that with a conservative coefficient of multiple determination of R^2 = 0.998 (Table 3), the model summary shows that 99.8% of the variations in the profitability of Nigerian banks are explained by the banks internal factors in our model. These internal factors are the management controllable factors, the bank specific financial ratios representing size, asset composition and quality, and capital adequacy.

The regression result presented in Table 3 reveals that not only do capital adequacy and asset composition have strong positive relationships with bank profitability, they also impacts significantly on bank profitability. Given that the t-Statistics of 92.089 and 114.533 > t* 2, we confirm a statistical significant impact of capital adequacy and asset composition captured as ratios of total equity and total loans and advances to total asset. This confirmation is strengthened with the perfect significance value of 0.000 < the 0.05 significance value. Our result is in line with the findings of Javaid et al. (2011), Imad et al. (2011), Gull et al. (2011), Goddard et al. (2004) and Naceur (2003) whose empirical results found strong evidence that loans and equity are positively related and have strong influences on profitability.

Conclusion

Our econometric analysis revealed major outcomes in

bank profitability in Nigeria. The major outcome of this study is that higher total assets may not necessarily lead to higher profits. The negative coefficient of size indicates that this relation might be negative due to diseconomies of scale suffered by banks due to uncontrollable increased size. Higher loans and advances contribute towards profitability. This reveals that more dependence on one major asset, may lead to profitability but with less significant impact on overall profitability. Overall we conclude that asset composition and capital adequacy are the major endogenous factors under the control of management that determines the profitability of banks in Nigeria.

Banks in Nigeria should endeavor to manage adequately the liquidity and profitability trade-off while diversifying their asset in a way to remain profitable and sustainable. However, further research is needed to clear the grey areas especially over a longer period of time. In addition variables such as cost efficiency, credit risk, and exogenous factors such as inflation, GDP and market concentration could also be incorporated to ascertain the determinants of bank profitability in Nigeria.

REFERENCES

Abreu M, Mendes V (2000). Commercial Bank Interest Margins and Profitability: Evidence for Some EU Countries, presented on the 50th International Altantic Economic Conference. (www.iaes.org/conferences/past/charleston_50/prelim_program/index.htm)

Alkassim FA (2005). "The profitability of Islamic and conventional banking in the GCC countries: A comparative study. www.failaka.com/downloads/Profitability_Islamic_Banking.pdf. Accessed 09/08/11

Angbazo, L. (1997), "Commercial Bank Net Interest Margins, Default Risk, Interest-rate Risk and Off-Balance Sheet Banking." J. Bank. Financ. 21(1):55-87.

Athanasoglou PP, Delis MD, Staikouras CK (2006). "Determinants of Bank Profitability in the South Eastern European Region" Munich Personal RePEc Archive MPRA Paper No. 10274, http://mpra.ub.uni-muenchen.de/10274. Accessed 25/09/11.

Badola BS, Verma R (2006). "Determinants of Profitability of Banks in India: A Multivariate Analysis" Delhi Business Review 7(2):79-88.

Barajas A, Steiner R, Salazar N (1999). "Interest Spreads in Banking in Colombia 1974–96" IMF Staff Papers 46:196-224.

Berger A (1995). "The Relationship between Capital and Earnings in Banking," J. Money Credit Bank. 27:432-456.

Bashir A (2000). Determinants of Profitability and Rates of Return Margins in Islamic Banks: Some Evidence from Middle East. Paper presented at ERF's Seventh Annual Conference, 26-29 October 2000, Amman, Jordan.

Berger A, Hanweck G, Humphrey D (1987). "Competitive Viability in Banking: Scale, Scope and Product Mix Economies," J. Monetary Econ. 20:501-520.

Bikker JA, Hu H (2002). "Cyclical Patterns in Profits, Provisioning and Lending of Banks and Procyclicality of the New Basle Capital Requirements", BNL Quart. Rev. 221:143-175.

Bourke P (1989). 'Concentration and Other Determinants of Bank Profitability in Europe, North America, and Australia', J. Bank. Financ. 13(1):65-79.

Boyd JH, Runkle DE (1993). "Size and Performance of Banking Firms. Testing the Predictions of Theory," J. Monet. Econ. 31:47-67.

Demirguc-Kunt A, Huizinga H (1997). Determinants of Commercial Bank Interest Margins and Profitability: Some International Evidence. Working Paper, Development Research Group, World Bank, Washington D.C.

Fraker GT (2006). Using Economic Value Added (EVE) to Measure and Improve Bank Perfromance. RMA-Arizona Chapter. Online available at: http://www.maaz.org/pictures/measuringbankperformance.pdf. Accessed 21/09/11.

Goddard J, Molyneux P, Wilson JOS (2004). "The Profitability of European Banks: ACross-Sectional and Dynamic Panel Analysis" The Manchester School 72(3):363-381.

Goddard J, Molyneux P, Wilson JOS (2004). "Dynamics of Growth and Profitability in Banking" J. Money Credit Bank. 36:1069-1090.

Gull S, Irshad F, Zaman K (2011). "Factors Affecting Bank Profitability in Pakistan" Romanian Econ. J. 14(39):61-87.

Guru BK, Staunton J, Balashanmugam B (1999). Determinants of Commercial Bank Profitability in Malaysia. University Multimedia Working Papers, Kuala Lumpur, Malaysia. Available at: http://afbc.banking.unsw.edu.au/afbc/papers/guru.pdf Accessed: 21/09/11.

Hassan MK, Bashir AH (2003). Determinants of Islamic Banking Profitability. Paper presented at International Seminar on Islamic Wealth Creation on 7-9 July 2003, organized by IRTI-Islamic Development Bank and Centre for Middle Eastern and Islamic Studies, University of Durham, United Kingdom.

Imad Ramadan Z, Qais Kilani A, Thair Kaddumi A (2011). "Determinants of Bank Profitability: Evidence from Jordan, Int. J. Acad. Res. 3(4):180-191.

Javaid S, Anwar J, Zaman K, Ghafoor A (2011) Determinants of Bank Profitability in Pakistan: Internal Factor Analysis, J. Yasar Univ. 23(6):3794-3804.

Kosmidou KF, Pasiouras MD, Zoponoudis C (2003). Assessing Performance Factors in the UK Banking Sector: A Multicriteria Methodology", paper presented at the 4th annual conference of International Economics and Finance Society on "Finance and the International Economy", 28-29 November, London.

Koutsoyiannis A (2003). Theory of Econometrics, 2nd ed. London, Palmgrave Publishers.

Molyneux P, Thorton J (1992). "Determinants of European Bank Profitability; A Note" J. Bank. Financ. 16:1173-1178.

Naceur SB (2003). 'The Determinants of the Tunisian Banking Industry Profitability: Panel Evidence,' Universite Libre de Tunis Working Papers.

Naceur SB, Goaied M (2001). "The Determinants of Commercial Bank Interest Margin and Profitability: Evidence from Tunisia" Working paper 856365 htpp://www.papers.ssrn.com/sol3/papers.cfm. Accessed 25/9/11.

Onwumere JUJ (2008). Business and Economic Research Methods, Enugu, Vougasen Limited.

Scott JW, Arias JC (2011). "Banking Profitability Determinants" Bus. Intell. J. 4(2):209-230.

Pasiouras F, Kosmidou K, Gaganis Ch. (2005), A pooled study of the internal and external determinants of Australian banks profits and margins, Working Paper, Financial Engineering Laboratory, Department of Production Engineering and Management, Technical University of Crete.

Smirlock M (1985). 'Evidence of the (non) Relationship Between Concentration and Profitability in Banking', J. Money Credit Bank. 17(1):69-83.

Stienherr A, Huveneers Ch. (1994). "On the Performance of Differently Regulated Financial Institutions: Some Empirical Evidence", J. Bank. Financ. 18(2):271-306.

Analysis of the effectiveness of capital expenditure budgeting in the local government system of Ondo State, Nigeria

Olurankinse Felix

Department of Accounting, Adekunle Ajasin University, Akungba – Akoko, Ondo State, Nigeria.
E-mail: olurankinsefelix@yahoo.com.

Year in year out, Nigerians always hear of billions and trillions of naira budgeted as capital expenditure in our annual budget. This amount undoubtedly continues to increase with each passing year, but the society is always at a loss as to where the money was invested. There seems to be wide disparity between budget proposal and accomplishment. The government at all levels are accused of disregard for budgetary provisions, late passage of budget, involvement in extra-budgetary activities, late release of capital vote and selective implementation of budget. This paper therefore investigates whether or not there is a significant difference between the mean of budgeted capital and expended capital using some infrastructures in some selected local government. The paper adopts a basic research approach where data were obtained from secondary sources, mainly from published materials which include annual financial statements and publication of approved budget estimates covering the period of study. A stratified random sampling was adopted in selecting the sample. A method of descriptive analysis was used in analyzing the data. The method includes measures of central tendencies and test of equality among the means of budgeted capital and expended expenditure on each project per local government. This test uses the student t-test of differences of means. The outcome of the paper shows that there was a positive and significant relationship between budgeted capital and actual expenditure. The implication of this is that an increase in budgeted capital will lead to an increase in capital expenditure on that infrastructure.

Key words: Infrastructures, budgeted capital, expended capital, disparity, local government areas.

INTRODUCTION

One of the reasons why government engage in budgeting is scarcity of resources which always leads to claims and demands outweighing the resources to satisfy them. There are different types of resource scarcity that the government can face, however, irrespective of the type of scarcity facing the government; choice must still be made about what constitutes government priorities at any particular period (Olurankinse, 2010).

Onimode (1999) was of the opinion that the choice should be made through democratic budgeting which allows the participation of the people in the determination of government priorities. However, in practice, the choice that is made is not of the people but of the dominant individuals within and outside government. The desire and expectations of the citizens from their government is that available resources be used efficiently and effectively to provide the highest level of public services possible. By measuring its level, efficiency and outcomes of a programme's effort, performance indicators can guide government resource allocation and communicate to the people, the goods, objectives and effectiveness of public programmes.

The effectiveness of capital expenditure is measured in terms of what proportion of the budget was actually spent and these calls for comparison between the amount set aside for a particular project in the annual budget and the actual amount of the physical infrastructures on ground. The need for this comparison is very crucial as it helps to measure deviation so as to take necessary control and to forestall further wastages and extravagant spending. (Adubi, 2002)

CONCEPTUAL FRAMEWORK

There have been views that the experience of public sector failure in Nigeria is not an indictment of fiscal management theory, but a reflection of the political and economic environment resulting from the absence of fiscal transparency and probity in the management of government finances. Kopts and Craig (1998) defined fiscal transparency as openness toward the public at a large about government structure and function, fiscal policy intentions, public sector accounts and projections." According to Akintoye (2008), It involves ready access to reliable comprehensive, timely, understandable and internationally comparable information on government activities. Today, because of scarce resources, the management of money is more important than ever for public and private entities, budgeting plays an enormous role in controlling operations efficiently and effectively.

Effectiveness can be explained in terms of what is achieved and the number of goods and services produced. It is about whether targets are met or not. Performing effectively means that the right work is being completed. If a team is working really hard but not delivering what is needed, then they are not effective.

Effectiveness is measured by setting out clear objectives before work starts and then evaluating whether the objectives have been met or not (Olofin, 2003).

There are constitutional provisions spelling out the financial power of each arm of government. For instance, the 1999 Nigerian constitution section 81 (1) rests all executive powers in the chairman requiring him to prepare estimate of the revenue and expenditures of local government for the next financial year and lay them before the councilors for authorization before spending can take place. Under the same constitution, only the legislative arm has the power to authorize expenditure of public funds (Bamori, 2004).

In order to ensure financial prudence and accountability, the constitution provides for the annual auditing of the public accounts. The audited accounts of the local government councils are submitted to the public account committee of the state assembly for consideration. It is important that the priorities of government are established as this will drive the most appropriate measures to be used and lead to the best effectiveness. If institutions lead to a well conceived budget, the quality of expenditures depends on four conditions: Delivery units receiving budgeted funds on time; adequate processes and controls with respect to the use of these resources; procurement methods generating value for money and government accountable for its managements of public funds (Ola and Effiong, 1999).

An effective mechanism to make progress on this front would be to develop financial reporting information which will be useful for all managers in the government. Making budget process more responsive to priorities required the establishment of priorities across expenditure. This according to Asiodu (2000) is based on three policy elements namely:

(a) Fiscal rules applying variously to limits on budget deficit, expenditures, taxes, debts etc.
(b) Strengthening the medium term perspectives of the budget process by identifying both the current and future impact and cost associated with spending programme.
(c) Aligning budget allocation with policy priorities to reduce budget fragmentation.

Having identified the different entities responsible and involve in the budgetary process, the following are recipes for bringing about effective execution of the budget:

(i) There must be competent and dedicated expert who should collect, process, analyses and apply data adequately to the budgetary process;
(ii) There must be effective and strong communication network in the entire budgetary process.
(iii) All involve in the planning in budgetary process should have regard for law and order, laid-down rules and regulations;
(iv) There should be honesty of purpose, respect for each view points and less suspicious of each other view point and action;
(v) Datelines, conditions and standards set for each of the units involves in the budgetary process should be standardized and not having double or triple standards;
(vi) The critical role of the legislature in the budget process is the authorization of expenditure proposed by the chief executive and legislature of fiscal measure to generate revenue. Therefore, debates and final consideration by the legislature should be objective and less partisan. It should be noted however, that political consideration cannot be completely removed from budgetary process.
(vii) Since the legislature have the power of the purse, it should not take advantage of such powers to unduly delay the authorization of the proposed expenditure by the chief executive of any of the three tiers of government.
(viii) The budgetary personnel must have the capability through some built- in mechanism to check certain uncertainties in the economy, particularly, in view of the prevailing economic conditions. Political will is sometimes lacking to do this.
(ix) There must be an up- to –date knowledge of the

progress and weaknesses of implementation processes. If up- to- date reports are not available, it becomes difficult to maintain effectiveness in the economy.
(x) The chief executive should bear in mind always his constituency that is, the entire local government area. Therefore, his proposed policies and the execution of such policies should be non-partisans.
(xi) Infrequent revisions of plans and targets could create uncertainties and if the economy is not kept in control, it could be disastrous for future planning and budgeting.
(xii) On the whole, attitude of justice, fairness and willingness to work together are crucial to the effective and successful implementation of budget. Planning and budgetary process, no matter how sophisticated the model adopted, will not work except those involved in all these processes are dedicated, diligent and honest in their respective roles.

The capital budget is largely concerned with the creation of long-term assets" (World Bank Institute, 2008). One test of a capital outlay is whether it adds substantially to the value of the assets of government (Olurankinse, 2011). It is one most appropriate means for planning for capital projects; supported by a capital improvement program. The term capital improvement refers to projects of relatively large size, nature and/or long life usually a minimum of fifteen to twenty years. Such expenditures are designed to provide new or additional governments facilities for public services. Since the objective is to provide major public facilities that have a relatively long life within the limits of available public resources, capital budgeting should involve planning, programming and formulation of policies in terms of the desired levels of public service to be provided goals and objectives. These goals and objectives should be related to population and economic levels and economic trends and projections to ascertain future demands for public services and facilities (Adubi and Oladapo, 2005).

MATERIALS AND METHODS

The study is a time series analysis and so a survey design was used. The population for this paper consists of the eighteen local governments in Ondo state. To reduce data to a manageable proportion, a stratified random sampling approach was adopted in selecting the sample. Data were obtained through secondary source, mainly from annual financial statements and publication of approved budget estimates from nine local governments. The use of student t-test of differences of means was employed in analyzing the data. The following local government areas of Ondo State were sampled:

i. Ondo West Local Government Area (NDW).
ii. Idanre Local Government Area (IDR).
iii. Ile-Oluji Local Government Area (LEL).
iv. Akure South Local Government Area (AKS).
v. Akoko Northwest Local Government Area (AKNW). vii. Okitipupa Local Government Area (KTP).
viii. Owo Local Government Area (WWW).

Model specification

The broad objective of this study is to find out if there is a significant difference between budgeted capital expenditure and the actual expenditure on some infrastructures with a view to determining their level of effectiveness. The research hypothesis can be summarized as finding the proportions of the budgeted capital actually spent on project. These projects are Education, Health, Agriculture and Social Development and Culture. This analysis was carried out using data from nine local government areas for the period of 12 years. This, therefore, calls for a construction of a microeconomic model which can be specified as follows:

$$PRO_{ni} = f(CBA_{ni}) \quad (1)$$

Where PRO = Particular capital project value observed, CBA = Capital Budget Allocation on the particular project, n = period = 1999 to 2010, i = individual local government. The projects are:

VEDM = Value of educational materials.
VHE – Value of health equipment.
VAI = Value of agricultural inputs.
VSDCF = Value of social development and cultural facilities.
U = Stochastic (random) error term.
i = 1, 2, 3, ..., 9 = the 9 local government areas.
The model is expressed exclusively as:

$$PRO_{ni} = \alpha_{oi} + \alpha_{1i}CBA \quad (2)$$

The model in Equation (2) is therefore a micro-determinant model where the parameters (α_1) are propensities. That is; αo = constant term, an autonomous determinant of capital Project. This may be termed as those factors (legal or illegal) that do determine capital project implementation outside the budgeted allocation for the project. α_1 = The parameter that measures the marginal propensity to spend budgeted allocation on education. α_2 = Parameter measuring the marginal propensity to spend budgeted allocation on Health. α_3 = Parameter measuring the marginal propensity to spend on Agriculture. α_4= Parameter measuring marginal propensity to spend budgeted allocation on social development and cultural facilities.

Marginal propensity is the rate of change in a variable with respect to unit increase in another variable. For the purpose of this paper, it can be defined as the rate of change in capital budget allocation with respect to changes in each of the projects. That is, what proportion of a unit increase in capital budget allocation will be devoted to each of the projects in the foregoing. It is therefore the first derivatives of Equation (1) with respect to each variable.

Estimation technique

This study adopts one method of analysis, namely descriptive techniques. The descriptive analysis include measures of central tendencies, mean, median, mode and the test of equality among the means of budgeted capital allocation and expended capital on each project per local government. This test uses the student t-test of differences of means. The formula for the t-test is given as:

$$t = \frac{\bar{X_1} - \bar{X_2}}{\sqrt{\delta\ 1/N_1 + 1/N_2}} \qquad \text{where } \delta = \sqrt{\frac{N_1\delta_1^2 + N_2\delta_2^2}{N_1 + N_2 - 2}}$$

ANALYSIS AND RESULTS

The result of the data is presented in Tables 1.

Table 1. t-test of equality of means.

	VEDM	VHE	VAI	VSDCF
Ondo West				
Exp. Mean	9.808	24.04	17.96	19.78
Obs. Mean	2.436	50.46	12.61	5.77
t-stat.	3.053	0.97	1.63	2.25
Prob.	0.005	0.340	0.13	0.03
Akoko N.W				
Exp. Mean	4.05	53.95	15.27	6.69
Obs. Mean	56.4	25.06	5.73	4.17
t-stat.	0.94	0.89	1.41	0.77
Prob.	4.05	0.38	0.17	0.45
Akoko S.W				
Exp. Mean	25.44	24.03	2.08	146.65
Obs. Mean	25.45	19.38	6.302	70.89
t-stat.	0.0003	0.369	0.782	0.641
Prob.	0.99	0.72	0.44	0.52
Akure South				
Exp. Mean	4.59	18.87	17.48	23.6
Obs. Mean	1.47	17.96	3.99	5.33
t-stat.	1.935	2.34	1.39	1.52
Prob.	0.007	0.03	0.17	0.14
Idanre				
Exp. Mean	2.97	68.10	11.018	6.912
Obs. Mean	1.65	40.81	5.66	2.42
t-stat.	1.16	0.64	0.723	1.34
Prob.	0.258	0.52	0.477	0.19
Ile-Oluji				
Exp. Mean	5.2466	51.07	8.16	16.98
Obs. Mean	28.595	19.3867	1.993	8.823
t-stat.	0.902	1.1457	1.914	0.988
Prob.	0.3764	0.2642	0.068	0.3337
Odigbo				
Exp. Mean	5.157	55.57	8.45	21.02
Obs. Mean	2.1606	123.93	4.16	6.388
t-stat.	1.422	0.943	1.183	1.1969
Prob.	0.1689	0.3558	0.249	0.2433
Okitipupa				
Exp. Mean	3.18	111.45	25.97	17.41
Obs. Mean	3.142	48.02	6.44	3,261
t-stat.	0.0116	1.096	1.883	2.391
Prob.	0.9908	0.284	0.073	0.02
Owo				
Exp. Mean	3.59	8.996	2.896	5.665

Table 1. Contd.

Obs. Mean	4.25	14.85	3.549	7.295
t-stat.	0.357	0.665	0.390	0.827
Prob.	0.723	0.512	0.700	0.416

Table 2. Hypothesis testing for t-test.

Local government	VEDM	VHE	VAI	VSDCF
Ondo West	Reject	Accept	Accept	Reject
Akoko N.W	Accept	Accept	Accept	Accept
Akoko S.W	Accept	Accept	Accept	Accept
Akure South	Reject	Reject	Accept	Accept
Idanre	Accept	Accept	Accept	Accept
Ile-Oluji	Accept	Accept	Reject	Accept
Odigbo	Accept	Accept	Accept	Accept
Okitipupa	Accept	Accept	Reject	Reject
Owo	Accept	Accept	Accept	Accept

Critical value = 1.782, Level of significance = 0.95. Source: Authors Computation 2011.

Test of equality of means using t-test

This study prefers the use of t-test because of the small sample nature of the observation (1999 to 2010). The results of the t-test are presented in Tables 1. The common hypothesis being tested is:

H_0: There is no significant difference between the mean of budgeted capital and expended capital for project "n".

Exp. Mean = Expected (budgeted) mean of capital allocation for the projects. Obs. Mean = Observed (actual expenditure) on the projects. VEDM, VHE, VAI, VSDCF, as earlier defined.

The test is conducted at 95% level of significance. The rule of thumb is to reject the null hypothesis if the t-statistics is greater than the critical value from the t-table at (N1 + N2 – 2) degree of freedom. The critical value at 95% level of significance and (12 + 12-2 = 22) degree of freedom is 1.782. This is also equivalent to rejection of the null hypothesis if the probability is less than or equal to 0.05. The results in Table 1 is interpreted as summarized in Table 2.

Acceptance of the null hypothesis implies that there is no significance difference in the budgeted allocation and the expended allocation on the particular project for the particular local government. It implies that on the average, all budgeted allocations are spent on the particular project without diversion of fund. On the other hand, rejection of the null hypothesis implies that there is a significance difference between the budgeted allocation and the amount actually spent on the project.

FINDINGS

The result of the student t – test as presented in Table 2 shows that majority of the local governments show a high level of effectiveness in terms of spending the allocation on the appropriate projects. This is evidenced by the ratio of the percentage of the acceptance of the null hypothesis in relation to the overall hypothesis tested. Thirty six (4 hypotheses per each Local government X 9 Local governments) hypotheses were tested in all. The result as contained in Table 2 shows that twenty nine representing 80.6% were accepted while seven representing 19.4% were rejected. The acceptance of the majority of the Null hypotheses show that in all the local government under study, budgeted capital allocation were expended on the appropriate capital projects except for four local governments.

(i) In Ondo West local government the value of educational materials (VEDM) does not justify the budgeted allocation to it. Likewise, the value of social development and cultural facilities are below the budgeted amount.
(ii) In Akure South local government, the values of education materials and health equipment purchased fall below the capital budget allocated to the projects respectively.
(iii) In Ile-Oluji Local Government, only the value of agricultural inputs falls below the budgeted allocation to the project.

(iv) In Okitipupa Local Government, only the value of social development and cultural facilities falls below the capital budget to the project on the average. This shows that capital allocation was effectively executed.

Conclusion

This study has empirically analyzed the effectiveness of capital expenditure budgeting in some selected local governments of Ondo State. The result of the empirical analysis shows that there is effectiveness in capital budget allocation and expenditure in these local governments. Nine local governments were sampled out for the study. All the nine local governments can be said to have shown effectiveness in capital budget allocation and expenditure except for few projects. Reasons adduced for budget effectiveness are highlighted below:

(i) The issue of budgeting was taken seriously. Every spending was in adherence with budgetary provisions.
(ii) There was total absence of extra-budgetary spending; a situation where a budget officer disburse money without recourse to budgetary provisions.
(iii) There was a good coordination between plan and budget. Performances were measured against proposal on regular basis for the purpose of detecting variances.
(iv) There was timely approval and release of capital votes and budget were implemented to the latter.
(v) Expected revenues and incomes were adequately provided for. There was no issue of under or over provision for either revenue or expenditure.

REFERENCES

Adubi AA (2002). Plan-Budget Link in Nigeria: An Exploratory Investigation. NCEMA Policy Analysis Series 8(2),(Downloaded from www: http /1– 17..//inweb18.worldbank.org on2/3/2007).

Adubi L, Oladapo K (2005) Performance measurement and the need for Comparison. Manage. Account. Rev., 6(2): 40-49.

Akintoye IR (2008). Budget and Budgetary Control for Selected Food Beverages Companies in Nigeria. Eur. J. Econs. Financ. Adm. Sci., (Downloaded from http://www.enrojournalsn,com on12/5/2009).

Asiodu P (2000). Budget Implementation. NCEMA Policy Analysis Series, 6(1): 7–10.

Bamori J (2004). Development in Management Accountancy. New York, U.K. Heinemann Publishers Ltd., 235p.

Kopt N, Craig K (1998). Transparency, Probity and Accountability in fiscal Operations. Calif. Manage. Rev., 34(6): 35-47

Ola ROF, Effiong OJ (1999) Public Financial Management in Nigeria. Apapa, Lagos. Amfitop Nigeria Ltd., 293p.

Olofin K (2003). Making Budget Process more responsive to priorities (downloaded from http://business management suite 101.com/articles.efn/management-efficiency-effectiveness and economy. 18/5/2010).

Olurankinse F (2010). Analysis of capital expenditure budgeting in Ondo State local government. Paper presented at the 3-days workshop on pre-budgeting organized by Ondo State government in conjunction with United Nations organization.

Olurankinse F (2011) Inter local government capital budget execution Comparism. Am. J. Econs. Bus. Adm. New York, 3(3): 506-510.

Onimode B (1999). Towards Effective Budgeting Under a Democratic System. Bullion Central Bank of Nigeria (CBN) 24(1): 72–81.

World Bank Institute (2008). Public Sector performance. The Critical Role of Evaluation. Evaluation Department (Downloaded from http on 19/12/2009)

Accounting practices of SMEs in Zimbabwe: An investigative study of record keeping for performance measurement (A case study of Bindura)

Nelson Maseko* and Onias Manyani

Department of Accountancy, Faculty of Commerce, Bindura University of Science Education, Zimbabwe.

Contemporary research is emphasizing the development of sound accounting systems in SMEs in order to improve financial management in these entities. This research investigated accounting record keeping practices for performance measurement employed by SMEs in Zimbabwe, using Bindura as a case. The survey research design was used. The target population comprised of 100 SMEs operating retail shops, manufacturing firms and suppliers of various services in Bindura. A structured questionnaire was used to collect primary data from the respondents which was analysed to generate frequencies and percentages. The study revealed that the majority of SMEs do not keep complete accounting records because of lack of accounting knowledge and as a result there is inefficient use of accounting information in financial performance measurement. The study recommended that national regulators must develop specific accounting guidelines for SMEs and develop accounting training programmes for entrepreneurs in small businesses. The study also recommended mandatory record keeping, to improve accounting practices of SMEs in Zimbabwe.

Key words: Small- and medium-sized entities (SMEs), record keeping, accounting practices, accounting concepts, profit measurement, international financial reporting standard for small- and medium-sized entities (IFRS for SMEs).

INTRODUCTION

Small and medium-sized entities (SMEs) play important roles in the economic growth and sustainable development of every nation, (Moore et al., 2008). The government of Zimbabwe has identified entrepreneurship development as a major policy thrust to achieve economic development. This is evidenced by a number of institutions established by the government to provide funding and improve operational efficiency in the SMEs sector, (Reserve Bank of Zimbabwe, 2009). The major advantages to any economy of developing SMEs have been identified as sources of innovation and business evolution (Wynarczyk et al., 1993). The development and growth of SMEs in Zimbabwe can provide solutions to the problem of high unemployment facing the country because these entities have low start-up costs, low risk and can exploit untapped knowledge bases of creativity in the population for new product development. Zindiye et al. (2008) approximated that there are 40 000 manufacturing entities in Zimbabwe, most of which are SMEs, and further postulated that SMEs account for the employment of at least 57% of the Zimbabwe population. Ncube and Greenan (2004) estimated that there are about 609 SMEs in the manufacturing sector of Harare. SMEs dominate all service sectors of the economy excluding banking.

Accounting systems provide a source of information to owners and managers of SMEs operating in any industry for use in the measurement of financial performance. The importance of financial performance measurement to any business entity, big or small, cannot be over-emphasized. In any sense, profit can analogously be viewed as the life-blood of a business and hence the accounting bases,

*Corresponding author. E-mail: nmaseko@buse.ac.zw.

Abbreviations: GAAP, Generally accepted accounting practices; **IASB,** international accounting standard board; **IAS,** international accounting standard; **IFRS,** international financial reporting standard; **SME,** small- and medium-sized entity; **ZIMRA,** Zimbabwe revenue authority; **VAT,** value added tax.

concepts and principles adopted ought to capture and report all the relevant accounting information to ensure reliability in its measurement. Reported profits reflect changes in wealth of owners and this can explain why major economic decisions in business are centred on financial performance as measured by profitability, (Cooley and Edwards, 1983). It has been recognised that appropriate accounting information is important for a successful management of any business entity, whether large or small (European Commission (EC), 2008).

It is crucial therefore that the accounting practices of SMEs supply complete and relevant financial information needed to improve economic decisions made by entrepreneurs. This research therefore focuses on investigating the types of accounting records being kept and maintained by SMEs, their completeness and the availability of accounting skills and knowledge to capture and process accounting information which can be used to measure performance in SMEs. The study is aimed at achieving the following objectives:

1. To investigate the types of accounting records being kept and maintained by SMEs.
2. To investigate the extent to which accounting information is being used in measuring financial performance by SMEs.
3. To analyze the completeness of accounting records being kept by SMEs as a source of information for economic decision making.
4. To assess the need for specific regulation of accounting and financial reporting practices of SMEs in Zimbabwe.

LITERATURE REVIEW

Definitions of a small- and medium-sized entity

Evidence from literature reveals that there is no universally agreed definition of an SME across all academic disciplines. This is so because no single definition can capture all the dimensions of a small and medium-sized entity, nor can be expected to reflect the differences between entities in different industrial sectors or countries at different levels of development. Most definitions are however based on size and they use fundamental bases such as number of employees, financial position or annual turnover (Beck et al., 2005; Ghafoor and Iqbal, 2007; Zindiye et al., 2008). However, none of these bases are pegged at the same level across disciplines and national boundaries (Holt, 2008).

In virtually every jurisdiction, from the largest economies to the smallest, over 99% of companies have fewer than 50 employees (Pacter, 2009) quoted in South Africa Institute of Chartered Accountants (SAICA), (2010). In Zimbabwe, the Ministry of SMEs (2000) defines a small enterprise as a business that employs not more than 50 people while operating as a registered entity and a medium enterprise as one employing up to 75 and 100 people. The Small Enterprises Development Corporation (SEDCO) (2010) does not differentiate between small and medium entities but defines a small and medium enterprise as a firm that has not more than 100 employees with maximum annual sales of up to US$830 000.

According to the Hong Kong Institute of Certified Public Accountants (2005) an entity is considered to be an SME in Hong Kong if it does not exceed any two of the three criteria pegged as total annual revenue of HK$50 million, total assets of HK$50 million, at the reporting date, and 50 employees.

The International Accounting Standards Committee Foundation (IASCF) (2007) defines an SME as an entity that does not have public accountability and thus publishes general purpose financial statements for external users.

SMEs are entities which do not have the onerous requirement of filing their financial statements with any regulatory body for the purpose of issuing financial instruments. These entities do not hold assets in any fiduciary capacity for a group of outside investors (banks, insurance entities, security brokers, funds, etc) but the owners, who usually are also managers. However, Sian and Roberts (2006) went further to differentiate a micro-entity from an SME. They defined micro-entities as the smallest entities within the SME spectrum and that these entities have less than 10 employees (including those that do not have any employees).

It can be seen from the foregoing definitions that there is no one universally agreed definition of an SME. However, for the purpose of this research, an SME is considered as an entity that employs less than 100 people, generating less than US$800 000 in annual turnover and holding assets only for the owner-managers. The majority of the entities that participated in this study can well be described as micro-entities, according to Sian and Roberts (2006) as they employ less than 10 employees including the owner.

Accounting practices and financial reporting of SMEs

In most jurisdictions, the law requires all or many of the SMEs to prepare financial statements and, often, to have them audited. Normally, the financial statements are filed with the government, posted on a website or are made available on request (EC, 2008). In Zimbabwe, all companies are required to keep proper books of accounts in compliance with Section 140 of the Companies Act (Chapter 24:03) and to prepare and submit tax returns based on these financial statements to the tax authority, Zimbabwe revenue authority (ZIMRA), in compliance with various pieces of tax legislation. A study by Lalin and Sabir (2010) concludes that regulations are the main drivers why SMEs prepare financial statements.

Holmes and Nicholls (1998) conclude that the volume of accounting practices in SMEs is dependent on a number of operating environmental factors that include size of the business, business age and industrial grouping. They further argue that most owners and managers of SMEs engage public accountants to prepare required information and that owners and managers search for additional information, but only to a limited extent. Ismail and King (2007) conclude that the development of a sound accounting information system (AIS) in SMEs depends on the owners' level of accounting knowledge. Keasy and Short (1990) and Bohman and Boter (1984) report that small firms use professional accounting firms for preparation of annual reports and for other accounting needs. Marriot and Marriot (2000) argue that the professional accountants should develop their services to also include graphic presentations and comments and interpretation of the amounts in financial statements. Evaraert et al. (2006) and Jayabalan and Dorasamy (2009) however argue that the high cost of hiring professional accountants leaves SME owner-managers with no option but to relegate accounting information management. Zhou (2010) proposes the use of accounting software by owner-managers in SMEs to improve accounting practices but laments that developers of accounting software are yet to produce the medium-sized software for SMEs.

An early study of users of financial statements in SMEs (Page, 1984) revealed that owners, managers, tax authorities and lenders are the main users. According to Olson et al. (2004), contemporary studies are discovering that the number of users of accounting information in SMEs is increasing to include venture capitalists and customers in supply-chains. Wichman (1983) concludes that accounting and marketing pose major challenges to management of SMEs and recommends that managers or owners in SMEs must learn about accounting or hire experts. Walhlstedt (1996) believes that conventional accounting reports play a significant role in SMEs but argues that the reports must be adjusted in order for them to be understood, proposing the use of the cash basis rather than the accruals basis.

McMahon (1999) argues that financial reporting practices in SMEs seem to fall short of what is dictated by various external financial reporting imperatives that exist for them, further arguing that owner-managers appear particularly reluctant to produce financial reports which might become accessible to outside parties either directly or through the offices of regulatory authorities.

Profit measurement and the accounting concept of capital maintenance

Different entities adopt different concepts of capital in reporting their financial performance and position. They can choose between financial and physical concepts of capital. Under the financial concept of capital maintenance, a profit is earned only if the financial (or monetary) amount of the net assets at the end of the period exceeds the financial (or monetary) amount of net assets at the beginning of the period, excluding any distributions to and contributions from equity owners during the period, (Framework, para.104a). On the other hand, profit, under the physical capital maintenance concept, is earned only if the physical productive capacity (or operating capability) of the entity at the end of the period exceeds the physical productive capacity at the beginning of the period, after excluding any distributions to and contributions from equity owners during the period, (Framework, para.104b).

According to the Framework (para. 109) all price changes affecting the assets and liabilities of an entity are viewed as changes in the measurement of physical productive capacity. Such price changes are treated as capital maintenance adjustments, making part of equity not profit. The concept of capital chosen indicates the goal to be attained in determining profit even though there may be some measurement difficulties in making the concept operational (Von and Wingard, 2009).

According to a study by Tanwongsval and Pinvanichkul (2008), SMEs ranked 'assessing profitability' second on the continuum of reasons for preparing financial statements well after 'sole purpose of tax preparation' which was ranked first. Cooley and Edwards (1983) report that SMEs considered maximization of net income (profit) to be the most important financial objective. Page (1984) also argues that owners in SMEs focus on profitability and the measures of net profit and net current assets when they are evaluating their firms.

Measurement issues

'Measurement' is defined as the process of determining the monetary amounts at which the elements of the financial statements are recognised and reflected in the financial statements, (Framework, para.99). There are a number of measurement bases which are employed to different degrees and in varying combinations by entities when preparing their financial statements (von and Wingard, 2009). The four common bases of measurement employed in financial statements include the historical cost basis, current cost basis, realisable value basis and present value basis.

Historical cost

Under the historical cost basis of accounting, assets are

recorded at the amount of cash or cash equivalents paid or the fair value of the consideration given to acquire them at the time of their acquisition. Liabilities are recorded at the amount of proceeds received in exchange for the obligation, or in some circumstances (for example, income taxes), at the amounts of cash or cash equivalents expected to be paid to satisfy the liability in the normal course of business, (Framework, para.100a). Historical cost is the most commonly adopted basis by entities in preparing their financial statements and it is used in combination with other measurement bases, (para.101). Von and Wingard (2009) argue that a major disadvantage of the historic cost concept is that it follows the financial capital maintenance concept (in nominal monetary units only) and as such overstates profit in a period of rising prices, which could lead to an erosion of capital.

Current cost

Under the current cost basis of accounting, assets are carried at the amount of cash or cash equivalents that would have to be paid if the same or an equivalent asset was acquired currently. Liabilities are carried at the undiscounted amount of cash or cash equivalents that would be required to settle the obligation currently (Framework, para.100b). The physical capital maintenance concept requires the adoption of the current cost basis of measurement (Von and Wingard, 2009).

Realisable value

Under the realisable (or settlement) value basis of accounting, assets are carried at the amount of cash or cash equivalents that could currently be obtained by selling the asset in an orderly disposal. Liabilities are carried at their settlement values; that is, the undiscounted amount of cash or cash equivalents expected to be paid to satisfy the liabilities in the normal course of business (Framework, para.100c).

Present value

Under the present value basis of accounting, assets are carried at the present discounted value of the future net cash inflows that the item is expected to generate in the normal course of business. Liabilities are carried at the present discounted value of the future net cash outflows that are expected to be required to settle the liability in the normal course of business (Framework, para.100d).

The selection of the measurement basis and concept of capital maintenance will determine the accounting model used in the preparation of financial statements.

Accounting bases

Cash basis accounting

In cases when an entity is a micro or even a very small entity, it might be more appropriate to use cash basis accounting (EC, 2008). Cash basis means that cost or income is accounted for at the equivalent amount of cash paid or received for it. This means that an entity recognises a transaction only when cash is received or paid. The cash book or the receipts and payment accounts is the main book in this system. In modern businesses, especially in retail shops, a point-of-sale or cash register machine is used.

Accrual basis accounting

It is based on the accruals concept of accounting which states that revenue and costs are accrued (that is, recognized as they are earned or incurred, not as money is received or paid), matched with one another so far as their relationship can be established or justifiably assumed, and dealt with in the statement of comprehensive income for the period to which they relate (Framework, para. 22). Profit under this type of accounting, is the difference between realized revenues ('realized' in the sense that invoices have been issued) and associated costs, measured either by historic costs or by current costs.

This involves accruing any receipts which have been earned in the financial year and accruing any payments which relate to purchases made in the financial year. The corollary of this is that any receipts received or payments made in the current financial year which relate to accruals made in the last financial year, will not affect the current year's profit.

An entity may make a choice between the two bases of cash or accruals or apply both depending on the nature of its business transactions. However, in some jurisdictions, entities may be required to adopt one prescribed basis. For example, in Zimbabwe, Section 14 of the Value added tax (VAT) act (Chapter 23:12) requires that all registered operators account for both cash and credit supplies (sales and purchases) using the accruals (invoice) basis of accounting. The cash (payment) basis is only available to registered operators who apply to Zimbabwe revenue authority (ZIMRA) for exemption from using the accruals (invoice) basis.

Financial record keeping

Financial records, for example the sales day book (sales journal), purchases day book (purchases journal), cash receipt book, cheque payments book, petty cash book, general journal, nominal ledger, debtors' ledger and creditors' ledger must be kept and maintained in a sound accounting system (McMahon, 1999).

However, not all SMEs may need to keep and maintain all the previous mentioned financial records but an entity has to decide this on the basis of its needs. When the entity makes the judgement of what financial records to maintain, it also needs to take into account whether some financial records are compulsory to be kept by regulatory authorities like ZIMRA.

Tax accounting in SMEs

Income tax systems in most OECD countries are accrual based (EC. 2008). Under cash accounting, income tax is paid on revenues only when cash is received, and input costs are claimed only when cash is paid out. Cash accounting systems targeted at SMEs to compute taxable income based on entries of revenues actually received and costs actually incurred. Cash basis can significantly reduce compliance costs depending on the additional supporting documentation that SMEs as taxpayers are required to keep and maintain. Other simplification measures may include simplified book-keeping requirements (McMahon, 1999).

In Zimbabwe the tax authority, ZIMRA, introduced a presumptive tax system which covers all SMEs and informal traders not registered for tax. The Zimbabwe VAT system requires businesses to keep and maintain proper books of accounts including the filing of tax invoices. Most SMEs qualify to compulsorily register for VAT under Section 23 of the VAT act (Chapter 23:12). However, the number of SMEs operating in the economy cannot be verified but it is estimated that 90% of all registered tax payers in Zimbabwe are SMEs (Ngorima, 2009)

Current issues in small and medium-sized entities (SMEs) financial reporting: International financial reporting standard (IFRS) for SMEs

On 9 July 2009, the IASB published an international financial reporting standard (IFRS) designed for use by small and medium-sized entities (IFRS for SMEs). This is the first set of international financial reporting requirements developed specifically for SMEs. SMEs are estimated to represent more than 95 per cent of all entities, according to the IFRS foundation (2010). Since the early 1970s, IFRSs have been designed to meet the needs of entities whose securities trade in public capital markets. This has affected the scope of issues covered in IFRSs, the amount of implementation guidance and the volume of disclosures (Institute of Chartered Accounting of Zimbabwe (ICAZ, 2010). SMEs generally have fewer resources, limited access to capital markets, less business complexity and fewer external users of its financial statements, compared to larger listed entities.

Users of financial statements of SMEs will be more interested in current liquidity and short-term cash flows than long-term forecasts of cash flows and earnings (Sian and Roberts, 2006). The complexities posed by full IFRSs in financial reporting by SMEs led countries like the UK to develop a standard of its own that was used by SMEs in financial reporting; the financial reporting standard for smaller entities (FRSSE), with extant local accounting standards applicable to all non-listed entities. Kenya, by contrast, is a country that adopted IFRSs in full and these have been applicable to all listed and non-listed entities since 1999 (Sian and Roberts, 2006). In Hong Kong the small and medium-sized entity financial reporting framework and financial reporting standard (SME-FRF and SME-FRS) was issued in August 2005 (HKICPA, 2008).

The introduction of an IFRS specifically for SMEs was necessitated by many challenges faced by these entities in adopting full IFRSs in financial reporting, the main of which was the excessive disclosure requirements, based on a cost-benefit analysis for SMEs (Nazri, 2010).

One major interest of SMEs that adopted full IFRSs was to reduce the cost of preparing financial statements according to the Instite of Chartered Accountant in England and Wales (ICAEW, 2008). Full IFRSs were designed for financial reporting that meets the needs of equity investors in large entities with shares trading on public capital markets. The full IFRSs cover a wide range of issues, including a sizeable amount of disclosures for easy understanding by a wide range of users in these large public companies. Users of the financial statements of SMEs do not usually have similar needs, but, rather are more interested in assessing shorter-term cash flows, liquidity and solvency (McMahon, 1999).

Also, many SMEs complained that full IFRSs impose a burden on them - a burden that has been growing as IFRSs have become more detailed and more countries have begun to use them (IFRS foundation, 2010). Concerns have been raised about the burden to financial statement preparers and the relevancy of the resulting information to lenders, vendors, credit rating agencies, family investors, development agencies and others who use SME financial statements (ICAZ, 2010). A fundamental change in the way companies, and SMEs in particular, report financial information to their lenders and insurers is also critical to minimise credit risk and business failure (ICAEW, 2008).

For small businesses, the cost of complying with IFRSs could be greater than the benefit received. A full set of accounts that comply with IFRSs are less relevant for the small business user who is most likely to be the owner-manager (Stern and Barbour, 2005), quoted in Stainbank (2008).

The introduction of an IFRS for SMEs in July 2009 by the IASB was a welcome development in many countries, especially in developing countries (Juping, 2010;

Table 1. Size of entity.

Industrial sector	Annual revenue base (US$)			
	Below 50 000 (micro)	50 000-100 000 (small)	Above 100 000 (medium)	Total
Retail (shops)	2	21	3	26
Manufacturing	4	10	5	19
Other service	8	7	1	16
Total	14	38	9	61
Percentage (%) frequency	23	62	15	100

Table 2. Legal ownership of SMEs.

Industrial sector	Family business	Sole proprietor	Partnership	Limited company	Total
Retail (shops)	13	8	2	3	26
Manufacturing	4	4	2	9	19
Other services	2	5	7	2	16
Total	19	17	11	14	61
Percentage (%) frequency	31	28	18	23	100

Nazri, 2010; Sheridan, 2009) but its impact on improving financial reporting by SMEs is yet to be verified. The South Africa Institute of Chartered Accountants (SAICA, 2002:4), in Stainbank (2008), acknowledged that it is neither reasonable nor practicable to require small entities to comply with reporting standards that are based on general purpose international financial reporting standards. In response to this expert call, the South African Department of Trade and Industry had to address the issue of differential reporting by SMEs through corporate law reforms which commenced in 2004 (Stainbank, 2008).

In Zimbabwe, the IFRS for SMEs was adopted in 2009 when it was first published by the IASB, (ICAZ, 2010). The new IFRS for SMEs is expected to improve the information content and format of financial statements presented by SMEs. Chimanikire (2011) advocates for change in the local law to permit the smooth adoption of the new standard. The researchers believe that the new standard came to address only financial reporting issues in SMEs but record keeping practices will remain a challenge. Poor record keeping practices will hamper performance measurement and the subsequent reporting which the new standard seeks to improve. In this light, it is envisaged that efforts to improve record keeping practices will eventually increase the chance of some SMEs adopting the IFRS for SMEs at some future point.

MATERIALS AND METHODS

The researchers used the survey method. As widely accepted, the survey method is a fact-finding study that involves adequate and accurate interpretation of findings (Cooper and Schindler, 2003). The study was carried out by gathering data from primary sources in order to achieve the research objectives. The target population comprised of 100 registered SMEs in Bindura. Based on the research objectives, a survey questionnaire was developed. The questionnaire was divided into three sections: Profile of the entity, accounting practices and perceptions about performance measurement. The questionnaire was pre-tested using 5 owner-managers of retail shops, 5 owner-managers of manufacturing entities and 3 operators of entities supplying other services.

A total of 100 questionnaires were distributed through networks of friends and colleagues to retail shops (selling groceries, clothing, hardware, pharmaceuticals and farming implements), manufacturing entities (including metal fabricators, panel beaters, carpentry workers in cottage industry, building contractors, textiles, bakeries and other food processors) and a variety of other service providers (including hairdressers, law firms, insurance agents, business consultants and those offering secretarial services). A total of 68 of the distributed questionnaires were returned and of these 61 were accepted as complete for the purpose of data analysis. With relevant collected data, analysis was then conducted based on the research objectives and conclusions drawn.

RESULTS

The results obtained from the survey through questionnaires are presented in this section. Table 1 shows that the majority of SMEs (62%) generate annual revenue of between US$50 000 and US$100 000 and that most of the SMEs are in the retail sector operating shops. Entities offering other services are mainly generating below US$50 000 in annual revenue. Table 2 shows that the largest number of SMEs (31%) is family businesses, followed by sole traders (28%) and limited companies (23%) respectively, with partnerships com-prising the smallest number (18%) of SME businesses.

Table 3 shows that in 40 of the 61 SMEs that participated in the study, owner-managers were

Table 3. Preparers of accounts and financial statements in SMEs.

Industrial sector	Full-time Accounting officer	Consultant	Owner-manager	Total
Retail (shops)	3	5	18	26
Manufacturing	4	4	11	19
Other services	2	3	11	16
Total	9	12	40	61
Percentage (%) frequency	15	20	65	100

Table 4. Accounting records kept by SMEs.

Industrial sector	Purchases day (order) book	Sales day (receipt) book	Expenditure (bills) book	Payroll records	Asset register
Retail (shops)	22	26	7	18	8
Manufacturing	6	9	11	7	12
Other services	7	2	8	2	4
Total	35	37	26	27	24
Percentage (%) frequency	58	62	43	45	40
Ranking	2	1	4	3	5

Table 5. Financial statements (or accounts) prepared by SMEs.

Industrial sector	Statement of income	Statement of financial position	Statement of cash flows	Statement of changes in equity	None
Retail (shops)	8	3	3	7	5
Manufacturing	6	3	3	4	0
Other services	4	1	1	3	6
Total	18	7	7	14	11
Percentage (%) frequency	30	12	12	23	18
Ranking	1	4	4	2	3

preparers of accounts and financial statements, 12 used hired consultants to prepare financial statements and only 9 employed full-time accounting officers. Respondents were asked to choose accounting records they kept in SMEs from a given list. Table 4 shows that the sales day (receipt) book ranked highest with 62% and the purchases day (order) book ranked second with 58%. The payroll records book ranked third with 45%, the expenditure (bills) book ranked fourth and the asset register book ranking last (fifth) with 40%. All of the SMEs in the retail shops business kept sales day (receipts) books and most of the SMEs in the manufacturing sector (12 out of 18) kept asset registers.

Respondents were also asked to select from a given list of financial statements those that they prepared for SMEs. Table 5 shows that the statement of income ranked highest with thirty percent and the statement of changes in equity ranked second with 23%. Eighteen percent of the SMEs did not prepare any financial statement or account. The statement of financial Position and the statement of cash flows both ranked forth with 12%.

Over and above accounting records kept, respondents were also asked to select from a given list, ledgers or books of accounts they kept and maintained for SMEs. Table 6 shows that the cash book ranked highest with 53% and the receivables account second with 32%. The payables account ranked third with 28% the non-current assets account ranked fourth with 22 and 13% of the SMEs responded not to have kept any book of accounts or ledger.

Incidence of calculating profit

Table 7 shows that 78% of the SMEs did not calculate profit while only 22% responded to have calculated profit.

Table 6. Books of accounts/ledgers kept and maintained by SMEs.

Industrial sector	Receivables accounts	Payables accounts	Cash book	Non-current assets accounts	None
Retail (shops)	2	5	19	3	4
Manufacturing	13	9	7	8	3
Other services	4	3	6	2	1
Total	19	17	32	13	8
Percentage (%) frequency	32	28	53	22	13
Ranking	2	3	1	4	5

Table 7. Responses to calculation of profits.

Respondents	Responses		Total
	Yes	No	
SMEs (%)	78	22	100

Table 8. Reasons given for calculating profit.

Reasons	Percentage responses
Tax purposes	13
Profit sharing	27
Financial reporting	28
Other	32
Total	100

Table 9. Accounting bases adopted.

Accounting basis	Responses (%)
Cash basis accounting	72
Accrual basis accounting	28
Total	100

Respondents' perceptions about reasons for calculating profit

Table 8 shows that 13% of the SMEs indicated that they calculated profit for tax purposes, 27% for profit sharing reasons, 28% for financial reporting while 32% gave other reasons for calculating profit. For the purpose of this research, only financial reporting is construed for performance measurement.

Accounting basis adopted

Table 9 shows that 72% of the SMEs adopted the cash basis of accounting with 28% adopting the accruals basis of accounting.

Challenges faced in keeping proper accounting records

Table 10 shows that the majority of SMEs (62%) attributed the challenges they faced in keeping proper accounting records to lack of accounting knowledge, 18% of SMEs indicated cost and time constraints as challenges while 12% cited lack of guidelines or specific accounting regulations for SMEs as contributing to

Table 10. Challenges faced by SMEs.

Challenges	Percentage responses
Lack of accounting knowledge	62
Cost and time constraints	18
Lack of guiding accounting rules	12
Other	8
Total	100

Table 11. Suggestions to improve accounting practices of SMEs.

Suggestions	Percentage responses
Bookkeeping training	36
Hire consultant	25
SME accounting guidelines	12
Mandatory record keeping	7
Other	20
Total	100

challenges they faced in keeping proper accounting records. Eight percent of the SMEs cited other challenges.

Respondents' suggestions given to improve accounting practices of SMEs

Table 11 shows that most of the SMEs (36%) suggested book-keeping training as a way to improve their accounting practices. Twenty five percent of the SMEs suggested they would hire consultants and twelve percent suggested having guidelines or specific accounting regulations in place to improve their accounting practices. Twenty percent gave other suggestions.

DISCUSSION

The results confirm that SMEs do keep subsidiary books of accounts, especially to capture sales and cost of sales. There is however little accounting information captured on operating expenses as evidenced by a few number of SMEs keeping books to record expenses. SMEs in the retail shops business are keeping sales day books for controlling inventory and those in the manufacturing sector keep records for non-current assets as owners try to safeguard their assets. Record keeping in SMEs is therefore not being done for the purpose of capturing accounting information for performance measurement but for security and control. This is supported by only 27% of SMEs preparing financial statements to report financial performance.

The results also reveal that the accounting basis adopted by an entity has a bearing on the accounting records kept. The study reveals that SMEs are more comfortable with the cash basis, supporting the propositions of Walhlstedt (1996) for the adoption of cash basis accounting in SMEs. Cash accounting is easy and straight forward as compared to the accruals accounting, which is complex, as it requires understanding of double-entry bookkeeping and accounting processes. Accruals basis accounting requires the recording of revenue and expenses for all transactions regardless of whether cash is received or not. Estimation and apportionment of revenue and expenses is also needed under the accruals basis in order to apply the matching concept in reporting period performance and this requires accounting skills which are lacking in SMEs.

The results also confirm the findings of McMahon (1999) that most SMEs do not prepare a complete set of financial statements with some not preparing any financial statement at all. An entity may fail to prepare financial statements even with well-maintained books of accounts because the preparation of financial statements requires accounting kills and this, as revealed by the results, is lacking in 62% of SMEs. The need to prepare a complete set of financial statements increases as an entity grows, especially into medium size. It is at the medium size that entity financial performance reporting will not only be limited to internal users but also to external users like lenders. Owner-managers dominate preparers of financial statements in SMEs and according to Wichman (1983), most of the owner-managers are not financially literate and they may be resorting to this practice to avoid the cost of hiring accountants, confirming the findings of Everaert et al. (2006). This means that, in the absence of statutory requirements to prepare financial statements, for example from tax authorities, SMEs could do without financial reporting because the chief users (owners) do not value financial reporting, basing on their perspectives of performance measurement.

Owner-managers in SMEs do not value the use of profitability in measuring performance but are compelled to calculate profits for tax purposes. Any entity should calculate profit as a measure to protect its capital from being depleted. Cash should not be mistaken for profit as an entity may have huge cash balances but having its asset base or productive capacity depleted by losses.

CONCLUSION AND RECOMMENDATIONS

The study revealed that SMEs do not keep complete accounting records because of lack of accounting knowledge and the cost of hiring professional accountants. As a result, there is inefficient use of accounting information to support financial performance measurement by SMEs in Zimbabwe. This study recommends that the regulators should come up with some SME-specific accounting guidelines and provide template forms for capturing accounting information by SMEs. The ministry responsible for SMEs should initiate accounting training programmes for entrepreneurs running small businesses. Further, this study recommends that record keeping in SMEs must be made mandatory to improve their accounting practices and increase chances of them formalizing their business operations.

ACKNOWLEDGEMENTS

The researchers would like to thank all the participants who contributed their accounting experiences in this study.

REFERENCES

Beck T, Demirguç-Kunt A, Levine R (2005). SMEs, Growth, and Poverty: Cross-country Evidence. World Bank mimeo.
Bohman H, Boter H (1984). Planning in small and medium-sized firms – The challenges and premises of the strategic planning. Dept. Bus. Admin. Econs. Umea Univ. Sweden.
Chimanikire R (2011). IFRS for SMEs simplifies good financial reporting In: The Chartered Secretary. 2011(2):17-19.
Companies Act (Chapter 24:03). Govt. Printers. Harare.
Cooley P, Edwards C (1983). Financial objectives of small firms. Am. J. Small Bus., 8(1): 28-31.
Cooper DR, Schindler PS (2003). Business research methods. Irwin: McGraw-Hill. NY.
European Commission (Enterprise and Industry Directorate-General). Final Report of the Expert Group: Accounting System for small enterprises – Recommendations and good Practices. November 2008.
Everaert P, Sarens G, Rommel J (2006). Outsourcing of Accounting Tasks in SMEs: An extended TCE Model. W.Paper. Univ. Gent. Kuiperskaai, Belgium.
Ghafoor Z, Iqbal M (2007). Role of the Internet in SME growth strategies: Case studies of Swedish companies. Thesis. Lulea Univ.
Ministry of SMEs (2000). Small and Medium Enterprises (Zimbabwe). Govt. Printers, Harare.
Holmes S, Nicholls D (1988). An analysis of the use of accounting information by Australian small business. J. Small Bus. Manage., 26(2): 57-68.
Holt G (2008). IFRS for SMEs In: Student Accountant. Kaplan-ACCA. London.
Hong Kong Institute of Certified Public Accountants (HKICPA 2008). Small and Medium-sized Entity Financial Reporting Framework and Financial Reporting Standard.
Institute of Chartered Accountants in England and Wales (2008). A blueprint for SME financial reporting to accelerate economic recovery: The Accounts Review Solution IN: Accountancy Age 2009.
Institute of Chartered Accountancy Zimbabwe (ICAZ 2010). Small and Medium-sized Entities news. (Available on www.icaz.org.zw, retrieved 6 Sept 2010).
International Accounting Standards Committee Foundation (IASCF 2007). Exposure Draft of a proposed IFRS for SMEs. February 2007. IASC Foundation Pubs. London.
IASB (2009). International Financial Reporting Standard for Small and Medium-sized Entities. 9 January. IASC Foundation Pubs. London.
Ismail NA, King M (2007). Factors influencing the alignment of accounting information in small and medium sized Malaysian firms. J. Infor. Sys. Small Bus., 1(1-2): 1-20.
Jayabalan J, Dorasamy M (2009). Outsourcing of Accounting Functions amongst SME companies in Malaysia: An Exploratory Study. J. Acc. Bus. Pub. Interest., 8(2): 96-114.
Juping C. Simpler (2010). SME financial reporting wanted In: The Business Times. 3 Jan. 2010. Singapore.
Keasy K, Short H (1990). The accounting burdens facing small firms: An empirical research note. J. Acc. Bus. Res., 20(80): 307-313.
Lalin H, Sabir RI (2010). Research on Usage and Usefulness Perception of Financial Accounting Practices in Less Developing Countries: A case of Cambodia. Proceedings of the 7th Intl. Conf. Innov. Manage., 1881-1885.
Marriot N, Marriot P (2000). Professional accountants and the development of management accounting service for the small firm: Barriers and possibilities. J. Mgt Acc. Res.,11: 75-492.
McMahon RGP (1999). Putting SME Financial Reporting into Theoretical and Practical Perspective. Res. Paper Series 98-10. The Flinder Univ. South Aus. Adelaide.
Moore WC, Petty JW, Palich CH, Longernecker JG (2008). Managing small business: An entrepreneurial emphasis, 14th ed.
Nazri M (2010). A standard for SME Financial Reporting In: SME Toolkit Malaysia. Intl. Fin. Corp. Aug., 2010.
Ncube LB, Greenan JP (2004). Entrepreneurial careers of women in Zimbabwe. J. Vocat. Edu. Res., 28(1).
Ngorima M (2009). Expert Calls for redrafting of Tax Law In: The Chartered Secretary, pp. 7-8.
Olson O, Blomskvisk M, Dergard J, Jonsson C (2004). Accounting and Entrepreneurship: A Review and Discussion of the Scientific Literature. Paper Presented at the 4th Asia-Pacific Interdisciplinary Research in Accounting Conference. 4-6 July. Singapore.
Page MJ (1984). Corporate financial reporting and the small independent company. J. Acc. Bus. Res., 15(3): 271-280.
Reserve Bank of Zimbabwe (2009). Surviving the new economic environment: Practical advice and policy initiatives to support the Youth, Women Groups and other vulnerable members of the society - January 2009 Monetary Policy Statement sup.
Sheridan B (2009). IFRS for SMEs - A Solution? In: Deloitte Financial Reporting Services, July 2010.
Sian S, Roberts C (2006). Micro-entity Financial Reporting: Some Empirical Evidence on the Perspectives of Preparers and Users. Infor. Paper prepared for Small and Medium-sized Practices Committee. IFAC. NY.
Small Enterprise Development Corporation (SEDCO) of Zimbabwe (2010). Small and Medium Enterprise. (Available on www.sedco.co.zw accessed 21/07/11).

South African Institute of Chartered Accountants (SAICA 2010). IFRS for SMEs, May 2010.
Stainbank L (2008). The Development of Financial Reporting for SMEs in South Africa: Implication of Recent and Impending Changes. Afr. J. Acc. Econ. Fin. Banking, 3(3): 1-17.
Tanwongsval V, Pinvanichkul T (2008). Accounting Information Requirements and Reporting Practices of Thai SMEs. King Mongkut Univ. Tech., pp. 59-74.
Value Added Tax Act (Chapter 23: 12). Govt. Printers. Harare.
Von WR, Wingard C (2009). GAAP Handbook 2009: Financial Accounting and Reporting Practice. Eds. LexisNexis Butterworth. Durban.
Wahlstedt K (1996). In search of unbiased accounting measurement for use in small business management. Doc. Thesis. Dept. of Econs. Swedish Univ. Agric. Sci. Uppsala, Sweden.
Wichman H (1983). Accounting and marketing – key small business problems. Am. J. Small Bus., 7(4): 19-26.
Wynarczyk KP, Watson R, Storey DJ, Short H, Keasy K (1993). The Managerial Labour Market in Small and Medium-sized Enterprises. Routledge
Zhou L (2010). The Research on Issues and Countermeasures of Accounting Information of SMEs. Intl. J. Bus. Manage., 5(3): 223-225.
Zindiye S, Roberts-Lombard M, Herbst G (2008). An empirical investigation into the factors affecting the performance of SMEs in the manufacturing sector of Harare, Zimbabwe. Mcom. Thesis. Fort Hare Univ. SA.

The evidence of management motivation to revalue property plant and equipment in Tunisia

Mohamed Ali Azouzi* and Anis Jarboui

Department of Financial and Accounting, Universities Higher Institute of Business Administration (ISAAS), ISAAS, BP 1013 - 3018 Sfax-Tunisia.

This article deals with the relationship between emotions and accounting method. Specifically, it examines the links between cognitive biases and use of assets revaluation. Indeed, in order to improve the explanatory power of the positive theory of accounting, we integrated the behavioural dimension in the analysis of accounting choices: our goal is to show the role of these biases on the choice of revaluation (negativity through the loss of optimism and complacency). All four cognitive biases were measured means of a questionnaire consisting of several items. The selected sample is composed of 120 Tunisians managers. Our results suggest that the presence of a revaluation is always positively correlated with the executives' suggestibility in relation to the behavioural biases.

Key words: Loss aversion, optimism, overconfidence, assets revaluation.

INTRODUCTION

Companies have long engaged in a results management (Strong and Meyer, 1987; Brown et al., 1992; Francis et al., 1996; Cotter et al., 1998; Holgate and Ghosh, 2000). Indeed, without violating accounting rules, managers have the opportunity to influence the form and content of financial statements by taking advantage of gaps in their accounting and managerial discretion (Barton, 2001). The aim of these accounting manipulations was to intentionally deviate from the results reported to a desired level in order to capture personal gain tomislead investors or to influence contracts dependent on accounting numbers.

The financial literature advances several motivations for earnings management, some refer to the positive theory of accounting (Watts and Zimmerman, 1986), based on the use of accounting numbers to handle contractual issues, and relate mainly to the debt contract (Defond, 1994, Dichev and Skinner, 2002), the contract compensation (Gaver et al., 1995) and political costs. The study of assets revaluation is part of research in positive theory of accounting. The positive theory focuses on the analysis of accounting choices observed within firms. Research in the positive theory of accounting consists mainly of two families work (Cormier, 2002): Studies testing the assumptions of the political contract Accounting theory (initiated by Watts and Zimmerman, 1978) and studies on information contained in accounting numbers. The study is part of the revaluation so clearly in the positive current accounting.

Work from the positive theory looked for explanatory factors of the revaluation (contractual, political costs, signs (Dumontier and Raffournier, 1988; Saada, 1995; Thauvron, 2000; Mard, 2006; Piera, 2003).

However, revaluation choice is at the Chief Executive Officer (CEO) discretion, one can legitimately question the motivations of a practice which has no direct impact on cash flow. Our idea is inspired by the behavioural approach and aims to demonstrate the role of emotional biases in accounting choice.

*Corresponding author. E-mail: mohamed_azouzi@yahoo.fr.

HYPOTHESES TO BE TESTED

The analysis of the revaluation practice is traditionally

discussed in reference to the characteristics of firms. The few empirical studies have identified the view that the revaluation practice is always positively correlated with: restrictive covenants in loan agreements, investment opportunities of firms, asset specificity and firm size (Piera, 2003).

However, CEO enjoys considerable latitude as to choice of accounting policies and methods of a company whose practice of revaluation. Moreover, CEO objectives pursued can be broken down between a search for security or survival and a desire for growth or acceptance of risk (Julien and Marchesnay, 1987). These objectives justified his accountants' choices whose practice of assets revaluation.

In this context, managers can use the flexibility afforded by accounting variables to manage the results to their advantage. The aim of these accounting manipulations was to avoid the violation of restrictive clauses of the contracts of debt that would be costly, benefit from lower funding costs that could result in additional debt and reduce the perceived risk of Bankruptcy. The objective of this study is to enrich the theory of positive accounting theory by introducing the dimension in accounting analysis of the determinants of asset revaluation (loss aversion, optimism and overconfidence). For that, it is expedient to introduce the one hand, the main assumptions of the positive theory of accounting and to show the impact of behavioral biases on the choice of the leader of the revaluation of the other.

The alternative theory: Positive accounting theory and signals theory

Henderson and Goodwin (1992: 78 to 79) reported that there are three main unfavourable effects of upward revaluation on the financial statements. First, lower reported profits result from an increase in depreciation expenses from depreciable asset revaluation. Second, lower gains on the sale of the revalue assets come from an increase in its revaluating amount. Third, some financial ratios decrease. Return on total assets (ROA) is reduced due to the decrease in reported profits and the increase in the value of assets. Return on equity (ROE) is also reduced due to the decrease in reported profits and the increase in shareholders' equity.

Although there are some disadvantages, many firms decide to revalue their assets. In order to examine the hidden motivations for this accounting procedure, positive accounting is applied.

Positive accounting theory

In summary, positive accounting theory is applied to explain the motivations for asset revaluation. It means that the firms will change their accounting methods to recognize their assets from historical cost to fair value in order to minimize their contracting costs. The asset revaluation can be used as a tool to lower the debt/equity ratio in order to avoid default costs (debt hypothesis). Upward revaluations help avoid violations of debt covenants (Whittred and Chan, 1992; Brown et al., 1992), and improve the firm's borrowing capacity by reporting a lower leverage ratio (Brown et al., 1992; Cotter and Zimmer, 1995; Lin and Peasnell, 2000; Jaggi and Tsui, 2001). Moreover, it is also used as a signal to indicate growth opportunity as well as liquidity problem.

Leverage hypothesis: To avoid default costs, managers have incentives to adopt accounting procedures that enable them to get around debt covenants that are generally represented in terms of debt/equity ratio such as increasing assets, reducing liabilities, increasing revenue, and decreasing expenses etc.

The asset revaluation is an accounting procedure that can be used to increase shareholders' equity for as long as the asset is held. Management decides to revalue in order to avoid a technical default that incurs debt violating costs or renegotiation costs. For this reason, a firm with a higher in debt ratio is expected to revalue its assets (Begley, 1990; Brawon et al., 1992; Nichols and Buerger, 2002; Richardson et al., 2002; Piera, 2004, 2007).

The previous losses hypothesis: To avoid past losses, CEO are encouraged to use assets revaluation to create a special reserve revaluation to improve equity. Whittred and Chan (1992) and Cotter and Zimmer (1995) on the other hand, found that companies, which revalued their fixed assets were those that experienced declining cash flows from operations as well as an increase in secured debts (Janes, 2003 ; Stulz and Shin, 2000).

Firm size hypothesis: Managers of large firms apply assets revaluations to reduce the return on equity and on assets as well as the potential capital gains obtained from sales of assets, and thereby reduce their political costs (Zimmerman, 1983; Gaeremynck and Veugelers, 1999 ; Piera, 2004).

Signals theory

Signalling hypothesis is constructed from the information asymmetry which causes inappropriate investment decision of investors. Information asymmetry means the differences in the quantity and quality of a firm's information available to a firm's manager which is compared with the information that is available to others, especially investors. The asset revaluation can be applied as a signal of future performance of the firm in order to resolve information asymmetry and eliminate underinvestment problem.

Kim (2001) argues that the choice of accounting policy reflects the agency conflicts within the firm and information asymmetry in favor of the officer. Accounting choices (including assets revaluation) are used as a signal of future performance of the company and the effectiveness of its CEO (Richardson, 1998; Paek and Press, 1997, Gull and Jaggi, 1998; Chaney and Lewis, 2000, Chen and Chung 2002).

CEO BEHAVIOURAL BIAS AND ASSETS REEVALUATION

CEO loss aversion and assets revaluation

Schleifer and Vishny (1989) argue that managers opt for revaluation (increasing their firms' size) in a twofold reduction of personal risk and roots. This allows them to build a social recognition within and a good reputation among shareholders.

Tondeur (2002) adds that leaders opt for assets revaluation with the objective of minimizing the restrictive clauses in contracts for loans and the risk of bankruptcy of their firms. One explanation is that the individual, by nature, seeks to maximize and improve well-being constantly (Helliar et al., 2005; Albouy and Schatt, 2010; Nosic and Weber, 2008). It is particularly annoying to see its financial assets to deteriorate in each period. Individuals working in the financial world have already met most of its needs and tend to self-esteem that wishes to satisfy (Maslow, 1989). So any leader could be threatened by the loss of social status seeks to enhance its work at the head of his company through an accounting choices such as assets revaluation.

Cressy (2000) also postulates that the higher level of wealth or financial health of a company is growing risk aversion has its individual level decrease. In other words, the manager opted for a revaluation of assets by valuing the assets of his company in order to minimize the degree of loss aversion to his house and with partners from the firm. This choice provides a safety margin needed to achieve strategic objectives.

Finally, the leader through the asset revaluation indicates the performance of his firm and reduces the takeover. This kind of conservatism is a way to thwart a potential loss of control (Barberis and Thaler, 2002). This shows that the loss aversion of the manager is positively correlated with the choice of the assets revaluation. Hence it is necessary to set up the following hypothesis:

H_1: The more CEO is risk aversion, the more he opted for assets revaluation.

CEO optimism and assets revaluation

Heaton (2002) emphasizes that leader's optimistic estimate that the market assesses the value of his shares. This optimism builds a sense of involvement of leaders and encourages them to overstate the assets of their firms (Gervais et al., 2002). This promotes the practice of assets revaluation.

Hackbarth (2004) adds that CEO optimistic tends to use debt rather than equity. This leader was optimistic interest to report their good management through its easy to use debt (Fairchild, 2007; Robin and Yun, 2011; Malmendier et al., 2010). In this context, we can consider the interest of leaders is to reassure creditors choosing accounting methods that reduce the apparent level of debt. The revaluation of assets, increasing the value of equity and assets reduces the level of indebtedness of the firm, whether in relation to the amount of capital or assets.

Leaders optimistic future performance of their firms tend to engage in positive revaluations to reduce the political costs that their company supports it, since it allows them to reduce the return on assets and equity, and the potential gain resulting from the resale of assets (Missonier, 2003).

Parfet (2000) shows that the ability of a company to present a stable and predictable performance is a sign of good management. So all optimistic leader seeks to show that good management through its accounting choices whose practice of revaluation. Therefore, it is interesting to suggest the following hypothesis:

H_2: The more CEO is optimistic, the more he opts for assets revaluation.

CEO Overconfidence and assets revaluation

Hawinks et al. (2001), stresses that decisions over investment resulting from overexposure to media executives need to be first choice as a thought-driven procedural logic or at least in the computational interest of shareholders. In other words, every CEO overconfident on seeking ways to restore its human's capital with the assets revaluation.

Bouchie and Vernier (2009), adding CEO overconfident will be subject to confirmation bias which will lead him to seek information that confirms prior beliefs in light of past experience. This implies that any leader overconfident on research accounting choices that confirm its forecast that the practice of assets revaluation.

An executive receives much more confident about investment opportunities (Baker et al., 2004; Heaton, 2002; Malmendier and Tate, 2005). The funding of these growth opportunities requires the use of external financing (debt) expensive. So to meet the expectations of creditors in terms of financial strength, the leaders opted for assets revaluation.

Malmendier and Tate (2005) argue that overconfidence is a negative attitude that influences the capacity

Table 1. Sample used in analyses.

Initial BVMT sample for 2007	50
Financial firms	(22)
Other non financial firms	117
Insufficient data to psychological characteristics	(12)
Insufficient data to assets revaluation	(13)
Final sample	120

assessment of the alternatives for any individual as the overstatement of private information (Fairchild, 2007; Chuang et al., 2009; Hirshleifer et al., 2010; Ben-David et al., 2010). This implies that a leader chosen automation complacency revaluation of assets affine respect the principle of reliability and adequacy of financial information of their firms. This development leads us to test the following hypothesis:

H_3: The more CEO is overconfident, the more he opts for assets revaluation.

SAMPLE FORMATION AND VARIABLE MEASUREMENT

The Tunisian legal

Two schemes of revaluation have been used for the Tunisian legal:

1. Revaluation legal is applied to assets and liabilities as an index that represents the increase in the general level of prices. For depreciable assets, the new value is equal to the difference between the original value revalued and depreciation which are regulated by legal texts.
2. The second regime is the regime of free revaluation which is not regulated by laws; it follows essentially a practice inspired by the reassessment law.

The Finance Law of 2000 prohibits the re-evaluation and legal basis of this law which stipulates that Tunisian companies can make charges for revaluation. However, Accounting Standard No. 5 which addresses the tangible assets provides only the case of downward revaluation of fixed assets, thereby promoting respect for the principle of prudence.

In practice, a paradox occurs in the absence of an accounting standard that clearly addresses this phenomenon where Tunisian firms are used, to a great extent, in the technical revaluation of assets.

Data sample selection

The empirical tests are based for 120 non financial Tunisia firms for the fiscal years 2007. All financial firms (including banks) are excluded because this industry is regulated and is likely to have fundamentally different cash flow and characteristics. Firms with insufficient data to cognitive biases and financial characteristics. Financial characteristics data are obtained from annual report of the BVMT. Psychological characteristics are collected by the questionnaire (Table 1).

Measurement of variables

The objective of this section is to determinate whether variable measurement (endogens and exogenesis).

Revaluation choice (dependents variables)

The choice of accounting policy and therefore the technique of revaluation Y is a dichotomous variable that take 1 if the firm opts for a reassessment and 0 if not.

Measuring emotional bias (principals independents variables)

Method: The questionnaire focuses on the score of emotional bias (optimism, overconfidence and lost aversion). The questions were inspired from the questionnaire formulated by Fern Hill society and Industrial Alliance: every item is coded a Likert scale in 5 points ("*never accepted =1*" *à* "*accepted very well =5*").

Participants: Table 2 consisted of 120 Tunisian CEO representatives and 120 firms (70 males, 45 females, 5 unreported), ranging in age from 25 to 58. Once an informed consent was obtained from the participants, test booklets were provided, which included the Fern Hill inventory and a scannable answer sheet. The participants were given an unlimited amount of time to complete the paper based inventory.

Control variables (auxiliary independents variables)

Prior research, suggest a significant association between accounting method, leverage ratios (LEV), previous losses (PL), listing (LFTSE) and firm size (LNSIZE) (Godard, 2001; Missonier, 2003; Mard, 2004; Tondeur, 2000).

Table 2. Questionnaire participants.

		N	Percentages
Age	25-30 years	25	20.83
	31-40 years	31	25.83
	40-49 years	36	30.00
	Over 50 years	28	23.34
Sex	Males	70	58.33
	females	45	37.50
	unreported	5	4.17
Diplomat	Bac	20	16.66
	Bac+2	30	25.00
	Bac+4	60	50.00
	DAS/HDSS	10	08.34

Leverage ratio: Prior research and empirical studies have found a positive relation between accounting method and leverage ratios. Leverage (LEV) is defined as the ratio of total debts to total debts plus total assets (Brown et al., 1992).

Previous losses: It is a dichotomous variable that take 1 if firms has made a significant previous losses and 0 otherwise. This measure was adopted by Whittred and Chan (1992), Cotter and Zimmer (1995) and Gaeremynck and Veugelers (1999).

Firm size: Firm's size may affect the accounting practice. We measure it as the log of firm's total assets (LNSIZE) (Bujadi and Richardson, 1997).

Listing firm of the Tunisia stock exchange: It is a dichotomous variable that take 1 if firms is listed in the Tunisia Stock Exchange and 0 otherwise.

The model

$Y = \alpha + \alpha_1\, LAV^{*} + \alpha_2\, OP^{*} + \alpha_3\, OVER^{*} + a_4$ LEV**$+ \alpha_5$ PL**$+ \alpha_6$ LNSIZE**$+ \alpha_7$ LFTSE**$+ \xi$

Where: Y: revaluation choice. LAV: score of lost aversion. OP: score of optimism. OVER**:** score of overconfidence. LEV**:** Leverage ratio. PL**:** 1 if firm has made previous losses and 0 otherwise. LNSIZE**:** firm's size. LFTSE**:** firm's listed in the Tunisia Stock exchange. Ξ: the error. *Principals variables. **Auxiliary variables.

Given that the dependent variable is binary, the appropriate analysis would be an application of logistic regressions. In this study, empirical data will be processed using two analytical techniques: descriptive analysis and multivariate analysis. From these statistical tests, we expect that firms that choose assets revaluation that have debt ratios and sizes of the highest, which carry significant losses earlier and are overconfident-optimistic-loss aversion managers. Also, we expect that companies that do not resort to the practices of fair value, those that are characterized by the presence of rational leaders, are small and have a low debt level (Table 3).

EMPIRICAL RESULTS

We will verify the relationship between CEO emotional characteristics and choice of asset revaluation.

Descriptive analysis

Table 4 shows the test results of mean differences. We recall that this test is relevant in determining the differences in average variables (relating to accounting choices) between business users and non-users of revaluation assets. However, the information obtained shows that P-value is significant for each difference.

The results indicate the presence of a significant mean difference between the two groups in the sample for all variables. Indeed, the variables LAV, OP and OVER successively on cognitive biases officer (with the loss aversion, optimism and overconfidence officer) show the existence of a significant difference between the two groups.

Note that the leaders choosing the revaluation of assets are averse to losses relative to those not using this accounting technique (at 5%). This result confirms our first hypothesis H_1, as well as most empirical studies (Tondeur, 2002; Barberis and Thaler, 2002). These studies have linked the use of cover reassessment of the leader against the risk of bankruptcy and the takeover. This explains why the leader loss aversions are more motivated to manage their risk through assets revaluation.

Table 3. Variables description.

Class	Phenomena	Measure	Variables	Predictions
Dependents variables				
Accounting Policy Choice	Choice assets revaluation	1 if CEO choice assets revaluation and 0 otherwise		**Y**
Principals Independents variables				
Lost aversion	Loss rumination and reputation	Score obteined by the questionnaire	**LAV**	**+**
Optimism	CEO overestimate capacity of her firms	Score obteined by the questionnaire	**OP**	**+**
Overconfidence	CEO overestimate her personal competences	Score obteined by the questionnaire	**OVER**	**+**
Auxiliary independents variables				
Leverage ratios	Disciplining CEO	Leverage ratios = total debts /(total debts +total assets)	**LEV**	**+**
Previous losses	Signaled financial situation of the firms	1 if the firms has made previous losses and 0 otherwise	**PL**	**+**
Firm Size	Signaled performance of the firms	Ln (total assets)	**LNSIZE**	**+**
Listing firm of the Tunisia Stock Exchange	Signaled disclosure quality of the firms	1 if the firm is listed and 0 otherwise	**LIFTSE**	**+**

Table 4. Descriptive statistics.

Variables	Revaluating firms				Non-revaluating firms				t-statistics
	n	Minimum	Maximum	Mean (S.D)	n	Minimum	Maximum	Mean (S.D)	
LAV	58	0.39483	0.94422	0.6546 (0.64568)	62	0.39720	0.94181	-0.0150 (0.85200)	p-value
OP	58	0.54740	1.2052	0.7791 (0.96541)	62	0..54592	1.2064	-0.0972 (0.85334)	4.827**
OVER	58	0.16632	0.70741	0.3140 (0.81873)	62	0.16440	0.70933	-0.1229 (0.67507)	5.276*
LNSIZE	58	2.01267	3.69521	13.7126 (2.30759)	62	2.01307	3.69481	10.8587 (2.34235)	3.198**
LEV	58	0.22980	0.34123	0.6089 (0.17582)	62	0.22918	0.34191	0.3234 (0.13055)	6.718*
PL	58	0.26835	0.59762	0.7069 (0.45916)	62	0.26823	0.59734	0.2742 (0.44975)	10.144*
LIFTSE	58	0.05306	0.40071	0.5172 (0.50407)	62	0.05244	0.40131	0.2903 (0.45762)	5.214**

*,**, *** Significance at respectively 10, 5% and 1%.

The results emerge as a positive and significant difference at the 10% between the two groups in the sample for the variable optimistic leader. In fact, leader's revaluation practitioners are more optimistic than non-users of the accounting technique. According to the second Hypothesis H_2, this result suggests a positive association between optimism and choice of the assets revaluation. Indeed, leaders optimistic tend to go into debt rather than resorting to equity to signal their good management through their easy recourse to debt (Hackbarth, 2004). They reassure creditor's interest in choosing accounting methods that reduce the level of debt which is the apparent assets revaluation. Table 4 shows the presence of a positive and significant difference at 5% between the two groups regarding the variable trust officer. Leaders using the revaluation are

Table 5. Pearson correlation.

	REV	LAV	OP	OVER	LNSIZE	LEV	PL	LIFTSE
REV	1							
LAV (p- value 2-tailed)	0.406** (0.000)	1						
OP (p- value 2-tailed)	0.437** (0.000)	0.194* (0.034)	1					
OVER (p- value 2-tailed)	0.282** (0.002)	0.034 (0.713)	0.138 (0.132)	1				
LNSIZE (p- value 2-tailed)	0.526** (0.000)	0.300** (0.001)	0.185* (0.043)	0.108 (0.241)	1			
LEV (p- value, 2-tailed)	0.683** (0.000)	0.312** (0.001)	0.327** (0.000)	0.193* (0.034)	0.566** (0.000)	1		
PL (p- value, 2-tailed)	0.433** (0.000)	0.416** (0.000)	0.183* (0.046)	0.146 (0.112)	0.268** (0.003)	0.367** (0.000)	1	
LIFTSE (p-value 2-taieled)	0.231* (0.011)	0.080 (0.388)	-0.025 (0.787)	0.140 (0.129)	0.113 (0.219)	0.324** (0.000)	0.300** (0.001)	1

*, ** Respectively significant at 10 and 5%.

suggestible to biases of overconfidence more than non-users of this accounting method. This implies the presence of a significant positive correlation between overconfidence and the choice of the leader of the revaluation. Thus, an officer sees a lot more confident about investment opportunities (Baker et al., 2004; Heaton, 2002, Malmendier and Tate, 2005). Funding for these growth opportunities requires recourse to external financing (debt) expensive. So to meet the expectations of creditors in terms of financial strength, the leaders opted for a revaluation of assets.

The results also highlight the presence of a positive and significant difference between the two groups regarding the variables: firm size (LNSIZE), leverage ratios (LEV), previous losses (PL) and listing (LIFTSE) relating to the financial situation of the company. Consistent with our theoretical predictions of these variables are positively and significantly associated with the choice of the revaluation.

Multivariate analysis

Since the dependent variables are qualitative, an application of logistic regression requires the absence of multicollinearity between the explanatory variables. This phenomenon can be detected by examining the correlation matrix of Pearson. The results of this test, as presented in Table 5, show that the correlation coefficients are significantly smaller than 0.8 which is the line drawn by Kennedy (1985). Hence the correlation between independent variables is acceptable. The Pearson correlation among variables are presented in Table 5.

To verify if the results are not affected by a particular variable, several model specifications are available (Table 6). The first model contains behavioral variables related to Leaders (LAV, OP, OVER), four are made by adding a financial variable strongly correlated with the choice of the revaluation (LNSIZE, LEV, PL, LIFTSE). The objective here is to determine empirically the effect of leader psychological profile on these accounting choices that the assets revaluation.

Overall, the multivariate results confirm those obtained by univariate analysis. Thus, the level of officer loss aversion (LAV) is positively and significantly associated with the choice of the assets revaluation (coefficient significant at 1%). This result is explained by the fact that the individual, by nature, seeks to maximize and improve their well-being constantly. So any leader threatened by the risk of loss of social status, seeks to enhance its work at the head of his company through an accounting choice as the revaluation of assets.

The sign of coefficient on OP measuring the manager's level of optimism is consistent with that suggested by the Hypothesis H_3 (at 1%). Indeed, firms opting for a revaluation of assets are managed by leaders optimistic. These leaders optimistic chosen risky projects which affect the specific risk of the firm (Weber et al., 2007).

Hence in order to minimize the risk level of their business leaders from companies with financial constraints opted for a assets revaluation by increasing the value of equity and assets. The interest is optimistic leaders to reassure creditors choosing accounting methods (revaluation) which reduce the apparent level of debt.

The results regarding the impact of overconfidence officer show a positive association And significant (at 5% level) between over-

Table 6. The binary logistic regressions.

Variables (expected sign)	Model 1	Model 2	Model 3	Model 4	Model 5
LAV (+)	0.000*** (1.899)	0.001*** (1.714)	0.005*** (1.606)	0.009*** (1.478)	0.009*** (1.493)
OP (+)	0.000*** (1.360)	0.000*** (1.690)	0.002*** (1.471)	0.001*** (1.606)	0.002*** (1.635)
OVER (+)	0.002*** (1.180)	0.004*** (1.169)	0.029** (1.008)	0.034** (1.035)	0.035** (1.035)
LNSIZE (+)		0.000*** (0.613)	0.039** (0.346)	0.019** (0.391)	0.020** (0.398)
LEV (+)			0.001** (7.313)	0.001*** (7.242)	0.003*** (7.034)
PL (+)				0.039** (1.508)	0.052** (1.467)
LIFTSE					0.828 (0.167)
Constant	0.000*** (-1.511)	0.000*** (-9.105)	0.000*** (-9.015)	0.000*** (-10.480)	0.000*** (-10.542)
Cox and Snell ratios R^2	0.383	0.512	0.570	0.586	0.586
X^2 of the model	58.031	27.951	15.242	4.653	0.047
- 2 log likelihood	108.191	80.239	64.997	60.345	60.297
N	120	120	120	120	120

**, ***Respectively significant at 5 and 1%.

confidence (OVER) of the officer and the assets revaluation. Thus, an officer sees a lot more confident about investment opportunities (Baker et al., 2004; Heaton, 2002, Malmendier and Tate, 2005). Funding for these growth opportunities requires recourse to external financing (debt) expensive. So to meet the expectations of creditors in terms of financial strength, the leaders opted for an assets revaluation.

The firm size (LNSIZE) has a positive and significant influence on the choice of the revaluation. This result is consistent with theoretical developments. Indeed the leaders of large companies are more concerned by the revaluation of their assets to reduce the political costs. This finding is confirmed by research Gaeremynck and Veugelers (1999) and Missonier (2004). The leverage ratios (LEV) is associated positively and significantly (at 1% level) with the choice of the revaluation. This result confirms the predictions of positive accounting theory and suggests that firm's use debts are more than others from the assets revaluation (Whittred et al., 1992; Brown et al., 1992; Cotter et al., 1995; Black et al., 1998; Cotter, 1999, Lin et al., 2000). Managers are encouraged to adopt accounting procedures that allow them to circumvent the restrictive covenants limiting the ability to leverage their businesses, though assets revaluation is a way to reduce transaction costs of the company.

The regressions show a positive and significant association between the presence of previous losses and the choice of the revaluation (at 5%). This result implies that firms have made significant previous losses are most affected by the revaluation. This finding suggests that the leaders of the Tunisian companies are resorting to revaluation to recover part of the capital lost due to realized losses

Finally, we note the presence of a positive and not significant between the listing of the company (LIFTSE) and the choice of the revaluation. This is explained by compliance with the law regarding disclosure of financial information.

Conclusion

This article examines the impact of cognitive biases in their choice of accounting methods (revaluation). Exploratory in nature, this work has attempted to fill a gap in research in accounting, with a survey of executives in large private enterprises in Tunisia. Analyses of data collected showed the importance of emotions Tunisian leaders in the explanation of their accounting choices. Indeed, the empirical analysis of the relationship of emotions with the reassessment shows the positive impact of cognitive bias frames Tunisian companies on quality, reliability and relevance of accounting information disclosed. Given the effects and benefits of the personal, social and professional biases, the cognitive defects imply that it is important to control them.

REFERENCES

Albouy M, Schatt A (2010). La politique de dividende permet-elle de discipliner les dirigeants ? , LEG UMR Cnrs 5118 – FARGO, Centre de recherche en Finance, Architecture et Gouvernance des Organisations, Cahier du FARGO n° 1100603, Juin 2010.

Baker M, Ruback RS, Wurgler J (2004).Behavioral Corporate Finance: A Survey. SSRN, à paraître (2005) in B. Eckbo (Ed.), Handbook of Corporate Finance: Empirical Corporate Finance. SSRN_ID740946.

Ball R,Foster G (1982). Corporate Financial Reporting: a method-ological review of empirical Research. J. Account. Res., 20: 161-234.

Barberis N, Thaler R (2002). A Survey of Behavioral Finance . In forthcoming Handbook of the Economics of Finance, 1:1053-1128.

Barton J (2001). Does the use of financial derivatives affect earnings management decisions. Account. Rev., 76: 1-26.

Ben-David I, Graham JR, Harvey CR (2010).Managerial Miscalibration. SSRN Working Paper. Electronic copy available at:

http://ssrn.com/abstract=1640552.
Bujadi ML, Richardson AJ (1997). A Citation Trail Review of the Uses of Firm Size in Accounting Research. J. Account.Lit., 16: 1-27.
Chaney PK, Lewis CM (2000). Earnings management and firm valuation under asymmetric information. Working paper, www.ssrn.com.
Chang C, Lee AC, Lee CF (2009). Determinants of Capital Structure Choice : A Structural Equation Modeling Approach. The Quarterly Revi. Econ. Finance, 49: 197-213.
Chen X, Cheng Q (2002). Abnormal accruals –based anomaly and managers motivations to record abnormal accruals. SSRN Working paper, www.ssrn.com.
Cormier D (2002).comptabilité anglo-saxonne et internationale. Economica, www.amazon.ca, ISBN-10: 2717844902.
Cotter J, Stokes D, Wyatt A (1998). An analysis of factors influencing asset write downs. Account. Finance. 38: 157-179.
Cressy R (2000). Credit Rationing Risk Aversion Entrepreneurial gold? An Alternative Explanation for the Evans and Jovanovich Finding. Economics Letters, 66: 235-240.
Defond M, Jiambalvo J (1994). Debt convenant effects and the manipulation of accruals. J. Account. Econ., 17: 145-176.
Dichev ID, Skinner DJ (2002). Large sample evidence on the debt convenant hypothesis. SSRN working papers,www.ssrn.com.
Dumontier P, Raffournier B (1988).voluntary changes of accounting policies in the absence of restrictive clauses in loan contracts: the French case. Working Paper 88, June, ESA Grenoble.
Fairchild R (2007). Managerial Overconfidence, Agency Problems, Financing Decisions and firm performance. University of Bath School of Management, Working Paper Series 11.
Fern Hill is a wealth management company, www.fhpartenership.com
Francis J, Hanna JD, Vincent L (1996). Causes and effects of discretionary asset write offs. J. Account. Res.. 34: 117-134.
Gervais S, Heaton JB, Odean T (2002). The Positive Role of Overconfidence and Optimism in Investment Policy.Mimeo, University Of California, Berkeley.
Gul FA, Jaggi B (1998). Evidence of Accruals Management: A Test of the Free Cash Flow and Debt Monitoring Hypotheses. SSRN Working paper, www.ssrn.com.
Hackbarth D (2004). Managerial characteristics and capital structure decisions. Working Paper, Indiana University.
Hawkins SA, Hoch SJ, Meyers-Levy J (2001). Low-Involvement Learning: Repetition and Coherence in Familiarity and Belief. J. Consumer Psychol., 11: 1-11.
Heaton JB.(2002). Managerial Optimism and Corporate Finance. Financial Management, 31: 33-45.
Helliar C, Power D, Sinclair C (2005). Managerial "irrationality" in financial decision making, Managerial Finance, 31(4): 1-11.
Hirshleifer DA, Teoh SH, Low A (2010). Are Overconfident CEOs Better Innovators? SSRN Working Paper. www.ssrn.com.
Holgate P, Ghosh J (2000). Revaluation loophole? Accountancy. 125(1279): 88.
Janes TD (2003). Accruals, financial distress end debt covenants. Working paper, www.ssrn.com.
Julien PA, Marchesnay M (1987). Small Business , Paris, Vuibert.
Kim Y (2001). Disclosure and earnings management by seasoned equity offerings firms», Working paper, www.ssrn.com.
Malmendier U, Tate G (2005). CEO Overconfidence and Corporate Investment. J. Finance, 60(6): 2661-2700.
Malmendier U , Tate G, Yan J (2010). Managerial beliefs and corporate financial policies. Working Paper, UC Berkeley and UC Los Angeles.
Mard Y (2004). Performance management accounting: the influence of financial policy, performance and control. Congress of the Association francophone de comptabilité.
Maslow AH (1989).Towards a psychology of being». Fayard, Paris, 1989.
Nosić A, Weber M (2008). How Risky Do I Invest: The Role of Risk Attitudes, Risk Perceptions and Overconfidence. Working Paper University of Mannheim.
Paek W, Press E (1997). Discretionary accruals, managers incentives and stock prices. Www. Umi.com.
Parfet W (2000). Accounting Subjectivity and earnings management: prepare a perspective. Accounting Horizons 14(4): 481-488.
Piera FM (2003). factors explaining the positive revaluation of assets: the case Switzerland. Accounting, Control, Auditing, 9: 59-80.
Piera FM (2007). Motives for fixed-asset revaluation: An empirical analysis with Swiss data. Int. J. Account., 42: 186–205.
Richardson VJ (1998). Information asymmetry and earnings management: some evidence. Working paper, www.ssrn.com.
Richardson TI, WU M (2002). Predicting earnings management: The case of earnings restatements. Working paper, www.ssrn.com.
Robin KCH, Yun-Yi W (2011). A test of the different implications of the overconfidence and disposition hypotheses. J. Bank. Finance, 35(8): 2037-2046.
Saada T (1995). Determinants of accounting choices: study of practical French and Franco-American comparison. Accounting, Control, Auditing, 1 (2): 52-74.
Schleifer A, Vishny RW (1989).Value maximization and the acquisition process . J. Econ. Perspectives, 2(1): 7-20.
Strong JS, Meyer JR (1987). Asset write downs: managerial incentives and security returns. J. Finance. XLII (3): 643-663.
Stulz RM, Shin HH (2000). An analysis of divisional investment policies. Working paper, www.ssrn.com.
Thauvron A. (2000). The manipulation of accounting income before a public offering . Accounting, Control, Auditing, 6 (2): 97-114.
Tondeur H (2002). The terms of debt contracts. J. Account. French, 346: 35-36.
Vernier E. and Bouchie A. (2009), « Impact Des Résultats Passés Sur L'aversion Au Risque De L'investisseur». Laboratoire de Recherche sur l'Industrie et l'Innovation Université du Littoral Côte d'Opale, document de travail n°209, février 2009.
Watts R. and Zimmerman J. (1978). Towards a positive theory of the determination of accounting standards. The Accounting Review, 53: 112-134.
Watts R, Zimmerman J (1986). Positive Accounting Theory. (Englewood Cliffs, NJ: Prentice-Hall).

Goodwill impairment after business combination among Jordanian shareholding companies

Husam Al-Khadash[1]* and Asmahan Y. Salah[2]

[1]Hashemite University P.O. Box 330125, Postcode 13133, Hashemite University, Zarqa, Jordan.
[2]Central Bank of Jordan, Amman, Jordan.

This study examined whether external users of financial statements are capable of assessing goodwill impairment apart from management. This study aimed at investigating goodwill write-offs resulted from acquisitions among Jordanian shareholding companies in Amman Stock Exchange (ASE) during 1985 - 2005. This study tested for the notion that the seeds of the eventual goodwill write-off are planted at the time of the acquisition. The likelihood of a write-off is related to an initial overpayment as indicated by acquisition characteristics as well as some of post acquisition performance indicators. The results of this study provided some support for the hypothesis that predicts the relationship between goodwill write-offs and acquisition and performance indicators. However, the study revealed that external users will not be able to assess goodwill impairment effectively within the available information and disclosure.

Key words: Goodwill, international accounting standards, impairment and acquisition.

INTRODUCTION

Goodwill recognition and measurement were in dispute for several years ago. In 2004, the International Accounting Standards Board (IASB, 2006) introduced new standards that changed the overall treatment of goodwill. Pooling of interests method was eliminated as an acceptable accounting method for business combinations in favor of acquisition method. Furthermore, goodwill is no longer be amortized instead it is tested annually for possible impair-ment. This study aims at identifying factors affecting goodwill impairment regarding the acquisitions occurred among Jordanian shareholding companies in Amman Stock Exchange (ASE) during 1985 - 2005. The metho-dology of investigation is based on the model of Hayn and Hughes (2005).

The importance of this study may be attributed to the recent enactments in accounting for goodwill as well as the need to determine goodwill deterioration externally which is of great importance to auditors and investors. Furthermore, Jordan has witnessed an increasing tendency of banks and firms to be combined which make this study to be essential.

The aim of the study is to examine whether external users of financial statements are capable of assessing goodwill deterioration, this is in accordance with the purpose of adopting International Financial Reporting Standard No. 3 (IFRS 3) Business Combinations; that is to provide users with the most useful information. One way to address the question at hand is to determine whether goodwill write-offs are predictable. Goodwill writing-off involves the extreme elimination of this asset from the balance sheet either through immediate writing-off or through amortization as in previous accounting treatments or through goodwill impairment as the new standards suggest.

If using the financial statements and the market information enable predicting goodwill write-offs, the investors and auditors will have sufficient information to value goodwill. Moreover this may indicate that there are some factors may affect goodwill write-offs other than management choice. Consequently, if goodwill write-offs are predictable, then any deterioration in its value can also be predictable (Hayn and Hughes, 2005).

The amendments in acquisitions and goodwill accounting improved the financial reporting because it adjusted the way goodwill is treated. The users of financial

*Corresponding author. E-mail: husam@hu.edu.jo.

statements will be better able to understand the investments made in those assets and subsequent performance of those investments. Since overpayments are a substantial component of goodwill it seems that it is reasonable to assume that in the years after the acquisition, the lack of coverage in future returns becomes evident and leads to write-offs of goodwill. If goodwill overpayment affects its subsequent writing-off, then it is appropriate to examine the probable effect of overpayment indicators on goodwill write-offs however; this is the essence of this study.

The core objective of the study is to determine the factors that affect goodwill impairment in the shareholding companies in Jordan. This study seeks to reveal whether those factors enable external users such as auditors and investors to predict goodwill write-off and hence goodwill impairment apart from management. This is an examination of management reporting quality, moreover it enables outside parties understanding the issues related to goodwill (Hayn and Hughes, 2005). The study also aims to highlight the market reaction to the acquisition release which may provide an insight of the success of the acquisition.

The balance of this study is organized as follows: the next section includes literature review related to goodwill. In the third section the methodology of investigation is illustrated, this includes the model of investigation as well as an explanation for each variable in it. Also it describes the sample and data used in the study. The statistical analysis results are displayed in the fourth part of the study. Finally the main conclusions are included in the fifth section of the study.

LITERATURE REVIEW

The concept of goodwill has developed in latest decades since the first definition of goodwill reflected it as a residual amount. Essentially goodwill is a residual that cannot be transferred to a new owner without also selling the other identifiable intangible and tangible assets (Sundararajan, 1995). Goodwill is difficult to measure regarding the factors that initially lead to the existence of it; in essence goodwill is what is left over after properly valuing everything else (Johnson and Petrone, 1999).

The definition of goodwill

At first goodwill was thought of as special properties of a business that make its relationships with customers more valuable than other businesses in the same field. The first definition describing goodwill was emerged in the 1880s whereas goodwill considered being the difference between the purchase price and the book value of an acquired company's assets (Johnson and Tearney, 1993).

Sundararajan (1995) discussed the two manners goodwill may be presented through; the first is the residuum approach that considers goodwill as a leftover amount. Goodwill represents the excess of purchase price over the fair market value of the acquiree's net assets and cannot be identified separately. The second is the excess profit approach where goodwill is the difference between the combined company's profits over normal earnings for a similar business. The second definition states that goodwill is the present value of the projected future excess normal earnings that may be generated by the acquiree. This concept is difficult to measure given the uncertainty related to the future earnings as well as the difficulty attributed to the probable discount rate to use (Sundararajan, 1995).

Under IFRS 3 goodwill is the excess of the cost of a business acquisition over the fair value of the net assets thereof. The fair value is defined as the amount for which an asset could be exchanged or a liability settled between knowledgeable, willing parties in an arm's length transaction.

Goodwill and business combination

Goodwill is an asset that cannot be determined unless an acquisition takes place (Ramanna, 2007). Firms may undertake business combinations for several reasons; the main reason is related to the expansion issue. Although firms can expand through internal growth as investment projects are carried out, external growth is usually used (in the form of business combinations).

Generally, business combinations are events or transactions in which two or more business enterprises or their net assets are brought under common control as a single accounting entity. Under IFRS 3 business combinations are considered to be acquisitions whereby one entity (the acquirer) obtains control over the net assets and synergies of another entity (the acquiree) in exchange for the transfer of assets, incurrence of liabilities or issuance of stocks.

Two methods are used in business combinations namely: pooling or uniting of interests and purchase or acquisition method. The main difference between the two methods is that goodwill arises only under the purchase method; the new treatment for acquisitions prohibits the use of pooling of interests. Acquisitions are complex and high risk processes unless there is logic to a takeover that leads to a planned approach to growth (Hopkins et al., 1999).

Several previous studies addressed the notion of business combination and its different methods reflecting the changes in the accounting treatment of acquisitions. Ayers et al. (2002) demonstrated that pooling of interests accounting results in substantially stronger reported performance and financial condition than purchase accounting.

Farhan (2002) studied banking mergers and acquisitions

in Jordan; he examined whether business combinations are useful and profitable for banks. He found that small banks should merge in order to form solid and large banking entities that may increase their share in the market as well as their contribution to the national economy growth.

An important aspect connected to business combinations is the impact of acquisitions on shareholders returns. Several previous studies examined this issue using event studies technique. Kusnadi and Sohrabian (1999) explored the impact of acquisitions on shareholders returns within the insurance sector. Their findings revealed that the acquiring firms do not obtain any significant abnormal returns. On the other hand Duso et al. (2006) proved the positive relationship between acquisitions and the profitability.

Accounting for goodwill

In 1997 the Financial Accounting Standards Board (FASB) enacted Concepts Statement No.6 in which the board decided that goodwill is an asset (Johnson and Petrone, 1999). Prior to the development of accounting standards on goodwill, there were many options related to goodwill accounting, these options were varied between asset based methods as capitalization and the elimination methods as the immediate write-off against reserves (Lewis and Pendrill, 2004). Amortization is another option that was widely used moreover it enables companies to match the cost of intangible assets over the period deemed to benefit from their acquisition.

Under International Accounting Standard No. 22 (IAS 22) Accounting for Business Combinations which was replaced by IFRS 3- the amortization was undertaken through goodwill's useful life, a specific number of years or subject to a maximum of twenty years. A lot of problems are related to the amortization method; it is difficult to determine the useful life of goodwill even when using specific years, the difficulty is attributed to the arbitrariness of such process as indicated in IFRS 3.

The impairment option is the current treatment of goodwill and which was allowed by IFRS 3 wherein goodwill is written-down to recoverable amount through the income statement. Impairment exists when the carrying amount of goodwill exceeds its fair value and is non recoverable, that is the book value is larger than the undiscounted cash flows expected from the goodwill's use and the eventual disposal. Goodwill deterioration may be determined regarding the indicators of goodwill overpayment and post acquisition performance indicators such as the firm return on assets (ROA). ROA is an important measure of performance and the change in its value may be a useful indicator in analysis as well.

Write-off in accounting is the expensing of goodwill that has been estimated to have no future benefits. This means that goodwill will be recorded as an expense on the current period's income statement rather than keeping it on the balance sheet as an asset. Write-down is a partial write-off where only part of the value of the asset is removed from the balance sheet.

IFRS 3 maintained the same amendments of goodwill and business combination accounting adopted by FASB in 2001. The amendments are represented in both the Statement of Financial Accounting Standards No.141 (SFAS 141) Business Combinations and the Statement of Financial Accounting Standards No.142 (SFAS 142) Goodwill and Other Intangible Assets.

There are few differences between IFRS 3 and US standards. The cost of an acquisition must be measured at the date of the acquisition that is the date the acquirer obtains control of the acquiree net assets. Conversely, under US standards the cost is measured at the date of the announcement. Furthermore, under IFRS 3 the cost of acquisition is determined either in cost or with reference to IAS 39 Financial Instruments: Recognition and Measurement while the cost of acquisition is determined in US standards regarding the equity method.

In SFAS 142 goodwill is allocated among reporting units, which are operating segments of an enterprise, while in IFRS 3 goodwill shall be allocated to cash-generating units. A cash-generating unit is defined in IAS 36 Impairment of Assets as the smallest identifiable group of assets that generates cash inflows that are largely independent of the cash inflows from other assets or groups of assets. The cash-generating units may be similar to or smaller than reporting units mentioned in SFAS 142.

Most of researches concentrated on the usefulness of the new standards as compared to the previous practices. Hitz and Kuhner (2002) analyzed the usefulness of impairment charge in decision making through comparing the net income prior and after goodwill write-offs to the economic income. They favored the goodwill impairment method over the amortization method. Chen et al. (2004) proved that the new rules of goodwill accounting outperform the previous enactments. On the other hand Wiese (2005) favored the amortization approach. Chambers (2006) concluded that that goodwill accounting under SFAS 142 does not improve financial reporting compared to amortization-based accounting.

Carlin et al. (2007) discussed the adoption of IFRS 3, which seemed to be complex and of great risk according to their conclusion. Zhang and Zhang (2006) predicted that management is motivated to allocate more purchase price to goodwill. The exposure draft of SFAS 142 includes some indicators of goodwill overpayment. First, the existence of more than one bidder may cause the value allocated to goodwill to be overstated (Ruback, 1983). Second, the means of payment is an important indicator when evaluating goodwill overpayment. When the payment is made in form of stock-for-stock acquisitions rather than cash payment, then the existence of goodwill overpayment becomes evident (Loughran and Vijh, 1997).

Third, the higher proportion of goodwill to the acquisition price may suggest the existence of overpayment. Finally, the difference between the acquisition price and the acquiree's market value is another factor that is suggested to be a reason for overpayment, the higher the difference, the more likelihood of goodwill overpayment.

In Jordan there is no study directly related to the issue of goodwill impairment, nevertheless, there is few researches demonstrated some issues of this study as the work of Waked (2005). He studied the effect of merging Jordanian shareholding companies on their financial performance. He concluded that in general there is no difference between the financial performances of merging firms before and after the acquisition but there are some significant differences in the firms ROA ratios.

METHODOLOGY OF THE STUDY

Management usually is the main responsible of performing goodwill write-offs. Determining goodwill write-offs by external users is what this study aims at, by using the goodwill write-off model which was developed by Hayn and Hughes (2005). This study depends on the acquisitions occurred among Jordanian firms within the period 1985 - 2005 in order to explain the main indicators that lead to goodwill impairment.

Goodwill write-off prediction model

Hayn and Hughes (2005) investigated if acquisition factors enable outside parties to predict the goodwill impairment pattern. Their work was actually inspired by the well-developed hazard model forecasting bankruptcy attributed to Shumway (1999) that served as guidance for them to develop the first model predicting goodwill write-off.

The goodwill write-off model was developed in accordance to the bankruptcy predicting model depending on two main things. First, bankruptcy is determined when the financial viability of the firm is getting worse similarly goodwill exists when there is a financial deterioration in the cash-generating unit. Second, the explanatory variables determine bankruptcy are varying with time resembles some of the explanatory variables that may affect goodwill write-offs, so both of models are interrelated in accounting for time.

Following is the model used in this study,

$$Pr\ (\text{Write-off})_{i,\ t} = f\ (\text{acquisition characteristics}_{i,\ A},\ \text{performance indicators}_{i,\ n}).$$

$$\text{WRITE-OFF}_{i,t} = \alpha + \beta_1 \text{PREM}_{i,A} + \beta_2 \text{BID}_{i,A} + \beta_3 \text{GW\%}_{i,A} + \beta_4 \text{STOCK}_{i,A} + \beta_5 \text{ANRET}_{i,A} + \beta_6 \text{ROA}_{i,n} + \beta_7 \Delta\ \text{ROA}_{i,n} + u_{i,t}$$

where:

WRITE-OFF= goodwill write-off.
PREM= the payment of a premium.
BID= the existence of more than one bidder.
GW = the percentage of goodwill to the acquisition price.
STOCK= using of stock as a mode of consideration in the acquisition.
ANRET= the abnormal return.
ROA= Return on assets.
Δ ROA= Change in return on assets.

The subscripts i and A denotes the firm and acquisition year respectively, while the subscript t represents the write-off year if there is any.

The dependent variable in the model is the goodwill write-off. This variable is a dichotomous that receives the value 1 if the firm experienced the write-off of goodwill and if there is no write-off, the variable receives the value 0. Consequently, if the firm takes write-off then t is the year of the write-off and n ranges from A+1 to t, years following the write-off are eliminated from the sample. On the other hand for non write-off group during 1985 - 2005 which is the sample period, n ranges from A+1 up to the year 2006 wherein the last data available. The study excludes the acquisitions that occurred in the year 2006 because of the non availability of data of post acquisition performance indicators at the time of analyzing the data.

The study use a binary logistic model, the difficulty of such model is attributed to its non-linear likelihood functions, as well as it involves varying characteristics of its independent variables. This model includes each firm year as a separate observation. Since the acquisition variables are not observable for each firm-year, past years values are substituted for missing values, this does not present an econometric problem [1]. Logistic models in which several observations exist for each individual, usually account for the lack of independence between observations that is the characteristic of panel data. This is resolved here because this model assumes that the number of independent observations used to estimate the model is the number of the firm-years in the data.

Performing correct descriptive statistics requires adjusting the sample size assumed by the logit program to account for the lack of independence between firm-year observations. For the write-off model each firm's entire life span is one observation thus the correct value of (n) for descriptive statistics is the number of acquisitions in the sample not the number of firm years. So to estimate the hazard model, each year in which the firm keeps goodwill without writing-off is included in the analysis.

The null hypothesis H_0 of this study is that there is no prediction power for the hazard model in goodwill write-off and hence goodwill impairment is not affected by the acquisition characteristics or by the performance factors. On the other hand the alternative hypothesis that is H_1 assumes the existence of some prediction effect of the independent variables on goodwill write-off.

The details of the econometric properties of the hazard model are described in Shumway's article (1999).

Variables of acquisition characteristics

The goodness of goodwill that indicates whether any overvaluation exists is determined at the time of the acquisition. The first variable in the goodwill write-off model is the payment of a significant premium. This represents the extent to which the acquirer is optimistic about the future performance of the acquired firm based on the current market operations which may contribute in overvaluation of goodwill. This variable is measured through firstly considering the average market value of the acquired firm.

After computing the average market value it is subtracted from the acquisition cost that embraces two components; the acquisition price and incurred liabilities. Eventually the premium is determined as the difference between the acquisition cost and the average market value of the acquired firm to the average market value of the acquired firm's equity over the pre-acquisition period.

The second variable related to the goodness of goodwill is the bidding action. The tendency of the acquisition price tends to be driven up during the acquisition when more than one bidder aspires to the acquisition rather than when the target firm is acquired through a fire sale or distress where goodwill seemed to be understated. This is a dummy variable denoted as 1 where there is more than one bidder and receives the value 0, otherwise. Goodwill is the third acquisition variable represented as a percentage of the amount imputed to goodwill to the acquisition price. Overpayment may be connected to this variable more than others in the model whereas the higher the ratio of goodwill to acquisition price the higher the probability of overpayment.

The fourth variable in the model is the use of stock as a means of payment. Since using stock may produce higher value than if those shares were sold for cash, the acquirer usually is aware of the potential loss of cash more than the dilutive effects of stock. The value of this variable ranging from 0 to 1 depending on the use of cash in the transaction where 0 indicates that it was all cash transaction, 1 means pure stock transaction (Hayn and Hughes, 2005).

The fifth indicator of goodwill overvaluation is the cumulated acquisition period abnormal return. This variable is generated as a market reaction to the acquisition announcement. This variable may serves as an estimator of acquisition success, if the abnormal returns were much less than those expected then the acquisition price might be overvalued (Kusnadi and Sohrabian, 1999).

The last variable may be estimated through the practice of event study analysis that is the statistical approach commonly used in researches to measure the impact of a particular information release on returns. The measure of the unexpected return that results from the announcement of acquisition is measured as the difference between the actual stock return and the return that might have been expected given the performance of the market (Kothari and Warner, 2004). This is accomplished through using the index model, which holds that the daily stock returns are determined by a market factor and a firm-specific factor. The index model is shown below:

$$r_t = \alpha + b\, r_{mt} + e_t$$

Where:

r_t: is the stock return given period t.
r_{mt} : is the market's rate of return during the period t.
e_t: is the part of a security's return resulting from firm-specific events.
b: is the measure of sensitivity to market return.
α : is the average rate of return the stock would realize in a period with a zero market return.

The general strategy to estimate this variable is to determine the cumulative abnormal return around the date of acquisition. The first step is to estimate the parameters α and b by using the regression analysis in a 250 trading day's period. Then the abnormal returns of each firm surrounding the acquisition date are computed for 21 days. Using the following formula:

$$e_t = r_t - (\alpha + b\, r_{mt})$$

Finally the abnormal returns are compounded to estimate the cumulative abnormal return.

Variables of post acquisition performance

This study includes two post acquisition performance explanatory variables. The first post acquisition indicator used in the model is the Return on Assets (ROA). This represents an important performance indicator that in its most simplified form equals income over assets. However; it may be disaggregated to more meaningful components, in relation with sales it may be considered as the profit margin times the asset turnover so that it possess a very indicative insight to the purpose of the study (Epstein and Mirza, 2005).

The second performance variable is much related to the first one since it represents the change in return on assets (Δ ROA). This variable highlights the situation of any deterioration occur in the performance of the firm and draws the direction of the firm's total return on assets (Hayn and Hughes, 2005). The performance indicators and the acquisition characteristics are combined together to estimate the hazard model of goodwill write-off. The study uses the statistical package SPSS to test the main hypothesis that assumes the independent variables as variables with no power in predicting goodwill write-off.

Sample and Data

This study examines the acquisitions that took place among Jordanian firms in the period 1985 - 2005 however, there are some conditions must be met by acquisitions in order to be included in the sample. First, both of the involved parties in the acquisition process are shareholding companies listed in ASE. Second, Acquisition characteristics data were available at the acquisition date. Fourth, business combinations that used the pooling of interests method were erased from the sample keeping only those acquisitions gave rise for goodwill to be included.

Given the above conditions, only 20 cases are included in the analysis whereas the original population was 52 acquisitions. Nine of them were in 1985-1989 while six occurred after 2005 and the remainders were in 1990s. There is no common trend in the attitude of acquisitions in Jordan perhaps it was remarkable that the acquisitions of 1985 - 1989 were mainly among the insurance sector. On the other hand the intensity of acquisitions beyond the year 2000 were concentrated in the industrial sector. The sample of the study includes 20 acquisitions with 89 firm-years.

The sources of data collection were multiple given the numerous data required, the information about the closing prices and the market values for the intended firms and the general market index were obtained from ASE. While the data about the study's performance indicators were obtained from the ASE company guides. The data related to the amount of goodwill, number of bidders, the acquisition price, the liabilities incurred the use of stock in the acquisition and goodwill write-offs were obtained from a various sources. The Ministry of Industry and Trade is the main source of data and the other sources are: ASE and The Central Bank of Jordan (for those acquisitions related with banks).

The descriptive statistics of the final sample that includes 20 acquisitions are drawn in Table 1 wherein each variable statistics in the goodwill write-off model are displayed. The table draws the mean, median, maximum value, minimum value and the standard deviation for each variable. As mentioned earlier the number of observations is adjusted to the number of acquisitions instead of the number of firm years in the descriptive statistics.

Table 1 indicates the data statistics for the overall sample whether performed goodwill write-off or not. It is displayed in the table that 80% of the acquisitions performed the write-off. Goodwill is an important asset in the acquisition process, as Table 1 indicates its mean value is 60.66% of the acquisition price which is relatively high. The acquisitions with multiple bidders constitute 20% of the sample while 35% of the acquisitions used the stock as the primary method of payment. The abnormal return of the acquisition period mean value is -0.21 which is a small negative number that affirms the notion of overpayment since the firms (on average) do not generate positive returns as expected. The performance indicators illustrate reductions in the values of return on assets.

The acquisition variables of the model were included in the model because of the possibility of being related to goodwill write-off and the main issue is the existence of overpayment. The lower part of Table 1 divides the sample into two groups: the write-off group which are those firms that performed write-off before the year 2006, and the non-write-off group which includes the firms with no goodwill write-off prior to 2006. The table displays the mean and median for each group and the t-statistic of differences in mean values.

Table 1 indicates that the premium of the write-off group is higher than of the non-write-off group but the t-statistics shows that the

Table 1. Descriptive statistics of variables of goodwill write-off model.

N = 20 acquisitions			80 % of acquisitions resulted in goodwill write-off 35 % of the acquisitions performed the write-off during the first year		
Variable	**Mean**	**Median**	**Standard deviation**	**Maximum**	**Minimum**
Acquisition indicators					
PREM	37.43	32.47	29.01	98.18	4.23
GW as a % of acquisition price	60.66	50.50	18.08	90.00	40.60
% of acquisitions with multiple bidders	20				
% of stock acquisitions	35				
ANRET as a%	-0.21	-0.51	8.46	32.29	-12.58
Performance indicators: variables are measured at the end of the second year following the acquisition year.					
ROA as a %	3.06	2.97	3.18	7.60	-1.84
Δ ROA as a %	-2.15	-1.85	3.15	4.30	-8.50
	Write-off group (n = 16)		**Non-write-off group (n = 4)**		
	Mean	**Median**	**Mean**	**Median**	**Difference in mean values (t-statistics)**
Acquisition indicators					
PREM	37.78	32.47	36.02	36.44	1.76 (0.150)
GW as % of acquisition price	64.79	61.00	44.15	44.00	20.64 (4.348)
% of stock acquisitions	12.5		50		
% of acquisitions with multiple bidders	37.5		25		
ANRET as a %	-0.04	-0.52	-0.88	-0.50	0.84 (0.345)

difference is not significant using two-tailed test. Furthermore, goodwill percentage of the acquisition price for the write-off group (64.79% on average) is much higher than for the non-write-off group (44.15% on average), a statistically significant difference. This may assure that the higher the value attributed to goodwill the higher the probability of overestimation of the acquisition price.

The announcement period abnormal returns are on average small negative numbers for both groups, and this is consistent with previous studies as Kusnadi and Sohrabian (1999). They found that the acquiring firms do not obtain any significant abnormal returns in the acquisition announcement period.

RESULTS

The analyses are performed to test for two main hypotheses; the first is the examination of the prediction power of the model and the second is to predict goodwill write-off using the results of the analysis. The study is based on a binary logistic regression model because the ordinary least squares (OLS) regression is inappropriate for explaining dependent variables that are dichotomous. It aims at estimating whether there is any relationship between the goodwill write-off and the variables that were observed at the time of the acquisition, and other variables observed beyond the acquisition event.

The model of the study is a binary logistic model whereby the regress receives only two values namely; 1 and 0. The analysis was orientated toward examining the existence or absence of the goodwill write-off based on the independent variables which are divided into two groups; acquisition variables and post acquisition performance indicators. Second, the other goal of estimating the goodwill write-off model is to rank the relative importance of independents based on their significance in determining goodwill write-off.

With reference to the criteria of selecting the sample of the study, 20 acquisitions were included in the analysis making the number of observations (n) to be 20 acquisitions and 89 firm-years. The first part of the analysis demonstrates the prediction of goodwill write-off.

The null model results

The analysis in Table 2 shows the first step in the binary logistic model that describes a "null model", that is model with no predictors and just the intercept. The first step, called step 0, includes no predictors and just the intercept, and step 1, where the explanatory variables are included with the intercept.

The overall percentage that was correctly predicted given the null model is 82.0. The coefficient for the constant (B) is -1.518 with a standard error 0.276. The null hypothesis that the constant equals zero is rejected because the calculated p-value is smaller than the critical

Table 2. The null model results.

			Write-off		Percentage correct
			0.00	**1.00**	
Step 0	**Write-off**	0.00			100
		1.00	73	0	0
	Overall percentage		16	0	82.0

		B	**S.E**	**Wald**	**df**	**Sig.**	**Exp (B)**
Step 0	Constant	-1.518	0.276	30.236	1	0.000	0.219
The initial -2 log likelihood				83.847			
Score test results							

			Score	**df**	**Sig.**
Step 0	Variables	PREM	0.100	1	0.752
		GW	30.364	1	0.000
		BID	0.264	1	0.607
		STOCK	9.646	1	0.002
		ANRET	0.874	1	0.350
		ROA	8.511	1	0.004
		ΔROA	6.498	1	0.011
	Overall statistics		39.716	7	0.000

P value at the level of significance 0.05 (Table 2). Hence, the analysis concludes that the intercept is not zero. The initial -2 log likelihood (-2LL) is 83.847, however this number is not informative itself but it will be compared with -2 log likelihood in step1.The intercept analysis findings are not of interest except that it shows the difference of including the independent variables in the model.

Table 2 displays also the results of the score test. When looking at the p-values, the variables that are expected to be significant at the level of 0.05 in the model are: GW, STOCK, ROA and ΔROA considering the other variables to be statistically insignificant regarding their p-values that exceed 0.05. When looking at the final component of Table 2, the overall statistics are predicted to be statistically significant given the level of significance that equals zero. The results demonstrated above are the results of Step 0 that is the first step in the binary logistic regression. The score test predicts the attitude of the independent variables in the model but it is just a preliminary prediction, which signifies that the results may be changed in the next step of the analysis that is step1.

As mentioned earlier the study uses the binary logistic regression model for two main targets one of them is to estimate whether there is any prediction relationship between goodwill write-off and the independent variables, which is the main goal of the study. This may be achieved through examining the overall test of the model coefficients. Thus if the model tests explored that the model failed to fit the data then the null hypothesis of no prediction power of the independent variables will be accepted.

The second target of the analysis is ranking the relative prediction power of the regressors which will not be meaningful if the tests of the overall model were negative. The null hypothesis may be rejected even if no one of regressors possesses any prediction power, if the model fits the data.

The overall model tests

This section includes what is frequently the most interesting part of the output that is the overall test of the model that is performed in step 1 wherein the predictors are included. Four tests are performed namely; Omnibus tests of model coefficients, Hosmer and Lemeshow test, R-squares and the -2log likelihood test. The following table represents the four tests.

With reference to Table 3 the first of the four tests is Omnibus tests of model coefficients, this is the chi-square statistic; the statistics for the step, block and model are the same because the analysis does not use stepwise logistic regression or blocking. The value given in the sig. column is the probability of obtaining the chi-square statistics given the null hypothesis is true. The null hypothesis is rejected given the level of significance less than 0.05, which indicates that the model is statistically significant.

Second, Hosmer and Lemeshow test provides a formal test for whether the predicted probabilities match the observed probabilities. The null and alternative hypotheses that are tested against this test are:

Table 3. The overall model tests.

First Test: Omnibus Tests of Model Coefficients					
		Chi-square	**df**	**Sig.**	
Step 1	Step	37.299	7	0.000	
	Block	37.299	7	0.000	
	Model	37.299	7	0.000	
Hosmer and Lemeshow test					
Step		Chi-square	df	Sig.	
1		5.574	8	0.695	
R-squares					
Step		-2 log likelihood	Cox and Snell	Nagelkerk	Pseudo
1		46.549	0.342	0.561	0.445

H_0: Logistic model is appropriate.
H_1: Logistic model is not appropriate.

In this case a large p-value indicates a good match; the goodwill write-off model analysis generates a 0.695 p-value, which indicates a good match. The Hosmer and Lemeshow test is also used in this study to predict the write-off pattern, which will be discussed later in the chapter.

Third, R-squares; the R^2 measures in binary logistic regression are not the same for OLS regression R^2. Nevertheless a number of logistic R-squared measures have been proposed. The R-square measures are not goodness of fit tests but rather attempt to measure strength of association. There are a lot of types for R^2 in the binary logistic regression, this study uses three types: Cox and Snell's R- square, Nagelkerke's R –square and Pseudo R-square. Cox and Snell's R- square is an attempt to imitate the interpretation of multiple R-square based on likelihood. With reference to Table 3 Cox and Snell's R- square is 0.342, which cannot be interpreted, as on OLS regression furthermore its maximum value does not reach one.

Nagelkerke's R-square is a further modification of the Cox and Snell's R-square and its maximum value may reach to the value 1 contrary to Cox and Snell's R-square. The Nagelkerke's R-square is 0.561, which is an indicator of a moderate association. Finally, Pseudo R square is not generated directly through the SPSS analysis instead it is measured through using this formula:

$$(I0 - (I + C)) / I0$$

Where:

I0: is the -2log likelihood for the null model.
I+C: is the -2log likelihood in the full model: intercept plus covariates.

The Pseudo R-square in the study is 0.445, which indicates a moderate prediction relationship. But actually R-square is of less importance in the logistic regression, since there is no direct equivalent of R-square in logistic regression to that used in OLS (Dufty, 2007).

The final goodness of fit test is -2log likelihood that has approximately a chi-square distribution; -2LL can be used for assessing the significance of the logistic regression analogous to the use of the sum of squared errors in OLS regression. The reduction in -2LL is an indicator that including the independent variables is appropriate. This reduction is equal to the Chi-square. In this study the -2LL has been reduced from 83.847 to 46.549, which means that the independent variables were useful.

After considering the goodness of fit tests, the first objective of the analysis was demonstrated. The model adequately fits the data, which indicates that there is a prediction power for the regressors. The next discussion will turn the attention to the second objective related to measure the significance of the variables in the model and rank their relative significance.

Acquisition variables versus performance indicators

After considering the analysis of the overall model, the analysis of independent variables significance is to be discussed through this section. This is through considering first the results of parameters significance and then rank their relative prediction power in goodwill write-off and hence goodwill impairment.

With reference to the score test analysis, the null model predicts goodwill, the use of stock as a mode of consideration and the performance indicators to be significant in the goodwill write-off prediction. But this may be changed after conducting the analysis of step 1. The results of the binary logistic regression are displayed in Table 4.

As Table 4 indicates; only goodwill and ΔROA are the significant variables among all independent variables because their p-value is less than 0.05, thus other variables are not powerful in predicting the goodwill write-off. Those results do not signify that the null hypothesis of no

Table 4. Variables in the equation.

	B	S.E	Wald	Sig.	Exp (B)
PREM	-0.004	0.017	0.071	0.790	<1
GW	17.292	6.061	8.138	0.004	>1
BID	-1.357	1.489	0.830	0.362	<1
STOCK	1.128	1.375	0.674	0.412	>1
ANRET	-7.616	7.824	0.947	0.330	<1
ROA	7.997	9.533	0.704	0.402	>1
∆ROA	-25.101	10.623	5.583	0.018	<1
Constant	-11.054	3.317	11.14	0.001	<1

Classification table

			Predicted		
			Write-off		Percentage correct
Observed			0.00	1.00	
Step 1	Write-off	0	73	0	100
		1	7	9	56.3
	Overall percentage				92.1

Table 5. Estimates of the predictive model.

Variable	Prediction	Full model	Acquisition variables	Performance variables
Intercept		-11.158 (0.000)	-8.55 (0.000)	-1.06 (0.007)
Acquisition variables				
PREM	-	-0.004 (0.795)	-0.010(0.490)	
GW	+	17.413 (0.004)	14.227 (0.003)	
BID	_	-1.349 (0.368)	-1.155 (0.379)	
STOCK	+	1.171 (0.394)	0.429 (0.701)	
ANRET	_	-7.817 (0.318)	-2.986 (0.675)	
Performance variables				
ROA	+	8.350 (0.376)		-14.054 (0.064)
∆ROA	_	-24.882 (0.019)		-11.618 (0.237)
Pseudo R^2		0.442	0.335	0.120

prediction power of the model is accepted given that the overall model is significant.

The coefficients of B are not interpreted as for the OLS regression, what is important is the sign of the coefficient. The odds ratios (Exp (B)) of the independents that are the exponentiations of the coefficients are actually more important than the coefficients. As mentioned in the table only GW and ΔROA are the significant variables that may affect the goodwill write-off. The odd ratio for GW is greater than one, which corresponds to increase in the dependent variable; on the other hand the odd ratio for the ΔROA is less than one, which indicates the negative relationship with the dependent variable. The classification table represents the appropriateness of the goodwill write-off model and presented in Table 4. The overall correct predicted percentage after including the explanatory variables is 92.1% as compared to 82.0% of the null model. The percentage of 92.1% is relatively a high percentage, which indicates that the model adequately fit the data.

The goodwill write-off prediction model is displayed in Table 5 after the split of the regressors into two groups namely; the acquisition variables and the performance variables. Table 5 represents the analysis of the full model and the results of the model after considering each group in separate. It is clear from the table that the performance indicators are weak in predicting goodwill write-off when considering in separate from the acquisition variables. The acquisition variables outperform the performance indicators regarding the values of Pseudo

Table 6. Contingency table for Hosmer and Lemeshow test.

	Write-off = 0		Write-off = 1		
	Observed	Expected	Observed	Expected	Total
1	9	8.939	0	0.061	9
2	9	8.845	0	0.155	9
3	8	8.734	1	0.266	9
4	9	8.660	0	0.340	9
5	8	8.510	1	0.490	9
6	8	8.215	1	0.785	9
7	7	7.816	2	1.184	9
8	8	7.183	1	1.817	9
9	7	5.723	2	3.277	9
10	0	0.376	8	7.624	8

R-square, 0.335 as compared to 0.120. However, the model generates better results when combining both groups of variables.

The predictive ability of the model

The final part of the analysis represents the predictive ability of the acquisition and post acquisition variables using Hosmer and Lemeshow test. The firm-year observations are ranked by their fitted probability values and are partitioned into ten probability deciles. This analysis is displayed in Table 6. Under the null hypothesis of no predictive power for the model, actual write-offs should be distributed evenly across the deciles, with an expected percentage of 10% of the write-offs occurring in each decile. The deciles are ranked relative to the probability of occurrence from the lowest to the highest. The table shows that the occurrence of goodwill write-off tends to be greater as the estimated probability of the model increases, indicating that the goodwill write-off model has a predictive power.

Conclusion

This study conducted a binary logistic regression in order to estimate the results of the goodwill prediction model. The results obtained may be interpreted with respect to several aspects. The null hypothesis of no prediction power of the model is rejected because the model is statistically significant in all tests of goodness of fit.

Although the overall model generates good results in the significance testing; only two explanatory variables are considered to be significant; that are GW and ΔROA. This result may be attributed to the importance of the goodwill in acquisitions occurred in Jordan that on average constitutes 60.66% of the acquisition price, as well as the importance of ΔROA as an indicator of financial performance deterioration. This implies that the strength of the model is moderate which is consistent with the findings of Hayn and Hughes (2005).

The ROA is not significant in the goodwill write-off process. This may occur as a consequence of including information about the firm as a whole not the cash-generating unit. When goodwill is allocated to a cash-generating unit, its effect will be more meaningful. Hayn and Hughes (2005) found that the performance indicators on the firm level are both significant. Schultze (2005) argued that goodwill impairment could be a result of several factors other than the deterioration of financial performance.

Although goodwill is the only significant variable among the acquisition variables, those indicators outperform the effect of performance indicators on goodwill write-off when splitting the effect of each group separately. The study highlighted the market reaction to acquisitions as a component of acquisition variables. The study is consistent with many of previous studies that firms usually do not generate positive abnormal returns during the announcement period (Oler, 2005).

The aim of the analysis is to predict the effect of available disclosures in determining the goodwill impairment. The main finding of this study is that investors and auditors may not be able to determine the goodwill impairment effectively apart from management. Nevertheless, the value attributed to goodwill may serve as an important indicator in goodwill impairment because managements are motivated to drive up the price of goodwill (Zhang and Zhang, 2006).

When the value of goodwill is high relative to the acquisition price, the existence of overpayment becomes evident. Consequently, goodwill impairment must take place in the few years following the acquisition. The change in ROA is useful in determining the goodwill impairment since it is an indicator of the profitability performance. The study revealed that on average the firms ROA tends to decrease after acquisition which is the same finding of Martynova et al. (2006).

To the best of the researchers' knowledge this study is

considered to be one of the first studies that address the issue of goodwill impairment in Jordan. To validate the conclusion of this study further comprehensive researches are required in the post-IFRS 3 era in Jordan. The recommendations for the future research have to concentrate on the notion of tracing goodwill performance at the level of cash-generating units as implied by IFRS 3. This may give the analysis a more comprehensive view of the deterioration in the performance of goodwill.

Even though the study concluded that the external users could not have an adequate view for goodwill impairment within the available disclosure, IFRS 3 requires substantial additional disclosures. Therefore, other studies should concentrate on the effectiveness of the new information to the external users in determining the appropriateness of management determinations regarding goodwill impairment.

REFERENCES

Ayers B, Lefanowicz C, Robbinson J (2002). "Do Firms Purchase the Pooling Method". Working Paper, University of Texas, Austin.

Carlin T, Finch N, Ford G (2007). "Goodwill Impairment-An Assessment of Disclosure Quality and Compliance Levels by Large Listed Australian Firms". Working Paper, Macquarie Graduate School of Management.

Chambers D (2006). "Is Goodwill Impairment Accounting Under SFAS 142 an Improvement over Systematic Amortization of Goodwill." Working Paper, University of Kentucky.

Chen C, Kohlbeck M, Warfield T (2004). "Goodwill Valuation Effects of the Initial Adoption of SFAS 142". Working Paper, University of Wisconsin-Madison.

Dufty D (2007). "What is Logistic Regression." Working Paper, StatGun Statistics Consulting.

Duso T, Gugler K, Yurtoglu B (2006). "Is the Event Study Methodology Useful for Merger Analysis? A Comparison of Stock Market and Accounting Data". Working Paper, Humboldt University Berlin and WZB.

Epstein B, Mirza A (2005). "Interpretation and Application of International Accounting and Financial Reporting Standards". Chapter 11. John Wiley and Sons, INC.

Farhan M (2002). "Banking Merger and Acquisition: Jordan Case". Master Thesis, Amman Arab University.

FASB (2001). "Statement of Financial Accounting No.141-Business Combinations". Financial Accounting Standards Board.

FASB (2001). "Statement of Financial Accounting No.142-Goodwill and Other Intangible Assets". Financial Accounting Standards Board.

Hayn C, Hughes P (2005). "Leading Indicators of Goodwill Impairment". Working Paper, University of California-Los Angeles.

Hitz J, Kuhner C (2002). "The New Rules for the Accounting of Derivative Goodwill in Accordance with SFAS 141 and SFAS 142." The Audit, pp. 273-287.

Hopkins P, Houston R, Peters M (1999). "Purchase, Pooling and Equity Analyst's Valuation Judgements". Working Paper, Indiana University.

IASB (2006). "International Accounting Standard No. 36 –Impairment of Assets". International Accounting Standards Board.

IASB (2006). "International Accounting Standard No. 38 –Intangible Assets". International Accounting Standards Board.

IASB (2006). "International Financial Reporting Standards No. 3 – Business Combinations". International Accounting Standards Board.

Johnson J, Tearney M (1993). "Goodwill- An Eternal Controversy". The CPA Journal, 63(4): 58-69.

Johnson L, Petrone K (1999). "Is Goodwill an Asset?". Commentary, Financial Accounting Standards Board.

Kothari, S. and Warner, J. (2004). "Econometrics of Event Studies". Working Paper, University of Rochester.

Kusnadi J, Sohrabian A (1999). "The Impact of Insurance Mergers on Shareholder Returns". URL: http://www.csupomona.edu.

Lewis R, Pendrill D (2004). "Advanaced Financial Accounting". Chapter 13. Seventh Edition, Prentice-Hall.

Loughran T, Vijh A (1997). "Do Long-Term Shareholders Benefit from Corporate Acquisitions?" .J. of Finance. 52(5): 1765-1790.

Martynova M, Oosting S, Renneboog L (2006). "The long Term Operating Performance of European Mergers and Acquisitions". Working Paper, European Corporate Governance Institute.

Oler D (2005). "Does Acquirer Cash Level Predict Post-Acquisition Returns." Working Paper, Indiana University.

Ramanna K (2007). "The Implications of Unverifiable Fair-Value Accounting: Evidence from the Political Economy of Goodwill Accounting". Working Paper, Massachusetts Institute of Technology.

Ruback R (1983). "Assessing Competition in the Market for Corporate Acquisitions". J. of Financial Economics, 11(1-4): 141-153.

Schultze W (2005). "The Information Content of Goodwill-Impairments under FAS 142: Implications for External Analysis and Internal Control". Working Paper, Schmalenbach Business Review. 57: 276-297.

Shumway T (1999). "Forecasting Bankruptcy More Accurately: A Simple Hazard Model". Working Paper, University of Michigan Business School.

Sundararajan V (1995). "Accounting for Goodwill". Working Paper, the CPA Journal Online.

Waked M (2005). "The Impact of Merging Jordanian Shareholding Companies on their Financial Performance." Master Thesis, Al-alBayt University.

Wiese A (2005). "Accounting for Goodwill: The Transition from Amortization to Impairment- An Impact Assessment". Working Paper, University of Stellenbosch.

Zhang I, Zhang Y (2006). "Accounting Discretion and Purchase Price Allocation after Acquisitions". Working Paper, University of Minnesota.

The evaluation of the investment environment in the industrial activity in Jordan

Mohammed Al-Shoura[1] and Anas Al Bakri[2]

[1]School of Management, Faculty of Business, Middle East University (MEU), Jordan.
[2]Management and Marketing Department, Faculty of Business and Economics, Qatar University, Al Tarfa, Doha 2713, Qatar.

The aim of this paper is to evaluate the investment environment in Jordan from the perceptions of the workers in the industrial activity. Data was collected by a questionnaire which depended on five aspects; namely; economic infrastructure, the characteristics of the Jordanian economic environment, labor force, industrial free zones and the Jordan Investment Board and the promotion policies. 70 questionnaires were distributed to the workers of the Jordanian industrial activity out of 120 workers which represent the study sample. 40 questionnaires were valid to statistical analysis, which is equivalent to 57.1% of the study sample. The study used SPSS for analyzing data to estimate the averages, standard deviations, T-test, percentages and frequencies. Statistical analysis showed that the characteristics of the economic infrastructure, the economic investment environment, and the industrial free zones have positive impact on attracting foreign investments. The study highly recommends that in order to improve water supply service, there is a need for greater exploitation of ground water, expanding of current dams and maintaining water piping networks. Another recommendation is reviewing the investment legislation so as to modify the investment encouragement laws which includes a guarantee for more incentives for foreign investments.

Key words: Foreign investments, investment environment, economic infrastructure.

INTRODUCTION

The third world countries have been recently competing to pave the way for attracting foreign investments in order to realize the economic development. The encouragement of such investment is related to several factor; providing a stable economic and political environment, a convenient infrastructure, freedom of trade competition, and the guarantee of investment protection. Furthermore, it is essential to provide man power, natural resources and rules that guarantee the intellectual property, invention rights and motives for investors. Jordan is a third world country that has very limited potentials. In the late eighties, Jordan faced many economic crises because of the retreat of external aids and the decrease of the money transferred by Jordanians abroad. Furthermore, the exports market of Jordanian products and the demand on Jordanian man power declined. Other reasons of these crises include the deficiency in the Jordanian balance of payment and the general budget, the retreat of gold reserves and foreign currency, the retreat of economic growth, the increase of unemployment, the decline of Jordan Dinar exchange, the increase of inflation and the degradation of the standards of living relative to the individual portion of the gross domestic product (Economic and Social Commission for Western

Asia (ESCAWA, 2003). As a result, Jordan has adapted many economic reform programs to insure a stable and an attracting environment for local and foreign investments. Jordan has also invested through many development projects and it has also depended on new legislations that provide motives and exemptions for foreign and local environments.

The significance and importance of the study

This study sheds some light on the investment environment in Jordan, the Jordan Investment Board and Investment Motives. It also provides a diagnosis of the advantages and disadvantages of the Jordanian investment environment.

Despite the great efforts done to attract more foreign and local investments, it investment is still limited compare to other countries. Therefore, this study aims at evaluating the investment situation in Jordan from the point of view of the personnel in the Jordan Investment Board and the Jordanian industrial estates. As a result, the obstacles that stop the flow of investments to Jordan will be clarified through the study. The problem of this study can be summarized by asking the following questions:

1. Do the characteristics of the economic environment in Jordan motivate the foreign investment to be directed toward Jordan?
2. Do the number and qualifications of labor force in Jordan contribute in directing foreign investments toward Jordan?
3. Do the industrial estates and free zones play a significant role in directing foreign investments to Jordan?
4. Do the policies of promotion in Jordan and the Jordan Investment Board play an important role in attracting foreign investments?
5. Does the infrastructure of Jordan economy contribute in attracting foreign investments?

The objectives of the study

The main objective is to clarify the point of view of the personnel towards the situation of investment environment in Jordan through:

1. The characteristics of the Jordanian economic environment and its role in attracting foreign investment.
2. The role of the labor force in Jordan in directing foreign investments toward Jordan.
3. The role of the industrial estates and free zones in attracting foreign investments to Jordan.
4. The role of the policies of promotion in Jordan and the Jordan Investment Board in attracting foreign investments.
5. The characteristics of infrastructure of Jordan economy and its role in attracting foreign investments.
6. Some suggestions are presented so as to improve the investment environment in Jordan.

Hypothesis of the study

The First hypothesis: The characteristics of the economic environment in Jordan do not motivate the foreign investment to be directed toward Jordan.
The second hypothesis: the labor force in Jordan does not contribute in directing foreign investments toward Jordan.
The third hypothesis: The industrial estates and free zones do not play a significant role in directing foreign investments to Jordan.
The fourth hypothesis: The policies of promotion in Jordan and the Jordan Investment Board do not play an important role in attracting foreign investments.
The fifth hypothesis: The infrastructure of Jordan economy does not contribute in attracting foreign investments.

The study population

The study population includes the high and media personnel in the Jordan Investment Board and industrial estates, who have a direct relationship with foreign investments. They are estimated by 120 personnel.

The study sample

The equation used to decide the size of the study sample is given as follows (Geller and Brian, 2003):

$$n = Z^2_{(a/2)} / \{4E^2 + [Z^2_{(a/2)} / N]\}$$

Where: n is the size of sample, E is an accepted error, Z is the normal distribution, and N is the statistical population. Error is assumed to be in the range of 5 to 10% (average error=7.5%). Depending on this estimated error, the number of personnel in the study sample is 56 which represent 45% of the study population. Consequently, the stratified random sample is used where seventy questionnaires were distributed to 70 personnel in the Jordan Investment Board and industrial estates which represent 58% of the study population. Fifty questionnaires were restored which represent 71% of the distributed questionnaires. After revision, 10 questionnaires were excluded due to their invalidity for analysis. Therefore, 40 questionnaires were considered for analysis.

Table 1. Description of the study sample (The personnel's demography).

Variable	Interval	Frequency	Percentage
Gender	Male	27	67.5
	Female	13	32.5
Age	≤30 years	13	32.5
	31-40 years	16	40.0
	41-50 years	9	22.5
	≥ 50	2	5.0
Qualification	High school or less	2	0
	Diploma	1	7.5
	Bachelor	20	50.0
	Graduates studies	17	42.5
Experience	< 5 years	10	25.0
	5-10 years	11	27.5
	11-15 years	9	22.5
	≥ 16 years	10	25.0
	Total	40	100.0

Table 2. The rating level according to Likert scale.

The average	The rating level
4.5 - 5	Very high
3.75 - less than 4.5	High
3 - less than 3.75	Medium
2 - less than 3	Weak
1 - less than 2	Very weak

DATA COLLECTION

Secondary data

It is the statistical data which are collected from the official directorates and institutions which are concerned about local and foreign investments. The economic and financial brochures of the Central Bank of Jordan (2011, 2012) are an example.

Primary data

They were collected by using the following method. First, the demographic data of the personnel such as gender, age, educational level, social status and experience (Table 1).

Second, the characteristics of economic environment are given in Table 5. Third, the characteristics of labor force in Jordan are given in Table 7. Fourth, the characteristics of the industrial estates and free zones are given in Table 9. Fifth, the Jordan Investment Board and promotion polices are given in Table 11. Sixth, the economic infrastructure is given in Table 13. Likert penta scale was used as follows: (1 = strongly agree, 2 = agree, 3 = don't know, 4 = disagree, 5 = strongly disagree). Table 2 explains the rating level for results depending on Likert scale:

Validity and stability of the method

Three foreign investment referees evaluated the questionnaires and consequently some modifications were done in the light of their notes. In order to prove the stability of the method, the measure of internal consistency (Cronbach-alpha method) was used. The index validity was used for the whole aspects of the method and the study by calculating of squares of coefficients of the whole method when it is applied on a preliminary sample study (out of the study sample), which consists of 12 investors. The coefficient of internal consistency was calculated to be 0.92 according to Cronbach-alpha equation. Table 3 gives the coefficients of internal consistency according to Cronbach-alpha equation for the five aspects of the study.

The statistical methods used in the study

In order to describe the characteristics of the sample, the SPSS program was used to analyze the data to find the frequencies and the percentages. Furthermore, the

Table 3. Coefficients of internal consistency according to Cronbach's-alpha equation for the aspects of the study.

Aspects	Internal consistency
The economic infrastructure	0.78
The economic environment	0.74
Labor force	0.82
Free zones and industrial estates	0.77
The Jordan Investment Board and promotion	0.80

average and the standard deviation were used to measure the degree of evaluation of the items of questionnaire. T-test was used to test the hypothesis of study.

LITERATURE REVIEW

Many studies discussed the factors that influence the flow of investments. Most important studies were Hijazin study (1996), discussed the factors that impede the foreign investments in Jordan; the weakness and instability of the economic structure, the legal environment, the weakness of the Jordanian policy of promotion and the weakness of the Jordan Investment Board. However, the study explained that the factors of security and political stability, the social environment, the low wages of employees encourage foreign investment.

Gharaibah and Azzam's study (1997) entitled "The determinants of foreign investments in the Jordanian economy" aimed at analyzing the situation of the Jordanian economy so as to measure all the factors that motivate more foreign investments. The study also discussed the types and the natures of the foreign investments and the Jordanian investment environment. Furthermore, this study applied a standard model which found out that the national income and growth, the political stability, trade conditions and local exchange play an important role in attracting foreign investments. The study of Hassan (1997) aimed at estimating the gap of the growth of the Jordanian economy during the years 1996 to 2001. It also estimated the productivity of the foreign capital during the years 1973 to 1975. This study also predicted the future and the need of the foreign capital in Jordan. Moreover, it considered the achievements of the second economic reform program during the years 1992 to 1996. The study showed that the Jordanian economy would suffer from the domination of foreign trade gap (foreign exchange) during the years 1996 to 2001. This study stressed on the positive effects of the foreign capital on the growth of the Jordanian economy. So, this study came to the conclusion that the Jordanian economy needs more foreign capital flow to ensure more growth rate of the economy. In the study of Muheesen (1999), the role of foreign investment in Amman Stock Exchange was introduced due to the increase of the non Jordanian investors who participate in the capital of the general joint-stock companies. On the other hand, the study found the strong and direct relationship between the stock price and the non Jordanian investors' shares. This direct relationship is also clear between the shares of the non Jordanian investors and the foreign net balance in the banking system. The legislation of the new laws concerning Amman Stock Exchange and the freedom of capital transfers paved the way for more foreign investments in Amman Stock Exchange.

"The investment conditions in Jordan and Egypt" is the title of a study issued by the Jordan Investment Board in 2001. Thirty investors in Egypt mentioned many reasons that prevented them from the investment in Jordan. High rates of taxes, customs duties, complicated project license, complex customs procedures, lack of transparency, the long routine, the high cost finance and the unqualified employees are the major obstacles against investment in Jordan. In addition, the study of Abdusalam (2002) dealt with the situation of foreign investment in Egypt especially after applying the economic reform policy in 1991. The study concluded that many obstacles face the investment in Egypt, such as the weakness of promotion policy, the deficiency of the taxes, legislative and managing systems, and the shortage of the research and development by comparison with other countries. Furthermore, in their study, Gyapong and Karikari (1999) made a comparison between the economic system of Ivory Coast and Ghana. The study clarified how the Ivory Coast succeeded through its economic policies in attracting more foreign investment during the years 1960 to 1980, compared with the economic policies of Ghana which did not motivate foreign investments to come to the country. On the other hand, the researchers Alvin and Densil (2002) discussed the efforts which were done by the developing countries to improve their economy to attract foreign investments. The researchers constructed a statistical model which was consisted of explanation elements on the flow of the foreign investment such as interest rate, the average of economic growth, the average of individual's income and the balance of payment. The study came to the conclusion that the average of the individual income and interest rate are the major factors of attracting foreign investments.

In another comparative study between Bahrain and North Ireland, Gilmore et al. (2003) investigated the motivations introduced and the degree of satisfaction of the foreign investments from the point of view of the general managers. They also explained the reasons that stand behind preferring a country for executing projects over other countries. Furthermore, the study mentioned that all projects in Bahrain are joint ones, while in Ireland they are not. Moreover, both countries shared the main factors which attract investments (to different degrees) such as taxes, infrastructure and political stability. However, low wages is not an obstacle against foreign investments. The study of Metwally (2004) analyzed the relationship between the foreign investments and the economic growth in Jordan, Egypt and Oman. Most foreign investments in these countries come from the European Union. The study also showed that the rate of the economic growth in these countries has a positive effect on the flow of the foreign investments to different degrees.

THEORETICAL FRAMEWORK OF THE STUDY

Investment is defined as the use of the capital to get profits. It is also defined as the concession of the current consumption to get future returns. On the other hand, it is economically defined as the appropriation of the capital to gain new productive methods and develop them to increase the production power.

All the previous definitions stress that the investment is considered as a total addition to the productive capital used in the production and services to gain more profits. However, we should pay more attention to the negative effects of the political economic and social factors on investment. The World Trade Organization (WTO, 1997) defines "the direct foreign investment" as the ownership of a production line in the host country by a foreign investor, which enables him to manage it and gain profits.

The characteristics of foreign investments

According to Geel (1982), foreign investment is characterized by:

(1) Long-term investment.
(2) The ownership of a total or a partial project by a foreign investor.
(3) The investor has a partial or a total domination on managing and organizing the projects financially and technologically.
(4) The possibility of transforming experiences from the mother country to the host country.

The determinants of foreign investments

The economic factors

The investors take into consideration the economic situation of the host country such as the local production, inflation, market volume, the natural and basic recourses, external trade, foreign exchange, trade balance, public debts, open economy and the role of the public and private sectors in the economy. All the previous factors are necessary for attracting foreign investments.

The labor force

Training and qualifying of human resources are important in increasing the ability of the country inorder to attract foreign investments. Furthermore, the success of any investment project, the realization of more profits and the adaptability with market needs cannot be fulfilled without the human resources.

The infrastructure

The decrease of transport, communications, electricity, water, education and health services are considered to be repulsive factors of foreign investments (Hijazin, 1996; Gharaibeh and Azzam, 1997).

The investment promotion

It is a set of activities that motivate the capable and interested businessmen as well as the investment corporations to participate in the projects of investment. This should happen with the cooperation of the corporations in the host country. The investment promotion is considered one of the integral elements of the investment environment and a connecting link of all the investment parties to provide them with the information they need and it also encourages more foreign and local investments. Some organizations such as the United Nations Investment Development Organization (UNIDO) carry out many investment promotion activities. Training courses for the personnel who are working in the investment aspects, the financial support for countries willing to establish centers for the investment promotion or improving current promotion methods are some of these activities.

Some characteristics of the investment environment in Jordan

In Jordan, many investment sectors have witnessed services and infrastructure improvements. Here are some examples of the improved sectors:

1. Communication services: The infrastructure of the wired and wireless communications sectors and the

sector of the information technology have developed in Jordan during the last few years. 373 companies work in this sector which expects a growth in its products markets by 10% in the few coming years.

2. Water sector: Jordan is one of the ten countries which suffer a shortage of water. One third of water resources in Jordan are not regenerated. Moreover, the average of the individual consumption of water in Jordan is about 200 m^3/year whereas in Syria, for example, it reaches about 800 m^3/year (9 folds of individual consumption of water in Jordan). On the other hand, the annual world average of water consumption is about 7700 m^3/year, while in North America it reached about 110000 m^3/year. For these reasons, Jordan's consequent governments adapted the projects of constructing dams to collect rain water. However, the problem is still in existent.

3. Transport services: The land carriage has been notably developed and expanded into wide areas in Jordan during the last years. The Gulf of Aqaba, on the other hand, is the Jordan main port for sea carriage. It has also witnessed a development by building special pavements and providing them with appropriate transport equipments. This development has also included the air transport, represented by the Royal Airlines. Planes of the Royal Jordanian Airlines reach directly to 47 cities in Europe, Middle and Far East, North America and Africa. There are also 26 airlines companies and 3 airports.

4. Education and Health: Jordan has been highly concerned with providing the essential infrastructure for schools and high education institutes. The percentage of educated people in Jordan has risen to be 87% in 2005. This is due to the compulsory education for the elementary and preparatory levels. On the other hand, the achievements of the health sectors include giving people the health services in public and private hospitals, clinics and health centers. The number of hospitals in Jordan is about 98, 42 among them are public hospitals.

5. The economic environment: In an attempt to deal with the economic crisis and to readjust economic structure, the Jordanian government adapted many economic reform programs with the corporation of the International Bank and International Monetary Fund (IMF) in the late eighties, precisely 1989. However, this cooperation was blocked because of the second Gulf war in 1990, which forced the government to adapt the second economic reform program to cover the years 1992 to 1998.

To give the private sector more opportunity and to adapt the third reform economic program which started in 1998 and ended in 2003 to fight poverty and unemployment, Jordan adapted the privatization program. However, this program didn't fulfill all its objectives. Consequently, the government adapted the fourth reform program for the years 2002 to 2004. The main objective was to offer a stable economic structure and to control inflation. This program encourages more foreign investments (Economic and Social Commission for Western Asia, ESCAWA, 2003).

The Jordanian finance sector, which is flexible and able to adapt with the economic condition, has a major role in forming a stable economic environment. It is also considered one of the basic fundaments that create an attracting investment environment. The stock exchange is a connecting link between individuals, saving institutions and the production projects through issuing stocks. Thus, the stock exchange is considered one of the elements of investment environment. Amman Stock Exchange has been established to increase the national savings and guarantee the best use of it in a way that guarantees correct, easy and quick dealings.

The Jordanian external trade policy depending on the philosophy of free economy, the Jordanian external trade policy has been able to reinforce Jordan's economic and trade relations with the Arab countries through signing the Arab free trade zone agreement and other dual free trade agreements. Jordan has also joined the joint agreement with European Union and the free trade agreement with USA. Jordan is also a member of the World Trade Organization and it signed many free trade agreements with Singapore and IFTA countries. Jordan signed over 32 dual investment agreements in order to develop the investment environment in Jordan. In December 1999, Jordan became the 135 member of the WTO. This membership facilitates penetration of the Jordanian products and services into the World markets (Economic and Social Commission for Western Asia, ESCAWA, 2003).

During the early nineties, Jordan started privatizing the public sector corporations gradually. This lead to the increase of the flow of foreign investment (ESCAWA, 2003). The Jordanian government sold all its portions in 64 companies. Cement Company, Communication Corporation, Public Transport Corporation, Arab Potash Company and Water Authority are examples of such companies. The gross yield of privatization reached more than one billion Jordan Dinar. The privatization program contributes to the attraction of foreign investments which exceeds one billion JD for privatized programs, especially the communication, water and transport sectors. In addition, Jordan suffers from a shortage in natural resources and the essential elements for growth such as petroleum and gas. However, Jordan is developed in the production of some minerals like phosphate, potash and manganese and other unexploited resources like oil shale and tar.

Table 4 shows the following: The amount of foreign investment was 438 million Dinar in the year 2004. Then in 2007 it decreased and kept on decreasing till it reached the lowest value (83.714) million Dinar in 2007. Then it raised in 2011 and 2012 due to the new laws and legislations which encourage the foreign investment (The annual report of the Jordan Investment Board, 2011,

Table 4. Investment in Jordan (2000-2012).

Year	Foreign investment /Dinar million	Local investment /Dinar million
2000	75.7	271.8
2001	124	257.1
2002	154.8	326.8
2003	184.1	364.6
2004	438.3	354.8
2005	409.1	472.2
2006	131.3	169.6
2007	83.7	177.9
2008	95.6	322.6
2009	267.2	473.6
2010	266.5	468.3
2011	320	422.4
2012	276.9	388.9

Resource: Jordan Investment Board (2012).

2012). The local investment raised from 354.895 million Dinar in 2004 to 473.694 million Dinar in 2009.

STATISTICAL ANALYSIS AND TEST OF HYPOTHESIS

First hypothesis

The Jordanian economic environment does not attract foreign investments in Jordan. The first hypothesis was expressed in 13 items in Table 5 which refers to positive evaluation of the Jordanian economic environment. The evaluation of these items was higher than the degree of neutrality (3) which represents the average of five level scale used in the present study. Table 5 gives the values of average and standard deviation for the opinions of personnel in the Jordan investment boards, the industrial estates and the free trade zones about the suitability of Jordanian economic environment for the attraction of foreign investments. In order to prove or disprove the first hypothesis test T was used at significance level 0.05. It is clear from Table 6 that the general average of items of Table 5 equals 3.76 and that the value of T equals -3.481 and statistical significance level equals 0.001. This confirms negation of the null hypothesis and affirmation of the alternative hypothesis that the positive characteristics of Jordanian economic environment attract foreign investments in Jordan.

Personnel affirmed that the following factors have positive role in the attraction of foreign investments: the stability of exchange rate of Dinar, the availability of foreign currency, free economic policies, programs of economic reformation in Jordan, the efficiency of the banking system and the availability of insurance service.

On the other hand, the degree of satisfaction of personnel was moderate with privatization policies, rate of taxes and fees, and stock exchange. Personnel affirm that inflation levels have negative effect on foreign investments. Furthermore, the evaluation of the effect of the size of budget disability and external indebtedness was positive, so these factors have no bad effects on foreign investments. However, dissatisfaction of foreign investors with inflation levels is due to its high levels in latter time which leads to the increase of investment expenses. Table 5 indicates that the rating level of personnel answers according to Likert scale is high (-3.75 less than 4.5) for more than half of the answers. This is a further support of our analysis of the first hypothesis.

Second hypothesis

Jordanian man power does not attract foreign investments in Jordan. The second hypothesis was expressed in 6 items in Table 7 which refers to positive evaluation of Jordanian man power. The evaluation of these items was higher than the degree of neutrality (3) which represents the average of five level scale used in the present study. Table 7 gives the values of average and standard deviation for the opinions of personnel in Jordan investment boards, industrial estates and free trade zones about the role of number and quality of Jordanian man power in attraction of foreign investments. In order to prove or disprove the second hypothesis test T was used at significance level 0.05. It is clear from Table 8 that the general average of items of Table 6 equals 3.29 and that the value of T equals -2.928 and statistical significance level equals 0.004. This confirms the negation of the null hypothesis and the affirmation of the alternative hypothesis that the positive characteristics of Jordanian man power do attract foreign investments in Jordan.

The Jordanian man power is characterized by high scientific and technical levels which are suitable for foreign investments in Jordan. Furthermore, the system of working hours and vacations is acceptable for investors, and the legislations applied in Jordan guarantee the right of persons in the investment process. Table 7 indicates that the rating level of answers of personnel in Jordan investment boards, industrial estates and free trade zones according to Likert scale is medium (-3 less than 3.75) for most of the answers. This is a further support of our analysis of the second hypothesis.

Third hypothesis

Industrial estates and free trade zones do not attract foreign investments in Jordan. The third hypothesis was expressed in 6 items in Table 9 which refers to the positive evaluation of the role of industrial estates and

Table 5. Personnel evaluation of Jordanian economic environment.

Item	Average	SD	Rating level
Free economic policies in Jordan provides suitable economic environment for investment.	4.38	0.67	High
The availability of foreign currency and its exchange are attractive for investment.	4.33	0.62	High
The attendance of Jordan to World Trade Organization is attractive for investment.	4.32	0.62	High
Stability of exchange rate of Dinar stimulates investments.	4.22	0.80	High
The Banking system in Jordan is effective in servicing investments.	4.15	0.77	High
Programs of the economic reform improve Jordanian economic environment for investment.	4.10	0.63	High
Privatization policies improve the Jordanian economic environment.	3.78	0.97	High
Jordanian Stock Exchange is effective and respects the benefits of investors.	3.78	0.92	High
The service of Jordanian insurance sector is suitable for investment.	3.43	0.98	Medium
The current Jordanian external indebtedness hinders flow of investment into Jordan.	3.23	0.92	Medium
Taxes and fees in Jordan stimulate the flow of investments into Jordan.	3.23	1.33	Medium
The acceptable economic inflation levels in Jordan encourage the flow of investments into Jordan.	3.18	0.96	Medium
The general budget disability in Jordan has negative effect on the flow of investments into Jordan.	2.83	1.01	weak

Table 6. The values of general average and T test of the items of the first hypothesis (Jordanian economic environment).

Aspect	Average	SD	Value of T	Significance level	Result
Jordanian economic environment	3.76	0.45	-3.481	*0.001	Negation of null hypothesis

*at significance level of $\alpha = 0.05$.

Table 7. Personnel evaluation of Jordanian man power.

Item	Average	SD	Rating level
Jordanian man power is characterized by high scientific level which is suitable for foreign investments in Jordan.	3.70	0.99	Medium
Technicians in Jordan are well qualified for investments.	3.48	1.11	Medium
The system of working hours and vacations in Jordan is suitable for investments.	3.30	1.22	Medium
Legislations applied in Jordan guarantee the right of both personnel and investors.	3.30	1.02	Medium
The number of man power in Jordan is sufficient for investments.	3.03	1.12	Medium
The month salaries in Jordan are suitable for investments.	2.95	1.20	weak

free trade zones in providing attractive investment environment in Jordan. The evaluation of these items was higher than the degree of neutrality (3) which represents the average of five level scale used in the present study. Table 9 gives the values of average and standard deviation for the opinions of personnel in Jordan investment boards, industrial estates and free trade zones about the role of industrial estates and free trade zones in the attraction of foreign investments. In order to prove or disprove the third hypothesis test T was used at significance level 0.05. It is clear from Table 10 that the general average of items of Table 9 equals 4.09 and that the value of T equals -2.008 and statistical significance level equals 0.048. This confirms negation of the null hypothesis and affirmation of the alternative hypothesis that industrial estates and free trade zones attracts foreign investments in Jordan.

The evaluation of the role of industrial estates and free trade zones was positive. The credit of some of these as qualified industrial zones contributes to various investments in Jordan. Investments in these industrial zones provide a way for reaching external markets because they provide facilities for encouraging investment in Jordan, well qualified labors and high competing products for external markets. Table 9 indicates that the rating level of answers of personnel in Jordan investment boards, industrial estates and free trade zones according to Likert scale is high (-3.75 less than 4.5). This is a further

Table 8. The values of general average and T test of the items of the second hypothesis (Jordanian man power).

Aspect	Average	SD	Value of T	Significance level	Result
Man power in Jordan	3.29	0.85	-2.928	*0.004	Negation of null hypothesis

*at significance level of α = 0.05.

Table 9. Personnel evaluation of industrial estates and free trade zones in Jordan.

Item	Average	SD	Rating level
Investment in industrial estates and free trade zones in Jordan provides a way for reaching external markets.	4.30	0.56	High
Industrial estates and free trade zones in Jordan facilitate investment in Jordan.	4.18	0.81	High
The location of the industrial estates and free trade zones in Jordan is suitable for investment.	4.10	0.81	High
Well qualified personnel are available in industrial estates and free trade zones in Jordan	4.00	0.88	High
Products of industrial estates and free trade zones in Jordan have competitive quality in external markets.	4.00	0.78	High
The credit of some industrial estates as qualified zones strengthens the position of investments in Jordan.	3.95	0.96	High

Table 10. The values of general average and T test of the items of the third hypothesis (industrial estates and free trade zones in Jordan).

Aspect	Average	SD	Value of T	Significance level	Result
Industrial estates and free trade zones in Jordan	4.09	0.60	-2.008	*0.048	Negation of null hypothesis

*at significance level of α = 0.05.

Table 11. Personnel evaluation of Jordan Investment Board and promotion policies.

Item	Average	SD	Rating level
Jordan Investment Board facilitates of investors dealings.	4.30	0.76	High
Jordan Investment Board promotes investments opportunities in Jordan in external markets.	4.13	0.82	High
Jordan Investment Board provides accurate information for investors.	3.93	0.89	High
Jordan investment Board makes national and international exhibitions and promotion programs for Jordanian products.	3.90	1.01	High
Jordan Investment Board has well qualified personnel to manage and carry out promotion process.	3.75	0.90	High
Jordan mass media contributes to the clarification of investments opportunities in Jordan.	3.62	1.13	medium

support of our analysis of the third hypothesis.

Fourth hypothesis

Jordan Investment Board and promotion policies do not attract foreign investments in Jordan. The fourth hypothesis was expressed in 6 items in Table 11 which refersto positive evaluation of role of Jordan Investment Board and promotion policies in providing attractive investment environment in Jordan. The evaluation of these items was higher than the degree of neutrality (3) which represents the average of five level scale used in the present study. Table 11 gives the values of average and standard deviation for the opinions of personnel in Jordan Investment Board, industrial estates and free

Table 12. The values of general average and T test of the items of the fourth hypothesis (Jordan Investment Board and promotion policies).

Aspect	Average	SD	Value of T	Significance level	Result
Jordan Investment Board and promotion policies	3.94	0.71	-3.004	*0.004	Negation of null hypothesis

*at significance level of α = 0.05.

Table 13. Personnel evaluation of Jordanian Investment Board and promotion policies.

Item	Average	SD	Rating level
Communication service is available in Jordan.	4.60	0.55	Very high
Suitable education is available in Jordan.	4.38	0.77	High
Satisfactory health service is available in Jordan	4.18	0.93	High
Good hotels and restaurants are available in Jordan.	4.10	0.96	High
Air transport is available in Jordan.	3.90	0.78	High
Technical services are available in Jordan.	3.83	0.87	High
Suitable electricity service is available in Jordan.	3.78	0.97	High
Land carriage is available in Jordan.	3.70	0.82	Medium
Sea carriage is available in Jordan.	3.60	0.96	Medium
Satisfactory sanitary service is available in Jordan.	3.58	1.11	Medium
Water supply service is available in Jordan.	2.40	1.26	weak

Table 14. The values of general average and T test of the items of the fourth hypothesis (Jordanian Investment Board and promotion policies).

Aspect	Average	SD	Value of T	Significance level	Result
Jordanian economic infrastructure	3.82	0.53	-2.778	*0.007	Negation of null hypothesis

*at significance level of α = 0.05.

trade zones about the role of Jordanian Investment Board and promotion policies in attraction of foreign investments. In order to prove or disprove the fourth hypothesis test T was used at significance level 0.05. It is clear from Table 12 that the general average of items of Table 11 equals 3.94 and that the value of T equals -3.004 and statistical significance level equals 0.004. This confirms negation of the null hypothesis and affirmation of the alternative hypothesis that Jordan Investment Board and promotion policies attract foreign investments in Jordan.

The evaluation of the role of Jordan Investment Board and promotion policies was positive. Jordan investment board facilitates investment dealings, provides accurate information for investors, and promotes investments (in Jordan) in external markets. Jordan Investment Board makes national and international exhibitions and promotion programs by well qualified personnel. Jordan mass media contributes to clarification of investments opportunities in Jordanian market. Table 11 indicates that the rating level of answers of personnel according to Likert scale is high (-3.75 less than 4.5) for almost all answers. This is a further support of our analysis of the fourth hypothesis.

Fifth hypothesis

Jordanian economic infrastructure does not attract foreign investments in Jordan. The fifth hypothesis was expressed in 11 items in Table 13 which refers to positive evaluation of the role of Jordanian economic infrastructure (local and international communications, health service, land carriage, air transport, sea carriage, education, electricity and water supply). The evaluation of these items was higher than the degree of neutrality (3) which represents the average of five level scale used in the present study. Table 14 gives the values of average and standard deviation for the opinions of personnel in Jordan Investment Board, industrial estates and free trade zones about the role of Jordanian economic infrastructure in attraction of foreign investments. In order to prove or disprove the fourth hypothesis test T was used at significance level 0.05. It is clear from Table 14 that the general average of 11 items of Table 13 equals 3.82 and that the value of T equals -2.778 and statistical significance level equals 0.007. This confirms negation of the null hypothesis and affirmation of the alternative hypothesis that Jordanian economic infrastructure attracts foreign investments in Jordan.

Personnel of the sample study express their opinions that the Jordanian economic infrastructure has many positive characteristics that encourage foreign investments to be involved in the Jordanian economic environment is ready to welcome investors as it is seen from Table 13 where the rating level of answers of personnel according to Likert scale is high (-3.75 less than 4.5) for almost all answers. This is a further support of our analysis of the fifth hypothesis.

Conclusions

(1) The characteristics of the economic environment in Jordan encourage the foreign investment to be directed to Jordan. Such characteristics include : the relative stability of Dinar exchange rate, suitable circulation of the foreign currency, open economic policies, the economic reform programs and the efficiency of the banking and insurance services.
(2) The educational and technical qualifications and the sufficient numbers of the man power in Jordan attract the foreign investment to Jordan. In addition to the acceptable system of the working hours and the vacations, the legislations guarantee the rights of all the parts of the economic operation.
(3) The Jordanian industrial estates and free zones play an important role in the encouragement of foreign investment. They participate in reinforcing the different kinds of investment by offering facilities to encourage investment in Jordan. These industrial estates and free zones have proper locations and high competitive abilities in the foreign markets.
(4) The Jordan Investment Board together with the promotion policy applied in Jordan play a role in attracting foreign investment by creating a comfortable and an attracting investment environment facilitating the deals of the investment. They also provide the investors with the accurate needed information. Furthermore, they promote for the opportunities of investment in Jordan through the local and international exhibitions executed by a qualified staff who manage the promotion process. The role of the Jordanian mass media in clarifying the investment aspects in the Jordanian markets cannot be denied.
(5) The characteristics of the economic infrastructure in Jordan have many advantages, which help in attracting foreign investment. For example, the services of the local and international communication, the health services, the air transport, land and sea carriage, education, water and electricity affect the economic infrastructure positively. These services help in attracting foreign investment.

Recommendations

Depending on the previous conclusions, some recommendations that may enhance the advantages of the Jordanian investment environment will be introduced.

(1) Improving water services through the exploitation of ground water in Disi Deposit, expanding dams and repairing water networks.
(2) Adapting financial and monetary policies that restrain the inflation and improving the economic environment especially through new legislations.
(3) Modifying the investment legislations by a team of public and private sectors, the thing that realize more foreign investment in the manufacturing of textiles, electronic products and the sector of information technology. Moreover, the foreign investor needs such as human resources and Arab experts should be satisfied without many complications.
(4) Establishing more vocational colleges and corporations and improving the working ones so as to provide investors with qualified human resources.
(5) Constructing specialized investment units in foreign countries and organizing a promotion campaign to promote for the Jordanian high quality products.

REFERENCES

Abdusalam M (2002). The situation of foreign investment in Egypt especially after applying the economic reform policy in 1991.
Alvin GW, Densil AW (2002). "Attracting FDI to developing countries: A changing role for government?". Int.J.Public Sector Manag., 15(5): 361 - 374.
Central Bank of Jordan (CBJ) (2012). Central bank Bulletin, Quarter Publish, Retrieved 15/July/2012, central bank website. Amman, Jordan.
Central Bank of Jordan (CBJ) (2011). Central bank Bulletin, Quarter Publish, Retrieved 15/July/2012, central bank website. Amman, Jordan.
Economic and Social Commission for Western Asia, ESCAWA (2003).
Geller G, Waarade B (2003). Statistic, 6 Edition, p.315.
Gharaibah H, Azzam A (1997). "The determinants of foreign investments in the Jordanian economy, Yarmouk J. 13(1):22-24, 33-51.
Gilmore A, Aodheen D, Carson D, Cummins D (2003). Factors Influencing Foreign Direct Investment And International Joint Venture, International Marketing Review , Northern Ireland 20(2):195-215.
Gyapong A, Karikari J (1999), Direct Foreign Investment Strategies And Economic Performance In Ghana And Ivory Coast, J. Econ. Dev. 24(1):133-147.
Hassan H (1997). "The gap of the growth of the Jordanian economy during the years 1996-2001", unpublished master thesis, Yarmouk University.
Hijazin A (1996). "The factors that impede the foreign investments in Jordan; the weakness and instability of the economic structure, the

legal environment", unpublished master thesis, the University of Jordan.
Metwally A (2004). Analyzed the relationship between the foreign investments and the economic growth in Jordan, Egypt and Oman.
Muheesen F (1999). The role of foreign investment in Amman Stock Exchange, Bank. J. 18(8):49-55.
The annual report of the Jordan Investment Board (2011). Amman-Jordan, unpublished statistics Jordan Investment Board.
The annual report of the Jordan Investment Board (2012). Amman-Jordan, unpublished statistics Jordan Investment Board.
The Jordan Investment Board (2001) "The investment conditions in Jordan and Egypt". Retrieved 10/July/2012.
World Trade Organization (WTO) report (1997). Trade and foreign direct investment, USIA Electronic J. 2(2).

Auditors' perceptions on impact of mandatory audit firm rotation on auditor independence –Evidence from Bahrain

Kousay Said and Hussein Khasharmeh

Department of Accounting, College of Business Administration, University of Bahrain, P.O. Box: 32038, Kingdom of Bahrain.

The current study examined several issues regarding auditor independence from the perspective of an emerging market such as Bahrain. Factors affecting the ability of auditors to remain independent include long audit tenure, financial dependence on a single audit client, non-audit services provided to audit clients, ex-auditor employment with an audit client and the existence of audit committees. It is therefore timely to examine the importance of auditor independence in the provision of reliable and credible financial information. The current study uses a questionnaire survey to examine auditors' perceptions of the impact of mandatory audit firm rotation on auditor independence. The results of the study revealed that the majority of auditors agreed that MAR could safeguard auditor independence. The results also reveal that there is *a* significant relationship between mandatory audit firm rotation and auditor independence. Analyses of variance (ANOVA) were also conducted to test for the possibility of confounding effects arising from participants' background and experience. None of these variables were found to have a confounding effect on the experimental results. The results also reveal that the adoption of rotation rules wasn't given enough attention among the auditing firms in Bahrain.

Keywords: Mandatory audit firm rotation (MAR), auditor independence, Gulf Cooperation Countries (GCC), European Commission (EC) Government Accounting Office (GAO), Company Accounting Oversight Board (PCAOB).

INTRODUCTION

The concept of mandatory audit rotation (MAR) is not new. There has been considerable interest in MAR as a means of strengthening auditor independence, reducing the incidence of audit failure, improving the quality of audit and protecting investors and other users of financial statements. Mandatory audit firm rotation sets a limit on the number of years a public accounting firm may audit a company's financial statements. After a predetermined period, an accounting firm is no longer eligible to serve as the company's auditor for a set time interval and a rotation of firms is required. A mandatory audit rotation rule which sets a limit on the maximum number of years an audit firm can audit a given company's financial statements has been proposed as a means to preserve auditor independence and possibly to increase investors' confidence in financial reports.

In October 2010, the European Commission (EC) issued a Green Paper to address financial market regulatory reform in reaction to the 2008 global financial crisis. The proposed regulations, issued in November 2011, included mandatory rotation of audit firms after six years (with an extension to nine if joint audits are used), with a cooling- off period of four years.

In the United States (US), the Government Accounting Office (GAO), which was delegated by the Securities and Exchange Commission (SEC) to study the issue of MAR, concluded that there is no clear evidence regarding the potential benefits of a MAR rule (GAO, 2008). However The Public Company Accounting Oversight Board (PCAOB) issued a concept release in August 2011 on ways to enhance auditor independence, objectivity and professional skepticism. The concept release included mandatory audit firm rotation on as one alternative for consideration. In discussing that alternative, they did not specify or indicate a specific term (PCAOB, 2011). Horwath (2012) pointed out that 94% of the comment letters received by the PCAOB were against rotation. There are certain G20 jurisdictions have introduced mandatory audit firm rotation including: (IESBA 2012)

1. Brazil- for listed companies excluding banks;
2. China - for state owned entities and financial enterprises;
3. India - for banks, insurance companies, provident trust funds and public sector entities;
4. Indonesia – five- year rotation for the central bank, and six - year rotation for public and private companies;
5. Italy – nine - year rotation for all listed companies;
6. Saudi Arabia – all listed companies excluding banks; and
7. Turkey –eight - year rotation for banks, seven -year rotation for insurance companies, Five – year rotation for energy companies and all listed companies.
8. In Bahrain, it is not mandatory to switch auditing firms. In fact, in 2006, the Central Bank of Bahrain (CBB) took a position against a notion in the parliament to mandate such a requirement on the ground that small markets are distorted by such decisions.

Experience has shown that switching of auditing firms takes place in very rare cases and generally occurs only after an audit failure. The (Central Bank of Bahrain) CBB does require audit partner rotation for financial institutions at least every five years. Auditing firms claim that they follow such a practice for other firms in accordance with their own internal policies. Auditors are not prevented from joining a client firm at any time, even immediately after formulating an audit opinion (CBB).

Some countries have repealed mandatory audit firm rotation in its entity, but nine smaller jurisdictions still require rotation, including: Laos, Morocco, Oman, Paraguay, Portugal (comply - or -explain), Qatar, Serbia, Tunisia and Uzbekistan (IESBA 2012).

Lack of auditor independence is believed to be the reason for financial reporting failure. One of the arguments which could impair auditor independence is the long-term relationship between auditor and its clients. For example Anderson had been auditing Enron's financial statements since its inception in 1985. In fact, Anderson was given permanent office space at Enron's headquarter. He also share a similar culture with Enron's colleagues such as wearing the same business attire, sharing office birthdays, having lunch together and joining Enron's trips (Arel et al., 2005). This close relationship may create a conflict of interests for the auditor which can adversely affect his independence.

Accountants have long recognized that auditor independence is critical to the validity of auditors as a profession. The independence of auditors should be the bedrock of the audit environment. Auditor independence is very crucial to public confidence in financial reporting. Arens et al., (1999) as cited by Nur and Meslina, (2009) defined independence as "taking unbiased viewpoint in the performance of audit tests, the evaluations of the results and the issuance of audit reports". Independence includes the qualities of integrity, objectivity and impartiality. An auditor should maintain objectivity and be free from conflict of interest in performing audit engagement. The EC Green Paper states that situations where a company has appointed the same audit firm for decades seem incompatible with desirable standards of independence. Accordingly, the Green Paper recommended that the mandatory rotation of audit firms should be considered.

Mandatory audit rotation has always been proposed as a solution to enhance auditor independence. It is argued that mandatory audit firm rotation will significantly increase auditor independence because the client no longer has a tactical threat of changing auditors in circumstances when they disagree with the auditor's professional judgment (Tackett et al., 2004). The auditor will not be burdened from pleasing the client's management and at the same time will reduce the auditor's concern over losing the client. Mandatory audit firm rotation would require the clients to replace their external auditor at a certain time, usually after a few years. Section 207 © of Sarbenes Oxlay Act (SOA) define the term "mandatory rotation" as the imposition of a limit on the period of years on which a particular registered public accounting firm may be the auditor of record for a particular issuer. SOA's reforms directly related to auditors include the establishment of the Public Company Accounting Oversight Board (PCAOB), increased audit committee responsibilities, and mandatory rotation of lead and reviewing audit partners after five consecutive years on an engagement (Arel, et al., 2005). Breeden (2012) believed that companies should re-propose their audit engagement at least once every five or six years.

Several prior studies have attempted to draw conclusions of MAR in terms of Audit quality. The majority of the published empirical papers are based on settings where mandatory rotation is not in place, with few exceptions which are characterized by some relevant limitations (Ruiz-Barbadillo et al., 2009; Kim and Yi, 2009; Firth et al., 2012). In December 2011, the American Institute of Certified Public Accountants (AICPA) issued a comment letter that the PCAOB refrain from imposing mandatory audit rotation. The AICPA letter supported the PCAOB's goals to enhancing auditor independence, objectivity and professional skepticism.

Whether audit firm rotation should be made mandatory is an issue that has been debated for almost five decades in the US and around the world (Kwon et al., 2010). Proponents of mandatory Audit firm rotation have argued that a new auditor would bring to bear greater skepticism and a fresh perspective that may be lacking in long-standing auditor-client relationship. The proponents added that when a company has been a client of an audit firm for a number of years, the client can be viewed as a source of a perpetual annuity, potentially comparing the auditor's independence. However; others concluded that mandatory audit firm rotation might not be the most efficient way to strengthen auditor independence (GAO, 2003).

Objectives of the Study

The main objective of this study is to explore whether mandatory audit firm rotation should be implemented in Bahrain, and the effects of such a requirement on auditor independence. The following research objectives have been developed:

1. To explore current audit appointment practices by listing companies in Bahrain.
2. To look into the opinion of auditing firms in Bahrain on potential effects provided by implementing mandatory audit firm rotation (auditor independence).
3. To investigate their views in implementing mandatory audit firm rotation in Bahrain.

Significance of the study

The motivation of the current study evolved for a number of reasons. First, most of the literature on audit firm rotation focuses on developed countries. The current study, therefore, addresses this issue in developing countries, the case of Bahrain. Second, as far as the current researchers are aware, no such study was carried out with special reference to Bahrain. The results of the study are hoped to increase knowledge about how listed companies and audit firms in Bahrain reflect mandatory audit rotation through their reporting practices. Third, because Bahrain is a member of GCC, they share a number of specific structural economic features. Key common features of GCC are: a high dependency on oil as expressed in the share of oil (and gas) revenues in total fiscal and export revenues; young and rapidly growing national labor forces; and the heavy reliance on expatriate labor in the private sector. In addition, listed companies are subjected to similar reporting requirements. The companies' laws in these countries require all legal entities to submit an annual report which includes a director's report, auditor's report, and financial statements, and to have their accounts prepared in accordance with International Financial Reporting Standards issued by the International Financial reporting Standards. Thus, GCC are expected to benefit from the results of the current study.

It is believed that this study would supplement literature by providing answers to the following research questions:

RQ1: Does mandatory audit firm rotation improve auditor independence?
RQ2: To what extent the auditors' perceptions of the impact of mandatory audit firm rotation on the auditor independence is influenced by demographic characteristics.

The remainder of the study is proceeds as follows: Section 2 provides for the Bahrain auditing environment. Section 3 provides a review of the controversy and literature review about mandatory audit firm rotation and hypotheses development. Section 4 provides for methodology (data collection, population of the study and testing hypotheses). Section 5 presents the statistical analysis and findings of the study. Section 6 highlights the conclusion and recommendations.

The Bahrain auditing environment:

Some important features of the audit market in Bahrain must be understood to perceive the context in which this study was undertaken.

As of the end of February 2008, audit services in Bahrain are provided by 24 accounting firms. Five of these are considered local; four are operating as foreign branches; and the remaining are linked to international firms. The Big Four; i.e., Ernst & Young (E&Y), Deloitte &

Touche (D&T), KPMG, and Price water house Coopers (PWC) have a strong presence in Bahrain. D&T and KPMG operate as a joint venture, whereas the other two operate as branches of international firms. BDO Jawad Habib and E&Y are the only two firms registered with the United States (US)

The Central Bank of Bahrain (CBB) requires financial institutions to be audited by one of the big audit firms. Audit services are regulated by the Amiri Decree Number 26 of 1996, which requires auditors to obtain a license to practice and set the minimum requirements for a license. In effect, audit firms got two licenses, one to practice auditing and the second specifically to offer auditing services to financial institutions.

Appointments of auditors, as per article (205) paragraph (e) of the Bahrain Commercial Companies Law Number 21 of 2001, should be made on a yearly basis at firm's annual stockholder meetings. However in practice, boards of directors are empowered by annual meetings to appoint auditors and to determine their remuneration. This practice is subject to criticism on the grounds that an auditor's role is to mitigate agency problems that might exist between the board and the shareholders.

The CBB's authority is based on article, (61) paragraph (a), of The Central Bank of Bahrain and Financial Institutions Law Number 64 of 2006, which states: "Every Licensee shall appoint one or more qualified and experienced external auditors for its accounts for every financial year. Prior written approval by the Central Bank will be required before appointing an auditor." This approval is needed annually. In cases where in a decision has been taken to replace the external auditors before the end of the year, the respective financial institutions are also required to inform the CBB about the reasons for this decision.

Auditors and Accounting Standards Module was first issued in October 2010 under otherwise excepted by the Central Bank of Bahrain (CBB). Specialized licensees must ensure that the audit partner responsible further audit does not undertake that function more than 5 years in succession. Specialized licensees must notify by CBB of any change in audit partner.

Auditors appointed by specialized licensees must be independent. Auditors who resign or are otherwise removed from office are required to inform the CBB in writing of the reasons for the termination of their appointment.

The appointment of auditors normally take place during the course of the firm's annual general meeting, specialized licensees should notify the CBB of the proposed agenda. The CBB's approval of the proposed auditor does not limit in any way shareholders rights to subsequently reject the board choice. The CBB is considering the proposed (re) appointment of an auditor, takes into account the expertise, resources and reputation of the audit firm, relative to the size and complexity of the licensee. Specialized licensees must notify the CBB as soon as they intended to remove their external auditor. Specialized licenses must ensure that the replacement auditor is appointed (subject to CBB approval), as soon as reasonably practicable after a vacancy occurs, but no later than three months.

The external auditor of specialized licensees must inform the CBB in writing, should it resign or its appointment as auditor be terminated, within 30 calendar days, of the event occurring, setting out the reasons for the resignation or termination. Unless otherwise exempted by the CBB, specialized licensees must ensure that auditor partner responsible for their audit does not undertake that function more than five years in succession. Article 61 (d) of the CBB law imposes conditions for the auditor to be considered as independent. Before a specialized licensee appoints an auditor, it must take responsible steps to ensure that the auditor has the required skills, resources and experience to carry out the audit properly, and is independent of the licensee. For an auditor to be considered independent, it must, among things, comply with the restrictions in Section AA-1.5. In that, specialized licensees must not provide regulated services to their auditor.

Article 217 prohibits an auditor from being a chairman or a member of the board of directors of the licensee he audits; must not hold any managerial position in the licensee he audits and acquiring any shares in the licensee he audits, or selling any such shares he may already own, during the period of his audit. Furthermore, the auditor must not be a relative (up to the second degree) of a person assuming management or accounting duties in the licensee. These arguments may be applied and/or linked to Bahrain. In the light of the increasing focus on the stock exchange market of Bahrain as important avenue for attracting foreign investments and to encourage local residents to invest in shares, Bahraini companies may engage in mandatory audit firm rotation as a mean to enhance the quality of audit. And this will help to enhance the company's ability to raise capital at the lowest cost possible (Healy and Palepu, 1993; Lev, 1992).

In Bahrain, it is not mandatory to switch audit firms. In fact, in 2006, the CBB took a position against a motion in the parliament to mandate such a requirement on the ground that small markets are distorted by such decisions. Experience has shown that switching of audit firms takes place in very rare cases and generally occurs only after an audit failure.

The CBB does require auditors of financial institutions to switch auditing partners at least every five years. Auditing firms claim that they follow such a practice for other firms in accordance with their own internal policies. Auditors are not prevented from joining a client firm at any time, even immediately after formulating an audit opinion.

Literature review and hypotheses development

Many studies have been conducted in the area of mandatory audit firm rotation (Mautz and Sharaft, 1961; Pierre St. and Anderson 1984; Dopuch et al., 2001; Gietzmann and Sen 2001; Davis et al., 2002; Geiger and Raghunandan, 2002; Carcello and Najy, 2004; Kaplan 2004; Arel et al., 2005; Chi et al., 2005; Gavious 2007; and Wibowo and Rosietta, 2009).

The close relationship between auditors and clients causes the auditor and the client to have a chance to compromise amounting and reporting method. This decreases the auditor's independence and thus, decreeses the audit quality. It is suggested in the literature review that extended auditor – client relationships can have a detrimental effect on auditor independence because an auditor's objectivity about a client decreases overtime (Mautz and Sharaft, 1961; Dopuch et al., 2001; Kaplan, 2004; Chi et al. 2005; Gavious, 2007). Proponent of audit firm rotation argued that mandatory audit rotation enhances auditor independence because managers cannot directly threaten auditors with their dismissal and cannot promise future income arising from their continued appointment (Kwon et al., 2010). Metcalf Committee indicated that mandatory audit firm rotation is a way to bolster auditor independence (US Senate, 1976). Regulators have suggested a link between auditor tenure and reductions in earnings quality and recommended imposing such a requirement (Commission on Auditors' Responsibilities, 1978; Division for (Certified Public Accountants (CPA) firms, 1992). There are more audit failure and lawsuits in the early years of audit engagement. The major financial reporting failures at Enron and WorldCom, as well as apparent failures at Quest, Tyco, Adelphia, and others, led to the financial reporting reforms contained in Sarbanes-Oxley Act of 2002. Many of the audit failures and legal issues occur in the early years of audit engagement, and thus, the longer the tenure; the audit quality will be better (Pierre St. and Anderson, 1984). Carcello and Nagy (2004) proposed that the probability of fraudulent financial reporting is highest early in the audit firm's tenure and is not substantially higher for instances of long standing audit engagement.

Others argue that even though the auditor rotation costs more, this increases the auditor's independence relatively more than the costs Gietzmann and Sen (2001). Audit rotation causes audit risk, below standard audit implementation, because an auditor has not comprehensively understood his client (Beatty, 1989; Craswell et al., 1995).

However, other views were adopted, in which auditing profession has argued that mandatory audit firm rotation would reduce the auditor incentives to invest in specific industries, destroys the knowledge of client companies that an audit firm usually accumulates over the period of years, distorts the competition in the market and increase the cost of an audit (AICPA, 1992).

GAO's (2003) study concluded that mandatory audit firm rotation may not be the most efficient way to strengthen audit independence and improve audit quality. It appears from the literature that politicians, regulators, analysts and small audit firms favor mandatory audit firm rotation as a solution to the perceived lack of objectivity and independence of auditors, whereas academicians, companies, and large audit firms tend to be against mandatory audit firm rotation because changing auditors is costly (Kwon, et al., 2010).

According to the literature review and based on the above discussion, the arguments in favor of mandatory audit firm rotation can be summarized as follows:

1. If auditors continue to audit the entity for too long, they risk developing too close relationship with the client and compromising independence.
2. Periodically having a new auditor would bring a fresh look to the public company's financial reporting and help the auditor appropriately deal with financial reporting issues because the auditor's tenure would be limited under mandatory audit rotation.
3. Mandatory audit firm rotation would help in the more even development of the auditing profession, helping smaller and medium – size audit firm rotation.

The arguments against mandatory audit firm rotation can be summarized as follows:

1. New auditors may miss problems in the period under review because they lack adequate experience with the client to notice either unusual events or important changes in the client's environment.
2. There are not enough large audit firms to address the audit requirements of large companies, making auditor rotation impracticable at the ground level.
3. The rotation would only prevent auditors from building in-depth institutional knowledge of a client and its business.

Without empirical evidence, it is neither clear whether mandatory rotation would not really ensure audit quality by strengthening auditor independence nor obvious whether the rotation rule would hamper audit quality because of insufficient knowledge of clients. Therefore, any generalization of such findings to a regime with mandatory audit rotation should be implemented with caution, because this study aims to examine the effects of mandatory audit firm rotation and each of auditor independence, the study focuses upon the previous studies about auditor independence.

Mandatory audit rotation and auditor independence

In this part we focus on the relationship between auditor independence and audit firm rotation. The independence of auditors is a key factor in evaluating the reliability of auditor's report. This feature has several implications. The first is for political nature: It is the auditor independence can enhance the credibility of published financial reporting and then add value for several categories of stakeholders. The second implication directly involves the profession: the trait of independence is the best way of demonstrating to the regulator and the public that the auditors are performing their task according to ethical principles, such as objectivity and integrity. (Cameran, et al., 2005).

The auditor who has not comprehensively understood client tends to depend on the estimation and information supplied by client (Gul et al., 2009). The relationship between tenure and independence is negatively hypothesized because the longer the tenure, the relationship between the auditor and the client is closer and thus, the auditors tends to be less critical/less independent (De Angelo, 1981).

Opponents of mandatory audit rotation argue that there are other factors motivating the auditor to maintain his independence, such as the need to preserve reputation and client revenue. Ernst & Young (2013) believe that mandatory firm rotation is not an effective way to enhance auditor independence.

We now pointed out some previous studies relating to auditor independence.

O'Leary, 1996 analyzed in his study the concept of independence and the relative consequences that mandatory rotation may have. The respondents to the study consider the cost of rotation to overweigh any benefits. The results of the study (63% of public listed companies and 37% of auditors) consider the introduction of mandatory rotation as a useful means of improving the perception of auditor independence.

Dopuch et al (2001), study aimed to assess whether mandatory rotation and / or retention of auditors increases their independence. The results support the hypothesis that the auditor compromises his independence most often in the no rotation / no retention regimes. On the other hand, the results are consistent with assumption that mandatory rotation coupled with retention increases the auditor's independence. They added that mandatory rotation limits the repeated interaction between manager and auditor that can lead to collusion, so this rule can improve an auditor's independence stand alone or in conjunction with mandatory rotation.

Gietzmann and Sen (2002) studied the tradeoff between the concerns of the auditors to be reappointed by the client and the costs that mandatory rotation rule implies. In other terms, the auditor receiving high fees from the client is interested in a renewal of the engagement and this can impair the auditor's incentive to be independent. The authors concluded that a long standing relationship can induce the auditor to give much more importance to the economic interest in preserving the client than to independence. The authors suggested that in the case of market concentration the proposal for mandatory rotation may be justifiable.

In 2002, and in a 2004 update, the independent academics of SDA Bocconi School of Management studied the impact of mandatory audit rotation in Italy (SDA Bocconi School of Management, 2002) and conducted that the policy seems to lead to additional cost, greater concentration of work among the largest audit firms, negative impact on audit quality (most noticeably in the years immediately after the rotation) and is ignored by the stock market (Cameran et al., 2005). Suriana (2006) carried a study to provide some viewpoints on whether mandatory audit firm rotation should be implemented in Malaysia.

The study examined the value provided by mandatory audit firm rotation from the perspectives of Chief Finance Officer of published companies in Malaysia. The study is based on a survey using questionnaires in order to gather information. The results indicate that mandatory audit firm rotation will enhance auditor independence as perceived by the respondents. However, the respondents believe that the costs overweigh its intended benefits. Kighir A. E. (2013) conducted a study to examine the relationship between audit firm rotation and auditor independence in Nigeria. The study found that there is no statistical significant relationship between audit firm rotation and auditor independence. Table 1 provides a comprehensive overview of research papers addressing the impact of mandatory audit firm rotation on auditor independence.

In summary, so far the extant literature, although very broad, was unable to provide direct and univocal empirical evidence in support or against the introduction of a MAR rule. There is a clear need to research this issue further in settings where the MAR rule is already in place and where the actual incentives of the auditor become more evident. Thus our paper aims at partially filling this gap. For users of financial reports, independence element is very important factor in the audit function; the more the auditor's independence is maintained, the more reliability of the financial statements provided by auditing firms.

Various findings drawn from previous studies, together with what has been discussed above it can be concluded that most prior research was carried out in developed countries.

Hence, there is a need to examine the impact of the MAR on auditor independence in one of the emerging economies; kingdom of Bahrain, In the light of that, and to accomplish the objectives of this research and to answer the research questions, the following hypotheses are formulated:

H01: There is no statistically significant relationship between mandatory audit firm rotation and auditor independence.

Table 1. Finding prior research survey on the impact of mandatory audit firm rotation on auditor independence.

Author/year	Sample	Method	Results
O'Leary & Radich, 1996	Australia, 300 companies, 180 audit partners	Survey research	63% of public listed companies and 37% of auditors consider mandatory audit firm rotation as a useful means of improving the perception of independence.
Summer, 1998	n/a	Analytical research	Mandatory rotation undermines the incentives for building up a reputation for independence by destroying quasi-rents from an ongoing relation
Vanstraelen, 2000	Belgian, companies submitted to the Belgian National Bank (1992-1996)	Archival research	Long-term auditor-client relationships significantly increase the likelihood of an unqualified opinion or significantly reduce the auditor's willingness to qualify audit reports. Further, auditors are more willing to issue an unqualified audit report in the first two years of their mandate than in the last year of their mandate
Hussey & Lan, 2001	UK, 776 CFOs	Survey research	The perception of audit independence would be enhanced by prescribing the rotation of auditors even if the concerns about audit quality and costs are predominant and overall opinion on the rotation rule is negative
Stefani, 2002	n/a	Analytical research	Positive effects of mandatory audit firm rotation on auditor independence
Gietzmann & Sen, 2002	n/a	Analytical research	Positive effects on independence exceed the costs of mandatory audit firm rotation, when there are only a few but very large audit clients on the audit market.
Iyer & Rama, 2004	USA, 124 CPAs employed as CFO or CEO, controller or treasurer in industry of AICPA	Survey research	Respondents with short audit tenures were more likely to indicate that they could persuade the client's position in case of disagreement.
Cameron *et al.* (2005) referring to SDA Bocconi School of Management, 2002	Italy, managers, internal auditors, auditors and managerial accountants	Survey research	Mandatory auditor rotation results in positive effects on perceived independence
Hatfield, Jackson & Vandervelde, 2006	USA, 155 CPAs	Experimental research	Neither partner rotation nor firm rotation may eliminate the effects of client pressure
Moody, Pany & Reckers, 2006	USA, 49 judges	Experimental research	Mandatory audit firm rotation enhances auditor independence perceptions compared to partner rotation. Further, judges consider auditors less likely to be liable for fraudulently misstated financial statements when firm rotation is involved in a minimally compliant corporate governance environment.
Kaplan & Mauldin, 2008	USA, 163 MBA students as nonprofessional investors	Experimental research	Compared to audit partner rotation, audit firm rotation does not strengthen 'independence in appearance' among nonprofessional investors.

Table 1. cont'd

Ebimobowei & Keretu, 2011	Nigeria, 172 auditors and investors	Survey research	Mandatory audit firm rotation increases the quality of audit reports as well as the independence of auditors, even though also the audit costs increase.
The Canadian Institute of Chartered Accountants 2012		Archival research	Depending upon the length of the rotation period, will eliminate or significantly reduce the institutional familiarity threats since a change in the audit firm must occur.

H02: There is no significant difference between respondents in their perceptions of auditor independence and mandatory audit firm rotation attributed to demographic characteristics variables.

METHODOLOGY

Our study used two sources of data collection: primary and secondary sources. The primary source of data is based on survey methods using questionnaires in order to gather the information related to this study. The benefit of using this method is that the researchers can contact participants who might be inaccessible (Cooper and Schindler, 2003). In addition, the data are collected using primary sources in order to gather the perceptions of the respondents. According to Cooper and Schindler, primary sources are always the most authorative because the information has not been filtered or interpreted by a second party.

Therefore, survey is one of the most appropriate methods used in collection of primary data. Secondary data is information collected come from official journals, articles, newspapers, text books and internet. Analyses of variance (ANOVA) were also conducted to determine whether auditors' perception of the impact of MAR on the auditor independence was influenced by demographic characteristics.

The questionnaire comprises three sections. Section one contains some demographic information and the current audit practices while section two includes questions about potential effects of mandatory audit firm rotation upon audit independence, and section three composes questions about overall opinions on requiring mandatory audit firm rotation. The questionnaire was revised in the light of a feedback from professionals who are working at universities and audit firms. Respondents were asked to express their opinions on the potential effects of mandatory audit firm rotation upon audit independence using a Liker Scale of five points ranging from 1 "strongly agree" to five "strongly disagree".

The data used in this study are obtained from a sample of auditors who are practicing in audit firms in Kingdom of Bahrain. We consider auditors as entire authorized and approved individuals and not specific auditing firms. Also, the increasing use of the word auditors in our study does not by any means refer to both external and internal auditors. That is to say the word auditors in this study refer only to external auditors. Though both types of auditors are required to be independent, the degree of the independence for external auditors is far too strong and mandatory.

The data used in this study are obtained from a sample of auditors who are practicing in audit firms in Kingdom of Bahrain. The number of auditing firms in Bahrain is about 25 firms. We asked each auditing firm to provide us with the number of auditors who are qualified to fill the questionnaire, and the total number of auditors received from all auditing firms in Bahrain was 102. Accordingly, 102 questionnaires were distributed with a response rate of 64.7%. (Appendix contains a list of auditing firms in Bahrain).

The questionnaire comprises three sections. Section one contains some demographic information and the current audit practices.; section two includes questions about potential effects of mandatory audit firm rotation upon audit independence, and section three composes questions about overall opinions on requiring mandatory audit firm rotation. The questionnaire was revised in the light of a feedback from professionals who are working at universities and audit firms. Respondents were asked to express their opinions on the effects potential effects of mandatory audit firm rotation upon audit independence using a Liker Scale of five points ranging from 1 "strongly agree" to five "strongly disagree".

The internal consistency of the questionnaire reliability was measured by using Cronbach's coefficient alpha statistical test as shown in Table 2. The analysis provides an indication of the average correlation among all the items that made up the scale. The results in the Table demonstrate that all indices obtained were considered high (0.766). A sample scale that shows alpha value above 0.70 is considered reliable (Bryman and Cramer, 2001). Therefore, the indices for the questionnaire reliability are generally considered adequate for this research.

RESULTS

Statistical Analysis

Demographics

Analyzing the first section of the questionnaire reveals the demographic background of the respondents, which are examined by looking at the Position; experience; professional qualifications; type of audit firm and number of employees' descriptive analysis regarding demography variables is shown in figures 1 to 4 below:

Table 2. Reliability Statistics

Cronbach's Alpha	Cronbach's Alpha Based on Standardized Items	N of Items
.766	.769	11

Table 3. Respondents distribution according to demography variables

Position	Frequency	Percentage (%)
partners;	8	12.12
managers	7	10.60
auditors	51	77.28
Experience		
	Frequency	**Percentage (%)**
Less than 5 years	24	36.4
5 – less than 10	26	39.4
10 – less than 15	8	12.1
15 – 20	4	6.1
More than 20	4	6.1
Qualification		
B.S.C.	24	36.4
Graduate degree	12	18.2
CPA/CA/ACCA/CFA/CMA	44	66.7
Others	2	3
Company's auditor		
BIG 4	24	36.4
Non-BIG 4	42	63.6
No. of employees		
Up to 50	46	69.7
Above 50	20	30.3

Table 3 summarizes the job title of the respondents' auditors. Of the 66 auditors analyzed, eight auditors (12.12%) are partners; seven auditors (10.6 %) are managers; with the remaining fifty-one auditors (77.28 %) who is working as seniors in audit firms.

Auditors are varied in years of experience which are classified into three categories for the purpose of this research; less than five years, between 5 to 20 years, and above 20 years of work experience. Table 3 shows that 63.6% of the respondents have over 5 years experience and this result indicates that the extent of experience and maturity that may be reflected positively upon the work.

Respondents were requested to report their professional qualifications and academic degree. Table 3 shows that the majority of the respondents (66.7%) have professional certificate, followed by B.S.C. with 36.4% and graduate degree with (18.2%). These results indicate highest academic level that respondents have, and this may be positively reflected upon the importance of the information given by the respondents. Respondents' auditors are affiliated with several audit firms. Table 3 shows that 36.4% of the auditing offices are BIG 4 and the remainders (63.6%) are associated with local audit firms.

Moreover, Table 3 shows that the number of employees working in audit offices is 50 employees on average with 69.7% and 30.3% above 50 employees. This results indicate that the auditing offices are working very well and are established themselves in the market. (Table 2).

Table 4 shows the distribution of respondents according to current audit practice. It is apparent that the auditors provide other services other than audit service to the

Table 4. Respondents distribution according to current audit practices

Services provided to audit clients (other than audit)	Frequency (%)		Frequency (%)	
	yes	%	No	%
Financial system design and implementation	36	54.5	30	45.5
Taxation	12	18.2	54	81.8
Accounting services	64	97	2	3
Internal audit services	50	75.8	16	24.2
Management functions or human resources	26	39.4	40	60.6
Legal services	36	54.5	30	45.5
Other non-audit services	34	51.5	32	48.5

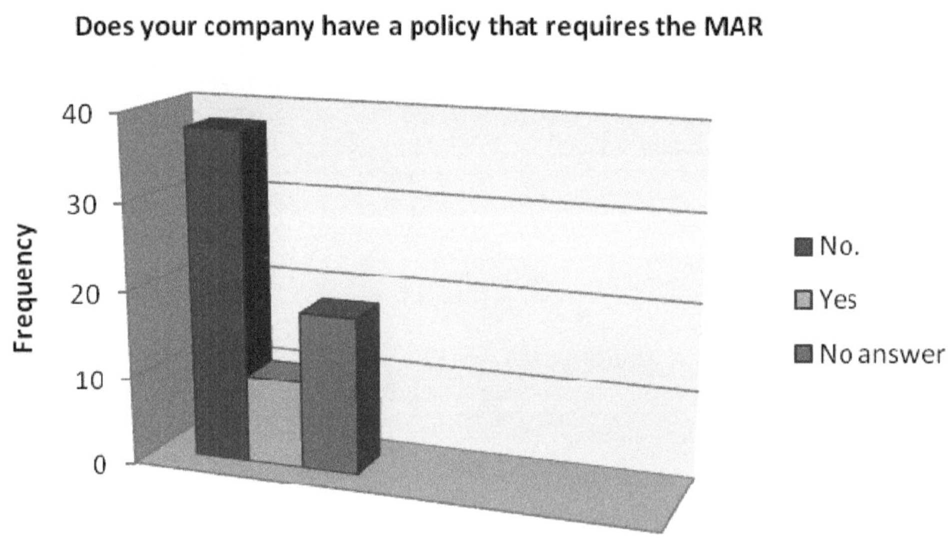

Figure 1. Respondents' answers regarding MAR policy

and legal service with (54.5%) for each.

Respondents were asked to indicate their perceptions regarding mandatory audit firm rotation rules. Figure 1 shows that 38 of the respondents (57.6%) do not require the MAR rule whereas 10 (15.2%) of the respondents have a policy that require the mandatory audit firm rotation rule and 18 (27.3%) have no answer. Figure 2 indicates that 40 of the respondents (60.6%) have no answer regarding the number of years that should the mandatory firm be permitted to once again compete for audit services followed by choice of three to less than five years and then five years to less than eight years.

The results regarding what should be the limit on the mandatory firm's audit tenure period also indicates that the choices "three to less than five years" and "five years to less than eight years" have 33.34% for each (Figure 3).

Figure 4 regarding the statement "do you believe that mandatory firm's should be applied uniformly for audits of all public companies regardless of the nature or size of the public company" indicated that the respondents were not in agreement, in which 50 % have no answer, 45.45% answer Yes, and 4.54 % answer No.

Auditors' perceptions on effects of audit firm rotation on perceived auditor independence

Respondents are requested to express their opinions on eleven statements using a Likert -scale of 5 points ranged from 1 "strongly agree"; to 5 "strongly disagree". This study defines any factors with the mean values up to 2.0, at least "agree" or "strongly agree" upon; in the range of 2.1 to 3.0, are "uncertain" and 3.1 or above indicating that the respondents either "disagree" or "strongly disagree" that MAR would enhances auditor independence.

Table 5 shows the means and standard deviations for each question individually and all questions together that

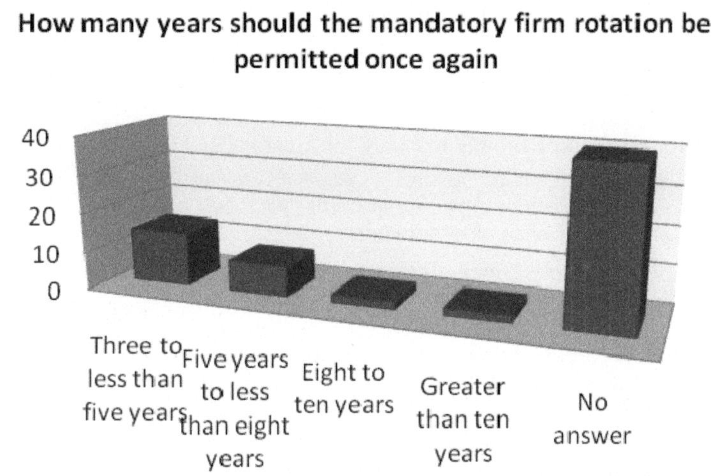

Figure 2. Respondents' answers regarding number of years permitted.

Figure 3. Respondents answer regarding limit on mandatory firms audit tenure

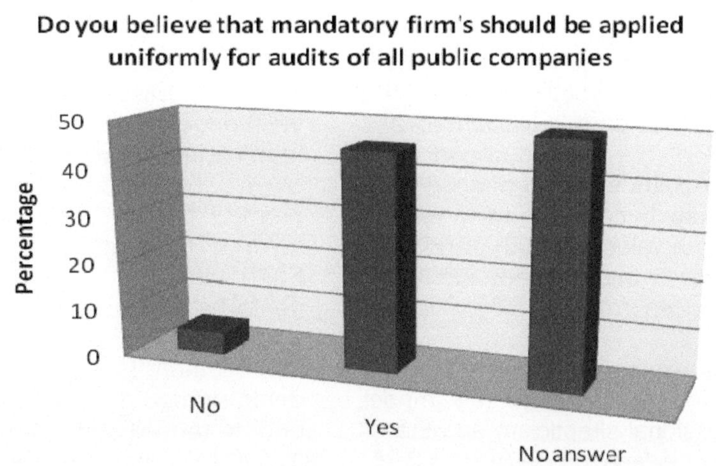

Figure 4. Respondents' answers regarding implementing MAR.

Table 5. Effects of audit firm rotation on perceived auditor independence

Question No.	Questions	Mean	Std. Deviation	t-Value	P-Value
1	Auditor's independence is a key priority not only for auditors, but also for management and investors..	1.67	.53	25.266	0.000
2	Under mandatory audit rotation, the audit firm will be more independent and objective in performing services.	2.15	.89	19.452	0.000
3	The longer audit tenure may adversely impact auditor objectivity and professional skepticism and therefore, impair the appearance of independence.	2.75	.89	25.018	0.000
4	A long term auditor-client relationship can induce an auditor to give much importance on the economic interest in preserving the client than to independence.	2.75	.99	22.556	0.000
5	Mandatory audit rotation would decreases auditors' incentive to compromise their independence through biased reporting in favor of management,	2.45	.86	23.117	0.000
6	Mandatory rotation would increase auditor's willingness to resist pressure from management.	2.45	.70	28.260	0.000
7	There are other factors motivating the auditor to maintain his independence, such as the need to preserve reputation and client revenue.	2.15	.96	18.120	0.000
8	Mandatory rotation will increase the auditor's potential for dealing more appropriately with financial reporting that may materially affect client's financial statements.	2.45	.83	24.137	0.000
9	Auditor's tenure exceeding five years is not significantly perceived as reducing auditor independence.	2.75	.93	24.110	0.000
10	Mandatory audit rotation can impair independence because it undermines the incentive to build up a reputation for honesty or because of the interest of the auditor in maintaining the client for the recovering of the initial investment.	3.27	.93	28.370	0.000
11	Mandatory audit rotation would decrease management's ability to influence the auditors.	2.33	.88	21.471	0.000
	Average mean & standard deviation for all first hypothesis questions together	**2.5**	**.86**	**29.110**	**0.000**

t-distribution with 65 degree of freedom ,for level of significance of .05 , the table critical value is 1.66.

test the hypothesis. The analysis indicates that the means range from 1.67 - 3.27. The standard deviation range from .53 –.99 which means that there is agreement among respondents about the hypothesis and the variances are low since the standard deviation of any question is less than half of the related mean. The respondents express that Auditor's independence is a key priority not only for auditors, but also for management and investors (mean=1.67, p-value= 0.000), and that under MAR, the audit firm will be more independent and objective in performing services (mean=2.15, p-value= 0.000).

Furthermore, respondents express their opinions and agree that the longer audit tenure may adversely impact auditor objectivity and professional skepticism and therefore, impair the appearance of independence (mean=2.75, p-value= 0.000). The respondents express that a long term auditor-client relationship can induce an auditor to give much importance on the economic interest in preserving the client than to independence (mean=2.75, p-value= 0.000). The respondents express the MAR would decreases auditors' incentives to compromise their independence through biased reporting in favor of management (mean=2.75, p-value= 0.000). And that MAR would decreases auditors' incentives to compromise their independence through biased reporting in favor of management (mean=2.45, p-value= 0.000). Furthermore, the results in table 3 suggest that respondents have expressed their opinions on the MAR would increase auditor's willingness to resist pressure from management (mean=2.45, p-value=0.000). The respondents agreed that there are other factors motivating the auditor to maintain his independence, such as the need to preserve reputation and client revenue (mean=2.15, p-value= 0.000), and that MAR will increase the auditor's potential for dealing more appropriately with financial

Table 6. Respondents distribution according to overall opinions on requiring mandatory audit firm rotation

Answer No.	There should be compulsory rotation of audit firm after a fixed number of years	Frequency	Percentage (%)
1.	Yes, I believe it enhances auditor quality, independence and objectivity and should be implemented.	30	45.5
2.	Yes, it can work if rotation period is long enough.	24	36.4
3.	No, the benefits of mandatory audit firm rotation would exceed the costs of implementing such a requirement.	8	12.1
4.	No answer.	4	6.1
	Regarding your public company's (or firm's) overall current opinion on whether or not your company supports requiring mandatory rotation of registered public accounting firms		
1	The company (firm) supports requiring mandatory rotation of public accounting firms at this time provided that the period of time for rotation is reasonable. (Please provide the principal reason for supporting mandatory rotation below.)	22	33.3
2	The company (firm) supports the concept of requiring mandatory rotation, but believes more time is needed to evaluate the effectiveness of the various requirements of the Sarbanes-Oxley Act of 2002 for enhancing audit quality.	14	21.2
3	The company (firm) does not support requiring mandatory rotation of public accounting firms. (Please provide the principal reason for not supporting mandatory rotation below.)	4	6.1
4	No answer	26	39.4

reporting that may materially affect client's financial statements (mean=2.45, p-value= 0.000). furthermore, respondents believe that Auditor's tenure exceeding five years is not significantly perceived as reducing auditor independence (mean=2.75, p-value= 0.000). Respondents were uncertain that MAR can impair independence because it undermines the incentive to build up a reputation for honesty or because of the interest of the auditor in maintaining the client for the recovering of the initial investment (mean=3.27, p-value= 0.000), and that MAR would decrease management's ability to influence the auditors. The results suggest that auditor tenure impacts the auditor independence, where auditors have relations with the client that add much pressure on his opinion, hence this might prevent him from issuing a qualified report that might lead to losing his client, and MAR will enhance auditor independence . Accordingly, the average mean for all questions together of the hypothesis equal 2.5 with standard deviation of .86 which is less than half of the mean. This means that no dispersion views among respondents about the questions of the hypothesis. Also, the analysis shows that the *t value is (*29.110*) which is* greater than the table critical value of t (1.66), and the p-value is 0.000 less than the value of significance of 0.05 ($p<0.05$), This result indicates that *there* is a statistically *significant relationship* between MAR and auditor independence, which means that the null hypothesis is rejected, and that there is a statically significant correlation between MAR of external auditors and audit independence at value of significance ($p<0.05$). This result is highly consistent with the findings of prior research on the correlation between MAR and auditor independence (Hussey and Lan, 2001; Stefani, 2002; Cameron et al. 2005; Moody et al. 2006; Ebimobowei and Keretu, 2011).

Auditors' perceptions of importance of mandatory audit rotation

Table 6 reports respondents' perceptions as to the importance of mandatory audit firm rotation. The analysis indicates that 45.5% believes that audit firm rotation would enhance auditor quality, independence and objectivity and should be implemented, 36.4% believe that it can work if rotation period is long enough, whereas 12.1% believes that the benefits of mandatory audit firm rotation would exceed the costs of implementing such a requirement.

Regarding the question "your public company overall current opinion on whether or not your company supports requiring audit mandatory rotation of registered public accounting firms". The table shows that 33.3% of the respondents supports requiring mandatory rotation of public accounting firms at this time provided that the period of time for rotation is reasonable, 21.2% believes that the company (firm) supports the concept of requiring mandatory rotation, but believes that more time is needed to evaluate the effectiveness of the various requirements of the Sarbanes-Oxley Act of 2002 for enhancing audit quality and 6.1% believes that the company (firm) does not support requiring mandatory rotation of public accounting firms.

Auditors' background variables and perceptions of MAR and auditor independence

It has been argued that respondents' background variables could affect perceptions of auditor independence. In this section, the relationships between the background variables such as auditors' position, working experience, qualification, and audit firm and perceptions of auditor independence are examined.

ANOVA was conducted to determine whether auditors' perceptions of the impact of MAR on the auditor independence was influenced by demographic characteristics. The results of the tests are presented in table 7 below.

Table 7 shows that respondents' positions did not have any significant impact on the perceptions of auditor independence. However, respondents' perceptions of the MAR will increase the auditor's potential for dealing more appropriately with financial reporting (statement 8 with $p < .05$), and that MAR can impair independence (statement 10 with $p < .05$) seems to be affected by the respondents' position. It was found also that experience has a significant impact on auditors' perceptions on some statement related to the impact of the MAR on the auditor independence at (statements 8 with $p < .05$). The results also reveal that perceptions of auditors' independence were not affected by respondents' qualifications only on some statement (statements 2, 8, and 11 with $p < .05$). Furthermore, it was found that type of audit firm has no impact on auditors' perception of the impact of MAR upon the auditor independence. In the light of on the above findings, Hypothesis 2, is not rejected since the evidence presented indicates that respondents' demographic characteristics have no significant impact on perceptions of auditor independence, but can be rejected only for the respondents' position (statement 8 and 10), experience (statement 8) and qualification (statements 2, 8, and 11).

Summary and Conclusion

The main purpose of this study is to presents the opinions of sample of auditors who are practicing in audit firms in Kingdom of Bahrain on potential effects provided by implementing mandatory audit firm rotation (auditor independence). It is believed that this study would supplement literature by providing answers to the following research questions. 1) Does mandatory audit firm rotation improve auditor independence? And 2) to what extent the auditors' perceptions about the impact of mandatory audit firm rotation on the auditor independence is influenced by demographic characteristics. Data for the study were collected by distributing an administered questionnaire to the sample study that consist all auditors working in audit firms in Bahrain. We started our study by asking auditors the most basic question: Does your company have a policy that requires the mandatory audit firm rotation rules? 57.6 percent of the respondents 'indicated that they don't have such a policy. Nearly 40 percent of the respondents agreed with the statement that mandatory firm's should be applied uniformly for audits of all public companies regardless of the nature or size of the public company with audit tenure period of three to less than eight years. As a contribution to previous research, the perceived effects of mandatory audit firm rotation on auditor independence found in this study was compared with the perceived effects found in previous studies by the first hypothesis. The Average mean and standard deviation for all first hypothesis questions together resulted in rejection to the null hypothesis. This means that there is a statistically significant relationship between mandatory audit firm rotation and auditor independence and that coincide by finding of prior studies. The average mean of all questions together of the hypothesis is 2.5 with average standard deviation of .86 which is less than half of the mean. This indicated that there is no dispersion existed among respondents about the questions of the hypothesis. Also, the analysis shows that the *t value is (29.110)* which is greater than the table critical value of t (1.66), and the p-value obtained is 0.000 which is less than the value of significance at ($p<0.05$), these results confirm that there is a statistically significant relationship. This study investigates auditors' opinions on requiring mandatory audit firm rotation. 45.5 percent of the respondents believe that mandatory audit firm rotation will enhances auditor independence and should be implemented. Moreover 36.4 % of them see it works if rotation period is long enough. Respondents were also asked their overall current opinion on "whether or not your company supports requiring mandatory rotation of registered public accounting firms", 33.3% of the respondents indicated agreement on this issue. While only 6.1% believes not.

Another relevant question addressed by this study is to what extent the auditors' perceptions of the impact of mandatory audit firm rotation on the auditor independence is influenced by demographic characteristics? Analysis of variance (ANOVA) was conducted to answer this question. As shown in table 7, it was found that respondents' positions do not have any significant impact upon the perceptions of auditor independence except for (statement 8 with $p < .05$), and (statement 10 with $p < .05$) seems to be affected by the respondents' positions. It was found also that experience has a significant impact on auditors' perceptions on some statement related to the impact of the MAR on the auditor independence at

Table 7. Analysis of differences in perceptions of MAR and auditor independence with demographic Variables

Question No.	Questions	ANOVA Test Significant Level			
		Position	Experience	Qualification	Audit Firm
1	Auditor's independence is a key priority not only for auditors, but also for management and investors..	0.482	0.948	0.831	0.979
2	Under mandatory audit rotation, the audit firm will be more independent and objective in performing services.	0.870	0.241	0.004*	0.749
3	The longer audit tenure may adversely impact auditor objectivity and professional skepticism and therefore, impair the appearance of independence.	0.502	0.255	0.470	0.116
4	A long term auditor-client relationship can induce an auditor to give much importance on the economic interest in preserving the client than to independence.	0.864	0.774	0.969	0.319
5	Mandatory audit rotation would decreases auditors' incentive to compromise their independence through biased reporting in favor of management,	0.864	0.979	0.920	0.331
6	Mandatory rotation would increase auditor's willingness to resist pressure from management.	0.325	0.902	0.936	0.616
7	There are other factors motivating the auditor to maintain his independence, such as the need to preserve reputation and client revenue.	0.110	0.987	0.428	0.229
8	Mandatory rotation will increase the auditor's potential for dealing more appropriately with financial reporting that may materially affect client's financial statements.	0.018*	0.041*	0.002*	0.071
9	Auditor's tenure exceeding five years is not significantly perceived as reducing auditor independence.	0.321	0.951	0.671	0.377
10	Mandatory audit rotation can impair independence because it undermines the incentive to build up a reputation for honesty or because of the interest of the auditor in maintaining the client for the recovering of the initial investment.	0.006*	0.481	0.573	0.991
11	Mandatory audit rotation would decrease management's ability to influence the auditors.	0.343	0.027	0.005*	0.197

(statements 8 with $p < .05$). The results also reveal that, perceptions of auditor independence were not affected by respondents' qualifications only on some statement (statements 2, 8, and 11 with $p < .05$). Furthermore, it was found that type of audit firm has no impact on auditors' perceptions of the impact of MAR on the auditor independence.

We also conclude that the adoption of rotation rules wasn't given enough attention among the auditing firms in Bahrain. For that, 27.3 % of respondents' don't know "whether their company have a policy that requires the mandatory audit firm rotation rules". 60.6% don't know how many years the mandatory firm should be permitted to once again compete for audit services. In asking the respondents their beliefs regarding whether MAR should be applied uniformly for audits of all public companies regardless of the nature or size of the public company, 54.5% indicate no answer. Also 39.5% of respondents' don't know "whether or not their company supports requiring mandatory rotation of registered public accounting firms.

This study is subject to a number of limitations that need to be acknowledged, which are mainly related to its research design. Firstly, the study only examined the perceptions of one groups of financial statement users" auditing firms located in Bahrain". The findings from the study can be generalized only to this group. Future studies could investigate the perceptions of other users such as institutional and private investors, audit committees and members of regulatory bodies. Secondly, the findings of such a study may not be generalized to different countries at different stages of development or with different business environments and cultures. A comparative study of MAR practice for different countries with emerging capital markets might also be fruitful. Therefore, it would be interesting to replicate this study in other GCC countries or Middle Eastern countries.

Thirdly, as this study focused on the impact of mandatory audit rotation on auditor independence in Bahrain, further research may be directed towards examining the impact of MAR upon audit quality and on the cost of audit rotation. The results are based on a limited number of respondents, we cannot assume that the views of non respondents are similar to the study finding .However, variables other than those included in the questionnaire of the study may affect the mandatory audit rotation.

ACKNOWLEDGMENT

We thank an anonymous reviewer and the helpful comments and suggestions on an earlier draft of this paper made by many of our colleagues at the University of Bahrain.

Conflict of Interests

The author(s) have not declared any conflict of interests.

REFERENCES

AICPA (American Institute of Certified Public Accountants) (1992), "Statement of position regarding mandatory rotation of audit firms of publicly held companies".

Arel B, Brody RG, Pany K (2005). "Audit firm rotation and audit quality", The CPA Journal, January.

Arens AA, Loebbecke JK, Iskandar TM, Susaela SD, Isa S, Boh M (1999). Auditing in Malaysia; An integrated approach, Kuala Lumpur, Malaysia, Prentice Hall.

Beatty RP (1989), "Auditor reputation and the pricing of initial public offering', The Accounting Review 64(10):693-709.

Breeden R (2012). "Proposals for auditor independence and audit firm rotation", Available at: blogs.law.harvard.edu/.../2012/.../proposals-for-auditor-independence.

Bryman A, Cramer D (2001). Quantitative Data Analysis with SPSS Release 10 for Windows, London: Routledge.

Cameran M, Vincenzo DD, Merlotti E (2005). "The audit firm rotation rule: A review of the Literature", pp. 1-67. Avaiable at: http://ssrn.com/abstract=825404.

Carcello JV, Nagy AL (2004) 'Audit firm tenure and fraudulent financial reporting', Auditing: J. Practice Theory, 23(2):55-69.

Central Bank of Bahrain (CBB) Rulebook, Volume 5, Auditors and Accounting Standards Module.

Chi W, Hueng Y, Xie H (2009), "Mandatory audit-partner rotation, audit quality and market perception: Evidence from Taiwan". Canterbury Account. Res. 26(2):359-390.

Cooper DR, Schindler PS (2003). Business research methods .(8th Ed).New York ,McGraw-Hill.

Craswell AT, Francis dan JR, Taylor SL (1995), "Auditor brand name reputations and industry specialization", J. Account. Econ. (20): 297-322.

Davis R, Soo B, Trompeter G (2002). "Auditor tenure, auditor independence and earnings management", Working Paper, Boston College, Boston, MA.

Dopuch N, King R, Schwartz R (2001). "An experimental investigation of retention and rotation requirements", J. Account. Res. 39: 93-118.

Young E (2013). "Q&A on mandatory firm rotation – point of view". Available at: www.ey.com/...mandatory...rotation/.../point_of-view_our_perspective.

Firth M, Rui OM, Wu X (2012). "How do various forms of auditor rotation affect audit quality? Evidence for China", Int. J. Account. 47(1):109-138.

Gavious I (2007). "Alternative perspectives to deal with auditors' agency problem", Critical perspectives on Accounting, 18:451-467.

Geiger M, Raghunandan K (2002), "Auditor tenure and audit quality", Auditing: J. Practice Theory, 21:187-196.

General Accounting Office (GAO) (2003), "Required study in the potential effects of mandatory audit firm rotation". Report to the Senate Committee on Banking, Housing, and Urban Affairs and the House Committee on Financial Services. Washington, DE: GAO.

Gietzman MB, Sen PK (2002), "Improving auditor independence through selected mandatory rotation", Int. J. Audit. 6:183-210.

Government Accounting Office (GAO) (2008). "Continued concentration in audit market for large public companies does not call for immediate action", Available at: http://www.gao.gov/products/GAO-08-163.

Gul FA, Fung SYK, Jaggi B (2009). "Earnings quality: Some evidence on the role of auditor tenure and auditors' industry expertise", J. Account. Econ. 47(3): 265-287.

Healy PM, Palepu KG (1993). "The effects of firms' disclosure strategies on stock prices", Account. Horizons. 7(1):1-11.

Horwath C (2012), "Audit firm rotation- A good or bad proposal, April 9. Available at:
www.crowehorath.net/...horwath.../audit_firm_rotation_a-good_o...

IESBA (2012). International Ethics Standards Board for Accountants (IESBA) meeting Agenda Paper 4 from the June 18-20, 2012 materials.

Kaplan R (2004). "The mother of all conflicts: Auditor and their clients', Illinois Public Law Legal Theory Research Paper Series, Research Paper, No. 04-13, May.

Kim JB, Yi CH, (2009). "Does auditor designation by the regulatory authority improve audit quality? Evidence form Korea", J. Account. Public Policy 28(3): 207-230.

Kwon KSoo, Lim YD, Simmnett R (2010). "Mandatory audit firm rotation and audit quality: Evidence from the Koorean audit market", Available at; www.asb.unsw.edu.au/../..Lim%20-20%Mandatory%20Audit%20Firm

Lev B (1992), "Information disclosure strategy", Calif. Manage. Rev. 34(4): 9-32.

Mautz R, Sharaf H (1961). "The philosophy of Auditing", Sarasota, FL: American Accounting Association.

Nur B, Meslina A (2009). "Auditor independence: Malaysian Accountants' perceptions', Int. J. Bus. Manage. 4(12): 129-141.

O'Leary C (1996). "Compulsory rotation of audit firms for public companies?", Accountancy Ireland, April.

PCAOB (Public Company Accounting Oversight Board) (2011), "Concept release on auditor independence and audit firm rotation (PCAOB Release No. 2011-009", August 16, 2001; PCAOB Rulemaking Docket Matter 37), Available at: http://pcaobus.org/Rules/Rulemaking/Docket037/Release_2011-006.pdf.

Pierre KSt, Anderson J (1984). "An analysis of the factors associated with lawsuits against public accountants", Account. Rev. 59:242-263.

Ruiz-Barbadillo E, Gomez-Aguilar N, Carrera N (2009). "Does mandatory audit firm rotation enhance auditor independence? Evidence from Spain", Auditing: J. Practice Theory. 28(1):113-135.

SDA Bocconi School of Management, (2002). "The impact of mandatory audit rotation on audit quality and on audit pricing: The case of Italy",

Academic Research, Unpublished.
Suriana Mamat (2006), "Mandatory audit firm rotation, the perception of Malaysian public listed companies", Master thesis, University Teknologi Mara, Malaysia, December.
Tackett J, Wolf F, Claypool G (2004) Sarbanes-Oxley and Audit Failure; A critical Examination, Managerial Audit. J. 19:3.

Appendix

Listed Audit Firms in Bahrain
•KPMG Fakhro
•Ernst & Young
•Deloitte & Touche Bahrain
•PricewaterhouseCoopers
•PKF Bahrain
•Horwath Bahrain
•Moore Stephens International Ltd
•National Audit Office
•Grant Thornton
•Talal Abu-Ghazaleh & Co
•BDO Jawad Habib
•Assure Consulting WLL
•Abdulaal Gulf Audit
•Al Mezan Bureau
•Al-Mudhaffar Public Accountants
•HLB R. Yassa & Co (N & Co) Chartered Accountants
•Nabeel Al Saie - Public Accountants
•Jawad Habib & Co
•Dynamic Structures
•Accounting & Auditing Organization for Islamic Financial Institutions
•Raafat Yassa & Co Chartered Accountant
•Saba & Co
•El Sayed El Ayouty & Co
•Xpress Accounting - Bahrain
•Al atheer Audit and Consulting

Rotation of independent auditors and analysis of their reports before and after rotation in Brazil

Mr Lopo Martinez Antonio[1] and Aldecir Bassetti[2]

[1]Fucape Business School, Vitória, Brazil
[2]UNESC, Colatina, Brazil

The aim of mandatory rotation of audit firms by public companies is to preserve the independence of the external auditor and reduce errors and fraud associated with the auditing of financial statements. Nevertheless requiring this rotation periodically is a controversial subject, since it involves the commercial and professional relationship of auditors with their clients and the market for auditing. This study focuses on the effect of rotation on the reports issued by audit firms, comparing them before and after the mandatory rotation established by the Brazilian Securities Commission (CVM), effective as of 2004. For this purpose, the auditor´s report was analyzed on the financial statements of 151 listed companies for the period of 2003 to 2006 that changed audit firms as required by the CVM's rules. According to the results, the rotation of independent auditors did not assure the preservation of independence, nor is there any evidence of an increase in the quality of auditing. However, it was noted that the requirement for periodic rotation led to reduced concentration in the auditing market, with increased participation of small audit firms.

Key words: Auditing; auditor rotation; audit opinion; mandatory rotation.

INTRODUCTION

There is a growing demand for transparency and trustworthiness from companies, regardless of the size or sector. Stakeholders (government, financial institutions, employees, suppliers and customers) increasingly want reliable information about companies, to provide greater security in their decisions (Cunha et al., 2009). Among other obligations, publicly traded corporations in Brazil, the subject of this study, are required to submit their financial statements to the Brazilian Securities Commission.

According to Boynton, Johnson and Keel (2002), although the audited company is the audit firm's client, the "responsibility of the auditors to the users of their opinion is significant." The many accounting and financial scandals and failures that have occurred in the past two decades (Enron/Arthur Andersen, World Com., Parmalat, among others) have prompted growing questions in the capital market about the independence, ethics and quality of auditing services (Reis, 2009).

In response to this rising concern the Brazilian Central Bank issued BACEN Resolution 2,267, which required financial institutions in the Brazilian market to rotate their auditors every four years (Oliveira and Santos, 2007). Following an imposition by the Central Bank, the CVM issued Instruction 308, requiring all listed Brazilian firms to rotate independent auditors every five years, starting with the 2004 fiscal year (Batista et al., 2009).

The imposition of these limits on independent auditor tenure by the Central Bank and the CVM was prompted by the belief that the provision of external auditing by a single firm for a long period of time can jeopardize the quality of the service, due to an overly cozy relationship. Other countries have also imposed mandatory auditor rotation, such as Italy, Greece and Austria (Oliveira and Santos, 2007). The advocates of mandatory auditor rotation argue that the new auditors will be more skeptical and will carry out their work with greater independence (Nagy, 2005). In contrast, opponents of mandatory rotation claim that quality does not only come from independence, but also involves factors such as specific knowledge of the client and its business sector, which is enhanced by long-term relationships (Ghosh and Moon, 2005).

With the enactment of Law 11,638 in 2007, which introduced important changes in the basic Law of Corporations (Law 6,404/1976), the CVM issued Deliberation 549/08, relaxing the requirement of Instruction 308/99 and allowing listed companies not to substitute their independent auditors until the issuance of their opinions for the year ended December 31, 2011 (Reis, 2009). Nevertheless, many firms had already changed auditors due to application of the previous deadline. According to Assunção and Carrasco (2008), in a study carried out at the behest of the CVM, a change in the audit firm caused by mandatory rotation increases the chances expression of reservations in the report issued auditors on the financial statements. This article further investigates this issue – of whether or not the new audit firm tends to be more rigorous in interpreting accounting rules in Brazil after the requirements for rotation, by carrying out a quantitative analysis profile of the reports issued before and after the compulsory rotation of independent auditors.

THEORETICAL FRAMEWORK

Review of the literature

Various studies have been published on the effects of rotating auditors, in Brazil and other countries. In the international context, Johnson et al. (2002) found evidence that short relationships between auditors and clients (two to three years) are more associated with lower quality of financial reports than medium-term relationships (four to eight years). In contrast, Myers et al. (2003) reported evidence of higher earnings quality with longer auditor tenure and interpreted their results as indicating that longer auditor tenure on average results in auditors placing greater constraints on extreme management decisions in the reporting of financial performance, that is, greater independence.

In turn, Nagy (2005) found evidence in line with the findings of Johnson et al. (2002), reporting that longer relationships are not related to reduced quality of auditing, but rather tend to improve it. Barbadillo et al. (2009) studied Spanish financial institutions, which were required to rotate auditors every nine years from 1988 to 1995, seeking evidence that this requirement was associated with an increase in the issuance of going-concern opinions of distressed banks. Their results provided empirical support for the arguments of opponents of mandatory rotation.

Finally, in a study focused on Taiwan, Chi et al. (2009) found that the policy established in that country requiring rotation had a mixed effect in terms of constraining managers' extreme use of accruals to increase or decrease earnings, but that in the perception of investors it enhanced auditor independence. In Brazil, Formigoni et al. (2007) analyzed the contribution of auditor rotation to the Independence and quality of the services provided and concluded that this rotation does not have a relevant effect on either the quality or independence. Likewise, Braunbeck (2008) studied the influence of auditor rotation on the quality of auditing from the perspective of investors. The findings indicated that the self-regulatory governance mechanisms combined with the quality control policies and procedures of large international audit firms in general neutralize the negative effects of the development of an overly cozy relationship between auditor and client, thus arguing against mandatory rotation.

Martinez and Reis (2010) studied the effects of auditor rotation on the propensity to manage earnings and found there were no significant differences in the proxy for earnings management and the rotation of independent auditors. They further found that the quality of auditing not only results from auditors' independence; it also depends on the knowledge of the client built up over the years of a relationship and the specific knowledge of the client's business sector. Likewise, Oliveira and Santos (2007) performed a survey among 127 financial market analysts about the effects of rotation and concluded that in the opinion of the respondents, this rotation does not assure greater independence or reduce the risk of accounting errors and fraud.

In contrast to the above findings, the work of Assunção and Carrasco (2008), carried out at the request of the CVM, concluded that auditor rotation is favorable to the market because after a change, the new auditors tend to be more conservative, increasing the probability of issuing an opinion with reservations.

Finally, Costa and Azevedo (2008) found inconclusive evidence regarding the effects of rotation. While they found statistically significant evidence that a change in audit firm decreases the likelihood of earnings management, they found no significant differences in this respect between when this change was voluntary and mandatory, thus rejecting the hypothesis that compulsory rotation decreases the level of earnings management. Almeida and Almeida (2007) investigated if Brazilian firms audited by one of the Big Four international firms (Deloitte Touche Tohmatsu, Ernst and Young, KPMG and Price water house Coopers) are more or less likely to engage in earnings management. They found that companies audited by one of the Big Four are less likely to manage earnings. Mendes, Niyama and Ito (2007) investigated the quality of Brazilian auditing by comparing Brazilian auditing rules against international standards, concluding that in general Brazilian rules adhere to international ones. Cupertino and Martinez (2007) performed a study of the level of accruals and if this level could be an indicator for the need to investigate by oversight authorities, finding that the level of accruals can act as a good yardstick in this respect.

Independence of auditing

Independence is an essential feature of effective auditing, being directly associated with the quality of the service and thus the reliability and usefulness of the information contained in financial statements. In the Brazilian literature, Azevedo (2007), Nagy (2005) and Oliveira (2005) all state that the relationship of auditing firms with their clients for extended periods can reduce the independence that should by definition prevail in the work of independent auditors.

In the international setting, Boynton, Johnson and Kell (2002) claim that independence is the philosophical foundation of the auditing profession. The American Association of Certified Public Accountants (AICPA) defines independence as the "ability to act with integrity and exercise objectivity and professional skepticism" (AICPA, 2010). In Brazil, auditing standards are established by the Federal Accounting Council. In 2010 it issued NBC PA 290 – Independência – Trabalhos de Auditoria e Revisão, which covers the requirements for independence of audit work and for limited or special revision of the financial statements. The main purpose was to bring Brazilian practices in line with the international standards issued by the International Federation of Accountants (IFAC).

With globalization of the capital markets, firms are increasingly issuing securities for trading on exchanges outside their home markets, requiring preparation of financial statements and their submission to independent auditing according to the rules in multiple jurisdictions (Santos et al., 2009). In the United States, auditing procedures and standards have traditionally been established by the Auditing Standards Board (ASB), through the issuance of Statements on Auditing Standards (SAS). According to AICPA (2009). The ASB was established in 1978 as the highest authority to establish auditing standards in the USA. In recent years, there has been increasing convergence of these standards with those in the international arena (IFAC, 1997). But the accounting rules in the USA are also subject to the dictates of the Sarbanes-Oxley Act of 2002, which altered the hierarchy of auditing procedures and set up the Public Company Accounting Oversight Board (PCAOB), with which audit firms and certified public accountants must be registered to be able to perform services to listed companies.

According to PCAOB (2009) and as prescribed by SAS #1, the main objective of independent auditing of financial statements is to express an opinion on their adequacy, in all material respects, in conformity with USGAAP. In the international realm, the IFAC has been trying to harmonize the auditing standards and practices adopted in the 120 member countries of the Federation. Brazil participates, through the CFC and IBRACON (Brazilian Institute of Independent Auditors). In 1999 a supranational body was created called the International Forum for Accounting Development (IFAD), with the aim of institutionally coordinating and supporting the harmoni-zation and implementation of international accounting and auditing standards in the member countries of the IFAC. Under the coordination of the IFAC and IASB (International Accounting Standards Board), these accounting and auditing standards were to be revised and harmonized by 2005 (Nasi, 2002).

In 2005, the International Auditing and Assurance Standar-ds Board (IAASB), another body of the IFAC, coordinated the ISA Clarity Project, for the purpose of revising and updating International Standards on Auditing (ISA) and issuing new ones, set to take effect at the end of 2009. Then, in January 2006 the IAASB issued a revised version of its Handbook of International Auditing, Assurance and Ethics Pronouncements, containing updated ISAs and quality control standards (International Standards on Quality Control – ISQC). ISQC #1 establishes the standards and guidelines regarding the responsibilities for the quality control system of firms that perform financial audits.

Audit report

The final product of the financial statement audit is the independent auditor's report. According to Almeida (2006, p. 41), the audit is "materialized through the auditor's report, by which the professional who conducted the auditing work issues an opinion regarding the adequacy of the object of study." CFC Resolution 953/03 (item 11.3.1.1), defines the "Independent Auditor's Report" as "the document by which the auditor expresses an objective opinion on the financial statements indicated therein." CFC Resolution 820/97 establishes four categories of audit reports: a) report without reservation; b) report with reservation; c) report with adverse opinion and d) report with abstention from opinion. Various authors have examined the effects of this classification framework, among them Almeida (1996), Attie (1998) and Franco and Marra (2001).

CFC Resolution 953/03 revised the basic structure of the standardized report, dividing it into three paragraphs: introduction, extension and opinion. Due to the convergence of Brazilian accounting standards to international ones, CFC Resolution 1,231/09 changed this basic structure to: introduction, responsibility of management, responsibility of the auditors and opinion.

Report without reservation or clean report

According to CFC Resolution 953/03 (item 11.3.2.1), a report without reservation is defined as that in which "the auditor is convinced that the accounting statements were prepared in harmony with the provisions contained in item 11.1.1.1 [GAAP] in all material aspects."

Report with reservation

The same Resolution, in item 11.3.4.1, establishes that a report with reservation is one "issued when the auditor concludes that the effect of any discordance or restriction on the extent of the work is not so great as to require an adverse opinion or abstention from expressing an opinion." Attie (1998, p. 73) defines it as follows: A report with reservation is issued when one or more numbers in the financial statements do not adequately reflect the correct position, according to the fundamental principles of accounting, or when the auditor cannot obtain sufficient evidence to verify such numbers.

Report with adverse opinion

Item 11.3.5.1 of CFC Resolution 953/03 defines a report with adverse opinion as one issued when the auditor believes "the financial statements are not adequately represented, as of the dates and for the periods indicated, according to the provisions contained in item 11.1.1.1 [GAAP]." When issuing an adverse opinion, the independent auditor must describe the reasons and nature of the divergences observed that corroborate the adverse opinion, as well as the consequences on the equity and financial position and profit/loss for the year.

Report with abstention from opinion

According to item 11.3.7.1 of the Resolution, the auditor must abstain from issuing an opinion. When there is uncertainty regarding a material fact, whose outcome can significantly affect the equity and financial position of the entity, as well as the result of its operations and the auditor must add a paragraph of emphasis in the report, referring to an explanatory note from management, which describe more comprehensively the nature and when possible, the effect of the uncertainty. When issuing a report with abstention from opinion, the independent auditor does not avoid responsibility to mention any significant deviation that would be included as a reservation and that can influence the decision of users of financial information.

METHODOLOGY

This is an exploratory and empirical study, based on research of the international and Brazilian literature and the standards and rules issued by international and national professional bodies and on content analysis of the reports of the independent auditors of a sample of listed Brazilian firms. Raupp and Beuren (2004) point out that in accounting, qualitative research is very common, since accounting deals exclusively with numbers, it can more accurately be described as a social science as opposed to an exact one.

The reports consulted of the independent auditors of 167 listed Brazilian companies, obtained from the CVM website, for the period of 2003 to 2006, during which these firms either had to rotate auditors due to CVM Resolution 308/99 or did so voluntarily. Of these 167 firms, 16 did not have complete data available, so the final sample consisted of 151 listed firms. The audit reports was compared of these 151 companies in the year before the change in audit firm and that after the rotation, irrespective of which year the shift occurred. In the financial statements of these 151 companies were identified the independent audit firms in the years before and after the rotation.

Then the firms were segregated into the "Big Four" (Price water house Coopers, Deloitte Touche Tohmatsu, KPMG and Ernst and Young) and other firms, to check for any changes in the relative participation of the big international firms versus smaller audit firms.

The audit reports was also classified according to the four categories defined above: without reservation, with reservation, with adverse opinion and with abstention from opinion and counted the number of paragraphs contained in the reports and how many of these paragraphs contained an emphasis of matter. The resulting data was analyzed utilizing frequency distributions and statistical coefficients, displayed in tables. As mentioned, according to Assunção and Carrasco (2008) in a study performed at the behest of the CVM, mandatory auditor rotation increases the chance that auditors will express reservations on the financial statements. To test this claim in the Brazilian setting, It was formulated the following two hypotheses:

Hypothesis 1: After the auditor rotation, there was increase in reports with reservations.

Hypothesis 2: After the auditor rotation, there was an increase in emphasis of matter paragraphs.

The aim is to contribute to the national and international debate about the legal and/or regulatory requirements for rotation of independent auditors.

Table 1. Firms engaged to audit the financial statements – before rotation Auditor

Auditor	Absolute frequency	Relative frequency (%)
Pricewaterhouse Coopers Auditores Independentes	38	25.19
Trevisan Auditores Independentes	19	12.58
BKR - Lopes, Machado Auditores S/C	17	11.26
Ernst and Young Auditores Independentes S.S.	11	7.28
Deloitte Touche Tohmatsu Auditores Independentes	10	6.62
KPMG Auditores Independentes	10	6.62
Boucinhas and Campos + Soteconti	4	2.65
Martinelli Auditores Independentes S.C.	4	2.65
Rokembach and Cia. Auditores S/C	3	1.99
Alonso, Barretto and Cia. Auditores Independentes	2	1.33
Bendoraytes, Aizenman and Cia	2	1.33
Gama and Cia Auditores Independentes S/C	2	1.33
HLB Audilink and CIA. Auditores	2	1.33
Veeck and Cia – Auditores	2	1.33
Actus Auditores Independentes S/S	1	0.66
Adelino Dias Pinho	1	0.66
AKW Auditores Independentes S/S Ltda	1	0.66
Auditór Auditores Independentes S/C	1	0.66
BDO Trevisan Auditores Independentes	1	0.66
Claudio Bianchessi and Assoc.Aud. S/C	1	0.66
Directivos S/C Auditores Independentes	1	0.66
Ecopal SC Auditores Independentes	1	0.66
Elmiro José Hallmann	1	0.66
ETAE Auditores Independentes S/C	1	0.66
Exacto Auditoria S/S	1	0.66
Francisco Assis de Sousa Auditor Independente	1	0.66
Imatéo Auditoria e Consultoria S/C	1	0.66
Instituto Nacional de Auditores	1	0.66
Justus Auditores Independentes	1	0.66
Maion and Cia. S/C Auditores Independentes	1	0.66
Narazzaqui and Cia. – Auditores	1	0.66
Nardon, Nasi - Auditores Independentes	1	0.66
Performance Auditoria e Consultoria Empresarial S/C	1	0.66
Santa and Souza Auditores Independentes	1	0.66
Teixeira and Associados Auditores Independentes	1	0.66
Terco Auditores Independentes S/C	1	0.66
Tufani, Reis and Soares Auditores Independentes	1	0.66
Units Auditores Independentes	1	0.66
Walter Hever Auditores Independentes	1	0.66
TOTAL OF 40 AUDIT FIRMS	**151**	**100.00**

ANALYSIS OF THE RESULTS

Firms engaged to audit the financial statements before rotation

The audit firms was first identified, retained to audit the financial statements of the sample companies before the rotation. The statistics are shown in Table 1.

In the period before the change in the independent auditor, 40 audit firms worked for the 151 companies in the sample. The audit firm with the most clients was Pricewaterhouse Coopers Auditores Independentes, with 38 clients, or 25.19% of the companies. The percentages of all the other audit firms were less than half this rate, with the most significant being Trevisan Auditores Independentes, which audited 12.58% of the companies, BKR - Lopes, Machado Auditores S/C, at 11.26%, Ernst and Young Auditores Independentes S.S., with 7.28% and Deloitte Touche Tohmatsu Auditores Independentes and KPMG Auditores Independentes, both with 6.62%. Boucinhas and Campos, Soteconti Auditores Independentes and Martinelli Auditores Independentes S.C both worked for four companies, or 2.65% of the sample, while Rokembach and Cia. Auditores S/C was retained by 1.99% companies. Alonso, Barreto and Cia – Auditores Independentes, Bendoraytes, Aizenman and Cia, Gama and Cia Auditores Independentes S/C, HLB Audilink and Cia. Auditores and Veeck and Cia – Auditores all had two clients, or 1.33% of the sample, while the rest each audited the books of one company apiece, or 0.66% of the total.

Firms engaged to audit the financial statements after rotation

It was then identified the breakdown of the audit firm engagements after the rotation. The results are shown in Table 2.

In the second period all the companies in the sample had changed auditors, either because of the new rule or spontaneously. The number of audit firms retained by the 151 sample companies increased to 54 from the 40 in the previous period. In this case, the most popular independent auditor was Deloitte Touche Tohmatsu Auditores Independentes, with a frequency of 16.56%, followed by Performance Auditoria e Consultoria Empresarial S/C with 9.27%, KPMG Auditores Independentes with 7.95%, Ernst and Young Auditores Independentes S.S. with 7.28%, Price water house Coopers Auditores Independentes and Trevisan Auditores Independentes, each with 5.30% and BDO Trevisan Auditores Independentes, with 3.31%, Audimar Auditores Independentes S/C and Directa Auditores, each with 2.65%, and Imer Puerari and Cia. Auditores, Mazars and Guérard Auditores Independentes S/C and PS Contax and Associados. Aud. Independentes. S/S, all with 1.99%. All the rest of the audit firms had one client only, for a frequency of 0.66%

Representation of the big four audit firms before and after rotation

As could be expected, in Table 3 among the 151 companies analyzed, the Big Four audit firms together represented a substantial share of the audit market, both before and after the rotation. This concentration in the Brazilian market is likely due to the reputation of the leading four international audit firms, with their clients' choices being influenced by a desire to convey greater security to investors. However, the combined percentage of the Big Four fell from 45.71% of the sample companies before the rotation to 37.09% afterward, indicating that the rotation requirement increased the opportunity for smaller independent auditors.

Classification of the audit report before and after the rotation

It can be seen from Table 4 that before the rotation, 78.81% of the companies analyzed received a "clean" opinion, that is, an audit report without reservations, meaning there was no relevant fact of concern. The remaining 21.19% of the companies received an opinion with reservation, while none received an adverse opinion or a report with abstention from opinion. These statistics changed little after the rotation. In this case, 79.47% of the companies analyzed received a report without reservations, while 19.87% received one with reservation, meaning there was at least one fact that raised the concern of the independent auditor. There was also one case where the auditor identified transactions of the client company with subsidiaries whose books had not been audited, preventing the issuance of an opinion on the financial statements of the parent company.

Number of paragraphs contained in the audit reports– before rotation

Table 5 shows that 151 audit reports received by the companies in the sample before the rotation contained a total of 688 paragraph, with the greatest frequency being reports containing three paragraphs (33.11%, or 50 companies), followed by reports containing four paragraphs (29.14%, or 44 companies), reports containing five paragraphs (14.45%, or 22 companies) and reports with six paragraphs (10.60%, or 16 companies). The rest of the sampled companies received audit reports containing seven or more paragraphs, with one report being 13 paragraphs long. The average number of paragraphs before the rotation was 4.55.

Number of paragraphs contained in the audit reports– after rotation

Table 6 shows that after the rotation, the audit reports of the 151 companies in the sample contained a total of 786 paragraphs. The largest percentage of these contained five paragraphs (60 companies, 39.74%), followed by 47 reports containing four paragraphs (31.13%) and 21 reports with six paragraphs (13.90%). Companies receiving reports with seven and eight paragraphs each represented 5.30% of the sample (8 companies), while

Table 2. Firms engaged to audit the financial statements – after rotation

Auditor	Absolute frequency	Relative frequency (%)
Deloitte Touche Tohmatsu Auditores Independentes	25	16.56
Performance Auditoria e Consultoria Empresarial S/C	14	9.27
KPMG Auditores Independentes	12	7.95
Ernst & Young Auditores Independentes S.S.	11	7.28
Pricewaterhouse Coopers Auditores Independentes	8	5.30
Trevisan Auditores Independentes	8	5.30
BDO Trevisan Auditores Independentes	5	3.31
Audimar Auditores Independentes S/C	4	2.65
Directa Auditores	4	2.65
Imer Puerari & Cia. Auditores	3	1.99
Mazars & Guérard Auditores Independentes S/C	3	1.99
OS Contax & Assoc. Auditores Independentes S/S	3	1.99
Audiva - Auditores Independentes S/C.	2	1.33
BKR - Lopes, Machado Auditores S/C	2	1.33
Boucinhas & Campos + Soteconti Auditores Independentes S/C	2	1.33
Martinelli Auditores Independentes S.C	2	1.33
RBA Global - Auditores Independentes S/S	2	1.33
Rodyo's Auditores Independentes S.S	2	1.33
Sigmac Auditores	2	1.33
Soltz, Matoso & Mendes Auditores Independentes	2	1.33
Terco Grant Thornton Auditores Independentes	2	1.33
Veeck & Cia – Auditores	2	1.33
Actus Auditores Independentes S/S	1	0.66
AFM Auditores Independentes	1	0.66
Alonso, Barreto & Cia - Auditores Independentes	1	0.66
Audicont – Auditores e Consultores Ltda	1	0.66
Audiplan Auditores Independentes	1	0.66
Bendoraytes, Aizenman & Cia. Auditores Independentes	1	0.66
Binah SP Auditores Independentes	1	0.66
BKS Auditores	1	0.66
Bordasch Auditores Associados	1	0.66
Cerutti & Machado Auditores Associados	1	0.66
Cokinos & Associados - Auditores Independentes S/C	1	0.66
Directivos Auditores Independentes	1	0.66
DRS Auditores	1	0.66
Fernando Motta & Associados Auditores Independentes	1	0.66
Gama & Cia Auditores Independentes SC	1	0.66
Guimarães e Associados Auditores e Consultores S/C	1	0.66
HLB Audilink & Cia. Auditores	1	0.66
Horwath Tufani, Reis & Soares Auditores Independentes	1	0.66
IGAF LM Auditores Independentes	1	0.66
João Valério e Moura Filho Auditor Independente	1	0.66
Loudon Blomquist Auditores independents	1	0.66
Macro Auditores Independentes	1	0.66
Maion & Cia. S/C Auditores Independentes	1	0.66
Moore Stephens Lima Lucchesi Auditores Independentes	1	0.66
Moreira & Associados Auditores	1	0.66
Padrão Auditoria S/S	1	0.66
Quorum Auditores Independentes	1	0.66

Table 2. cont'd

R & R Auditoria e Consultoria	1	0.66
Sacho Auditores Independentes	1	0.66
SGS Auditores Independentes S/C	1	0.66
Sicom Auditores Independentes	1	0.66
TOTAL OF 54 AUDIT FIRMS	**151**	**100.00**

Table 3. Big Four audit firms

Auditor	Before rotation	After rotation
Pricewaterhouse Coopers Auditores Independentes	25.19%	5.30%
KPMG Auditores Independentes	6.62%	7.95%
Deloitte Touche Tohmatsu Auditores Independentes	6.62%	16.56%
Ernst and Young Auditores Independentes S.S.	7.28%	7.28%
TOTAL	**45.61%**	**37.09%**

Table 4. Classification of the independent auditor's report

Classification of the audit report	Absolute frequency – Before	Relative frequency (%)	Absolute frequency – After	Relative frequency (%)
Without reservation	119	78.81	120	79.47
With reservation	32	21.19	30	19.87
With adverse opinion	0	0.00	0	0.00
With abstention from opinion	0	0.00	01	0.66
TOTAL	**151**	**100.00**	**151**	**100.00**

Table 5. Number of paragraphs

Number of paragraphs	Absolute frequency	Relative frequency (%)
03	50	33.11
04	44	29.14
05	22	14.56
06	16	10.60
07	10	6.62
08	03	1.99
09	03	1.99
11	02	1.33
13	01	0.66
TOTAL	**151**	**100.00**

four companies received reports containing nine or more paragraphs and the reports of three companies had only three paragraphs. The average for the sample after the rotation was 5.205 paragraphs.

Companies receiving audit reports containing an emphasis of matter paragraph

Also it was investigated the presence of paragraphs in

Table 6. Number of paragraphs

Number of paragraphs	Absolute frequency	Relative frequency (%)
05	60	39.74
04	47	31.13
06	21	13.90
08	08	5.30
07	08	5.30
03	03	1.99
09	02	1.32
14	01	0.66
11	01	0.66
TOTAL	**151**	**100.00**

Table 7. Existence of an emphasis of matter paragraph before rotation

Emphasis paragraph	Absolute frequency	Relative frequency (%)
Yes	78	51.66
No	73	48.34
Total	**151**	**100.00**

Table 8. Existence of an emphasis of matter paragraph after rotation

Emphasis paragraph	Absolute frequency	Relative frequency (%)
Yes	78	51.66
No	73	48.34
Total	**151**	**100.00**

the audit reports containing an emphasis of matter comment. The results before the rotation are shown in Table 7. It can be seen that the audit reports of 51.66% of the companies analyzed contained an emphasis paragraph.

Table 8 shows the number of reports with emphasis paragraphs after the rotation.

The statistics on emphasis paragraphs were exactly the same after the rotation, indicating that the change in audit firms did not cause any change in the matters held by the auditors to deserve emphasis.

CONCLUSION

The mandatory rotation of audit firms has received increasing attention from regulators in recent years , as a way to strengthen auditor independence and improve professional skepticism . Proponents suggest that it would prevent the development of excessively close relationships between the auditor and the audited company administration and limiting the economic dependence of auditors of the companies they audit . Opponents have a number of considerations about the mandatory rotation of audit firms, including that it would be detrimental to audit quality, weaken the role of the board of directors and audit committees , would increase the total costs for preparers of financial statements and would be very difficult to implement in a complex global environment .

The objective of this work was to analyze empirically the impact of auditor rotation on the audit reports issued on the financial statements, using a sample of 151 listed Brazilian firms, obtained from the website of the Brazilian Securities Commission (CVM), during the period of 2003 to 2006, when a requirement for periodic auditor rotation came into effect.

Comparison of the independent auditors engaged by these companies in the year before and the year after the rotation showed an increase in the number of audit firms from 40 to 54, indicating the rotation requirement provided a chance for more audit firms to work among this sample of companies. Nevertheless, the Big Four continued to predominate after the rotation, although their combined percentage in the sample declined from 45.61% to 37.09%. With respect to the classification of the report issued, the rotation policy did not have a significant effect on the rigor of the opinions, as reflected in the percentage issued with reservations, indicating there was no increase in the level of independence. The same result was found regarding the number of paragraphs containing emphasis of matters, again indicating the rotation policy did not enhance the independence of audit firms.

Due to the learning curve that audit firms must face in each new audit, audits may be less efficient in early labor. Audit firms can obviously and effectively manage transitions effectively, but this is not without cost or risk, both the auditor and the company incur costs at the beginning of the work with an external auditor. The cost of mandatory audit firm rotation may be aggravated because of the particular circumstances of a company. For example, changing an auditor in the middle of a great deal of capital or loan is complicated and expensive. The imposition of a specific date for the completion of the rotation of the audit firm could further worsen the situation under volatile market conditions. From this paper, there is no evidence that mandatory audit firm rotation increases audit quality. In fact, our studies have shown that it may affect it negatively. One of the advantages of hiring an audit firm for the long term is that the auditor obtains knowledge and so meaningful understanding of the company over time, as well as its risks, which can improve audit quality. Hiring for a longer period may allow the audit firm to develop expertise and credibility to the organization, demonstrating, over time, your accounting technical expertise, the quality of their audit work and his knowledge of the company's business. Hiring for a longer period may also result in a greater respect for the judgment of the auditor when the auditor makes inquiries about the conclusions of the management of the audited company. The results presented here are informative in character. A more comprehensive analysis is necessary to reach more solid conclusions on the effect of requiring auditor rotation on the quality of auditing and the profile of reports in the Brazilian market.

The restricted number of observations is also a limitation, as it was chosen only to study companies that changed auditors against a backdrop of the new rule requiring rotation (although not all the companies that changed did so because the maximum tenure of their incumbent auditor had expired).

One avenue for further study would be identification of the reasons for emphasis paragraphs and their absolute frequency.

Another would be to analyze the audit reports of Brazilian companies with dual listing (on the BM and FBovespa and NYSE) that either by regulatory requirement or spontaneously changed audit firms.

Conflict of Interests

The author(s) have not declared any conflict of interests.

REFERENCES

Almeida JF, Almeida JGC (2007). Auditoria e earnings management: um estudo empírico nas empresas de capital aberto auditadas pelas Big Four e demais firmas de auditoria. In: VII CONGRESSO USP DE CONTROLADORIA E CONTABILIDADE, 519, São Paulo. Anais eletrônicos.

Almeida KN (2006). Uma análise crítica dos pareceres dos auditores independentes sobre demonstrações contábeis de empresas brasileiras. 2006. 125 f. Dissertação (Mestrado em Ciências Contábeis) - Programa Multiinstitucional e Inter-Regional de Pós-Graduação em Ciências Contábeis - UnB, UFPB, UFPE e UFRN, Brasília.

Assunção J, Carrasco V (2008). Avaliação da Rotatividade dos Auditores Independentes. Rio de Janeiro: Departamento de Economia da Pontifica Universidade Católica do Rio de Janeiro.

Attie W (1998). Auditoria: conceitos e aplicações. 3rd ed. São Paulo: Atlas.

Azevedo FB (2007). Efeito da troca da firma de auditoria no gerenciamento de resultados das companhias abertas brasileiras. 2007. 56 p. Master's Dissertation in Accounting – Fundação Instituto Capixaba de Pesquisas em Contabilidade, Economia e Finanças – FUCAPE, Vitória.

Barbadillo ER, Aguilar NG, Carrera N (2009). Does Mandatory Audit Firm Rotation Enhace Auditor Independence? Evidence from Spain. J. Practice Theory. 28(1):113-135.

Boynton WC, Johnson RN, Kell WG (2002). Auditoria. Translation by José Evaristo do Santos. São Paulo: Atlas.

Braunbeck GO (2008) De emendas e sonetos: o mercado quer o rodízio de auditores? In: VIII CONGRESSO USP DE CONTROLADORIA E CONTABILIDADE, 170,. São Paulo. Anais eletrônicos.

Chi W, Huang H, Liao Y, Xie H (2009). Mandatory Audit Partner Rotation, Audit Quality, and Market Perception: Evidence from Taiwan. Contemporary Account. Res. 26(2):91-359.

Costa FM, Azevedo F (2008). Efeito da troca da firma de auditoria no Gerenciamento de resultados das companhias abertas brasileiras. Available at: <http://www.anpcont.com.br//docs/congressoll/02/CUE373.pdf>.

Cupertino CM, Martinez AL (2007) Procedimentos de revisão analítica para seleção de empresas para auditoria: abordagem pelo nível de accruals discricionários. In: VII CONGRESSO USP DE CONTROLADORIA E CONTABILIDADE, 421,.

Formigoni H, Antunes M, Paulo E, Leite RS (2007). A contribuição do rodízio de auditoria para a independência e qualidade dos serviços prestados: um estudo exploratório baseado na percepção de gestores de companhias abertas brasileiras. In: VII CONGRESSO USP DE CONTROLADORIA E CONTABILIDADE, 614,. São Paulo.

Franco H, Marrq E (2001). Auditoria contábil. 4th ed. São Paulo: Atlas,

Ghosh A, Moon D (2005). Auditor Tenure and Perceptions of Audit Quality. Account. Rev. 80:2.

Johnson VE, Khurana IK, Reynolds JK (2002). Audit-Firm Tenure and the Quality of Financial Reports. Contemporary Account. Res. 19:4

Martinez AL, Reis GM (2010). Audit Firm Rotation and Earnings Management in Brazil (July 14, 2010). Available at SSRN: http://ssrn.com/abstract=1640260.

Mendes MC, Niyama JK, Ito EHY (2007). Controle de qualidade dos serviços de auditoria independente: um estudo comparativo entre as normas brasileiras e as normas internacionais. In: VII CONGRESSO USP DE CONTROLADORIA E CONTABILIDADE, . São Paulo.

Myers JN, Myers LA, Omer TC (2003). Exploring the Term of the Auditor-Client Relationship and the Quality of Earnings: A Case for Mandatory Auditor Rotation? Account. Rev. 78:3.

Nagy YAL (2005). Mandatory Audit Firm Turnover, Financial Reporting

Quality, and Client Bargaining Power: The Case of Arthur Andersen. Account. Horizons. 19:2.

Nasi AC (2002). A globalização das normas contábeis e de auditoria. Fenacon em Serviços .

Oliveira AQ, Santos NM (2007). Rodízio de Firmas de Auditoria: a experiência brasileira e as conclusões do mercado. Revista de Contabilidade e Finanças, São Paulo, 18(45):91-100,.

Oliveira LM, Diniz Filho A (2001). Curso Básico de Auditoria. São Paulo: Atlas.

Reis GMR (2009). O rodízio de auditores independentes e a análise se existe ou não impactos no gerenciamento de resultados das empresas auditadas. 2009. Master's Dissertation in Accounting – Faculdade de Ciências Contábeis, Universidade Federal da Bahia, Salvador.

Ethics and postsecondary accounting curriculum in Bahrain: Perspective from faculty members

Kousay Said and Khaled Ibrahim Al-Tarawneh

Department of Accounting, College of Business Administration, University of Bahrain, P.O. Box: 32038, Kingdom of Bahrain.

Recent corporate scandals have led to renewed calls for ethics education for the accounting profession. Academic institutions employ variety of teaching methods and place a substantial level of emphasis when teaching ethics to accounting students. We report on a questionnaire survey of accounting faculty members at Bahraini universities to investigate the perceptions on the issue of incorporating ethics into accounting curriculum. Our survey results on faculty members show that ethics should be taught to accounting students as an extremely important topic. Respondents are considering the development of abilities needed to deal with ethical dilemmas as highly significant issue. Offering ethics as integrated with other accounting courses is the most popular option. Most faculty members expressed an interest in teaching ethics.

Key words: Accounting ethics, ethics education accounting curriculum, accounting scandals, stand-alone courses, Bahrain.

INTRODUCTION

Prior research on accounting ethics indicates that there is no agreement on the need for ethics education for accounting students (Piper et al., 1993; McDonald and Donleavy, 1995; Peppas and Diskin, 2001). Corporate scandals such as that at Enron and the fall of Arthur Andersen have led to renewed calls for ethics education for the accounting profession. It is argued that among other things failures by accounting firms and individual accountants contributed to the financial scandals (O'Leary, 2009). The problems are also attributed to a stagnant accounting curriculum that has remained significantly unchanged over the last fifty to sixty years (Russell and Smith, 2003). Those who blame the accounting profession for corporate malfeasance see education as a necessary intervention to remedy the situation. The personal values and ethical perceptions of accounting student are attributes that can indicate their moral reasoning ability. Therefore, it is important that ethical values and positive perceptions are to be taught to these students through an intervention at the college level.

Ethics education may enable students to determine what is ethically right or wrong although they may fail to behave ethically due to inability to identify ethical issues (Chan and Leung, 2006). Wright (1995) contends "education is the best means to develop good ethical behaviour in the modern business environment." Many researchers criticize accounting educators for failure to coherently include ethics as part of the accounting curriculum (Russell and Smith, 2003; Price Water House Coopers, 2003). Many others demonstrate an inherent weakness in the area of ethical and moral reasoning (Evans and Marcal, 2005; Trevino and Nelson, 2004; Rynes et al., 2003; Rest et al., 1999 and Adkins and Radtke, 2004). Ozdogan and Eser (2007) explored the ethical sensitivity of students of business subjects in different universities in Turkey; their findings suggested that while accounting students have a higher level of moral awareness than non-accounting students, taking an ethics course made no significant difference to the ethical sensitivity of participants. Thus, it is especially important that the accounting education system be better designed to assist students in developing these essential skills. This will require significant action from both the institutions offering accounting degrees and the accounting authoritative bodies who legislate and monitor accounting practices in order to improve teaching methods and increase the instructional time devoted to ethical material. Accordingly, some researchers suggested that ethics should be integrated in the curriculum without having a stand-alone course (William and Becker, 2011; Ghaffari et al., 2008; Blanthorne et al., 2007; AACSB International, 2007; Armstrong et al., 2003; Alam, 1999). Other researchers suggested that a separate stand-alone course in ethics should be included in the accounting curriculum (Fisher et al., 2007; Bean and Bernardi, 2007; Benner, 2002; Nicklaus, 2002; Swanson, 2004; Fisher and Swanson, 2005; Gray et al., 1994; Armstrong, 1993).

As a contribution to the above stream of research, this study intends to elicit the perceptions of accounting educators on ethics but from a Middle-Eastern perspective. This research paper anticipates to provide an additional perspective in addition to the findings of previous studies on accounting ethics. Most of the previous research on ethics was based on western point of views with respect to the basic assumptions regarding ethics. For example, in western universities, especially in Britain and the USA, accounting students learn among other things the opinions of Friedman (1970) and Drucker (1981) with respect to corporate social responsibilities and their belief that the focus of business should be on business activities and consequently teaching ethics is not an important issue. Given the fact that the majority of business scandals were happening in western economies and the fact that ethics are behavioral reflection to the norms, values, and beliefs carried by individuals or corporations in a particular society, it merits researching accounting ethical concerns in non-western societies such as the Middle-East region. Therefore, an interesting research question is to investigate whether prior research findings regarding ethical issues in accounting education would hold true in other places such as Bahrain.

The purpose of this paper is to provide some common understanding of accounting faculty perceptions on the issue of incorporating ethics into accounting curriculum. In doing so, this paper updates prior research by presenting a current and more comprehensive view of accounting ethics education as reported by accounting faculty members in Bahrain. Tying our study to previous literature based on an extensive literature review, we examine whether Bahraini's faculty perceptions are consistent with the perceptions of faculty members investigated in previous research. This examination covers many ethical issues such as whether ethics should be included in the curriculum, why ethics should (or should not) be included, how ethics should be taught, what should be taught, and where in the curriculum ethics should be taught. We also report information about how and where faculty members currently teach ethics and the degree to which faculty members believe this coverage is sufficient.

Objectives

As a contribution to previous research on accounting ethics, this study seeks to elicit the perceptions of accounting academics in Bahrain related to six main questions concerning ethics in accounting:

1. Is it important to teach ethics for accounting students?
2. What are the perceived benefits of teaching ethics to students?
3. How is it integrated in the curriculum?
4. What are the barriers facing ethics integration?
5. What are the important topics to be covered?
6. What teaching methods would be followed to deliver ethics to students?

Significance of the study

To the best of the authors' knowledge, this is the first exploratory survey conducted in the Arabian Gulf region and in Bahrain in specific regarding integrating ethics into accounting curriculum. Bahrain is a member of International Federation of Accountants (IFAC) which releases Code of Ethics for Professional Conduct. Furthermore, Bahrain adopted International Financial Reporting Standards (IFRS) since 2002 that requires highest level of standardization and improvements in accounting profession. Thus, ethics education has become an important issue for the country. The findings of this study may be providing some helpful hints to those who legislates code of ethics for professional conduct in Bahrain.

In addition, this study fits into the wider literature by comparing the results of previous studies conducted in different countries. The findings of this study anticipate to provide some helpful insights to the accounting education systems in general as well as to increase the awareness of accounting educators to the importance of addressing ethical issues according to the findings and the recommended teaching strategies. In addition, this study may provide particular attention to potential differences among countries which may lead to insightful findings and interesting conclusions.

The findings generated from this study will be an evidence to support or refute the findings of prior research on ethics. Outcomes from this study may bring the attention of accounting practitioners in Bahrain to the importance of ethics in accounting education, and are helpful in developing closer network with academics to insure a positive future for the development of accounting ethics education at Bahraini universities. Finally, the results might provide basis for further studies that seek development in accounting ethics education.

LITERATURE REVIEW

Prior research on accounting ethics education can be classified into four groups of studies:

1. Studies that have been conducted on the importance of teaching ethics in accounting.
2. Studies that have been conducted on highlighting the perceived benefits of teaching ethics in accounting.
3. Studies that have shown how to integrate ethics into the accounting curriculum.
4. Studies that have suggested curriculum development for the accounting education.

The importance of teaching ethics in accounting education

The evidence on the impact of ethical interventions in this context of accounting curriculum is somewhat mixed – different studies have reached different conclusions as to the effectiveness or otherwise of, particularly, classroom-based interventions on individuals' moral development and decision-making processes.

O'Leary (2009) undertook a two-part study in which a class of students was given scenarios on which to make an ethical decision, the questionnaire being completed by students both before and after following an ethics course. Analysis of the data showed that students were responding more ethically after the intervention and students confirmed their own belief that the intervention had been effective. Thomas (2012) found that accounting students approaching the end of the programme made more ethical decisions than first-year accounting students and Dellaportas (2006) demonstrated that accounting students exposed to a 12-week intervention included within a course on professionalism showed significantly increased levels of moral awareness. Gammie and Gammie (2009) also demonstrated changes in moral awareness in the context of examining the implications of gender differences. Exercises designed to heighten student awareness of ethics, such as that developed by Radtke (2004) have also been used to good effect to allow students to identify what constitutes an ethical dilemma, as well as how to respond to it.

Over the past two decades a vast number of research papers and notes were conducted on the importance of teaching ethics in accounting curricula. Sugahara and Boland (2011) perceived opinions of faculties that primarily teach accounting in Japanese tertiary schools in 2009 and the results indicate that over 90% of accounting faculties believe that ethics should be taught within the accounting curriculum. Blanthorne et al. (2007) surveyed perceived opinions of academicians in the United States and found that 95% of them agreed on teaching ethics to accounting students. Likewise, Madison and Schmidt (2006), Evans and Marcal (2005) and Adkins and Radtke (2004) raised questions to their respondents concerning the importance of ethics in accounting programs and found significant support to this issue. Another study by Bampton and Cowton (2002) surveyed perceived opinions of academicians in the UK and found that 87% of them agreed that teaching ethics will improve students' ethical reasoning skills. Jennings (2004) believes that accounting students should be taught ethics because of the role that accountants played in recent scandals such as Enron, World Com., and Arthur Andersen. Lawson (2002), in a survey of business faculty at five institutions, asked the general question of "should ethics be taught" and found universal acceptance.

Major professional accounting organizations such as the American Institute of Certified Public Accountants (AICPA), Institute of Management Accountants (IMA), Institute of Internal Auditors (IIA) and International Federation of Accountants (IFAC) include ethics and values in their professional examinations by holding their members accountable to a professional code of ethics and requiring continuing professional education requirements for their memberships (AICPA, 2009; IMA, 2010; IIA, 2010; IFAC, 2010). Since accounting students are professionally motivated to earn professional credentials, many accounting curricula focus on these professional codes of conduct (Jennings, 2004). Table 1 summarizes relevant prior research related to the main questions of this research paper. Column 2 of Table 1 panel (A) shows prior research findings related to the importance of teaching ethics. The first hypothesis of this study intends to compare the importance of teaching ethics found by this study with that found by previous researchers.

The perceived benefits of accounting ethics education

Kelly (2004) pointed out that the recent challenges to the accounting profession raised by the recent corporate scandals and the indictment and conviction of Arthur Andersen have brought about the requirement that accountants must adhere to the highest ethical standards. It is the responsibility of educational institutions to foster and reinforce adherence to these

Table 1(Panel A). Findings of prior research surveys on ethics.

Researchers	Importance of teaching ethics	Perceived benefits	Barriers for ethics integration curriculum
Sugahara and Boland (2011)	Mean (3.45)		
Madison and Schmidt (2006)	4.36		
Adkins and Radtke (2004)	3.29	c- Develop ability to deal with ethical conflicts facing profession. (mean: 3.46) g-Identify moral implication of accounting Issues. (mean: 2.87) i- Develop sense of moral obligation. (mean: 3.28) f- Learn to deal with uncertainties of Profession. (mean: 3.48) h- Set the stage for change in ethical behavior. (mean: 2.91)	
Blanthorne et al (2007)		- Ethical development is crucial to the accounting Profession. (mean: 4.64) - Public trust needs to be reestablished due to recent scandals. (mean: 4.42) - The profession may lose the right to regulate itself if ethical lapses continue. (mean: 4.14)	-Lack of faculty interest (mean: 3.04) -Lack of faculty qualification (mean: 2.95) -Ethics education does not suit accounting curriculum. (mean: 3.01) -Lack of classroom instructional materials. (mean: 2.64) - Ethics cannot be taught. (mean: 2.48) -ethical values should be left to family, church, etc. (mean: 2.22)
Karnes and Sterner (1988)	3.53		- Financial constraints. (mean: 3.53) Curriculum constraints. (mean: 2.88) -Faculty constraints. (mean: 3.38) -Lack of subject matter/ materials. (mean: 3.45) -May teach how to act unethically. (mean: 4.08)

ethical standards. To be considered ethical leaders, executives must be both moral persons and moral managers (AACSB, 2004). Improving the level of individual accountants' ethics may be the most effective way to improve business ethics. The threat of fines, loss of a professional license or imprisonment when violating the Sarbanes- Oxley Act of 2002 may have a deterrent effect for some, but these methods clearly have not been completely proven to be effective for others. It may be through education rather than government regulation that ethics in the accounting profession will improve (AACSB, 2004). Recently, a substantial number of research papers have been conducted on the role of ethics in accounting education (McPhail, 2001; O'Connell, 2004; Moriceau, 2005; Swanson, 2005; Blanthorne et al., 2007). These studies have used different research methods in different cultures, but they share a common assumption that ethical matters in accounting are of widespread social concern and that accounting educators must address such matters in their teaching. As Albrecht and Sack (2000) claimed, accounting programs should ensure that students have the necessary tools they need to succeed in their accounting profession. Accounting curricula, however, are being criticized for not focusing enough on values, ethics and integrity. Chan and Leung (2006) reported that students may have the ability to determine what is ethically right or wrong, but may fail to behave ethically due to an inability to identify ethical issues. They found that accounting students who had a core course of 'Ethics in Accounting' in their accountancy degree curriculum, showed higher ethical sensitivity ability, compared to the students who had taken only a few hours of integrated ethical interventions of their entire curriculum coverage. Column 3 of Table 1 panel (A) shows relevant prior research findings with respect to the perceived benefits of teaching ethics to accounting students. The second hypothesis of this study intends to examine the degree of consistency between the results of this study and prior research findings with respect to the perceived benefits of teaching ethics.

Integrating ethics into accounting curriculum

In 2004, the International Federation of Accountants (IFAC) included International Education Standard 4 (IES4): Professional Values, Ethics and Attitudes in the suite of educational standards that 164 member bodies in 125 countries agree to meet. In addition, higher education accreditation bodies such as the Association to Advance Collegiate Schools of Business (AACSB) accreditation requires the inclusion of ethical reasoning skills into accounting courses (Williams and Elson, 2010). Ethical theories, codes of conduct, questions and dilemmas have been added to the content of popular accounting textbooks, and many universities have included some ethics to their accounting curricula.

Prior research on teaching ethics for accounting students focuses on many issues including whether or not ethics can be taught (Geary and Sims, 1994), how best to teach it in terms of methodology and approach (Massey and Van Hise, 2009) and the level at which ethics is being integrated into accounting curriculum (McNair and Milam, 1993; Fisher, Blanthorne and Kovar, 2007; Ghaffari et al., 2008).

Accounting educators and practitioners continue to believe that ethics coverage is important for developing students' skills towards moral and ethical reasoning. For example, Armitage and Poyzer (2010) compare the views of practitioners and accounting professors concerning the inclusion of ethics in auditing courses. Although neither group rated ethics as the most important element in an auditing course, both had ethics as one of the top 5 most important topics.

The question of whether ethics can be integrated effectively into the accounting curriculum has also been explored empirically with mixed results. Some empirical evidence suggests that ethics interventions can change reasoning and behavior (Trevino and Nelson, 2004; Rynes et al., 2003; Rest et al. 1999), while other intervention studies suggest otherwise (Lampe, 1996; Ponemon, 1993).

The difficulty of ethics integration is ascribed to many barriers that face education institutions.

Resource-related reasons that have been debated in prior research for not teaching ethics are space and time in the curriculum (Mintz, 1990; Langenderfer and Rockness, 1989), lack of ability, proper training, willingness of the faculty (Gunz and McCutcheon, 1998; Mintz, 1990), and lack of rewards or encouragement (McNair and Milam, 1993; Cohen and Pan, 1989; Adkins and Radtke, 2004; Blanthorne et al., 2007). Finally, some researchers argue that ethical development is best left to institutions outside of formal education, like the family or spiritual or religious institutions (Blanthorne et al., 2007).

In order to contribute to previous studies on ethics integration, this study used a list of barriers that have been used frequently in prior studies as possible reasons for not integrating ethics into accounting education. Bahraini educators will be asked to indicate their agreement level, using a five- point Likert scale, over the importance of these reasons as barriers to ethics integration. Reasons that are perceived as important barriers by Bahraini educators will be compared to significant barriers found in previous research. The third hypothesis of this current study intends to investigate whether perceived barriers by Bahraini educators are not significantly different from those found in previous research (Adkins and Radtke, 2004; Blanthorne et al 2007). Column 4 of Table (1) Panel (A) shows prior research significant barriers along with their corresponding means.

Curriculum development of accounting ethics education

The focus of this section is on how accounting ethics should be taught to students. Should it be taught as a separate course or be integrated in other courses? Should it be as a compulsory or elective course in the student's study plan? At what level should it be taught? These questions are of major concern for those who are involved in the development of accounting curricula. Only few research papers were found to address these questions in their investigations. For example; McNair and Milam (1993) conducted a survey on whether to have a stand- alone course on ethics or to integrate ethics along with other courses and they found only 8.3 percent of their respondents favored a stand- alone accounting ethics course.

Fisher and Swanson (2005) and Fisher and Schmidt (2007) criticized academia's narrow focus on teaching professional codes of conduct and recommended that accounting programs offer a stand- alone ethics course at the beginning of an accounting program to deliver the message that ethics is an important topic in an accounting program. They criticized the integrated course approach for not delivering enough academic bases in ethics to enable students have the knowledge and critical thinking skills to address ethical issues. Likewise, Dellaportas (2006) also believed that a discrete course in ethics and accounting should be included in accounting programs.

Madison and Schmidt (2006) reported that 30 percent of surveyed accounting chairpersons supported a

Table 1 (Panel B). Findings of prior research surveys on ethics.

Researchers	Ethics Delivery Stand- alone versus Integration	Teaching Methods	Content Topics
McNair and Milam (1993)	8.3% Favor Stand- alone	Lecture (91.1% 4.83) Code of Ethics (53.5% 4.80) Written Case (48.4% 5.45) Video Vignette (29.9% 4.85) Written Vignette (24.4% 4.66)	
Madison and Schmidt (2006)	30.5% favor Stand- alone 69.5% favor integration		
Adkins and Radtke (2004)	59.1% ethics necessary for accounting students		
Blanthorne et al (2007)	2% favor stand- alone 98% favor integration 79.2% in all courses 18.9% in some courses		- Ethical issues faced by the profession. .(Mean = 4.56) --Understand professional moral obligations. (Mean = 4.41) - Ethical decision-making process/models. (Mean = 4.16) - The pursuit of personal excellence (Mean = 3.74) - Classical ethical theories. (Mean = 2.98)
Karnes and Sterner (1988)	8.5% favor stand- alone		

required ethics course in accounting and integration across the curriculum, as compared with 70 percent who favor integration only. Ghaffari et al. (2008) conducted a similar survey of accounting programs in the U.K. which was limited to the question of integration versus stand-alone coverage. Their findings were highly consistent with Madison and Schmidt (2006).

Moreover, Gaffari et al. (2008), Blanthorne et al. (2007), AACSB International (2007), Armstrong et al. (2003) and Alam (1999) have generally concluded that accounting faculty overwhelmingly agreed to integrate ethics with some accounting courses.

It seems that previous studies have conflicting results with respect to the way of delivering ethics education to students. Whether to deliver it in a stand- alone course or to keep it embedded in other courses is an interesting contribution to prior findings. Column 2 of Table (1) panel (B) summarizes relevant prior studies that show percentages of their respondents who favor a stand-alone course versus integrated course.

Where, When, What, and How to Deliver Ethics

Once it becomes evident that ethics education is an appropriate objective in the accounting profession, the overarching series of questions then becomes where, when, and how it should be taught. In his commentary on the issue, Wyatt suggests that college students be taught about the internal pressure and challenges associated with public accounting. He says that, in his experience, "Undergraduate students are probably at their peak of idealism, so educators should exploit this opportunity to reach students" (Wyatt, 2004). Wyatt also argues that students should be prompted to discuss case studies, and professors should not teach singular correct answers. Along with this, Wyatt says that accounting ethics education should revolve around the philosophical concepts that are the foundation of the ethical standards in accounting, rather than around the "thou shalt not" that are commonly emphasized". Doing so will enhance the student's understanding of how professional judgment realistically functions for a professional accountant.

In reality, colleges and universities have thus far instituted accounting ethics in a variety of capacities, from none at all to mandatory accounting-specific ethics courses. Procario-Foley and McLaughlin (2003) point out the inconsistencies in academia; some schools are providing ethics training for business students through programs like The Arup Program in Social Ethics for

Business at Georgetown University, yet some schools do not require even a course in business ethics. While this can partly be blamed on funding available for such programs, it also points out the academic community's lack of a definite stance on the issue. The three courses requirement that NASBA originally proposed (one being business-specific and one accounting-specific) was rejected by the Association to Advance Collegiate Schools of Business (AACSB), a move that was criticized by many in the academic community (Bean and Bernardi, 2007). Bean and Bernardi note that this points to the "increasing acknowledgment of the need for ethics education for business students, which should be discipline specific rather than the current practice of incorporating ethics on a piecemeal basis throughout the curriculum".

The issue of where business ethics should be taught also needs to be addressed in the context what department or school should teach it becomes easier. Familiarity with business practice is needed for teaching ethics. The students are primarily business/accounting majors. These two facts argue for its inclusion in the business school as opposed to the philosophy or religion department.

Accounting ethics is like business policy in the sense that it addresses issues raised in each of the major functional courses. Because of this multidisciplinary aspect, a logical argument can be made that accounting ethics, like business policy, should reside in the accounting department of the business school. The question of when to teach business ethics is best viewed in terms of what it is and why it is taught. One argument maintains that in an undergraduate accounting program, in which students often have little or no accounting experience, the functional courses should precede accounting ethics (as they often precede business policy). This provides students with a background in accounting practice for applying what they learn in the accounting ethics course. An opposite argument holds that the ethical principles involved can and should be applied in each of the major functional areas. Thus they should be taught before these functional studies begin, because they will better inform courses in accounting, marketing, and so forth.

Both arguments have some meet. However, the opportunity for students to apply ethical principles in each of their functional courses, and thus to reinforce and test the approaches taught in accounting ethics, is attractive. For this reason, my recommendation is placement early in the undergraduate accounting curriculum (Dellaporats, 2006).

The question of who should teach business ethics is a troublesome one. Because it includes both a body of knowledge and applications of this knowledge to business situations, a reasonably qualified teacher of this subject would need the mastery of a certain number of philosophical writings and principles and also familiarity with business as practiced in a variety of industries. Yet, there is no specific program that prepares teachers with this dual background. Adkins and Radtke (2004) offer that perhaps accounting faculty members do not feel qualified to teach ethics, or may not be interested in incorporating ethics into an already full curriculum. They argue that most faculty members are not formally trained in ethics. This is not surprising, considering accounting faculty's training is technically oriented. However, a lack of ethical training does not necessarily undermine its importance in the field; instructors teach accounting students about the technical aspects of the accounting workplace, so it would seem natural that they should also teach ethical principles that apply to the accounting workplace as well.

For accounting educators to overcome this lack of expertise, there are ways of overcoming this by having an ethics dissertation; taking ethics courses; attending continuing professional education on ethics, studying the ethics literature, and being involved in ethics research (Bean and Bernardi, 2007). The normal route to full credentials as a college or university teacher is the completion of a doctoral degree in one's subject area. At present, there are no doctoral programs in business ethics. However, there is ample precedent for the development of new subject areas and their gradual professionalization. Thirty years ago, there were no doctoral programs in strategy or in computer science. Today, both are considered by many to be full-fledged disciplines. The pattern seems to be that faculty with an interest and a competence in a related area pursue additional reading and research and become the de facto experts in the new field. Over time, journals are established, conferences are held, proceedings are published, textbooks are written, and doctoral programs are established.

The current state of business ethics, measured by such developments, suggests considerable progress toward the establishment of a discipline. Courses are being taught, journals and books are being published, and experts are making their appearance. Thus, the question of who should teach business ethics may be gradually answering itself. For the present, the minimum qualifications would seem to include knowledge of the major writers and principles in ethics and familiarity with business practice

METHODOLOGY

Sample

The community based research of this study were lecturers teaching core accounting courses, such as financial accounting, management accounting, auditing and taxation for the accounting bachelor degree programme at seven selected public and private universities in Bahrain at a total of 70 accounting instructors.

Table 2. Type of institution of higher education.

Institution	Educators	Percent
Public University	16	39
Private University	20	48.8
Public University College	5	12.2
Total	41	100.0

Table 3. Reliability statistics.

Cronbach's Alpha	Cronbach's alpha based on standardized items	Number of items
.860	.879	68

Table 4. Years of working experience of respondents.

Experience	Number of educators	Percent
Less than 5 years	5	12.8
5 to 10 years	19	48.7
More than 10 years	15	38.5
Total	39	100.0

Research Instrument

Separate questionnaires were designed to get feedback from accounting instructors at different universities based on a careful review of the accounting and business ethics literature, with consideration for current topics related to ethics instruction, such as those of AACSB, IAESB, and IFAC activities.

The questionnaire design

The questionnaire is designed into eight parts. The first three parts include demographic information, questions related to whether the respondents have ethics in their accounting programs. The fourth, fifth and sixth parts include questions concerning the benefits and limitations of teaching or not teaching ethics to accounting students. The seventh part includes questions regarding how and when to teach ethics. Faculties were asked to indicate whether to have a stand-alone course or integrate ethics along with other accounting courses and to indicate at what educational level they think that ethics should be taught. The final part includes questions regarding what should be taught. The respondents were asked to indicate their perceptions with respect to a set of topics that are assumed to cover accounting ethics.

Instructor was contacted to ascertain willingness to participate in the study. Accordingly, questionnaires with covering letter were personally handed over directly by the authors, 65 questionnaires were distributed to accounting instructors in the seven universities. Only 55 completed the questionnaire, from which 14 were not usable, so only 41 questionnaires (63% response rate) were usable for the purpose of this exploratory study. Table 2 presents information on listed universities. It shows that most respondents are from private universities at 48.8 %, followed by those from public university at 39% and those from public college at 12.2%. The academic ranks of respondents are as follows: 46.3% assistant professors; 17.1% associate professors; 9.8% full professors and 26.8% others.

The internal consistency of the questionnaire reliability was measured by using Cronbach's coefficient alpha statistical test which provides an indication of the average correlation among all the items that made up the scale. The results in Table 3 demonstrate that all indices obtained were considered high (above 0.80). A sample scale that shows alpha value above 0.80 is considered reliable (Bryman and Cramer, 2001). Therefore, the indices for the questionnaire reliability are generally considered adequate for this research.

Table 4 shows the level of experience for the respondents. The majority of respondents have 5-10 years of teaching experience (48.7%). This is followed by those with more than 10 years of teaching experience (38.5 %), and finally those with less than 5 years of teaching experience. Two respondents did not disclose their years of working experience (12.8%).

To ensure that our sample is unbiased, Slovin's Formula is used to calculate the minimum sample size .n in a 65 total population with a margin of error 10 %: n=N/ (1+ (N*e^2)) = 70(1+ (65*0.1*0.1)) = 41.1 people

Table 5 shows the rank of the participated accounting educators. The table demonstrates that the majority of the respondents were assistant professors who comprised 46.3% of the respondents. This is followed by 26.8% for others who are master degree holders. Then, associate professors were 17.1% and full professors were 9.8%.

Table 5. Rank of respondents.

Rank	Full Prof	Associate	Assistant	Other	Total
Number	4	7	19	11	41
Percent	9.8%	17.1%	46.3%	26.8%	100%

Table 6. The relationship between accounting ethics education and corporate scandals.

Statements	SD	D	N	A	SA	Mean	SD	Sig
(a)Incorporating ethics into the accountancy curriculum will reduce the incidence of financial scandals	1(2.4)	2(4.9)	5(12.2)	16(39)	12(29.3)	4.00	.986	.000
(b)Failure to teach ethics in the accounting curriculum contributed to recent business scandals	1(2.4)	5(12.2)	5(12.2)	17(41.5)	8(19.5)	3.72	1.059	.000
(c)Current high-profile financial statement fraud cases, including Enron and WorldCom, galvanize more interest in and demand for accounting ethics education	0	1(2.4)	3(7.3)	24(58.5)	13(31.7)	4.20	.679	.000
(d)Do not think that a lack of ethics education in the accounting curriculum contributed to recent accounting scandals	6(14.6)	13(31.7)	10(24.4)	10(24.4)	1(2.4)	3.33	1.095	.000
(e)Strengthening the credibility of financial reporting	1(2.4)	0	1(2.4)	8(19.5)	31(75.6)	4.66	.762	.000
(f) Promoting responsible corporate governance	1(2.4)	1(2.4)	4(9.8)	16(39)	19(46.3)	4.24	.916	.000

Hypotheses

As a contribution to prior research, this study investigates three main hypotheses to support or refute prior findings with respect to the main research questions. Building on the summary in Table 1, the following hypotheses need to be investigated:

H01: The perceptions of Bahraini faculty members are not significantly different from the perceptions of faculty members found in prior research with respect to the importance of teaching ethics to accounting students.
HO2: The perceived benefits of accounting ethics education by Bahraini faculty members are not significantly different from the perceived benefits by faculty members of prior research.
HO3: The perceptions of Bahraini faculty members toward barriers of integrating ethics into accounting curriculum are not significantly different from the perceptions of faculty members of prior research.

Research questions that are less debatable will be discussed using descriptive statistics and will be compared to statistics from prior research.

ANALYSIS AND FINDINGS

Importance of teaching ethics accounting

Accounting educators in Bahrain were asked to rank their agreement/disagreement to a set of statements addressing the effect of teaching ethics in accounting on improving financial reporting, enhancing corporate governance and reducing corporate scandals. Respondents were asked to indicate their answers using a five-point Likert scale, with 5 indicating "strongly agree" and 1 indicating "strongly disagree." Table 6 shows that the majority of the respondents believed that ethical development is critical to the profession, necessary to re-establish public trust after recent accounting scandals, and an important step toward making sure that the profession does not lose the right to self-regulate.

Nearly 70 percent of the respondents agreed with the statement that incorporating ethics into the accountancy curriculum will reduce the incidence of financial scandals (statement a in Table 6 and 61 percent of the respondents' believed that Failure to teach ethics in the accounting curriculum contributed to recent business scandals (statement b). When asking educators whether they agree that "current high-profile financial statement fraud cases, including Enron, WorldCom, HIH, Fannie Mae, Xerox, Tyco, Ford Pinto, etc., have created more interest in accounting ethics education", (statement c), 91% of the respondents indicated agreement on this issue. Statements (e) and (f) were used to cast on other benefits showing the importance of incorporating ethics into accounting education. For statement (e), 95.1% of the respondents agreed on the importance of accounting ethics education in "strengthening the credibility of financial reporting" and for statement (f), 85.3% of the respondents agreed on the importance of ethics in "promoting responsible corporate governance". In general, these findings are consistent with the results of the above prior research except the fact that educators in Bahrain (61%) believed that lack of ethics education contributed to recent corporate accounting scandals. This result is inconsistent with the finding of Fisher et al. (2005), one of few studies which found that lack of ethics education did not contribute to recent scandals.

Table 7. Ranking of Perceived benefits of teaching ethics to accounting students.

Benefits	Mean (SD) Rank	Agree Percent	Neutral Percent	Disagree Percent
a) Increasing the demand for individuals possessing accounting ethics education and skills	4.07 (.848) 3	85.5	9.7	4.8
b) Satisfying society's demand for ethical education and practice	3.38 (.964) 10	68.3	24.4	7.3
c) Help students solve moral and ethics issues facing the accounting profession and the business community	4.00 (.894) 4	73	20.3	6.7
d) Preparing students to engage in fraud examination	3.63 (1.280) 9	58.5	24.4	17.1
e) Make students more desirable in the marketplace	3.90 (.892) 6	68.3	26.9	4.8
f) Preparing students to deal with the uncertainties of the accounting profession	3.73 (.949) 8	63.4	31.7	4.9
g) Help students solve moral and ethics issues facing the accounting profession and the business community	3.95 (.947) 5	64	31.1	4.9
h) Can improve students' ethical attitudes and behavior	3.78 (.947) 7	73.2	12.2	14.6
I) Ethical development is crucial to the accounting profession	4.64 (0.73) 1	92.5	5.7	1.8
j) Overall, I believe ethics should be taught as integral part of accounting curriculum	4.46 (.745) 2	90.2	7.4	2.4

In order to test our first hypothesis, an overall mean for all perceived means for all statements is found (4.06) with average standard deviation of 0.91. This calculated mean is compared with the weighted mean (3.86) for the perceived importance of ethics education found in prior research. Since the calculated t-value for this comparison is 1.41 then we cannot reject the null hypothesis at $\alpha = 0.05$. This means that the findings of this study with respect to the perceived importance of teaching ethics in accounting are not significantly different from its perceived importance found in prior research.

The perceived benefits of accounting ethics education

Given the increased demand for incorporating ethics into the accountancy curricula, this study also investigates the rationale for teaching ethics in accounting education, but from the perspective of accounting educators in Bahrain. One part of the questionnaire includes ten benefits of teaching ethics in accounting education that proven to be significant in prior research. Then, respondents were asked to indicate their agreement or disagreement over these benefits and to rank their importance using a five-point Likert scale. Table 7 shows the results of the respondents' ranking to the perceived benefits.

The vast majority of respondents (92.5%) agreed that "accounting student's ethical skills development is crucial to the development of the accounting profession" (Benefit I in the table). This benefit was ranked first with the highest agreement mean of 4.64. This result is highly consistent with the finding of prior research (Blanthorne et al., 2007).

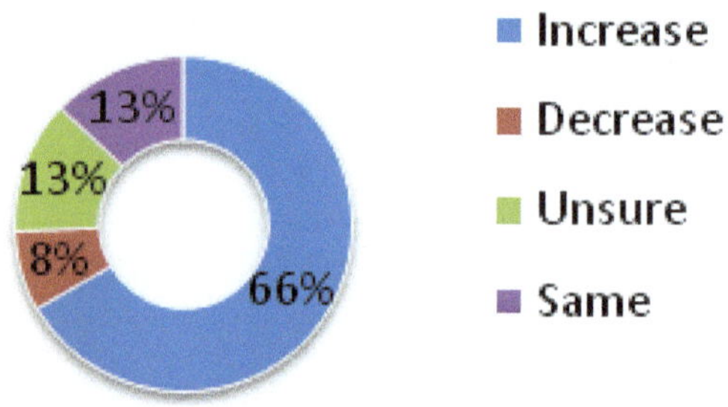

Figure 1. Expectations of future accounting scandals.

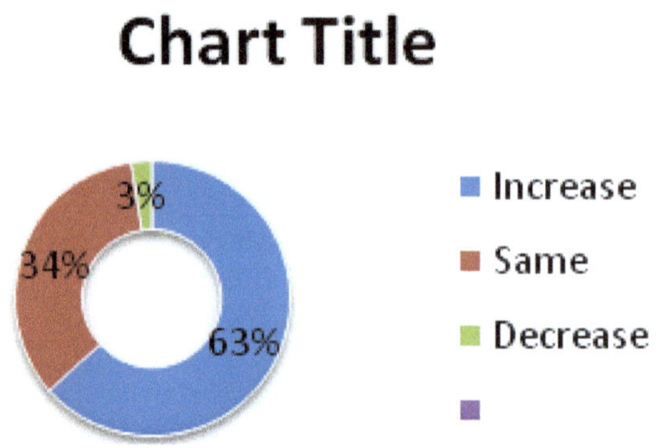

Figure 2. Expectations of the demand on accounting ethics as a result of scandals.

The table also shows that (benefit j) which states that "ethics education must be taught as an integral part of the accounting curriculum" ranked secondly by 90.2% of the respondents with the second highest agreement mean of 4.46. The thirdly ranked perceived benefit of teaching ethics to accounting students is (benefit a) which states that "ethics education will increase the demand for individuals possessing accounting ethics education and skills" with a mean rating of 4.07 and an agreement by 85.5% of the respondents. In general, the mean responses for all listed benefits are greater than 3 which imply that Bahraini accounting educators would rather see accounting ethics in the accounting curriculum in a much more positive light.

One of the dimensions of accounting ethics that are not clearly addressed by previous research is to investigate whether ethical accounting scandals will resume in the future and to what extent. Figure 1 indicates that 63.4% of the respondents believe that accounting scandals will be increased, 12.2% believe that the scandals will remain the same, 12.2% were unsure, and only 7.3% of the respondents believe that accounting scandals will be decreased in the future. Respondents were also asked to indicate whether the existence of scandals increases or decreases the demand on accounting ethics. Figure 2 shows that more than half of the respondents (63.4%) believe that the demand for accounting ethics will be increased with the existence of more scandals, while 34.3 % of the respondents believe that there is no effect of the scandals on the demand for ethics accounting. Only 2.6% of the respondents believe that demand on ethics will be decreased with the existence of scandals.

The second hypothesis of this research posits that there are no significant differences in the perceived benefits of teaching ethics by Bahraini educators from those perceived benefits by prior research's educators. In order to investigate this hypothesis, the mean responses for the perceived benefits in Table 7 were compared to the mean responses found in prior studies for the same benefits. Column 3 of Table (1) panel A shows prior research perceived benefits along with their corresponding means. The comparison is made based on an overall mean for those prior research benefits that are found to be the same as in Table 7. The overall mean of the benefits of prior research is weighted for the number of respondents in each research study. The overall mean of the benefits in table (7) is 4.09 with an average

Table 8. Accounting educators perceptions toward integrating ethics into accounting curriculum.

	Educators	Percent
Panel A: do you integrate ethics into your curriculum?(N=41)		
No	16	39.0
Yes	25	61.0
Total	41	100.0
Panel B: If No, when are you planning to do so? (N=16)		
Within one year	2	12.5
Within two years	9	56.25
Within five years	3	18.75
Do not plan to offer such coverage	2	12.5
Total	16	100.0
Panel C: if yes, how do you integrate accounting ethics into your curriculum?(N=25)		
Offer a separate course on business ethics	4	16.0
Integrate ethics coverage in most of the courses (including accounting and auditing courses).	21	84.0
Total	**25**	**100.0**

standard deviation of 0.868. Benefit a, benefit d, and benefit e were excluded because they have no match with prior research. The weighted overall mean of prior research is 3.05 based on the perceived benefits mentioned in Table 1. Since the calculated t-value is 7.66, then the null hypothesis should be rejected at $\alpha = 0.05$. This means that there are statistically significant differences between the perceived benefits found in this study and those found in previous studies. This result is not surprising because most prior research benefits were perceived with means of 3 or less, while benefits of this study were perceived with means of 3 or more. However, the rejection of this hypothesis may indicate that educators in different countries may perceive the benefits of teaching ethics differently.

Perceptions on integrating ethics into the accounting curriculum

Educators in Bahrain were asked to indicate their perceptions towards integrating ethics into the accounting curriculum. The results were encouraging as displayed in Table 8 panel A, in the sense that 61 % of the respondents reported that they do integrate ethics into accounting curriculum, whereas 39 % of the respondents do not currently cover ethics in their curricula. Those who were not covering ethics were asked when they will do so. Panel B of table (8) shows that the majority (56.25%) of those who did not cover ethics will do so within one or two years which may indicate their positive perception to the importance of ethics. As in panel C, the majority of respondents (84%) who reported that they are covering ethics into their accounting curricula, are embedding ethics in other accounting and auditing courses. Only 16% of them were teaching ethics in a separate course. These results are highly consistent with those of prior research on whether and how to integrate ethics into accounting education (Fisher et al., 2005; Trank and Rynes, 2003; Waddock, 2005; Madison and Schmidt, 2006; Ghaffari et al., 2008).

In the light of pervious results, we also asked accounting educators to indicate their agreement or disagreement using a 5- point Likert scale on the potential severity of a number of barriers in integrating accounting ethics into the accounting curriculum. These barriers were depicted from the findings of prior research (Gunz and McCutcheon, 1998; McCutcheon, 1998; Fisher et. al., 2005; Ghaffari et. al., 2007; Adkins and Radtke, 2004; Blanthorne et al., 2007).

Table 9 shows that the mean responses for all listed barriers, except for the last three, are greater than 3. That is; respondents reported that lack of faculty with sufficient training in ethical issues (3.76); and Lack of faculty interest and engagement (3.70) as sever obstacles. In addition, other listed barriers with means over 3.0 are all important to be considered, such as lack of student interest (3.59), lack of instructional materials (3.56), lack of administration interest and support (3.51), lack of faculty time (3.20), and lack of financial resources (3.08). The mean responses for the last three listed barriers including "ethics cannot be taught to students (2.21), the influence of family, religion and other institutions in society (2.46), and the technical nature of accounting education (2.49)" were not considered as impediments to the integration of ethics into the curriculum. These results

Table 9. Barriers of integrating ethics into accounting curricula.

Panel D: Indicate the severity and possible influence of certain barriers in integrating ethics into accounting curriculum	Mean (SD)	Agree Percent	Neutral Percent	Disagree Percent
Lack of faculty interest and engagement	3.70 (1.137)	65.9	14.6	19.5
Lack of student interest	3.59 (1.140)	63.4	19.5	17.1
Lack of faculty with sufficient training in ethical issues.	3.76 (1.113)	61	24.4	14.6
Lack of administrative interest and support	3.51 (1.143)	51.3	34.1	14.6
Lack of instructional materials (books and cases) specific to accounting and ethics	3.56 (1.379)	63.4	14.6	22
Lack of financial resources	3.08 (1.289)	39	26.8	34.2
Lack of faculty time	3.20 (1.091)	41.5	31.7	26.8
Ethics education is inappropriate because it does not suit with the technical nature of accounting education	2.49 (1.227)	51.3	22	26.7
The influence of family, religion and other institutions in society, are sufficient to provide guidance. "In another word students already know rights from wrong and accounting ethics courses are unnecessary	2.46 (1.206)	29.2	9.8	61
Ethics can't be taught to students	2.21 (1.376)	20.3	9.8	69.9

suggest that the primary obstacles facing delivery of ethics accounting education is a staffing problem. Few faculty members are trained for teaching ethics. Other barriers are institutional in nature (that is Time constraint, administration, and student...etc).

In order to contribute to previous studies on ethics integration, this study investigates whether significant barriers that have been used frequently in prior studies as possible reasons for not integrating ethics into accounting education would hold true in Bahrain. Therefore, reasons that are perceived as important barriers by Bahraini educators are compared to significant barriers found in previous research.

The third hypothesis posits that there are no significant differences over perceived barriers by Bahraini educators and those perceived barriers found in previous research (Karnes and Sterner, 1988; Adkins and Radtke, 2004; Blanthorne et al., 2007).

Column 4 of Table (1) panel (B) shows relevant studies of prior research that mentioned significant barriers along with their corresponding means. An overall weighted mean for those barriers is calculated (2.87) and then compared to the overall mean found in this study (3.03) using significant barriers in Table 9. Since the calculated t-value is 0.83 then the null hypothesis cannot be rejected even at α = 0.01 which means that the findings of this research with respect to the barriers facing ethics integration are highly consistent with the findings of prior research.

This conclusion indicates that obstacles facing ethics integration into accounting curriculum are of global concerns.

Table 10. How should ethics be taught?

Panel A: In what way do you think ethics should be taught?	**Yes**		**No**		**Not sure**		**Total**	
	educators	percent	Educators	Percent	educators	percen t	Ed	%
Accounting ethics should be taught as a separate course	10	24.4%	29	70.7%	2	4.9%	41	100
Accounting ethics it should be taught as embedded in other courses	34	82.9%	5	12.2%	2	4.9%	41	100

Table 10 b.

Panel C: At what level should a separate course in ethics be taught?	**educators**	**percent**
Graduate	16	39.1%
Undergraduate	22	53.7%
Both graduate and undergraduate	32	73.2%
If Undergraduate, which year?*		
First year	2	5.1%
Second year	5	12.8%
Third year	6	15.4%
Fourth year	21	53.8%
All years	4	10.3%

Table 10 c.

Panel D: Which courses should accounting ethics be embedded in?	**educators**	**percent**
Accounting information systems	23	56.1
Cost and management accounting	24	58.5
Taxation	34	82.9
Auditing	38	92.7
Financial Accounting	32	78
Ethics should be taught in all accounting	28	68.3

Ethics delivery and placement in the curriculum

The seventh part of the questionnaire includes questions related to how and when to teach ethics in the accounting curriculum. Respondents were asked to indicate their perceptions regarding ethics integration versus discrete using a five point Likert scale with five indicating strongly agree and one indicating strongly disagrees. Their responses with respect to the curriculum development are presented in Table 10. Panel (A) of Table 10 shows that 82.9% of the respondents believe that accounting ethics should be embedded in other accounting courses, while only 24.4% of the respondents encourage the use of a separate course. These percentages are highly consistent with finding of prior research such as Madison and Schmidt (2006) and Blanthorne et al. (2007).

In addition, if accounting ethics is be taught as a separate course, respondents were asked to indicate whether to include ethics in the accounting curriculum or as a college requirement in the student study plan. Panel (B) of Table 10 indicates that 51.4% of the respondents preferred that it should be as a separate course in the accounting curriculum, while 56.1% of them preferred to see it as a separate course in the business curriculum and not necessarily in the accounting curriculum. Therefore, it seems that Bahraini educators are indifferent with respect to having ethics as major requirement or college requirement. Furthermore, 70.7% of the respondents who favored accounting ethics as a separate course strongly support the notion that accounting ethics is to be offered as a compulsory course, while only 26.8% indicated that accounting ethics

Table 11. Topical content of accounting ethics course.

Whether ethics is separate or embedded course, please indicate the level of importance of each the following ethics accounting topics	Rank	Mean	SD
Responsibility of business in society	1	4.70	.516
Fundamentals of ethics and professional codes of conduct	2	4.54	.674
Earnings management and income smoothing issues *Islamic codes of ethics*	3	4.49	.553
Identification of ethical issues	4	4.43	.712
Evaluating ethical issues	5	4.41	.706
Ethical decision making skill	6	4.40	.810
Islamic codes of ethics	7	4.27	.708
Corporate governance and public interest	8	4.17	.946
Forensic accounting and auditing	9	4.20	1.123
Issues of conflicts of interest, such as principal-agent conflict interest and self review threats	10	4.02	.961

should be offered as an elective course. So far none of these findings is in conflict with the domain of prior findings. However, the debatable issues are related to the content and methods of delivering ethics to students the following two sub-sections are intended to show findings of this study along with findings of prior research.

Course content

Educators in Bahrain were presented with a list of ethical topics taken from prior studies and were asked to indicate their perceptions to the importance of these topics using a 5- point Likert scale where (5) indicating highly important and (1) indicating least important. The results in Table 11 indicate that there is a strong view from all respondents that all listed ethics topics are important to accounting ethics education. The means of responses for all listed topics are greater than 4 suggesting a high degree of importance. The table also shows a ranking for the topics according to their mean responses. That is, respondents place the highest degree of importance to the topic 'responsibility of business in society' (mean = 4.70) which ranked 1st. This is followed by the topic 'fundamentals of ethics' (mean = 4.54) which ranked 2nd. The table shows the rest of ranks for other topics where 'issues of conflict of interests' (mean = 4.02) is ranked 10th. Respondents were also asked to suggest any ethics related topics other than those included in the questionnaire. Only three of them (less than 1%) offered comments suggesting the covering of 'the Sarbanes-Oxley Act', 'adherence to taxation rules' and 'corporate environmental and social responsibility'. However, due to the low percentage achieved for this aspect, this part is ignored for further comments.

Teaching methods

Respondents were presented with a list of commonly used teaching methods that have been utilized in previous studies. They were asked to indicate their suitability for teaching ethics using a 5- point likert Scale. Table 12 shows the means of their responses and their ranks. The results indicate that the most suitable methods are as follow: written case studies (mean = 4.55); textbooks (mean = 4.24); normal classroom lecture (mean = 4.17); and research projects (mean = 4.10). Other commonly used methods such as: class debates; guest speakers; videos; and written exercises are also considered suitable teaching methods with means of 3.98, 3.85, 3.80 and 2.89 respectively.

These findings are in line with prior research results (Blanthorne et al., 2007; Ghaffari et al., 2008) by showing case studies as the most useful technique followed by the use of textbooks and class room lectures.

However, when compared with past research, the results may indicate that accounting faculty may make progress toward teaching ethics in the way they believe it should be taught. For example, the use of case studies is a viable technique since most students have heard of recent scandals and can easily link ethical and moral issues to the details of the presented case study.

SUMMARY AND CONCLUSION

The main purpose of this study is to provide a more comprehensive view of teaching accounting ethics at the college-level as reported by accounting faculty members at Bahraini universities.

As a contribution to previous research on accounting ethics, this study examines faculty perceptions as to whether ethics should be included in the curriculum, why ethics should (or should not) be taught, how and where in the curriculum ethics should be taught and what to teach in the curriculum.

Data for the study were collected by distributing an administered questionnaire to accounting educators in

Table 12. In your opinion, how suitable are the following ways of delivering ethics education in accounting at either graduate level or undergraduate level?

Ethics should be learned using	Rank	Mean	SD
Real written case studies	1	4.55	.830
Textbooks	2	4.24	.972
Normal classroom lecture	3	4.17	.932
Research projects	4	4.10	1.010
Class debate	5	3.98	.961
Guest speakers	6	3.85	1.027
Videos	7	3.80	1.188
Written exercise	8	2.89	1.269

public and private universities in Bahrain.

We started our study by asking accounting educators the most basic question: Should ethics be taught? Investigating this question in light of recent scandals highlights the importance of ethics inclusion into accounting education. Following the methodology of prior research, this study investigates first the relationship between ethics education and corporate scandals. Nearly 70 percent of the respondents agreed with the statement that incorporating ethics into the accountancy curriculum will reduce the incidence of financial scandals and 61 percent of the respondents believed that failure to teach ethics in the accounting curriculum contributed to recent business scandals. When asking educators whether they agree that "current high-profile financial statement fraud cases have created more interest in accounting ethics education", 91% of the respondents indicated agreement on this issue. As a contribution to previous research, the perceived importance of teaching ethics found in this study was compared with the perceived importance found in previous studies by the first hypothesis. The generated t-value of such comparison resulted in non-rejection to the null hypothesis. This means that there is no significant difference in the perceived importance of teaching ethics by this study and that perceived by prior researchers.

This study also investigates the rationale for teaching ethics in accounting education, but from the perspective of a group of accounting educators in Bahrain. Respondents were presented with ten benefits of teaching ethics to accounting students that proven to be significant in prior research and were asked to indicate their agreement or disagreement over these benefits and to rank their importance to accounting students using a 5-point Likert scale. The majority of the respondents believed that ethical development is critical to the profession, necessary to re-establish public trust after recent accounting scandals, and an important step toward making sure that the profession does not lose the right to self-regulate. These results were also compared with perceived benefits found in previous studies in order to detect any differences related to changing countries. This comparison was made by the second hypothesis which was rejected because of its high t-value. This result means that there are statistically significant differences between the perceived benefits found in this study and those found in previous studies.

One of the dimensions of accounting ethics that are not clearly addressed by previous research is to investigate whether ethical accounting scandals will resume in the future and to what extent. The results indicate that 63.4% of the respondents believe that accounting scandals will be increased in the future.

This study also investigates the perceptions of Bahraini accounting educators with respect to incorporating ethics into the accounting curriculum. The goal, here, is to update prior research on this aspect. The results suggest that 67% of the educators favor inclusion of ethics in the curriculum. The majority of respondents (84%) who reported that they are covering ethics into their curricula are embedding ethics in other accounting and auditing courses. These results imply that educators are aware of the importance of ethics to professional organizations, and consequently believe that the inclusion of ethics in the curriculum is important, especially in terms of topics related to professional practice.

In order to contribute to previous studies on ethics integration, this study investigates whether significant barriers that have been used frequently in prior studies as possible reasons for not integrating ethics into accounting education would hold true in Bahrain. Therefore, reasons that are perceived as important barriers by Bahraini educators are compared to significant barriers found in previous research. The third hypothesis investigates the existence of any significant differences of perceived barriers by Bahraini educators and those perceived barriers found in previous research. Since the calculated t-value is only 0.83 then the null hypothesis cannot be rejected even at $\alpha = 0.01$ which means that the findings of this research with respect to the barriers facing ethics integration are highly consistent with the findings of prior research. This conclusion indicates that obstacles facing ethics integration into accounting curriculum are of global concerns.

Respondents were asked to indicate their perceptions regarding ethics integration versus discrete course. Their responses indicate that 75% of the respondents believe that accounting ethics should be embedded in other accounting courses, while only 24.4% of the respondents encourage the use of a separate course. In addition, if accounting ethics is taught as a separate course, respondents were asked to indicate whether to include ethics in the accounting curriculum or to include it as a college requirement in the student study plan. The results indicate that 51.4% of the respondents preferred that it should be included as a separate course in the accounting curriculum, while 56.1% of them preferred to see it as a separate course in the business curriculum and not necessarily in the accounting curriculum. Therefore, it seems that opinions among accounting educators are not significantly different concerning the introduction of ethics into accounting curriculum as a separate course. Moreover, 70.7% of the respondents who favored accounting ethics as a separate course strongly support the notion that accounting ethics is to be offered as a compulsory course, while only 26.8% indicated that accounting ethics should be offered as an elective course.

Another relevant question addressed by this study is whether the ethics course should be offered at the graduate, undergraduate, or at both levels. The results indicate that about 73.2% of accounting educators see that accounting ethics should be offered at both level, whereas 53.7 % believed that it should be offered at undergraduate level, and 39.1% of the respondents see that accounting ethics should be offered at the graduate level.

Respondents were also asked at what level of the undergraduate program they believe a separate ethics course should be taught. The results show that 53.8% of the respondents agree that ethics should be offered in the fourth year, 12.8 % of them believe that it should be offered in the third year, 5.1 % of them believe that it should be in second year, only 2.6 % see that it should be offered in the first year, and 10.3% of respondents believed that the course should be offered in all four years. The argument in support of this result is that students are more mature at their fourth year to understand how to develop ethical and moral reasoning. In addition, about 68.3% of the respondents believed that accounting ethics should be integrated into every accounting course.

Educators were presented with the suggested ethical topics and were asked to indicate their perceptions to the importance of these topics. The results indicate that there is a strong view from all respondents that all listed ethics topics are important to accounting ethics education. Respondents place the highest degree of importance to three topics: 'responsibility of business in society', 'fundamentals of ethics', and 'earning management and income smoothing issues'. Regarding how ethics should be taught, respondents believe that the case method is the best method of delivery, and they may be incorporating case analysis more than in the past. In general, these results indicate our respondent's strongly view ethics courses as being important to be taught and included in to the accounting curriculum.

Limitations of the study

The reported results and implications require consideration of the study's limitations. The results are based on a small sample of respondents .We cannot assume that the views of non respondents are similar to the study finding. While measures were taken to ensure data quality, some responses were found to lack the required quality and were excluded.

ACKNOWLEDGMENT

We thank an anonymous reviewer and the helpful comments and suggestions on an earlier draft of this paper made by many of our colleagues at the University of Bahrain and from other universities.

REFERENCES

Armstronga MB (1993). 'Ethics and professionalism in accounting education: A sample course', *J. Account. Educa.* 11: 77–92.

Adkins N, Radtke RR (2004). 'Students' and faculty members, perceptions of the importance of business ethics and accounting ethics education: Is there an expectations gap?', *J. Bus. Ethics*, 51: 279–300.

Alam KF (1999). 'Teaching Business Ethics', *Ethics and Accounting Education* ,2(3): 261-272.

Albrecht WS, Sack RJ (2000). 'Accounting education: Charting the course through a perilous future', *American Accounting Association*.

Armstrong MB (1987). 'Moral development and accounting education', *J. Account. Educa.* (Spring): 27–43.

Association of Chartered Certified Accountants (ACCA). (2007)'Consultation on New Qualification', *Available at: https: / /*www.accaglobal.com.

Association to Advance Collegiate Schools of Business (AACSB) International. (2004)'Ethics education in business schools: Report of the ethics education task force to AACSB International's board of directors', *AACSB*, St. Louis, MO'.

Bean DF, Bernardi RA (2005)'Accounting ethics courses: A professional necessity', *The CPA J.* 75 (12): 64-65.

Benner J (2002)'MBA accreditation body resists professors call for required ethics course', *AFX Global Ethics Monitor Online*, November 14

Blanthorne C, Kovar SE, Fisher DG (2007)'Accounting Educators' Opinions about Ethics in the Curriculum: An Extensive View', *Issues in Account. Educa.* 22(3): 355-390.

Chan SYS, Leung P (2006)'The effects of accounting students' ethical reasoning and personal factors on their ethical sensitivity', *Managerial Audit. J.* 21(1): 436-457.

Cohen JR, Bennie NM (2006)'The applicability of a contingent factors model to accounting ethics research', *J. Bus. Ethics*. 68: 1–18

Cohen JR, Pant LW (1989)'Accounting educators' perceptions of ethics in the curriculum', *Issues in Accounting Education* ,4 (Spring): 70-81.

Dellaportas S (2006) 'Making a difference with a discrete course on accounting ethics', *Journal of Business Ethics*, 65(4): 391-404

Evans FJ, Marcal LE (2005)'Educating for ethics: Business deans' perspectives', *Bus. Society Rev.* 110 (3): 233–248.

Fisher D, Blanthorne C, Kovar S (2007)'Accounting educators' opinions about ethics in the curriculum: A profile', *Issues in Account. Educa.* 22: 355-389.

Fisher D, Swanson L, Schmidt J (2007)' Accounting Education Lags CPE Ethics Requirements: Implications for the Profession and a Call to Action', *Account. Educa.* 16 (4): 345-363.

Fisher DG, Swanson DL (2005)'Accounting Ethics Education and Unfounded Faith in Integration Across the Curriculum: If We Don't Know Where We're Going, Any Road Will Take Us There', Unpublished Working Paper, Kansas State University, March.

Friedman M (1970)'The Social Responsibility of Business Is to Increase Its Profits', *New York Times. Magazine*, September 13, 1970.

Gammie E, Gammie B (2009) 'The moral awareness of future accounting and business professionals: the implications of a gender divide', *Pacific Account. Rev.* 21(1): pp.48-73

Geary WT, Sims RR (1994)'Can Ethics be Learned', *Accounting Education'*,3: 3-18.

Ghaffari F, Kyriacou O, Ross B (2008)'Exploring the Implementation of Ethics in U.K. Accounting Programs', *Issues in Account. Educa.* 23: 183-198.

Gray R, Bebbington J, McPhail K (1994)'Teaching ethics in accounting and the ethics of accounting teaching: Educating for immorality and a possible case for social and environmental accounting education', *Account. Educa.* 3(1): 51-75.

Gunz S, McCutcheon J (1998)'Are academics committed to accounting ethics education?', *J. Bus. Ethics* 17: 1145-1154.

Jennings MM (2004)'Incorporating ethics and professionalism into accounting education and research: A discussion of the voids and advocacy for training in seminal works in business ethics', Issues in Account. Educa. 19 (2): 7-26.

Karnes A, Sterner J (1988). The role of ethics in accounting education', *Account. Educators J.* (Fall): 18–31.

Langenderfer HQ, Rockness JW (1989)'Integrating ethics into the accounting curriculum: Issues, problems, and solutions', *Issues in Account. Educa.* 4 (Spring): 58-69.

Madison L, Schmidt J (2006)'Survey of Time Devoted to Ethics in Accountancy Programs in North American Colleges and Universities', *Issues in Account. Educa.* 21(2): 99-109.

Massey DW, Van Hise' J (2009)'Walking the Walk: Integrating Lessons from Multiple Perspectives in the Development of an Accounting Ethics Course', *Issues in Account. Educa.* 24(4): 481-511.

McNair F, Milam E (1993)' Ethics in Accounting Education: What is Really Being Done', *J. Bus. Ethics.* 12: 797-809.

McPhail K (2001)'The other objective of ethics education: Re-humanizing the accounting profession. A study of ethics education in law, engineering, medicine and accountancy',. *Journal of Business Ethics*, 34 (3 / 4).

Mintz S (1990)'Ethics in the management accounting curriculum', *Manage. Account.* (6): 51-54.

Moriceau J (2005)'What can we learn from a singular case like Enron?', *Critical Perspectives on Accounting* ,16: 787–796.

Nicklaus D (2002)'Is a bigger dose of ethics needed in business schools?', *St. Louis Post Dispatch*, December 18.

O'Connell BT (2004)'Enron.con: "He that filches from me my good name ... makes me poor indeed" *Critical Perspectives on Account* 15: 733–749.

O'Leary C (2009) 'An Empirical Analysis of The Positive Impact of Ethics Teaching on Accountancy Students', *Accounting Education: An Int. J.* 18 (4): 505-520

Ozdogan FB, Eser Z (2007) 'Ethical sensitivity of college students in a developing country', *J. Teaching Int. Bus.* 19(1): 83-99

Piper T, Gentile MC, Daloz S (1993)' Can Ethics Be Taught?', *Boston, MA: Harvard Business School.*

Ponemon LA (1993)' Can ethics be taught in accounting?', *J. Account. Educa.* 11: 185–209.

Procario-Foley, E. G. and McLaughlin, M. T.: 2003'A propaedeutic for a framework: Fostering ethical awareness in undergraduate business students', *Teaching Bus. Ethics,* 7(3): 279-301.

Rest JR (1986)'Moral Development: Advances in Research and Theory', *New York, NY*: Praeger Publishers.

Russell K, Smith C (2003)'Accounting educations role in corporate malfeasance: It's time for a new curriculum!', *Strategic Financ.* 85(6): 47-51.

Rynes SL, Trank CQ, Lawson AM, Ilies R (2003)'Behavioral coursework in business education: Growing evidence of a legitimacy crisis', *Acad. Manage. Learning Educa.* 2: 269-283.

Sugahara S, Boland G (2011)'Faculties' Perceptions of Ethics in the Accounting Curriculum: A Japanese Study', *Research on Professional Responsibility and Ethics in Account.* 15, ISBN: 978-1-78052-004-9.

Swanson DL (2004)'The buck stops here: Why universities must reclaim business ethics education, in D. Reed & R. Wellen (eds.), Special Issue on Universities and Corporate Responsibility', *Journal of Academic Ethics*, 2 (1): 43-61.

Thomas S (2012) 'Ethics and Accounting Education', *Issues Account. Educa.* 27 (2): 399-418

Trank CQ, Rynes S (2003) 'Who moved our cheese? Reclaiming professionalism in business education', *Academy of Management Learning Educa.* 2(2): 189–205.

Trevino L, Nelson K (2004)'Managing Business Ethics: Straight Talk About How to Do It Right', *Hoboken*, NJ: Wiley.

Waddock S (2005) 'Hollow men and women at the helm . . . hollow accounting ethics', *Issues Account. Educa.*, 20(2): 145–150.

William F, Becker A (2011)'Ethics In The Accounting Curriculum: What Is Really Being Covered?', *Am. J. Bus. Educa.* Volume 4, Number .

Williams JL, Elson R (2010)'Improving Ethical Education in the Accounting Program: A Conceptual Course', *Acad. Educa. Leadership J.* 14(4): 107-116.

Wyatt AR (2004)'Accounting professionalism—they just don't get it!', *Accounting Horizons*,18

Audit expectation gap and MBA accounting students' knowledge on auditor(s)' responsibilities: Evidence from a public university in Kumasi Ashanti Region of Ghana

Frank Yao Gbadago

Department of Accounting Studies Education, College of Technology Education University of Education, Winneba, Kumasi, Ghana.

Auditing has become a critical indispensable part of business and corporate life in today's world and it is receiving great entrenchment in national legal status of almost every nation. However, there are evidences that suggest that users of financial statements and the public at large do not have knowledge about auditors' responsibilities and this has resulted in what has become known as audit expectation gap. This study sought to investigate the level of knowledge of final year MBA (Accounting) students on auditors' responsibilities and what auditors do vis-a-vis the companies' code, International Standards on Auditing as well as the professional guidelines on auditing in one of the public universities in Kumasi, the capital town of Ashanti Region of Ghana. The study used structured self-administered questionnaire to gather information from the final year MBA (Accounting) students. The data collected were analyzed using descriptive and inferential statistics with the help of MS Excel package. The study revealed that the mean knowledge of the students' on auditors' responsibilities was 4.25 suggesting that only 25% of the final year MBA (Accounting) students know for sure what auditors' responsibilities are. The study therefore recommended that policy makers, the university education administrators and regulators such as National Accreditation Board of Ghana together with the faculties take a closer look at Teaching and Learning of Accountancy and business Studies especially Auditing in Higher Education. It was further suggested that the universities review their syllabi on auditing courses to include the responsibilities, duties and roles of auditors, so as to examine these sections regularly to encourage students to read and understand it properly. Finally, the study proposed further research to cover most of the public universities in Ghana in the near future.

Key words: Audit expectation gap, final year MBA (Accounting), auditors' responsibilities, knowledge, teaching and learning in higher education.

INTRODUCTION

Auditing could be explained to mean an independent examination of records and financial statements of an entity and expression of opinion by a qualified person known as an auditor as to whether records and financial statements as prepared by management of the entity reflects the true and fair state of affairs of the entity and that the financial statements are prepared in accordance with the applicable regulatory frameworks and standards (ICAG, 2008; Omane-Antwi, 2009; Okafor and Otalor, 2013). Auditing has become a critical indispensable part of business and corporate life (Okafor and Otalor, 2013) in today's world and it is receiving great entrenchment in national legal status books (i.e. companies' codes) of almost every nation if not all with other ancillary legislations (corporate governance codes) as well (Saladrigues and Grañó, 2014). This explains why it is widely thought in all business schools in our colleges and universities as one of the compulsory electives. It is said to have begun as far back as early 15th centuries during the days of Pacioli, Lucas (Omane-Antwi, 2009). Auditing of an entity and its operations achieve various purpose or roles (Lee et al., 2007; Kim et al., 2010; Okafor and Otalor, 2013; Ramlugun, 2014) which could be grouped mainly as primary purpose and secondary purpose (ICAG, 2008; Omane-Antwi, 2009; Kim et al., 2010) as discussed below.

The primary purpose of an audit is to express an opinion on the truth and fairness of the financial statements and the underlying books of accounts. This gives credence to the various users of the financial statements most importantly the owners (shareholders) of the business entity. Again, it gives creditability to management, the appointed agents entrusted with the stewardship and/or management of the organization's resources.

The secondary purpose of auditing, however is to prevent errors and frauds, detect and prevent errors and frauds inherent in the entity's operating system, identifying internal control weaknesses and to suggest improvement to the internal control systems (Kim et al., 2010). The achievement of the above foregoing objectives are fundamental reasons for instituting good corporate governance systems in organizations and it is primarily the responsibility of the entity's management. Thus, auditing helps to achieve good corporate governance in organizations.

On a larger scale, auditing based on its assurance and confidence and trust repose leads to effective allocation of resources within an economy and across continents (Lee et al., 2007; Okafor and Otalor, 2013; Saladrigues and Grañó, 2014; Ramlugun, 2014). Given the significance of auditing, there is therefore the need for all financial information users including the general public to have kin interest in audit and what auditors do.

However, since the end of Andersen, Enron, Worldcom etc debacle and the 2008 financial crisis, the performance and functions of auditors have been in the public domain attracting varying comments and opinions according to Charitou et al. 2004 (as cited by Appiah, 2013; Ramlungun, 2014; Lee et al., 2007). A close analysis of these comments suggests that both the users and the public have different expectations of auditor(s), their duties and responsibilities (Lee et al., 2007; Noghondari and Foong, 2009; Onumah et al., 2009; Agyei et al., 2013; Saladrigues and Grañó, 2014).

There is therefore difference in expectation(s) in respect of what users of audited financial information and the public expect of the auditor(s). That is, the level of audit performance, how the auditor(s) actually performed their audits, the effectiveness of an audit engagement(s) as well as the auditors' ability to detect and prevent fraud coupled with what the auditor believes is his responsibilities as supported by the various auditing standards and status (Lee et al., 2007). This is what is termed audit expectation gap or simply put expectation gap (Millichamp, 1996; Lee et al., 2007; ICAG, 2008; Noghondari and Foong, 2009, Omane-Antwi, 2009; Agyei et al., 2013). Though audit expectation gap has been empirically established to exist in Ghana (Onumah et al., 2009; Agyei et al., 2013) just like other studies elsewhere, it appears no Ghanaian study (based on information available to the researcher) has been able to investigate the audit expectation gap among accounting students in Ghana. Therefore, the objective of this study is to contribute to this call by being one of the few that have taken that audacious step in filling this gap. To the researcher investigating expectation gap among accounting students is decisive at this time because, sooner, these students will be at the fore front of auditing and accounting profession in Ghana, being the auditors and accountants, as such the earlier they are exposed to this profession threatening quandary may lead to its early elucidation. This is the motivation for this current study given the importance of expectation gap to the audit practice (profession) and industry (i.e. users of financial information) and its consequence on trust and confidence of the public and users of audited financial information. It is imperative that the findings of this study will help change the nature of training given to future auditors and accountants at their incubation period thereby helping to tackle this gap problem through education (Dixon and Woodhead, 2006; Onumah et al., 2009; Olagunju and Leyira, 2012; Agyei et al., 2013; Ramlugun, 2014). The rest of the paper is organized thus: the next immediate section provides a brief review of relevant related existing literature followed by discussion of the methodology used for the study. Thereafter, the empirical results are discussed followed by conclusions and recommendations based on the findings of the study.

REVIEW OF RELATED LITERATURE

As accounting attempts to provide a comprehensive information about economic and/ or financial activities of business enterprise via financial statements to various users there is the need for an independent person known as an auditor to express an opinion on the financial statements together with the underlying records and books of accounts prepared by the managements (directors) of the reporting entity to be presented to the various users whether it presents a true and fair view of the state of affairs of the reporting entity (Okafor and Otalor, 2013) or otherwise. Auditing is said to have started when shareholders and other stakeholders of businesses attempt to find out whether managements of their business enterprises were operating their entities and/ or resources made available to them within the laid down rules, regulations, practice, norms and/ or to achieve agreed targets (profitability) etc (Kim et al., 2010). Thus, the need for an audit primarily started when the separation of ownership and control in business entities (in which shareholders nominate directors to run the affairs of their entities) commenced (Millichamp, 1996; Watson and Head, 1998; ICAG, 2008 and Omane-Antwi, 2009; Kim et al., 2010). There are abundant body of literature that suggest that while the shareholders (who are the owners of the business entity) have the goal of value maximization as their primary objective, the managers (appointed employees) do have different objectives which are mostly self gratification and are opposing to that of the shareholders. This situation is theoretically referred to as "agency problem" (Millichamp, 1996; Watson and Head, 1998; ICAG, 2008; Omane-Antwi, 2009). To accord the shareholders and other stakeholders the assurance that their entities were being; effectively operated, have effective and robust internal control systems in place capable of safe guarding assets and resources, the entity's business objectives are being achieved, that the financial reports on the operations are reliable and free from material misstatements, fraud and misappropriation of assets are being prevented and are likely to be detected by the Internal Control Systems (ICS) and the cost of doing business are being minimized, a third party who is independent needs to give an opinion to attest to all of the above (Kim et al., 2010; Saladrigues and Grañó, 2014). This is what brought about the concept of auditing. Auditing is thus seen as an important tool in corporate governance for remedying the agency problem. That is to realign the appointed agents' objectives with that of the shareholders to ensure that there is that goal congruence (Watson and Head, 1998; Kim et al., 2010) within the entity.

From the above discussions, shareholders and stakeholders expect the auditor(s) to meet their expectations. Bearing this in mind, any audit performance short of these perceived expectations of users of financial information would be seen as substandard performance (Lee et al., 2007; Noghondari and Foong, 2009; Agyei et al., 2013). Conversely, auditor(s)' regulatory frameworks such as the companies law, auditing standards and ethical guidelines define the roles, responsibilities and duties of the auditor(s) and in some cases indicated the sort of audit work and programmes to be carried out in varying audit engagements which may far differ from the public's perceived responsibilities expect of the auditor. This situation is usually referred to as audit expectation gap (Porter, 1993; Epstein and Geiger, 1994; Millichamp, 1996; Leung and Chau, 2001; Lin and Chen, 2004; Fadzly and Ahmad, 2004; Chowdhury et al., 2005; Dixon et al., 2006; Lee et al., 2007; ICAG, 2008; Noghondari and Foong, 2009, Omane-Antwi, 2009; Agyei et al., 2013; Saladrigues and Grañó, 2014). The auditors' failure to meet the public's perceived expectations undermines the public's confidence in the auditor as well as the audit function (Limperg, 1932; Porter, 2005 (as cited in Lee et al., 2007) supported by Agyei et al. (2013). The fear is if that confidence is betrayed, the audit function will be destroyed as it becomes futile exercise then as observed by Limperg, 1932 (as cited in Lee et al., 2007; Agyei et al., 2013). This is because the stakeholders and users of audited financial statements need to put reliance on the audited financial statements for purposes of entity's economic performance evaluation, investment decisions among others as postulated by Godsell (1992) (as cited by Lee et al., 2007) and Libby et al. (2008).

Host of studies both theoretical and empirical put forward that audit expectation gap does exist suggesting that the public mostly the users of audited financial statements and the auditors have different expectations about audit performance (Liggio, 1974; Humphrey et al., 1993; Gloeck and De Jager, 1993; Porter, 1993; Epstein and Geiger 1994; Millichamp, 1996; Leung and Chau, 2001; Lin and Chin 2004; Fadzly and Ahmad, 2004; Chowdhury et al., 2005; Dixon et al., 2006; Lee et al., 2007; ICAG, 2008; Noghondari and Foong, 2009, Omane-Antwi, 2009; Agyei et al., 2013; Saladrigues and Grañó, 2014). As observed by Lee et al. (2007) and Noghondari and Foong (2009), most of the above mentioned studies happened in the developed economies (Liggio, 1974; Humphrey et al., 1993; Gloeck and De Jager, 1993; Porter, 1993; Epstein and Geiger 1994; Leung and Chau, 2001; Lin and Chin 2004; Fadzly and Ahmad, 2004; Chowdhury et al., 2005; Saladrigues and Grañó, 2014) while just a few were done in the developing economies like South Africa (McInnes, 1994 as cited in Noghondari and Foong, 2009), Egypt (Dixon et al., 2006), Nigeria (Adeyemi and Oloowokere, 2011; Olagunju and Leyira, 2012; Okafor and Otalor, 2013). However, in recent times, there has been emergence of empirical studies in Ghana investigating the audit expectation gap. Notably among them are Onumah et al. (2009) and Agyei et al. (2013) based on information available to the researcher. The few Ghanaian studies available only examined the existence of audit expectation gap among financial information users and auditors. For example, Onumah et al. (2009) evaluated the gap among the preparers and users of audited financial statements and observed that whereas financial statements users have significantly different perceptions about assurances provided by auditors' reports, the views of company accountants are somehow quite close to those of auditors. Also, Agyei et al. (2013) in a similar manner looked at expectation gap among users (specifically stock brokers) and auditors and affirmed that there exists audit expectation gap in Ghana particularly in respect to auditors' responsibility relating to fraud detection and prevention and soundness of internal control systems of the audited entities. There after proposed to the audit profession regulators to formulate such standards, rules and regulations that adequately guide the auditors in fulfilling the reasonable expectations of various user groups. It appeared; the Ghanaian studies (Onumah et al., 2009 and Agyei et al., 2013) like most other studies elsewhere observed that the wrong perceptions of the users of financial information about auditors' responsibilities continued to account for the existence of the audit expectation gap among the stakeholders of financial statements. However, analyzing Onumah et al. (2009)'s assertion that the views of company accountants are quite close to those of auditors further, one could conclude that since the company accountants do receive the same training and education like that of the auditors, that is why they do have the same views just like the auditors. Also, Humphrey (1997) and Epstein and Geiger (1994) in their studies concluded that the technicality of terms and concepts used in auditing by the auditors, users' inability to appreciate the nature and limitations of audit respectively are responsible for the existence of audit expectation gap. Also, Agyei et al. (2013) indicated that the shift in audit objectives and responsibilities in late 20th century from fraud detection to verification of financial statements, largely accounted for some of the audit expectation gap. It is apparent from the foregoing that lack of knowledge (Noghondari and Foong, 2009; Okafor and Otalor, 2013; Ramlugun, 2014) on the responsibilities of auditors on the part of the users, lack of tact by the auditors and the auditing profession to get users to appreciate their roles, duties, responsibilities, what they are required to do within the arm-bit of the regulatory legal status and other frameworks continue to give credence to the audit expectation gap's existence. To minimize the expectation gap's persistence and possible escalation (Onumah et al., 2009), educating both the users and auditors may be seen as the best solution (Noghondari and Foong, 2009; Olagunju and Leyira, 2012; Okafor and Otalor, 2013; Agyei et al., 2013; Ramlugun, 2014) more importantly the young and upcoming ones still in schools. This therefore sets the scene for the current study on audit expectation gap among the final year MBA (Accounting) students in Ghana as a case.

Now that the auditing profession assumes a growingly new dynamisms following the Andersen, Enron, Worldcom etc debacle and the 2008 financial crisis coupled with the frequent legal battles and public calls for tighter regulations and monitoring as well as new International Standards on Auditing (ISAs) as being thought in business schools and colleges all over the world, an empirical study among accounting students in one of the public universities of Ghana to ascertain the level of their knowledge on the responsibilities of the auditor (existence of audit expectation gap) may be seen as one of the novelty in contributing to body of literature on the current issue specifically in Ghana and beyond. It is believed this may help to shape how accountancy and auditing is thought in our colleges and universities going forward. Also, it is necessary to find out if the current teaching of accountancy and auditing at the business schools of our universities and colleges are able to correct the erroneous perceptions about the responsibilities of auditors beginning from the classroom. If it cannot then to suggest remedial actions necessary for bridging this gap considering the challenges the expectation gap posts (Okafor and Otalor, 2013) to auditors and audit profession as a whole in Ghana and elsewhere.

In practice, the auditor performs an audit engagement(s) in strict adherence to the following regulatory frameworks as explained below;

a) The engagement contract(s) which indicates the terms of reference upon which the auditor is appointed. The engagement contract or letter sets out the extent of work to be undertaken by the auditor for the client and reminds the client of the liabilities of both parties (Millichamp, 1996; ICAG, 2008; Omane-Antwi, 2009). According to ISA 210 (as cited in ICAG, 2008; Omane-Antwi, 2009), engagement contract usually covers the functions of the auditor and the responsibilities of the directors, discovering of fraud and defalcations, details of other services, charges, reporting authority as well as the time frame within which the report is expected. The golden rule to auditors is that they should avoid being side tracked.

b) The provisions of the local legislation governing auditors as provided in the Companies Code, 1963 (Act 179). In Ghana, auditor's duties and responsibilities are governed by Act 179. Thus, he is said to have performed his duties if he had complied with the Act specifically Section 136 (1).

c) The Ethical and Professional Guidelines. This serves as a conceptual frame work that requires the auditor in performance of his audit engagement to maintain highest integrity, professional competence while remaining objective, confidential, and exercising due care (IFAC Handbook, 2007as cited in ICAG, 2008; Omane-Antwi, 2009).

d) The international Standards on audit (ISA), stipulates the attitude the auditor should assume in the course of his audit performance (ISA 200 and 240). Thus, he is said to have performed his duties if he is seen to have assumed the recommended attitude and skillfulness.

As it were, one is tempted to assume that anyone with education in accounting, finance, business, and commence should possess adequate knowledge and awareness on the responsibilities, roles, functions, duties of an auditor(s) as well as what auditors do. Stated differently, can audit expectation gap exist among those with prior training (academic qualification) and education in accounting and auditing? Though, studies have been done to ascertain existence of audit expectation gap among users and preparers of financial statements in Ghana, no such studies were done among MBA accounting students to evaluate the audit expectation gap with the view to eliminate it. As such, this study accordingly used research participants (respondents) from one of the public universities in Kumasi capital town of Ashanti Region of Ghana where their level of knowledge and awareness on the responsibilities, roles, functions, duties of an auditor(s) as well as what auditors do within the legal and regulatory framework were tested.

METHODOLOGY

This study used a survey approach where sets of self-administered questionnaire were used as the data collection instrument which was administered to the research respondents during one of their free periods by their course representatives. Self-administered structured questionnaire was used because of its ability to collect data of high quality within shortest possible time with minimal costs as well as not requesting the physical presence of the researcher. The instrument comprises close-ended questions in four sections which were pre-tested to improve its clarity and potency.

The population for the study was every Ghanaian student studying Master of Business Administration (MBA) (Accounting) in final year. The final year MBA class was selected and used for this study because it is assumed that, as they are in final year and had taken Auditing and Assurance course among others as parts of their core electives, they might have had a palpable level of knowledge in auditing as well as know the responsibilities of an auditor as required by the legal status books and other regulatory frameworks and hence provide an opportunity to ascertain if appreciable level of knowledge (Onumah et al., 2009) is capable of mitigating audit expectation gap among financial information (statements) users in Ghana. However, due to the vastness of the population, a purposive and convenient sampling approach was then adopted, where a final year MBA (Accounting) Students of one of the Public Universities in Kumasi the capital town of Ashanti region of Ghana was conveniently chosen for the study. For the purposes of anonymity and/ or confidentiality the name of the university is withheld and instead referred to here as UGX, Kumasi. The class size was forty-eight (48) students. The 48 copies of set of research questionnaire were first submitted to the course representative (rep). The course rep there after administered the research questionnaires to the respondents to complete and return them on their own. Out of 48 copies of research questionnaire given out, only 17 copies representing 35.42% of copies were returned answered and were used for data analysis. Though the response rate was low, it is considered as acceptable for this study. As this rate is typical in most surveys using self-administered questionnaire as data collection instrument which are posted or left with the respondents to return upon completion as posited by Robertson and McCloskey (2002), generally have about 30% response rate on the average depending on the context and location. This was somewhat consistent with the observations of some prior studies bordering on the current research issue having response rates as 23.07, 30, 32.30, 30.60% by Lee et al. (2007), Fadzly and Ahmad (2003) and Best et al. (2001) (as cited in Lee et al., 2007; Ramlugun, 2014), respectively.

The questions in the instrument were closed-ended with responses. Closed ended questions were used because, to the researcher, this best obtain the needed data within the shortest possible timeline within which respondents were expected to complete the instruments. The responses provided were analyzed by the help of MS Excel package. Descriptive and inferential statistics were used in presenting findings of the study as depicted in the ensuing section.

RESULTS AND DISCUSSION

Demographic characteristics

The study respondents were made of 82.35% males and 17.65% females indicating dominance of males in the sample used (Table 1).

The respondents' ages range between 25 years to 42 years with 30 years, 33 years and 38 years group all having 11.76% each age representation of the sample. The average age however is 33.5 years even though about 11.76% of the respondents did not provide any responses as shown in Table 2.

The coefficient of variation and standard deviation are 0.16 and 5.21 respectively as shown in Table 3, suggesting that the average age of the respondents is 33 ½ years.

The respondents' educational background is mainly first degree (94.15%) in business and accounting related qualifications as shown in Table 4. This explains why they have chosen their current line of study which is MBA (Accounting).

Further, the working or job responsibilities of the respondents include preparation of payroll, handling accounts payable and receivable, financial statements preparation to overall responsibility for accounting functions for their employers, filing of returns and co-ordinating annual and other statutory audits and reviews among others. That is the respondents mainly work as accounting and finance personnel of their respective entities that they are currently engaged in. The number of years of working experiences of the respondents is as shown in Table 5.

The study revealed that, the respondents have one to fifteen (1-15) years' number of years working experience with an average years and standard deviation as 2.43 years and 3.82 respectively with a coefficient variation of 1.57, suggesting that the average number of years of working experiences of the respondents is 2.43 years.

Table 1. Gender of the respondents.

Gender	Frequency	Percentage (%)
Male	14	82.35
Female	3	17.65
Total	17	100.00

Source: Field Survey, January, 2015.

Table 2. Ages of respondents.

Age	Frequency	Percentage (%)
25 Yrs	1	5.88
27 Yrs	1	5.88
29 Yrs	1	5.88
30 Yrs	2	11.76
32 Yrs	1	5.88
33 Yrs	2	11.76
34 Yrs	1	5.88
35 Yrs	1	5.88
37 Yrs	1	5.88
38 Yrs	2	11.76
40 Yrs	1	5.88
42 Yrs	1	5.88
No response	2	11.76
Total	**17**	**100.00**

Source: Field Survey, January, 2015.

Table 3. Statistics on respondents' ages.

	Statistics
Class Mean	33.50
Standard Deviation	5.21
Median	33.50
Coefficient of Variation	0.16

Source: Field Survey, January, 2015

However, about 65% of the respondents have not worked outside their current sector of engagement. That is only about 35% of the respondents have ever worked outside accounting and finance profession.

As put forward by Onumah et al. (2009), Agyei et al. (2013), Okafor and Otalor (2013) and Ramlugun (2014), adequate knowledge about auditors' responsibilities and duties as recommended by the legal status, international standards on auditing (ISA) and professional guidelines will greatly eradicate audit expectation gaps. The findings on the level of knowledge of the respondents on the responsibilities, roles, duties and what auditors are supposed to do are as depicted in Table 6.

The study revealed that 71% of respondents knew that it is not the responsibility of the auditor (s) to prepare the

Table 4. Educational background of respondents.

Education	Frequency	Percentage (%)
SSCE	0	-
O' Level	0	-
A' level	0	-
Diploma	0	-
Degree	16	94.12
Not Applicable	1	5.88
Total	17	100.00

Source: Field Survey, January, 2015.

Table 5. Number of years of working experiences of respondents.

Years of working experience	Frequency	Percentage (%)
1-5 yrs	5	**29.41**
6-10 yrs	10	**58.82**
11-15 yrs	2	**11.76**
16-20 yrs	0	-
21-30 yrs	0	-
31 & above	0	-
No response	0	-
Total	17	100.00

Source: Field Survey, January, 2015.

financial statements of their clients while about 29% did not know. That is though all the respondents have studied accounting and Forensic Auditing and Assurance in the course of their studies; about 29% did not know that it is not the responsibility of the auditor(s) to prepare the entity's financial statements. On auditor's guarantee for the audited financial statements' completeness and accuracy, 53% exhibited knowledge and awareness whereas 35% did not know. Interestingly, 6% indicated they are not sure. As aspiring accountants and auditors, they are expected to know what auditors do and what auditors' responsibilities are. Further, on auditor's verification of accounting transactions of the audit clients, the study revealed that about 65% of the respondents are of the view that an auditor should verify all transactions while 29% indicated otherwise. The mean response however is 4.25. In practice, however, due to voluminous nature of accounting transactions, auditors are most of the time constrained to use sampling techniques and judgments coupled with assessed inherent risks to determine the number of transactions to be verified during an audit.

The study also revealed that while 82.35% of the respondents agreed that auditors are responsible for verifying the estimates in the financial statements, 5.88% did not agree while 11.76% did not provide any response. Further, on errors, fraud, theft detecting and prevention

Table 6. Number of years of working experiences of respondents.

No	Variables	Frequency									
	The auditor's responsibility is:	**YES**	**%**	**No**	**%**	**Not Sure**	**%**	**No response**	**%**	**Total**	**Total (%)**
1.	To prepare the company's financial statements	5	29.41	12	70.59	0	-	0	-	**17**	**100**
2*.	To guarantee the complete accuracy of audited financial statements	9	52.94	6	35.29	1	5.88	1	5.88	**17**	**100**
3.	To verify every accounting transaction	11	64.71	5	29.41	0	-	1	5.88	**17**	**100**
4*.	To verify the accounting estimates in the financial statement	14	82.35	1	5.88	0	-	2	11.76	**17**	**100**
5.	To prevent fraud and errors in the company	5	31.25	10	62.50	0	-	1	6.25	**16**	**100**
6.	To detect all frauds and errors in the company	6	35.29	10	58.82	0	-	1	5.88	**17**	**100**
7.	To detect theft (other than petty theft) which has been committed by employees & directors	4	23.53	10	58.82	2	11.76	1	5.88	**17**	**100**
8.	To guarantee that a company whose financial statements have been given an unqualified ('clean') audit report is financially sound	10	58.82	5	29.41	2	11.76	0	-	**17**	**100**
9.	To plan the accounting and internal control system	5	29.41	9	52.94	3	17.65	0	-	**17**	**100**
10.	To interpret the financial statements to enable users evaluate whether to invest in the company	6	35.29	4	23.53	5	29.41	2	11.76	**17**	**100**
11*.	To performs his duties in accordance with the Companies code, 1963 (Act179), ISA, Ethical guidelines, engagement contracts etc	12	70.59	2	11.76	2	11.76	1	5.88	**17**	**100**
12*.	To obtain reasonable and material evidence in the performance of his audit work	9	52.94	2	11.76	4	23.53	2	11.76	**17**	**100**

Source: Field Survey, January, 2015. Note: * denotes auditors' responsibilities in accordance with regulatory and legal frameworks.

(65, 59, 59%) indicated that the auditor is not responsible for any of the above respectively. However, somewhat consistent with audit practice and norms as well as theories being taught, 71 and 53% agreed that auditors are to perform their duties in accordance with the auditing regulatory frameworks and to obtain reasonable and material evidence in the performance of their audit.

The inferential statistics on the findings as depicted in Table 6 regarding the respondents' knowledge and/ or awareness of auditors' responsibilities and what is expected of auditors are shown in Table 7. The mean knowledge of the respondents of what is and is not auditors' responsibilities is 4.25 with mean standard deviation and coefficient variation of 1.24 and 0.29 respectively. This implies that, on the average about four students out of a sample size of 17 final year MBA (Accounting) students know of auditors' responsibilities. That is only about 25% of the accounting students know for sure what auditors' responsibilities are. This confirms existence of audit expectation gap (Onumah et al., 2009; Agyei et al., 2013) even among MBA (Accounting) students in Ghana. The findings are very alarming to accounting and auditing profession in Ghana as well as accounting and auditing education in the Business Schools and Colleges of our universities in Ghana.

The primary focus of this study was to investigate audit expectation gap among the final year MBA (Accounting) students in one of the public universities in the Kumasi Metropolis, an emerging economy with the view to suggest how the gap among the students who are aspiring accountants and auditors can be elucidated and subsequently among the users of audited financial statements. The study thus established that, there does exist, audit expectation gap even among final year MBA (Accounting) students in Ghana.

The implications post by the findings of this study are very convoluted as it is a wake-up call

Table 7. Number of years of working experiences of respondents.

	Variables The auditor's responsibility is:	Mean	Stand. Dev	Median	Coeff. of Var
1.	To prepare the company's financial statements	4.25	5.68	2.50	1.34
2*.	To guarantee the complete accuracy of audited financial statements	4.25	3.95	3.50	0.93
3.	To verify every accounting transaction	4.25	4.99	3.00	1.17
4*.	To verify the accounting estimates in the financial statement	4.25	6.55	1.50	1.54
5.	To prevent fraud and errors in the company	4.25	4.99	3.00	1.17
6.	To detect all frauds and errors in the company	4.25	4.65	3.50	1.09
7.	To detect theft (other than petty theft) which has been committed by employees & directors	4.25	4.03	3.00	0.95
8.	To guarantee that a company whose financial statements have been given an unqualified ('clean') audit report is financially sound	4.25	4.35	3.50	1.02
9.	To plan the accounting and internal control system	4.25	3.77	4.00	0.89
10.	To interpret the financial statements to enable users evaluate whether to invest in the company	4.25	1.71	4.50	0.40
11*.	To performs his duties in accordance with the Companies code, 1963 (Act179), ISA, Ethical guidelines, engagement contracts etc	4.25	5.19	2.00	1.22
12*.	To obtain reasonable and material evidence in the performance of his audit work	4.25	3.30	3.00	0.78

Source: Researcher's Computation based on Field Survey, January, 2015.

for our universities administrators, policy makers and the regulators of accounting and auditing profession to relook at the auditing and accounting study and education again in various institutions.

Though this study cannot be said to be without limitations especially in respect to the sample size, it could be seen as one of the few pioneers that lead the way in studying audit expectation gap among final year MBA (Accounting) students in public universities in an emerging economy specifically Ghana.

CONCLUSION AND RECOMMENDATIONS

The results of this study confirmed the existence of audit expectation gap even among final year MBA (Accounting) students of a public university in Ghana specifically Kumasi, the capital town of Ashanti Region, an emerging economy. This calls for a closer look at accounting and auditing education in our business schools and colleges of universities in Ghana by policy makers and administrators of Teaching and Learning in Higher Education. Also, the lead role expected of ICAG as the regulator of accountancy and auditing training and licensing is being call upon. Based on the findings of this study, the researcher wishes to make the following recommendations. Firstly, the current syllabi in respect of auditing and accountancy courses in the business schools and colleges of the universities should be reviewed to ensure clear inclusion of the responsibilities, duties, roles of auditors and what auditing entails with conscious efforts to ensure that they are core part of examinations to ensure students make efforts to read and understand them. Also, the professional Accountancy Body in Ghana responsible for training, education, regulating and practice of accounting and auditing (that is ICAG) should liaise with the business schools and colleges of the Universities in Ghana. Also, the study recommended that policy makers, the university education administrators, regulators such as National Accreditation Board of Ghana together with the faculties take a closer look at Teaching and Learning of Accountancy and business Studies especially Auditing in Higher Education. This will help in a long way to correct the findings of the current study. Though this study adds to extant body of knowledge on audit expectation gap and thus fills the current research gaps on current issue more importantly in Ghana, it has some limitations such as, the smallness of the sample size and the use of only one public university in Kumasi instead of covering more public universities in Ghana. This may largely affect the validity of generalization of the findings. A Further study is therefore recommended in the near future to cover most of the universities in Ghana with larger sample size.

Conflict of Interests

The author has not declared any conflict of interest.

REFERENCES

Adeyemi SB, Oloowokere JK (2011). Stakeholders' perception of audit performance gap in Nigeria. Int. J Account Financ. Rep. 1(1):159-160.

Agyei A, Aye BK, Owusu-Yeboah E (2013). An Assessment of Audit Expectation Gap in Ghana. Int. J. Acad. Res. Account., Financ. Manage. Sci., 3(4):112-118.

Appiah KO (2013). Corporate Governance and Corporate Failure: Evidence from Listed UK Firms. PhD Thesis, Loughborough University, UK.

Best PJ, Buckby S, Tan C (2001). Evidence of the audit expectation gap in Singapore. Manage. Auditing J., 16(3): 134-144.

Chowdhury R, Innes J, Kouhy R (2005). The public Sector Audit Expectation Gap in Bangladesh. Manage. Auditing J. 20(8): 893-905.

Charitou A, Neophytou E, Charalambous C (2004). Predicting Corporate Failure: Empirical Evidence for the UK. European Accounting Review, 13(3):465-497.

Companies Code, 1963 (Act 179).

Dixon R, Woodhead A (2006). An Investigation of the Expectation Gap in Egypt. Manage. Auditing J., 3(21): 293-302.

Epstein M, Geiger M (1994). Investor Views of Audit Assurance: Recent Evidence of the Expectation Gap. J. Accountancy, 177(1): 60-66.

Fadzly M, Ahmad Z (2004). Audit Expectation Gap: The Case of Malaysia. Manage. Auditing J. 19: 897-915.

Gloeck JD, De Jager H (1993). The audit expectation gap in the Republic of South Africa. School of Accountancy Research Series. Research Report Volume 93, Number 1, University of Pretoria.

Godsell D (1992). Legal Liability and the Audit Expectation Gap. Singapour Accountant, 8: 25-28.

Humphrey C, Moizer P, Turley W (1993). The Audit Expectation Gap in Britain: An Empirical Investigation. Accounting and Business Research, 23: 395-411.

ICAG (2008). "Auditing and Internal review, Study Manual". Accra, Ghana, Black Mask Ltd.

Kim KA, Nofsinger JR, Mohr DJ (2010). "Corporate Governance". Third Edition, USA, Pearson.

Lee TH, Gloeck JD, Palaniappan AK (2007). The Audit Expectation Gap: An Empirical Study in Malaysia. Southern Afr. J. Account. Audit. Res. 7: 1-15.

Leung P, Chau G (2001). The Problematic Relationship between Audit Reporting and Audit Expectations; Some Evidence from Hong Kong. Adv. Int. Account. 14:181-206.

Libby R, Libby PA, Short DG, Kanaan G, Gowing M (2008). "Financial Accounting". (3rd Canadian Edition), McGraw-Hill Ryerson Ltd, Montreal, Canada.

Liggio C (1974). The Expectation Gap: The Accountant's Waterloo. J. Contemporary Bus. 3: 27-44.

Limperg T (1932). The Social Responsibility of the Auditor, Reproduced in Limperg Institute; (1985). The New Zealand, Limperg Institute.

Lin Z, Chen F (2004). An Empirical Study of Audit 'Expectation Gap' in The People's Republic of China. Int. J Auditing, 8: 93-115.

McInnes WM (1994). The audit expectation gap in the Republic of South Africa. Account. Bus. Res., 24:282-283.

Millichamp AH (1996). "Auditing" 7th Edition, London, UK, Letts Educational.

Noghondari AT, Foong SY (2009). Audit Expectation Gap and Loan Decision Performance of Bank Officers in Iran. International Journal of Accounting, Auditing and Performance Evaluation, 5(3):310–328.

Okafor C, Otalor IF (2013). Narrowing the Expectation Gap in Auditing: The Role of the Auditing Profession. Res. J. Financ. Account. 4(2):43-52.

Olagunju A, Leyira MC (2012). Audit Expectation Gap: Perspectives of Auditors and Audited Account Users. Int. J. Dev. Manage. Rev. Volume 7.

Omane-Antwi KB (2009). "Auditing Theory and Practice (The Auditing Compendium)". Tema, Ghana, Digibooks Ghana Ltd.

Onumah MJ, Nana Yaw, SS, Babonyire A (2009). The audit expectation gap concept: Examining views on auditors' reports from Ghana. Accounting in Emerging Economies (Research in Accounting in Emerging Economies, Volume 9. Emerald Group Publishing Limited, pp. 321-343.

Porter B (1993). An Empirical Study Of The Audit Expectation-Performance Gap. Account. Bus. Res. 24: 49-68.

Ramlugun VG (2014). Audit Expectation Gap: Evidence from Mauritius. Res. J. Econ. Bus. Stud., 3(5): 18-28.

Robertson C, McCloskey M (2002). "Business Statistics, Amultimedia guide to concepts and applications". Arnold, London, UK, pp. 91-92.

Saladrigues R, Grañó M (2014). Audit Expectation Gap: Fraud Detection and Other Factors. Eur. Account. Manage. Rev. 1(1): 120-142.

Watson D, Head T (1998). "Corporate Finance Principles and Practice". England, Pearson Education Ltd.

Investigating the use of the four perspectives of balanced score card (BSC) as technique for assessing performance by Nigerian banks

Mohammed Ibrahim

Department of Accounting, Gombe State University, Gombe, Gombe State, Nigeria.

This paper explores the use of BSC as technique for assessing performance in the Nigerian banking industry. The population of the study comprised 21 banks operating in Gombe State, Nigeria. A purposive sampling technique was adopted to arrive at the sample of eleven banks. A survey technique was used to obtain data for the study. Fifty five copies of questionnaire were distributed to the executive staff of the sampled banks (5 each to every selected bank), out of which forty three copies were duly completed and returned. Descriptive statistics and Kruskal-Wallis ANOVA was used as techniques for data analysis. The study concludes that Nigerian banks relied heavily on financial performance measures followed by customer performance measures as technique for assessing their performance. The study recommended that Nigerian banks should enhance their performance measurement systems by balancing their performance measures within the four perspectives of BSC. This will check the skewness of the CAMEL's rating approach (C = capital adequacy, A = asset quality, M = management quality, E = earning quality and L = liquidity), which uses financial measures to assess banks performance in Nigeria.

Key words: Balanced scorecard (BSC), bank, performance, performance measurement, Nigeria.

INTRODUCTION

Banks serve vital intermediary role in a market-oriented economy and have been seen as the key to investment and growth. Most studies have argued that the financial sector is vital for the socio-economic development of any country. For example, studies by Beck et al. (2000) and Levine (2003) suggest that a well developed and sound financial system can contribute significantly to economic growth by recognizing the important role financial intermediaries play in bridging the disequilibrium between savings and investment needs within an economy. They argue that economic growth can be sustained only if scarce resources are mobilized efficiently and transformed effectively into productive investments, and this function is efficiently conducted by the financial intermediaries. Furthermore, Hamid (2008) observes that a developing economy, like Nigeria, requires the services of a well-functioning banking system in order to realize its socio-economic objectives. Hussey (1999) posits that a bank is a commercial institution licensed as a taker of deposit and is concerned mainly with making and receiving payments on behalf of its customers, accepting deposits and making short-term loans to private individuals, companies and other organizations. However, pperformance measurement is an integral part of management accounting (Emmanuel and Otley, 1995). At present, management accountants do more management activity and less accounting dealing with costs (Burns et al., 2004). The position of manager or management accountant is now similar to that of an internal business consultant (Siegel and Sorenson, 1994).

Companies around the globe have stuck to the traditional measures of financial performance until in the late 1980s when increased globalised competition has forced them to consider non-traditional measures (Ghalayini and Noble, 1996). Furthermore, the operating environment and the nature of business operations have become increasingly future-orientated. This has recently set new requirements for management accounting to become more future and business-oriented, which in turn has led to the use of forward-looking accounting information including non-financial measures. The requirements of the customers keep changing and a satisfied customer today may be lost in the future if his changing requirements are not met. In order to retain the customer, therefore, his changing requirements must be satisfied by way of innovation in products, services and processes (Ahmed et al., 2011).

However, in order to adapt to internal and external changes, the method of monitoring performance should be dynamic. Kaplan and Norton (1992) developed an innovative multi-dimensional corporate performance scorecard known as the BSC. It provides a framework for selecting multiple key performance indicators that supplement traditional financial measures with operating measures of customer satisfaction, internal business processes, and learning and growth activities.

In both research and practice, the BSC has received much attention, particularly as a strategic performance measurement system in many industries, including hospitality, health, manufacturing and banking (Beechey and Garlick, 1999). In the same vein, BSC is a framework which has been widely used during the last decade for performance measurement in different disciplines (Lee et al., 2008; Luu et al., 2008). It has been observed that most of the successful organizations are adopting BSC (Rigby, 2001; Fernandes et al., 2006).

However, according to Etim and Agara (2011), despite widespread adoption of BSC, there appears to be no significant documentation on the translation of BSC in any Nigerian firm that could serve as a reference point for replication in spite of the success already recorded by companies that have implemented it. The study relating to BSC in Nigeria is the one conducted by Iwarere and Lawal (2011) which empirically evaluated the performance of facility maintenance of public organizations in Nigeria and recommended that public organizations in Nigeria should adopt four key aspects of the BSC that focus on four related perspectives of organizational and management performance such as financial performance measures; internal process; customer satisfaction and workforce support. In addition, Etim and Agara (2011) empirically explore how the strategic management performance model called BSC, has faired among firms that have introduced/adopted the model in Nigeria. They concluded that for Nigerian organizations to participate in the global economic arena, the adoption of BSC is imperative. The foregoing discussion suggests that there are relatively few empirical studies on the use of BSC as technique for assessing performance in Nigeria. It is against this bedrock that this study intends to examine the use of BSC as a technique for assessing performance in the Nigerian banking industry. Thus, this study hypothesized that Nigerian banks do not use all the four perspectives of BSC as technique for assessing performance. The paper is thus organized into five sections. Section one which is the introduction. Section two, which is the next section, reviews related literature on the subject matter of the study. Section three discusses the methodological issues of the paper, while section four presents and discusses the results obtained from the data generated for the study and finally, section five gives the conclusion of the paper.

The concept of performance

The term performance has been defined by different authors in different ways. According to Drucker (1954), when discussing the issue of performance, the issues of effectiveness and efficiency are interrelated and that efficiency refers to the ability of an organization to do things right, while effectiveness is about doing the right things. Kohli and Jaworski (1996) observe that organizational performance consists of cost-based performance measures, which reflect performance after accounting for the costs of implementing a strategy (profit measures), and revenue-based performance measures, which do not account for the cost of implementing a strategy (sales and market share). Aluko (2003) defines performance as the execution or accomplishment of work, tasks or goals to a certain level of desired satisfaction and that organizational performance is defined in terms of the ability of an organization to satisfy the desired expectations of three main stakeholders comprising owners, employees and customers. An institution that persistently makes a loss will ultimately deplete its capital base, which in turn puts equity and debt holders at risk. Moreover, since the ultimate purpose of any profit-seeking organisation is to preserve and create wealth for its owners, the bank's return on equity (ROE) needs to be greater than its cost of equity in order to create shareholders' value. Dauda (2010) highlighted that organization performance is determined by the demand for its product or services. Many organizations put in place methods and strategies that could enable them attract customers and improve the quality and quantity of their product.

From the foregoing definitions, it can be deduced that performance is the efficient and effective use of resources by an organization for the accomplishment of its objective or goal leading to increase in the following: share price, sales, market share, sustainable profitability, net present value, earnings, generating cash flows, risk-taking, leverage and demand of its product or service and satisfying the desired expectations of its three main stakeholders comprising owners, employees and customers.

The concept of performance measurement

Though the term performance measurement has been used since the late 1970s, there has not been a universally accepted definition for it. An aged saying indicates that what gets measured gets managed (Schmenner and Vollmann, 1994). Performance measurement is the process of ensuring that an organization pursues strategies that lead to the achievement of overall goals and objectives (Nanni et al., 1992). According to Cheng (2008), performance measure can be defined as the system by which an organization monitors its operations and evaluates whether the organization is attaining its goals. Besides, to fully utilize the function of the performance evaluation, it is necessary to set up a series of indicators that properly reflect the performance of the organization.

Given the aforementioned definitions, it can be inferred that performance measurement is multidimensional, comprising the ways and manners through which the operations of an organization overtime are monitored and assess with a view to determining whether the organization is attaining its goals in terms of value delivery to customers and other stakeholders.

The financial measures of performance

Financial measures have long been used to effectively evaluate the performance of business organizations. Financial measures are required by legislation and have been in existence for many years. All businesses, therefore, use some form of financial measurement systems. The term traditional performance measurement system, however, has been coined to describe performance measurement systems where the overall focus is financial and, as a consequence, the scorecard is dominated by financial-outcome-related measures. However, prior to 1992, various absolute and relative accounting measures were being utilized for performance evaluations. Prominent accounting measures were total income, operating profit, net profit, cash flows, return on investment, residual income, and value added income (Garrison et al., 2003; Kaplan and Atkinson, 2005; Horngren et al., 2006). Although the use of financial performance measures is important in performance measurement, there has been growing criticism of financial measures as they are historic in nature and lack futuristic outlook (Schoenfeld, 1986; Dearden, 1987; Emmanuel and Otley, 1995; Kaplan and Norton, 1996).

From the foregoing, despite the heavy criticisms of the use of financial measures of performance by companies, some organizations still consider it as the most effective tool for measuring performance. However, it is as a result of the heavy criticisms on the use of financial performance measures that some have argued for the inclusion of non-financial performance measures.

The non-financial measures of performance

Prior to the 1980s, management accounting control systems tended to focus mainly on financial measures of performance, where only those items that could be expressed in monetary terms were considered, while product quality, delivery, reliability, after sales service and customer satisfaction were not given prominence in the measurement (Drury, 2004). Also, Fisher (1995) states that there are three main reasons for the emergence of non-financial performance measures: the limitations of traditional financial performance measures, competitive pressures, and the growth of other initiatives. Chartered Institute of Management Accountant (2005) as cited in Agyei-Mensah (2009) defines non-financial performance measures as measures of performance based on non-financial information which may originate in and be used by operating departments to monitor and control their activities without any accounting input. Non-financial performance measures provide managers with timely information centred on the causes and drivers of success and can be used to design integrated evaluation systems (Kaplan and Norton, 1996; Banker et al., 2000).

From the above discussion, one can see that the proponents of non-financial measure of performance consider it to be the best measure of performance which focuses on the future performance rather than on historical information due to increasing competition, changing organisational roles, changing external demands and the power of information and communication technology.

The concept of balanced scorecard

French people began using a measure called "the tableau de board", or the dashboard of measure, which included both financial and non-financial measures (Stewart and Hubin, 2001). The emphasis on quality in the American continent during the 1980s made Canadian companies to include non-financial measures also in

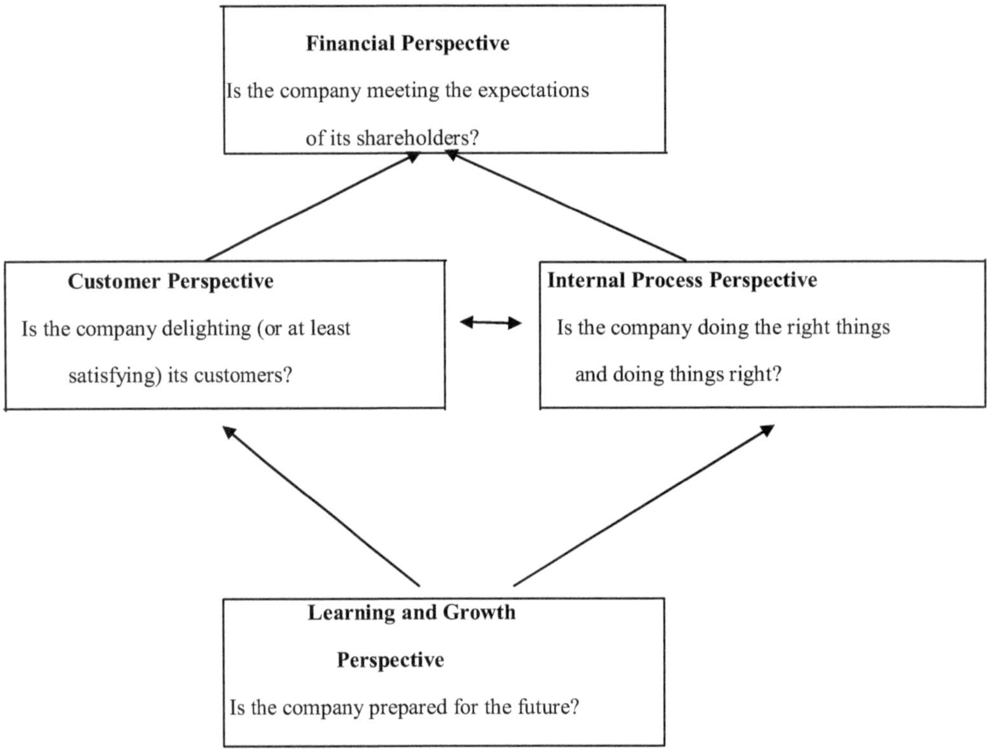

Figure 1. Four perspectives of BSC. Source: Kaplan and Norton, 1992 pp 136.

evolving their business strategy. This was the initial conception of the balanced scorecard (Stewart and Hubin, 2001). The BSC arose out of the need to improve the planning, control and performance measurement functions of management accounting. Because of the rise in popularity of the BSC, and benefits attributed to its use, Atkinson et al. (1997) state that the BSC is a significant development in management accounting that deserves intense research attention. French and the Canadians were the first to use the BSC in a different form. The BSC balances the financial indicators with non-financial drivers of performance. It allowed measuring the business performance in a more balanced way by considering both financial and non-financial measures (Ishtiaque et al., 2007).

Within the BSC framework, four categories of measures are identified in order to achieve balance amid the financial and the non-financial, between internal and external and between current performance and future performance (Kaplan and Norton, 1992). These perspectives are not mutually exclusive to one another; rather, they affect each other in quite a high degree as shown in Figure 1.

The financial measures typically focus on profitability related measures (the basis on which shareholders, in turn, typically gauge the success of their investments), such as return on capital, return on equity and return on sales among others (Kaplan and Norton, 1992; Lipe and Salterio, 2000). Measures that are closely related to customers include results from customer surveys, sales from frequent customers, and customer profitability. The customer perspective is a core of any business strategy that describes the unique mix of product, price, service, relationship, and image that a company offers (Kaplan and Norton, 2001). Out of the four BSC perspectives, the customer is at the core of any business and is crucial to long-term improvement of a company's performance (Kaplan and Norton, 1992; Pineno, 2002).

In addition, the internal process measures are typically based on the objective of most efficiently and effectively produced products or services that meet customer needs. For example, such measures may include order conversion rate, on-time delivery from suppliers, cost of non-conformance, and lead time reduction (Kaplan and Norton, 1996). Furthermore, Kaplan and Norton (1996) suggested that measures of employee capabilities, information systems capabilities and employee motivation and empowerment are examples of performance measures relating to learning and growth perspective. In the same vein, the innovation and learning perspective includes three broad constructs: human capital, measured by employee skills (Ellingson and Wambsganss, 2001; Libby et at., 2004; Ullrich and Tuttle, 2004) and know-how, organization capital measured by sharing of worker knowledge, shared vision, objectives and values, information capital measured by knowledge management capabilities and accessibility of information (Kaplan and Norton, 2004).

Empirical study on the use of BSC as performance indicators

Balanced Scorecard (BSC) is a framework which has been widely used during the last decade for performance measurement in different disciplines (Epstein and Wisner, 2001; Lawson et al., 2006; Idalina et al., 2007; Lee et al., 2008; Luu et al., 2008). It has been observed that most of the successful organizations are adopting BSC (Silk, 1998; Malmi, 2001; Rigby, 2001; Fernandes et al., 2006). In addition, increase use of BSC can be seen in recent researches like: in supply chain integration (Bhagwat and Sharma, 2007 Chang, 2009), research and development projects (Eilat et al., 2008; Asosheh et al., 2010), university performance evaluation (Wu et al., 2011). According to Kuang – Hua (2005), BSC is the most influential managerial concept in the last 75 years.

The use of BSC can be seen through several other similar studies. Malmi (2001) investigated how BSC is applied in Finish companies and why companies adopt it. The study document that BSC is used in two different ways. The first approach is management by objectives and the second is to use BSC as an information system. Also, the idea of linking measures together based on assumed cause-and-effect relationship was not well understood by the early adopters of BSC. In addition, Anand et al. (2005) analyzed the practice of the organizational performance management system of India with a focus on BSC from 2002 – 2003 using a survey method. The study finds that about 45.28 per cent of the companies are using BSC. Also, initiating the change process in the organization 50 per cent, broadening of the performance measures 45.8 per cent, and facilitating the integration of business plans with the financial plans 45.8 per cent are the major motivations for the implementation of BSC in corporate India. Similarly, Ishtiaque et al. (2007) conducted a survey in Bangladesh to identify the use of BSC and found that the number of hours spent for training per employee, on time deliveries, delivery cycle, throughput time and set up time are the performance measures used by the firms. They recommend that frequent in house and outdoor development sessions should have to be arranged and product and service innovations and modifications need to be encouraged and customer complaints need to be resolved quickly. Furtheremore, Ahmed et al. (2010) conducted a survey on commercial banks in Pakistan to know the extent to which the BSC was being applied. The study concluded that the commercial banks were using all the perspectives of the BSC without knowing that they were using them. Al-Matarneh (2011) conducted a survey to determine the ability of Jordanian industrial companies to apply the BSC for evaluating their overall performance and the availability of the necessary data for that. The results show that there is recognition by the Jordanian industrial companies of the importance of implementing the BSC in assessing their overall performance. They also found that the Jordanian industrial companies realized the importance of using the operational measurements (non-financial) for assessing their overall performance and they can afford the cost of applying the BSC and they have the necessary human resources to implement it. The study recommends that the Jordanian industrial companies should use the BSC as a means to rationalize the decisions of managers and guide their behaviour and performance evaluation and that the Jordanian industrial companies should attract experts from developed countries to apply the BSC. Moreover, Ahmed et al. (2011) conducted a survey to know what measures are used by the commercial banks in Pakistan to evaluate their performance within the four perspectives of the BSC. The study results show that: first, the common most financial measures used by the commercial banks in Pakistan are return on investment, percentage growth in revenue and profit per account; second, the measures for customer satisfaction are number of complaints, number of new customers and number of appreciation letters; third, the measures for internal process are improvement in response time to customers queries, introduction of new products and services, reduction in waiting time and number of new facilities, and lastly measures for learning and growth are feedback from employees, employees' suggestions, labour turnover and number of trained employees.

From the foregoing, the BSC has been applied by companies in both developed and developing economies cutting across various industries. But its application in the Nigerian context received little attention. This study, therefore, tries to fill this gap by studying the use of BSC in assessing performance in the Nigerian banking industry.

THEORETICAL FRAMEWORK

The theory that explains this work is the contingency theory of performance measurement. The contingency theory and contemporary performance measurement unlike the traditional approach to performance measurement where performance measurement is comparable across industries and measures are alike; contemporary performance measurement pays attention to particular characteristics of a company. Though BSC follows the same approach, they may only be comparable with one another. The actual choice of performance measures differs not only among companies active in different industries but also among companies competing within the same industry. These differences may stem not only from the fact that some managers conduct the affairs of their company so as to achieve only a satisfactory and not the maximum level of the objectives (Cyer and March, 1963). Or, as theory of limited rationality says, they may emerge because human beings differ in their abilities to process and understand large quantities of information.

Table 1. Descriptive statistics on the use of performance indicators under each of the four perspectives of BSC.

		Financial perspective	Customers' perspective	Internal process perspective	Learning and growth perspective
N	Valid	43	43	43	43
	Missing	0	0	0	0
Mean		4.1023	4.0047	3.3442	3.9256
Median		4.2000	4.0000	3.4000	4.0000
Mode		4.60	4.20	3.00	4.20
Std. Deviation		.57466	.53539	.63744	.68316
Minimum		2.60	2.40	1.80	2.40
Maximum		5.00	5.00	4.60	5.00

Source: Generated by the researcher using SPSS 19.0 from questionnaire response, 2012.

Contingency theory of management accounting can be used as theoretical foundations to explain these differences. The contingency approach to management accounting is based on the premise that there is no universally appropriate accounting system, which applies equally to all organizations in all circumstances (Otley, 1980). Since a performance measurement system is considered part of the management accounting system or at least depends on its part, the contingency approach to performance measurement can be formulated in the same way. It is based on the premise that there is no universally appropriate performance measurement system applicable to all organizations in all circumstances. Instead, a contingency theory attempts to identify specific aspects of a performance measurement system that are associated with certain defined circumstance and to demonstarte appropriate matching (Rejc, 2003).

METHODOLOGY

The study evaluates the use of BSC as a technique for assessing performance. The research focuses on all the twenty one (21) banks operating in Gombe State, Nigeria. A judgemental/purposive sampling technique was adopted to arrive at the sample of eleven (11) banks. A survey technique was therefore used to obtain relevant data for the study. This was done by means of questionnaire administered on the banks' executives. The questionnaire was adopted by the researcher from Kaplan and Norton (1996) approach, with some modifications. A five (5) item scale (Strongly Agree (SA) = 5 Points, Agree (A) = 4 Points, Undecided (UD) = 3 points, Disagree (DA) = 2 Points, and Strongly Disagree (SD) = 1 Point) was used to measure the respondents' views on the use of BSC as a technique for assessing performance. Furthermore, the questionnaire was administered directly by the researcher and his research assistants on the banking executives (Branch Managers, Operations Managers, Heads Customer Service, Marketing Managers and Branch Accountants) because it is believed that they are in a better position to provide the right information about how banks measure their performances.

The data generated for this research were first analyzed using Descriptive Statistics to ascertain the level of agreement or disagreement with the statement in the questions. Under the Descriptive Statistics, percentages, means, medians, modes, standard deviations, minimum points and maximum points were used in data analysis.

i. Mean value of 3.50 is benchmarked as minimum

ii. Minimum acceptable values for median and mode stand at 3.50

In addition, Kruskal Wallis Test was carried out to compare the perception of the banks on the four perspectives of the BSC, with a view to finding which of the four perspectives is given much attention by them. The Kruskal Wallis Tests were utilized because the study variables were not amenable to quantifiable measurements. Thus, this justifies the use of this tool for analysis. The Statistical Package for Social Sciences (SPSS) version 19.0 was used to carry out the analyses.

RESULTS AND DISCUSSION

The data collected in the study using questionnaire are presented and interpreted from which inferences were drawn. Of the fifty five (55) copies of questionnaire administered to the respondents of the sampled banks, forty three (43), representing 78%, were filled and returned, while twelve (12), representing 22%, were not returned. Table 1 presents the results of analysis of the use of the four perspectives of BSC as technique for assessing banks'performance.

Table 1 presents the elements of descriptive statistics on the use of performance measures under each of the four perspectives of BSC in assessing performance of banks in Nigeria. From the table, it can be seen that the modal and the median responses are high for all the four perspectives of BSC with the exception of the internal process perspective which has 3.00 and 3.4000 as its mode and median respectively. This implies that majority of the respondents opted for agreement and strong agreement with the statements on financial, customer and learning and growth perspectives of BSC.

However, there is low inclination toward internal business process perspective. Furthermore, it could be deduced from the table that the respondents place a major weight on the use of performance measures under financial perspective (mean = 4.1023), followed by customer perspective (mean = 4.0047), learning and growth perspective (mean = 3.9256) and internal process perspective (mean = 3.4884). The mean scores of financial, customer and learning and growth perspectives of BSC stand above cut-off value mean of 3.5000, and

Table 2. Kruskal Wallis test on the four perspectives of BSC.

Perspectives of BSC	N	Mean rank
Financial perspective	5	15.60
Customers' perspective	5	13.80
Internal process perspective	5	3.00
Learning and growth perspective	5	9.60
Total	20	

Source: Generated by the researcher using SPSS 19.0 from questionnaire response, 2012. Kruskal-Wallis Statistics KW = 13.474. P-value is 0.004.

this indicates a high score on the use of performance indicators under the three perspectives of BSC and low performance on the use of performance indicators under internal process perspective.

Moreover, the standard deviation around the mean value in all the four perspectives of BSC is insignificant. Even the internal process perspective which has the mean below the cut-off mean value, its standard deviation is still insignificant (.63744). Additionally, all the four perspectives have 5 as their maximum value and the minimum values of 2.60, 2.40, 1.80 and 2.40 for financial, customer, internal process and learning and growth perspectives, respectively.

The four perspectives of the BSC

This sub section compares the perception of the banks on the four perspectives of the BSC, with a view to finding which of the four perspectives is given much attention by them. The results are presented in Table 2.

Table 2 shows Kruskal Wallis Test of 13.474 and P-value of 0.004. This suggests that, there is significant variation by the respondents on the four perspectives of BSC. The table also indicates that financial perspective has the highest mean rank of 15.60 followed by customer perspective with a mean rank of 13.80 and learning and growth perspective with mean rank of 9.60. The internal process perspective has the least mean rank of 3.00.

The above discussion suggests that, the banks focus more on financial perspective followed by customer perspective and learning and growth perspective, but they put less emphasis on internal process perspective of BSC. This means that, on the average, Nigerian banks are utilizing financial, as well as, non-financial measures for their performance evaluation systems, without any formal recourse to the BSC. This finding correlates with the finding of Ahmed, Bowra et al. (2010) who conducted a survey on commercial banks in Pakistan and concluded that the commercial banks were following all the four perspectives of BSC without knowing that they were following them. Similarly, it is consistent with the findings of Anand et al. (2005) who found that the financial perspective of BSC has been found to be the most important perspective followed by the customer perspective and learning and growth perspective.

CONCLUSION AND RECOMMENDATIONS

In this paper an attempt was made to explore the use of BSC as technique for assessing performance by Nigerian banks. The concept of performance, performance measurement, financial and non-financial measures of performance and the concept of balanced scorecard have been discussed. Other issues such as the four perspectives of the BSC and empirical studies on the use of BSC as technique for assessing performance were also highlighted.

From the analysis of related literature, analysis and interpretation of data and results of hypothesis test, the researcher concludes that, for the fact that Nigerian banks relied heavily on financial performance measures followed by customer performance measures as a technique for assessing their performance, a comprehensive view of their performance cannot be guaranteed without incoporating all the four perspectives of BSC.

Lastly, Nigerian banks should enhance their performance measurement systems by balancing their performance measures within the four perspectives of BSC. This will check the skewness of the CAMEL's rating approach (C = capital adequacy; A = asset quality; M = management quality; E = earning quality and L = liquidity), which uses financial measures to assess banks' performance in Nigeria.

Conflict of Interests

The author has not declared any conflict of interest.

REFERENCES

Agyei-Mensah BK (2009). The Impact of Contingent Factors on Performance Measures in the Rural Banks of Ashanti Region of Ghana, Available at: http://ssrn.com/abstract=1960479 (Retrieved 22/12/2011).

Ahmed Z, Bowra ZA, Ahmad I, Nawaz M, Khan MS (2010). Balanced Scorecard: Is it a Spontaneous Performance Measurement Tool, Interdiscipl. J Contemporary Res. in Bus., 2(2): 99-10.

Ahmed Z, Bowra ZA, Ahmad I, Nawaz M, Khan MS (2011). Performance Measures used by the Commercial Banks in Pakistan within the four Perspectives of Balanced Scorecard, J Money, Investment and Banking, 21: 12-20.

Al-Matarneh GF (2011). Performance Evaluation and Adoption of Balanced Scorecard in Jordanian Industrial Companies, Eur. J Econ., Financ. Admin. Sci. 35:1-10.

Aluko MAO (2003). The Impact of Culture on Organizational Performance in Selected Textile Firms in Nigeria, Nordic J Afr. Stud., 12(2):164-179.

Anand M, Sahay BS, Saha S (2005). Balanced Score Card in Indian Companies, Vikalpa, 30(2):1-15.

Asosheh A, Nalchigar S, Jamporazmey M (2010). Information Technology Project Evaluation: An Integrated Data Envelopment Analysis and Balanced Scorecard Approach, Expert Systems with Applications, 37:5931-5938.

Atkinson AA, Balakrishan R, Booth P, Cote JM, Groot T, Malmi T, Roberts H, Uliana E, Wu T (1997). New Directions in Management Accounting Research, J Manag. Account. Res., 9: 79-101.
Banker RD, Potter G, Srinivasan D (2000). An Empirical Investigation of an Incentive Plan that includes Non-Financial Performance Measures, The Accounting Review, 75(1): 65-92.
Beck T, Levine R, Loayza N (2000). Finance and the Sources of Growth, J Financ. Econ., 58(1&2):261-300.
Beechey J, Garlick D (1999). Using the Balanced Scorecard in Banking, The Australian Banker, 133: 28-30.
Bhagwat R, Sharma MK (2007). Performance Measurement of Supply Chain Management: A Balanced Scorecard Approach, Computers & Industrial Engineering, 53: 43-62.
Burns J, Hopper T, Yazdifar H (2004). Management Accounting Education and Training: Putting Management in and taking Accounting out, Qualitative Research in Accounting and Management, 1(1):66-84.
Chang HH (2009). An Empirical Study of Evaluating Supply Chain Management Integration using the Balanced Scorecard in Taiwan, Service Industries J, 29: 185-202.
Cheng CB (2008). Performance Evaluation for a Balanced Scorecard System by Group Decision Making with Fuzzy Assessment, Int. J Appl. Sci. Eng., 6(1): 53-69.
Cyer RM, March JG (1963). A Behavioural Theory of Firm. Engliwood, Prentice-Hall, pp 332.
Dauda YA (2010). Employee's Market Orientation and Business Performance in Nigeria: Analysis of Small Business Enterprises in Lagos State, Int. J. Market. Stud., 2(2): 1918-7203.
Dearden J (1987). Measuring Profit Centre Managers, Harvard Business Review, 65(5): 84-88.
Drucker PF (1954). The practice of Management, Newyork, Harper & Row Inc.
Drury C (2004). Management and Cost Accounting (6th Ed.), London, Book Power.
Eilat H, Golany B, Shtub A (2008). Research & Development Project Evaluation: An Integrated Data Envelopment Analysis and Balanced Scorecard Approach, Omega, 36: 895-912.
Ellingson DA, Wambsganss JR (2001). Modifying the Approach to Planning and Evaluation in Governmental Entities: A Balanced Scorecard Approach, J. Public Budgeting, Account. Financ. Manage. 13(1): 103-120.
Emmanuel C, Otley D (1995). Readings in Accounting for Management Control, London, Chapman and Hall.
Epstein MJ, Wisner PS (2001). Using a Balanced Scorecard to Implement Sustainability, Environmental Quality Management, 11(2):1-10.
Etim RS, Agara IG (2011). The Balanced Scorecard: The new Performance Management Paradigm for Nigerian Firms, Int. J Econ. Dev. Res. and Investment, 2(3): 64-73.
Fernandes KJ, Raja V, Whalley A (2006). Lessons from Implementing the BalancedScorecard in a Small and Medium Size Manufacturing Organization, Technovation, 26: 623-634.
Fisher J (1995). Use of Non-financial Performance Measures, in Young, S. M. (ed),Readings in Management Accounting, Englewood Cliffs, Prentice Hall, pp. 329-335.
Garrison RH, Noreen EW, Seal W (2003). Management Accounting, New York, McGraw Hill.
Ghalayini AM, Noble JS (1996). The Changing Basis of Performance Measurement, Int. J Operations and Production Management, 16(8):63-80.
Hamid KT (2008). An Assessment of the Relationship between Corporate Governance and Internal Control System in the Nigerian Banking Industry, An Unpublished Ph. D. Thesis Submitted to the Department of Accounting, Bayero University, Kano, for the award of Ph. D. Degree in Accounting.
Horngren CT, Datar SM, Foster G (2006). Cost Accounting: A Managerial Emphasis. (12th Ed), New Jersey, Prentice-Hall Inc.
Hussey R (1999). Oxford Dictionary of Accounting, (2nd ed.), London, Oxford University Press. pp 43.
Idalina DS, Lucas R, Paula A (2007). Developing Sustainability Balanced Scorecards for Environmental Services: A Study of three Large Portuguese Companies, Environmental Quality Management, 16(4): 13-34.
Ishtiaque AA, Khan H, Akter S, Fatima ZK (2007). Perception Analysis of Balanced Scorecard: An Application over a Multinational Corporation of Bangladesh, J Bus. Stud., 28(2): 238-268.
Iwarere HT, Lawal KO (2011). Performance Measures of Maintenance of Public Facilities in Nigeria, Res. J Bus. Manag., 5(1): 16-25.
Kaplan RS, Norton DP (1992): Balanced Scorecard: Measures That Drive Performance, Harvard Business Review, 70(1):71-79.
Kaplan RS, Norton DP (1996). Using the Balanced Scorecard as a Strategic Management System, Harvard Business Review, 74(1): 75-85.
Kaplan RS, Atkinson AA (2005). Advanced Management Accounting. (3rd Ed), New Jersey: Prentice-Hall Inc.
Kaplan RS, Norton DP (2001). The Strategy Focused Organization: How Balanced Scorecard Companies Thrive in the New Business Environment, Boston: Harvard Business School Press.
Kaplan RS, Norton DP (2004). Measuring the Strategic Readiness of Intangible Assets, Harvard Business Review, 82(2): 52-63.
Kohli AK, Jaworski BJ (1996). Market Orientation: Review, Refinement and Roadmap, J Market. focused Management, 1(2):119-135.
Kuang-Hua H (2005). Using Balanced Scorecard and Fuzzy Data Envelopment Analysis for Multinational Research & Development Project Performance Assessment, J. Am. Acad. Bus., Cambridge, 7: 189-196.
Lawson R, Stratton W, Hatch T (2006). Scorecarding Goes Global, Strategic Finance, 87(9): 34-41.
Lee AHI, Chen WC, Chang CJ (2008). A fuzzy Analytic Hierarchy Process and Balance Scorecard Approach for Evaluating Performance of Information Technology Department in the Manufacturing Industry in Taiwan, Expert Systems with Applications, 34: 96-107.
Levine R (2003). More on Finance and Growth: More Finance, More Growth? Federal Reserve Bank of St. Louis Review, 85(4): 31-46.
Libby T, Salterio SE, Webb A (2004). The Balanced Scorecard: The Effects of Assurance and Process Accountability on Managerial Judgment, Accounting Review, 79(4): 1075-1094.
Lipe MG, Salterio S (2000). The Balanced Scorecard: Judgmental Effects of Common and Unique Performance Measures, The Accounting Review, 75(3): 283-298.
Luu TV, Kim SY, Cao HL, Park YM (2008). Performance Measurement of Construction Firms in Developing Countries, Construction Management and Economics, 26(4): 373-386.
Malmi T (2001). Balanced Scorecards in Finnish Companies: A Research Note. Management Accounting Research, 12: 207-220.
Nanni AJ, Dixon JR, Vollmann TE (1992). Integrated Performance Measurement: Management Accounting to Support the New Manufacturing Realities, J Manag. Account. Res., 4: 1-19.
Otley DT (1980). The Contingency Theory of Management Accounting: Achievement and Prognosis. Accounting, Organization and Society, 5(4):413-428.
Pineno CJ (2002). The Balanced Scorecard: An Incremental Approach Model to Health Care Management, J Health Care Finance, 28(4): 1-69.
Rejc A (2003). Traditional Versus Contemporary Performance Measurement: Evidence from Large Suvenian Companies. Economic and Business Review, 5: 117-135.
Rigby D (2001). Management Tools and Techniques: A Survey, California Management Review, 43(2): 139-160.
Schmenner WR, Vollmann ET (1994). Performance Measures: Gaps, False Alarms and Usual Suspects, Int. J. Oper. Prod. Manag., 14(12):58-69.
Schoenfeld HM (1986). The Present State of Performance Evaluation in Multinational, in Holzer HP, Schoenfeld HM (ed), Managerial Accounting and Analysis in Multinational Enterprises, Berlin, Walter De Gruyter Publishers, pp. 217-252.
Siegel G, Sorenson JE (1994). What Corporate America Wants in Entry-level Accountants, Management Accounting, 76(3):26-31.
Silk S (1998). Automating the Balanced Scorecard, Management Accounting, 79 (11): 38-44.
Stewart AC, Hubin JC (2001). The Balanced Scorecard: Beyond Reports and Rankings, Planning for Higher Education, 29(2):37-42.
Ullrich MJ, Tuttle BM (2004). The Effects of Comprehensive Information

Reporting Systems and Economic Incentives on Managers Time planning Decisions, Behavioural Research in Accounting, 16:89-105.
Wu HY, Lin YK, Chang CH (2011). Performance Evaluation of Extension Education Centres in Universities based on the Balanced Scorecard, Evaluation and Program Planning, 34: 37-50.

Canonical relationship between performance indicators based on Brazil, US and IFRS accounting standards of Brazilian and United Kingdom companies

Roberto Carlos Klann[1] , Ilse Maria Beuren[2] and Nelson Hein[1]

[1]Universidade Regional de Blumenau, Blumenau, SC, Brazil.
[2]Universidade Federal do Paraná, Curitiba, PR, Brazil.

The aim of the article is to identify canonical correlations among performance indicators calculated from a base of accounting statements prepared in accordance with United States Generally Accepted Accounting Principles (US GAAP), Brazilian accounting standards (BR GAAP) and International Financial Reporting Standards (IFRS). Descriptive research with a quantitative approach was carried out. A research sample of 50 companies was selected, including 17 Brazilian companies listed on the Bovespa's Board of Corporate Governance and 33 English companies listed on the London Stock Exchange, all of which trade American Depositary Receipts on the New York Stock Exchange. The results demonstrate divergence between companies and indicators in relation to differences calculated in performance indicators as well as statistically significant canonical correlations in both groups researched. The performance indicators of Brazilian and English companies were not affected in any significant way, despite divergences between BR GAAP and US GAAP and between IFRS and US GAAP. However, stands out as the main limitation that no company listed on Bovespa was found in the lists of European stock exchanges, which was necessary in order to verify the differences in these companies' indicators in the conversion of their accounting statements from BR GAAP to US GAAP and IFRS. This required the adoption of an alternative (i.e., canonical correlations). The main implication of this study is that the impact of IFRS adoption by Brazilian companies may be less than the expected, in terms of improvement of accounting quality and cost of adoption. The article advances research on a comparative study of the financial disclosures made according to Brazilian, American and international accounting standards, supported by an analysis of performance indicators calculated from accounting statements prepared from and based on these standards.

Key words: Performance indicators, accounting statements, BR GAAP, US GAAP, IFRS, canonical correlations.

INTRODUCTION

The separation between capital and management has brought asymmetric information problems, which in this study are analysed from an external investor perspective. The differences between what is shown to foreign and domestic investors can be configured as an asymmetric information problem within the scope of Agency Theory.

The publication of audited accounting statements is one example of how accounting information functions as a reducer of information asymmetry. Therefore, accounting plays an important role in the reduction of information asymmetry in the context of Agency Theory. However, it also confronts information asymmetry problems in its financial disclosures from the perspective of the accounting standards of other countries.

Disclosure and the harmonisation of accounting standards have been the objects of several studies over the past few years. Various international bodies have issued accounting standards, such as the Financial Accounting Standards Board (FASB), the Federation des Experts Comptables Europeens and the Confederation of Asian and Pacific Accountants. However, the one that stands out in terms of harmonization is the International Accounting Standards Board (IASB), which has been aligning accounting standards with the objective of eliminating information asymmetry in accounting.

The intention of this article is to advance research in this direction by means of a comparative study of the financial disclosures made according to Brazilian, American and international accounting standards. To this end, we analyse performance indicators calculated from accounting statements prepared from and based on these standards. The study seeks to identify the differences between the performance indicators of Brazilian companies, calculated based on the accounting statements provided to the São Paulo Stock Exchange (BOVESPA) and New York Stock Exchange (NYSE), and those of English companies calculated based on accounting statements sent to the London Stock Exchange (LSE) and to the NYSE.

Therefore, this study refers to firms of two countries (Brazil and England) based on three accounting statements (BR GAAP, US GAAP and IFRS). The choice of these two countries is a result of their contextual differences in terms of legal systems, importance of capital markets, investor protection mechanisms and quality of accounting education in addition to the characteristics of the accounting regulations in each country. These factors may contribute to a comparison of the differences between the information highlighted by companies based on local accounting standards and International Financial Reporting Standards (IFRS) in relation to performance indicators.

Brazil can be characterised by a legal system based on code law, with developing capital markets and rule-based accounting standards, while England has a legal system predicated on common law, strong capital markets and principles-based accounting standards. Thus, one can identify which of these two contexts presents greater information asymmetry between what companies evidenced to local stakeholders (local GAAPs) and to external stakeholders (IFRS).

Moreover, no studies have applied canonical correlation analysis to examine the differences in accounting information using performance indicators calculated on financial statements prepared based on different sets of accounting standards, in this case, BR GAAP, US GAAP and IFRS. This analysis can help determine the gain in accounting information quality through the adoption of IASB standards.

The use of canonical correlation analysis in this case is indicated by providing a broader perspective of the effects of different sets of accounting standards in relation to companies' performance indicators, which would not occur if the analysis were carried out by pairs, indicator by indicator.

Significant canonical correlations between the differences in the performance indicators of Brazilian and English companies would mean that the international accounting convergence process does not offer significant improvements to accounting information quality in relation to the disclosure of Brazilian companies. In this case, efforts towards convergence might be useless.

Put another way, the absence of canonical correlations between these differences could represent an opportunity to improve accounting information quality in Brazilian companies through the adoption of IASB standards.

Based on this, the following research question was designed: Are there statistically significant canonical correlations between performance indicators calculated from a base in accounting statements prepared according to BR GAAP and US GAAP and to IFRS and US GAAP? Therefore, the objective of the article is to identify canonical correlations between performance indicators calculated from a base in accounting statements prepared according to Brazilian and American accounting standards and to International and American accounting standards.

The article is structured as seven topics, starting with the introduction to the study. This is followed by a theoretical inquiry into the efforts made towards the harmonisation of accounting standards, the principal divergences in accounting standards on an international scale and performance indicators calculated from a base in accounting statements. Evidence of the method and procedures used in the research is then given. This is followed by a presentation of the results of the research, highlighting canonical correlations between the investigated performance indicators calculated from the three accounting standards. Finally, the conclusions of the research are presented.

Harmonisation of accounting standards and accounting quality

Several studies have examined the convergence of international accounting standards and the impact on accounting information quality. There are many approaches being used for that, such as earnings management, timely loss recognition and value relevance.

Since the 1980s, several international studies have sought to identify the quantitative impact of international accounting differences in different countries as well as interpret their causes using economic and cultural approaches (Gray, 1980, 1988; Weetman and Gray, 1990, 1991). Gray (1980) showed the tendency for companies in France and West Germany to be relatively conservative in earnings measurement compared with UK companies. Weetmann and Gray (1990) also found more conservative bias in earnings measurement under US GAAP compared with UK principles.

The adoption of IFRS by European Union countries since 2005 has increased international accounting convergence studies. Bartov et al. (2005) compared international and US standards and concluded that IFRS is a high quality set of accounting standards that is equivalent to US GAAP in terms of value relevance. Barth et al. (2008) examined whether the application of International Accounting Standards (IAS) was associated with higher accounting quality. They found that applying IAS generally leads to higher quality of accounting amounts. Daske et al. (2008) analyzed the effects of market liquidity, cost of capital, and Tobin´s q in 26 countries using a sample of firms that were mandated to adopt IFRS. Their results show increases in market liquidity, decrease in firm´s cost of capital, and increase in equity valuations.

On the other hand, Holthausen (2009) pointed out several factors that impact the financial reporting outcomes beyond the adoption of IFRS, as incentives, enforcement, ownership structure, and market and legal forces. Dechow et al. (2010) discussed the causes of various measures of earnings qualities have been used by researchers lately. They pointed out that the quality of earnings is a function of the firm´s fundamental performance, what is one area for future work.

More recently, Barth et al. (2012) examined whether application of IFRS by non-US firms results in accounting amounts comparable to those resulting from application of US GAAP by US firms. They concluded although application of IFRS has improved financial reporting comparability with US firms, significant differences remain.

Previous research tends to indicate that the adoption of IFRS has improved the quality of accounting information. The differences observed among accounting systems and the impact of IFRS adoption may be related to institutional factors such as the legal system (Ball et al., 2000), capital market development (Ding et al., 2007; Jeanjean and Stolowy, 2008), the country's economic development (Kang and Pang, 2005) and differences between local accounting standards and IFRS (Barth et al., 2008).

Leuz (2003) examined companies trading in Germany's New Market in 1999 and 2000. He found no differences in information asymmetry between companies using IAS and those using US GAAP. Bartov et al. (2005) also found no significant difference in the value relevance of US GAAP and IFRS.

Ball et al. (2000) found differences in the timeliness of the reporting of losses and conservatism based on whether companies are from a common law or code law country. Considering Brazil to be a code law country and England and the US as common law countries, we expect there to be no correlation between differences in performance indicators, when comparing BR GAAP with US GAAP and IFRS with US GAAP, which may mean higher or lower information asymmetry in the financial statements of Brazilian companies.

Lang et al. (2006) compared reconciled earnings for non-US companies with the earnings of US companies from 1991 to 2002. They found that companies from countries with weaker investor protection have less informative and more managed earnings, which can mean a lower quality of accounting information. Ali and Hwang (2000), Ball et al. (2000) and Hung (2001) all showed that in countries such as that, accounting quality and transparency are lower.

Nobes (1998) and Radebaugh et al. (2006) pointed out that differences in accounting systems exist because accounting needs differ among nations. Therefore, it would be expected that there is no correlation between differences in the performance indicators of Brazilian and English companies.

Bae et al. (2008) identified 21 key items to measure the compliance of local accounting standards to IASB standards, analysing the differences in 49 countries. They found that the UK has greater compliance between local accounting standards and IASB standards (of the 21 items analysed, only one was divergent). By contrast, Brazil had 12 differences from IASB standards. These results reinforced the expectation of no correlation between differences in the performance indicators of Brazilian and British companies when comparing BR GAAP with US GAAP and IFRS with US GAAP.

Thus, the following research hypotheses were formulated and tested by means of statistical analysis:

H_1: There is statistically significant canonical correlation between the performance indicators of Brazilian companies, calculated based on BR GAAP and US GAAP.

H_2: There is a statistically significant canonical correlation between the performance indicators of English companies, calculated based on IFRS and US GAAP.

There being no evidence to reject H_1 and H_2, it could be concluded that the differences between Brazilian and American accounting standards are similar to the differences between American and international accounting standards. It can then be inferred whether

Brazilian accounting standards are more or less adequate compared with American standards and international accounting standards.

Principal divergences in accounting standards on an international scale

Most studies of differences in international accounting standards point in the same direction, attributing such differences to the legal characteristics and systems of each country. Commenting on the probable motivations for different accounting practices in member countries of the European Community, Castro (1998) listed the following motives: cultural influence, level of governmental control, structure of property and amassing of capital and peculiarity in accounting principles.

According to Weffort (2005), the causes of different accounting practices can be classified as the characteristics and necessities of the users and preparers of information, the way that the society is organised, cultural aspects and external factors. This can be accompanied by asymmetric information. Depending on their locations, users can have different impressions of the same company. Table 1 shows the principal differences between the recommendations of the IASB, the FASB and the Brazilian Accounting Standards for the recognition and measurement of differences in the valuation of company resources.

The divergences presented in Table 1 can influence the value constants of accounting statements. The same company can present different compositions of assets and liabilities and divergent results when analysing its accounting statements sent to different markets or countries. These differences end up altering the values of performance indicators, which are calculated from these statements.

In conclusion, a company can present very different indicators of liquidity, indebtedness or profitability depending on the statements analysed. However, the calculation of performance indicators is part of the analysis of accounting statements, which seeks to extract this information from reports on the economic and financial situations of organisations.

RESEARCH METHOD AND PROCEDURES

The research carried out here is characterised as descriptive research. In this sense, this research sought to analyse the performance indicators of Brazilian and English companies for verifying the existence of canonical correlations between them.

In relation to its approach to the problem, research can be characterised as quantitative. This comparability of information is what allows for the quantitative analysis of data. Therefore, in order to apply it, the existence of a set of more or less comparable elements is indispensable.

The research population is composed of 81 Brazilian companies listed at Levels 1 and 2 in the New Market of Corporate Governance of Bovespa (www.bovespa.com.br) in January 2007 and 1,306 English companies (not necessarily made up of English capital but listed on the LSE) (www.londonstockexchange.com) in January 2007.

Initially, the intention was to compare Brazilian companies listed on Bovespa with those on a European stock exchange. However, no company listed on Bovespa was found on the lists of European stock exchanges. The intention was also to verify the differences in the indicators of these companies in the conversion of their statements from BR GAAP to US GAAP and IFRS. Since only companies that negotiate their shares on European stock exchanges were identified, which do not need to convert their statements into IFRS, this approach was compromised and the study took advantage of this second alternative.

In Brazil, companies listed at the Levels of Corporate Governance of Bovespa were selected, because they were considered to possess greater commitment to information transparency, thus transmitting greater reliability. In the case of English companies, we opted to use companies listed on the LSE as it has the greatest number of companies listed that need to publish accounting statements elaborated from a base in IFRS.

The sample selected for the research was of the intentional type in which, according to Richardson (1999), the elements of the sample are intentionally related according to the characteristics prescribed in the plan and hypotheses of the research. The criterion used was that sample companies negotiate American Depositary Receipts (ADRs) on the NYSE. Based on this, 17 Brazilian companies listed at the Bovespa Governance levels were selected along with 33 English companies listed on the LSE, making a total sample of 50 companies.

Data were collected by means of accounting reports sent to Bovespa, to the LSE and to the NYSE by the companies in the sample. Based on these reports, various economic and financial indicators related to the theoretical foundation of the work were calculated (Table 2).

Performance indicators were calculated based on the accounting statements of the Brazilian companies for 2005, sent to Bovespa and to the NYSE. Percentage differences were then taken between the indicators of the accounting statements sent to Bovespa and those sent to the NYSE. An identical procedure was then applied to the English companies, based on accounting statements sent to the LSE and NYSE. These performance indicators were chosen because they are the most important accounting indicators according Brazilian literature (used by analysts and investors from Brazil (Iudícibus, 1998;

Table 1. Principal differences between IFRS, US GAAP and Brazilian accounting standards.

Elements	Divergences in recognition and measurement
R&D expenses	IASB – generally recognised as a period expense. Activated only in specific cases (IAS 38). FASB – all R&D expenses must be taken as a result immediately, without exceptions (SFAS 2). BRAZIL – must be capitalised as an asset and amortised during the expected period of future economic benefits, no longer than 10 years.
Re-evaluation of Assets	IASB – is admitted for some specific assets. IAS 16 accepts re-evaluation as an alternative treatment in order to avoid material divergence between the cost and the respective economic market value. FASB – prohibits any type of re-evaluation. BRAZIL – permits re-evaluation, including negative. The proposal to modify corporate law foresees re-evaluation only in cases of corporate re-organisation.
Accounting of financial leasing	IASB – the essence must prevail over the form. The asset must be registered by the leaser as a fixed asset and it should correspond with a liability obligation (IAS 17). FASB – follows the same line as the IASB, but has criteria defined by characterising leasing as a financial operation. In this case, the contract must have at least one of these requirements: transference of the property of the asset to the leaser, a bargain buying price, the contractual period must be greater than 75% of the useful economic life of the asset or the present value of the minimum leasing payments must be greater than 90% of the marker value of the asset leased on the date when the operation began (SFAS 13). BRAZIL – are accounted as rent, in obedience to fiscal legislation, both for the lessee and the leaser.
Accounting of goodwill	IASB – goodwill acquired must be capitalised as an asset and amortised during the period of useful life, no longer than 20 years. In the case of wanting to adopt a period longer than this, the impairment test must be made annually. Internally generated goodwill cannot be capitalised (IAS 38). FASB – must be capitalised as an asset and subjected annually to the impairment test, taking it as the result of the difference between the determined value of the goodwill and what is effectively capitalised (SFAS 142). BRAZIL – treated as a premium, must be declared an asset and amortised according to its useful life, no longer than 10 years. Fiscal legislation permits the inclusion of goodwill as an asset that must be amortised up to five years.
Responsibilities for employee retirement benefit plans	IASB – accounting through a competence regime, with recognition of a passive actuarial and of a financial asset evaluated by fair value (IAS 19). FASB – similar to IASB standards (SFAS 87 and SFAS 88). BRAZIL – essentially observes IAS 19, starting in 2001, but only for public companies authorised by the CVM (Deliberation 371/00). Others adopt a cash basis.
Financial instruments	IASB – derivatives must be registered as resource items in the balance sheet, as assets and liabilities by fair value and, usually, adjustments to fair value must be recognised when they occur as a result, except those derivatives classified as hedges (IAS 39). FASB – standards identical to the IASB (SFAS 133). BRAZIL – only financial institutions subordinate to the control and inspection of the Central Bank adopt international accounting rules. Public companies are subject only to disclosure by explicative notes of market values – for options, futures, terms and swaps. Other anonymously owned companies, subordinate to Law n. 6.404/76, are not obligated to make any kind of disclosure of these instruments.
Stock-based compensation	IFRS – cost is recognised in earnings when service is received. US GAAP – refer exclusively to employee payments. Two rules are applied: intrinsic value or fair value. Cost is recognised in earnings on which the employee worked. BRAZIL – no clear rules regarding about its calculation or recognition, only minimum standards of disclosures in notes.
Treatment of pensions and post-retirement benefits	IFRS – require accounting for post-retirement and layoff benefits. US GAAP – present more detailed guidance for post-layoff benefits. BRAZIL – less distinction between defined benefit plans and defined contribution plans, not as treatment for insured benefits. Also, the non-recognition of a usable surplus of benefit plans as assets of the sponsoring company, among others.

Table 1. Cont'd

Valuation of inventory	IFRS – methods include FIFO and weighted average. Reversals of losses are allowed. US GAAP – methods include FIFO, LIFO and weighted average. Reversals of losses are not allowed. BRAZIL – methods include FIFO and weighted average. Reversals of losses are allowed. Inventories should be adjusted to market value when less than the carrying value.
Balance sheet	IFRS – does not define a specific format but requires segregation between current and non-current assets and liabilities. Presentation by order of liquidity is only preferable when presenting more trustworthy information (IAS 1). US GAAP – can present a classified balance sheet or not. Items presented separately generally follow a decreasing order of liquidity (APB Opinion n. 22). BRAZIL – assets and liabilities are divided into circulating and non-circulating groups and presented in decreasing order of liquidity within these groups.

Source: adapted from Niyama (2005, pp. 55–83) and PriceWaterhouseCoopers (2006, pp. 12–25).

Table 2. Performance indicators used in the research.

Indicators	Formula	Comments
Current liquidity (CL)	CL = CA / CiL	Where the acronyms CA and CiL denote short-term assets and short-term debts.
General liquidity (GL)	GL = (CA + LTRA) / (CiL + DLTL)	Where LTRA is Long-term Realisable Assets and DLTL is Demandable Long-term Liabilities (long-term debts).
Indebtedness (IND)	IND = TL / NW	Where TL is Total Liabilities (short- and long-term debt) and NW is Net Worth (capital invested by shareholders and bond investors).
Financial dependence (FD)	FD = TL / TA	Where TA means Total Assets.
Fixed permanent capital (FPC)	FPC = PA / (NW + DLTL)	Where PA is Permanent Assets.
Profitability of Net Worth (PNW)	PNW = NP / (NW – NP)	Where NP is the Net Profit of the exercise.
Return on Assets (ROA)	ROA = OP / (TA – NP)	Where OP denotes Operating Profit.

Source: research data.

Assaf, 2002).

Moreover, the existence of canonical correlations between the performance indicators of both groups was analysed (Bovespa and NYSE; LSE and NYSE). Canonical regression was developed by Bartlett (1938) as an extension of the canonical correlation analysis of Hotteling (1935, 1936). Whereas canonical correlation analysis focuses on "correlation between linear combinations of two sets of variables, canonical regression deals with the estimation of a regression equation that corresponds to the largest, or first, canonical correlation" (Estrella, 2007, p. 724). This correlation measures the degree of association that exists between two sets of variables (here, the secondary indicators of BR GAAP and US GAAP, IFRS and US GAAP). Thus, the regression is a generalisation of a multiple linear regression, or this is a particular case of the primary.

In the matrices $X_{17\times7}$ and $Y_{17\times7}$, we have the table of the 17 Brazilian companies and their seven respective accounting indicators. The matrices $W_{33\times7}$ and $Z_{33\times7}$ contain the table of the 33 English companies and their seven accounting indicators.

Concerning statistical inference, there is a test to verify whether the matrices X, Y, W and Z are correlated among themselves. However, this test is only applied when the vectors are normal multivariates. When multivariate normality is valid, it is also possible to construct statistical tests to evaluate the significance of canonical variables. As the software used in the article was the 5.1 version

Table 3. Percentage differences in performance indicators calculated based on the accounting statements remitted to Bovespa and the NYSE.

Percentage Difference in Indicators – 2005 (Bovespa to NYSE)	IND	FD	FPC	GL	CL	ROA	PNW
Aracruz Celulose & Papel S/A	0.38	0.17	0.02	-0.14	-0.12	-0.09	0.85
Banco Bradesco S/A	0.06	0.01	0.44	-0.00	-0.49	-0.55	-0.13
Banco Itaú Holding Financeira s/A	0.32	0.03	-0.53	0.01	-0.47	-0.38	0.20
Brasil Telecom Participações S/A	0.49	0.14	-0.13	0.01	0.20	1.01	-1.21
Braskem S/A	-0.30	-0.09	0.13	-0.06	-0.01	-0.40	-0.49
Cia. Brasileira de Distribuição	0.02	0.01	-0.02	0.05	-0.07	-0.64	-0.08
Cia. Energética de Minas Gerais – CEMIG	0.35	0.13	-0.05	0.02	-0.06	0.56	0.59
Cia. De Saneamento Básico do Estado de São Paulo – SABESP	-0.37	-0.18	-0.07	0.81	0.01	-0.11	-0.13
Cia. Vale do Rio Doce	0.38	0.17	0.03	-0.03	-0.25	0.05	0.13
CPFL Energia S/A	0.29	0.10	-0.04	0.02	0.00	-0.15	0.26
Gerdau S/A	0.06	0.02	-0.01	-0.00	-0.02	0.05	0.15
Gol Linhas Aéreas Inteligentes S/A	0.08	0.05	0.20	-0.09	-0.01	-0.14	-0.06
Perdigão S/A	-0.01	-0.00	0.03	-0.01	-0.02	-0.01	-0.01
Sadia S/A	-0.04	-0.01	0.08	-0.03	0.05	0.11	0.13
Ultrapar Participações S/A	-0.05	-0.03	0.05	-0.00	0.08	-0.08	-0.02
Unibanco Holdings S/A	0.05	0.00	0.04	0.01	-0.41	-0.58	0.19
Votorantim Celulose & Papel S/A	0.13	0.06	-0.01	-0.06	-0.08	-0.11	-0.15
Mean	0.11	0.03	0.01	0.03	-0.10	-0.09	0.01
Empresa	IND from Bovespa (1)		IND from NYSE (2)			Difference [(1 : 2) – 1]	
Aracruz Celulose and Papel S/A	1.26		0.92			0.38	

Source: research data.

of *Statgraphics*, these tests were already conducted by default.

Correlation and determination were effected through the use of the following formulas:

$$r = \sqrt{\frac{SQ(\mathrm{model})}{SQTotal(running)}} \Rightarrow r^2 = \frac{SQ(\mathrm{model})}{SQTotal(running)},$$

where SQ(model) denotes the sum of the squares referent to the model of regression adjusted to the data and SQTotal is the sum of the squares in their totality.One limitation of this research is that no company listed on Bovespa was found in the lists of European stock exchanges, which was necessary in order to verify the differences in these companies' indicators in the conversion of their accounting statements from BR GAAP to US GAAP and IFRS.

Another limitation results from the performance indicators chosen, since the results cannot be the same if the indicators differ from those selected. However, this is something that a future study with other research strategies can address.

Description and analysis of data

There were percentage differences in the performance indicators of Brazilian companies calculated based on the statements sent to Bovespa and the NYSE. Similarly, there were also percentage differences in the performance indicators of English companies based on the statements sent to the LSE and to the NYSE. Moreover, the existence of canonical correlations between performance indicators was assessed for both groups (Bovespa and NYSE, LSE and NYSE).

Percentage differences in performance indicators according to Brazilian standards

Performance indicators were calculated based on the 2005 accounting statements of Brazilian companies remitted to Bovespa and to the NYSE. Later, percentage differences between the accounting statement indicators remitted to Bovespa and those sent to the NYSE were recorded. These differences are presented in Table 3, which were calculated this way.

Table 3 demonstrates that the percentage variations in the performance indicators are heterogeneous; there are positive and negative variations. Furthermore, some companies have significant differences in particular indicators and irrelevant ones in other indicators. For example, Aracruz Celulose S/A has a positive variation in PNW of 85%. In other words, this indicator, calculated according to the accounting statements remitted to the NYSE, is 85% higher than the indicator calculated based

Table 4. Percentage differences in performance indicators calculated based on the accounting statements remitted to the LSE and the NYSE.

Percentage difference in indicators – 2005 (LSE to NYSE)	IND	FD	FPC	GL	CL	ROA	PNW
Abbey National	0.61	0.01	0.51	-0.01	-0.01	0.00	1.90
Amvescap	0.52	0.25	-0.02	0.00	0.00	0.26	0.48
Astrazeneca	1.20	0.66	-0.29	0.06	0.00	1.40	2.80
Barclays	0.12	0.00	0.03	0.00	0.00	-0.10	0.38
BP	0.09	0.03	0.00	-0.02	0.00	0.05	0.31
British Airways	-0.23	-0.05	0.03	0.05	-0.09	0.06	-0.48
British Sky Broadcasting Group	-26.00	0.38	-0.06	-0.04	-0.07	0.12	-1.39
BT Group	-1.13	-0.16	-0.04	0.15	0.03	-0.02	-2.30
Cadbury Schweppes	0.67	0.18	-0.01	-0.09	0.01	0.10	1.37
Corus Group	0.26	0.11	-0.02	-0.08	0.00	0.03	0.39
Diageo	1.46	0.42	-0.04	0.07	0.00	0.57	2.26
Gallaher Group	2.24	0.08	0.02	-0.06	-0.02	0.04	-1.60
Glaxosmithkline	2.73	0.76	-0.26	0.22	0.00	1.45	15.22
HSBC Holdings	0.01	0.00	-0.02	0.00	0.00	0.00	0.11
Imperial Chemicals Industries	-5.51	0.52	-0.12	-0.02	-0.03	0.57	-5.30
Imperial Tobacco Group	11.53	0.26	0.08	0.08	-0.07	0.32	-3.23
Intercontinental Hotels Group	0.37	0.15	-0.05	0.33	-0.02	0.67	1.58
International Power	0.05	0.02	-0.02	0.02	0.11	0.04	0.55
Lloyds TSB Group	0.08	0.00	-0.01	0.00	0.00	0.00	1.36
National Grid	1.01	0.03	0.10	-0.34	-0.35	0.59	-1.89
Pearson	0.05	0.03	-0.02	0.02	-0.01	0.08	0.82
Prudential	0.35	0.01	0.51	0.01	0.00	0.02	-0.15
Reed Elsevier	0.97	0.21	0.02	-0.04	0.00	0.18	1.76
Royal Bank of Scotland Group	0.13	0.01	0.07	0.00	0.00	0.00	0.47
Scottish Power	0.17	0.05	0.03	-0.07	-0.10	0.09	-0.23
Signet Group	0.65	0.37	-0.35	-0.13	-0.13	0.21	0.58
Smith & Nephew	0.15	0.07	0.01	-0.06	-0.02	0.04	0.24
Spirent Communications	-0.52	-0.16	-0.44	0.55	0.60	-1.91	-1.92
Tomkins	1.89	0.52	-0.21	-0.13	0.17	0.73	2.42
Unilever	0.77	0.17	0.01	-0.01	-0.01	0.21	2.65
United Utilities	-0.05	-0.02	0.02	0.15	-0.11	0.16	0.47
Vodafone Group	-0.52	-0.39	0.02	1.23	-0.09	0.38	-0.38
Wolseley	0.14	0.05	-0.04	0.00	-0.05	0.05	0.22
Mean	-0.17	0.14	-0.02	0.05	-0.01	0.19	0.59
Empresa	IND from LSE (1)		IND from NYSE (2)			Difference [(1 : 2) – 1]	
Abbey National	65.57		40.76			0,61	

Source: research data.

on the statements sent to Bovespa. On the other hand, Brasil Telecom Participações S/A presented a negative variation of 121% in this same indicator. Perdigão and Ultrapar had minimum variations of approximately 1 and 2%, respectively.

Percentage differences in performance indicators according to IFRS

The performance indicators for English companies were calculated based on their 2005 accounting statements sent to the LSE and the NYSE. Later, percentage differences between the accounting statements indicators sent to the LSE and remitted to the NYSE and those sent to the NYSE were recorded. These differences are presented in Table 4, which were calculated this way.

The percentage differences in performance indicators calculated based on IFRS in relation those based on US GAAP seem to be significant or not depending on the indicator and company analysed. For example, for the PNW indicator, we observe positive differences of

Table 5. Variables used for the analysis of canonical correlations.

indicator	bovespa	nyse	lse
CL	CL (SP)	CL (NYSE)	CL (LSE)
GL	GL (SP)	GL (NYSE)	GL (LSE)
IND	IND (SP)	IND (NYSE)	IND (LSE)
FD	FD (SP)	FD (NYSE)	FD (LSE)
FPC	FPC (SP)	FPC (NYSE)	FPC (LSE)
PNW	PNW (SP)	PNW (NYSE)	PNW (LSE)
ROA	ROA (SP)	ROA (NYSE)	ROA (LSE)

Source: elaborated for this article.

Table 6. Coefficients of the first canonical variables U_1 and V_1 for each case analysed.

Indicator	Vector a_1	Vector b_1	Vector c_1	Vector d_1
CL	-0.142026	0.000136	0.357904	0.347224
GL	0.255925	0.352222	0.125954	0.105145
IND	-0.529735	0.0433868	0.212702	0.237947
FD	0.107004	0.241373	-0.577028	0.545090
FPC	-1.318900	-0.856630	0.683714	0.626723
PNW	0.191667	-0.067966	-0.205875	-0.382328
ROA	-0.261411	-0.015583	-0.136117	0.123756

Source: research data.

1,522% for Glaxosmithkline and 280% for Astrazeneca. On the other hand, we can also see negative differences of 530% for Imperial Chemicals and 323% for Imperial Tobacco. This heterogeneity of differences can also be seen in the other indicators. Depending on the company and indicator analysed, there may or may not be significant distortions.

Analysis of canonical correlations between the calculated performance indicators

In order to carry out a global analysis of the impact of the divergences in accounting standards on a company's performance indicators, we analysed canonical correlations. The indicators calculated based on accounting statements prepared according to the standards of countries whose stock exchanges were used in the study were used as variables, as seen in Table 5.

Using the statistical software *Statgraphics* (version 5.1), the coefficients of the first canonical variables U_1 and V_1 were determined for each case analysed, as demonstrated in Table 6.

Table 6 presents four vectors: a_1, b_1, c_1 and d_1, with i = 1, 2, ..., 7 ("i" is an indicator of its sub-index). The vectors a1 and b1 (with i = 1, 2, ..., 7) establish the relationship between Bovespa (called SP) and the NYSE. The values listed in the a_1 and b_1 vector columns are the coefficients of each variable (CL, GL, IND, FD, FPC, PNW, ROA). The c_1 and d_1 vectors (where i = 1, 2, ..., 7) establish the relation between the NYSE and the LSE. The values listed in the c_1 and d_1 vector columns are the coefficients of each variable (CL, GL, IND, FD, FPC, PNW, ROA).

The canonical regression is also known as "first correlation" because it organises crossed regressions between the analysed variables (Timm, 2002). Therefore, it is possible to establish seven regression equations between each of the indicators analysed. However, there is no reason for analysing them all because only the first regression is important, since it has the highest correlation coefficient.

If the equation was calculated with the values of CL, GL, IND, FD, FPC, PNW and ROA for a company listed in Bovespa, the values were multiplied by each of their related coefficients, added (or subtracted, if they were negative), and then the same carried out for the NYSE, the result between U1 and V1 would be similar. Thus, this creates a relation that sets a cloud of data to another cloud of data. Thus, the first canonical variables were described between the values of Bovespa and the NYSE:

$U_1(SP) = -0.1420265\ CL(SP) + 0.255925\ GL(SP) + \ldots - 0.261411\ ROA(SP)$

and

$V_1(NYSE) = 0.000136\ CL(NYSE) + 0.352222\ GL(NYSE) + \ldots - 0.0155833\ ROA(NYSE)$

The coefficient of canonical correlation between these two groups of data is 99.88% (Table 7). Therefore, the performance indicators calculated based on accounting statements elaborated in BR GAAP are strongly related to those calculated from accounting statements elaborated in US GAAP.

Using an identical procedure, and taking the data between the NYSE and the LSE, we arrive at the following:

$U_1 = 0.0357904\ CL(NYSE) + 0.125954\ GL(NYSE) + \ldots - 0.136117\ ROA(NYSE)$

and

$V_1 = 0.347224\ CL(LSE) + 0.105145\ GL(LSE) + \ldots + 0.123756\ ROA(LSE)$

In this case, the coefficient of canonical correlation (also high) reached 99.22% (Table 8), which shows that a strong relationship exists between the indicators calculated from accounting statements prepared in IFRS and US GAAP.

Conclusions

The objective of the article was to identify canonical

Table 7. Canonical correlation coefficients of Brazilian companies.

Number	Eigenvalue	Canonical Correlation	Wilks Lambda	Chi-Square	D.F.	P-Value
1	0,997705	0,998852	8,97877E-11	196,635	49	0,0000
2	0,992839	0,996413	3,91197E-8	144,981	36	0,0000
3	0,992189	0,996087	0,00000546267	102,999	25	0,0000
4	0,965656	0,982678	0,00069933	61,7558	16	0,0000
5	0,931028	0,964898	0,0203626	33,0995	9	0,0001
6	0,534313	0,730967	0,295231	10,37	4	0,0346

Source: research data.

Table 8. Canonical correlation coefficients of England companies.

Number	Eigenvalue	Canonical Correlation	Wilks Lambda	Chi-Square	D.F.	P-Value
1	0,984409	0,992174	0,00000176399	324,574	49	0,0000
2	0,952385	0,975902	0,000113143	222,628	36	0,0000
3	0,935976	0,967459	0,00237623	148,035	25	0,0000
4	0,770145	0,877579	0,0371147	80,6967	16	0,0000
5	0,724752	0,851323	0,16147	44,6742	9	0,0000
6	0,399105	0,631748	0,586635	13,0672	4	0,0110
7	0,0237314	0,15405	0,976269	0,588429	1	0,4430

Source: research data.

correlations between performance indicators calculated based on three accounting systems (Brazilian, American and international). In terms of the global analysis of the impact of the divergences in accounting standards on companies' performance indicators, we found correlation coefficients of 99.88 and 99.22%, respectively, in the two related groups (BR GAAP and US GAAP, and IFRS and US GAAP). This indicates a strong relationship between the performance indicators calculated from accounting statements elaborated in BR GAAP and those calculated from accounting statements elaborated in US GAAP. It also shows a strong relationship between the indicators calculated from accounting statements prepared in IFRS and US GAAP.

The influence on performance indicators due to divergences between international and American accounting standards was greater than that observed between Brazilian and American accounting standards. These minor differences can be explained by turning to the historical origins of the sample countries. In Brazil, there has been a strong influence from Anglo-American audit firms, which came to the country bringing a strong tradition of audit procedures and manuals and the habit of training companies on accounting standards and procedures. These aspects have given the accounting procedures adopted in Brazil certain similarities to those established in US GAAP.

Concerning the research hypotheses formulated, the hypothesis $H_1$and H_2 are accepted based on the presented statistical analysis. H_1 presupposed statistically significant canonical correlations between performance indicators based on BR GAAP and US GAAP of Brazilian companies. H_2 did the same between performance indicators based on IFRS and US GAAP of English companies.

It can be concluded that, in a general way, the performance indicators of Brazilian and English companies are not affected in a significant way, despite divergences between Brazilian and American accounting standards and between international and American accounting standards. Therefore, the main implication of this study is that the impact of IFRS adoption by Brazilian companies may be less than the expected, in terms of improvement of accounting quality and cost of adoption. By comparing the canonical correlations of the sampled Brazilian and English companies, it can be stated that the relationship of the indicators calculated from accounting statements converted from BR GAAP to US GAAP is greater than those converted from IFRS to US GAAP. Therefore, based on the sample researched and performance indicators considered, greater divergences are noted between international standards and American standards than between Brazilian accounting standards and American standards.

However, the results of this research cannot be generalised, as they only relate to the sample of Bovespa and LSE companies surveyed and the considered indicators. The canonical correlations presented could have been affected by the length of samples, which when extended may increase or decrease the effects of the differences between accounting standards. The performance indicators selected may also have influenced the research findings, since relating the financial statements of groups of accounts depends on the consequences of applying different accounting standards. It is thus still necessary to consider that each company may present larger or smaller values in accounting amounts that are more or less affected by differences in accounting standards. Moreover, the value relevance and importance of any performance measures can differ from Brazil to England due to various factors, including the differences in the underlying accounting methods. Another limitation of our study is related to the year 2005 that may not be ideal, since this is the first year of mandatory adoption of IFRS in EU.

Conflict of Interests

The authors have not declared any conflict of interests.

REFERENCES

Ali A, Hwang L (2000). Country-specific factors related to financial reporting and the value relevance of accounting data. J. Account. Res. 38(1):1-21.

Assaf NA (2002). Estrutura e análise de balanços: um enfoque econômico-financeiro (7a. ed.). São Paulo: Atlas.

Bae K-H, Tan H, Welker M (2008). International GAAP differences: the impact of foreign analysts. Account. Rev. 83(3):593-628.

Ball R, Kothari S, Robin A (2000). The effect of international institutional factors on properties of accounting earnings. J. Account. Econ. 29(1):1-51.

Barth ME, Landsman WR, Lang MH (2008). International Accounting standards and accounting quality. J. Account. Res. 46(3):467-498.

Barth ME, Landsman WR, Lang MH, Williams C (2012). Are IFRS-based and US GAAP-based accounting amounts comparable? J. Account.Econ. 54(1):68-93.

Bartlett MS (1938). Further aspects of the theory of multiple correlation. Proceedings of the Cambridge Philosophical Society. 34:33-40.

Bartov E, Goldberg SR, Kim M (2005). Comparative value relevance among German, US, and International Accounting Standards: a German stock market perspective. J. Account. Audit. Financ. 20(2):95-119.

Bolsa de Valores de São Paulo (BOVESPA) (2007). Available as of January 3th, 2007, at http://www.bovespa.com.br/principal.asp.

Castro NJL (1998). Contribuição ao estudo da prática harmonizada da contabilidade da União Européia. Tese de doutorado não-publicada, Universidade de São Paulo, São Paulo, Brasil.

Daske H, Hail L, Leuz C, Verdi R (2008). Mandatory IFRS reporting around the world: early evidence on the economic consequences. J. Account. Res. 46 (5):1085-1142.

Dechow P, Ge W, Schrand C (2010). Understanding earnings quality: a review of the proxies, their determinants and their consequences. J. Account.Econ. 50(2-3):344-401.

Ding Y, Hope O-K, Jeanjean S, Stolowy H (2007). Differences between domestic accounting standards and IAS: measurement, determinants and implications. J. Account. Public Policy 26(1):1-38.

Estrella A (2007). Generalized canonical regression. Econ. J. 115(505):722-744.

Financial Accounting Standards Board (FASB). SFAS 2 Accounting for Research and Development Costs, Available as of April 20th, 2008, at http://www.fasb.org/st/summary/stsum2.shtml.

Financial Accounting Standards Board (FASB), SFAS 13 Accounting for Leases, Available as of April 20th, 2008, at http://www.fasb.org/st/summary/stsum13.shtml.

Financial Accounting Standards Board (FASB), SFAS 87 Employers' Accounting for Pensions, Available as of April 20th, 2008, at http://www.fasb.org/st/summary/stsum87.shtml.

Financial Accounting Standards Board (FASB), SFAS 88 Employers' Accounting for Settlements and Curtailments of Defined Benefit Pension Plans and for Termination Benefits, Available as of April 20th, 2008, at http://www.fasb.org/st/summary/stsum88.shtml.

Financial Accounting Standards Board (FASB), SFAS 133 Accounting for Derivative Instruments and Hedging Activities, June 1998, Available as of April 20th, 2008, at http://www.fasb.org/pdf/fas133.pdf.

Financial Accounting Standards Board (FASB), SFAS 142 Goodwill and Other Intangible Assets, Available as of April 20th, 2008, at http://www.fasb.org/st/summary/stsum142.shtml.

Generally Accepted Accounting Principles in the United States, Accounting Principles Board (APB) Opinion 22 - Disclosure of Accounting Policies, Available as of April 20th, 2008, at http://cpaclass.com/gaap/apb/gaap-apb-01.htm.

Gray SJ (1980). The impact of international accounting differences from a security analysis perspective: some european evidence. J. Account. Res. Oxford. 18(1):64-76.

Gray SJ (1988). Towards a theory of cultural influence on the development of accounting systems internationally. Abacus, Sidney. 24(1):1-15.

Holthausen R (2009). Accounting standards, financial reporting outcomes, and enforcement. J Account. Res. 47 (2), 447-458.

Hotteling H (1935). The most predictable criterion. J. Educ. Psycol. 26(2):139-142.

Hotteling H (1936). Relations between two sets of variates. Biometrika. 28(3-4):321-377.

Hung M (2001). Accounting standards and value relevance of earnings: an international Analysis. J. Account. Econ. 30(3):401-420.

International Accounting Standard Board (IASB), IAS 1 Presentation of Financial Statements, Available as of April 20th, 2008, at http://www.iasplus.com/standard/ias01.htm#2007sept.

International Accounting Standard Board (IASB), IAS 16 Property, Plant and Equipment, Available as of April 20th, 2008, at http://www.iasb.org/NR/rdonlyres/C10C2381-6B52-4C4A-92D4-7874C40040D0/0/IAS16.pdf.

International Accounting Standard Board (IASB), IAS 17 Accounting for Leases, Available as of April 20th, 2008, at http://www.iasplus.com/standard/ias02.htm.

International Accounting Standard Board (IASB), IAS 19 Employee benefits, Available as of April 20th, 2008, at http://www.iasplus.com/standard/ias19.htm.

International Accounting Standard Board (IASB), IAS 38 Intangible Assets, Available as of April 20th, 2008, at http://www.iasplus.com/standard/ias38.htm.

International Accounting Standard Board (IASB), IAS 39 Financial Instruments: Recognition and Measurement, Available as of April 20th, 2008, at http://www.iasb.org/NR/rdonlyres/1D9CBD62-F0A8-4401-A90D-483C63800CAA/0/IAS39.pdf.

Iudícibus Sde. (1998). Análise de balanços (7a. ed.). São Paulo: Atlas.

Jeanjean T, Stolowy H (2008). Do accounting matters? An exploratory analysis of earnings management before and after IFRS adoption. J. Account. Public Policy 27(6):480-494.

Kang T, Pang YH (2005). Economic development and the value-relevance of accounting information – a disclosure transparency perspective. Rev. Account. Financ. 4(1):5-31.

Lang M, Wilson W, Raedy J (2006). Earnings management and cross-listing: are reconciled earnings comparable to US earnings? J.

Account. Econ. 42(1-2):255-284.
Leuz, C. (2003). IAS Versus US GAAP: Information asymmetry-based evidenced from Germany's new market. J. Account. Res. 41(3):445-472.
London Stock Exchange (LSE). List companies. Available as of January 5th, 2007 ,at http://www.londonstockexchange.com/statistics/companies-and-issuers/companies-and-issuers.htm
Niyama JK (2005). Contabilidade internacional. São Paulo: Atlas.
Nobes C (1998). Towards a general model of the reasons for international differences in financial reporting. Abacus 34(2):162-187.
PriceWaterhouseCoopers (PWC). Semelhanças e diferenças IFRS x USGAAP x práticas contábeis adotadas no Brasil. Available as of November 21th, 2006, at http://www.pwc.com.br.
Radebaugh L, Gray S, Black E (2006). International accounting and multinational enterprises (4a ed.). New Jersey: John Wiley & Sons.
Richardson RJ (1999). Pesquisa social: métodos e técnicas (3a. ed.). São Paulo: Atlas.
Timm NH (2002). Applied multivariate analysis. New York: Springer Verlag.
Weetman P, Gray SJ (1990). International financial analysis and comparative corporate performance: the impact of UK versus US Accounting principles on earnings. J. Int. Finan. Manage. Account. 2(2):111-130.
Weetman P, Gray SJ (1991). A comparative international analysis of the impact of accounting principals on profits: the USA versus the UK, Sweden and the Netherlands. Account. Bus. Res. Kingston. 21(83):363-379.
Weffort EFJ (2005). O Brasil e a harmonização contábil internacional: influências dos sistemas jurídico e educacional, da cultura e do mercado. São Paulo: Atlas.

24

The market impact of mergers and acquisitions on acquiring firms in the U.S.

Ronald Stunda

Valdosta State University, U.S.

Previous studies have examined acquiring firms undergoing mergers and acquisitions along with the impact that these events have on firm security prices. These studies have had mixed results. Some indicate negative impact on stock prices while others conclude that there is a positive effect. This study extends these previous studies by increasing both the number of firms sampled and the years evaluated. The first finding indicates that when acquiring firms are compared to firms not engaged in M&A activities, the acquiring firms' stock price effect is significantly negative, while the non-M&A firms' stock price effect is significantly positive. When the acquiring firms are evaluated by industry membership, findings suggest that firms engaged in M&A activities in all industries evaluated exert a significantly negative effect on stock prices, with the exception of the oil and gas industry along with the banking and financial services industry. These two industries were found to have a significantly positive effect on stock prices. These findings are important because they provide investors, managers and others with additional insight to the effects of mergers and acquisitions, from the acquiring firm's perspective, on security prices. This study indicates that firms in certain industries may be more positively impacted, from a stock price perspective, than firms in other industries.

Key words: Mergers, acquisitions, security prices, acquiring firms.

INTRODUCTION

Wall Street dealmakers are off to a busy start to 2014, as some of corporate America's most recognizable names have become involved in multi-billion-dollar mergers and acquisitions (M&A). American Airlines and US Airways announced they would be merging in an $11 billion deal, while private equity firm 3G and Warren Buffett's Berkshire Hathaway announced a $28 billion joint acquisition of food conglomerate H.G. Heinz. These two deals follow a $24.4 billion leveraged buyout of Dell by private equity firm Silver Lake Partners and the firm's founder, Michael Dell.

According to data from *Deallogic*, U.S. companies have spent $219 billion on M&A in 2013, a sharp increase from 2012, when firms spent just $85 billion during the same period. The uptick in mergers and acquisitions is said to have begun during 2009, with a near doubling over the previous year (2008). In 2014, U.S. firms are on pace to have the biggest year in M&A activity since 2000.

While all this activity may have the potential of benefiting shareholders of acquired firms — as well as lots of Wall Street investment bankers — what does it say about the acquiring firms and the overall health of the economy? Since the later part of the 20th century, M&A has tended to come in waves, spurred by the availability of credit, changes in government policy, or bursts of private-sector innovation. Deregulation, for instance, motivated a wave of mergers in the airline industry in the 1970s and the consolidation of the banking industry in the 1990s. But perhaps the most important factor in motivating these bursts of M&A is economic conditions, particularly the strength of the stock market. Mergers in particular are often financed with stock, and high stock values give companies the resources with which to make purchases.

According to *Forbes Magazine* (3/7/14), the stock market has been doing pretty well for a few years now, with the Standard and Poor's (S&P) 500 up more than 138% since its bear-market lows of 2008. So why are we now seeing the M&A boom? Surely one reason is that today's market is heavily fortified by quantitative easing. *Forbes* goes on to state that the Federal Reserve has taken unprecedented action to keep interest rates low in both the short and long term, and those efforts have kept stock prices high despite the weak economy. In other words, given central bank stimulus, a rising stock market is not quite the indicator it used to be.

In addition to predicting M&A activity, the stock market is also considered a leading indicator of economic growth, meaning increases in GDP generally follow bull markets. This is because stock prices reflect investors' expectations for a company's future income. A high stock price today represents investors' belief in big profits tomorrow. Taken in the aggregate, a surging stock market index is a predictor of increases in GDP down the line.

Forbes is quick to point out that the huge gains seen in stock prices since 2009 have also not been followed by robust economic growth. It is noted that this is probably because Fed action has done more to promote stock price increases than economic fundamentals. But this is exactly why we should be encouraged by this fast start to M&A activity in 2014, especially if it keeps up in the coming months. It may mean that recent stock market gains are once again reflecting confidence about future profits, and not just central bank stimulus.

Recent empirical studies (Girma, 2008; Hu, 2009; Yen and Andre, 2010; Kemal, 2011; Chatterjee, 2011), as detailed below, indicate that M&A activity may in fact have a negative impact on the acquiring firm's profits and subsequent stock price. But yet, given what has been described above, it appears that M&A has in fact helped to lift the stock market, and ultimately, acquiring firms' bottom lines and stock prices. So what impact does M&A in fact have on the stock price of acquiring firms? To resolve this issue, individual mergers and acquisitions must be analyzed and their impact on security prices evaluated.

PURPOSE

This study examines the market response to mergers and acquisitions from the acquiring firms' perspective. As previously noted, data provided from *Deallogic*, indicate that mergers doubled from 2008 to 2009 and increased to 158% in 2013 over 2012. *Forbes* magazine indicates that the market impact of these activities have been confounded by the effect of efforts by the Federal Reserve. This study will seek to analyze M&A activities of acquiring firms in the U.S. over a selected study period (2009-2012) and compare the market price effect to similar size firms in the same industries not engaging in M&A activities over the same study period. In addition, the M&A acquiring firms' study period will also be related to a base study period (2004-2007) for the same firms when they were not in the M&A process. The analyses of these results will help us better focus on the market effect of mergers and acquisitions, and if, in fact, they will help lift the overall economy in the long run.

LITERATURE REVIEW

Over the decades, there have been several extant studies conducted on the effect of M&A activities. Holmstrom (2001) found that mergers and acquisitions of acquiring firms improved not only the productivity but the corporate governance mechanism of U.S. firms. Olinger et al. (2006) found that mergers and acquisitions in the U.S. rose during the period from 1980-1999 mainly due to leveraged hostile takeovers and buyouts. Kemal (2011) found that the effects of M&A activities on the acquiring firm included a worsening of financial ratios, particularly those relating to liquidity, along with a pronounced drop in security prices. Chatterjee (2011) also notes a reduction in security prices of acquiring firms in the U.S. possibly as a result of direct and indirect acquisition costs. Altunbas and Ibanes (2004), on the other hand, found evidence of improvement in acquiring firms' return ratios and security prices. Hu (2009) examines post-acquisition periods of acquiring firms and finds mixed financial results with some acquiring firms posting a worsening security price effect while others showing a positive effect. This finding is furthered by Girma (2008) who finds post-acquisition security prices higher for predominantly larger firms and negative for predominantly smaller firms, though the sample size is small. Some firms have abnormal positive returns while other firms have abnormal negative returns. Hu (2009) concludes that the industry and year of acquisition play a role in subsequent return on the acquiring firm.

From a profitability perspective, Mantravadi and Reddy (2008) found evidence that acquiring firms experience increases in profitability; however, the impact is strongest for firms in textile, banking and finance, and healthcare. Wong et al. (2009) conducted research focusing on security returns of acquiring firms, but their research was limited to firms in the Asian markets. Their findings indicated that the buying firms' market shares receive abnormal positive returns in periods after the M&A announcement. In contrast to this study, Yen and Andre (2010) surveyed a limited number of mergers and acquisitions in the U.S. and found that acquiring firms either suffer losses as the result of the activity, or at best, breakeven. Yen and Andre (2010) also found no evidence of immediate positive returns on security prices of the acquiring firms, and in fact discovered an associated decline in security prices among these firms, although corporate governance procedures seemed to improve.

One of the explanations of how such studies might have such differing results associated with mergers and acquisitions is offered by Williams (2010). Williams (2010) indicated that researchers often overlook the marketing synergies that may result from mergers and acquisitions, which lay at the heart of either failure or success of the endeavor by the acquiring firm. Williams (2010) found that horizontal integration offers the best chance at success and profitability of acquiring firms. Also, Williams (2010) discovered that the more established the acquiring firm is (that is, more long-lived) the greater likelihood it has of realizing increased profitability. Williams (2010) also notes limitations in time periods studied. Ismail et al. (2011) also suggest that reasons for conflicting results from various studies on M&A activities may be because of the scope (which is limited in both numbers of mergers and acquisitions and time frames covered) of the studies and most of the above studies focus on a single industry, with the exceptions of Hu (2009) and Mantravadi and Reddy (2008), which assess U.S. acquiring firms' security prices by industry for limited time periods. Also, Ismail et al. (2011) find that past studies do not adequately assess firm size or time in industry, both of which might have an effect on results.

Recent merger and acquisition literature is conflicted in its analysis of the results associated with acquiring firms. Some studies indicate a negative impact on the acquiring firm and its stockholders (Girma, 2008; Hu, 2009; Yen and Andre, 2010; Chatterjee, 2011; Kemel, 2011), while other studies find abnormal positive results (Altunbas and Albanes, 2004; Hu, 2009; Girma, 2008; Wong et al., 2009). Because M&A activities have hit new highs over recent years, it is important that we obtain a better understanding of the effect of such activities on the acquiring firm and their stockholders. This study will attempt to do just that by analyzing the effect of mergers and acquisitions on the acquiring firms' stock price by year and industry from 2009-2012, thus increasing the scope of the study and providing a broader base by which to statistically measure any security price impact of mergers and acquisitions on acquiring firms.

Hypothesis development

As previously noted, extant studies assessing the effects of mergers and acquisitions contain many varying results. These studies indicate minimal, negative and even positive impact on stock prices of acquiring firms. In order to better place in perspective the stock price effect of mergers and acquisitions, acquiring firms that have engaged in M&A activities between 2009-2012 are compared to similar size firms that have not engaged in M&A activities over the same period. This time period was selected because it represents the post-financial crisis period of the U.S. Economic recovery was said to have begun in the first quarter of 2009 (*U.S. Bureau of Labor Statistics*). By utilizing both increased sample periods and total numbers of firms (in continuance of the Ismail et al., (2010)'s study) and comparing to a control group of non-M&A firms, the results of this study can then be compared to past studies and assessed for areas of conformity and departure. This gives rise to the first hypothesis, stated in the null form:

H1: The share price responses to unexpected earnings of acquiring firms engaged in merger and acquisition activities is not significantly different from those of firms not engaged in merger and acquisition activities.

Some past merger and acquisition studies (Hu, 2009; Mantravadi and Reddy, 2008), which assess U.S. acquiring firms' security prices by industry for limited time periods indicate that the effect of M&A activities on security prices varies by industry, with certain industries showing a greater effect than others. In order to assess this phenomenon, the group of acquiring firms that have engaged in M&A activities between 2009-2012 is broken down by major industry and the industry effect is analyzed. This gives rise to the second hypothesis, stated in the null form:

H2: The share price responses to unexpected earnings of acquiring firms engaged in merger and acquisition activities is not significantly different when assessed by industry category.

Still other studies in the area of mergers and acquisitions attribute the effect of M&A activities on stock prices to time-specific metrics (Ismail et al., 2011; Williams, 2010). In order to assess this, a sensitivity analysis is conducted for both acquiring firms engaging in M&A activities during the study period 2009-2012, and firms not engaging in M&A activities during this same time period. These two groups of firms are then compared to a base study period (2004-2007). This study period was selected since it:

1. Represents a time period when mergers and acquisitions were slightly down in the U.S.; and
2. It represents a time period prior to the onset on the

Table 1. Sample of acquiring firms engaged in M&A activities, 2009-2012.

	Number of acquiring firms
Total U.S. firms	2,049
Firms eliminated due to insufficient Compustat data	123
Firms eliminated due to insufficient CRSP data	208
Total sample firms	1,718

Sources: EDGAR, Compustat, CRSP.

Table 2. Sample of acquiring firms engaged in M&A activities by industry 2009-2012.

Industrials	**301**
Oil/Gas	288
Utilities	244
Real Estate	229
Transportation	204
Banking/Financial Services	196
Healthcare	177
Other	79
Total sample firms	1,718

Source: Compustat.

Table 3. Sample of firms not engaged in M&A activities by industry 2009-2012.

Industrials	**290**
Oil/Gas	215
Utilities	199
Real Estate	150
Transportation	188
Banking/Financial Services	202
Healthcare	158
Other	98
Total sample firms	1,500

Source: Compustat.

financial crisis in the U.S. Results would provide additional information on whether the effect is time-specific. This gives rise to the third hypothesis, stated in the null form:

H3: The share price responses to unexpected earnings of acquiring firms engaged in merger and acquisition activities and those not engaged in such activities is not significantly different when compared to the same firms in a base study period.

Sample selection

The aim of this study is to investigate the share price behavior of publicly traded firms that are identified as the acquiring firm in a merger and acquisition in the U.S. A database was assembled for the study years 2009-2012 utilizing a Lexis-Nexis and Electronic Data-Gathering, Analysis and Retrieval (EDGAR) search. The database was compiled to capture all announced mergers and acquisitions along with the announcement release date. The availability of earnings and security return information was then assembled for these firms using Compustat and Center for Research on Security Prices (CRSP) data bases for earnings and security price information respectively. Table 1 indicates the total number of U.S. firms identified as the acquiring firm in a merger and acquisition activity. It also indicates the numbers of firms disqualified for insufficient Compustat and/or CRSP data for the study years.

Table 1 reflects the total sample of acquiring firms during a merger and acquisition during the study period 2009-2012.

In order to assess any industry differences among the acquiring firms, a further database was compiled detailing the above M&A firms by industry. Table 2 indicates the industry breakdown of the 1,718 firms in the study sample.

Table 2 reflects the acquiring firms presented in Table 1 broken done by major industry during the study period 2009-2012.

Because some prior studies indicate that the stock reaction to M&A activities of acquiring firms may perhaps be firm or time-specific, an additional sample is assessed of firms not engaged in M&A activities during the study period, that are the same general size and from similar industries. This sample consists of 1,500 firms identified by industry in Table 3.

Table 3 reflects a sample of similar firms not engaged in merger and acquisition activities during the study period 2009-2012. This sample is used for comparative purposes.

Although the above hypotheses and sample selection overcome deficiencies of past studies (that is, expanded sample, expanded time periods, more full analysis of industries and comparison to a base period), they do not overcome all of the criticisms posed by Ismail, et al. (2011) who find that past studies do not adequately assess firm size or time in industry, both of which might have an effect on results. To the extent these issues are not addressed, their absence poses a limitation to the overall findings of the study.

METHODOLOGY

Ordinary least squares (OLS) regression was used to test the models for all hypotheses. The reason for using OLS measurement was to remain consistent with the approach used by prior researchers (Williams, 2010; Kemal, 2001; Altunbas and Albanes, 2004; Holmstram, 2001), thus insuring comparability to prior studies. Cross-sectional dependence and heteroskedasticity are not likely to be present in stock return metrics since sample firms are not affected by common event dates (Binder, 1985; Bernard, 1987; Grammatikos and Yourougou, 1990). However, whenever a set of multiple regression variables are employed, there is a probability of the presence of multicollinearity within the set of independent variables which may be problematic from an interpretive perspective. To assess the presence of multicollinearity, the Variance Inflation Factor (VIP) was utilized. This approach was used in Hu (2009), Andre (2010), Kemel (2011), Ismail et al. (2010) and Wong et al. (2009). When the VIP factor exceeds a value of 10, multicollinearity is said to be present (O'Brien, 2007).

Hypothesis one methodology

The purpose of the test of the first hypothesis is to assess the relative information content of unexpected earnings to share prices in a cross sectional analysis of all 1,718 acquiring firms involved in merger and acquisition activities for the study period 2009-2012. In addition, an assessment of unexpected earnings to share prices in a cross sectional analysis of all 1,500 firms of similar size and industry not involved in similar M&A activities is also made during the same study period. The results of both groups are then analyzed for any similarities or differences. The following regression model (similar to that used in Williams, 2010; Kemal, 2001; Altunbas and Albanes, 2004; Holmstram, 2001) is used to test empirical results:

$$CAR_{it} = a + b_1UEM_{it} + b_2UENM_{it} + b_3MB_{it} + b_4B_{it} + b_5MV_{it} + e_{it} \quad (1)$$

Where: CAR_{it} = Cumulative abnormal return firm i, time t
A = Intercept term
UEM_{it} = Unexpected earnings for firm i, time t, for all merger firms in sample
$UENM_{it}$ = Unexpected earnings for firm i, time t, for all non-merger firms in sample
MB_{it} = Market to book value of equity as proxy for growth and persistence
B_{it} = Market model slope coefficient as proxy for systematic risk
MV_{it} = Market value of equity as proxy for firm size
e_{it} = error term for firm i, time t

The coefficient "a" measures the intercept. The coefficient b_1 is the earnings response coefficient (ERC) for all merger firms in the sample (1,718). The coefficient b_2 is the ERC for all non-merger firms in the sample (1,500). The coefficients b_3, b_4, and b_5, are assessed for any potential contributions to the ERC for all firms in the sample. To investigate the effects of the information content of earnings on security prices, there must be some control for variables shown by prior studies to be determinants of ERC. For this reason, the variables represented by coefficients b_3 through b_5 are included in the study. Unexpected earnings (UE_i) is measured as the difference between the actual earnings (EA_i) and security market participants' expectations for earnings proxied by consensus analyst following as per Investment Brokers Estimate Service(IBES) (EXi). The unexpected earnings are scaled by the firm's stock price (P_i) 180 days prior to the forecast:

$$UE_i = \frac{(EA_i - EX_i)}{P_i} \quad (2)$$

For each cross sectional sample firm, an abnormal return (AR_{it}) is generated for event days –1, 0, and +1, where day 0 is defined as the release date of the M&A activity identified by EDGAR. The Dow Jones News Retrieval Service (DJNRS) is also reviewed to insure that confounding factors, such as change of corporate ownership or form, or management change, are minimized by excluding any firms which contain these events. The market model is utilized along with the CRSP equally-weighted market index and regression parameters are estimated between –290 and –91. Abnormal returns are then summed to calculate a cumulative abnormal return (CAR_{it}). Hypotheses 1 is tested by examining the coefficients associated with the unexpected earnings of the two samples (that is, b_1, and b_2).

Hypothesis two methodologies

The purpose of the test of the second hypothesis is to assess the relative information content of unexpected earnings to share prices in a cross sectional analysis of all 1,718 acquiring firms involved in merger and acquisition activities by industry membership for the study period 2009-2012. This test will help determine if certain industries demonstrate stronger security price reaction while undergoing M&A activities. In assessing empirical results by industry, a regression model similar to the one used in hypothesis one, and in conformance with that used in Hu (2009) and Mantravadi and Reddy (2008), is replicated. The following model used is:

$$CARit = a + b_1UEI_{it} + b_2\,UEG_{it} + b_3UEU_{it} + b_4UER_{it} + b_5UET_{it} + b_6UEB_{it} + b_7UEH_{it} + B_8UEO_{it} + b_9MB_{it} + b_{10}B_{it} + b_{11}MV_{it} + e_{it} \quad (3)$$

Where: CARit = Cumulative abnormal return firm i, time t
a = Intercept term
UElit = Unexpected earnings for firm i, time t, for all industrial firms in sample
UEGit = Unexpected earnings for firm i, time t, for all oil/gas firms in sample
UEUit = Unexpected earnings for firm i, time t, for all utility firms in sample
UERit = Unexpected earnings for firm i, time t, for all real estate firms in sample
UETit = Unexpected earnings for firm i, time t, for all transportation firms in sample
UEBit = Unexpected earnings for firm i, time t, for all banking/financial services firms in sample
UEHit = Unexpected earnings for firm i, time t, for all healthcare firms in sample
UEOit = Unexpected earnings for firm i, time t, for all other firms in sample
MBit = Market to book value of equity as proxy for growth and persistence
Bit = Market model slope coefficient as proxy for systematic risk
MVit = Market value of equity as proxy for firm size
eit = error term for firm i, time t

Hypothesis three methodology

While hypothesis one assess differences on security prices among acquiring firms engaged in M&A activities versus those not engaged in M&A activities during the same time period, it does not adequately assess the effect of time-specific differences. In order

Table 4. Stock price effect of merger and non-merger firms, test of hypothesis 1.

a	b_1	b_2	b_3	b_4	b_5	Adj. R^2
.04	-.04	.07	.12	05	.19	.195
(.60)	(2.47)[a]	(2.59)[a]	(.38)	(.44)	(.29)	

Model: $CAR_{it} = a + b_1UEM_{it} + b_2UENM_{it} + b_3MB_{it} + b_4B_{it} + b_5MV_{it} + e_{it}$; b_1 = information content of all acquiring firms in the sample (1,718); b_2 = information content of all non-merger firms in the sample (1,500); b_3 = control variable for growth and persistence; b_4 = control variable systematic risk; b_5 = control variable firm size; a = significant at .01 level; study period = 2009-2012.

to assess this, a comparison must be made of the relative information content of unexpected earnings to share prices in a cross sectional analysis of all 1,718 acquiring firms involved in merger and acquisition activities for the study period 2009-2012 to the same firms in periods which they are not undergoing M&A activities (2004-2007). These results are then assessed against the relative information content of unexpected earnings to share prices in a cross sectional analysis of all 1,500 firms not involved in merger and acquisition activities for the study period 2009-2012 compared to the same firms in a similar base period (2004-2007). Results are then compared to help determine if time is a factor in determining the effect of stock price changes, thus overcoming the criticism of prior studies by Williams (2010), and Ismail et al. (2011). The following regression model is used:

$$CAR_{it}= a + b_1D_1UE_{it} + b_2D_2UE_{it} + b_3MB_{it} + b_4B_{it} + b_5MV_{it} + e_{it} \quad (4)$$

Where: CAR_{it} = Cumulative abnormal return firm i, time t
a = Intercept term
D_1UE_{it} = Dummy variable for unexpected earnings for firm i, time t, for all merger firms in sample where 1= 2009-2012, 0= 2004-2007
D_2UE_{it} = Dummy variable for unexpected earnings for firm i, time t, for all non-merger firms in sample where 1= 2009-2012, 0= 2004-2007
MB_{it} = Market to book value of equity as proxy for growth and persistence
B_{it} = Market model slope coefficient as proxy for systematic risk
MV_{it} = Market value of equity as proxy for firm size
e_{it} = error term for firm i, time t.

RESULTS

Hypothesis one results

Results for Hypothesis one are indicated in Table 4. Findings indicate that when assessing the impact of mergers and acquisitions from the acquiring firm's perspective for the time period 2009-2012, there tends to be a significant negative impact on stock prices of the acquiring firms, quite possibly as a result of associated high acquisition costs as posited by Hu (2009; Yen and Andre, 2010). Firms not engaged in merger or acquisition activities during the same period tend to reflect a significant positive impact on stock prices. This finding runs contra to extant research (Altunbas and Albanes, 2004; Girma, 2008; Hu, 2009; Wong et al., 2009), that indicates minimal to positive security price impact of acquiring firms. Hypothesis one, which suggests no difference between the two sample groups must, therefore, be rejected.

In addition, whenever a set of multiple regression variables are employed, there is a probability of the presence of multicollinearity within the set of independent variables which may be problematic from an interpretive perspective. To assess the presence of multicollinearity, the Variance Inflation Factor (VIP) was utilized. Values of VIP exceeding 10 are often regarded as indicating multicollinearity. In the test of hypothesis 1, a VIP of 1.2 was observed, thus indicating the non-presence of significant multicollinearity.

Table 4 reflects the results of the assessment of information content through the running of the regression formula above. For the total sample of firms engaged in mergers and acquisitions (b_1 variable) the Earnings Response Coefficient is negative (-0.04) and significant at the .01 level. For the total sample of firms not engaged in merger and acquisition activities (b_2 variable) the Earnings Response Coefficient is positive (0.07) and significant at the .01 level. This indicates that firms undergoing merger activities during the study period have a negative effect on stock prices while those not in the process of merger activities have a positive effect on stock prices. Other variables assessed in the model are not significant at traditional levels.

Hypothesis two results

As indicated in Table 5, the response coefficients b_1 through b_8 represent unexpected earnings for all acquiring firms engaged in M&A activities during the study period 2009-2012, broken down by industry. Only firms falling into the oil/gas and banking and financial services industries tend to have positive impact on se-curity prices at conventional significance levels. All other industries reflect a negative security price association at conventional significance levels. This result helps to clarify previous studies that reflect positive security price association while other studies reflect negative security price association. Clearly, when an industry analysis is conducted it is evident that some industries on whole reflect a move in one direction while other industries reflect a move in an opposite direction. These results could be as a result of the size of the firms in the industries or the duration of the firms in the industries

Table 5. Stock price effect of merger firms by industry, test of hypothesis 2.

a	b_1	b_2	b_3	b_4	b_5	b_6	b_7	b_8	b_9	b_{10}	b_{11}	Adj. R^2
.05	-.05	.10	-.08	-.15	-.11	.09	-.13	-.07	.08	.02	.15	.201
(.42)	(2.36)[a]	(2.41)[a]	(1.97)[b]	(1.59)[c]	(1.46)[c]	(2.40)[a]	(2.51)[a]	(1.96)[b]	(.35)	(.51)	(.24)	

Model: $CAR_{it} = a + b_1UEI_{it} + b_2 UEG_{it} + b_3UEU_{it} + b_4UER_{it} + b_5UET_{it} + b_6UEB_{it} + b_7UEH_{it} + b_7UEO_{it} + b_8MB_{it} + b_9Bit + b_{10}MV_{it} + e_{it}$; b_1 = information content for industrial firms; b_2 = information content for oil/gas firms; b_3 = information content for utility firms; b_4 = information content for real estate firms; b_5 = information content for transportation firms; b_6 = information content for banking financial services firms; b_7 = information content for healthcare firms; b_8 = information content for all other firms; b_9 = control variable for growth and persistence; b_{10} = control variable systematic risk; b_{11} = control variable firm size; a = significant at .01 level; b = significant at .05 level; c= significant at .10 level; study period = 2009-2012.

Table 6. Stock price effect of merger and non-merger firms compared to a base study period, test of hypothesis 3.

a	b1	b2	b3	b4	b5	Adj. R2
.05	-.03	.07	.11	.04	.22	.223
(.60)	(2.45)[a]	(.59)	(.36)	(.49)	(.21)	

Model: $CAR_{it} = a + b_1D_1UE_{it} + b_2D_2UE_{it} + b_3MB_{it} + b_4B_{it} + b_5MV_{it} + e_{it}$; b1 =dummy variable for information content of all acquiring firms in the sample (1,718); b2 = dummy variable for information content of all non-merger firms in the sample (1,500); b3 = control variable for growth and persistence; b4 = control variable systematic risk; b5 = control variable firm size; a = significant at .01 level; study period = 2009-2012 if D_1/D_2 =1, 2004-2007 if D_1/D_2 = 0.

which they comprise, as posited by Ismail et al. (2011). Hypothesis two, which suggests that the security price effect of acquiring firms engaged in M&A activities are not significantly different across industry must, therefore, be rejected. The Variance Inflation Factor (VIP) was again utilized to assess multicollinearity in the regression model. In the test of hypothesis 2, a VIP of 1.8 was observed, thus indicating the non-presence of significant multicollinearity. Table 5 reflects the results of the assessment of information content by industry through the running of the regression formula above. Only the oil and gas industry (b_2 variable) (.10) and the banking and financial services industry (b_6 variable) (.09) reflect an increase in stock prices while undergoing merger and acquisition activities during the study period. These results are significant at the .01 level. All other industries reflect a decrease in stock prices while undergoing merger and acquisition activities during the study period. Other variables assessed in the model are not significant at traditional levels.

Hypothesis three results

As indicated in Table 6, the response coefficient b_1 is a dummy variable that represents the effect of the unexpected earnings for all acquiring firms engaged in M&A activities during the study period of 2009-2012 when compared to a base period outside the time frame of the M&A activities represented by years 2004-2007. Coefficient b_2 represents a dummy variable indicating the effect of the unexpected earnings for all firms not engaged in M&A activities during the study period of 2009-2012 when compared to the same base period of 2004-2007. The b_1 variable is significantly negative, while the b_2 variable is positive but not significant at conventional levels. These results indicate that when varying time periods are assessed, acquiring firms engaged in M&A activities possess significantly negative security price effects while engaged in those activities relative to periods when they are not undergoing M&A activities. With respect to firms not undergoing M&A activities, time period differences are not significantly different with regards to impact on security prices. Hypothesis three, which suggests that the security price effect of acquiring firms engaged in M&A activities are not significantly different from those of firms not engaged in M&A activities across time, must therefore, be rejected.

The Variance Inflation Factor (VIP) was again utilized to assess multicollinearity in the regression model. In the test of hypothesis 3, a VIP of 1.9 was observed, thus indicating the non-presence of significant multicollinearity. Table 6 reflects the results of the assessment of information content of comparing firms engaged in merger and acquisition activities for the study period 2009-2012 (b_1 variable) compared to firms not engaged in merger and acquisition activities during a base period of 2004-2007 (b_2 variable) through the running of the regression formula above. For the total sample of firms engaged in mergers and acquisitions (b_1 variable) the Earnings

Response Coefficient is negative (-0.03) and significant at the .01 level. For the total sample of firms not engaged in merger and acquisition activities during the base period (b_2 variable) the Earnings Response Coefficient is positive (0.07) and significant at the .01 level. This indicates that the timing element for non-merger firms is inconsequential in associating with firms undergoing merger activities. Other variables assessed in the model are not significant at traditional levels.

Conclusion

The first finding indicates that when acquiring firms, totaling 1,718, are compared to firms not engaged in M&A activities, totaling 1,500, during the study period 2009-2012, the acquiring firms' stock price effect is significantly negative, while the non-M&A firms' stock price effect is significantly positive. Chatterjee (2011) finds that direct costs of the acquisition, such as the purchase price itself, along with indirect costs such as legal, accounting and other costs, may be responsible for some of the downward pressure on the stock price subsequent to the acquisition.

When the acquiring firms are evaluated by industry membership, findings suggest that firms in all industries evaluated exert a significantly negative effect on stock prices, with the exception of the oil and gas industry along with the banking and financial services industry. These two industries were found to have a significantly positive effect on stock prices. This could be as a result of firm size or duration in the industry as posited by Ismail et al. (2011).

In order to assess if time periods were a factor in sample differences, samples from both the acquiring firms and non-M&A firms for the study period 2009-2012 were compared against a base period when neither was undergoing merger or acquisition activities, 2004-2007. Findings suggest that for the non-merger sample, there is no significant difference between the time periods. However, for the acquiring firms' sample, the 2009-2012 period reflects significantly negative stock price effects as compared to the 2004-2007 base period. This could be as a result of the post-recession hype in acquisitions and loose Fed policies as posited by *Forbes*.

These findings are important because they provide investors, managers and others with additional insight into the effects of mergers and acquisitions, from the acquiring firm's perspective, on security prices. In particular are the results of the analysis of these firms by industry. This study indicates that firms in certain industries may be more positively impacted, from a stock price perspective, than firms in other industries. In other words, perhaps through the industry's sheer size of its firms or the length in the firms in those industries, some industries are able to overcome handicaps that place a drag on the security prices of other industries and their associated firms.

Conflict of Interests

The author has not declared any conflict of interests

REFERENCES

Altunbas Y, Ibanes D (2004). Mergers and acquisitions and bank performance. The Role of Strategic Similarities, September, 2011.

Bernard V (1987). Cross-sectional dependence and problems in inference in market-based accounting research. J. Account. Res. 25: 1-48.

Binder J, (1985). Measuring the effects of regulation with stock price data. R and J. Econ.16:167-183.

Chatterjee R (2011). Mergers and acquisitions: the impact on share price. J. Inst. of Manag. Stud. 11:123-148.

Girma S (2008). The impact of mergers and acquisitions on earnings and stock prices. J. Globalization and Labor Markets (Spring): 63-82.

Grammatikos T, Yourougou P (1990). Market expectations of the effects of the Tax Reform Act of 1986 on banking organizations. J. Bank. Financ. 14:1171-1187.

Holmstram B (2001). Corporate governance and merger activity in the U.S. J. Econ. Perspect.15:158-172.

Hu Y (2009). The long-term performance of acquiring firms. J. Int. Bus. pp.66-83.

Ismail A, Abdou F Annis C (2011). Industry differences associated with mergers and acquisitions. J. Int. Bus., September: 84-101.

Kemal M (2001). Post-merger profitability, a case of banks. Int. J. Bus. Social Sci. 5:22-41.

Mantravadi P, Reddy A (2008). Post-merger performance of acquiring firms from different industries. Int. Res. J. Financ. Econ. 15:44-67.

O'Brien R (2007). Rules regarding variance inflation factors, J. Qual. Quantity pp.673-690.

Olinger M, Chambers B, Nelson K (2006). Mergers and acquisitions lead to higher labor productivity. Am. J. Sociol. 87:35-47.

Williams J (2010). A case of merger and acquisition blind spot. Allied Acad. Financ. Stud. J. pp.15-29.

Wong B, Cheung K, Mun T (2009). The effect of merger and acquisition announcements on security prices of acquiring firms. Int. J. Econ. Financ. 2:119-132.

Yen T, Andre P (2010). The effects of ownership structure of acquiring firms. J. Bus. Policy Res. 5:59-76.

25

Ethics education in management accounting studies: Evidence from business schools in Ghana

Randolph Nsor-Ambala[1] and Joseph Mensah Onumah [2]

[1]Department of Accounting, Henley Business School, University of Reading, UK.
[2]Department of Accounting, University of Ghana Business School, Legon, Ghana.

Management accounting in recent times, and perhaps rightly so, has begun to gain recognition as a profession separate and complimentary to financial accounting. Evidence exists to suggest that management accountants are exposed to a unique set of ethical challenges within industry and that a significant high number of management accountants have engaged in unethical practices in performing their jobs. For the accounting profession as a whole, the growing number of corporate failures has created a credibility crisis that requires a deliberate intervention to mitigate. If this is not addressed sooner, the accounting profession stands the risk of losing relevance. Scholarship on ethical issues in accounting practice have either focused mostly on financial accounting or have sought to combine ethical issues for financial and management accounting. Various arguments have been made in recent times of the need to treat ethical issues in behavioural studies as context-specific and therefore separate ethical considerations in management accounting from financial accounting. This study adopts an approach, following various literature, that effective ethics education can help practitioners deal appropriately with ethical issues at the work place, and explores students' and faculty members' perceptions on current practices in ethics education. As expected, faculty and students differ significantly on a wide range of issues on ethics education in management accounting. Based on the insights provided from this study, appropriate recommendations have been made to improve ethics education in management accounting.

Key words: Management accounting, ethics education, ethics, accounting scandals.

INTRODUCTION

Even though most research on ethics have focused on general business ethics, rather than ethical issues on functional areas of management (Bampton and Cowton (2002a), research on accounting ethics has gained significant relevance in recent times perhaps owing to concerns around the credibility of organizational reporting vis-à-vis the spectacular corporate scandals and failures (Adkins and Radtke, 2004) as well as concerns about appropriateness of executive mitigating unethical behaviour in business practice (Loeb, 1998) with mixed results (Adkins and Radtke, 2004). Research on ethics has been on the increase, particularly in developed countries (Bampton and Cowton, 2002a).This surge in empirical studies on organizational ethical dilemmas have mostly taken place in developed countries with very few studies about business ethics in developing countries including Africa. Even in developed countries that have experienced phenomenal increase in academic attention to ethical issues, studies have raised concern that ethics education remains on the periphery and in most cases has not been comprehensively integrated into mainstream educational curriculum (Bampton and Cowton, 2002b).

Hopper et al. (2009) and Needles (1976) argue for contextual studies (in line with contingency theory) on behavioural issues to strengthen the generalization power of any given theory. Tsamenyi et al. (2004) and Hopper et al. (2009) call for more empirical studies on behavioural, social and developmental issues in Africa. Tsamenyi et al. (2004) and Hopper et al. (2009) particularly make a compelling case for further empirical studies on management accounting issues in Africa.

Hopper et al. (2009) argue that even though many contextual factors and issues may not be unique to developing countries, developing countries still remain largely distinctive such that it will be wrong to categorise accounting research about developing countries as 'exotic and irrelevant' to mainstream accounting studies. Hopper et al. (2009) argue for more research in management accounting in developing countries aimed at fostering understanding that encourages local solutions to local challenges rather than wholesale adoption of western proposed solutions based on alien values. Bampton and Cowton (2002a), and Armstrong (1993) argue that ethics education will be more relevant if it moves a step beyond general business ethics education into purposively-designed ethics curriculum integrated into the various functional areas (or subjects) of management such as management accounting. This may be effective in bridging the gap between ethics theory and relevant business practice and perhaps more helpful in improving general ethical behaviour vis-à-vis, the current trend of significantly high unethical and partially unethical management accountants in business practice (Evan et al., 2001).

Following the scholarly interest in business ethics and accounting ethics education, most business schools, at least in developed countries, have attempted to integrate business ethics into their curriculum (Loeb, 1998), even though the focus seems to be on general business ethics (Cole and Smith, 1995) with an approach to education that treats ethics as peremptory, with a lack of commitment from academics (Gunz and McCutcheon, 1998) resulting in relatively limited discussion of critical ethical issues in the classroom (Adtkins and Radtke, 2004). Duska and Duska (2003) argue for ethics education in accounting. Where research has attempted to explore ethical issues among financial and accounting practitioners, the focus has been on ethical issues in financial accounting and auditing (Shah, 1996), with very limited literature, albeit evolving, on ethical issues in management accounting (Amstrong, 1985). This skew poses a challenge in that studies on ethical issues in management accounting are equally relevant to general business practice and investor value growth especially following the recent scandals within public and private organizations that provide evidence of laxity in governance, breaches of control systems, and deliberate misreporting of managerial performance in order to earn underserved executive compensation (Armstrong, 1985). Management accountants face significant ethical dilemmas at work. Fisher and Lovell (2000), for instance categorizes 45 ethical issues that management accountants face at the work place.

Because management accounting is integrated into the management process and concerned with supporting managerial decision making around planning, resource accountability and control, competitive strategy, resource allocation and performance evaluation, it may be appropriate to posit that ethical issues in management accounting have a more pronounced effect on resource allocation, investment value, business success and effectiveness. Management accounting is quite distinct in purpose and operational methodology from financial accounting and therefore exposed to varied considerations of ethical issues. Indeed the creation of separate professional bodies of management accountants emphasizes this difference. As an example, financial accountants are governed by an established framework of regulations that perhaps provides a guiding framework for decisions involving ethical concerns. Management accounting on the other hand, has no set of standards or regulations on operational methodology and any efforts at developing a professional code of ethics is affected by this inherent limitation. Management accountants may therefore be more exposed to scenarios requiring ethical considerations on a regular basis than financial accountants; and more worrying, management accounting may probably involve more situations of unethical conduct (due to the absence of standards or regulations) than financial accounting. As well, if education in ethics can mitigate unethical behaviour in organizations (McNeel, 1994) and if this effect is more pronounced if education in ethics moves beyond general business ethics to integrating ethics into specific subjects related to the functional areas of management (Bampton and Cowton, 2002b), then more studies are required about ethics education in management accounting.

Research problem

Studies confirm that accountants lag behind other college graduates in moral development (e.g. Shaub, 1995). As well, the various accounting scandals may have created a credibility crisis for the accounting profession, which remains till today (Adkins and Radtke, 2004) and hopefully studies on ethics education may go a long way to help accountants regain their credibility and re-affirm their relevance.

This study attempts to explore current practices in ethics education in management accounting within the context of a developing country. Specifically, this study explores how ethical issues are integrated into teaching of management accounting in universities in Ghana.

Beyond the explicit relevance of further studies in ethics education in management accounting (Bampton and Cowton, 2002a), and in Africa (Hopper et al., 2009), the choice of management accounting was based on two further reasons. Firstly, this study ties into a broader study on business ethics the researchers are undertaking. Secondly, because management accounting, compared to financial accounting, ties in more easily with general business management (Bampton and Cowton, 2002a), studies on ethics education in management accounting lends itself more easily to borrowing from theoretical prepositions existing in the literature on general business ethics to explain any observations and findings.

This study adds to the growing literature on business ethics by focusing on a scarcely researched subject area (ethics education in management accounting), in Africa. Despite the numerous calls for more empirical studies in Africa, very little of such studies take place. With the attention Africa is receiving from multinational organisations and private investors, following the economic crisis in western economies, relevant empirical studies are required to guide government policy and business decisions.

Africa as a place of inquiry presents an intriguing set of challenges and opportunities. Africa presents an opportunity for new knowledge that, perhaps, may have a greater positive correlation with social development than in advanced countries. If the purpose of research is to promote social development and human progress, then a compelling case arises for continuous empirical studies in Africa.

The rest of the study is organised as follows. The next section discusses the conceptual basis and the existing literature relevant to this study. The third section discusses the research methodology. The fourth section presents the research findings. Section five presents the conclusions of the study, possible limitations of the research and makes recommendations as well as suggestions for future research.

LITERATURE REVIEW AND CONCEPTUAL BASIS

Adkins and Radtke (2004) compare the perception of students to faculty members regarding the relevance of business ethics and accounting ethics education and find that students attach more importance to both business ethics and the goals of accounting ethics education than faculty members. Albrecht and Sack (2000) as well as various accounting professional bodies have emphasized the need for increased discussions of ethical issues in the class room. McNeel (1994) find evidence that ethics education can positively influence moral development especially during business practice.

Stevens et al. (1993) argue that more studies have investigated students' perception of ethical issues (Cole and Smith, 1995) than faculty members' perception. Adkins and Radtke (2004) argue that even for the few studies that have compared students' perception on ethical issues with faculty members' perception (Stevens et al., 1993; Cole and Smith, 1995), none performs the comparative analysis using matched data based on the same survey instrument.

Stevens et al. (1993) find evidence to suggest that students' perception on ethical issues are significantly influenced by faculty members especially during student faculty interactions, because most students see faculty members as role models and mentors with more information and awareness on professional ethical standards and recent accounting scandals (Adkins and Radtke, 2004). If students' perception on ethical issues are heavily influenced by faculty members, then it is safe to posit that if lecturers spend less time engaging students with discussions on ethical issues, students may assume that such issues are either irrelevant in real business practice, or may not be in a position to make the right ethical choices when confronted with real life issues within an organisation.

Various studies confirm that women are generally more ethical and take ethical issues more seriously (Arlow, 1991). Several studies also find that relatively older persons take ethical issues more seriously (Deshpande, 1997).

Research on ethical behaviour in management accounting is still evolving. Mihalek et al. (1987) find evidence to suggest that a significant number of management accountants have engaged in report manipulation due to organizational pressure and inadequate exposure to a code of ethics. Evans et al. (2001) find evidence to suggest that most management accountants, within organizations are dishonest and partially honest rather than totally honest in their reporting behaviour to their superiors. Studies have confirmed that management accountants engaging in budget slacking and/or padding (Hopwood 1972), knowingly attribute managerial failures and other corporate failures to the wrong reasons such as "unforeseen or uncontrollable events" and deliberately delay the submission of reports with the intention to shift stakeholder interest, and, consciously use technical jargons, sophisticated numbers etc, to confuse stakeholders. Various reasons account for this behavioural orientation and include monetary motivation as well as organizational contextual factors, environmental factors and personality traits. Irrespective of the reason, the concerning trend of not totally honest reporting behaviour among management accountants is worrying and may imply that the quality of managerial decision making around competitive strategy and resources allocation are inefficient with direct adverse effect on investor value.

Bampton and Cowton (2002a) study practices around ethics education in management accounting in a developed country (UK) and find a surprisingly low level of ethics education either explicitly or implicitly in management accounting modules. Despite the attempt by Business schools to incorporate ethics education, in some form at least, into the school curriculum, there are still challenges with the methods employed to teach ethics. Saul (1981) for instance argues that efforts at emphasizing relevance for ethics education in Business schools, is more an attempt to impress the external public and not a genuine desire to mainstream ethics education. Kahn (1990) argues that the lack of genuine efforts to mainstream ethics education re-enforces the gap between 'practical ethics' and academia. Kahn (1990) argues that whereas traditional academic studies on ethics serve a normative purpose, organizational ethics represents a more contextual study of ethics such that even though equally relevant, are more effective if approached differently. Mintz (1990) finds evidence to suggest that ethics is not appropriately integrated into management accounting courses and leading textbooks do not adequately cover ethics. Hajjawi (2008) finds similar results in Palestine universities.

Several studies have shown a positive relationship between ethics education and ethical behaviour at the work place (Jaffe and Tsimerman, 2005). Jaffe and Tsimerman (2005) argue that the ethical behaviour of future organisational leaders can be positively influenced by comprehensive ethics education of current students because current students made future business leaders.

RESEARCH METHODOLOGY

This study employs a survey method, using self-administered semi-structured questionnaires (with a mix of closed-ended and opened-ended questions) to explore the extent of coverage of ethical issues in management accounting education among universities in Ghana. The use of questionnaires in behavioural studies in financial and management accounting is well documented (Bampton and Cowton, 2002a, Adkins and Radtke, 2004). Concerns about social desirable response bias, that often affects most behavioural studies in accounting, will be mitigated because the questions asked are not personal (Randall and Gibson, 1990). To improve the internal validity of the questionnaire, it was piloted among some PhD students and amended based on suggestions provided.

The issues examined by the questionnaire are broadly grouped into four. The first section explores teaching practices on management accounting in Ghana. This is an attempt to replicate the studies by Bampton and Cowton (2002a) in Ghana. However this study deviates from Bampton and Cowton's (2002a) in that it measures ethics education from the perspective of both the student and the faculty members, using matched data from the same survey questions. Issues examined include the extent to which management accounting ethics is included in degree courses, whether it is integrated into existing courses or taught separately, which issues are addressed, and challenges faced in management accounting ethics education.

The section after this attempts to measure students' and faculty members' perception about the relevance and essence of education in management accounting ethics and borrows from frameworks proposed by Callahan (1980), Loeb (1998), and Adkins and Radtke (2004).

The next section measures demographic data and investigates any significant relationship between demographics and identified trends from section one and section two of the questionnaire. To explain identify trends, this study will draw on theories on general business ethics. The section thereafter attempts to measure students' and faculty members' ability at ethical issue recognition and judgment using a scenario construct that investigates manipulation of reports; approving questionable expense sheets, ignoring company policy; granting questionable credit (Sweeney and Costello, 2009).

The questionnaires were addressed to university management accounting lecturers and students. No sampling strategy was applied in selecting faculty members as the population of management accounting lecturers is not large. Questionnaires were delivered by hand (by the researchers or a support assistant) to faculty members, and permission was sought from faculty members to distribute questionnaires to students. Generally, management accounting lecturers were supportive of the research and provided assistance in targeting students studying management accounting. This study was conscious of its ethical responsibility to survey participants and ensured voluntary participation, informed consent, no harm to participants, confidentiality and anonymity of participants as well as privacy to participants. As an example, an introductory page to the questionnaire explained that participation was voluntary, with a brief of the essence of the research, that participation was anonymous and did not request for names or any form of identification. All responses were directly collected from respondents and no student handed over his/her response to a faculty member. Most students had responded to questionnaires before hence could discount the myths that accompany its administration. The findings of this research are presented below.

DATA ANALYSIS AND FINDINGS

There are about 25 tertiary institutions offering a bachelor's degree in accounting in Ghana. Questionnaires were administered to 20 of these institutions. Twenty faculty members in twenty institutions responded to the questionnaire (a response rate of 100%). In each of the twenty institutions ten questionnaires were administered to management accounting students. In all 200 students were sampled and the response rate was 70%.

80% of the faculty respondents were males whereas 57% of the student respondents were females. 70% of faculty respondents were lecturers, 25% were senior lectures and one (5%) was a teaching assistant. Majority of the student respondents (86%) were less than 22 years old, and 64% were third year undergraduate students. Most faculty respondents (65%) were between the ages of 35 to 50. Very few lecturers and students had practicing experience in management accounting: 70% of faculty members had no such experience compared to

Table 1. Coverage of ethics in management accounting modules.

Coverage	Lecturers		Students	
	N	%	*n*	%
Not covered	14	70%	109	78%
Explicit	2		10	
Implicit	1		3	
Explicit and implicit	3		12	
Ethics covered	6	30%	25	18%
No response	-	0%	6	4%
Total	20	100%	140	100%

Source: Research study.

99% for student respondents.

ETHICS COVERAGE IN MANAGEMENT ACCOUNTING

Management accounting is offered as a compulsory module towards the award of a bachelor's degree in accounting across all the universities sampled. 65% of the universities (13 institutions) offered management accounting in the third year of study (i.e. Level 300); 10% (2) offered it as a compulsory course in the third and fourth year, and the remaining 25% offered it as a compulsory module in the final or fourth year (level 400). 50% of two-year postgraduate taught-courses offer management accounting as a compulsory module in the first year and the other 50% offer it as a compulsory module in the second year.

As to the inclusion of ethics, a significant portion of faculty members (70%) and students (78%) indicated that ethics education is not incorporated into management accounting modules. Non response bias will have resulted in a situation where only lecturers who actually incorporate ethics into management accounting education will have responded. The evidence presented below therefore, does not suggest non response bias because (a) there was a relatively significant number of negative responses and (b) a comparison of early respondents and negative respondents did not reveal any significant differences (Table 1).

The introduction of ethics education in management accounting has been quite recent, mostly between the past two to five years. Only one institution had incorporated ethical issues in the management accounting module for more than five years. Only one faculty member indicated an increasing trend of coverage of ethical issues in management accounting studies (in terms of credit hours dedicated). The other five faculty members incorporating ethics education in management accounting studies mentioned that the trend of coverage had remained unchanged. All faculty members who included ethics education in management accounting studies were optimistic that ethics education in management accounting will increase significantly within the next five academic years because of (a) improvements in the availability of study materials that address ethical issues in, management accounting studies; (b) the growing interest by the accounting and management accounting profession in ethical issues and (c) the growing interest of students in ethical issues.

Various questions were included to measure the seriousness attached to ethics education by the institutions that incorporate ethics education into management accounting studies. These included an exploration of the credit hours dedicated to ethical issues in management accounting studies and the inclusion of ethical issues in module assessments and examinations. The institutions that incorporated ethics education in management accounting studies, dedicated very little time to ethics education (about 8%); citing 'inadequate time' (67%) and the existence of a general ethics course (50%) as the main reason(s).86% of students cited the growing disconnect between industry and academia as the main reason for the little or no focus on ethical issues in management accounting; other students(21%) suggested the lack of interest by lecturers., with a few of them (9%) citing the lack of adequate experience by faculty members to deal with ethical issues in management accounting.

Four out of the six faculty members (67%) who incorporated ethics education confirmed that the time allotted to studies of ethical issues in management accounting was inadequate. All students who indicated that ethics education was incorporated agreed with faculty members that the time allotted was very inadequate.

The inclusion of ethical issues in assessments and examinations in management accounting is not consistent. 40% of students indicated that ethical issues were never assessed and 20% of students indicated that it was sometimes assessed. 50% of faculty members sometimes included ethical issues in module assessment but not always and one (1) faculty member has not yet included ethical issues in module assessment but intends to do so in the future. Interestingly, 2 faculty members

Table 2. Reasons for ethics coverage in management accounting.

	Mean[i] Rank	N	n%
Lecturers' personal interest	1.5	6.0	100%
Ethics is very important	1.8	6.0	100%
Mandatory from the University	2.0	2.0	33%

Source: Research study.

(33%) indicated that ethical issues are always assessed. Considering the fact that 10 students were sampled from each institution, it was expected that at least 20 students will confirm same. Only ten students from these institutions confirmed this assertion; perhaps suggesting a general challenge by students in identifying ethical issues. Faculty members who included ethics in management accounting teaching provided various reasons for the inclusion (Table 2).Only two universities mandated the incorporation of ethical issues in management accounting studies. The inclusion of ethical issues in management accounting was mostly as a result of lecturer's personal interest.

Faculty members who did not include ethics education in management accounting studies suggested that there was no need for a separate focus on ethical issues in management accounting studies (71%), there are no ethical issues peculiar to management accounting studies (64%), inadequate study support materials (64%) and ethics education is adequately covered in other accounting modules (57%).

29% of faculty members who currently do not include ethics education in management accounting will 'with certainty' consider including ethics education in future management accounting modules; with 43% undecided and 14% to consider integrating ethics education in management accounting studies depending on (1) the availability of study materials, (2) the revision of the course outlines to make time available and (3) the continuous non-existence of a general ethics course.

Students and faculty members differ significantly on the need for a separate focus on ethical issues peculiar to management accounting studies. A significant number of lecturers (50%) do not consider a separate focus on ethical issues in management accounting as very relevant because they do not perceive that there are ethical issues peculiar to management accounting studies. However 71% of students consider ethics education in management accounting studies as very relevant(very important or quite important), hence requiring a separate focus irrespective of whether there is a general course on ethics or not.

GOALS AND RELEVANCE OF ETHICS EDUCATION

Even though all faculty members and students agreed that ethics can be taught to students, only 30% of lecturers were very convinced ('absolutely' and 'to a great extent') that ethics education at the tertiary level will help accounting students to solve moral and ethical dilemmas facing the accounting profession. However a significantly more percentage of students (93%) were convinced that ethics education was critical ('absolutely' and 'to a great extent') in helping students deal with ethical dilemmas at work.

As regards the need for a separate focus on ethical issues in management accounting, students and faculty members differed.50% of faculty members considered it as 'moderately important' or only important to 'some extent', however 71% of students considered it as 'very important' or 'quite important'. 45% of faculty members prefer a combined ethics course for management and financial accounting and 61% of students prefer a compulsory ethics course integrated into management accounting studies.

Faculty and students also differed on the appropriate level at which ethical issues in management accounting should be discussed. Students generally prefer discussions on ethical issues to start earlier (at level 100) compared to faculty members (at level 300).

There are significant differences between lecturers and students in this study, on the expected outcome of ethics education in management accounting (as seen in Table 3).Whilst most lecturers agreed that ethics education should focus on the history of ethics in accounting vis-à-vis the general fields of ethics, most students disagreed and rather preferred ethics studies to focus on real life ethical conflicts and dilemmas in management accounting practice.

CAPACITY TO IDENTIFY ETHICAL ISSUES

The use of scenarios in ethics studies helps to focus on the most important factors in the decision making by respondents and measure multiple variables simultaneously in a standardized manner across respondents using a precise description of a social situation that makes the decision making situation more real.

Scenarios are widely used in business ethics studies (Randall and Gibson, 1990); Weber (1992) and to be effective as exploratory tools, they must avoid ambiguity (Randall and Gibson, 1990), must be interesting to the participants using precise language to describe real life situations that participants are familiar with and must reflect realistic ethical dilemmas (Weber, 1992) relating to the phenomenon being studied.

The scenario illustrated practical ethical dilemmas faced by management accountants at the work place and should be familiar to most third year and final year students in management accounting (Flory et al., 1992). The scenario exposed ethical issues about (1) approving a questionable expense report, (2) manipulating company books, (3) bypassing company policy and (4) extending questionable credit which have been identified as the most recurring ethical issues faced by management accountants at the work place. The scenario ended with action decisions taken by a hypothetical management accountant in response to ethical dilemmas. Faculty members and students were asked to identify the existence of ethical issues if any, and whether they agreed with the action decisions of the hypothetical management accountant.

The essence of the scenario was to measure the ability of faculty members and students in recognizing ethical issues and exercising ethical judgments and intentions. This is critical to understanding the capacity of faculty members in appropriately handling ethical discussions in management accounting studies as well as current student's preparedness to deal with ethical dilemmas at the work place because the ability to recognize ethical issues is critical catalyst to making the right ethical decision.

10% of faculty members and 42% of students could not identify the existence of ethical issues in the scenario presented. Only 10% of faculty members and 5% of students correctly identified all the four ethical issues involved in the scenario. 75% of faculty members and 87% of students could only partially identify the ethical issues involved; with most of them identifying only one ethical issue. The most identified ethical issue was manipulation of company records, bye-passing company policy as well as approving questionable credit. 40% of faculty members and 66% of students suggested they will act in a similar manner as the hypothetical management accountant. Whereas faculty members mostly cited the potential financial benefits to the organisation as a justification for their ethical intentions, students cited the need to be a team player, else the potential fallout with colleagues and management (i.e. work place attrition and job security) who may lose their bonuses if they act otherwise.

DISCUSSION AND IMPLICATIONS

Overall, the focus of ethics education in management accounting studies is very limited; with very few lecturers incorporating ethics education in management accounting studies. Where ethics education was incorporated, it was driven mainly by the personal interest of the lecturer in the subject area (Table 3).

As to the mode of delivery, a combination of explicit and implicit modes of instruction was used but the overall quality and seriousness of the instruction was limited. Specifically, (a) the time allotted to ethics education as part of management accounting studies was significantly low and inadequate; (b) and module assessment did not regularly include ethics issues. Whereas faculty members explained the inadequacy of the time allotted for ethics in management accounting studies to time constraints, and the existence of a general course in ethics, students cited the growing disconnect between academia and practice, lack of faculty interest and lack of adequate experience as the main reason (Table 4).

Most lecturers did not include ethics education in management accounting studies because they did not see the relevance of a separate focus for ethical issues in management accounting studies for the reasons that (a) ethics education was covered in other areas of study and management; (b) there were no ethical issues peculiar to management accounting; and (c) there were inadequate support materials.

Students and faculty members agreed that ethics education is very relevant; that ethics can be taught to tertiary students; but the time allotted for its education is inadequate.

Higher education research has confirmed significant discrepancies between students and faculty members on a lot of issues including perceptions about the effective mode of instruction (Miron, 1988).Students generally prefer a separate focus of ethical issues in management accounting studies irrespective of whether a general course in it exists or not; but lecturers disagree on the relevance of this approach, instead preferring a combined ethics course for financial and management accounting. Even though faculty members agree that ethics can be taught, they are relatively less convinced, compared to students, of the effectiveness of ethics education in helping to solve the moral and ethical dilemmas in accounting practice.

Faculty and students disagree on the most appropriate level to begin such education in management accounting studies. Whereas faculty members prefer ethics education to begin at senior years of tertiary education, students prefer it to begin at relatively earlier levels.

Students and faculty also disagree on what the goals of ethics education in management accounting should be. Students disagree that the goals should be to help students appreciate and understand the history and composition of all aspects of accounting ethics and their relationship to the general field of ethics.

Even though a surprisingly high number of lecturers and students were unable to comprehensively identify ethical issues and make the right ethical judgment in the earlier scenario presented, the situation was more pronounced for students. A relatively higher proportion of

Table 3. Expectations from ethics education.

		Sample	SD	D	SWD	N	SWA	A	SA	Mean
Ethics education is relevant	Lect.	*n=20*	0%	0%	0%	14%	0%	29%	57%	1.7
	Studt	*n=140*	0%	0%	0%	0%	0%	30%	70%	1.3
Including ethics education in management accounting courses/modules is critical	Lect.	*n=20*	0%	14%	0%	0%	0%	57%	29%	2.3
	Studt	*n=140*	0%	0%	0%	0%	0%	20%	80%	1.2
Ethics education in financial accounting should be separated from ethics education in management accounting	Lect.	*n=20*	29%	29%	0%	0%	14%	29%	0%	4.7
	Studt	*n=140*	0%	0%	0%	0%	0%	50%	50%	1.5
The goals of ethics education in MA should be to help students relate management accounting education to moral issues	Lect.	*n=20*	0%	0%	14%	14%	14%	43%	14%	2.7
	Studt	*n=140*	0%	0%	0%	0%	30%	30%	40%	1.9
The goals of ethics education in MA should be to help recognize issues in management accounting that have ethical implications	Lect.	*n=20*	0%	0%	14%	0%	14%	71%	0%	2.6
	Studt	*n=140*	0%	0%	0%	0%	20%	0%	80%	1.4
The goals of ethics education in MA should be to help students develop a sense of 'moral obligation' or responsibility.	Lect.	*n=20*	0%	0%	0%	29%	0%	71%	0%	2.6
	Studt	*n=140*	0%	0%	0%	0%	30%	40%	30%	2.0
The goals of ethics education in MA should be to help students deal with real life ethical conflicts and dilemmas in management accounting practice.	Lect.	*n=20*	0%	0%	0%	14%	29%	29%	29%	2.3
	Studt	*n=140*	0%	0%	0%	0%	0%	0%	100%	1.0
The goals of ethics education in management accounting should be to set the stage for change in ethical behaviour.	Lect.	*n=20*	0%	0%	0%	14%	29%	43%	14%	2.4
	Studt	*n=140*	0%	0%	0%	0%	0%	50%	60%	1.6
The goals of ethics education in MA should be to help students understand the history of ethics and its relationship to the general field of ethics.	Lect.	*n=20*	0%	0%	14%	14%	29%	29%	14%	2.9
	Studt	*n=140*	10%	10%	50%	0%	0%	10%	20%	4.2
The goals of ethics education in management accounting should be to help students learn to deal with exercising judgment in MA practice.	Lect.	*n=20*	0%	0%	0%	0%	29%	71%	0%	2.3
	Studt	*n=140*	0%	0%	0%	0%	0%	30%	70%	1.3

Where SD=Strongly Disagree, D=Disagree, SWD=somewhat disagree; N=Neutral, SWA=somewhat agree, A=Agree, SA=Strongly Agree. SD, D, SWD, N, SWA, A, SA are represented as 7,6,5,4,3,2,1 on the Likert scale. Source: Research Study.

Table 4. Identifying ethical issues and making right ethical judgment.

Respondents		Ethical Recognition (Is there an ethical issue?)			Identified Ethical Issue (What are the ethical issues?)					Ethical Judgment (Will you act in a similar manner?)	
		Yes	No	No Response	Fully Identified	Partly Identified			None	Appropriate Ethical Judgment	Inappropriate Ethical Judgment
					ALL	3	2	1			
Lecturers	n=20	18	2		2	3	5	7	3	12	8
	n%	*90%*	*10%*	*0%*	*10%*	*15%*	*25%*	*35%*	*15%*	*60%*	*40%*
Students	n=140	81	59		7	17	43	61	12	47	93
	n%	*58%*	*42%*	*0%*	*5%*	*12%*	*31%*	*44%*	*9%*	*34%*	*66%*

Source: Research study.

students were unable to identify ethical issues and make the right ethical judgment. Considering the fact that faculty members are a critical link in enlightening students on ethical issues, this trend may be disturbing. More-so, a number of studies have suggested that senior level students are relatively more ethical than lower level students (Ludlum et al., 2013), and may qualify as subject-surrogates for ethics studies in the real work environment because no significant difference(s)exists (Ludlum et al., 2013). Holding that to be true, the relatively inability by a significant number of senior level accounting students to identify ethical issues and make the appropriate ethical judgment is worrying and may perhaps confirm the relevance of students' desire for ethics studies to begin at earlier stages of study.

The results of this study suggest multiple implications for business schools. Given the importance of ethics in the field of accountancy and the growing evidence of the need to improve the mode of instruction of its education in accounting modules, it is impossible to have a holistic view of the effectiveness or otherwise of ethics education, without considering the views of both faculty and students. Examining the perspectives of faculty members as well as students on management accounting ethics education can provide useful insights to guide policy and organizational decisions. Secondly understanding the areas of difference in perceptions may be the starting point to mitigate any discrepancies and help improve accountancy education. Lastly, it is likely that similar discrepancies exist in other areas of study and instruction. Therefore this study provides the impetus for similar studies in other phenomenon.

Conflict of Interests

The authors have not declared any conflict of interests.

REFERENCES

Adkins N, Radtke RR (2004). Students' and faculty members' perceptions of the importance of business ethics and accounting ethics education: Is there an expectations gap? J. Bus. Ethics. 51(3):279-300.

Arlow P (1991). Personal characteristics in college students' evaluations of business ethics and corporate social responsibility, J. Bus. Ethics, 10(1):63-69.

Armstrong P (1985). Changing management control strategies: the role of competition between accountancy and other organisational professions, AOS 10(2):129-148.

Bampton R Cowton CJ (2002a), The teaching of ethics in management accounting: Progress and prospects, Business Ethics: A Eur. Rev. 11(1):52-61.

Bampton R, Cowton CJ (2002b). Pioneering in ethics teaching: The case of management accounting in universities in the British Isles, Teach. Bus. Ethics. 6(3):279-295.

Callahan D (1980), Goals in the teaching of ethics, In Ethics Teaching in Higher Education (pp. 61-80), Springer US.

Cole BC, Smith DL (1995), Effects of ethics instruction on the ethical perceptions of college business students, J. Educ. Bus. 70(6):351-356.

Deshpande SP (1997), Managers' perception of proper ethical conduct: The effect of sex, age, and level of education, J. Bus. Ethics 16(1):79-85.

Duska RF, Duska B (2003), Accounting Ethics, Malden, Massachusetts: Blackwell Publishing.

Evans III JH, Hannan R, Krishnan R, Moser DV (2001), Honesty in managerial reporting, Account. Rev. 76(4):537-559.

Fisher CM, Lovell A (2000), Accountants' responses to ethical issues at work. Oxford: Chartered Institute of Management Accountants.

Flory SM, Phillips Jr TJ, Reidenbach RE, Robin DP (1992). A multidimensional analysis of selected ethical issues in accounting, Account. Rev. pp.284-302.

Gunz S, McCutcheon J (1998), Are academics committed to accounting ethics education? J. Bus. Ethics 17(11):1145-1154.

Hajjawi O (2008), Pioneering in teaching business ethics: The case of management accounting in universities in Palestine, Eur. J. Econ. Finan. Admin. Sci. 14:149-157.

Hopper T, Tsamenyi M, Uddin S, &Wickramasinghe D (2009), Management accounting in less developed countries: what is known and needs knowing, Account. Audit. Accountability J. 22(3):469-514.

Hopwood AG (1972), An empirical study of the role of accounting data in performance evaluation, Empirical Research in Accounting: Selected Studies, Supplement J. Account. Res. 10:156-82.

Jaffe ED, Tsimerman A (2005), Business ethics in a transition economy: Will the next Russian generation be any better? J. Bus. Ethics 62(1):87-97.

Kahn WA (1990), Toward an agenda for business ethics research, Acad. Manage. Rev. 15(2):311-328.

Loeb S (1998), A separate course in accounting ethics: An example, Adv. Account. Educ. 1:235-250.

Ludlum MP, Moskaloinov S (2004), Right and wrong and cultural diversity: Replication of the 2002 Poll on Business Ethics, J. Educ. Bus. 79(5):294-298.

McNeel SP (1994), College teaching and student moral development, Moral Development in the Professions: Psychol. Appli. Ethics 27:49.

Mihalek PH, Rich AJ, Smith CS (1987), Ethics and management accountants, Manage. Account. 69:34-36.

Mintz S (1990), Ethics in the management accounting curriculum, Manage. Account. 71(12):51-54.

Miron M (1988), Students' evaluation and instructors' self-evaluation of university instruction, Higher Educ. 17(2):175-181.

Needles BE (1976), Implementing a framework for the international transfer of accounting technology, Int. J. Account. Educ. Res. 12(1).

Randall DM, Gibson AM (1990), Methodology in business ethics research: A review and critical assessment, J. Bus. Ethics 9(6):457-471.

Saul GK (1981), Business ethics: Where are we going? Acad. Manage. Rev. 6(2):269-276.

Shah AK (1996), Creative compliance in financial reporting, Account. Organ. Soc. 21(1):23-39.

Shaub MK (1995), An analysis of the association of traditional demographic variables with the moral reasoning of auditing students and auditors, J. Account. Educ. 12(1):1-26.

Stevens RE, Harris OJ, Williamson S (1993), A comparison of ethical evaluations of business school faculty and students: A pilot study, J. Bus. Ethics 12(8):611-619.

Sweeney B, Costello F (2009), Moral intensity and ethical decision-making: An empirical examination of undergraduate accounting and business students, Account. Educ. 18(1):75-97.

Tsamenyi M, Bennett M, Black J (2004), Perceived purposes of budgets in organizations in a developing country: field study from Ghana, J. Afr. Bus. Stud. 5(1):73-92.

Weber J (1992), Scenarios in business ethics research: Review, critical assessment, and recommendations, Bus. Ethics Q. 2:137-160.

[i]Respondents were asked to rank the various reasons for inclusion of ethical issues in management accounting studies with 1 representing most important, etc. The Mean Rank is calculated as a summation of the various ranks received per variable divided by the number of ranks.

Permissions

All chapters in this book were first published in JAT, by Academic Journals; hereby published with permission under the Creative Commons Attribution License or equivalent. Every chapter published in this book has been scrutinized by our experts. Their significance has been extensively debated. The topics covered herein carry significant findings which will fuel the growth of the discipline. They may even be implemented as practical applications or may be referred to as a beginning point for another development.

The contributors of this book come from diverse backgrounds, making this book a truly international effort. This book will bring forth new frontiers with its revolutionizing research information and detailed analysis of the nascent developments around the world.

We would like to thank all the contributing authors for lending their expertise to make the book truly unique. They have played a crucial role in the development of this book. Without their invaluable contributions this book wouldn't have been possible. They have made vital efforts to compile up to date information on the varied aspects of this subject to make this book a valuable addition to the collection of many professionals and students.

This book was conceptualized with the vision of imparting up-to-date information and advanced data in this field. To ensure the same, a matchless editorial board was set up. Every individual on the board went through rigorous rounds of assessment to prove their worth. After which they invested a large part of their time researching and compiling the most relevant data for our readers.

The editorial board has been involved in producing this book since its inception. They have spent rigorous hours researching and exploring the diverse topics which have resulted in the successful publishing of this book. They have passed on their knowledge of decades through this book. To expedite this challenging task, the publisher supported the team at every step. A small team of assistant editors was also appointed to further simplify the editing procedure and attain best results for the readers.

Apart from the editorial board, the designing team has also invested a significant amount of their time in understanding the subject and creating the most relevant covers. They scrutinized every image to scout for the most suitable representation of the subject and create an appropriate cover for the book.

The publishing team has been an ardent support to the editorial, designing and production team. Their endless efforts to recruit the best for this project, has resulted in the accomplishment of this book. They are a veteran in the field of academics and their pool of knowledge is as vast as their experience in printing. Their expertise and guidance has proved useful at every step. Their uncompromising quality standards have made this book an exceptional effort. Their encouragement from time to time has been an inspiration for everyone.

The publisher and the editorial board hope that this book will prove to be a valuable piece of knowledge for researchers, students, practitioners and scholars across the globe.

List of Contributors

Husam Aldeen Al-Khadash
Department of Accounting, Hashemite University, P.O. Box 330125, Postcode 13133, Hashemite University, Zarqa, Jordan

Sulieman Al-Beshtawi
Department of Accounting, Al-Mafraq, University, Zarqa, Jordan

Noor Azizi Ismail
College of Business, Universiti Utara Malaysia, Sintok 06010 Kedah, Malaysia

Azlan Zainol Abidin
College of Business, Universiti Utara Malaysia, Sintok 06010 Kedah, Malaysia

Francois Aubert
Faculté des Sciences Économiques et de Gestion, Université d'Auvergne Clermont 1, B. P. 54, 41 Bd. Francois Mitterrand, 63002 Clermont-Ferrand Cedex, France

Anthony Adekunle Owojori
Department of Educational Foundations and Management, Faculty of Education University of Ado-Ekiti, Nigeria

Ishola Rufus Akintoye
Department of Accounting, Olabisi Onabanjo University, Ago-Iwoye, Ogun State, Nigeria

Felix Adidu
Department of Business Administration, Delta State University, Abraka, Delta State Nigeria

Nabila Zribi
Faculty of Economics and Management of Sfax, University of Sfax-Tunisia, Route Saltania 4 Km, 3081 Sfax-Tunisia

Younes Boujelbène
Faculty of Economics and Management of Sfax. University of Sfax-Tunisia, Higher Institue of Business Administration of Sfax, Route from the Areport 4 Km, Sfax. BP1013-3018 Sfax-Tunisia

Adekunle A. Owojori
Accounting and Business Education, University of Ado-Ekiti, Ado-Ekiti, Ekiti State, Nigeria

Ishola R. Akintoye2
Department of Accounting, Banking and Finance, Osun State University, Nigeria

Felix A. Adidu
Department of Business Administration, Western Delta University, Oghara, Delta State, Nigeria

Okpanachi Joshua
Department of Economics and Management Sciences, Faculty of Arts and Social Sciences, Nigerian Defence Academy,Kaduna, Nigeria

Ilse Maria Beuren
Universidade Regional de Blumenau - PPGCC/FURB, Rua Antonio da Veiga, 140, Sala D 202, Bairro Victor Konder -Caixa Postal 1507, CEP 89012-900 - Blumenau/ SC, Brasil

Roberto Carlos Klann
Universidade Regional de Blumenau - PPGCC/FURB, Rua Antonio da Veiga, 140, Sala D 202, Bairro Victor Konder -Caixa Postal 1507, CEP 89012-900 - Blumenau/ SC, Brasil

PHAM Duc Hieu
University of Commerce, Ha noi, Vietnam

Youssef RIAHI
Department of Finance and Strategy of Businesses, Institute of Higher Management of Tunis, University of Tunisia, 23 Impasse 5 Rue 4267 DEN 2011, Tunis- Tunisie

Mounira BEN ARAB
Department of Finance and Strategy of Businesses, Institute of Higher Management of Tunis, University of Tunisia, 23 Impasse 5 Rue 4267 DEN 2011, Tunis- Tunisie

R. K. Uppal
D. A. V. College, Malout (Punjab), India

W. U Ani
Department of Banking and Finance, Michael Okpara University of Agriculture, Umudike, Abia State, Nigeria

D. O Ugwunta
Department of Banking and Finance, The Renaissance University, Enugu, Nigeria

I. J Ezeudu
Department of Banking and Finance, Michael Okpara University of Agriculture, Umudike, Abia State, Nigeria

G. O. Ugwuanyi
Department of Accountancy, Institute of Management and Technology, Enugu, Nigeria

Olurankinse Felix
Department of Accounting, Adekunle Ajasin University, Akungba - Akoko, Ondo State, Nigeria

Nelson Maseko
Department of Accountancy, Faculty of Commerce, Bindura University of Science Education, Zimbabwe

Onias Manyani
Department of Accountancy, Faculty of Commerce, Bindura University of Science Education, Zimbabwe

Mohamed Ali Azouzi
Department of Financial and Accounting, Universities Higher Institute of Business Administration (ISAAS), ISAAS, BP 1013 - 3018 Sfax-Tunisia

Anis Jarboui
Department of Financial and Accounting, Universities Higher Institute of Business Administration (ISAAS), ISAAS, BP 1013 - 3018 Sfax-Tunisia

Husam Al-Khadash
Hashemite University P.O. Box 330125, Postcode 13133, Hashemite University, Zarqa, Jordan

Asmahan Y. Salah
Central Bank of Jordan, Amman, Jordan

Mohammed Al-Shoura
School of Management, Faculty of Business, Middle East University (MEU), Jordan

Anas Al Bakri
Management and Marketing Department, Faculty of Business and Economics, Qatar University, Al Tarfa, Doha 2713, Qatar

Kousay Said
Department of Accounting, College of Business Administration, University of Bahrain, P.O. Box: 32038, Kingdom of Bahrain

Hussein Khasharmeh
Department of Accounting, College of Business Administration, University of Bahrain, P.O. Box: 32038, Kingdom of Bahrain

Mr Lopo Martinez Antonio
Fucape Business School, Vitória, Brazil

Aldecir Bassetti
UNESC, Colatina, Brazil

Kousay Said
Department of Accounting, College of Business Administration, University of Bahrain, P.O. Box: 32038, Kingdom of Bahrain

Khaled Ibrahim Al-Tarawneh
Department of Accounting, College of Business Administration, University of Bahrain, P.O. Box: 32038, Kingdom of Bahrain

Frank Yao Gbadago
Department of Accounting Studies Education, College of Technology Education University of Education, Winneba, Kumasi, Ghana

Mohammed Ibrahim
Department of Accounting, Gombe State University, Gombe, Gombe State, Nigeria

Roberto Carlos Klann
Universidade Regional de Blumenau, Blumenau, SC, Brazil

Ilse Maria Beuren
Universidade Federal do Paraná, Curitiba, PR, Brazil

Nelson Hein
Universidade Regional de Blumenau, Blumenau, SC, Brazil

Ronald Stunda
Valdosta State University, U.S

Randolph Nsor-Ambala
Department of Accounting, Henley Business School, University of Reading, UK

Joseph Mensah Onumah
Department of Accounting, University of Ghana Business School, Legon, Ghana